Vietnam War

Vietnam War

THE ESSENTIAL REFERENCE GUIDE

James H. Willbanks, Editor

 ABC-CLIO

Santa Barbara, California • Denver, Colorado • Oxford, England

Library of Congress Cataloging-in-Publication Data

Vietnam War : the essential reference guide / James H. Willbanks, editor.
  p. cm.
Includes bibliographical references and index.
ISBN 978–1–61069–103–1 (cloth : acid-free paper) — ISBN 978–1–61069–104–8 (ebook)
1. Vietnam War, 1961–1975. 2. Vietnam War, 1961–1975—Sources. I. Willbanks, James H., 1947–
DS557.7.V5668   2013
959.704′3—dc23   2012032418

ISBN: 978–1–61069–103–1
EISBN: 978–1–61069–104–8

17 16 15 14 13   1 2 3 4 5

This book is also available on the World Wide Web as an eBook.
Visit www.abc-clio.com for details.

ABC-CLIO, LLC
130 Cremona Drive, P.O. Box 1911
Santa Barbara, California 93116-1911

This book is printed on acid-free paper ∞

Manufactured in the United States of America

This book is dedicated to all who fought to defend South Vietnam
and
to my son, Russell Willbanks, a veteran of the wars in both Iraq and Afghanistan

Contents

Overview of the Vietnam War

The war in Vietnam was the United States' longest war and certainly one of the most contentious. The fighting between the United States and the government of South Vietnam on one side and North Vietnam and the Viet Cong (VC) on the other lasted from the mid-1950s until the mid-1970s and spread into Laos and Cambodia.

1950–1967

The United States first became involved in Vietnam in 1950 when it began supporting France in the latter's effort to defend its colonial presence in Vietnam. Within the context of the Cold War, this assistance to France was extended as part of the effort to contain communism. Despite American aid, the French were eventually defeated by the Communist-dominated Viet Minh. The Geneva Conference in 1954 resulted in the partition of Vietnam along the 17th Parallel with Ho Chi Minh's Democratic Republic of Vietnam (DRV) holding sway in the north and the State of Vietnam governing the south. In an effort to counter Ho, the United States supported the anti-Communist regime in Saigon headed by Ngo Dinh Diem.

Diem's corrupt and unpopular regime was unable to deal with the insurgency that grew in the south after Diem refused to conduct the elections in 1956 that had been called for by the Geneva Accords. Additionally, his repressionist policies alienated the South Vietnamese people. With U.S. approval, a group of South Vietnamese generals launched a coup; their removal and murder of Diem resulted in a series of revolving-door governments and more political instability. The Communists stepped up their attacks and North Vietnamese Army units began traveling down the Ho Chi Minh Trail to join the fight in the fall of 1964. In 1965, the United States sent in combat troops to prevent the South Vietnamese government from collapsing in the face of the Communist insurgency. By late 1967, after a rapid escalation of the U.S. commitment, there were nearly 500,000 American troops in South Vietnam and bitter fighting raged all over the country.

The war in Vietnam caused deep divisions on the home front in the United States and contributed to the social upheaval of the 1960s. The failure to achieve any meaningful progress against the VC and North Vietnamese, the spread of the antiestablishment counterculture, the graphic coverage of the fighting by the media, and the credibility gap that developed between successive presidential administrations and the American public seriously undermined support for the war.

1967–1972

By late 1967, U.S. forces had dealt serious blows to the Communists, but the fighting

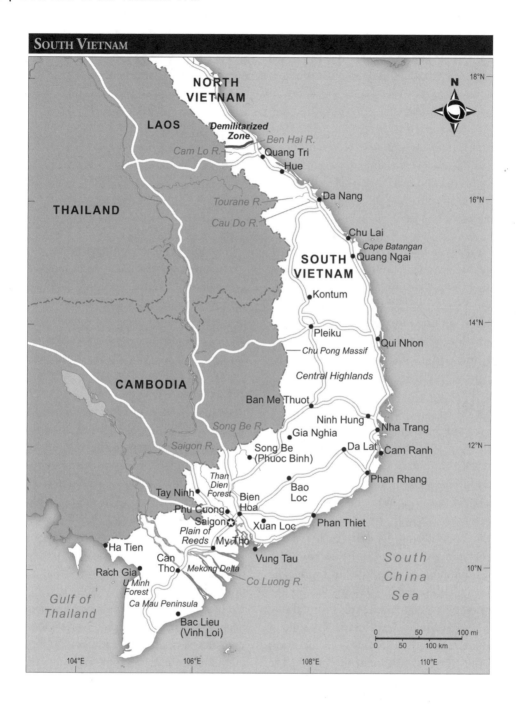

continued unabated. President Lyndon Johnson launched a public relations campaign emphasizing that progress was being made in order to bolster public support. In the midst of this campaign, the Communists launched the massive Tet Offensive on the Tet (New Year) holiday in 1968. Although American and South Vietnamese forces prevailed, the shock and scope of the attacks stunned the American public and convinced a demoralized Johnson not to run for reelection.

Richard Nixon was elected in 1968 largely because he promised to end the war and achieve "peace with honor." To do this, he announced that he would "Vietnamize" the war. This meant that the responsibility for the fighting would be shifted to the South Vietnamese so that U.S. forces could be disengaged. While this was being done, the fighting continued to rage. Neither massive bombing of both South Vietnam and North Vietnam nor the expansion of the war into Cambodia and Laos brought the war any closer to an end.

Dissatisfied with the bloody stalemate, North Vietnam launched a massive invasion of the south in the spring of 1972. Although initially successful, North Vietnamese forces were turned back by a massive application of American airpower. Nixon proclaimed Vietnamization a success. Meanwhile, Henry Kissinger had been conducting secret peace negotiations with Communist representatives in Paris. By October 1972, they had forged a tentative peace agreement. However, President Nguyen Van Thieu of South Vietnam voiced violent opposition to the terms, and the North Vietnamese angrily walked out of the negotiations. Nixon ordered a massive bombing campaign against Hanoi and Haiphong. After 18 days, the North Vietnamese agreed to return to the negotiating tables, but the agreement that was worked out was not substantially different from the one that had been agreed upon before the bombing.

1973–1975

The Paris Peace Accords were signed on January 27, 1973. The terms of the agreement called for an in-place cease-fire and the withdrawal of all U.S. troops by March 1973. There was no mention of the North Vietnamese troops left in South Vietnam when the cease-fire went into effect, but Nixon promised Thieu that the United States would support South Vietnam if Hanoi violated the terms of the cease-fire.

Despite Nixon's promises, the fighting continued after U.S. troops had all departed as the South Vietnamese and their opponents vied for control of the countryside. Nixon, beset by the Watergate Scandal, resigned in August 1974, and, subsequently, Congress reduced military aid to Vietnam. In December 1974, Hanoi launched a final offensive in the south. On April 30, 1975, North Vietnamese tanks crashed through the gates of the Presidential Palace in Saigon and South Vietnam surrendered.

The United States, although it had not been defeated on the battlefield, had lost the first war in its history. More than 58,000 Americans had been killed and over 300,000 wounded. South Vietnam had fallen to the Communists. The war had sharply divided American society and made Americans question the veracity of their own governmental institutions. The legacies of the war would last for many years to come.

James H. Willbanks

Causes of the Vietnam War

Immediate Causes

Tonkin Gulf Incidents

On August 2, 1964, the U.S. destroyer *Maddox*, engaged in a secret intelligence-gathering DESOTO Missions, reported that it was fired on by North Vietnamese torpedo boats in international waters. On August 4, the *Maddox* and another U.S. destroyer, the *C. Turner Joy*, reported a second attack. U.S. Navy commanders told Secretary of Defense Robert McNamara that unreliable radio and sonar contacts made it difficult for them to confirm the second attack. Nevertheless, President Lyndon Johnson, looking for a reason to retaliate against the Communists, claimed unprovoked aggression and ordered air strikes against North Vietnamese torpedo bases and oil storage depots.

The incident led to congressional passage on August 7, 1964, of the Tonkin Gulf Resolution, which authorized the president to take "all necessary measures to repel any armed attacks against the forces of the United States and to prevent further aggression" in Vietnam. The only dissenting votes in Congress were by Senator Wayne Morse of Oregon and Senator Ernest Gruening of Alaska. During the deliberations and discussions on the measure, Johnson did not inform Congress about the questionable circumstances of the second attack or of the covert operations the U.S. vessels had been conducting.

The Tonkin Gulf Resolution gave Johnson the authority to respond to any Communist aggression in any way he saw fit. Johnson's immediate response to the Tonkin Gulf incident was to launch retaliatory air raids on North Vietnamese coastal installations. However, the resolution ultimately gave Johnson sufficient authority to commit U.S. ground combat troops in Vietnam. The first contingent of U.S. Marines was committed in March 1965 to protect American air bases in South Vietnam. However, this was only the beginning of a rapid buildup that would result in nearly 550,000 U.S. troops in Vietnam by April 1969.

Operation ROLLING THUNDER

With his new powers under the Tonkin Gulf Resolution, Johnson initiated Operation ROLLING THUNDER, which was a series of bombing raids in North Vietnam. Its purpose was primarily to destroy the North Vietnamese will to fight, but it also sought to destroy industrial bases and surface-to-air missiles (SAMs) and to discontinue reinforcements and supplies along the Ho Chi Minh Trail.

Beginning in March 1965, Operation ROLLING THUNDER gradually escalated in intensity to force the Communists to negotiate. While half of North Vietnam's bridges were destroyed and many supply depots hit, this did not stop the flow of supplies from its Communist allies because the port of Haiphong and the Chinese border were off-limits to aerial attack. Restrictions on the bombing of civilian areas also enabled the Viet Cong (VC) to use these locations for military purposes, often siting antiaircraft guns at schools.

Operation ROLLING THUNDER, coupled with the ground troops that Johnson sent in increasing numbers, announced the beginning of the Vietnam War.

Intermediate Causes

The Failures of the Diem Regime

After the Geneva Accords, the United States, in an attempt to counter the Communist regime of Ho Chi Minh in North Vietnam, threw its support behind Ngo Dinh Diem, who had been named prime minister of the State of Vietnam by Emperor Bao Dai. In 1955, Diem was elected president in a disputed national referendum. When Diem announced that he would not conduct the elections called for in 1956 by the Geneva Accords, the United States supported this move, knowing that Diem most likely would have been defeated by Ho.

For a while it looked as if Diem could win support from his people and create a viable non-Communist state in South Vietnam. By 1957, Diem had impressed U.S. observers by using the army against gangsters and armed religious groups to consolidate his power. However, the United States' honeymoon with Diem would last only a few years.

Diem had no intention of introducing democracy and the social reforms urged by the United States. He relied heavily on his family to form the core of his political

structure. In an effort to consolidate power, Diem unleashed a savage campaign in urban areas to silence all potential political opposition and, at the same time, launched a merciless pacification program in the countryside. With the help of U.S. and British experts, in 1959 Diem began a wholesale resettlement program that forced the resident population into so-called agrovilles—and later, strategic hamlets—in an effort to weed out the Communists and control the population. Diem's inability to win the support of his people and the ineptness of his army in combating the growing South Vietnamese insurgency ultimately led to his overthrow. However, the demise of Diem did not help the situation. This led to an increase in American involvement in Vietnam that ultimately led to the commitment of U.S. ground troops.

Establishment of the National Liberation Front

With the 1956 elections called for by the Geneva Accords canceled by Diem, the Viet Minh cadre that had been left in the south after the country was partitioned launched an armed insurgency. Initially, Ho counseled patience, but in January 1959 the party congress in Hanoi voted to support the armed revolution in South Vietnam. To facilitate support of the coming struggle, Hanoi solicited aid, equipment, technicians, and advisers from the Soviet Union and the People's Republic of China. In September 1960, Hanoi announced a two-part program calling for socialist reform in North Vietnam and liberation of South Vietnam from the Saigon government and its American supporters.

With Hanoi's blessing, on December 20 some 20 organizations, opposed to the Diem regime and its support by the United States, merged with the former southern Viet Minh revolutionaries to form the

National Liberation Front (NLF), popularly known as the Viet Cong (VC). The group's objective was the overthrow of the Diem regime and the reunification of both Vietnams. From then on, the NLF prosecuted a very effective guerrilla war against the Diem regime.

Battle of Ap Bac

In early January 1963, South Vietnamese Army forces attacked VC guerrilla positions in a South Vietnamese village in the Mekong Delta, 40 miles southwest of Saigon. The South Vietnamese troops performed poorly, and the smaller VC forces took the day. Although U.S. military officials declared Ap Bac a victory because the VC left the area, American journalists who witnessed the battle declared it a debacle.

The poor performance of the South Vietnamese Army at Ap Bac demonstrated to the John F. Kennedy administration just how bad the situation was in Vietnam. It was clear that Diem and the South Vietnamese Army would have a difficult time combating the growing insurgency, and the Battle of Ap Bac pointed out only too clearly how far the South Vietnamese had to go to be able to defend themselves.

Persecution of Buddhists

Buddhism is the dominant religion in Vietnam. Although strongly anti-Communist, South Vietnamese Buddhists were increasingly alienated by Diem's repressionist regime. The situation came to a head on May 8, 1963, after the government prohibited Buddhists from carrying flags on Buddha's birthday. Crowds gathered in Hue to protest, and government troops fired into the crowd to disperse the dissidents, killing nine people. Diem's government blamed VC guerrillas for the deaths, but the Buddhist leadership organized protests against the Diem regime. The

Kennedy administration threatened to break with Diem over the issue of Buddhist repression, but the situation only worsened.

On June 11, 1963, in Saigon, Thich Quang Duc, a Buddhist monk from Hue, set himself on fire to protest the regime's policies. Vast demonstrations broke out in several cities, followed by the self-immolation of 6 more monks. On August 21, Diem's brother, Ngo Dinh Nhu, raided the Xa Loi Pagoda in Saigon, killing more than 30 monks. Similar raids were carried out in other cities. The persecution of the Buddhists convinced the Kennedy administration that Diem would never win the support of his own people and would thus not be able to build a government and army strong enough to prevail against the Communist insurgency.

The Assassination of Diem

By mid-June 1963, the military and political situation in South Vietnam had deteriorated to a new low and the United States threatened to break with Diem. When the Kennedy administration heard of an impending military coup, it made no move to prevent it. On November 2, 1963, Diem and his brother were ousted and murdered, and General Duong Van Minh became the leader of South Vietnam.

The death of Diem and his brother was followed by a period of intense political instability, which was characterized by a series of military governments that replaced each other in rapid succession. Meanwhile, the VC stepped up its campaign of hit-and-run attacks on government installations, military outposts, convoys, strategic hamlets, and district towns throughout South Vietnam. The Saigon government and its military, even with U.S. advisers, appeared incapable of dealing with the rapidly growing insurgency. The growing political and military instability in Vietnam would eventually result in the commitment of U.S. combat troops and a full-scale conflict that would become the United States' longest war.

Long-Term Causes

Containment and the Cold War

After the end of World War II, the ties that had bound together the Allies in the effort to defeat Germany and Japan began to give way to suspicion, hostility, and a new rivalry between East and West that eventually led to diplomatic struggles and armed confrontations. Ideological differences between the United States and the Soviet Union on a host of postwar issues, including the government of postwar Poland, led to a conflict that spread throughout Europe and the world. It appeared as though the Soviet Union posed a threat to the United States, and that communism would spread if not checked. What became known as the Cold War would be waged by means of economic pressure, selective aid, diplomatic maneuvering, propaganda, low-intensity military operations, and in some instances full-scale war.

In 1947, to gain support from Congress for aid to Greek and Turkish governments facing Communist insurgencies, President Harry S. Truman announced what became known as the Truman Doctrine, which pledged U.S. help to any government facing such a threat. This was the beginning of the containment policy, which held that the United States would take whatever measures necessary to contain the spread of communism. The situation worsened in 1949 when the Soviet Union successfully tested its own atomic bomb and the Communist forces of Mao Zedong triumphed in the Chinese Civil War. With the Communist victory in China and the Soviets on the march in Eastern Europe, the battle lines were clearly drawn.

When North Korean Communist forces attacked across the 38th Parallel in June 1950, the U.S. government decided that the Communist threat needed to be checked. The Cold War and the policy of containment would have a strong impact on American support for France in the Indochina War and on American prosecution of its own war in Vietnam, which began shortly after the French defeat at Dien Bien Phu in 1954.

The Indochina War

When Truman declared the policy of containment, there was already a war under way in Southeast Asia between French colonialists and Vietnamese nationalists led by Ho Chi Minh. From 1858 to 1897, the French had conquered Vietnam, Cambodia, and Laos in a piecemeal fashion, ultimately establishing colonial rule over Indochina. Under France, Vietnam was politically dominated and economically exploited, contributing to a deep-seated Vietnamese passion for independence and national unity.

This passion for independence reached a new height in the years after World War I. The Indochinese Communist Party (ICP), founded in 1930 by Ho and others, played a key role in the resistance against French rule. Ho was joined in the spring of 1940 by Pham Van Dong and Vo Nguyen Giap, who would figure prominently in both the war against the French and then the war against the Americans.

In September 1940 Japanese forces occupied Indochina. In 1941 Ho and the ICP formed a broad-based nationalist alliance, the League for the Independence of Vietnam (Viet Minh), to resist foreign rule. During what became known as the August Revolution, when the Japanese surrendered in August 1945, the Viet Minh seized the moment by occupying Hanoi and proclaiming the formation of the Democratic Republic of Vietnam (DRV) with Ho as president. When British troops assisted the French in driving the Viet Minh out of the city, Ho appealed to the United States for support, which Washington ignored. France refused to recognize the DRV, and in November 1946, fighting broke out between the Viet Minh and French troops; full-scale war soon followed.

Between 1946 and 1954, Viet Minh forces battled the French for control of Vietnam. At first the Viet Minh had a difficult time in coping with the better-trained and better-equipped French forces. However, in 1949 the Chinese Communist People's Liberation Army (PLA) pushed into southern China and forced the Chinese Nationalist regime to flee to Taiwan. When Mao Zedong announced support for the Viet Minh, Ho gladly accepted military aid and advice from Beijing.

Because it now looked as if communism were spreading, the United States threw its support behind the French. In February 1950 Truman extended diplomatic recognition to the French-backed State of Vietnam and committed $50 million in military assistance to the French in Vietnam for their fight against the Viet Minh. But even with U.S. aid and assistance, the French had a difficult time subduing the insurgency, and the war soon turned into a bloody stalemate. While the French had a firm hold on the south, where they had installed Emperor Bao Dai as the head of state, the Viet Minh controlled large areas of northern Vietnam.

In late 1953 General Henri Navarre, the French commander in Vietnam, came up with a plan to lure the Viet Minh into a large-scale battle at a remote base near the Lao border. General Giap responded by surrounding the French base at Dien Bien Phu, and after a 56-day siege, the French surrendered to the Viet Minh on May 7, 1954.

The Geneva Accords

In 1956 the United States, France, Great Britain, the Soviet Union, the People's Republic of China (PRC), Laos, Cambodia, the State of Vietnam, and the DRV met at Geneva, Switzerland, to determine the future of Vietnam. Although the Viet Minh wanted full independence and a strong role for the Communist party, Chinese premier Zhou Enlai convinced Ho to accept a temporary division of Vietnam at the 17th Parallel, with elections to be held in 1956 to resolve the issue of who would control all of Vietnam. The Viet Minh felt betrayed in not achieving what they had fought for, and Ho returned to Hanoi to reestablish the DRV and wait for the elections. France, Great Britain, the PRC, and the Soviet Union endorsed the Geneva Accords, but the Viet Minh did not sign them, nor did Ngo Dinh Diem, who became prime minister of the State of Vietnam.

The seeds of the American war in Vietnam were sown during the Indochina War. France's demise and the partitioning of Vietnam had set the stage for future U.S. involvement. Given the nature of the Cold War, the requirement to prevent the Communists from taking over Vietnam remained after the French were defeated. The United States shouldered the task and eventually became embroiled in the longest war of its history.

James H. Willbanks

Consequences of the Vietnam War

Immediate Consequences

Consequences for the United States

The war in Vietnam sparked a tide of social and economic discord that resulted in a near breakdown of the American body politic. These tensions tore at a social consensus that had been built in part on anti-communism and the global role of the United States. The war eroded confidence in public institutions and contributed to wide challenges to social order and authority in the 1960s. Unprecedented upheaval followed the May 1970 Cambodian Incursion, resulting in tragic student deaths at Kent State University and Jackson State University. The Vietnam War also heightened class tensions in the United States. Of the 2.5 million U.S. personnel who served in Vietnam, 80 percent were from working-class or poor backgrounds.

The Vietnam War had a devastating effect on the U.S. military, especially the ground forces. As the fighting wore on year after year, American military forces were stretched to the breaking point. President Lyndon Johnson refused to call up the reserves, and this resulted in multiple tours of duty for American service members, especially for the army and marines. With little progress being made in the war, morale and discipline problems began to increase.

Drug and alcohol abuse became a significant problem. The same racial unrest that occurred at home in the United States began to be felt in Vietnam. By the end of the war, the American military was demoralized and in desperate need of revitalization and reform.

The war also had a tremendous impact on the American economy. U.S. fiscal policies necessary to support the war in Vietnam exacerbated larger economic problems arising from Cold War military commitments. In order to finance the war, which ultimately cost the United States more than $170 billion, the Johnson administration ran budget deficits and refused to restrain an overheated economy. Johnson hoped to sustain domestic government programs while also paying for the war, leading to rampant inflation. In the final analysis, his policies added to the national debt, contributed to double-digit inflation by the 1970s, and took away resources needed for social services in the United States.

Despite the massive expenditure of blood and money in Vietnam, the United States, although never defeated on the battlefield, failed to achieve its stated objective of fostering a free and independent South Vietnam that could stand alone against the Viet Cong (VC) and North Vietnam. The Paris Peace

Accords paved the way for U.S. withdrawal from the war, but South Vietnam was left to its own devices, and ultimately Saigon fell to the Communists.

Casualties

The simplest and most brutal consequences from the Vietnam War can be seen in the form of casualty counts. During the Indochina War, the French lost some 76,000 dead and 65,000 wounded, while their allies lost 19,000 dead and 13,000 wounded. Viet Minh forces lost an estimated 250,000 dead and 189,000 wounded, while civilian deaths from the fighting are estimated at 250,000.

During the Vietnam War, the United States lost 58,159 killed and 304,000 wounded during 1959–1975. Some 74,000 of the wounded survived as quadriplegics or multiple amputees. In addition to the dead and wounded, there were over 2,200 American service members listed as missing in action (MIA).

The low estimate for South Vietnam's losses is over 110,000 killed in action and nearly 500,000 wounded. The number of Vietnamese civilians killed in the war may never be known, but the lowest estimate given is 415,000.

In April 1995, Hanoi announced that 1.1 million Communist fighters, including both VC guerrillas and North Vietnamese soldiers, had died between 1954 and 1975. An additional 600,000 were wounded in action.

Elsewhere in Southeast Asia, the casualty figures were also high. The Royal Lao Army and its guerrilla auxiliaries lost many thousands in the undeclared war in Laos, as did regular and irregular Thai forces fighting there. In addition to the Cambodians killed in the fighting and bombing in that country, at least two million other Cambodians were killed by the Khmer Rouge during 1975–1978.

Fall of South Vietnam

For the South Vietnamese, the most tragic consequence of the Vietnam War was the dissolution of their country. When the North Vietnamese tanks rolled onto the grounds of the Presidential Palace in Saigon on April 30, 1975, the Republic of Vietnam ceased to exist as a sovereign nation. Victorious, Vietnamese Communist leaders set forth three major goals: to unify the two zones into a single nation, to lead the entire Vietnamese people to socialism, and to ensure the national security of the state. In July 1976, a new Socialist Republic of Vietnam (SRV) was created, with its capital in Hanoi. In the south, the Communist authorities placed former South Vietnamese political and military leaders in "reeducation camps" for indoctrination or punishment.

The lives of the South Vietnamese changed forever. The United States had abandoned them, the Communists had overrun their country, and now they were under the control of the government in Hanoi. Even the name of their former capital, Saigon, was changed by the victors to Ho Chi Minh City. The fall of South Vietnam led to fundamental changes in the way of life in the south, and many could not accept the new reality, choosing instead to flee their homeland.

Boat People and Refugees

With the fall of South Vietnam, thousands of Vietnamese fled the country by sea. There was an immediate evacuation of 140,000 Vietnamese with ties to the defeated government and to the United States. Over the next 13 years, the first wave was followed by about 983,000 refugees to other countries. Some of this latter group were called "boat people" because they left Vietnam by sea. After 1978, Malaya and Thailand began turning away refugees, and incidents of piracy against the refugee boats increased. Tens of thousands of boat people were lost at sea; it is estimated that 10–50 percent of the refugees who attempted the ocean passage drowned or otherwise perished.

The acceptance and resettlement of the boat people and other refugees became an international political issue. From 1975 into the 1980s, between 1.5 million and 2 million refugees fled the Communist-led SRV, Cambodia, and Laos because of political instability and military conflict. Many of these Cambodian, Lao, and Vietnamese refugees flooded the United States. In 1978, one of the U.S. preconditions for normalization of relations with the SRV was that measures be taken to stem the flood of refugees. Still, the consensus among most Americans was that the United States had an obligation to aid refugees from the Vietnam War. Accordingly, President Jimmy Carter in June 1979 used his executive authority to raise quotas for immigrants from Communist countries and Southeast Asia to a high of 14,000 per month. From 1975 to 1986, more than half a million refugees from Vietnam, Cambodia, and Laos came to the United States. To date, about $5 billion in U.S. federal aid has been spent to help these refugees start a new life in the United States.

Intermediate Consequences
American Malaise
Even though South Vietnam fell after American troops had been withdrawn, the United States clearly failed in Vietnam. American troops had been withdrawn without achieving the stated objective of insuring a free and independent South Vietnam. After U.S. withdrawal, the South Vietnamese succumbed and the Communists took over all of Vietnam.

To many Americans and other observers around the world, it was clear that the United States had failed in Vietnam and that American foreign policy had been misguided, its government had been less than genuine, and its moral fiber had been found lacking. Such perceptions caused a painful national malaise in American society. Before the Vietnam War, American exceptionalism had been alive and well. Americans felt that the United States was a good nation led by well-meaning people. Previously, Americans had come to the aid of faltering European powers in times of trouble to save democracy from the hands of tyrants. Vietnam, however, was different. To many Americans, it seemed that the United States had chosen the wrong cause in Vietnam and, in so doing, had become the aggressor meddling in a Vietnamese civil war. America had been defeated; its leaders had lied; its soldiers had committed atrocities; and its society had nearly imploded from the pressures of the war. After the fall of South Vietnam, the United States languished in a period of self-doubt and recriminations. Americans no longer trusted their own government as they had before, and many Americans began to question the very concept of American exceptionalism and the place of the United States in world affairs.

Treatment of Vietnam Veterans
With the defeat in Vietnam, most Americans struggled to forget the war and the turmoil of the 1960s in an effort to get on with their lives. The war had been a traumatic experience for the nation, but it was over and most Americans simply chose to ignore the war and its consequences. With the American people in the throes of what one historian has called "national amnesia"

about Vietnam, the veterans of the war were shunted aside as unwelcome reminders of that which most Americans wanted to forget.

During the war, Vietnam veterans returned to their nation quickly and without ceremony. Unlike previous wars in which soldiers trained and fought together, the draft system placed most American soldiers into battle as single replacements. They went off to war and returned as individuals, many arriving at their homes only hours after leaving combat. They returned to a society that did not welcome them home. They were sometimes met with ridicule, scorn, or apathy from those who were either opposed to the war or ambivalent about it. Thus, many Vietnam veterans, who had done only what their country had asked them to do, found themselves abandoned and alone in a country that had forgotten them and their sacrifice. After the war, the situation worsened. The soldiers had participated in an unpopular war in which the objectives were not always clear, but, moreover, they had lost their war. They were made to feel as though they were to blame for America's defeat.

Rejection was made harder to take for Vietnam veterans because they could remember the great national welcome home afforded to their fathers after World War II. Traumatized and confused, these young men found that their sacrifice was held unworthy of national notice or pride. As a result, many veterans experienced great difficulty in adjusting to civilian life and felt alienated from the rest of society; some began to close off from the world, and many dealt with the trauma of war in a destructive manner, turning to drugs, alcohol, crime, and even suicide.

Government services for Vietnam returnees through the Veterans Administration (VA) were often inadequate because of a lack of political will to provide services for the veterans. For years, the government and the VA refused to admit that Vietnam veterans suffered any postwar problems. However, a significant number suffered from a sense of emotional numbness, nervousness, depression, nightmares, difficulty in developing close personal relationships, insomnia, and survivor guilt. In 1980 the American Psychiatric Association finally recognized their suffering as a bona fide psychological malady, but most veterans did not receive any treatment for their continuing problems until some 20 years after the war had ended. In psychological terms, these men suffered from posttraumatic stress disorder (PTSD). The recognition that their illness was a normal human reaction to witnessing the violence and destruction of war greatly helped in the treatment of thousands of Vietnam veterans.

Not all Vietnam veterans experienced difficulty in adjusting to society. The vast majority of soldiers returning from Vietnam got on with their lives. Many attended college under the GI Bill. Many veterans started their own businesses or became executives in America's largest companies. A number of veterans have served in Congress, and several have been elected governors of their states.

Still, many Vietnam veterans, feeling that their service was unappreciated by the rest of American society, bonded together into a special brotherhood of those who had been there. The Vietnam Veterans Memorial dedicated in Washington, D.C., on November 13, 1982, began as a project by veterans and finally provided a way for American society to recognize the sacrifices made during the Vietnam War.

Long-Term Consequences
Vietnam Syndrome

Former president Richard Nixon asserted that the United States suffered from a "Vietnam syndrome" in the aftermath of its defeat in Vietnam, by which many sought to avoid all foreign involvement. Indeed, Congress, on November 7, 1973, had passed the War Powers Resolution over Nixon's veto. The intent of this legislation was to limit the power of the president to commit U.S. forces to extended combat or risk of combat without congressional approval, either through a declaration of war as the Constitution provides or at least by specific enabling legislation.

The Vietnam syndrome remained a contentious issue into the 1980s and 1990s. When Ronald Reagan became president, he characterized the Vietnam War as a noble effort to defeat the forces of tyranny and asserted that the lack of success in Southeast Asia should not prevent Americans from seeking to help others elsewhere. Accordingly, Reagan launched an invasion of the tiny island of Grenada in 1983, ostensibly to rescue American medical students there, but also so that the nation and the military could feel good about themselves again. Reagan also approved American aid to the Contras, a force fighting an armed insurrection against the leftist Sandinista government in Nicaragua. A majority of members of Congress, evidencing the power of the "Vietnam syndrome," voted for legislation prohibiting the aid. These policy differences eventually led to some members of the White House staff receiving criminal convictions for arranging aid to the Contras in violation of federal law.

When President George H. W. Bush prepared to send U.S. forces to the Persian Gulf region to counter the Iraqi invasion of Kuwait in 1990–1991, he first built up a massive force, sought international and domestic approval, and then launched the attack. He feared that Americans would not accept high casualties and would not support a protracted war like that in Vietnam. The leaders of the campaign, General Norman Schwarzkopf and General Colin Powell, were Vietnam veterans who had learned from their experience to enter a war with overwhelming force, achieve attainable goals, and exit the conflict. The resulting war was quick and decisive, albeit for limited objectives.

However, the absence of a new American policy consensus on the use of U.S. military force was seen in the hesitancy of the Bush and Bill Clinton administrations on how to respond to bloody civil strife in the Balkans in the 1990s. Even with the September 11, 2001, attacks on the World Trade Center and the Pentagon, questions abound concerning the war against terrorism. With U.S. forces committed in Afghanistan today, the comparison between this conflict and Vietnam continue almost daily. It is clear that the specter of Vietnam still looms large in American foreign policy.

Vietnam under Communism

With the fall of Saigon in April 1975, Vietnam was reunified under Communist rule. However, the government in Hanoi inherited a country that had been ravaged by 30 years of constant warfare. Infrastructure lay in ruins, and millions of refugees wandered the countryside. Economically, Vietnam suffered from a botched attempt at agricultural collectivization, high inflation, and isolation from the West. With little hope for a better future, nearly 1.5 million Vietnamese fled Vietnam in the late 1970s, usually by boat, seeking sanctuary in the West. More than 1 million of these refugees arrived and settled in the United States.

Compounding the problems facing the government of unified Vietnam was a long simmering dispute with Cambodia. The tensions exploded into open warfare following repeated raids by the Khmer Rouge into Vietnamese territory and the massacre of ethnic Vietnamese in Cambodia. On December 25, 1978, Vietnam invaded Cambodia. By January 7, 1979, Phnom Penh had fallen and the Khmer Rouge leadership fled to the rural areas; Hanoi placed a pro-Vietnamese Communist in control and left an occupation force of 140,000 troops in place as the conflict continued.

In retaliation for the Vietnamese invasion of its client state of Cambodia, China launched military attacks against the northern provinces of Vietnam. Beijing ended the campaign after about a month, having taught the Vietnamese a "lesson." Although the fighting was brief, the casualties were high on both sides.

As a result of continued war and the occupation of Cambodia, Japan and several Western nations withheld economic aid from Vietnam, and the now isolated country remained one of the world's poorest nations. In the 1980s, famine struck Vietnam and inflation rates reached a high of 600 percent. Agricultural production continued to fall even as Vietnam achieved one of the highest birth rates in the world.

Doi Moi

In 1986, with Vietnam beset by serious social and economic problems, a new group of more liberal socialist leaders in the Vietnamese Communist Party Congress abandoned the attempt to maintain a purely planned economy and announced the new policy of *Doi Moi*, or renovation, to help Vietnam come out of its economic crisis. This program, loosely patterned after the policies being promoted in the Soviet Union at the time, consisted of six new policies, including the introduction of some aspects of a market economy and decentralization of state economic management.

In addition to these new policies, the Vietnamese pursued a rapprochement with the United States. The first steps included overtures to Washington in August 1987 concerning the issue of American soldiers missing in action (MIA). Since the end of the war, the United States had demanded a full accounting of the fates of MIAs as a precursor to normalized relations, but initially the Vietnamese had been less than forthcoming in addressing the issue. Negotiations over the MIA issue opened a new dialogue between Hanoi and Washington. The liberalization of policies in Vietnam, the withdrawal of Vietnamese occupation troops from Cambodia, and the other factors mentioned above combined with the end of the Cold War to open a new phase in relations between Vietnam and the United States. In 1991, the Vietnamese government allowed the United States to set up a temporary office in Hanoi to coordinate the efforts to account for American MIAs. In 1993, President Clinton lifted the trade embargo on Vietnam, and the United States fully normalized relations with the country one year later. Slowly, Vietnam has begun the process of modernization, but despite the modest successes of the *Doi Moi* programs, the country remains hindered by Communist policies and a tremendously inefficient government. Although foreign investment is on the rise, great problems still exist. The population of some 90 million remains very poor, with an annual per capita income in 2012 of only $1300. In the end, though, it seems that a free market economy will ultimately take over Vietnam. American and other foreign businesses, undaunted by the bewildering Communist bureaucracy, are flocking to Vietnam, attracted by its natural wealth and cheap workforce. Although Vietnam remains a one-party state under a Communist system of government, the influx of foreign investment and the other changes that have transpired in recent years threaten to drastically transform the nation.

James H. Willbanks

Communist Strategy

The extents to which opposing sides in war are able to develop and adapt their strategies and tactics often proves to be the deciding factor that determines the victor. As each side seeks to find and exploit weaknesses in the other, both belligerents also strive to strengthen their defenses. Because the Vietnam War lasted more than two decades, there was an extensive amount of time in which military strategy could adapt and evolve. Thus, any understanding of that conflict must be built upon an analysis of the military strategies developed and employed by those countries and groups involved.

In the following Defining Moments, Dr. Barney J. Rickman III explores two events in the Vietnam War that stand as examples of the evolution of Communist strategy. In the first, he demonstrates how the Tet Offensive was the result of skilled planning, available strategic reserves, and a change in viewpoint on the part of the Communist Viet Cong and North Vietnamese. In the second Defining Moment, Dr. Rickman explores North Vietnam's Easter Offensive. This offensive, launched in 1972, represented another step in strategic evolution, as it employed conventional forces rather than guerrillas, which had been the backbone of Communist forces throughout most of the war to that point. Although the military results of both offensives were less than optimal for the Viet Cong and North Vietnamese, each proved to have dramatic consequences that would contribute to the Communists' eventual victory.

Defining Moment 1: Tet Offensive

The Communist Tet Offensive of January 1968 was a major turning point in the Vietnam War. During celebrations marking the arrival of the Lunar New Year, or Tet, the Viet Cong (VC) launched assaults on over 100 cities across South Vietnam, including the capital Saigon. Because the Lunar New Year was the most important Vietnamese holiday, prior to 1968 both sides had observed a cease-fire during Tet to allow Vietnamese to observe the traditional practice of returning to their home villages. Assisted by North Vietnamese troops sent south, the VC committed some 84,000 troops to this action. The widespread urban offensive surprised the American military in its timing and its intensity. The Americans expected an offensive, but they misread both its scale and exact timing, which most assumed would come after Tet.

Nineteen VC even assaulted the U.S. Embassy in Saigon. They used a bomb to breach the high wall surrounding the embassy; then attacked the embassy itself for six hours. The VC captured Hue, the ancient capital of Vietnam's emperors.

They could not, however, hold these positions when faced with superior American firepower. Americans killed or wounded all the VC who assailed the embassy in Saigon. In the following weeks, the U.S. military and Army of the Republic of Vietnam (ARVN, South Vietnamese Army) dislodged the Communists from all areas initially seized, including Hue. VC and North Vietnamese losses during the Tet Offensive have been estimated at 58,000, while the United States lost 3,895 Americans by March 31. Losses for the ARVN totaled 4,954.

Because enemy losses were so much higher than American and South Vietnamese military deaths, U.S. leaders proclaimed Tet a clear defeat for the VC and North Vietnamese, but the effects of Tet were ambiguous. The VC and the North Vietnamese failed to achieve their primary objective of instigating what they called a "General Offensive, General Uprising." The Communist leaders expected the Tet Offensive would spark urban uprisings to topple the South Vietnamese government. The United States would then leave Vietnam. Although the uprisings failed to occur and U.S. firepower pulverized the VC, the enemy achieved their secondary objective: to demonstrate that they had not been "broken," despite the U.S. efforts from 1965 to 1967. The VC hoped to discourage Americans by showing that no area of South Vietnam was safe. The Communists had also dealt pacification efforts a serious blow.

The Communists had paid a heavy price, however, with half of their forces becoming casualties. The Tet Offensive all but wiped out the VC as an effective fighting force. The North Vietnamese bore the brunt of the war thereafter.

North Vietnam and the VC followed a strategy of protracted war. As in the Indochina War with the French (1946–1954), the forces of Ho Chi Minh sought to exhaust their opponent over the long term. Prior to Tet, this strategy was usually implemented through guerrilla attacks in the countryside, but at a minimum the enemy expected Tet to accelerate U.S. frustration with an expensive war so far from home. A March 1968 public opinion poll found that 78 percent of Americans worried that the United States was making little progress in Vietnam. The American shock over the Tet Offensive's size was exacerbated because two months prior to the massive VC attack, General William Westmoreland, commander of U.S. forces in Vietnam, had assured Americans that the war in Vietnam was going well.

Although the United States suffered far fewer losses in Tet than did the VC and North Vietnamese, American actions to dislodge the enemy further undermined the stability of South Vietnam. As with U.S. actions from 1965 to 1967, the application of overwhelming firepower hurt the enemy, but this firepower also caused widespread collateral damage. An estimated 14,300 South Vietnamese civilians died in February 1968, and almost one million became refugees. In addition to this dislocation, the Communists, although hurt by Tet, did not surrender. The VC retreated into the countryside and returned to their earlier guerrilla tactics.

Barney J. Rickman III

Defining Moment 2: Easter Offensive

In a dramatic shift from its past guerrilla tactics, in 1972 North Vietnam launched a conventional invasion into South Vietnam. In late March, 125,000 North Vietnamese troops in 14 divisions and 26 separate regiments poured into South Vietnam from three directions using 1,200 tanks and armored vehicles. On March 30, the B-5 Front attacked south across the Demilitarized

Zone (DMZ). On April 2 the B-2 Front attacked across the Cambodian toward An Loc, the capital of Binh Long Province, just 65 miles from Saigon. On April 3 the B-3 Front attacked Kontum in the Central Highlands in an attempt to cut South Vietnam in two. As had happened during the Tet Offensive (1968), the enemy surprised American and South Vietnamese forces by the timing and size of this operation. North Vietnam quickly took large sections of northern South Vietnam, but, as in 1968, superior American firepower halted the offensive, turning back the North Vietnamese attackers at An Loc and Kontum. In addition to air attacks on northern forces in the south, President Richard M. Nixon ordered the bombing of North Vietnam, especially the supply lines for the invasion. In May, Nixon expanded the bombing beyond the limits of Operation ROLLING THUNDER. During June the United States hit North Vietnam with 112,000 tons of bombs. By late June the Easter Offensive ended as battle lines in South Vietnam stabilized.

Like the Tet Offensive, the effects of the Easter Offensive were ambiguous. On the one hand, North Vietnam failed to topple the South Vietnamese government, and the North suffered huge human and material losses: North Vietnamese casualties from the offensive and U.S. bombing may have exceeded 100,000. North Vietnam also lost half of its tanks and heavy artillery. Despite these losses, North Vietnam and the Viet Cong (VC) expanded their areas of control within South Vietnam. Perhaps most importantly, North Vietnam demonstrated problems in Nixon's Vietnamization initiative, launched in 1969. The president had gradually been replacing U.S. troops with South Vietnamese forces for the ground war in

South Vietnam. Although some South Vietnamese units performed well, others collapsed in the face of enemy attacks. South Vietnam's military, moreover, remained dependent on the United States. Without U.S. air support, South Vietnam probably could not have blunted the enemy offensive. U.S. firepower to halt the invasion, however, also hit many South Vietnamese. South Vietnam's casualties surpassed 105,000.

After the Easter Offensive, both sides compromised to reach a cease-fire agreement. The United States and North Vietnam had begun peace talks in 1968, but these meetings had achieved little, as neither was willing to compromise. By mid-1972, however, both sides were willing to make concessions to break the stalemate. Nixon had earlier demanded that all North Vietnamese troops withdraw from South Vietnam before he would remove U.S. troops and end air operations in Vietnam. By 1972 the president accepted that Northern forces would remain in the South even after the United States halted its military intervention. For their part the North Vietnamese had earlier stipulated that they would accept a political process on the future of South Vietnam only if the government of Nguyen Van Thieu was removed first. The North Vietnamese feared that Thieu would manipulate future elections as South Vietnamese leaders had done in the past. In 1972 North Vietnam agreed that Thieu could remain in power during the cease-fire and the period leading up to new elections. In the Paris Peace Accords (January 1973), future elections in South Vietnam would be supervised by a three-part commission of delegates from Thieu's government, the VC, and various neutralist groups.

Barney J. Rickman III

Opposition to the War

Opposition to the Vietnam War came from all directions. Some protesters were young idealistic students; others were grieving spouses or parents who had lost a loved one in Vietnam. There were soldiers who had witnessed the carnage firsthand and African Americans and other minorities who decried Vietnam as a "white man's war" in which they should play no part. There were musicians who performed songs of protest and movie and sports stars who used their celebrity to raise public awareness. Politicians who opposed the war tried to influence government policy directly. Some opposed the war for purely practical reasons (such as the rising cost in both lives and money), while others viewed the conflict as morally reprehensible. Many groups practiced non-violent forms of civil disobedience, while a few asserted that violence would be necessary for change. Some individuals and organizations remained tightly focused on the war, while others saw the crisis in Vietnam as a reflection of a larger sociopolitical crisis at home.

In the two Defining Moment essays that follow, Dr. Barney J. Rickman III examines the antiwar movement from two very different angles. In the first, he discusses Students for a Democratic Society (SDS), one of the best known college-based protest organizations from that time. Founded in 1960, SDS attracted idealistic young people who not only opposed the war, but also sought to tackle larger topics such as social injustice and capitalistic greed. In the second essay, Dr. Rickman explores Senator Robert F. Kennedy's denunciation of the war. Kennedy, an immensely popular Democrat, couched his opposition in much narrower and far less radical terms than did the SDS.

Defining Moment 1: SDS Opposes the War

In November 1965 Students for a Democratic Society president Carl Oglesby explained why his organization opposed the war in Vietnam. Oglesby's speech, at an antiwar rally in Washington, D.C., represented the "radical" strand in the emerging antiwar movement. The radicals (also labeled the "New Left") believed capitalism predetermined U.S. foreign policy. Oglesby argued that U.S. leaders intervened abroad to "safeguard what they take to be American interests around the world against revolution or revolutionary change." The SDS president asserted that because the American standard of living required access to inexpensive raw materials, the United States acted abroad primarily to secure that access. Oglesby blamed Third World poverty on American affluence. It "is a crime that so few should have so much at the expense of so many." To the radicals, the war in Vietnam reflected deeper problems of injustice within the United States. To reduce poverty at home and abroad, radicals believed Americans must accept dramatic change or a "revolution" in their capitalist "system" to ensure a more equitable distribution of resources and wealth.

The opposition of SDS to the war reflected the group's origins and early development. Founded in 1960 to encourage students to address injustice, SDS initially focused on supporting the civil rights movement and reducing poverty in the United States. Motivated by John F. Kennedy's call for national service, early SDS members expected rapid improvements in the United States, but many became disillusioned. Shocked by the violence of some southern whites against nonviolent civil rights protest, some SDS members were further dismayed when many African Americans remained poor even after the decline of racial segregation. This disillusionment caused many SDS members to accept a Marxist-based critique of the U.S. economy.

Historians debate the effect of the radicals on support for the Vietnam War. Although the radicals drew attention to the war, their ideas and actions alienated many. Most Americans rejected the idea that capitalism required systematic change. Many Americans were offended further when some radicals justified violence as acceptable protest. In 1967 an SDS leader encouraged attacks on military draft centers. The most radical SDS members broke from SDS in 1969 to form the Weathermen, a group that accepted the use of arson and bombing to advance "revolution." According to polling data, radical ideas and actions may have been counterproductive. In 1966 and 1967, even as Americans increasingly worried about the war, many hesitated to advocate withdrawal because

they did not want to be associated with the radicals. This hesitancy grew as some radicals glorified the North Vietnamese and Viet Cong. This glorification peaked in 1972 when actress Jane Fonda, married to SDS founder Tom Hayden, traveled to North Vietnam. During the war and after, many Vietnam veterans despised the radicals and especially "Hanoi Jane" for their wartime actions.

Defining Moment 2: Sen. Robert F. Kennedy Questions the War

After the Tet Offensive in early 1968, Robert Kennedy made public his concerns about Vietnam. In his actions and arguments, Kennedy reflected the emerging "antiwar liberal" strand of opposition to the war. Kennedy did not initially oppose U.S. actions in Vietnam. As U.S. attorney general (1961–1964), Kennedy supported the actions of his brother, President John F. Kennedy, to preserve South Vietnam. Elected to the Senate in 1964, Kennedy in 1965 accepted President Lyndon B. Johnson's actions to "Americanize" the war. During 1966 and 1967, however, the senator from New York became increasingly concerned about Vietnam, and in 1968 he voiced his worries.

In his address, Kennedy demonstrated that he was not an antiwar "radical." Kennedy did not question the fairness of capitalism; he did not call for a "revolution" at home, nor did he glorify the Viet Cong. The senator further distinguished himself from the radicals in his approach to Americans who served in Vietnam. As the radicals became more militant in the late 1960s, some criticized and even assaulted returning veterans for having participated in the war. Antiwar liberals did not malign veterans. Kennedy argued that for "the sake of those young Americans who are fighting today, if for no other reason, the time has come to take a new look at the war in Vietnam."

Kennedy argued U.S. policy in Vietnam was flawed because the pervasive corruption of South Vietnam's government undermined popular support. The senator believed it was an "illusion that we can win a war which the South Vietnamese cannot win for themselves. ... People will not fight to line the pockets of generals. ... " The senator also worried that the widespread use of firepower to defeat the enemy was killing too many civilians.

Historians have argued that antiwar liberals had more effect on public opinion than did antiwar radicals. The liberals gave legitimacy to opposing the war by describing specific problems with U.S. policy. The antiwar liberals may have been one reason why support for the war declined, but some historians have asserted that two factors limited the influence of the antiwar liberals. First, the antiwar liberals divided over tactical issues, especially whether men opposed to the war should avoid the draft. Second, presidents Johnson and Richard M. Nixon used the Federal Bureau of Investigation (FBI) and other agencies against the antiwar movement. FBI "moles" infiltrated the movement not only for surveillance, but also to act in ways that would discredit the entire movement as "un-American."

Kennedy's opposition to Vietnam ended on June 4, 1968, when an Arab nationalist assassinated him for his support of Israel. The senator had just won the California primary. Had he lived, Kennedy probably would have been the 1968 Democratic nominee for president.

Barney J. Rickman III

The Tet Offensive and the Media

Media coverage of the Vietnam War remains a source of controversy in the United States. Nowhere is that controversy more evident than in discussions of the media's coverage of the Tet Offensive in 1968. Up until that point, the media had mostly provided the American people with fleeting glimpses of the North Vietnamese forces in action, since the People's Army of Vietnam (PAVN, North Vietnamese Army) and the Viet Cong (VC) stayed mostly in the dense jungle or paddy areas of South Vietnam. During the Tet Offensive, however, much of the fighting took place in urban areas, providing ample opportunity for the media to get graphic footage of the fighting. In particular, the attack on the U.S. Embassy in Saigon received an inordinate amount of attention from the media because the Western press was stationed nearby. Back in the United States, millions of Americans watched scenes and viewed photographs of the embassy attack and the bloody Battle of Hue, witnessing the tenaciousness of the enemy for the first time. Doubts about U.S. progress toward ending the war were heightened during this time and prompted President Lyndon B. Johnson's decision not to seek reelection.

Jerry Morelock, the author of the first essay, asserts that the media missed the big picture of the Tet Offensive while focusing on individual combat actions. He points out that the attack on the U.S. Embassy in Saigon was a minor, failed action that received a disproportionate amount of attention from journalists stationed nearby. In addition, he states that the nearly monthlong Battle of Hue provided the media with numerous opportunities to take gruesome photographs of dead soldiers and civilians, obscuring the fact that U.S. forces achieved a major military victory at Hue. Clarence R. Wyatt, the author of the second essay, argues that the Tet Offensive was not the turning point in public opinion about the war that many make it out to be. He points out that support for the war had been steadily declining since 1965, and that by October 1967, three months before Tet, the majority of Americans believed U.S. involvement in Vietnam was a mistake.

Perspective 1: Media Coverage Turns Tet into a Defeat

How would you characterize a battlefield fiasco in which the attacking forces were totally defeated, every objective they captured was retaken, and the attackers lost 40,000 of their best troops killed, with tens of thousands more wounded? In 1968 the media represented North Vietnam's disastrous Tet Offensive to the American public as a "victory" for the North Vietnamese Army (NVA).

Hanoi planned the 1968 Tet Offensive to precipitate a general uprising among South Vietnam's presumably disaffected population that would force Saigon to accept a coalition government. Yet the savagery wreaked by NVA general Vo Nguyen Giap's countrywide attack dismally failed to evoke the expected popular uprising. However, battlefield success is no guarantor of final triumph in war, as the aftermath of the Tet Offensive so starkly demonstrated. Although U.S. and South Vietnamese forces weathered and then overcame Giap's assault, the shock that reverberated through the American public precipitated a downward spiral in popular domestic support for the war that turned the Communists' battlefield defeat into a public relations victory that arguably won the war for Hanoi.

No one can—or should—question the veracity of media reporting of the Tet Offensive or the truthfulness of its coverage of the Vietnam War in general, for that matter. With rare exceptions, the reporting was factual and accurate. Contrary to what some may claim, the media did not intentionally lie about what they saw, heard, and reported from Vietnam. Yet, getting the facts right did not ensure that reporters got the story right. Media coverage of the Tet Offensive is likely the most egregious example of reporting the facts of individual combat actions while missing the more important story of the big picture that those combat actions represented. Out of the hundreds of combat actions that occurred during Tet, two in particular garnered excessive media coverage that, in turn, produced an unexpected domestic political impact far beyond the modest scope and size of the forces involved and the relatively small body count in each case: the Viet Cong (VC) sapper attack on the U.S. embassy in Saigon and the Battle of Hue.

The Tet attack on the U.S. embassy in Saigon was a minor, unsuccessful assault by a small group of VC sappers that became a sensationalized media icon, hyped as symbolizing the United States' failed strategy in Vietnam. The embassy was added to the VC target list almost as an afterthought, and only 19 enemy soldiers took part. In fact, all VC attackers were eliminated, and none actually made it inside the embassy building. Yet, what one U.S. participant characterized as "a piddling platoon action" took place only a short distance from the main quarters for the Western press corps—a proximity that virtually guaranteed extensive media coverage by reporters who were either too shocked or too timid to venture very far afield. When Americans picked up their morning papers a few hours after the last VC sapper was killed, the first inklings they had of the Tet Offensive were inaccurate headlines stating that the U.S. embassy had been "captured." The panicked, often confused news reports—coming on the heels of President Lyndon Johnson's and U.S. Vietnam commander William Westmoreland's claims that America was winning the war—delivered a shock from which the public never recovered.

The battle for Vietnam's ancient imperial capital of Hue, in contrast to the failed, six-hour "piddling" action at the embassy in Saigon, lasted 26 days—the longest sustained infantry combat of the war to that point. A major NVA Tet objective, Hue was quickly captured by NVA regulars supported by VC main force units, thereby precipitating brutal, house-to-house fighting by U.S. forces to retake a city that was essentially a fort. The nearly monthlong battle for Hue provided ample opportunity for reporters to illustrate their coverage with gruesome photographs of dead marines, soldiers, and civilians, many showing bodies grotesquely stacked in trucks and hauled away under heavy fire. Although American forces recaptured the city, killing 5,000 North Vietnamese while losing 216 U.S. dead, the lopsided body count tally could never overcome the 26 days of pessimistic reporting and the barrage of bloody, negative images. By February 26, 1968, the American public was, almost literally, "shell shocked" by the intense media coverage.

These two combat actions and how reporters chose to present them, more than any other events reported by the media from Vietnam, exerted a negative and lasting influence on American public opinion and attitude toward the war. Reporters may have gotten their facts right, but they clearly missed Tet's "big picture" story—with ultimately tragic results for the people of South Vietnam. Beyond its influence on public perceptions about the Vietnam War, media reporting also had an unintended and long-lasting secondary impact that is still felt today. Soldiers' experience with how they perceived that the media reported Vietnam left many veterans of the conflict wary and distrustful of reporters. Many, particularly army officers who later reached high rank, became embittered and resolved to keep reporters at arm's length, providing only information that they were required to hand over, and even than often reluctantly and grudgingly. Although the recent program of embedding reporters within military units in combat is a belated attempt to reestablish an atmosphere of trust and openness, it may be too little, too late for military personnel who trace their roots back to the Vietnam generation. They had assumed that their war in Vietnam would be reported by Ernie Pyle; instead, they got Dan Rather.

Jerry Morelock

Perspective 2: Blaming Media Coverage of Tet Is an Oversimplification

On the morning of February 1, 1968, a Viet Cong agent, a small man in a plaid shirt, was seized by South Vietnamese Marines in central Saigon. Soon, General Nguyen Ngoc Loan, chief of the National Police, approached the man, drew his pistol and, without a word, fired a single round into the man's head. The man in the plaid shirt collapsed, his life and soul pouring onto the dirty Saigon street.

This death was not memorable because of the prominence of either the killer or the killed. It didn't change the tide of battle. Rather, it is memorable because Associated Press photographer Eddie Adams and NBC cameraman Vo Suu captured the event. Within hours, the photo and the film had been seen by millions of people around the globe; millions of people had witnessed the last moment of life for the man in the plaid shirt.

The photo and the film have also become part of the mythology that has grown up around the 1968 Tet Offensive and its coverage, a mythology that encapsulates the controversy over the press's role in the Vietnam War. This myth says that Tet was a watershed in public support of the war. It portrays public opinion before the event as supportive of or at least apathetic toward the war and claims that afterward public opinion swung against the war. Those who view Tet this way point to press coverage as one of, if not the, prime catalysts of this shift. They blame the press for distorting the character of the offensive, exaggerating both Viet Cong and North Vietnamese success and American and South Vietnamese desperation. In his memoirs, General William Westmoreland attacked the press for misrepresenting the actual course of events. Robert Elegant, a former correspondent for *Newsweek*, in 1981 cited Tet as a particularly grievous example of how the press sapped the public's will to pursue the war. Most of these critics ascribe the press's actions to gross incompetence, liberal bias, or outright disloyalty.

But this view fails to understand what shaped the actions and coverage of the war by mainstream American news organizations, most especially coverage of the Tet Offensive. Journalists in Vietnam—especially from the major news organizations—were some of the best the profession had to offer. Just as was the case for young military officers, a tour in Vietnam was considered an essential boost for up-and-coming reporters, many of whom went on to become some of the biggest names in American journalism for the next generation.

This perception of the press also does not recognize the challenges of covering American involvement in Vietnam. Most of the military action in Vietnam involved relatively small units, lasted for anywhere from a few minutes to a few hours, and took place all across a difficult landscape. Also, military action represented just one aspect of a conflict that involved important political, social, and economic issues crucial to success or failure. At the height of the press presence in Vietnam, some 600 individuals held press credentials, a small number to cover such a widespread and complicated story. The nature of the challenge becomes even starker when one realizes that of those 600 or so people, only about 125 to 150 were actual news-gathering journalists; the remainder were drivers, couriers, and office personnel.

These logistical challenges led to the development by 1965 of a largely cooperative relationship between news organizations and the U.S. government and military on the ground in Vietnam. The press needed steady access to information in order to cover the war; the government and military realized that if they provided the press that information, it could have significant influence on coverage. Thus, news organizations came to depend on official sources to cover a complex and far-flung conflict, and the government and military were able to use the news media to feed that information to the American public.

Finally, those who contend that incompetent or biased coverage shattered the American people's confidence in the war effort fail to see that support had been declining steadily since the commitment of American ground troops in large numbers in the spring and summer of 1965. The changes of opinion associated with Tet in 1968 had long been in the works. Editorial opinion, even of news organizations that had long supported Vietnam policy, was growing openly skeptical by the fall of 1967. Concern in Congress also grew steadily. Senior administration officials also became increasingly doubtful. Defense Secretary Robert McNamara had grown so concerned that earlier that year he authorized the secret study that came to be known as the Pentagon Papers. Even President Lyndon B. Johnson, who announced his withdrawal from the presidential race on March 31, had been contemplating retirement for some time.

However, the strongest repudiation of the view that the Tet Offensive turned the public against the war comes from the American public itself. From July 1965 to late 1972, the up-or-down measure of public support for the war effort was the question "Do you believe United States involvement in the Vietnam War to have been a mistake?" Well before Tet, in October 1967, for the first time, more Americans answered "yes" than "no" to that question in the wake of a significant increase in American casualties and the imposition of a 10 percent income tax surcharge to pay for the war.

The scale and audacity of the Tet Offensive startled the American public, just as it did American leaders in Saigon and Washington. Tet also pushed the press's fragile logistical base to the limit, resulting in some confused coverage in the attack's earlier hours, as Peter Braestrup ably described in *Big Story*. But the public had come to question the government's effort in Vietnam months before. The American people did not need the press or the government to tell them that the cost of the war, in blood and in money, had reached a price that they were increasingly unwilling to pay—that their sons, husbands, and brothers continued to die in a confusing, inconclusive war. In March 1968 the weekly paper in the small town of Brewton, Alabama, turned from its previous support of the war after two young soldiers from the town died during the fighting. "Like hundreds of other communities across the country," the paper's editor said, "the war came too close when it got to Brewton."

Clarence R. Wyatt

U.S. Involvement in Indochina

Politics and war are inextricably linked, impacting one another throughout a conflict. The fortunes of war and politics in Vietnam —the rise and fall of governments and the fates of nations and people—were no different. A full understanding of the United States' involvement in Indochina, beginning almost immediately after the end of World War II and lasting for some 30 years, is impossible without significant consideration of the key political events and decisions that shaped America policy.

In the Defining Moments that follow, Dr. Barney J. Rickman III analyzes the roles of two major political decisions by two different American presidents and how they contributed to U.S. involvement in Vietnam. President Dwight D. Eisenhower's creation of the Southeast Asia Treaty Organization (SEATO) in 1954 was in direct response to attempts by Communist-supported movements in the area to gain control of different nations there. More than a decade before U.S. combat troops were deployed to Vietnam, American forces, both political and military, were being brought to bear in the region. The great escalation of American military involvement in Vietnam took place after the summer of 1964, when President Lyndon B. Johnson asked for and received permission from Congress to exercise his executive authority as he saw fit to deal with the growing Communist insurgency in South Vietnam. This "blank check" from Congress was given in response to alleged North Vietnamese attacks on U.S. Navy vessels in the Gulf of Tonkin. These two events, more than a decade apart, serve as critical turning points in American policy toward Indochina.

Defining Moment 1: SEATO

President Dwight D. Eisenhower created the Southeast Asia Treaty Organization (SEATO) as one of his many efforts to oppose the Viet Minh forces led by Ho Chi Minh. Because Ho advocated Marxism, Eisenhower dismissed Ho as an insincere nationalist. Like President Harry S. Truman, Eisenhower believed that a Vietnam controlled by Ho would be subservient to the Soviet Union. On April 7, 1954, Eisenhower publicly asserted that a Viet Minh victory would start a domino effect of spreading communism throughout Asia. Eisenhower further feared the domestic political damage of "losing" Vietnam to communism. After the 1949 Communist victory in the Chinese Civil War, Truman's political foes had lambasted the president for losing China to communism.

Eisenhower therefore chose to accelerate Truman's efforts to oppose Ho. In 1953 Eisenhower increased U.S. assistance to the

French war effort against the Viet Minh. During the Battle of Dien Bien Phu (April–May 1954), Eisenhower considered a possible military intervention to relieve the French garrison surrounded by Viet Minh forces. Eisenhower eventually rejected military action because neither the U.S. Congress nor Great Britain would support it. Eisenhower opposed France's willingness to discuss Vietnam at the Geneva Conference (May–July 1954), but the French rejected U.S. advice because French opinion had tired of war. The United States refused to sign the Geneva Accords that allowed Ho to control the northern half of Vietnam and created a process for reunification in 1956 via elections.

Despite the Geneva Accords, Eisenhower continued to oppose Ho. During 1954, the Central Intelligence Agency (CIA) began covert operations in North Vietnam to undermine Ho's regime. In public, the United States made new alliances by creating SEATO. Joining with Britain, France, and five other nations, the United States pledged to defend Southeast Asia from communism. Although SEATO lacked the requirement for military action included in the North Atlantic Treaty Organization (NATO), the pact provided a vehicle for the United States to help create an independent South Vietnam. SEATO included a provision that allowed members to protect Vietnam south of the 17th Parallel. This American-led effort to treat the 17th Parallel as an international boundary violated the spirit, and perhaps even the letter, of the Geneva Accords. The accords had considered the 17th Parallel a "military demarcation line [that] is provisional and should not in any way be interpreted as constituting a political or territorial boundary."

In 1954, Eisenhower decided to support Ngo Dinh Diem as the leader of South Vietnam. Pro-American and anti-Communist, Diem seemed the best available leader to build a new U.S. ally in the Cold War. Right from the start, however, the new nation experienced problems. Because Diem had not participated in the war against the French, he lacked Ho's nationalist credentials. Ho had also built the Viet Minh, an effective organization with a popular base. Diem, by contrast, came to power as prime minister of a French-created puppet regime. Prior to 1954, the French had attempted to legitimate their rule by using Vietnamese such as Bao Dai, the last emperor of Vietnam. Bao Dai appointed Diem as prime minister in 1954. As the French withdrew, Diem used the Vietnamese bureaucracy and military established by the French as a base for South Vietnam, but his government failed to garner popular support, especially among peasants. A fervent Catholic, Diem alienated the Buddhist majority. Diem also incited opposition by violating the Geneva Accords. In an attempt to weaken popular support for Ho in the south, Diem arrested many members of the Viet Minh, even though such action was prohibited by the Geneva Accords. Diem also silenced debate over his policies by arresting critics and shutting down newspapers. In 1955, Diem announced that he would not allow South Vietnam to participate in any reunification elections in 1956 as mandated by the Geneva Accords.

Barney J. Rickman III

Defining Moment 2: Tonkin Gulf Resolution

After the assassination of John F. Kennedy on November 22, 1963, President Lyndon B. Johnson faced decisions on what to do with an increasingly precarious South Vietnam. Like earlier presidents, Johnson refused to let South Vietnam collapse because of the feared domino effect it would have on Asia and the domestic political damage it would cause the presidency. In early 1964 Johnson increased covert actions against North Vietnam. These sabotage operations dated back to the 1950s and had been expanded by President Kennedy. Johnson hoped that these operations would convince North Vietnam to stop aiding the Viet Cong (VC), but the U.S. effort failed. In 1964 North Vietnam began sending its own troops down the Ho Chi Minh Trail to supplement VC efforts to topple South Vietnam.

On August 2, 1964, North Vietnamese torpedo boats attacked a U.S. destroyer off the coast of North Vietnam in the Gulf of Tonkin. The *Maddox*, which was involved in identifying North Vietnamese radar and intercepting radio messages from international waters, was not damaged. The *Maddox* returned to the area accompanied by another U.S. destroyer, the *C. Turner Joy*. On August 4, crewmen on the two ships thought they were under attack because of sonar and radar reports, but the captains later decided the initial reports were probably mistaken.

Johnson acted on the initial news of a second attack, using it to order a retaliatory air strike against North Vietnamese naval installations and to push through Congress a resolution that would allow him to expand military action in Vietnam to block Communist aggression. In response to Johnson's claim that U.S. ships had been clearly attacked twice, Congress passed the resolution with almost no debate. Johnson did not tell Congress about either the espionage activities of the U.S. ships or the increased covert assaults on North Vietnam. Even before Congress passed the resolution, Johnson ordered the first bombing attacks on North Vietnam on August 5.

As South Vietnam's political stability and military effectiveness continued to decline in 1965, Johnson used the Tonkin Gulf Resolution to justify a gradual increase in U.S. military activities. In February 1965 the president approved the start of a gradually escalating bombing campaign (later code-named Operation ROLLING THUNDER) against North Vietnam. In March the first U.S. combat troops arrived in South Vietnam to protect U.S. air bases; by April these troops started ground assaults on VC forces. In July Johnson approved a significant expansion of ROLLING THUNDER and ground operations within South Vietnam.

In 1965, however, Johnson hesitated to escalate openly the U.S. involvement in Vietnam. In the weeks following the start of ROLLING THUNDER, the administration denied that any major change in U.S. bombing policy had occurred. The administration later obscured the extent of Johnson's July decisions. Although the president admitted that he had approved sending an additional 50,000 troops to South Vietnam, Johnson did not explain that he had also approved another 50,000 troops to be sent by December for a total of 100,000 additional troops in 1965. The president acted this way because he wanted Congress and the American people to focus on his Great Society domestic initiatives. Johnson often acted on Vietnam with secrecy as he sought a delicate balance. On the one hand, Johnson remained committed to preserving South Vietnam; on the other, he did not want Vietnam to overwhelm his other priorities, especially the Great Society.

Barney J. Rickman III

A

Abrams, Creighton Williams, Jr. (1914–1974)

U.S. Army general; commander, U.S. Military Assistance Command, Vietnam (MACV), during 1968–1972; and celebrated combat leader. Born on September 15, 1914, in Springfield, Massachusetts, Creighton Williams Abrams Jr. grew up in a family of modest means in the semirural setting of nearby Agawam. Graduating from the U.S. Military Academy, West Point, in 1936, Abrams was posted to the famous 7th Cavalry Regiment at Fort Bliss, Texas. When World War II loomed, he volunteered for armored service, finding there a mode of warfare entirely congenial to his own hard-driving and imaginative style of leadership.

Abrams rose to professional prominence as commander of a tank battalion that often spearheaded General George Patton's Third Army during World War II. Abrams led the forces that punched through German lines to relieve the encircled 101st Airborne Division at Bastogne during the Battle of the Bulge, earned two Distinguished Service Crosses and many other decorations, and received a battlefield promotion to full colonel. He inspired General Patton to say that "I'm supposed to be the best tank commander in the Army, but I have one peer— Abe Abrams. He's the world's champion."

After World War II, Abrams served as director of tactics at the Armor School, Fort Knox (1946–1948); graduated from the Command and General Staff College (1949); and was a corps chief of staff at the end of the Korean War (1953–1954). He graduated from the Army War College in 1953 and then was promoted to brigadier general in 1956 and major general in 1960. Abrams held a variety of staff assignments during this period, and from 1960 to 1962 he commanded the 3rd Armored Division. In 1963 he was promoted to lieutenant general and was made commander of V Corps in Germany.

When American involvement in Vietnam intensified, in mid-1964 Abrams was recalled from Germany, promoted to full (four-star) general from far down the list of lieutenant generals, and made the army's vice chief of staff. In that assignment during 1964–1967 he was deeply involved in the army's troop buildup, a task made infinitely more difficult by President Lyndon Johnson's refusal to call up reserve forces. In tandem with U.S. Army chief of staff General Harold K. Johnson, with whom he shared a set of professional values rooted in integrity and concern for the soldier, Abrams made an effective steward of the army's affairs.

In May 1967 Abrams was assigned to Vietnam as deputy commander of MACV. In that position he devoted himself primarily to the improvement of South Vietnamese armed forces, crisscrossing the country to see firsthand what units and commanders were doing and what they needed in the way of training, support, and guidance. When, during the 1968 Tet Offensive the Army of the Republic of Vietnam (ARVN, South Vietnamese Army) forces gave a far better account of themselves than was expected, Abrams rightly received much of the credit.

U.S. Army general Creighton W. Abrams Jr. (1914–1974) was deputy commander of the U.S. Military Assistance Command, Vietnam (MACV) during 1967–1968 and its commander during 1968–1972. As chief of staff of the army from 1972 to 1974, Abrams worked to rebuild the army and laid the foundation for its later success. (Herbert Elmer Abrams/Center for Military History)

Soon after the beginning of the Tet Offensive, Abrams was sent north to Phu Bai to take command of fighting in I Corps. Operating out of a newly established headquarters designated MACV Forward, Abrams concentrated on the battle to retake Hue, forming in the process a close relationship with ARVN general Ngo Quang Truong, commander of the ARVN 1st Division. Abrams coordinated the efforts of a growing assortment of U.S. Army and U.S. Marine Corps elements and ARVN forces while working to improve the logistical system.

After a month of hard fighting, Truong's forces cleared Hue and raised the Republic of Vietnam (RVN, South Vietnam) flag over the Citadel. Truong praised Abrams

for knowing exactly what his forces were doing and supplying them with what was necessary if they aggressively accomplished their mission. Soon it was announced that Abrams would assume the top job in Vietnam.

General Abrams formally assumed command of MACV on July 3, 1968, having been in de facto command since shortly after the Tet Offensive. As commander of MACV, Abrams changed the conduct of the war in fundamental ways. His predecessor's attrition strategy, search-and-destroy tactics, and reliance on body count as the measure of merit were discarded. "Body count," Abrams said, "is really a *long* way from what's involved in this war. Yeah, you have to do that, *I* know that, but the *mistake* is to think that that's the central issue."

Instead Abrams stressed population security as the key to success. He directed a one-war approach, pulling together combat operations, pacification, and upgrading South Vietnamese forces into a coherent whole. "In the whole picture of the war," he observed, "battles really don't mean much." Under Abrams, combat operations had as their ultimate objective providing security for the population so that pacification, the most important thing, could progress. "That's where the battle *ultimately* is won," he said.

Abrams was a consummate tactician who proved to have a feel for this kind of war. He urged his commanders to reduce drastically so-called H&I (harassment and interdiction) fires, unobserved artillery fire that he thought did little damage to the enemy and a good deal of damage to innocent villagers. He also cut back on the multibattalion sweeps that gave Communist forces the choice of terrain, time, and duration of engagement. He replaced these with multiple small-unit patrols and ambushes that blocked the enemy's access to the people, interdicting their movement of forces and supplies.

Abrams's analysis of the enemy system was key to this approach. He had observed that to function effectively the enemy needed to prepare the battlefield extensively, pushing forward a logistics nose instead of being sustained by a logistics tail, as in common military practice. This meant that many enemy attacks could be preempted if their supply caches could be discovered and captured or destroyed. Abrams also discerned that Communist main forces depended heavily on guerrillas and the Viet Cong (VC) infrastructure in the hamlets and villages, not the other way around, and that digging out that infrastructure could deprive the main forces of the guides, bearers, intelligence, locally procured food and supplies, and other elements that they needed to function effectively. These insights were key to revising the tactics of the war.

By April 1970 Abrams's staff had developed a briefing titled "The Changing Nature of the War." Change had been under way since Tet 1968, said the study: "Although shifts in the level of violence, type of military operations, and size and location of forces involved are characteristics of this change, the allied realization that the war was basically a political contest has, thus far, been decisive." The significant aspect was what Abrams had done about acting on that realization. "For the first time in the war," said the analysis, "the enemy's traditional bases of power are being directly challenged—his political organization and his control of the population." That, it appeared, was where the outcome of the war would be decided, because "both sides are finally fighting the same war."

Abrams's force of personality and strength of character were, during his years in command, at the heart of the American effort in Vietnam. Over the course of the years his army was progressively taken away from him, withdrawn chunk by chunk until he was in a symbolic sense almost the last man left. Still, Abrams did what he could to inspire, encourage, and support the remaining forces, American and Vietnamese alike.

A diplomat, observing the skill with which Abrams orchestrated the complex endeavor, once remarked that he "deserved a better war." That wasn't the way Abrams looked at it, recalled his eldest son: "He thought the Vietnamese were worth it."

Abrams left Vietnam in June 1972 to become army chief of staff. In that position he set about dealing with the myriad problems of an army that had been through a devastating ordeal. He concentrated on readiness and on the well-being of the soldier, always the touchstones of his professional concern. Stricken with cancer, Abrams died in office on September 4, 1974. However, he had set a course of reform and rebuilding that General John W. Vessey, former chairman of the Joint Chiefs of Staff (JCS), later recalled: "When Americans watched the stunning success of our armed forces in DESERT STORM, they were watching the Abrams vision in action. The modern equipment, the effective air support, the use of the reserve components and, most important of all, the advanced training which taught our people how to stay alive on the battlefield were all seeds planted by Abe."

Lewis Sorley

References

Buckley, Kevin. "General Abrams Deserves a Better War." *New York Times Magazine*, October 5, 1969.

Colby, William, with James McCargar. *Lost Victory: A Firsthand Account of America's Sixteen-Year Involvement in Vietnam.* Chicago: Contemporary Books, 1989.

Davidson, Phillip A. *Vietnam at War: The History, 1946–1975.* Novato, CA: Presidio, 1988.

Palmer, General Bruce, Jr. *The 25-Year War: America's Military Role in Vietnam.* Lexington: University Press of Kentucky, 1984.

Sorley, Lewis. *A Better War: The Unexamined Victories and Final Tragedy of America's Last Years in Vietnam.* New York: Harcourt, Brace, 1999.

Sorley, Lewis. *Thunderbolt: General Creighton Abrams and the Army of His Times.* 2nd ed. Bloomington: Indiana University Press, 2008.

African Americans in the U.S. Military

African Americans have served in every war waged by the United States. Throughout the nation's history, African American soldiers, sailors, and marines have contributed conspicuously to America's military efforts. From the American Civil War through the Korean War, segregated African American units, usually officered by whites, performed in both combat and support capacities. In 1948 President Harry Truman ordered the military establishment to desegregate. Although the U.S. Navy and the U.S. Air Force accomplished integration by 1950, the U.S. Army, with the vast majority of African American servicemen, did not achieve desegregation until shortly after the Korean War ended in 1953. The Vietnam War thus marked the first major combat deployment of an integrated military and the first time since the turn of the century that African American participation was actually encouraged.

In 1962 President John F. Kennedy reactivated the President's Committee on Equal

U.S. Army private first class Jerome Alexander and Sp4c. George Lightfoot, Company B, 2nd Battalion, 1st Infantry, 196th Light Brigade, fire at a suspected Viet Cong position during a search and destroy mission some six miles west of the city of Tay Ninh. (National Archives)

Opportunity in the Armed Forces. Chaired by attorney Gerhard Gesell and known as the Gesell Committee, the panel explored ways to draw qualified African Americans into military service. In 1964 African Americans represented approximately 13 percent of the U.S. population but less than 9 percent of the nation's men in arms. The committee found uneven promotion, token integration, restricted opportunities in the National Guard and the Reserves, and discrimination on military bases and in surrounding communities as causes for low African American enlistment. Before the government could react to the committee's report, the explosion of U.S. involvement in Southeast Asia changed the problem. An expanded military, a discriminatory draft, and other government programs brought not only increased African American participation but also accusations of new forms of discrimination.

U.S. involvement in Vietnam unfolded against the domestic backdrop of the civil rights movement, which had begun in earnest in the mid-1950s and accelerated rapidly in the early 1960s. From the outset the use, or alleged misuse, of African American troops in Vietnam brought charges of racism. Civil rights leaders and other critics, including the formidable civil rights leader Dr. Martin Luther King Jr., described the Vietnam conflict as racist: "a white man's war, a black man's fight." King maintained that black youths represented a disproportionate share of early draftees and that African Americans faced a much greater chance of seeing combat.

The draft did indeed pose a major concern. Selective Service regulations offered deferments for college attendance and a variety of essential civilian occupations that favored middle- and upper-class whites. The vast majority of draftees were poor, undereducated, and urban blue-collar workers or were unemployed. This reality struck hard in the African American community. Furthermore, African Americans were woefully underrepresented on local draft boards. In 1966 blacks accounted for slightly more than 1 percent of all draft board members, and seven state boards had no black representation at all.

Project 100,000, a Great Society program launched in 1966, attempted to enhance the opportunities of underprivileged youths from poverty-stricken urban areas by offering more lenient military entrance requirements. The project largely failed. Although more than 350,000 men enlisted under Project 100,000 during the remainder of the war, 41 percent were African American, and 40 percent drew combat assignments. Casualty rates among these soldiers were twice those of other entry categories. Few Project 100,000 inductees received training that would aid their military advancement or create better opportunities for civilian life.

African Americans often did supply a disproportionate number of combat troops, a high percentage of whom had voluntarily enlisted. Although they made up less than 10 percent of American men in arms and about 13 percent of the U.S. population between 1961 and 1966, they accounted for almost 20 percent of all combat-related deaths in Vietnam during that period. In 1965 alone, African Americans represented almost one-fourth of the army's killed in action. In 1968 African Americans, who made up roughly 12 percent of U.S. Army and U.S. Marine Corps total strengths, frequently contributed half the men in frontline combat units, especially in rifle squads and fire teams. Under heavy criticism, army and marine commanders worked to lessen black casualties after 1966, and by the end of the conflict African American combat deaths amounted to approximately 12 percent, more in line with national population figures. Final casualty estimates do not support the assertion that African Americans suffered disproportionate losses in Vietnam, but this in no way diminishes the fact that they bore a heavy share of the fighting burden, especially early in the conflict.

Destructive riots in Harlem in 1964, in the Watts district of Los Angeles in 1965, and in Detroit in 1967 had negative effects on the military, but the widespread violent reaction to the April 1968 assassination of Dr. King brought the greatest racial turmoil to the armed forces. After that, racial strife, rarely an issue among combat units because of shared risk and responsibility, became most evident in rear areas and on domestic installations. At the naval base at Cam Ranh Bay in the Republic of Vietnam (RVN, South

Vietnam), white sailors donned Ku Klux Klan–like outfits, burned crosses, and raised the Confederate flag. African American prisoners, many of whom were jailed for violent crimes, rioted at the U.S. Army stockade at Long Binh in South Vietnam; one white soldier was killed and several others were wounded during the upheaval, which spread over weeks. The Marine base at Camp Lejeune, North Carolina, and the army's base at Fort Benning, Georgia, were among the important domestic posts to witness serious racial problems.

African Americans played a major role in the Vietnam War and in the process changed the complexion of the U.S. armed forces. Contrary to popular impressions, a large proportion of African American servicemen were well-trained, highly motivated professionals; some 20 received the Medal of Honor, and several became general officers. Despite the likelihood of seeing hazardous duty, they reenlisted at substantially higher rates than whites. In 1964 blacks represented less than 9 percent of all U.S. armed forces; by 1976 they made up more than 15 percent of all men in arms. Much remained to be done. Although the percentage of African American officers doubled between 1964 and 1976, they still accounted for less than 4 percent of the total.

David Coffey

References

Appy, Christian G. *Working-Class War: American Combat Soldiers & Vietnam*. Chapel Hill: University of North Carolina Press, 1993.

Binkin, Martin, Mark J. Eitelberg, et al. *Blacks and the Military*. Washington, DC: Brookings Institution, 1982.

Dougan, Clark, and Samuel Lipsman. *A Nation Divided*. The Vietnam Experience Series. Boston: Boston Publishing, 1984.

Goff, Stanley, and Robert Sanders, with Clark Smith. *Brothers: Black Soldiers in the Nam*. Novato, CA: Presidio, 1982.

Nalty, Bernard C. *Strength for the Fight: A History of Black Americans in the Military*. New York: Free Press, 1986.

Airpower, Role in War

More than half of the $200 billion that the United States expended to wage the Vietnam War went to support air operations, including those of the U.S. Air Force, the U.S. Navy, the U.S. Army, and the U.S. Marine Corps; allied aviation; and civilian contract airlines. Although occasionally pivotal, especially in supporting ground operations, airpower was never decisive. The role of airpower in the Vietnam War remains subject to controversy and myth.

Airpower enthusiasts perpetuate the myth that if U.S. air forces had been unleashed, quick and decisive victory would have followed. To support their contention, they point to the so-called Christmas Bombings (Operation LINEBACKER II) in December 1972. Advocates of airpower claim that air operations did all they were asked to do and that they could have been more effective had their hands not been tied.

The myth perpetuated by some in the antiwar movement is that a cruel technology was unleashed on the people of Indochina. They claim that the cities of the Democratic Republic of Vietnam (DRV, North Vietnam) were carpet bombed and that napalm was used indiscriminately throughout the war. Although many of these claims are the result of ignorance or shoddy scholarship, some, such as the contention that 100,000 tons of bombs fell on Hanoi during LINEBACKER II, border on the fanciful.

Indeed, from 1962 through 1973 the United States dropped nearly eight million tons of

Four Republic F-105 Thunderchiefs radar bombing a North Vietnamese target on the direction of a Douglas B-66 Destroyer. From 1962 to 1973, the United States dropped nearly 8 million tons of bombs on Vietnam, Laos, and Cambodia. This compares to 3.4 million tons dropped by the Allies in all of World War II. (Department of Defense)

bombs on Vietnam, Laos, and Cambodia. The Republic of Vietnam (RVN, South Vietnam) received about half that tonnage, making it the most-bombed country in the history of aerial warfare, a dubious distinction for an ally. The air campaign resulted in the U.S. Air Force losing 2,257 aircraft. Total air losses for the U.S. Air Force, the U.S. Navy, the U.S. Marine Corps, and the U.S. Army came to 8,588 fixed- and rotary-wing aircraft.

Although missions against North Vietnam caught the popular imagination and perhaps inspired the most controversy, the focus of air operations was South Vietnam. Nearly 75 percent of all sorties (one aircraft on one mission) were flown in support of U.S. and Army of the Republic of Vietnam (ARVN, South Vietnamese Army) ground forces. Indeed, many veterans claim that they owed their survival to close air support by the air force and marines. But airpower played a larger role than dropping bombs. Helicopters provided unprecedented mobility to American and allied forces by hauling troops and artillery to and from the battlefield. Medical evacuation helicopters carried wounded—many of whom otherwise would not have survived—to modern rear-area medical facilities, where specialists performed life-saving surgery. Air force transports kept far-flung outposts such as Kham Duc and Khe Sanh supplied, even when they were surrounded by Communist forces and cut off from land lines of communications. Twin-engine, propeller-driven, side-firing gunships, such as the Douglas AC-47 Spooky and, later, the Fairchild AC-119 Shadow/Stinger and Lockheed AC-130 Spectre, went aloft at night to prevent Communist forces from overrunning isolated Special Forces outposts. Boeing B-52 Stratofortress ARC LIGHT missions pounded supply caches and sometimes obliterated entire Communist regiments when they massed for an attack. These were particularly effective during the siege of Khe Sanh in 1968 and at An Loc in 1972.

The unprecedented weight of this effort indicates that the primary role for airpower in Vietnam was in support of ground operations. This ran counter to the tenets of U.S. Air Force doctrine that held that airpower could be better used in a strategic air campaign against North Vietnam. The argument

can be made that airpower played a strategically counterproductive role in South Vietnam. Images of napalm bursting over villages and huts, of denuded forests resulting from the use of Agent Orange, and of bombs tumbling from B-52s fed the claims of the antiwar movement. On a more rational level, the argument can be made that the ability of the air force to provide support for troops actually prolonged the war by making it possible for army and marine forces on the ground to remain engaged in a conflict that they really did not know how to win.

Airpower used outside South Vietnam in so-called out-country operations accounted for nearly another four million tons of bombs. Out-country operations included three major air campaigns over North Vietnam, a series of interdiction campaigns along the Ho Chi Minh Trail in Laos, and various air operations over Cambodia. Of all the campaigns conducted out of country, only Operation LINEBACKER I, the air response to North Vietnam's Spring Offensive of 1972, was an unmitigated success. The rest either failed or are subject to conflicting interpretations.

Operation ROLLING THUNDER, the bombing of North Vietnam from March 2, 1965, to October 31, 1968, was the longest air campaign ever conducted by the U.S. Air Force. ROLLING THUNGER was an effort at both strategic persuasion and interdiction. Although the vast majority of historians agree that ROLLING THUNDER failed to achieve its stated objectives, the most ardent airpower enthusiasts claim otherwise. They maintain that Hanoi was on the verge of defeat when the bombing was curtailed following the 1968 Tet Offensive. Critics contend that the shift from what had been a guerrilla war, albeit with increasingly conventional aspects, to what had become much more a conventional war by 1969 was indicative both of Hanoi's ability to move supplies and troops to South Vietnam and of the failure of ROLLING THUNDER.

LINEBACKER I, the air response to Hanoi's 1972 Spring Offensive, was the most successful employment of airpower in the Vietnam War. The strategy of using conventional airpower to stop a conventional invasion was effective. The nature of the war in South Vietnam had changed by the spring of 1972, and Hanoi's 14 divisions fighting inside South Vietnam needed up to 1,000 tons of supplies a day to continue their operations. Furthermore, LINEBACKER I was the first modern air campaign in which precision-guided munitions (so-called smart bombs) played an integral role in a coherent and effective strategy. The use of conventional airpower to stop a conventional invasion made it the classic example of a successful aerial interdiction campaign.

LINEBACKER II (the "Eleven-Day War" as it is called by some airpower enthusiasts) took place during December 18–29, 1972. Some 739 B-52 sorties dropped 15,000 tons of bombs on targets in and around Hanoi, Haiphong, Vinh, and other major North Vietnamese cities. Fighter-bombers added another 5,000 tons. The North Vietnamese launched virtually every SA-2 surface-to-air missile (SAM) in their inventory to shoot down 15 B-52s, 9 fighter-bombers, a U.S. Navy reconnaissance jet, and a U.S. Air Force Sikorsky HH-53 Jolly Green Giant helicopter.

Airpower advocates claim that LINEBACKER II brought North Vietnam to its knees. They further contend that if airpower had been used with equal resolve at any point after 1965, the war could have been concluded quickly and on terms favorable to the United States. Critics point out that just as the nature of the war in 1972 was different than it was earlier, U.S. demands on Hanoi were also different. By 1972 most

American troops had been withdrawn. All that the leaders in Washington wanted was to get the remaining U.S. troops out and get prisoners of war back and for the Saigon government to survive for a reasonable interval. With its air defenses in shambles, however, Hanoi had little reason to test U.S. resolve. The bombing compelled them to sign an agreement that basically allowed for the continued withdrawal of U.S. forces and the return of prisoners of war held in North Vietnam and South Vietnam.

The Ho Chi Minh Trail in southern Laos was subjected to a massive aerial interdiction effort that dwarfed ROLLING THUNDER and LINEBACKER I combined. Bombing of the trail began in 1965 with Operations BARREL ROLL, STEEL TIGER, and TIGER HOUND. None of these had much effect on what was still a guerrilla war in South Vietnam. But as the war steadily escalated and the flow of supplies became more critical, the bombing increased. On November 15, 1968, two weeks after President Lyndon Johnson ended ROLLING THUNDER, Operation COMMANDO HUNT began. Before the United States stopped bombing Laos in February 1973, nearly three million tons of bombs were dropped, mostly on the Ho Chi Minh Trail.

COMMANDO HUNT was a series of seven campaigns, each of about six months' duration. During this effort, gunships such as the four-engine Lockheed AC-130 Spectre roamed over the trail at night using infrared sensors and low-light–level television to find trucks, which were then destroyed by their computer-aimed 40-millimeter (mm) cannon or 105-mm howitzers. B-52s flew up to 30 sorties a day to dump bombs into interdiction boxes around Tchepone (a key transshipment point) and in the four passes leading from North Vietnam into Laos and from Laos into South Vietnam and Cambodia. During the day, when few trucks ventured onto the trail, fighter-bombers attacked suspected truck parks, storage areas, and antiaircraft gun emplacements. But in the final analysis this massive employment of airpower, while generating statistical success, failed to curtail the flow of troops and supplies moving from North Vietnam into South Vietnam and Cambodia. In fact, airpower never effectively shut down the Ho Chi Minh Trail.

Air operations over Cambodia made up the last component of the out-country air war. Beginning with the secret Operation MENU (March 18, 1969–May 26, 1970) bombing until August 15, 1973, when Congress mandated an end to air operations over Cambodia, about 500,000 tons of bombs fell on People's Army of Vietnam (PAVN, North Vietnamese Army), Viet Cong (VC), and Khmer Rouge base camps and supply dumps. Although it is difficult to determine the effectiveness of this bombing, the argument can be made that the MENU bombing helped prevent a major buildup of Communist forces that would have preceded an attack toward Saigon. Had such an attack developed, Vietnamization and the continued withdrawal of American troops might have been jeopardized. On the other hand, despite the dropping of half a million ton of bombs, the Khmer Rouge steadily increased its strength and extended its hold on the countryside to win the war in April 1975.

Despite what may seem to be a succession of failures, airpower did some remarkable things. There were noteworthy technical and tactical innovations introduced during the Vietnam War. These included aerial defoliation of jungles and crop destruction, the development and employment of propeller-driven side-firing gunships, and the use of forward air controllers (FACs) to coordinate air strikes in South Vietnam and northern Laos. One of the greatest success stories for the U.S. Air Force was the development of a superb long-range combat aircrew search-and-rescue (SAR) capability. Although the recovery of downed aircrews is a good operational capability to have when rescuing downed pilots is a highlight of an air war, this says something about the overall performance of airpower.

The United States was the first major power to lose a war in which it controlled the air but was not, however, the last. In the 1980s the Soviet Union experienced some of the same frustrations in its long and bloody war in Afghanistan. What Vietnam did indicate for airpower is that winning or losing in warfare is much more than a function of sortie generation and firepower on targets. Airpower incorporates many factors, including politics, national will and resolve, geography, time, and the weather. Above all, warfare, especially limited warfare, is an art. U.S. airpower leaders in Vietnam may have been masters of airpower, but they were not masters of the art of war.

Earl H. Tilford, Jr.

References

Berger, Carl, ed. *The United States Air Force in Southeast Asia, 1961–1973: An Illustrated Account.* Washington, DC: Office of Air Force History, 1977.

Clodfelter, Mark. *The Limits of Air Power: The American Bombing of North Vietnam.* New York: Free Press, 1989.

Frankum, Ronald B., Jr. *Like Rolling Thunder: The Air War in Vietnam, 1964–1975.* New York: Rowman and Littlefield, 2005.

Michel, Marshall L., III. *The Eleven Days of Christmas: America's Last Vietnam Battle.* San Francisco: Encounter Books, 2002.

Momyer, William W. *Airpower in Three Wars: World War II, Korea and Vietnam.* Washington, DC: U.S. Government Printing Office, 1978.

Morrocco, John. *Rain of Fire: Air War, 1969–1973.* The Vietnam Experience Series. Boston: Boston Publishing, 1985.

Morrocco, John, et al., eds. *Thunder from Above: Air War, 1941–1968.* The Vietnam Experience Series. Boston: Boston Publishing, 1984.

Attrition

Attrition was the military strategy adopted by General William Westmoreland, commander of the U.S. Military Assistance Command, Vietnam (MACV), to win the Vietnam War. Also referred to as the body count syndrome, attrition became the measure of progress of a war in which neither conquering and holding enemy territory nor winning total victory were U.S. objectives. To Westmoreland and his supporters, the attrition strategy had two strengths in the effort to find, fight, and destroy the enemy: it appeared to be the quickest way to end hostilities, and it also preserved the traditional mission of the U.S. infantry. The goal of the strategy was to cajole the Viet Cong (VC) and People's Army of Vietnam (PAVN, North Vietnamese Army) to fight a midintensity war. U.S. forces would then destroy their opponents at a rate faster than the Democratic Republic of Vietnam (DRV, North Vietnam) or VC could replace them. Unfortunately, and despite its elegant logic, the attrition strategy suffered from four basic problems.

First, it did not account for the American people's historical antipathy toward long-drawn-out conflicts, especially in the absence of a formal declaration of war. In the case of Vietnam, this national hostility toward gradualism collided with two revealing statistics: North Vietnam had 13 million people available for military service during the war, and unlike other nations, which historically capitulated when they lost 2 percent of their prewar population, Hanoi readily and consistently accepted losses closer to 3 percent and showed no signs of surrender. Given these numbers, U.S. military analysts determined by 1969 that the attrition strategy had failed. The analysts concluded that based on 1965 rates of attrition, North Vietnam could have continued the war until 1981. Westmoreland's strategy was thus tragically overly optimistic. After the Tet Offensive in early 1968, the American people turned against the war, but the strategy had yet to succeed.

A second problem with the attrition strategy was that it vainly tried to turn what was at first largely an insurgency in the jungles of Southeast Asia into a conventional European-style war. But the Vietnam War was a war unlike anything the United States had ever fought. U.S. forces did perform extremely well in large operations that matched their European-style training; however, if North Vietnamese troops suffered defeat in conventional battles, they quickly reverted back to irregular warfare in which they employed hit-and-run tactics that minimized contact with U.S. troops. As a result, the Vietnam War was a mismatch in paradigms. The U.S. Army's approach, which emphasized body counts and conventional warfare, did not match North Vietnam's Maoist, largely unconventional strategy. The consequence was a grinding (and lengthy) war of attrition rather than a quick war of annihilation.

A third problem with attrition was that it was not compatible with the U.S. Army's pacification program. Not only did the strategy pull U.S. troops away from the population centers, but it typically allowed Hanoi to determine when and where combat would occur. As a result, Communist commanders could control their own attrition rates to a level low enough to sustain the war indefinitely and thus fatigue U.S. forces to the point of defeat.

The fourth problem with the attrition strategy was that it indirectly eroded the moral fiber of American forces. As the war staggered on, distinguishing insurgents from civilians remained a problem. Some U.S. units became less concerned about inflicting civilian casualties. Furthermore, field commanders began padding reports of enemy dead to make themselves appear more efficient and thus enhance their own prospects for promotion in what they saw was a dead-end war.

Adam J. Stone

References

Krepinevich, Andrew F., Jr. *The Army and Vietnam*. Baltimore: Johns Hopkins University Press, 1986.

Lewy, Guenter. *America in Vietnam*. Oxford: Oxford University Press, 1978.

Palmer, General Bruce, Jr. *The 25-Year War: America's Military Role in Vietnam*. Lexington: University Press of Kentucky, 1984.

B

Bao Dai (1913–1997)

The last of the Nguyen emperors. Bao Dai, son of Khai Dinh, was born in Hue on October 22, 1913, and was named Nguyen Phuoc Vinh Thuy. Educated in France, he lived with a wealthy dignitary's family under the charge of nannies and tutors and was immersed in the French language as well as French history, music, and art. He did not return to Vietnam until the death of his father, whose funeral he attended in November 1925. On January 8, 1926, he was crowned emperor, taking the imperial name Bao Dai ("Keeper or Preserver of Greatness" or "Protector of Grandeur") before returning to France. The French government did not permit him to return to Vietnam until September 10, 1932.

Enthusiastic about forming a loyal alliance between the colonial power and his own government, Bao Dai was left with little maneuvering room. The 1884 Treaty of Protectorate gave France the ability to manage affairs as it wished, and the Agreement of 1925 stripped the Vietnamese court of most of its remaining authority, leaving emperors with little to do except issue ritual decrees. All other matters would be left to the French resident superior.

Undaunted, Bao Dai began a series of reforms. He hoped in that fashion to erect a modern imperial government and to convince France to establish a framework allowing limited independence for Vietnam under his rule. He fired most of his Francophile mandarin advisers in order to bring new blood into the Vien Co Mat, or cabinet. He established the Commission of Reform, abolished the requirement that people prostrate themselves in his presence, and dissolved his official harem. In 1933 he promulgated his Labor Charter, prohibiting requisitioned labor except in time of public emergency. The French stymied his zeal at every turn, however.

In March 1934 Bao Dai married a daughter of the wealthy Nguyen Huu Hao, Marie-Therese Nguyen, who became Empress Nam Phuong. As Bao Dai's enthusiasm for reform waned, he settled into a sedentary life, browbeaten also by his mother. He complained of debilitating migraine headaches and neurasthenia, characterized by fatigue, depression, worry, and localized pains without apparent causes. He spent ever more time at his villa in Da Lat on hunting expeditions that lasted for weeks. With little else to do, he traveled regularly around Vietnam on ceremonial visits. He became a playboy governor, interested primarily in gambling, women, and hunting; reportedly he shot a large percentage of Vietnam's tigers. As the years passed he was increasingly occupied with gambling on the French Riviera and jet-setting from one spa to another.

Bao Dai cooperated with the Japanese during their World War II occupation and in March 1945, at their behest, declared independence from France in proclaiming the Empire of Viet Nam. In the few months allotted to this government Bao Dai tried to deal with northern famine, supported

Bao Dai, the last of Nguyen emperors. After the start of the Indochina War, Bao Dai struck a deal with the French leading to the creation of the State of Vietnam, but the French never permitted it real independence, and Bao Dai soon succumbed to a playboy lifestyle. (Library of Congress)

extensive press freedoms, and called on his people for support. It was not to be. With the collapse of the Japanese government, the Viet Minh took control during the August Revolution and called on Bao Dai to abdicate. This he did on August 25, 1945, becoming simply First Citizen Vinh Thuy. Elected to a seat in the new Viet Minh legislature from his dynasty's ancestral home in Thanh Hoa Province, Vinh Thuy quickly became dissatisfied with his Communist overlords and left his country as part of an official diplomatic delegation to China.

Bao Dai remained in Chongqing (Chungking) until September 1946, when he moved to Hong Kong and remained there through late 1947 until he returned to Europe.

In June 1946 French high commissioner for Indochina Admiral Georges Thierry d'Argenlieu created the Autonomous Republic of Cochin China as a means to limit Viet Minh power and called on Bao Dai to serve as its head. Unenthusiastic, Bao Dai called instead for real Vietnamese independence. Émile Bollaert, d'Argenlieu's replacement, continued to urge Bao Dai to return to Vietnam as chief of state. Bao Dai did so, somewhat reluctantly, after signing the Elysée Agreements with French president Vincent Auriol on March 8, 1949. Now designated as an Associated State within the French Union, the State of Vietnam received official acknowledgment on January 29, 1950, when the Elysée Accords were ratified by the French National Assembly. Bao Dai took up residence in Saigon and remained head of this government through the partitioning of Vietnam by the 1954 Geneva Conference and the first year of existence of the Republic of Vietnam (RVN, South Vietnam). In this capacity Bao Dai institutionalized corruption by his dealings with Le Van "Bay" Vien, leader of the Binh Xuyen gang, the illicit activities of which included control of opium trafficking, gold smuggling, racketeering, prostitution, and gambling in South Vietnam.

Following the 1954 Geneva Accords, Bao Dai, then in France, named Ngo Dinh Diem as his premier. Later regretting this move, Bao Dai tried to regain control, finally authorizing one of his generals to lead a coup against Diem. This failed, and Diem then called for an election to determine whether the nation should be a monarchy or a republic. Held on October 23, 1955, the voting was supervised by Diem's henchmen; Diem won handily and became the president of South Vietnam.

Bao Dai spent much of the remainder of his life at his chateau near Cannes. His first wife died in 1968, and the next year he married Monique Baudot. From these two marriages he had two sons and four daughters. With most of his royal fortune gone, Bao Dai spent the final years of his exile in a modest Paris apartment. He died in a military hospital in Paris on July 30, 1997.

Cecil B. Currey

References

Chapuis, Oscar. *The Last Emperors of Vietnam: From Tu Duc to Bao Dai.* Westport, CT: Greenwood, 2000.

Currey, Cecil B. "Bao Dai: The Last Emperor." *Viet Nam Generation* 6(1–2) (1994): 199–206.

Karnow, Stanley. *Vietnam: A History.* 2nd rev. and updated ed. New York: Penguin, 1997.

Marr, David G. *Vietnam 1945: The Quest for Power.* Berkeley: University of California Press, 1995.

BARREL ROLL, Operation (1964–1973)

Allied air campaign carried out in northern Laos primarily to support ground forces of the Royal Lao Government and General Vang Pao's Hmong (mountain people) irregular forces, trained by the U.S. Central Intelligence Agency (CIA). The area of operation stretched from the Laotian capital of Vientiane on the border of Thailand north to the strategic Plain of Jars and then northeast to the Pathet Lao capital of Sam Neua in Sam Neua Province bordering the Democratic Republic of Vietnam (DRV, North Vietnam).

Operation BARREL ROLL was born out of the North Vietnamese government to support implementation of the July 1962 Geneva Accords, which declared Laos an independent and neutral state. In 1963, when Prime Minister Souvanna Phouma failed to create a coalition government as a result of Communist intransigence, he called for and received U.S. military aid in the form of arms and supplies, including North American T-28D Trojan aircraft. These trainers were adapted to a counterinsurgency role as fighter-bombers.

In June 1964, in response to a Pathet Lao and People's Army of Vietnam (PAVN, North Vietnamese Army) spring offensive in the Plain of Jars, allied air forces, with approval from President Lyndon Johnson, commenced Operation BARREL ROLL in support of Royal Laotian forces. The first attacks were on June 9 by U.S. Air Force North American F-100 Super Sabres against Communist antiaircraft artillery (AAA). Throughout its nine years, BARREL ROLL operated under a strange set of rules of engagement; all air assets were controlled by the U.S. ambassador in Vientiane.

America's three ambassadors during this time were, in succession, Leonard Unger, William H. Sullivan, and G. McMurtrie Godley. As head of the so-called Country Team (i.e., all the Americans in-country), they were responsible for directing all air operations in northern Laos. Although they did not develop the details, they did validate targets, usually with approval of the Laotian government. No target could be bombed without their permission. Attacks were often limited to specific areas to avoid hitting irregular units operating beyond the control of allied authorities.

At the outset, the U.S. Air Force established Headquarters 2nd Air Division/Thirteenth Air Force at Udorn, Thailand, 45 miles from Vientiane to support the Royal Lao Air Force (RLAF). This command was headed by a major general who reported directly to the Thirteenth Air Force commander and the 2nd Air Division commander in Saigon as well as to the U.S. ambassadors in Thailand and Laos. This officer established actual directives for daily BARREL ROLL missions. The Udorn headquarters unit was redesignated Seventh Air Force/Thirteenth Air Force in April 1966 when the Seventh Air Force was established at Tan Son Nhut Air Base.

The U.S. embassy in Vientiane also had an air staff that by the end of 1969 had grown to 125 personnel. There were also air operations centers in each of the five military regions of Laos. In turn, American-flown forward air controllers (FACs), known as "Ravens," were also assigned to support Hmong units as well as Royal Laotian air and ground forces. Ravens flew Cessna O-1 Bird Dogs, Cessna U-17 Skywagons, and T-28Ds during their six-month tours of duty. They also employed Douglas C-47 Skytrains as airborne battlefield command and control centers. These tours were hazardous and unofficial, since the United States and Laos maintained the fiction of adhering to the 1962 Geneva Accords that forbade belligerent forces of any nation in Laos.

Between 1965 and 1973, the war in Laos took on a regular pattern tied to the region's weather. The makeup of the warring forces in Laos was almost exactly the opposite of those in Vietnam. In this case, the Communists had the regular army troops, tanks, and trucks, while the Hmongs, who did the vast majority of the fighting for the allies, operated most often as guerrilla or irregular units. Indeed, because Royal Lao Army (RLA) troops were generally poor fighters, U.S. interests increasingly depended on General Vang Pao's youthful soldiers. However, attrition soon took its toll, and by the 1970s the United States was also depending on Thai volunteer forces.

Given the relative size and firepower of Hmong and Communist forces (increasingly PAVN regulars), it was the Hmongs who used the monsoon season (April–August) to take to the offensive; the Pathet Lao and PAVN, needing open roads, used the dry season (September–March) to launch counterattacks. Even though Vang Pao's forces were most often outnumbered and outgunned, with significant support from U.S. and RLAF airpower they not only held their own but often launched highly successful offensives deep into Communist territory.

By August 1966 Hmong forces had pushed to within 45 miles of the North Vietnamese border, only to be countered by 14,000 PAVN regulars and 30,000 Pathet Lao. By April of the next year the Communist counteroffensive had overrun several key Royal Lao and Hmong villages and defensive positions including several Lima sites (LSs), mountaintop strong-point bases. By diverting significant numbers of aircraft from Operation ROLLING THUNDER in North Vietnam, intensive U.S. air strikes halted Communist advances and allowed Vang Pao's forces to go on the offensive during the monsoon season of 1967.

However, the dry season of late 1967 and early 1968 witnessed another counterattack led by PAVN regulars using Soviet tanks and Soviet AN-2 Colt aircraft to overrun several allied towns and bases, including the key LS85 position only 25 miles from Sam Neua and 180 miles west of Hanoi. LS85 had an important 700-foot runway and tactical air navigation system built by U.S. Air Force personnel in 1966. In late 1967 this system was augmented with an all-weather unit manned by 19 U.S. Air Force personnel. Not only did PAVN forces capture and destroy the site in March 1968, but they killed 7 of the U.S. airmen.

The ebb and flow of events continued in 1968 and 1969. The Communists employed more and better Soviet tanks and artillery throughout. In spite of these additions, RLA and Hmong forces enjoyed their greatest victories in the summer of 1969. By September of that year, supported by hundreds of BARREL ROLL sorties, they had taken nearly all of the Plain of Jars, including Xieng Khouang. They captured enormous caches of ammunition, supplies, food, and fuel as well as 12 frontline tanks, 13 jeeps, and 30 trucks.

Unfortunately for the allies, the Communist counteroffensive that began in December 1969 retook all the lost territory, including Xieng Khouang and most of the high ground surrounding the Plain of Jars. So significant was it that in February 1970 Ambassador Godley was forced to beg President Richard M. Nixon for Boeing B-52 Stratofortress strikes to save the situation.

During February 17–18, 1970, B-52s flew 36 sorties and dropped 1,078 tons of bombs. During the first battle for Skyline Ridge, B-52s, supported by truck-killing night-raiding T-28Ds, AC-47s, Fairchild AC-119 gunships, and Lockheed AC-130 Spectres, flew nearly 3,000 sorties. By March 18, 1970, Communist forces had been beaten back from Vang Pao's base camp at Long Tieng.

The next year the Communists repeated their successes during the second battle for Skyline Ridge, only to be pushed back again by determined Hmong defenders and 1,500 American air sorties. Between August and November 1972 a third PAVN offensive pushed to within 16 miles of Long Tieng, only to be halted by massive B-52 and General Dynamics F-111 Aardvark strikes.

On November 10, 1972, cease-fire talks began between the Pathet Lao and the Royal Lao Government of Souvanna Phouma. Anticipating a cease-fire, Communist forces used the negotiation period to mop up Royal Lao outposts on the Plain of Jars. On February 21, 1973, Washington signed the cease-fire agreement and all but abandoned its Laotian allies. While B-52 sorties were flown on February 23 followed by tactical aircraft sorties in April, because of potential cease-fire violations they were futile gestures. The last BARREL ROLL sortie was flown on April 17, 1973.

Before the end of the war, allied aircraft had dropped more than three million tons of bombs on Laos, three times the tonnage dropped on North Vietnam. Of this number, 500,000 tons were dropped in northern Laos. From 1965 to 1968, allied aircraft flew fewer than 100 sorties per day on average over northern Laos. In 1969 this number jumped to approximately 300, but in 1970 it fell back to 200 and from 1971 to 1973 returned to pre-1969 levels. As with other Laotian air operations such as STEEL

TIGER and TIGER HOUND, the numbers and performance were impressive but in the end proved fruitless.

William P. Head

References

Berger, Carl, ed. *The United States Air Force in Southeast Asia, 1961–1973: An Illustrated Account.* Washington, DC: Office of Air Force History, 1977.

Momyer, William W. *Airpower in Three Wars: World War II, Korea and Vietnam.* Washington, DC: U.S. Government Printing Office, 1978.

Morrocco, John. *Rain of Fire: Air War, 1969–1973.* The Vietnam Experience Series. Boston: Boston Publishing, 1985.

Morrocco, John, et al., eds. *Thunder from Above: Air War, 1941–1968.* The Vietnam Experience Series. Boston: Boston Publishing, 1984.

Schlight, John. *The War in South Vietnam: The Years of the Offensive, 1965–1968.* Washington, DC: Office of Air Force History, 1988.

Tilford, Earl H., Jr. *Crosswinds: The Air Force's Setup in Vietnam.* College Station: Texas A&M University Press, 1993.

Bundy, McGeorge (1919–1996)

Academic, foreign policy expert, special assistant to the president for national security affairs (1961–1966), and a key figure in the development of U.S. Vietnam policy. Born on March 30, 1919, in Boston, Massachusetts, McGeorge ("Mac") Bundy graduated from Yale University in 1940. As a young man he assisted former secretary of war Henry Stimson in writing his memoirs. Bundy then served as dean of the faculty of arts and sciences at Harvard University (1953–1961) before joining the John F. Kennedy administration as national security

McGeorge Bundy was one of the young, brash, bright advisers who gave the administration of John F. Kennedy its reputation for intellectual prowess and ideological toughness. Bundy was also one of President Lyndon B. Johnson's "Wise Men" and a key figure in the development of U.S. Vietnam policy throughout the war. (Yoichi R. Okamoto/Lyndon B. Johnson Presidential Library)

advisor. Bundy continued in this post under President Lyndon B. Johnson until February 1966. Robert Komer, one of Bundy's deputies, handled Bundy's job on an interim basis until Walt W. Rostow permanently assumed the position.

Bundy was known for his intelligence, although some thought him smug, even arrogant. But he was one of the most powerful and influential advisers in both the Kennedy and Johnson administrations and as such held the respect and confidence of both presidents. During his five years as special assistant, Bundy was intimately involved in critical decisions on the Vietnam War.

He was part of Kennedy's inner circle during the Buddhist Crisis of 1963 and the coup against Ngo Dinh Diem, president of the Republic of Vietnam (RVN, South Vietnam), that November. Bundy sought to ensure the survival of a democratic independent South Vietnam, but he did not want the United States to take over the fight against the Communist insurgents.

After the assassinations of both President Diem and President Kennedy in November 1963 and the passage of the Gulf of Tonkin Resolution in August 1964, Bundy changed his views. By the end of that year, he favored an enlarged U.S. role, including a graduated bombing campaign against the Democratic Republic of Vietnam (DRV, North Vietnam) and the buildup of U.S. troops in South Vietnam. He was in South Vietnam when the Viet Cong (VC) attacked the U.S. barracks and helicopter base at Pleiku in February 1965, killing nine Americans and destroying five aircraft, an event that helped to confirm his belief that the U.S. military had to intervene. He supported retaliatory air raids on North Vietnam and believed that a strong military presence would strengthen the position of the United States and South Vietnam in peace negotiations.

Yet even in the midst of the 1965 troop buildup, Bundy feared that the Americanization of the war would overwhelm civil reform programs and pacification efforts in South Vietnam. During 1965 he urged Johnson to enhance the pacification effort by allocating more resources and improving its management. By 1965 Bundy also began to question the continuing military escalation. He resigned from government service because he had already served more than five years, and he questioned continuing escalation in Vietnam. He had played an influential role in centralizing American management of pacification programs in

Washington under Robert Komer and in Saigon under Ambassador William Porter.

As one of Johnson's so-called Wise Men, Bundy continued to advise the president after leaving the administration. During the critical post–Tet Offensive meeting with Johnson in March 1968, Bundy supported de-escalation and a new approach to the war.

After leaving government, Bundy served as president of the Ford Foundation until 1979, at which time he left to become a professor of history at New York University for 10 years. In 1990 he joined the Carnegie Corporation of New York as the chairman of its committee on reducing the danger of nuclear war. He was its scholar-in-residence at the time of his death of a heart attack in Boston on September 16, 1996.

Richard A. Hunt

References

Barrett, David M. *Uncertain Warriors: Lyndon Johnson and His Vietnam Advisers.* Lawrence: University Press of Kansas, 1993.

Bird, Kai. *The Color of Truth: McGeorge and William Bundy, Brothers in Arms: A Biography.* New York: Simon and Schuster, 1998.

Goldstein, Gordon M. *Lessons in Disaster: McGeorge Bundy and the Path to War in Vietnam.* New York: Times Books, 2008.

Halberstam, David. *The Best and the Brightest.* New York: Random House, 1972.

Hunt, Richard A. *Pacification: The American Struggle for Vietnam's Hearts and Minds.* Boulder, CO: Westview, 1995.

Preston, Andrew. *The War Council: McGeorge Bundy, the NSC and Vietnam.* Cambridge: Harvard University Press, 2006.

Bundy, William Putnam (1917–2000)

Vietnam policy maker (1961–1969). Born in Washington, D.C., on September 24, 1917, William (Bill) Putnam Bundy was the brother of influential presidential adviser McGeorge Bundy. Bill Bundy was educated at Yale University and Harvard University and married the daughter of Secretary of State Dean G. Acheson. A liberal Democrat, Bundy worked at the Central Intelligence Agency (CIA) until his appointment as assistant secretary of defense for international security affairs. He became deputy secretary of defense for international security affairs in 1961 and eventually assistant secretary of state for East Asian and Pacific affairs.

Bundy, a devoted yet unheralded bureaucrat, knew Southeast Asia well and, as a supporter of U.S. objectives in the region, helped to frame policy for the Republic of Vietnam (RVN, South Vietnam). As a Cold War warrior and advocate of military force, he favored covert operations and questioned President John F. Kennedy's firmness. Bundy supported South Vietnamese president Ngo Dinh Diem and opposed pressuring his regime. Bundy thought that the Communist threat warranted a U.S. response and favored U.S. troop deployments to South Vietnam.

By 1964 Bundy bore much of the responsibility for Vietnam policy making. Intolerant of in-house dissent, he labored to stave off doubters while proposing to strike the Democratic Republic of Vietnam (DRV, North Vietnam) through interdiction of the port of Haiphong and through air attacks on transportation routes, industrial areas, and military bivouac areas. Such action, he believed, would bolster the South Vietnamese but required congressional authorization in the form of a resolution, the rough draft of which Bundy coauthored by late May 1964. Once Congress ratified the Gulf of Tonkin Resolution that August, Bundy again recommended forceful measures against the Hanoi government until its leadership decided to disengage.

In November 1964 President Lyndon B. Johnson created a unit of eight intermediate-level State Department, Defense Department, and CIA functionaries chaired by Bundy. Instructed to examine U.S. policy choices for Southeast Asia, the group offered three approaches: Option A advanced limited bombing, additional reprisals, and greater resort to clandestine operations; Option B pleaded an all-out air campaign from the outset; and Option C, which Bundy backed, called for a graduated pressure but was noncommittal regarding the use of U.S. combat troops.

Situated between administration hawks and doves, Bundy supported the Johnson administration's Vietnam policy until leaving government in 1969. Even though he supported air raids against North Vietnam in 1965, he expressed reservations about South Vietnam's leaders, generals Nguyen Cao Ky and Nguyen Van Thieu. Bundy went along with a bombing pause, yet he belittled a peace initiative by Florentine law professor Giorgio La Pira and questioned W. Averell Harriman's appointment as ambassador-at-large, tasked with representing the United States at the Vietnam War peace negotiations.

In 1966 Bundy accompanied President Johnson to the Honolulu Conference and felt relieved once the president decided against disengagement following the Buddhist Crisis. However, disenchantment with the president's management style and the poor coordination of the war effort contributed to a growing pessimism about escalation that brought Bundy to the brink of hopelessness after the 1968 Tet Offensive. He left government service when Johnson left office in January 1969.

From 1969 to 1971, Bundy served as a senior research associate at the Center for International Studies at the Massachusetts Institute of Technology. He then joined the faculty of Princeton University, a position he retained from 1972 to 2000. Between 1972 and 1984, he was also an editor of *Foreign Affairs*. Bundy also published several books before he died in Princeton, New Jersey, on October 6, 2000.

Rodney J. Ross

References

Bird, Kai. *The Color of Truth: McGeorge and William Bundy, Brothers in Arms; A Biography*. New York: Simon and Schuster, 1998.

Halberstam, David. *The Best and the Brightest*. New York: Random House, 1972.

Herring, George C. *LBJ and Vietnam: A Different Kind of War*. Austin: University of Texas Press, 1994.

Sheehan, Neil, et al. *The Pentagon Papers: As Published by the New York Times*. New York: Bantam, 1971.

Bunker, Ellsworth (1894–1984)

U.S. ambassador to the Republic of Vietnam (RVN, South Vietnam), 1967–1973. Born on May 11, 1894, in Yonkers, New York, Ellsworth Bunker graduated from Yale in 1916 and entered the family sugar business. Not until midlife, after an extremely successful international business career, did he become a diplomat.

Named first to be U.S. ambassador to Argentina, Bunker later held that same rank in Italy and then in India. He was U.S. representative to the Organization of American States (OAS) at the time of the 1965 U.S. intervention in the Dominican Republic. Bunker played a key role in promoting a moderate civilian government there and worked closely with Lieutenant General Bruce Palmer Jr., the American commander of OAS forces. Bunker was lauded as a naturally skilled and highly effective diplomat.

Arriving in Saigon as U.S. ambassador in April 1967, Bunker established the practice

Ellsworth Bunker was the U.S. ambassador to the Republic of Vietnam (RVN) for six years, during 1967–1973. His open support for RVN president Nguyen Van Thieu drew criticism in some quarters. (Lyndon B. Johnson Presidential Library)

of sending periodic reporting cables to the president. These constitute an impressive record of sound judgment and wise counsel, including his insight into military matters. After General Creighton Abrams took command, Bunker often emphasized, as he did in an October 1968 cable, that U.S. authorities were stressing more heavily than ever before that there was only one integrated military effort rather than separate wars of big battalions, pacification, and territorial security.

On the political side, Bunker's reporting was both practical and timely. In May 1968 he cabled that most Vietnamese regarded peace negotiations with trepidation and expected few results to come from them. Bunker consistently urged that the United States not cease bombing the Democratic Republic of Vietnam (DRV, North Vietnam) until it provided a serious commitment to cease activity in the Republic of Vietnam (RVN, South Vietnam). The wisdom of this approach was demonstrated when, on the representations of W. Averell Harriman, the United States accepted vague assurances that reciprocity would be demonstrated, only to see the enemy subsequently deny that there had been any "understandings" while simultaneously violating their supposed terms.

Bunker developed great regard for the South Vietnamese during his years in their country. He also appreciated and stressed how the Vietnamese were taking on a growing share of the financial burden of prosecuting the war. He reported that in 1967 American support for the budget accounted for 40 percent of the total, in 1968 it was 24 percent, and in 1969 it was projected to be 16 percent. Furthermore, he believed that the Vietnamese reacted with great resolution and perseverance to the war.

Bunker's regard for President Nguyen Van Thieu also grew year by year. Bunker in turn enjoyed the wide respect of leaders of the South Vietnamese government. Bunker did draw criticism from some quarters for his open support for Thieu in the 1967 and 1971 elections, however.

Bunker served as ambassador to South Vietnam for six years, a longer time than any other senior American official, military or civilian, had been in continuous service there.

Between 1973, when he left his post, and 1978, Bunker performed an important last public service as chief negotiator of the Panama Canal Treaty. He died on September 27, 1984, in Brattleboro, Vermont.

Lewis Sorley

References

Bunker, Ellsworth. *The Bunker Papers: Reports to the President from Vietnam, 1967–1973*. 3 vols. Edited by Douglas Pike. Berkeley, CA: Institute for East Asian Studies, 1990.

Johnson, Lyndon B. *The Vantage Point: Perspectives of the Presidency, 1963–1969*. New York: Holt, Rinehart and Winston, 1971.

Kissinger, Henry. *White House Years*. Boston: Little, Brown, 1979.

Nixon, Richard M. *RN: The Memoirs of Richard Nixon*. New York: Grosset and Dunlap, 1978.

Schaffer, Howard B. *Ellsworth Bunker: Global Troubleshooter, Vietnam Hawk*. Chapel Hill: University of North Carolina Press, 2003.

C

Cambodian Incursion (April 29–July 22, 1970)

Joint U.S. Army and Army of the Republic of Vietnam (ARVN, South Vietnamese Army) invasion of officially neutral Cambodia. With progress in pacification, Vietnamization, and U.S. troop withdrawals, 1970 may have passed quietly were it not for the overthrow of Cambodia's neutralist Prince Norodom Sihanouk on March 18. Pro-U.S. prime minister General Lon Nol closed the port of Sihanoukville and sent his small army, the Forces Armées Nationale Khmer (FANK, Khmer National Armed Forces), against an estimated 60,000 Vietnamese Communist troops entrenched in three border provinces. On April 4, 1970, the Vietnamese Communist Party's Politburo directed Vietnamese Communist forces in the Republic of Vietnam (RVN, South Vietnam), in cooperation with Cambodian Communist forces, to seize control of the 10 Cambodian provinces that bordered South Vietnam. The Politburo's reference to "cooperation with Cambodian communist forces," which were extremely weak at that time, was essentially a facade. In his postwar memoirs, senior Vietnamese Communist leader Vo Chi Cong admitted that in April 1970 after Khmer Rouge leader Ieng Sary rejected a Vietnamese offer to send troops to "liberate" northeastern Cambodia, the Vietnamese disregarded Ieng Sary's response and sent several People's Army of Vietnam (PAVN, North Vietnamese Army) regiments into Cambodia from Vietnam's Central Highlands. The Vietnamese then informed Ieng Sary of their action after the fact. PAVN and Viet Cong (VC) forces went on to occupy two more Cambodian provinces and threaten Phnom Penh itself.

What became known as the Cambodian Incursion actually began in early April when Republic of South Vietnamese forces, ostensibly with Lon Nol's assent and unaccompanied by American advisers, mounted multibattalion raids against Communist bases in the Parrot's Beak next to the III Corps border. Surprised PAVN and VC forces withdrew deeper into the Cambodian jungles, but by April 20 the ARVN claimed to have killed 637 PAVN/VC troops while losing 34.

U.S. leaders viewed these raids with alarm, emphasizing to South Vietnamese president Nguyen Van Thieu the need to keep Cambodia neutral. But when Communist forces seriously threatened the new government in Cambodia, U.S. Military Assistance Command, Vietnam (MACV), commander General Creighton Abrams argued for a full ARVN intervention with U.S. combat support. On April 25, despite opposition from Secretary of Defense Melvin Laird and Secretary of State William Rogers, President Richard Nixon ordered both ARVN and U.S. ground forces into Cambodia to relieve pressure on FANK, to destroy Communist sanctuaries, and perhaps to capture the elusive headquarters of the Central Office for South Vietnam (COSVN), assumed to be located in the Fishhook area. Broader goals included demonstrating the progress of Vietnamization, buying time for additional U.S. troop

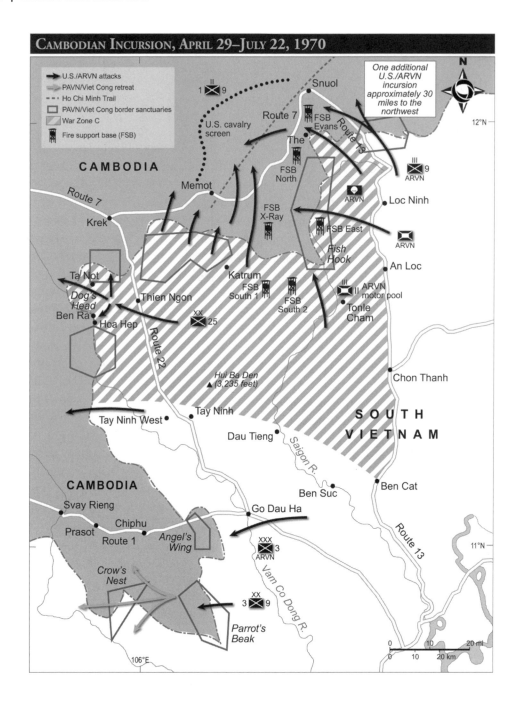

CAMBODIAN INCURSION, APRIL 29–JULY 22, 1970

One additional
U.S./ARVN
incursion
approximately 30
miles to the
northwest

Legend:
- U.S./ARVN attacks
- PAVN/Viet Cong retreat
- Ho Chi Minh Trail
- PAVN/Viet Cong border sanctuaries
- War Zone C
- Fire support base (FSB)

CAMBODIA

Snuol

Route 7   FSB Evans
The
FSB North
Memot   FSB X-Ray   ARVN   Loc Ninh
U.S. cavalry screen
Route 7
Krek   FSB East   ARVN
Fish Hook   An Loc
Ta Not   Katrum
Dog's Head   Thien Ngon   FSB South 1   FSB South 2   ARVN motor pool
Ben Ra   Hoa Hep   25   Tonle Cham
Route 22
Hui Ba Den
(3,235 feet)   Chon Thanh
Tay Ninh West   Tay Ninh
Dau Tieng   Saigon R.
Ben Suc   Ben Cat
CAMBODIA
Svay Rieng   Go Dau Ha
Chiphu   Angel's Wing   ARVN   3   Route 13
Prasot   Route 1
Crow's Nest
Vam Co Dong R.
3   9
Parrot's Beak

SOUTH VIETNAM

N   12°N   11°N
106°E   0 10 20 mi   0 10 20 km

withdrawals, and breaking the bargaining stalemate.

The Cambodian Incursion involved 50,000 ARVN and 30,000 U.S. troops and was the largest series of allied operations since Operation JUNCTION CITY in 1967. Troops were divided among three groups of operations: TOAN THANG (TOTAL VICTORY), conducted by ARVN III Corps and the U.S. II Field Force; CUU LONG (MEKONG), conducted by the ARVN IV Corps; and BINH TAY (TAME THE WEST), conducted by the ARVN II Corps and the U.S. I Field Force. The ARVN would operate more than 37.28 miles inside Cambodia, while U.S. forces would penetrate only 18.64 miles. Ordered by Abrams to be ready to move into the Fishhook on 72 hours' notice, Lieutenant General Michael S. Davison, II Field Force commander, met with Lieutenant General Do Cao Tri, ARVN III Corps commander, and Major General Elvy Roberts, commander of the U.S. 1st Cavalry Division (Airmobile), to select areas of operation. Roberts quickly assembled a joint task force but without clear guidance about the real objectives or the duration of the operation and lacking hard intelligence about the Communist situation.

Set for April 30, the hastily planned Fishhook invasion was delayed to allow ARVN forces to initiate Phase I of Operation TOAN THANG 42 on April 29, which was aimed at clearing Communist base areas in the Parrot's Beak. Because this operation was entirely run by the ARVN, it attracted little media attention. During the first two days, an 8,000-man ARVN III Corps task force, including two infantry divisions, four Ranger battalions, and four armored cavalry squadrons, killed 84 Communist soldiers while suffering 16 dead and 157 wounded.

Phase II began on May 2, with ARVN III Corps forces attacking south of Route 1 into the Parrot's Beak, while an ARVN IV Corps task force pushed north. The Communists broke contact after losing 1,043 killed and 238 captured; ARVN casualties were 66 killed and 402 wounded. Hundreds of individual and crew-served weapons and tons of ammunition were captured. In Phase III, which began on May 7, ARVN forces killed 182 retreating Communist soldiers near

Prasot and also discovered a 200-bed hospital and several supply caches.

The allies also rushed thousands of small arms and ammunition to Lon Nol's army, which quickly expanded to more than 100,000 men but retreated into urban areas and never launched a real offensive. When the ARVN linked up with FANK forces, it discovered that Khmer soldiers had murdered hundreds of ethnic Vietnamese. ARVN troops avenged these acts by looting several Cambodian towns. In Phase IV as ARVN forces began clearing Route 1 as far as Kompong Trabek, some 30 miles inside Cambodia, President Thieu began assembling an armed flotilla to sail up the Mekong to repatriate as many as 50,000 ethnic Vietnamese.

Ironically, while the ARVN was concerned with rescuing ethnic Vietnamese, the Cambodians asked them to relieve a FANK garrison under siege at Kompong Cham northeast of Phnom Penh. In Phase V of TOAN THANG 42, General Tri rushed a column of 10,000 men to accomplish this mission, but ARVN forces would have to retake Kompong Cham in June, inflicting and absorbing significant losses. When the Communists overran Kompong Speu southwest of Phnom Penh on June 13, a 4,000-man ARVN mechanized force quickly advanced to retake the town. ARVN and FANK troops then cleared Route 4 from Phnom Penh to Sihanoukville, which had been blockaded by the Republic of Vietnam Navy (VNN, South Vietnamese Navy). TOAN THANG 42 had upset Communist plans to overthrow the Lon Nol regime and accounted for 3,588 Communist killed or captured and the seizure of more than 2,000 weapons, 308 tons of ammunition, and 100 tons of rice.

The second stage of the Cambodian Incursion, called TOAN THANG 43–46, was a series of joint U.S.-ARVN operations aimed at clearing Communist sanctuaries located in the densely forested Fishhook area. Commanded by Brigadier General Robert H. Shoemaker, deputy commander of the 1st Cavalry Division, the initial task force consisted of the 1st Cavalry's 3rd Brigade (reinforced by a mechanized infantry battalion), the 11th Armored Cavalry Regiment (ACR), and the ARVN 3rd Airborne Brigade. TOAN THANG 43 began early on May 1, coinciding with President Nixon's televised announcement that the incursion would "guarantee the continued success of our withdrawal and Vietnamization program." Following extensive preparatory support by Boeing B-52 Stratofortress bombing, tactical air strikes, and artillery fire, an armada of U.S. helicopters inserted the ARVN Airborne troops into three landing zones (cleared by dropping 15,000-pound bombs) to block escape routes. The 1st Cavalry's 3rd Brigade and the 11th ACR then advanced across the border in what Roberts described as "a walk in the sun." On the first day, 1st Squadron, 9th Cavalry (1-9 Cavalry), gunships and ARVN Airborne troops accounted for 259 killed and 7 captured from the PAVN 7th Division.

General Davison then ordered the 11th ACR to move north to capture the Communist-occupied town of Snoul. When sporadic fire greeted the armored column, the town was leveled in two days of incessant bombardment. No dead PAVN soldiers were found, only the bodies of 4 civilians. As the expectation of open-battlefield victories faded, the mission of TOAN THANG 43 largely became one of seizing and destroying supply depots. After entering the Fishhook on May 2, the 1st Cavalry Division's 2nd Brigade stumbled into a massive but lightly defended supply base extending over 1.15 square miles of jungle and dubbed

"The City." Although not the COSVN, The City contained large weapons and ammunition caches and a training base with 18 buildings, including mess halls and a surgical hospital. Captured materials included more than 2,000 individual and crew-served weapons, two million rounds of ammunition, and nearly 40 tons of foodstuffs. By mid-June, allied forces in the Fishhook also captured or destroyed more than 300 trucks and other vehicles. TOAN THANG 43 accounted for 3,190 Communist soldiers killed or captured.

TOAN THANG 44 began on May 6 as the U.S. 25th Infantry Division's 1st Brigade, including two mechanized battalions, drove across the border west of Tay Ninh to search for Enemy Base Area 354. By May 14 in engagements south of the Rach Ben Go, the American forces accounted for 302 killed or captured and more than 300 weapons, 4 tons of ammunition, and 217 tons of rice seized. Also on May 6, the 1st Cavalry Division's 2nd Brigade initiated TOAN THANG 45, aimed at Enemy Base Area 351 located north of Phuoc Long Province. Facing only sporadic contact, the brigade uncovered the largest depot ever captured during the war, so huge that it was dubbed "Rock Island East." As at The City, the tonnage of supplies was so great that a road was built to remove them. By June, the entire 1st Cavalry Division was inside Cambodia and, amid frequent contact with Communist forces, uncovered many more weapons and supply caches as well as a vehicle-maintenance depot and an abandoned communications depot.

TOAN THANG 45 accounted for 1,527 Communist troops killed or captured and 3,500 weapons, 791 tons of ammunition, and 1,600 tons of rice seized. 1st Cavalry Division units repelled numerous harassing attacks as they rushed to meet the withdrawal deadline. Their last firebase in Cambodia was dismantled by June 27, and all troops were back inside South Vietnam by June 29.

Simultaneously with TOAN THANG 45, an ARVN 5th Division regiment and a squadron of the ARVN 1st Armored Cavalry Regiment launched TOAN THANG 46 against Enemy Base Area 350, north of Binh Long Province. ARVN forces discovered another surgical hospital and several major caches of supplies and ammunition. By June 20 increased Communist activity forced the termination of TOAN THANG 46 but not before it accounted for 79 Communist soldiers killed or captured and 350 weapons, 20 tons of ammunition, and 80 tons of rice seized.

ARVN IV Corps troops initiated Operation CUU LONG I, designed to open the Mekong River, on May 9. Within two days the ARVN 9th and 21st divisions, augmented by five armored cavalry squadrons, cleared both banks of the river, allowing a 100-ship convoy (including 30 U.S. vessels) to reach Phnom Penh and proceed north to Kompong Cham. By May 18 the convoy had repatriated nearly 20,000 Vietnamese held in refugee camps. Simultaneously, ARVN III Corps forces cleared Route 1 as far as Neak Luong.

In CUU LONG II, from May 16 to May 24, ARVN IV Corps troops joined FANK forces in recapturing Takeo, 25 miles south of Phnom Penh, and cleared Route 2 and Route 3, killing 613 Communist troops while suffering only 36 killed and 112 wounded. IV Corps forces then launched CUU LONG III, again joining with FANK forces to reestablish control over towns south of Phnom Penh and to evacuate more ethnic Vietnamese.

Two days after the Parrot's Beak and Fishhook incursions began, the allies decided to expand operations to attack Communist base areas in northeastern Cambodia facing II Corps. In this operation, designated Operations BINH TAY I–IV, allied forces included the ARVN 22nd and 23rd Infantry divisions, the 2nd Ranger Group, the 2nd Armor Brigade, and two brigades of the U.S. 4th Infantry Division. These operations are absent from most accounts of the incursion, perhaps because American participation was relatively brief and poorly executed. In fairness, Major General Glen D. Walker's 4th Infantry Division was over-extended, having recently relocated to Binh Dinh Province, leaving the ARVN in control of the western Central Highlands. Having no forward installations and only limited logistical and artillery support, the 3rd Battalion, 506th Infantry (3-506 Infantry), had to abort its initial insertion into Cambodia on May 4. The next day the 1st Battalion, 14th Infantry (1-14 Infantry), joined them in a successful insertion, but heavy hostile fire downed several helicopters. Joined by the 2-8 Infantry on May 6, 4th Division troops uncovered an abandoned PAVN training camp that included a 30-bed hospital and tons of supplies.

After his understrength battalions took significant casualties without making direct contact with Communist forces, Walker decided to turn the operation over to the ARVN. All 4th Infantry Division troops left Cambodia by May 16. When terminated on May 25, BINH TAY I had accounted for 212 Communist dead and the seizure of more than 1,000 weapons and 50 tons of rice. Allied casualties were 43 killed and 18 wounded.

In BINH TAY II, from May 14 to May 27, battalions of the ARVN 22nd Division swept across the border from Darlac Province searching for Enemy Base Area 701. Contact was limited, but the ARVN uncovered several more caches of weapons and supplies. In BINH TAY III, from May 20 to June 12, the ARVN 23rd Division searched for Enemy Base Area 740, located west of Ban Me Thuot. The most dramatic event was the destruction of a 10-truck convoy. In BINH TAY II and III, ARVN forces killed 171 while losing 30 dead and 77 wounded. In BINH TAY IV, from June 23 to June 27, an ARVN 22nd Division task force of military and civilian vehicles, supported by U.S. artillery and helicopter gunships, moved deep into Cambodia along Route 19 to reach a beleaguered FANK garrison at Labang Siek and managed to evacuate more than 7,000 Khmer soldiers and dependents across the border to Pleiku Province. All II Corps ARVN troops left Cambodia by June 27.

Although all American ground forces had departed Cambodia by June 30, President Thieu considered the survival of Lon Nol's regime vital to Saigon and would not be bound by the deadline. ARVN units continued operating up to 37 miles inside Cambodia into 1971, supported by U.S. long-range artillery, tactical air support, and B-52 bombings.

During the Cambodian Incursion the amount of supplies uncovered was 10 times more than that captured inside Vietnam during the previous year: 25,401 individual and crew-served weapons; nearly 17 million rounds of small-arms, 200,000 rounds of antiaircraft, and 70,000 rounds of mortar ammunition; 62,022 hand grenades; 43,160 B-40 and 2,123 107-millimeter (mm) or 122-mm rockets; 435 vehicles; 6 tons of medical supplies; and 700 tons of rice. The total was enough to supply 54 Communist main-force battalions for as much as a year. The human cost also was great: officially, at least 11,349 Communist, 638 ARVN, and 338 U.S. killed; 4,009 ARVN and 1,525 U.S. wounded; and 35 ARVN and 13 U.S. missing. In addition, 2,328 Communist soldiers rallied or were captured.

U.S. national security advisor Henry Kissinger believed that the Cambodian Incursion dealt a stunning blow to the Communists, drove main-force units away from the border and damaged their morale, and bought as much as a year for the survival of the South Vietnamese government. During 1970 and 1971 the ARVN held the initiative on all battlefields in South Vietnam. The incursion temporarily reduced the pressure on Lon Nol, lessened the dangers to withdrawing American troops, and showcased the improvement of the ARVN.

But while enhancing Vietnamization, the operations also exposed critical tactical and organizational deficiencies in the ARVN and its complete dependence on U.S. air support. The facade of renewed ARVN strength became evident during the disastrous Laotian incursion in February 1971.

The short-term gains from the Cambodian Incursion actually may have boomeranged. Knowing that American intervention would be limited in both time and scope, Communist forces avoided open confrontation and quickly returned to reclaim their sanctuaries and reestablish complete control in eastern Cambodia. The PAVN compensated for its temporary losses in Cambodia by seizing towns in southern Laos and expanding the Ho Chi Minh Trail into an all-weather network capable of handling tanks and heavy equipment, eventually enabling the PAVN to overrun much of southern Laos with massive conventional assaults. Furthermore, the continuing withdrawal of U.S. combat units from III Corps forced the ARVN to deploy an excess of troops there, thus reducing their strength in northern South Vietnam where the Communist threat grew incessantly. In the long run, the Cambodian Incursion posed only a temporary disruption of the march of Communist forces toward the domination of all of Indochina. Despite Nixon's boast in July 1970, the prospects for a "just peace" were as dim as ever.

Hanoi now believed that little could be gained through negotiations.

An unanticipated result of the Cambodian Incursion was to give the antiwar movement in the United States a new rallying point. Dissent was not limited to campus confrontations such as the tragedies at Kent State University in early May and at Jackson State later that month but also led to a series of congressional resolutions and legislative initiatives that would severely limit the executive power of the president. By the end of 1970, Congress had prohibited expenditures for U.S. forces operating outside of South Vietnam.

Finally, the widening of the battlefield in 1970 eventually left Cambodia the most devastated nation in Indochina. To avoid massive allied bombings, Communist forces spread deeper inside Cambodian territory, and Lon Nol's army, receiving only minimal U.S. assistance, would struggle futilely for five more years against both the Khmer Rouge and the PAVN. The Cambodian Incursion had turned the war into one for all of Indochina, and the departure of U.S. troops left a void too great for the ARVN or FANK to fill.

John D. Root

References

Davidson, Phillip A. *Vietnam at War: The History, 1946–1975.* Novato, CA: Presidio, 1988.

Military History Institute of Vietnam. *Victory in Vietnam: The Official History of the People's Army of Vietnam, 1954–1975.* Lawrence: University Press of Kansas, 2002.

Nolan, Keith William. *Into Cambodia: Spring Campaign, Summer Offensive, 1970.* Novato, CA: Presidio, 1990.

Shaw, John M. *The Cambodian Campaign: The 1970 Offensive and America's Vietnam War.* Lawrence: University Press of Kansas, 2005.

Stanton, Shelby L. *The Rise and Fall of an American Army: The U.S. Ground Forces in Vietnam, 1965–1975.* Novato, CA: Presidio, 1985.

Tran Dinh Tho. *The Cambodian Incursion.* Washington, DC: U.S. Army Center of Military History, 1979.

Vo Chi Cong. *Tren Nhung Chang Duong Cach Mang (Hoi Ky)* [On the Road of Revolution: A Memoir]. Hanoi: National Political Publishing House, 2001.

China, People's Republic of, Policy toward Vietnam

The People's Republic of China (PRC) has had a long and tumultuous history with Vietnam. A small Vietnamese state called Van Lang had been founded in this region as early as 2879 BCE. But in 111 BCE Van Lang, now called Nam Viet under the Trieus, was overrun by the Han dynasty and was gradually absorbed into the Chinese empire. Despite intensive Chinese influence and more than 1,000 years of Chinese rule, however, in 939 CE the Vietnamese reclaimed their independence from China and expanded south of the Red River Valley. This new state was called Dai Viet (Great Viet).

Although Dai Viet remained a tributary state of China and adopted many Chinese customs and practices, it retained its political autonomy until the nineteenth century. During this period Dai Viet successfully assimilated the Champa kingdom from the Chams and seized the Mekong Delta from the crumbling Khmer empire. At the end of the nineteenth century, however, Vietnam was conquered by France and was joined with the French protectorates of Laos and Cambodia into the Union of Indochina.

After World War II the Chinese Communists supported Ho Chi Minh's Viet Minh guerrillas against France. Following the

Following the defeat of Guomindang (Nationalist) forces, on October 1, 1949, in Beijing, Chinese Communist leader Mao Zedong officially proclaims the establishment of the People's Republic of China. (AP/Wide World Photos)

1949 Communist victory in the Chinese Civil War, Chinese aid to the Viet Minh increased. PRC support was vital to the Viet Minh. The Chinese not only supplied arms, many of them captured U.S. weapons supplied to the Guomindang (GMD, Nationalist) regime of China and captured during the civil war, but their long common border allowed the Chinese to set up training camps and base areas. Chinese military assistance played a key role in the Viet Minh victory in the 1954 Battle of Dien Bien Phu. The leaders of the Democratic Republic of Vietnam (DRV, North Vietnam) were not happy when, at the 1954 Geneva Conference, PRC premier Zhou Enlai pressured Ho Chi Minh to accept the "temporary" division of Vietnam at the 17th Parallel as well as a relatively long wait before national elections were to be held (two years). Zhou Enlai also agreed to recognize the states of Cambodia and Laos, in large part because the PRC sought to curtail Vietnamese influence over the remainder of Southeast Asia.

The promised elections were not held, however. The civil war in Vietnam was then renewed, and Hanoi adopted the people's war strategy favored by Chinese Communist leader Mao Zedong. The PRC was the first Communist state to recognize the National Front for the Liberation of South Vietnam (National Liberation Front [NLF]). The PRC also provided substantial material support to the insurgents, including considerable quantities of arms and help in the movement of supplies. Mao was determined to keep Hanoi in the fight, and after the early August 1964 Gulf of Tonkin Incident, China, which had been training the first North Vietnamese jet fighter regiment at a Chinese air base in southern China, arranged with the Vietnamese for the fighter regiment to fly their aircraft (36 MiG-17s) to a Vietnamese airfield north of Hanoi. A Chinese instructor pilot named Tao Minh flew with the regiment's lead element during the flight south to Vietnam.

The PRC leadership expressed outrage over U.S. escalation of the war in 1965, and in April of that year China signed an agreement with North Vietnam providing for the introduction into North Vietnam of Chinese air defense, engineering, and railroad troops to help maintain and expand lines of communications within North Vietnam. China later claimed that 320,000 of its troops served in North Vietnam during 1965–1971 and that 1,000 died there. The Vietnamese state that several Chinese engineering divisions built, maintained, and repaired roads and railroad lines from the Chinese border south to Hanoi from 1965 to 1969 and that the Chinese 68th, 168th, and 170th Air Defense divisions, along with a number of other antiaircraft units, were sent to Vietnam a year later and engaged U.S. aircraft from late 1966 through the end of the ROLLING THUNDER bombing campaign (late 1968) in the provinces located north and northeast of Hanoi. China probably provided some three-quarters of the total military aid given to North Vietnam during the war. Vietnamese figures show that the Soviet Union provided a total of 513,582 tons of military aid, including weapons, ammunition, equipment, and logistics supplies, during the period 1954–1975, while China provided nearly 1.6 million tons of military aid during the same period. However, the value of China's military aid probably represented only about one-quarter of the total value of all military aid received by North Vietnam. Chinese aid to North Vietnam between 1949 and 1970 is estimated at $20 billion. While China's government refused to allow Soviet aircraft to overfly Chinese airspace to Vietnam, it did permit the Soviets to ship military assistance to North Vietnam over its railroad network.

The PRC took a hard line during negotiations between Hanoi and Washington. For the first time, however, the Chinese did endorse a North Vietnamese peace plan for ending the war in 1971. Worsening Sino-Soviet diplomatic relations and warming Sino-American friendship did play a role in ending the Vietnam War during the early 1970s. Certainly President Richard Nixon's historic February 1972 visit to China shocked the North Vietnamese leadership and may have led it to put more pressure on Hanoi to reach a peace settlement, which was finally accomplished in January 1973.

Diplomatic relations between China and the Socialist Republic of Vietnam soon soured, however, leading to military clashes during the late 1970s. In November 1978 Vietnam signed a treaty of friendship and cooperation with the Soviet Union, and in early 1979 Vietnamese forces invaded Cambodia and installed a pro–Hanoi government there. In response and on behalf of the ousted Khmer Rouge government, Chinese troops invaded Vietnam the same year, and the two countries fought a short but costly border war that left the Sino-Vietnamese border virtually unchanged. During this entire period an estimated 1.4 million Vietnamese, many of them ethnic Chinese, fled Vietnam by boat. Approximately 50,000 of these so-called boat people perished at sea, while about one million settled abroad, including some 725,000 in the United States.

In the 1990s Sino-Vietnamese relations developed into a new phase of cooperation. This was largely the result of the collapse of communism in Eastern Europe and the dissolution of the Soviet Union in 1991, which left the two governments isolated in a much smaller and far less powerful Communist bloc. Apparently putting aside inherent conflicts and past confrontations, the governments of China and Vietnam thereafter maintained as smooth a relationship as they could manage. In the early 2000s both nations continued to foster a mutual rapprochement as trade and cultural exchanges increased. In December 2007 Hanoi and Beijing announced their intention to construct a major highway linking the two countries, which will go a long way toward demilitarizing their shared border and fostering improved economic and political relations.

Bruce Elleman and Spencer C. Tucker

References

Butterfield, Fox. *China: Alive in the Bitter Sea*. New York: Times Books, 1982.

Chen, King C. *China's War with Vietnam, 1979: Issues, Decisions, and Implications.* Stanford, CA: Hoover Institute Press, 1987.

Fairbank, John King. *The Great Chinese Revolution, 1800–1985.* New York: Harper and Row, 1992.

Hsü, Immanuel C. Y. *The Rise of Modern China.* New York: Oxford University Press, 1995.

Nguyen Van Minh, ed. *Lich Su Khang Chien Chong My Cuu Nuoc, 1954–1975, Tap IV, Cuoc Dung Dau Lich Su* [History of the Resistance War against the Americans to Save the Nation, 1954–1975, Vol. 4, A Historic Confrontation]. Hanoi: National Political Publishing House, 1999.

Spence, Jonathan D. *The Search for Modern China.* New York: Norton, 1990.

Ta Hong, Vu Ngoc, and Nguyen Quoc Dung. *Lich Su Khong Quan Nhan Dan Viet Nam (1955–1977)* [History of the People's Air Force of Vietnam (1955–1977)]. Hanoi: People's Army Publishing House, 1993.

Civil Operations and Revolutionary Development Support

Umbrella organization for U.S. pacification efforts in the Republic of Vietnam (RVN, South Vietnam). Civil Operations and Revolutionary Development Support (CORDS) organized all civilian agencies involved in the pacification effort in South Vietnam under the military chain of command. Established under the Military Assistance Command, Vietnam (MACV), on May 10, 1967, CORDS was placed under the direction of Robert Komer, a MACV civilian deputy commander. Komer, special assistant to President Lyndon B. Johnson, held the rank of ambassador and the military equivalent of three-star general and reported directly to MACV commander General William C. Westmoreland. Upon Komer's departure in November 1968, William

Colby, who had been the assistant chief of staff for CORDS, took direction of CORDS.

CORDS succeeded the Office of Civil Operations (OCO), originally created to assume responsibility over all civilian agencies working in South Vietnam under the jurisdiction of the U.S. embassy in Saigon. CORDS integrated American aid programs targeting the social and economic development of South Vietnam. These were viewed as the basis upon which to build the Vietnamese nation and win the hearts and minds of the Vietnamese people in the face of Communist political and military opposition. CORDS activities were primarily directed toward the 80 percent of the South Vietnamese population who lived in the rural villages and hamlets most vulnerable to the Viet Cong (VC). In this way, the Communists would be deprived of their traditional population base.

CORDS was organized into six operational divisions: Chieu Hoi, Revolutionary Development, Refugees, Public Safety, Psychological Operations, and New Life Development. The Chieu Hoi (Open Arms) program was designed to induce VC and People's Army of Vietnam (PAVN, North Vietnamese Army) soldiers to turn themselves in to the South Vietnamese government as *hoi chanh* ("returnees") through government propaganda campaigns and monetary payments. Returnees were given job training, welfare services, and resettlement assistance and were also integrated into Army of the Republic of Vietnam (ARVN, South Vietnamese Army) military units.

The Revolutionary Development (RD) division was organized into 59-member teams designed to provide security and promote economic development at the village level. RD teams were trained at the National Training Center in Vung Tau and assigned to villages throughout the country. Working through the U.S. Agency for International

Development (USAID), the refugee program was designed to resettle millions of displaced villagers across the country, often through the establishment of refugee resettlement centers, and to provide them security.

CORDS integrated all military and civilian personnel into a single chain of command by assigning them to the same missions through the establishment of CORDS advisory teams at the province level. During 1968, for example, in the 12 II Corps provinces some 4,000 CORDS personnel served under the operational command of CORDS deputy James Megellas, who held the military equivalent of major general and reported directly to Lieutenant General William R. Peers, commander of I Field Force, Vietnam. CORDS teams at the province level consisted of State Department, USAID, U.S. Information Agency (USIA), and U.S. Public Health Service personnel. In Khanh Hoa Province, for example, Team 35 had 87 military and 23 civilian personnel, including foreign service officers, public health nurses, and rural health and agricultural advisers. Priority projects in 1968 were the resettlement of Montagnard tribesmen and improving the quality and effectiveness of Regional Forces/Popular Forces (RF/PF) units to provide security at the village level.

With the war intensifying and the increasing vulnerability of civilian aid efforts in the countryside, providing security for what became known as nation building or pacification became a military priority. In September 1969 there were 6,464 U.S. military advisers assigned to CORDS, 5,812 of whom served in the field. Major efforts were made within the U.S. Army in particular (which had 95 percent of CORDS military advisers) to assign qualified military advisers to CORDS advisory teams. Three army civil affairs companies (the 2nd, 29th,

and 41st companies) were directly involved in pacification programs under CORDS administration. Major efforts were also made under both Komer and Colby to improve the effectiveness of RF/PF units by increasing both their manpower and their firepower equivalent to local VC units. By the end of 1969, RF/PF units numbered 475,000 men. Their effectiveness was a major factor in providing security at the village level in support of pacification efforts.

With the January 1973 Paris Peace Accords and the withdrawal of American armed forces, the rationale for the existence of CORDS was removed. CORDS ceased operations on February 27, 1973, and selected functions were assumed by the office of the special assistant to the ambassador for field operations, a civilian operation headed by George Jacobson, who had been assistant chief of staff of CORDS under Colby.

David M. Berman

References

Hickey, Gerald Cannon. *Free in the Forest: Ethnohistory of the Vietnamese Central Highlands, 1954–1976*. New Haven, CT: Yale University Press, 1982.

Hunt, Richard A. *Pacification: The American Struggle for Vietnam's Hearts and Minds*. Boulder, CO: Westview, 1995.

Wiesner, Louis A. *Victims and Survivors: Displaced Persons and Other War Victims in Viet-Nam, 1954–1975*. Westport, CT: Greenwood, 1988.

Colby, William Egan (1920–1996)

U.S. Army officer; ambassador; Central Intelligence Agency (CIA) station chief in Saigon; deputy to the commander of U.S. Military Assistance Command, Vietnam (MACV); and director of the CIA (1973–1976). Born on January 4, 1920, in St. Paul,

William Colby, shown here in 1973, was director of the U.S. Central Intelligence Agency during 1973–1976. Earlier Colby had headed the Civil Operations and Revolutionary Development Support (CORDS), the umbrella organization for U.S. pacification efforts in the Republic of Vietnam. (AP/Wide World Photos)

Minnesota, William Egan Colby graduated from Princeton University in 1940. He obtained a commission in the U.S. Army and in 1943 began working with the Office of Strategic Services (OSS). Colby's involvement with this organization, which included parachuting agents into Europe and assisting resistance forces during World War II, led to a 33-year intelligence career.

In 1947 Colby earned a law degree from Columbia University, and in 1950 he joined the CIA. In 1959 he became CIA station chief in Saigon. During the next three years Colby and other CIA officials experimented with various forms of security and rural development programs for the Republic of Vietnam (RVN, South Vietnam). From these endeavors the Citizens' (later Civilian) Irregular Defense Groups (CIDGs), the Mountain Scout Program, and the Strategic Hamlet Project emerged in 1961.

In 1962 Colby became chief of the CIA's Far East Division, a position he held until 1968. This new appointment forced him to concentrate not only on Southeast Asia, including Laos, Thailand, and Cambodia, but also on China and other areas, such as the Philippines. In this new position he stressed pacification as the key to overcoming Communist aggression in Vietnam.

In 1965 CIA analysts established the Hamlet Evaluation System (HES) to measure certain factors in the villages in the Republic of Vietnam (RVN, South Vietnam). These elements contributed to identifying the progress of pacification in the countryside. Despite this, an aggressive pacification strategy did not emerge until 1968.

In 1968 Colby returned to Vietnam and, with ambassadorial rank, succeeded Robert Komer as deputy to the commander of MACV for Civil Operations and

Revolutionary (later changed to Rural) Development Support (CORDS). While serving in this post, Colby oversaw the Accelerated Pacification Campaign. Initiated in November 1968, the campaign focused on enhanced security and development within South Vietnam's villages and included such components as the Phoenix Program and the People's Self-Defense Force.

From 1969 to 1970, planning for pacification and development shifted from the Americans to the South Vietnamese in accordance with the Richard M. Nixon administration's policy of Vietnamization. Then in 1971 the program shifted to a more self-oriented role for the villages of South Vietnam. A year later Colby returned to Washington, D.C., to become the executive director of the CIA and then served as CIA director from May 1973 until his retirement in November 1976.

Colby assumed leadership of the CIA during the worst crisis in its history, triggered in part by that agency's assistance of former agent E. Howard Hunt in his illegal break-ins, including that at the Watergate complex in June 1972. Colby's predecessor, James R. Schlesinger, had ordered the compilation of a list of CIA actions that might have violated its charter. Colby inherited that list and revealed to Congress the agency's involvement in illegal domestic surveillance programs, plots to kill foreign leaders and overthrow governments, use of humans as guinea pigs in mind-control experiments, and other violations of its charter. He believed that revealing to Congress the agency's unsavory side helped to save it from congressional abolition. This action earned Colby admiration from many in Congress and the public but also earned him the enmity of many Cold War warriors, which helped bring an end to his tenure as director in 1976.

In retirement Colby maintained that the United States and South Vietnam might have won the war if only they had fought the CIA's kind of war and countered Communist guerrilla tactics. In his 1989 memoir he argued that the Americans had employed incorrect strategy and tactics. He claimed that in the early 1970s Vietnamization was succeeding and pacification was building the base for a South Vietnamese victory, culminating in the defeat of the 1972 Communist offensive, with U.S. air and logistical support but no ground assistance. Colby believed that this chance for victory was thrown away when the United States sharply reduced its military and logistical support and then "sold out" the South Vietnamese government during negotiations in Paris. The final straw came when Congress dramatically cut aid to South Vietnam, making inevitable the 1975 Communist victory.

Colby also spoke out against the nuclear arms race, and in 1992 he spoke out in favor of cutting the defense budget and spending the money on social programs. Colby drowned in a canoeing accident off Rock Park, Maryland, on April 27, 1996.

R. Blake Dunnavent

References
Andradé, Dale. *Ashes to Ashes: The Phoenix Program and the Vietnam War*. Lanham, MD: Lexington Books, 1990.

Colby, William. *Honorable Men: My Life in the CIA*. New York: Simon and Schuster, 1978.

Colby, William, with James McCargar. *Lost Victory: A Firsthand Account of America's Sixteen-Year Involvement in Vietnam*. Chicago: Contemporary Books, 1989.

Con Thien, Siege of (September 4–October 4, 1967)

Site of major fighting during the later part of 1967, Con Thien (correct Vietnamese spelling: Con Tien) was located 14 miles from the coast of Vietnam and 2 miles south of the demilitarized zone (DMZ). A low hill just 525 feet in elevation, Con Thien overlooked one of the principal People's Army of Vietnam (PAVN, North Vietnamese Army) infiltration routes into the Republic of Vietnam (RVN, South Vietnam).

In the spring of 1967 the U.S. Military Assistance Command, Vietnam (MACV), ordered the construction of an anti-infiltration barrier across the DMZ. Manned strong points would occupy prominent terrain features overlooking infiltration routes. Artillery positions would provide fire support and house reaction forces needed to man the strong-point system. Con Thien was to be an important component of this anti-infiltration barrier.

By mid-1967, U.S. marines had established a formidable presence in the area. Dong Ha was the major logistics base in the region, and Con Thien provided a clear view of it. If the PAVN could seize Con Thien, they would be able to bring the Dong Ha base under artillery and rocket fire.

Con Thien remained a primary target for PAVN artillery. During September 1967 the PAVN subjected the marines at Con Thien to one of the heaviest shellings of the war. Con Thien's defenders came to expect 200 rounds of incoming artillery fire daily, and on September 25 more than 1,200 rounds fell there, killing 23 marines. PAVN ground activity increased under this artillery umbrella. On September 4 and 7, marines located and fought PAVN forces south of Con Thien. On September 10 the 3rd Battalion, 26th Marines, engaged a PAVN regiment in battle near Con Thien, spoiling a major attack. On September 13 a PAVN company attacked the perimeter at Con Thien but failed to breach the defensive wire.

The marines then sent two additional battalions to reinforce Con Thien. The PAVN

response was to blast the defenders with 3,000 incoming rocket, artillery, and mortar rounds during September 19–27. U.S. forces reacted to these attacks with one of the greatest concentrations of artillery and air firepower of the Vietnam War. PAVN forces were struck by what MACV commander General William C. Westmoreland called Operation NEUTRALIZE. This 49-day bombing campaign was orchestrated by Seventh Air Force commander General William M. Momyer and was known as SLAM (for Seek, Locate, Annihilate, and Monitor). During the period aircraft flew 4,200 sorties to drop 40,000 pounds of bombs, while the U.S. Navy fired 6,148 shells, and land artillery added another 12,577 shells. This intense bombardment was undoubtedly the major reason that the PAVN siege forces around Con Thien (101D Regiment of the 325th Division and the 803rd Regiment of the 324th Division) pulled back across the DMZ into the Democratic Republic of Vietnam (DRV, North Vietnam) during this time period, although an official Vietnamese account claims that the forces were withdrawn because of the effects of unusually heavy monsoon rains.

The constant combat took a heavy toll. In a one-month period, the 2nd Battalion, 4th Marines, saw its strength cut in half, from 952 to 462 men. On October 14 a PAVN ground force attacked 2nd Battalion's position, overran a company command post, and engaged the marines in hand-to-hand combat. By the end of October, the 2nd Battalion's strength was down to about 300 men.

Although fighting around Con Thien fell off after October, it remained a harsh environment. The monsoon provided endless drizzle and turned roads into quagmires. The threat of Communist artillery fire was constant, as was the possibility of massed infantry attacks. Neuropsychiatric, or shell shock, casualties were common.

Westmoreland described the fighting around Con Thien as a "crushing defeat" for the PAVN. MACV estimated PAVN deaths in the area of Con Thien during the autumn of 1967 at 1,117. The fighting had taken a heavy toll on the Americans as well. U.S. Marine Corps casualties totaled more than 1,800 killed and wounded.

Peter W. Brush

References

Coan, James P. *Con Thien: The Hill of Angels.* Tuscaloosa: University of Alabama Press, 2004.

Momyer, William W. *Airpower in Three Wars: World War II, Korea and Vietnam.* Washington, DC: U.S. Government Printing Office, 1978.

Pham Gia Duc. *Su Doan 325, 1954–1975*, Tap II [325th Division, 1954–1975, Vol. 2]. Hanoi: People's Army Publishing House, 1986.

Simmons, Edwin H., ed. *The Marines in Vietnam, 1954–1973: An Anthology and Annotated Bibliography.* 2nd ed. Marine Corps Vietnam Series. Washington, DC: History and Museums Division, U.S. Marine Corps Headquarters, 1985.

Telfer, Gary L. *U.S. Marines in Vietnam: Fighting the North Vietnamese, 1967.* Washington, DC: History and Museums Division, Headquarters, U.S. Marine Corps, 1984.

Containment Policy

Strategic policy by which the U.S. government endeavored to limit the expansion of communism during the Cold War. The doctrine of containment originated in the antagonism that developed between the United States and the Soviet Union during World War II and in the immediate postwar period. The doctrine gained potency from the historical lessons that American policy makers learned from the prewar era—that appeasement of aggression merely fueled increasingly more strident and unreasonable demands from dictators—and from the domino theory, the belief that the fall of one country to communism would lead to a chain reaction in neighboring nations.

George F. Kennan, a career foreign service officer stationed in Moscow from July 1944 to April 1946, was the architect of containment. On February 22, 1946, he sent the State Department what has since been called the Long Telegram, an 8,000-word analysis of Soviet actions and ideology asserting that the Soviet Union was driven by a traditional and instinctive Russian sense of insecurity and hostility blended with the rhetoric of messianic Marxism. The Soviet Union, Kennan said, represented a political force fanatically committed to the destruction of capitalist society. The Long Telegram received a positive reception in Washington and was distributed to officials, diplomats, and the military. The next year Kennan was selected to head the newly created State Department Policy Planning Staff, an exclusive study and reporting group charged with advising the secretary of state on foreign policy.

Kennan's containment doctrine was cogently expressed in his essay "The Sources of Soviet Conduct," published under the pseudonym "Mr. X" (although his authorship was soon revealed) in the July 1947 issue of *Foreign Affairs.* In the article, Kennan suggested "long-term, patient but firm and vigilant containment of Russian expansive tendencies." The Soviets, he believed, would eventually mellow or break up, but in the meantime the United States should "confront the Russians with unalterable counterforce, at every point where they show signs of encroaching upon the interests of a peaceful and stable world."

Kennan's views did not go unchallenged. Journalist Walter Lippmann wrote 12 critiques of the article that were later published as the book *The Cold War*. Kennan himself acknowledged deficiencies in the article, including the failure to show clearly that he meant "political containment of a political threat" rather than containment by military means.

Kennan's views were readily adopted by U.S. policy makers suspicious of Soviet actions and intentions. Containment, along with the domino theory, became the touchstone of U.S. Cold War policy, and its implementation through military as well as political and economic means can be seen in conflicts with the Soviet Union and, after 1949, the People's Republic of China (PRC). Examples of containment in action include the 1947 Marshall Plan for European economic recovery, the 1949 North Atlantic Treaty Organization (NATO), the 1948–1949 Berlin Airlift, the refusal to recognize the PRC, the 1950–1953 Korean War, and the Vietnam War.

Containment in Vietnam initially was linked with checking communism in Europe. During World War II President Franklin D. Roosevelt had favored the independence of France's Indochina colonies, but in the postwar period American leaders supported French colonialism because they needed France as a military ally to contain the Soviet Union in Europe. They also believed, erroneously, that because Ho Chi Minh was a Communist, he was controlled by Moscow and Beijing. Beginning in 1950 soon after the Korean War started in June, the United States provided France with direct military and economic assistance in the Indochina War.

Containment of communism seemed jeopardized by the 1954 French defeat at Dien Bien Phu and the de facto division of Vietnam at the Geneva Conference later that year. To contain the Communist threat, U.S. secretary of state John Foster Dulles took the lead in establishing the Southeast Asia Treaty Organization (SEATO) in 1955, which included the United States, France, and Britain in a defense alliance with Asian nations. In 1956 the United States assumed responsibility for training and supporting the military in the Republic of Vietnam (RVN, South Vietnam).

President John F. Kennedy continued the policy of Communist containment and increased the American presence in Vietnam. In May 1961 he authorized commando raids against the Democratic Republic of Vietnam (DRV, North Vietnam) and sent Special Forces advisers to South Vietnam. When Kennedy was assassinated in November 1963, the United States had about 16,000 troops in Vietnam. In the following years under President Lyndon B. Johnson, the number of U.S. troops increased to more than 500,000 men, and the war destroyed Johnson's presidency. In the end, the United States was unable to contain communism in Vietnam. On April 30, 1975, Communist forces captured Saigon and renamed it Ho Chi Minh City.

Kennan, the original author of the containment doctrine, regarded American involvement in Vietnam as a tragic mistake. He believed that Vietnam was a marginal area in the Cold War and thought that involvement there kept the United States from taking advantage of divisions within the Communist world. In 1966 he testified before Senator J. William Fulbright's hearings on the war that containment was designed for Europe and did not fit Asia. In the judgment of many historians, Kennan was right.

Kenneth R. Stevens

References

Gaddis, John Lewis. *Strategies of Containment: A Critical Appraisal of Postwar American National Security Policy.* New York: Oxford University Press, 1982.

Kennan, George F. *Memoirs, 1925–1950.* Boston: Little, Brown, 1967.

Lippmann, Walter. *The Cold War: A Study in U.S. Foreign Policy.* New York: Harper and Row, 1947.

Cooper-Church Amendment

U.S. legislation imposing restrictions on U.S. military action in Southeast Asia. The U.S. military incursion into Cambodia in late April 1970 provoked antiwar demonstrations across the United States and spurred the most serious congressional challenge to date of the president's war powers in Indochina. As passed by the U.S. Senate, the Cooper-Church Amendment, introduced by John Sherman Cooper (R-KY) and Frank Church (D-ID), would have barred funds for the support and maintenance of U.S. ground combat forces and advisers in Cambodia after June 30, 1970, and prohibited any combat activity in the air above Cambodia in support of Cambodian forces unless Congress approved such operations. The amendment also would have barred U.S. support for third-country forces, in particular forces of the Republic of Vietnam (RVN, South Vietnam), in Cambodia.

During the seven-week Senate debate from May 13 through June 30, 1970, the amendment and the military appropriations bill to which it was attached brought about heated discussion of the Richard M. Nixon administration's Asian policy and blocked Senate action on other major legislation. After numerous amendments were introduced to weaken it, the Cooper-Church Amendment was approved by a vote of 58 to 37 on June 30, 1970.

During the debate, Senator Robert Dole (R-KS), a leader of the anti–Cooper-Church forces, introduced an amendment to repeal the 1964 Gulf of Tonkin Resolution. It was overwhelmingly approved. The Nixon administration opposed the Cooper-Church Amendment but was neutral on the Gulf of Tonkin matter.

House and Senate conferees remained deadlocked for six months over the Cooper-Church Amendment. Eventually the Cooper-Church Amendment was attached to the supplementary foreign aid authorization bill but was later dropped from the bill. A revised Cooper-Church Amendment was added to the fiscal 1971 foreign aid authorization bill, clearing Congress on December 22, 1970. The bill was enacted on January 5, 1971. Unlike the earlier Cooper-Church Amendment passed by the Senate, the final version did not prohibit U.S. air activity over Cambodia. The amendment's approval came about six months after U.S. ground troops had pulled out of Cambodia.

President Nixon denounced the Cooper-Church Amendment and other antiwar amendments as harmful to his bargaining position with the Democratic Republic of Vietnam (DRV, North Vietnam). In February 1971 the Nixon administration supported the South Vietnamese invasion of Laos and eventually rode out the political storm over Cambodia. Still, the Cooper-Church Amendment and the proposal of even more restrictive amendments in the Senate put increasing pressure on the Nixon administration to end the war in Indochina. Senate debate also encouraged increased antiwar sentiment among the media, clergy, and other opinion leaders in the United States.

David C. Saffell

References

Herring, George C. *America's Longest War: The United States and Vietnam, 1950–1975*. 4th ed. New York: McGraw-Hill, 2001.

Morris, Roger. *Uncertain Greatness: Henry Kissinger and American Foreign Policy*. New York: Harper and Row, 1977.

Cu Chi Tunnels

Important Communist base area. The district of Cu Chi is located some 40 miles northwest of Saigon on the way to Tay Ninh. In 1966 Cu Chi lay astride the Viet Cong (VC) main supply line to Cambodia. Thus, it is not surprising that VC leaders decided to locate a headquarters complex here as well as to fortify the surrounding area. What was surprising to Americans was that the VC constructed these positions underground.

The interlocking series of tunnels and chambers, sometimes three or four levels in depth, were a marvel of military engineering, made possible by dense clay soil in the Cu Chi area. Stretching well over 100 miles, the tunnels contained hospitals, armories, classrooms, kitchens, living quarters, and even munitions factories. A complex series of ventilation shafts allowed occupants to survive underground for months at a time. Trapdoors at the surface were well concealed, and the tunnels themselves had many hidden doors and passages that enhanced their tactical advantage. Although they did not find it pleasant duty, VC soldiers were able to use the tunnel networks to considerable advantage.

On January 7, 1966, units of the U.S. 1st Infantry Division and the 173rd Airborne Brigade discovered this extensive network. This initial contact provided only a glimpse of the problems that tunnel fortifications would pose for U.S. forces at Cu Chi and across Vietnam. When the 25th Infantry Division established its base camp at Cu Chi later that spring, it assumed the task of clearing the tunnels. For several weeks the rear areas of the division were attacked by VC soldiers emerging from the tunnels, a type of envelopment from below.

U.S. personnel attempted different approaches to clearing the tunnels. These included tear gas, acetylene gas, and explosives. Soon U.S. commanders realized that the only way to clear them effectively was by hand. This task fell to a group of volunteers who became known as "tunnel rats." Because of the narrow tunnel passages, these men were almost uniformly small in stature and performed their duties with a minimum of equipment. Usually a tunnel rat went below with a pistol, a knife, and a flashlight. The tunnels proved to be physically and psychologically draining on American troops, and most tunnel rats served relatively short periods in this taxing assignment.

Tunnel networks were later discovered in other parts of Vietnam, but none were as extensive or as problematic as those at Cu Chi. By 1967 the tunnels had been cleared, but they served as an early example of the tactical ingenuity and tenacity facing U.S. forces in Vietnam. Today the Cu Chi tunnels are a major tourist attraction.

Richard D. Starnes

References

Bergerud, Eric M. *Red Thunder, Tropic Lightning: The World of a Combat Division in Vietnam*. Boulder, CO: Westview, 1993.

Mangold, Tom, and John Penycate. *The Tunnels of Cu Chi*. New York: Random House, 1985.

Stanton, Shelby L. *The Rise and Fall of an American Army: The U.S. Ground Forces in Vietnam, 1965–1975*. Novato, CA: Presidio, 1985.

D

Dak To, Battle of (June 17–November 22, 1967)

Series of battles in 1967 at the U.S. Special Forces camp at Dak To, northeast of Pleiku. On June 17, 1967, Dak To came under heavy mortar fire. During the next few days the 2nd Battalion, 503rd Infantry, 173rd Airborne Brigade, searched the slopes of Hill 1338 for the attackers. On June 22 Company A encountered a battalion of the People's Army of Vietnam (PAVN, North Vietnamese Army) 24th Infantry Regiment. The difficulty of fighting in the jungle-covered mountains became immediately evident. Commanders in helicopters could not see their units on the ground, artillery exploded in treetops rather than on the ground, and smoke from smoke grenades dissipated before reaching the top of the jungle and served only to identify for the enemy the location of American soldiers. In this battle, U.S. losses were 76 killed in action and 23 wounded. PAVN losses were estimated at 475 killed or wounded, although that number is disputed.

During July, companies from the 173rd Airborne Brigade continued to patrol near Dak To. Documents found in numerous PAVN camps indicated the presence in the area of three PAVN regiments with a mission to attack U.S. Army Special Forces camps blocking infiltration routes into the Republic of Vietnam (RVN, South Vietnam). On July 7 Company B, 4th Battalion, 503rd Infantry, met a strong PAVN force on Hill 830 and suffered 24 killed and

62 wounded. Contacts continued throughout the month.

In late 1967 the PAVN began moving more units south to prepare for the Tet Offensive. Units from the U.S. 4th Infantry and 1st Cavalry divisions, units from the Army of the Republic of Vietnam (ARVN, South Vietnamese Army), and other battalions from the 173rd Airborne Brigade deployed to Dak To. Facing the Americans in the Dak To area were four regiments (the 24th, 66th, 174th, and 320th regiments) of the reinforced PAVN 1st Division, led by the division commander Nguyen Huu An, who had commanded PAVN forces during the brutal fight against the U.S. 1st Air Cavalry Division in the Battle of the Ia Drang Valley in November 1965.

During the first nine days of November, companies from the 8th Infantry and 12th Infantry, 4th Infantry Division, and from the 173rd Airborne Brigade engaged in savage fighting near Hill 823. In the ensuing battles, paratroopers from the 4th Battalion, 503rd Infantry, killed about 125 PAVN soldiers but lost 15 killed and 48 wounded. Examination of PAVN dead revealed that the unit was composed of well-equipped fresh troops.

A major battle occurred on November 11 between the PAVN 66th Regiment and American units. On Hill 724 the 1st Battalion, 8th Infantry, fought off a PAVN attack that resulted in 92 PAVN troops killed. U.S. casualties were 18 killed and 188 wounded.

On Hill 223, Companies A, C, and D of the 1st Battalion, 503rd Infantry, 173rd

Airborne Brigade, encountered a PAVN battalion. Hit by mortar, rocket, and small-arms fire from the well-camouflaged PAVN, Companies A, C, and D were surrounded. Company C of the 4th Battalion, 503rd Infantry, arrived about 875 yards from the battle and relieved the 1st Battalion. U.S. casualties were 20 killed, 184 wounded, and 2 missing. PAVN losses were officially reported as 175 killed, but participants believed that no more than 80 were actually killed.

During November 12–15 units from the 1st and 2nd battalions, 503rd Infantry, encountered PAVN troops in well-constructed bunkers and trenches. In the ensuing battles, American troops lost numerous killed and found 85 PAVN troops dead. PAVN rockets meanwhile destroyed the ammunition dump at the Dak To fire-support base.

On November 19 the 2nd Battalion of the 503rd Infantry began moving up Hill 875, unaware that in front of them the PAVN 174th Regiment occupied bunkers and trenches connected by tunnels. As two companies advanced, PAVN troops closed behind them. Company A's command post was overrun, and the remnants of that company plus Companies C and D were surrounded. In late afternoon a U.S. Air Force fighter dropped a 500-pound bomb in the middle of Company C. The explosion killed 42 Americans (several of them officers) and wounded 45. Throughout November 20 the survivors repelled numerous PAVN attacks. That night three companies from the 4th Battalion, 503rd Infantry, arrived to reinforce the defenders. Units from the 4th Infantry Division and the ARVN 42th Infantry Regiment encountered PAVN troops west, south, and northeast of Dak To.

Not until November 22 did the 4th Battalion, along with two 4th Infantry Division companies, gain the crest of Hill 875. In the battle American casualties totaled 115 killed, 253 wounded, and 5 missing. Total PAVN losses since November 1 were estimated at 1,000.

In these engagements, known collectively as the Battle of Dak To, the PAVN failed to achieve one of its main objectives: the destruction of an American unit. The PAVN had, however, come close. Despite heavy losses, the Americans had achieved a victory. Three PAVN regiments scheduled to participate in the upcoming Tet Offensive were so mauled that they had to be withdrawn to refit. In his memoirs General Nguyen Huu An admitted that at the time of the 1968 Tet offensive, "After the battle of Dak To, the combat strength of [my] 1st Division had deteriorated, and we no longer possessed the strength to 'devour' an American infantry brigade."

Richard L. Kiper

References

Murphy, Edward F. *Dak To: The 173rd Airborne Brigade in South Vietnam's Central Highlands, June–November 1967.* Novato, CA: Presidio, 1993.

Nguyen Huu An and Nguyen Tu Duong. *Chien Truong Moi* [New Battlefield]. Hanoi: People's Army Publishing House, 2002.

Dau Tranh **Strategy**

Strategy reportedly devised by Vo Nguyen Giap, Ho Chi Minh, and Truong Chinh, leaders of the Democratic Republic of Vietnam (DRV, North Vietnam). The theory of a long war, or people's war, is incomprehensible to Western military and political leaders. Truong Chinh said that because war is the most acute form of struggle between man and man, people's warfare rather than weapons and techniques decides victory. People's warfare means mobilization of every person in the nation. Involvement of entire families becomes critical to *dau tranh* ("struggle") because the idea of a noncombatant is eliminated.

Dau tranh has two elements, political struggle and armed struggle. They are the jaws of the pincer movement and must work together against an enemy. Only then is victory possible, and that dualism forms the dogma. Armed struggle is the program of violence involving military actions and other forms of bloodshed. Political struggle is the systematic coercive activity involving individual and societal mobilization, organization, and motivation. Every action taken in war falls within the framework and scope of these two elements.

In one interpretation, *dau tranh* means "the people as instrument of war." The strategy has a threefold sequence of implementation: control the people, forge them into a weapon, and hurl the weapon into battle. *Dau tranh* is a political strategy in that any revolution is political. In that sense, violence is necessary to *dau tranh* but is not its essence. The strategy's goal is to seize power by disabling society through primarily organizational means. Organization becomes more important than ideology or military tactics. A united front, an organization of organizations, is the basic instrument of control.

The organizations become channels of communication. Organization leads to mobilization and then motivation. Victory goes to the side that is best organized, stays best organized, and most successfully disorganizes the other side. The *dau tranh* strategist never uses a real grievance to undermine the enemy because spontaneity is unpredictable. The strategist manufactures a grievance and follows a manufactured timetable to achieve a new social order.

Armed *dau tranh* is unlike ordinary military combat because it includes various military actions as well as assassinations, kidnappings, and other activities not usually associated with regular armed forces. This method is a program of violence that is always cast in a political context. *Dau tranh*'s strategic objective is to put armed conflict in the context of political dissidence so that available resources must constantly be divided between the armed and political methods.

Political *dau tranh* consists of three programs that move the abstract into reality. The first is action among the people, its most potent aspect being the village-level effort to gain support. In the Vietnam War, this program worked to limit American military response and to affect the American public's perception of the war, undermining support for the war and therefore undercutting American international diplomacy. This program required complete advanced planning and absolute control during execution.

The second program, action among the military, was a proselytizing effort aimed at individual enemy soldiers and civil servants. Its goal was to weaken the government of the Republic of Vietnam (RVN, South Vietnam). The third program, action among the people controlled by the National Front for the Liberation of South Vietnam (National Liberation Front [NLF]), also known as the Viet Cong (VC), exercised administrative and motivational control of liberated areas (the rudimentary beginning of Marxist society) and gave Communist forces a place to rest and recuperate in liberated areas.

Superior organization to allow more complete mobilization is the key to success in *dau tranh*. This kind of struggle channels the enemy's response and in effect dictates the enemy's strategy. The enemy is forced to fight under unfavorable terms. The devastation formerly directed at a target or confined to a battle zone is turned on the people themselves, for they have become the battlefield.

Countering the *dau tranh* strategy requires control of resources and population, which inevitably means deliberately inflicting civilian casualties. Moreover, *dau tranh* confuses the enemy's perception of the war and can channel that perception. This aspect of the strategy confused Americans about the essential nature of the war and its conduct and its outcome as well as the nature of their enemy.

Dau tranh succeeds only to the extent that it avoids or nullifies an enemy's total military, political, and economic strength.

Thomas R. Carver

References

Military History Institute of Vietnam. *Victory in Vietnam: The Official History of the People's Army of Vietnam, 1954–1975*. Lawrence: University Press of Kansas, 2002.

Pike, Douglas. *PAVN: People's Army of Vietnam*. Novato, CA: Presidio, 1986.

Truong-Chinh. *Selected Writings*. Hanoi: Gioi Publishers, 1994.

Vo Nguyen Giap. *People's War People's Army: The Viet Cong Insurrection Manual for Underdeveloped Countries*. New York: Praeger, 1962.

Dien Bien Phu, Battle of (March 13–May 7, 1954)

Set-piece battle that ended the Indochina War. The siege of Dien Bien Phu was the most famous battle of the Indochina War and one of the great battles of the twentieth century. In 1953 French military commander in Indochina General Henri Navarre decided to establish an airhead in northwestern Tonkin astride the main Viet Minh invasion route into Laos. Although not enthusiastic about the idea, Navarre believed that a strong base there would prevent an outright enemy invasion of Laos. The position would be located at the village of Dien Bien Phu, then held by a small Viet Minh garrison. Dien Bien Phu had a small airstrip and was some 185 miles by air from Hanoi.

In November 1953 Navarre in Saigon gave orders for the operation, dubbed CASTOR, to proceed. On November 20, 2,200 French *paras* (paratroopers), the cream of the French Expeditionary Corps, dropped into the valley north and south of Dien Bien Phu. They easily defeated the few Viet Minh there and began establishing defensive positions.

With a hubris not unknown to other French military commanders in Indochina, Navarre completely underestimated his enemy. He expected to use superior French artillery and airpower to destroy any Viet Minh forces attacking Dien Bien Phu and assumed that at most Viet Minh commander General Vo Nguyen Giap would commit one division to such an effort. Should this belief prove incorrect, Navarre was confident that the garrison could be evacuated. Even in retrospect, it is hard to believe that he could have so seriously underestimated his enemy, given prior experience and especially the 1951–1952 Battle of Hoa Binh.

Hardly anyone had heard of Dien Bien Phu when the French occupied it. Dien Bien Phu was an obscure village situated in a valley surrounded by hills on all sides. To leave the enemy the opportunity to be in control of the high ground surrounding the base was dangerous, but as Navarre put it later, when the French arrived, the Viet Minh did not have artillery there.

Colonel Christian Marie Ferdinand de la Croix de Castries (promoted to brigadier general during the subsequent battle) commanded French forces at Dien Bien Phu. An aristocrat with a reputation of a playboy (the French strong points were reportedly

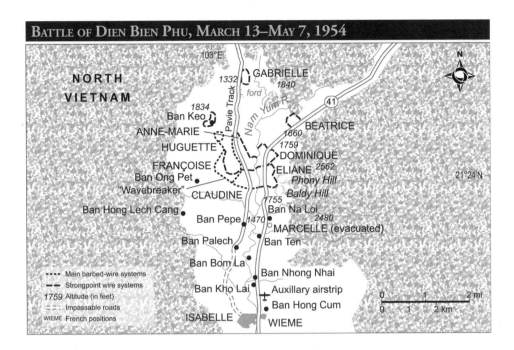

BATTLE OF DIEN BIEN PHU, MARCH 13–MAY 7, 1954

named for his current mistresses), de Castries had wide experience in Indochina and was regarded as a capable commander. During the subsequent battle, however, he at times showed signs of detachment, seeming to withdraw mentally.

By the end of the first week, the French had 4,500 men in the valley. They were entirely dependent on air supply by a small number of transport aircraft (three groups totaling 75 Douglas C-47s Dakotas). The French also had available 48 Martin B-26 Marauder and Privateer bombers and 112 Bearcat and Hellcat fighter-bombers. There were also a few helicopters. After the battle Navarre wrote in his memoirs that "The insufficiency of aviation was, for our side, the principal cause of the loss of the battle."

The Viet Minh, on the other hand, relied, as they had in previous battles, on the very primitive system of transport by human porters. Giap's troops later improved Route 41 leading to Dien Bien Phu to enable the roadway to handle trucks and artillery pieces.

At the end of April thanks to Chinese support, Giap had 14 transport companies with 800 trucks in a total of 1,200 to 1,300 vehicles. Nonetheless, the laborers (the "people's porters," Giap called them) remained the core of the Viet Minh supply system and were critical to the battle's outcome.

The French central command post was in Dien Bien Phu itself. Around it de Castries ordered the construction of a series of strong points: Beatrice, Gabrielle, Anne-Marie, Dominique, Huguette, Françoise, Elaine, and Isabelle. Unfortunately for the French, Isabelle was separated from the others; some three miles to the south, it was easily cut off and diverted a third of the French forces.

De Castries had originally planned a wider defensive ring, perhaps 30 miles in length, but the problems of bringing everything in by air shrank the perimeter. Fortifications were also woefully inadequate. The French assumed that they could use airpower and counter-battery artillery fire to knock out any Viet Minh artillery before it became a problem. Indeed, the French were contemptuous of Viet Minh artillery capabilities. The French made no effort to camouflage their own positions and placed their own guns in open pits without protective cover. The Viet Minh easily observed French work from the hills, but French light observation aircraft failed to detect the Viet Minh buildup.

The Chinese directly supported the Viet Minh by handling some of the artillery batteries and helping to draw up fire plans. Chinese general Vy Quoc Thanh was also at Dien Bien Phu as military adviser and to help plan the campaign.

The French flew in reinforcements, but these were negated because Giap had not only called off his northern offensive but also decided to commit all available divisions to attack Dien Bien Phu. Thus, the defenders would encounter a much larger force than the single division that Navarre had anticipated. Giap also worked to cripple the French airlift capacity. In daring raids in early March, Viet Minh commandos attacked French air bases at Gia Lam near Hanoi and at Do Son and Cat Bi airfields near Haiphong, destroying 22 aircraft.

Meanwhile at Dien Bien Phu, the French had undertaken patrols. Ominously these were routinely mauled by the Viet Minh, and de Castries's own chief of staff was killed just a few hundred yards from one of the strong points. The French then abandoned such patrolling as being counterproductive and providing little information about the enemy.

Giap now closed the ring on the French fortress. The 304th, 308th, 312th, and 316th divisions were brought to the area. The French called in airpower. Grumman F-8F Bearcats and Martin B-26 Marauder bombers attacked Viet Minh hill positions with bombs, napalm, and rocket fire, but

the positions were well disguised by natural camouflage and were difficult to identify. The French also flew in 10 M-24 Chaffee light tanks by air and assembled them in the fortress under fire, although these had little impact on the battle.

By mid-February de Castries had sustained casualties of almost 1,000 men. The Viet Minh meanwhile continued to build their strength. Bernard Fall estimates that the Viet Minh ultimately assembled at Dien Bien Phu some 49,500 combat troops and 31,500 support personnel, mostly unskilled porters. An additional 23,000 troops maintained supply lines back to the Chinese border. In mid-March the French had 10,814 men in the valley, of whom about 7,000 were front-line combat troops. Fully a third of the garrison was Vietnamese, although most of these were tribal Thai. The Viet Minh thus enjoyed a superiority of approximately 5 to 1 in manpower, and they also had greater firepower.

The siege of Dien Bien Phu officially opened on March 13 with a heavy Viet Minh bombardment. Although the French added 4,000 men during the siege, Giap more than offset this with manpower increases of his own. He also steadily improved both the quantity and quality of his artillery. Ultimately the Viet Minh deployed 20 to 24 105-millimeter (mm) howitzers, 15 to 20 75-mm howitzers, 20 120-mm mortars, and at least 40 82-mm mortars. They also had some 80 Chinese-crewed 37-mm antiaircraft guns, 100 antiaircraft machine guns, and 12 to 16 six-tube Katyusha rocket launchers. During the battle, the Viet Minh fired 103,000 rounds of 75-mm or larger-size artillery shells, most of it by direct fire, simply aiming down their gun tubes at the French positions. Approximately 75 percent of French casualties came from artillery fire.

By contrast, French artillery assets were entirely inadequate. The French had only

4 155-mm howitzers, 24 105-mm howitzers, and 4 120-mm mortars. In contrast to the Viet Minh, the French fired only 93,000 shells during the battle and, unlike the Viet Minh, had difficulty identifying their targets.

On the very first night of the siege, March 13–14, the Viet Minh took Beatrice. Gabrielle fell two days later. Giap's basic tactic was massive artillery fire followed by waves of infantry. The Viet Minh also brought the airstrip under fire to try to destroy F-8F Bearcat fighters there. One was destroyed on March 13, and two escaped to Vientiane. The next day three more got away to Cat Bi airfield; the remaining six were destroyed on the ground. The control tower was also badly damaged, and the radio beacon guiding planes there in bad weather was knocked out.

Pessimism now began to spread in the French command. In Hanoi, French commander in the north General René Cogny, who was never enthusiastic about the operation, now began to consider the possibility of losing the fortress. His resources were stretched thin, as Giap had sent the 320th Division, 3 autonomous regiments, and 14 regional battalions to disrupt the vital transportation link between Hanoi and Haiphong and divert French resources by attacking French outposts in the Tonkin Delta. The Viet Minh offensive there began on March 12, the day before the battle began at Dien Bien Phu. Thus, Cogny had to fight two battles at once. Navarre, who held to the primacy of central Indochina, refused all reinforcements to Cogny.

It is not surprising that de Castries's pleas for reinforcements fell on deaf ears. Even ammunition was in short supply, as Viet Minh sappers blew up French stocks.

On March 22 the French used their last four tanks to counterattack People's Army of Vietnam (PAVN, North Vietnamese Army) troops that had cut off Isabelle. This met up with units from Isabelle striking north. It was the first French success of the battle, but it cost 151 French dead, 72 wounded, and 1 missing. Viet Minh casualties were heavier, but Giap had a seemingly inexhaustible supply of manpower.

The arrival of the rainy season made conditions more miserable for attacker and defender alike and further complicated French resupply problems. C-47 transports still flew in supplies and evacuated wounded but at great risk. On March 26 one transport was shot down; two more were shot down on March 27. Late that same day one managed to land and pick up 19 wounded. This was the last flight in or out of Dien Bien Phu.

On March 26 Major Marcel Bigeard, who had parachuted into the fortress only 10 days before, commanded a successful attack against Viet Minh positions. Supported by artillery, fighter aircraft, and a tank platoon from Isabelle, the French *paras* sallied from the fortress to assault the Viet Minh. Bigeard later gave Viet Minh losses at 350 dead and more than 500 wounded as well as 10 taken prisoner. The raiders also captured 5 20-mm AA cannon, 12 .50-caliber machine guns, 2 bazookas, and 14 submachine guns and reclaimed 10 prisoners.

Having already endured about 6,600 killed and 12,000 wounded, Giap's force suffered from low morale, what Giap later called "right-wing tendencies." Discussions led by political cadres about courage, right thinking, and dedication helped to restore morale, as did a more important change in tactics. Giap abandoned the costly human-wave attacks in favor of attrition warfare, resembling World War I. He pushed forward trenches until the particular target strong point was cut off from outside support.

The last stage of the battle was fought without letup in an area of about a square mile around the airstrip. The Viet Minh attacked on April 29, and by May 4 French senior officers knew there was no longer any hope. The last French reinforcements, 165 men of the 1st Colonial Parachute Battalion, jumped into the garrison during May 5–6. They had come at their own insistence to share the fate of their comrades. This brought the cumulative total of the garrison to 16,544 men. By now most of the airdrops of supplies were falling into Viet Minh hands. The final Viet Minh assault occurred on May 6, accompanied by the explosion of mines and the firing of Katyusha rockets. The last French troops surrendered on the evening of May 7.

During the siege, more than half of the French troops had been rendered *hors de combat*: 1,600 dead, 4,800 wounded, and 1,600 missing. The Viet Minh immediately sent their 8,000 prisoners off on foot on a 500-mile march to prison camps; less than half of them would return. Of the Vietnamese defenders taken, only 10 percent would be seen again. The Viet Minh had also shot down 48 French planes and destroyed 16 others on the ground. Viet Minh casualties are estimated at approximately 7,900 killed and 15,000 wounded.

The French had two plans to rescue the garrison. Operation CONDOR called for an infantry thrust from Laos to link up with airborne forces sent from Hanoi. Operation ALBATROSS was a plan for the garrison to break out on its own. Navarre did not order Cogny to begin planning for this until May 3. Not until May 7 did de Castries decide to attempt to execute the plan, but it was then too late. Another plan, codenamed VULTURE, was also considered. This envisioned massive U.S. intervention in the form of air strikes, but President Dwight D. Eisenhower could not secure British support, and the plan was dropped.

The Battle of Dien Bien Phu was the death knell of the French in Asia. In Paris, Premier Joseph Laniel, dressed entirely in black, gave the news to the National Assembly. The Geneva Conference was already in progress to discuss a host of Asian issues, and the French defeat provided the politicians with an excuse to shift blame for the Indochina debacle to the military. Although France had not provided the troops or resources that the French military required to win the war, it could now blame the military for the defeat and extricate the nation from the Indochina morass. A new government under Pierre Mendès-France came to power to carry out that mandate. Almost immediately after the Indochina War, the French Army found itself transferred to Algeria to fight again. This time, the army promised, there would be no sellout.

Spencer C. Tucker

References

Bigeard, General Marcel. *Pour une parcelle de gloire*. Paris: Plon, 1975.

Fall, Bernard B. *Hell in a Very Small Place: The Siege of Dien Bien Phu*. New York: Lippincott, 1966.

Morgan, Ted. *Valley of Death: The Tragedy at Dien Bien Phu That Led America into the Vietnam War*. New York: Random House, 2010.

Porch, Douglas. *The French Foreign Legion: A Complete History of the Legendary Fighting Force*. New York: HarperCollins, 1991.

Roy, Jules. *The Battle of Dienbienphu*. New York: Harper and Row, 1965.

Simpson, Howard R. *Dien Bien Phu: The Epic Battle America Forgot*. Washington, DC: Brassey's, 1994.

Windrow, Martin. *The Last Valley: Dien Bien Phu and the French Defeat in Vietnam*. London: Weidenfeld and Nicolson, 2004.

Domino Theory

Foreign policy precept and a view held by many U.S. policy makers during the Cold War that if one country fell to communism, its neighbors were threatened with a chain reaction of Communist takeovers. The domino theory arose from fear that the withdrawal of colonial powers from Southeast Asia would lead to the fall of Vietnam and then the rest of Southeast Asia and perhaps India, Japan, the Philippines, and Indonesia.

Remembering the failure of appeasement before World War II, policy makers believed that unchecked aggression would eventually force a larger crisis, but firmness might deter Communist takeovers. The domino theory was also certainly influenced by the fall of China to the Communists in 1949 and the Korean War (1950–1953), which attempted to prevent a domino effect in East Asia. It was also likely informed by the rapid succession of Communist takeovers that occurred in Eastern and Central Europe in the immediate aftermath of World War II. In many ways, the theory was a natural extension of the containment policy, which had been operative—if not overtly expressed—since 1946.

The domino theory was first publicly expressed by U.S. president Dwight D. Eisenhower at a press conference on April 7, 1954, in anticipation of French defeat at Dien Bien Phu. Eisenhower explained that "You have a row of dominoes set up, you knock over the first one, and what will happen to the last one is the certainty that it will go over very quickly. So you have a beginning of a disintegration that would have the most profound influences."

Although the phrase "domino theory" was not used until Eisenhower's press conference, the idea was already in place as early as 1947. When the Soviet Union supported Azerbaijani separatists in Iran, Soviet client states backed a Communist rebellion in Greece, and the Soviet Union pressured Turkey to share control of the straits between the Mediterranean Sea and the Black Sea, President Harry S. Truman requested $400 million of aid for free peoples resisting subjugation by outside forces. Senator Arthur H. Vandenberg, a Michigan Republican, publicly warned that failure to support the president could result in a "communist chain reaction from the Dardanelles to the China Sea and westward to the rim of the Atlantic."

Asia and Vietnam occupied a central place in the domino paradigm. A 1950 study commissioned by President Truman emphasized Vietnam's strategic importance as a natural invasion route into Southeast Asia and anticipated repercussions for other countries in the region if Vietnam became Communist. U.S. aid for French operations in Vietnam began that year, soon after the Korean War began. Two years later National Security Council Report 124/2 (NSC-124/2) of June 24, 1952, warned that the loss of any one Southeast Asian country to communism would probably lead to the "relatively swift submission to or an alignment with communism by the remaining countries." President Truman announced during the Korean War that the United States was fighting in Korea "so we won't have to fight in Wichita, or in Chicago, or in New Orleans, or on San Francisco Bay."

Entering office in 1953, Eisenhower accepted the domino theory without reservation. In August 1954 following the French defeat at Dien Bien Phu and the temporary division pending elections of Vietnam along the 17th Parallel at the Geneva Conference, Eisenhower approved NSC-5429/2, which stated that the United States had to prevent further losses to communism in Asia through all available means.

Therefore, the U.S. Central Intelligence Agency (CIA) attempted a number of sabotage efforts against the Democratic Republic of Vietnam (DRV, North Vietnam). Additionally, in September 1954 the United States signed a treaty with Britain, France, Australia, New Zealand, Thailand, Pakistan, and the Philippines creating the Southeast Asia Treaty Organization (SEATO) to defend each other against attack. With part of Vietnam under communism, Eisenhower saw Laos as the next domino. During a foreign policy briefing the day before John F. Kennedy's 1961 inauguration, Eisenhower informed the president-elect that if Laos fell to the Communists, it was only a matter of time until the Republic of Vietnam (RVN, South Vietnam), Cambodia, Thailand, and Burma collapsed.

Presidents Kennedy and Lyndon B. Johnson also subscribed to the domino theory. Kennedy increased aid and the number of U.S. military advisers in Vietnam, which numbered about 16,000 when he was assassinated in November 1963. Johnson increased the number of U.S. troops in Vietnam to about 546,000. In a speech at Johns Hopkins University in April 1965, he said that retreat in Vietnam would not end conflict with communism in Southeast Asia. Echoing the lesson of appeasement for the generation that fought World War II, Johnson asserted that the "central lesson of our time is that the appetite of aggression is never satisfied. To withdraw from one battlefield means only to prepare for the next." Much later, in the 1980s, President Ronald Reagan revived the domino theory to justify his administration's policies that sought to overthrow the leftist Sandinista regime in Nicaragua. In 1990–1991 President George H. W. Bush again invoked the theory during the Persian Gulf War, which sought to prevent Iraq from annexing or toppling any more regional powers in the Middle East.

The eventual Communist victory in Vietnam in 1975 did not substantiate the domino theory in Southeast Asia. The neighboring states of Cambodia and Laos did fall to communism, but these nations were destabilized by the Vietnam conflict itself, and Cambodia is no longer Communist. Other Asian nations have remained safely non-Communist.

Kenneth R. Stevens

References

Berman, Larry. *Planning a Tragedy: The Americanization of the War in Vietnam.* New York: Norton, 1982.

Herring, George C. *America's Longest War: The United States and Vietnam, 1950–1975.* 4th ed. New York: McGraw-Hill, 2001.

E

EAGLE PULL, Operation (April 12, 1975)

U.S. air evacuation of personnel from Phnom Penh, Cambodia, in April 1975. On June 27, 1973, the U.S. Support Activities Group/ Seventh Air Force (USSAG/7AF), located at Nakhon Phanom Royal Thai Air Force Base, Thailand, published Contingency Plan 5060C (CONPLAN 5060C), code name EAGLE PULL, concerning the evacuation of Phnom Penh. Rescue units received the EAGLE PULL plan as Khmer Rouge units closed in on the capital, and it seemed that Phnom Penh and all of Cambodia would fall. But to the surprise of many, when the U.S. bombing stopped on August 15, 1973, the Cambodian Army repulsed the Khmer Rouge attack.

During the next 20 months, the USSAG/ 7AF changed EAGLE PULL to meet evolving circumstances. When one Cambodian town after another fell to the Khmer Rouge, EAGLE PULL focused only on evacuating Americans and a handful of others from Phnom Penh. A complex prioritization system that classified noncombatant evacuees according to sex, age, and physical condition was developed, and a U.S. Marine Corps ground security force was added to the plan.

On April 3, 1975, as Khmer Rouge forces again closed in on Phnom Penh, EAGLE PULL forces were placed on alert. An 11-man marine element flew into the city to prepare for the arrival of the evacuation helicopters. The marines designated a soccer field located a quarter of a mile from the American embassy as Landing Zone (LZ) Hotel. On April 10 Ambassador Gunther Dean asked that EAGLE PULL be executed no later than April 12.

At 8:50 a.m. on April 12, an Aerospace Rescue and Recovery Service (ARRS) HH-53 landed a four-man U.S. Air Force combat control team to coordinate the operation. Three minutes later, it guided in a U.S. Marine Corps Sikorsky CH-53 Sea Stallion with the first element of the marine security force. Marine and air force helicopters then carried 276 evacuees, including 82 Americans, 159 Cambodians, and 35 foreign nationals, to the safety of U.S. Navy assault carriers in the Gulf of Thailand. By 10:00 a.m., the marine contingency force, the advanced 11-man element, and the combat control team had been evacuated. There were no casualties in the operation.

Earl H. Tilford, Jr.

References

Benjamin, Milton R., and Paul Rogers Brinkley. "Farewell to Phnom Penh." *Newsweek*, April 2, 1975, 27.

Tilford, Earl H., Jr. *Search and Rescue in Southeast Asia, 1961–1975*. Washington, DC: Office of Air Force History, 1980.

Easter Offensive (1972)

The 1972 Easter or Spring Offensive carried out by the People's Army of Vietnam (PAVN, North Vietnamese Army) is frequently referred to as the Nguyen Hue

North Vietnamese artillery pounds ARVN positions during the 1972 Easter Offensive. The North Vietnamese–run offensive was an all-out invasion of South Vietnam to defeat the Saigon regime once and for all. (U.S. Army Center of Military History)

Campaign, so named for the Vietnamese ruler who defeated the Chinese in 1789, although technically the term "Nguyen Hue Campaign" was used by the Democratic Republic of Vietnam (DRV, North Vietnam) to refer only to the offensive campaign in the Binh Long–Tay Ninh area northwest of Saigon and not to the entire 1972 offensive. The Easter Offensive consisted of a massive coordinated three-pronged attack designed to strike a decisive blow against the government and armed forces of the Republic of Vietnam (RVN, South Vietnam). Within two weeks of the operation's beginning on Easter Sunday, large conventional battles were fought simultaneously on three major fronts. The PAVN employed conventional tactics and introduced weaponry beyond that of any previous campaign. This was the largest offensive ever launched by Hanoi and was a radical departure from North Vietnam's past strategy and methods of

warfare historically used in its attempt to conquer South Vietnam.

The North Vietnamese leaders decided to employ conventional tactics for this offensive for several reasons. First, they did not believe that the Americans, with only 65,000 troops left in Vietnam, could influence the situation on the ground; Hanoi believed that the political situation in the United States would not permit President Richard M. Nixon to commit any new troops or combat support to assist the ARVN. Hanoi hoped to discredit Nixon's Vietnamization and pacification programs and cause the remaining U.S. forces to be withdrawn quicker. Additionally, a resounding North Vietnamese military victory would humiliate Nixon, force the Nixon administration to negotiate a peace agreement favorable to Communist forces but that contained terms that might entice Nixon to accept it prior to November 1972 presidential elections, or perhaps even help to defeat Nixon's reelection bid, opening the White House to a more moderate Democratic Party president less disposed to further U.S. involvement in Vietnam.

PAVN general and North Vietnamese defense minister Vo Nguyen Giap was the reluctant architect of the 1972 Easter Offensive. Despite his own belief that this was not yet the time for an offensive, Giap prepared to carry out the Politburo's orders. The campaign was designed to destroy as many ARVN forces as possible, thus permitting the Communists to occupy key South Vietnamese cities and enabling PAVN forces to be in position to directly threaten the government of South Vietnamese president Nguyen Van Thieu. Giap hoped to achieve a knockout blow, but if that could not be achieved, he hoped to seize at least enough critical terrain to strengthen the North Vietnamese position in any subsequent negotiations.

Throughout 1971 Hanoi requested and received large quantities of modern weapons from the Soviet Union and China. These included MiG-21 jets, surface-to-air missiles (SAMs), T-54 medium tanks, 130-millimeter (mm) field guns, 160-mm mortars, 57-mm antiaircraft guns (including self-propelled guns), and for the first time heat-seeking shoulder-fired SA-7 Strella antiaircraft missiles. In addition, other war supplies such as spare parts, ammunition, vehicles, and fuels were shipped to North Vietnam in unprecedented quantities.

Giap's offensive plan called for a multidivisional attack across the demilitarized zone (DMZ) toward Hue and Da Nang, with other forces pressing in from the A Shau Valley in the west. Giap wanted to force President Thieu to commit reserves to protect his northern provinces, after which Giap would launch a second assault from Cambodia to threaten the South Vietnamese capital of

Saigon (present-day Ho Chi Minh City). Then Giap would launch the third attack in the Central Highlands to take Kontum and aim for the coast in Binh Dinh Province, thus splitting South Vietnam in two and leading to its collapse or, at the very least, a peace agreement on Hanoi's terms.

The North Vietnamese offensive began on Good Friday, March 30, 1972, when three PAVN divisions, reinforced by T-54 medium tanks, attacked south across the DMZ separating North and South Vietnam and along Highway 9 out of Laos toward Quang Tri and Hue in I Corps Tactical Zone. Three days later three additional divisions moved from sanctuaries in Cambodia and pushed into Binh Long Province, capturing Loc Ninh and surrounding An Loc, the provincial capital only 65 miles from the national capital of Saigon. Additional PAVN forces attacked across the Cambodian border in the Central Highlands toward Kontum in the II Corps Tactical Zone. Finally, two more PAVN divisions took control of several districts in Binh Dinh Province, along the coast of the South China Sea. In each case the PAVN assault was characterized by human-wave attacks backed by tanks and massive artillery support. Fourteen PAVN infantry divisions and 26 separate regiments (including more than 120,000 troops and some 500 tanks and other armored vehicles) participated in the offensive.

The PAVN thrusts were at first very successful, particularly in northern South Vietnam where they quickly overran the newly formed ARVN 3rd Division in Quang Tri. The PAVN also threatened both Hue and Kontum, but ARVN forces were able to stiffen their defenses 25 miles north of Hue, while defenders at Kontum were also successful in halting the PAVN assault there. ARVN forces at An Loc were besieged by the PAVN and sustained repeated ground attacks and massive artillery and rocket fire; nevertheless, the ARVN forces held out until the siege there was broken in July 1972.

President Nixon resumed the bombing of North Vietnam on May 8, 1972 (Operation LINEBACKER I) and ordered the mining of Haiphong Harbor as well as several other North Vietnamese ports. This took some of the pressure off ARVN forces, but intense fighting continued throughout the summer all over South Vietnam. In June, ARVN forces in Military Region I launched a counteroffensive that eventually resulted in the recapture of Quang Tri Province. The Easter Offensive had failed.

Although the combat performance of the ARVN had been uneven at best, the ARVN had held, supported by U.S. advisers and massive American airpower, including Boeing B-52 Stratofortress strikes that repeatedly broke up attacking Communist formations and reduced the odds against the ARVN. Estimates placed North Vietnamese casualties at more than 100,000 killed; in addition, North Vietnam lost at least half of its large-caliber artillery and tanks. However, the PAVN still controlled more territory in South Vietnam than before, and Hanoi believed that it was in a stronger bargaining position at the Paris negotiations. Nevertheless, the success of South Vietnamese forces in confronting the North Vietnamese onslaught was touted as proof that President Nixon's Vietnamization policy had worked.

James H. Willbanks

References

Andradé, Dale. *America's Last Vietnam Battle: Halting Hanoi's 1972 Easter Offensive.* Lawrence: University Press of Kansas, 2001.

Clarke, Jeffrey J. *Advice and Support: The Final Years; The U.S. Army in Vietnam.* Washington, DC: U.S. Government Printing Office, 1988.

Lavalle, A. J. C. *Airpower and the 1972 Spring Invasion.* U.S. Air Force Southeast Asia Monograph Series, Vol. 2, Monograph 3. Washington, DC: Office of Air Force History, 1985.

McKenna, Thomas P. *Kontum: The Battle to Save South Vietnam.* Lexington: University Press of Kentucky, 2011.

Military Arts Faculty, Military Science Institute. *Chien Dich Tien Cong Quang Tri 1972* [1972 Quang Tri Offensive Campaign]. Hanoi: Military Science Institute, 1976.

Military History Institute of Vietnam. *Chien Dich Tien Cong Nguyen Hue (Nam 1972)* [The Nguyen Hue Offensive Campaign (1972)]. Hanoi: Military History Institute, 1988.

Ngo Quang Truong. *The Easter Offensive of 1972.* Indochina Monographs. Washington, DC: U.S. Army Center of Military History, 1980.

Turley, Gerald H. *The Easter Offensive: The Last American Advisors, Vietnam, 1972.* Novato, CA: Presidio, 1985.

Willbanks, James H. *Abandoning Vietnam: How America Left and South Vietnam Lost Its War.* Lawrence: University Press of Kansas, 2004.

Willbanks, James H. *The Battle of An Loc.* Bloomington: Indiana University Press, 2005.

F

FARM GATE, Operation (1961–1967)

Extended U.S. air operation in Vietnam. Operation FARM GATE began on October 11, 1961, when President John F. Kennedy ordered the United States Air Force (USAF) to send a combat detachment to assist the Republic of Vietnam (RVN, South Vietnam) in its struggle against an increasingly aggressive Communist insurgency. Kennedy earlier had asked the military services to develop a counterinsurgency capability. The USAF had responded by forming the 4400th Combat Crew Training Squadron. Nicknamed "Jungle Jim," the unit relied on older propeller-driven aircraft to both train indigenous air forces and undertake limited combat missions in support of ground forces.

Code-named operation FARM GATE, the 155 officers and airmen of Detachment 2A, 4400th Combat Crew Training Squadron, arrived at Bien Hoa Air Base—some 10 miles from the South Vietnamese capital of Saigon (present-day Ho Chi Minh City)—in November 1961. Distinctive in their Australian-type bush hats, fatigues, and combat boots, the air commandos (as they were known) initially were restricted to training South Vietnamese airmen. Soon, however, the mission's eight North American T-28 Trojans, four Douglas A-26 Invaders, and four Douglas C-47 Skytrains became involved in other tasks.

FARM GATE'S expanding role in the war began shortly after the detachment's arrival in Vietnam when it started flying reconnaissance missions and providing logistical support to U.S. Army Special Forces. On December 6, 1961, the Joint Chiefs of Staff (JCS) authorized FARM GATE to undertake combat missions, provided that at least one Vietnamese national was carried on board strike aircraft for training purposes.

During 1962 the propeller-driven B-26s and T-28s of FARM GATE became the nucleus of an expanding American air effort in Vietnam. The emphasis continued to focus on training South Vietnamese airmen to bear the burden of combat. FARM GATE aircraft also flew air strikes; however, they were restricted by rules of engagement to missions that the Vietnamese were not able to undertake. Poor facilities, inadequate supplies, and the lack of a clearly defined role in the war contributed to morale problems within FARM GATE throughout the year.

Ever-increasing requests for air support as the war intensified led President Kennedy on December 31, 1962, to approve an expansion of FARM GATE. Its growth in 1963 brought organizational changes. In July the contingent at Bien Hoa became the 1st Air Commando Squadron (Provisional), part of the Pacific Air Force (PACAF). The squadron contained two strike sections of 10 B-26s and 13 T-28s plus support sections of four Helio Aircraft U-10 Super Couriers (used for psychological warfare) and six C-47s. In addition, there were small detachments of B-26s at Pleiku and Soc Trang. Although the PACAF wanted to drop the code name of FARM GATE, Washington disapproved on grounds that the change might cause confusion for the logistical facilities supporting the operation in Vietnam.

Despite the expansion of FARM GATE, the growing intensity of the ground war brought demands for combat operations that the air commandos were unable to fulfill. For example, between May and August 1964, 431 requests for air support went unanswered. The sortie rate for FARM GATE aircraft suffered from shortages of spare parts and structural problems with the wings of the B-26s.

Aircraft problems continued to plague FARM GATE during the early months of 1964. Following several structural failures, that spring FARM GATE's B-26s and T-28s were replaced by more modern Douglas A-1E Skyraiders. The growth of the American role in the war also led to the establishment of a second squadron of A-1Es (the 602nd Fighter Commando Squadron) at Bien Hoa in October.

FARM GATE underwent a major change in March 1965. Washington finally dropped the requirement that a South Vietnamese national be carried on combat missions. At the same time, Secretary of Defense Robert S. McNamara approved the replacement of South Vietnamese markings on the aircraft with regular USAF markings. The two FARM GATE squadrons of A-1Es were now flying 80 percent of all sorties in support of the Army of the Republic of Vietnam (ARVN, South Vietnamese Army).

As the USAF presence in South Vietnam increased in 1966, FARM GATE declined in importance. In January the two A-1E squadrons moved out of Bien Hoa. One went to Nha Trang and then transferred to Thailand at the end of the year. The other squadron flew out of Pleiku.

The last vestiges of FARM GATE disappeared at the end of 1967, when the squadron at Pleiku redeployed to Thailand. By this time, the war in South Vietnam had long since lost its counterinsurgency character and assumed a more conventional nature. The air commandos would find a more congenial environment for their special talents in Laos, where a different kind of war was being fought.

William M. Leary

References

Futrell, Robert F. *The United States Air Force in Southeast Asia: The Advisory Years to 1965*. Washington, DC: Office of Air Force History, 1981.

Schlight, John. *The War in South Vietnam: The Years of the Offensive, 1965–1968*. Washington, DC: Office of Air Force History, 1988.

Ford, Gerald Rudolph (1913–2006)

U.S. Republican congressman (1949–1973), vice president (December 1973–August 1974), and president of the United States (August 1974–January 1977). Born in Omaha, Nebraska, on July 14, 1913, Gerald Rudolph Ford's birth name was Leslie Lynch King Jr. He was reared in Grand Rapids, Michigan, and was adopted by his stepfather, at which time his name was changed. Ford received his bachelor's degree from the University of Michigan, where he played football, and received his law degree from Yale University in 1941. He served in the U.S. Navy as an ensign during World War II and was elected to the first of 12 consecutive terms in the House of Representatives in 1948.

Throughout his years in Congress, a tenure that was highlighted by service as his

Gerald Ford served as a member of the U.S. House of Representatives and vice president. He became president of the United States in August 1974 on the resignation of President Richard M. Nixon. (Gerald R. Ford Presidential Library)

party's minority leader (1965–1973), Ford developed an expertise in the area of defense appropriations and became a leader of the moderate Republican bloc. He was a consistent supporter of the U.S. commitment in Vietnam, differing with the Lyndon B. Johnson administration only in that Ford believed that more money and resources should be allocated there. As vice president, a position to which he was appointed by President Richard Nixon in October 1973 after the resignation of Spiro T. Agnew, Ford publicly defended the administration's record on Vietnam.

It was left to Ford, who became president upon Nixon's resignation on August 9, 1974, to preside over the final stage of the Vietnam War. Ford was also given the unenviable tasks of healing a country ripped apart by Vietnam and the Watergate Scandal, dealing with rampant inflation, and attempting to jump-start a nearly moribund economy.

Perhaps Ford's most controversial move came only weeks into his presidency when he granted Nixon a full and unconditional pardon on September 8, 1974. Many at the time decried the move, and some claimed that Ford had struck a deal with Nixon before becoming vice president the year before. In retrospect, however, Ford's decision might well have been for the best, as it spared the nation many more months of acrimonious proceedings related to Watergate. There is no credible evidence to suggest that Ford had made any deal with Nixon, although Ford's move might well have cost him the presidency in 1976.

As president, Ford moderated his earlier, more hawkish views on the Vietnam War. Only two weeks into his presidency, he ignored the advice of those—including Secretary of State Henry Kissinger—who counseled a harsh policy against draft dodgers and combat personnel who were absent without leave (AWOL). Ford formed the Presidential Clemency Board, which reviewed individual cases and assigned specific sanctions or acquittal.

In January 1975 Ford faced the final offensives of the Cambodian Khmer Rouge and the Democratic Republic of Vietnam (DRV, North Vietnam). Rather than risk political opposition to an American recommitment in Vietnam, the Ford administration took no serious steps to counter either attack. With no treaty commitment to Cambodia, it was relatively easy for Ford to order Operation EAGLE PULL, the abandonment of the U.S. embassy in Phnom Penh on April 11, 1975. But in a secret correspondence delivered before his resignation, President Nixon had promised Nguyen Van Thieu, president of the Republic of

Vietnam (RVN, South Vietnam), that if North Vietnam violated the 1973 truce, the United States would recommit troops to South Vietnam. Nevertheless, despite the advice of Kissinger and ambassador to South Vietnam Graham Martin, Ford refused to honor that pledge. Instead, after the North Vietnamese began their 1975 Spring Offensive (the Ho Chi Minh Campaign), Ford made only a halfhearted attempt to cajole Congress into appropriating monies for South Vietnam's defense. When Congress refused, Ford ordered the evacuation of all remaining U.S. military and embassy personnel. The April 29–30 evacuation of Saigon (Operation FREQUENT WIND) removed some 1,400 Americans and 5,600 Vietnamese.

The evacuations from Phnom Penh and Saigon as well as the May 1975 *Mayaguez* Incident, America's final military engagements of the Vietnam War, were all used against Ford during the 1976 presidential election. The evacuations were cited as evidence that the Ford administration did not adequately support U.S. allies, while the *Mayaguez* Incident was cited to show that Republican administrations, by choosing force over diplomacy in a crisis, had learned nothing from Vietnam.

Ford faced a complete Washington outsider in the 1976 election, former Georgia governor Jimmy Carter. Carter promised honest and transparent government, a foreign policy based on human rights, and a reinvigorated economy. Carter defeated Ford by a razor-thin margin. Ford's link to Nixon, his inability to resolve the country's economic problems, and his perceived missteps during the last throes of the Vietnam War all worked against him. Be that as it may, Ford was a decent and honorable man who brought a modicum of normalcy to a deeply divided and demoralized nation.

Ford entered private life in January 1977 and was a member of many corporate boards. He died on December 26, 2006, at his home in Rancho Mirage, California.

John Robert Greene

References

Brinkley, Douglas. *Gerald R. Ford.* New York: Times Books, 2007.

Ford, Gerald R. *A Time to Heal: The Autobiography of Gerald R. Ford.* New York: Harper and Row, 1979.

Greene, John Robert. *The Presidency of Gerald R. Ford.* Lawrence: University Press of Kansas, 1995.

FREQUENT WIND, Operation (April 29–30, 1975)

The final U.S. evacuation from the Republic of Vietnam (RVN, South Vietnam). Operation FREQUENT WIND began at 10:51 a.m. Saigon time on April 29, 1975. Before dawn that morning a heavy artillery and rocket barrage on Tan Son Nhut Air Base signaled that the final assault on Saigon was imminent. At first light, with shells still crashing onto the field, South Vietnamese aircrews began fleeing in their planes, leaving jettisoned bombs and fuel tanks strewn on runways. From his headquarters at the air base, Major General Homer D. Smith, head of the U.S. Defense Attaché Office (DAO), reported to Ambassador Graham A. Martin that the runways were unusable and that Americans and endangered South Vietnamese would have to be flown out by helicopter to ships waiting off the Vietnamese coast, Option IV in the evacuation plan.

Martin insisted on coming to Tan Son Nhut to see for himself and, even then, waited nearly two more hours before ordering the evacuation. Finally, at 10:51 the message was flashed: "Execute Frequent Wind

Option IV." Before the airlift could begin, however, a complicated series of ship-to-ship flights had to be carried out to load 865 marines who were to provide security for the evacuation.

The first Sikorsky CH-53 Sea Stallions landed at the DAO Tan Son Nhut compound at 3:06 p.m. The marines sprinted off, and waiting evacuees scrambled on. Six minutes after landing, the helicopters were airborne again, heading back to the fleet through a sky full of woolly clouds. By evening, nearly 4,500 Vietnamese and 395 U.S. citizens had been flown out of the air base. The marines began withdrawing at 10:50 p.m. The last to leave were demolition teams who blew up secret communications gear and then the DAO building itself, along with barrels containing more than $3.6 million in U.S. currency.

No large-scale airlift was planned from the U.S. embassy. Accordingly, Brigadier General Richard E. Carey, U.S. Marine in charge of the evacuation, was stunned when shortly before 4:00 p.m., word came that several thousand people, about half of them Vietnamese, were stranded in the embassy compound, and growing crowds were gathering outside. Carey issued new orders directing helicopters and 130 additional marines to the embassy, where around 5:00 p.m. the first evacuees were lifted out.

Only one CH-53 at a time could land in the embassy's courtyard parking area, while the rooftop pad accommodated only the smaller Boeing CH-46 Sea Knights. Darkness fell, and with it came thunderstorms that dispersed the crowds outside the walls and also made flying hazardous. To guide the CH-53s, an embassy officer used a slide projector to mark the landing area with a brilliant white rectangle of light.

A slow but steady stream of flights continued until about 11:00 p.m., paused while the marines were evacuated from the DAO, and then resumed after midnight. The task force commanders and officials in Washington were increasingly anxious to finish the operation, but no one knew how many Vietnamese remained in the embassy. Helicopters kept returning to the fleet with more Vietnamese, leaving an impression, one pilot recalled, that they were trying to empty "a bottomless pit."

Fearing that the operation might go on indefinitely, task force commanders and White House officials ordered the refugee flights stopped. At 4:30 a.m. Carey radioed to his pilots that only Americans were to be flown out from then on. A communications plane over Saigon relayed a presidential message ordering Ambassador Martin to board the next helicopter. Just before 5:00 a.m., Martin climbed onto a CH-46 and left. The handful of remaining Americans followed.

About 420 Vietnamese were still waiting on the parking lot. Among them were the embassy's firemen, who had volunteered to stay until the last flight in case of an emergency. Hundreds of other Vietnamese employed by the U.S. government, including many who worked for the Central Intelligence Agency (CIA) and the U.S. Information Agency, were abandoned elsewhere in Saigon because their American superiors failed to get them into the embassy or to Tan Son Nhut. Altogether, 978 Americans and approximately 1,100 Vietnamese were flown out of the embassy.

At daybreak only the marine security force remained. Barricading the stairs behind them, they climbed to the roof. One by one the last nine CH-46s dropped down, loaded, and left for the fleet. Master Sergeant Juan Valdez was the last to board. At 7:53 a.m. on April 30, the final helicopter lifted off the roof, turned, and flew eastward.

Arnold R. Isaacs

References

Herrington, Stuart A. *Peace with Honor?* Novato, CA: Presidio, 1983.

Isaacs, Arnold R. *Without Honor: Defeat in Vietnam and Cambodia.* Baltimore: Johns Hopkins University Press, 1983.

Fulbright, James William (1905–1995)

U.S. senator and outspoken Vietnam War critic. Born in Sumner, Missouri, on April 9, 1905, James William Fulbright received his BA in history from the University of Arkansas in 1925 and an MA from Oxford University in 1928 before earning a law degree from George Washington University in 1934. He then became an attorney in the antitrust division of the Department of Justice and taught law at the University of Arkansas. In 1939 he was appointed president of the university, a post he held until 1941. An ardent and lifelong Democrat, during 1943–1945 he represented Arkansas in the U.S. House of Representatives, authoring the Fulbright-Connally Resolution that ultimately facilitated the creation of the United Nations (UN). Fulbright then served in the U.S. Senate from 1945 to 1974.

In 1945, convinced that education brought out the good in the young and cultivated a desire to preserve the American republic, Fulbright, himself a Rhodes Scholar, took the lead in the establishment of Fulbright Fellowships, an international exchange program. Independent by nature, Fulbright disagreed with aspects of foreign policy of every U.S. president from Harry S. Truman to Richard M. Nixon but especially attacked the Lyndon B. Johnson administration on the Vietnam issue. In the early 1950s Fulbright also took a sharp public stand against

U.S. senator J. William Fulbright from Arkansas. Fulbright initially supported the Vietnam War and helped shepherd the Gulf of Tonkin Resolution through the Senate, but by 1966 he had turned against U.S. involvement and became one of its most outspoken critics. (Library of Congress)

Senator Joseph R. McCarthy and the excesses of McCarthyism, certainly a risky move at the time.

Although Fulbright helped shepherd the 1964 Gulf of Tonkin Resolution through the Senate, by 1966 he had concluded that the Vietnam War was primarily an insurgency against a corrupt and repressive Saigon government that did not deserve the backing of the United States. He believed that Vietnam had no bearing on the vital interests of the United States and that American involvement was undermining democracy and individual liberty at home as well as overseas. That same year, televised hearings held by Fulbright's Senate Foreign Relations Committee helped turn popular opinion against the war and endeared him to antiwar activists.

Johnson was furious at Fulbright's scathing criticism, but the senator kept up the pressure until the last American troops left Saigon in 1973.

Fulbright was defeated in his 1974 reelection bid and resigned from the Senate in December 1974. After leaving office he joined the law firm of Hogan & Hartson in Washington, D.C. Fulbright also stayed very active in international affairs and national politics. His greatest legacies during his long public service career are certainly his anti–Vietnam War stance and the Fulbright Fellowship, which to date has sponsored more than 250,000 individuals. Fulbright died in Washington, D.C., on February 9, 1995.

Brenda J. Taylor

References

Berman, William C. *William Fulbright and the Vietnam War: The Dissent of a Political Realist*. Kent, OH: Kent State University Press, 1988.

Woods, Randall Bennett. *J. William Fulbright, Vietnam, and the Search for a Cold War Foreign Policy*. New York: Cambridge University Press, 1998.

G

Geneva Conference and Geneva Accords of 1954

International conference held in 1954 that brought the Indochina War to an end. The Geneva Conference had begun on April 26, 1954, with negotiations directed toward converting the previous year's armistice in Korea into a permanent peace. Negotiations on that issue produced no result, however. Separate negotiations over the ongoing war in Indochina began on May 8, one day after the fall of the French bastion of Dien Bien Phu in northwestern Vietnam to the Viet Minh. The Indochina talks involved representatives—in most cases the foreign ministers—of France, the Democratic Republic of Vietnam (DRV, North Vietnam), the United States, the Soviet Union, China, Britain, Laos, Cambodia, and the State of Vietnam (later the Republic of Vietnam [RVN, South Vietnam]).

The United States and the State of Vietnam proposed that North Vietnamese forces (the Viet Minh) be disarmed and that the French-created State of Vietnam be left in control of all of Vietnam. Because North Vietnam was winning the war, while the State of Vietnam was a junior partner on the losing side, this proposal was simply ignored by those who were serious about an agreement, principally the representatives of France, North Vietnam, China, the Soviet Union, and Great Britain. Washington never really believed that there was a chance that its proposals would be accepted.

U.S. secretary of state John Foster Dulles was a restive participant in the first few days of the talks on Korea but then left the conference. He saw no likelihood of an agreement on Indochina that Washington could approve, and he disliked the idea of negotiating with Zhou Enlai (Chou En-lai), foreign minister and premier of the People's Republic of China (PRC). Washington did not recognize the PRC, and Dulles despised it. Indeed, when Zhou approached Dulles to shake hands during a recess in the first session over the issue of Korea, Dulles simply turned his back.

After Dulles's May 3 departure, the U.S. delegation in Geneva was headed at various times by Undersecretary of State Walter Bedell Smith or by U.S. ambassador to Czechoslovakia U. Alexis Johnson. Johnson was under orders from Dulles not to participate in the negotiations but instead to sit and listen.

On June 17, 1954, Pierre Mendès-France became France's premier and minister of foreign affairs. In a bold statement on June 20 he threatened to resign if he could not achieve an agreement in one month (i.e., by July 20). The accords were actually completed during the early morning hours of July 21, but the clocks had been stopped to allow a pretense that it was still July 20.

During the Geneva Conference, both China and the Soviet Union had put pressure on North Vietnam to conclude a settlement. They were eager to end the fighting in order to reduce world tensions and make it easier for them to break out of their international isolation. This pressure was instrumental in causing North Vietnamese leaders to accept an agreement under which the Viet Minh gave up large amounts of territory and population then under its control in exchange for a promise of later reunification. There have also been assertions that Moscow obtained something more concrete in exchange for its pressure on North Vietnam to accept the Geneva Accords: a promise that France would refuse to join the proposed European Defense Community (EDC), an organization that would have considerably strengthened the North Atlantic Treaty Organization (NATO). North Vietnamese foreign minister Pham Van Dong, who was less than certain that reunification of North Vietnam and South Vietnam would actually occur as promised in the accords, submitted to this pressure reluctantly. Some authors have stated that the North Vietnamese leadership believed that reunification would not occur as promised, but evidence for that assertion is questionable.

The accords included separate peace agreements for Vietnam, Cambodia, and Laos (signed by French, North Vietnamese, and Cambodian officers) and an unsigned declaration of the conference. There were also unilateral declarations by several governments.

The Laotian and Cambodian governments associated with the French Union were left in control of their respective countries except for two provinces of northeastern Laos, where the Pathet Lao (Laotian Communists) were to concentrate their forces pending a political settlement.

Vietnam was to be temporarily split in approximately equal halves. A demilitarized zone (DMZ) along the 17th Parallel separated the two areas. The portion north of the DMZ was to be governed by the DRV, and the portion south of the DMZ would be governed by the French Union until 1956. North Vietnam had slightly more than half the population of Vietnam, but this was also considerably less territory and population than the Viet Minh controlled at the time the agreement was signed. Authorities in each zone were forbidden to take reprisals against people who had supported the other side in the recent war. The two zones were to be reunified following internationally supervised elections in 1956, and most participants at the conference assumed that the Communist leaders of North Vietnam would win such elections if they were held.

During the 300-day period that it would take for all North Vietnamese armed forces to leave South Vietnam and for all French Union forces to leave North Vietnam, civilians could also move from one zone to the other if they so chose. Many northerners, mainly Catholics, went south; far fewer southern supporters of the North Vietnamese government moved north.

The accords forbade Vietnam, Laos, and Cambodia from participating in military alliances; this is why none became members of the Southeast Asia Treaty Organization (SEATO) when it was established a few months after the end of the Geneva Conference. The accords also limited the introduction of foreign troops and weapons into Indochina. As the Geneva Accords provisions for Vietnam collapsed over the following years, the restriction on foreign troops eventually became the only important part of the accords still taken seriously, the only issue in regard to which there continued to be at least a pretense of compliance and enforcement.

Supervision of the implementation of the Geneva Accords was left to the International Commission for Supervision and Control (ICCS), usually referred to as the International Control Commission (ICC). India, Canada, and Poland each supplied one-third of the ICC personnel, and India furnished the chairman.

Washington was not happy with the Geneva settlement. The widespread belief that the U.S. government pledged not to undermine the accords arises from misreading of a U.S. declaration of July 21, 1954. This stated only that the United States would not go so far as to use force or the threat of force in undermining the accords. Washington certainly hoped to prevent the reunification of Vietnam as called for by the accords but was not sure of its ability to do so. Years later after reunification had indeed been blocked, Washington began claiming that the Geneva Accords had proclaimed South Vietnam an independent country.

Ngo Dinh Diem, who in June 1954 became premier of the State of Vietnam, disliked the accords even more than did the Americans, but his position in his early months in office was weak. He did not at first have real control over the Vietnamese National Army or even the Saigon police. His representative at Geneva, Foreign Minister Tran Van Do, was unable to influence the shaping of the accords, and Diem obviously did not have the ability to block their implementation. Before the middle of 1955, however, Diem had attained effective control of most of South Vietnam, and in July of that year he declared his refusal to discuss with North Vietnam the holding of the 1956 elections. Diem endorsed the idea of reunification—he always said that Vietnam was one nation rather than two—but rejected the procedures established by the accords for achieving reunification.

Edwin E. Moïse

References

Arnold, James R. *The First Domino: Eisenhower, the Military, and America's Intervention in Vietnam.* New York: William Morrow, 1991.

Randle, Robert F. *Geneva 1954: The Settlement of the Indochinese War.* Princeton, NJ: Princeton University Press, 1969.

U.S. Department of State. *Foreign Relations of the United States, 1952–1954*, Vol. 16, *The Geneva Conference.* U.S. Department of State Publication 9167. Washington, DC: U.S. Government Printing Office, 1981.

Young, Kenneth T. *The 1954 Geneva Conference.* New York: Greenwood, 1968.

Goldwater, Barry Morris (1909–1998)

U.S. senator from Arizona (1953–1965, 1969–1987) and Republican Party candidate for president in 1964. Born in Phoenix in the U.S. Territory of Arizona on January 1, 1909, Barry Goldwater graduated from the Staunton Military Academy in Virginia in 1928. He then attended the University of Arizona for one year, leaving to run the family's department store upon the death of his father. Goldwater became president of the company in 1937.

During World War II, Goldwater served in the Army Air Forces in the Pacific theater, attaining the rank of lieutenant colonel; he later rose to the rank of major general in the reserves. After the war, in 1949 Goldwater was elected to the Phoenix City Council, and in 1952 he was elected U.S. senator. Among his varied committee assignments, he served as chair of the Armed Services Committee and the Senate Select Committee on Intelligence. In 1973 he voted against the War Powers Act, arguing that it was improper and probably illegal.

During his time in the Senate, Goldwater became an articulate champion of the conservative wing of the Republican Party. He became renowned as a plainspoken advocate of smaller, less intrusive government and

Senator Barry Goldwater was the leader of the conservative wing of the Republican Party in the 1960s and a strong supporter of U.S. involvement in Vietnam. He won his party's nomination for president in 1964 but lost the general election in a landslide to Democratic Party candidate and sitting president Lyndon B. Johnson. (Library of Congress)

the proponent of a hawkish stance vis-à-vis communism.

In 1964 Goldwater ran for the presidency as the Republican nominee. During the campaign he advocated a strong military establishment with a heavy reliance on airpower and a rollback of government-sponsored social welfare programs. He was also steadfast in his commitment to halting the spread of communism, and on more than one occasion he referred to Communist leaders as captors of enslaved peoples. Goldwater was very hawkish on the issue of the war in Vietnam. He thought that the United States should do whatever it took, short of nuclear weapons, to support U.S. troops in the field. He also believed that if the United States

was not prepared to make a major military commitment, including "carrying the war to North Vietnam," it should withdraw completely. He talked about the possibility of low-level atomic weapons to defoliate infiltration routes, but he never actually advocated the use of nuclear weapons in Vietnam. Nonetheless, the Democrats easily painted Goldwater as a warmonger, eager to use atomic weapons against the Democratic Republic of Vietnam (DRV, North Vietnam). This was undoubtedly a key factor in his crushing defeat at the hands of Lyndon Johnson, who took about 61 percent of the vote to only 39 percent for Goldwater. The 1964 campaign also witnessed one of the most memorable Cold War–influenced campaign commercials, the so-called Daisy Spot that featured a little girl picking petals from a daisy. She was overshadowed by an ominous countdown followed by a nuclear detonation.

As the war wound to a close, Goldwater remained a consistent critic of U.S. command decisions. He blamed America's defeat in Vietnam on the government bureaucracy and governmental officials who stood in the way of aiding the troops and commanders in the field.

In spite of his crushing loss in the 1964 election, Goldwater was credited with reinvigorating the conservative wing of the Republican Party and with greatly influencing Ronald Reagan, who was elected president 16 years later. Goldwater's campaign also marked the beginning of the end of the Democrats' dominance in the southern United States. After the election, Republicans made great inroads in what had previously been referred to as the "Solid South."

During his last year in office, Goldwater cosponsored the Goldwater-Nichols Military Reform Act, which gave military commanders greater flexibility on the battlefield and granted the chairman of the Joint Chiefs of

Staff (JCS) more influence as the president's principal military adviser. Goldwater did not run for reelection in 1986 and retired from the Senate in 1987. An accomplished photographer, he published several books of his photographs of the landscape and people of the southwestern United States. As he grew older, he came to moderate some of his views and criticized liberals and conservatives alike. Goldwater died in Paradise Valley, Arizona, on May 29, 1998.

Lauraine Bush and Paul G. Pierpaoli, Jr.

References

Goldberg, Robert Alan. *Barry Goldwater.* New Haven, CT: Yale University Press, 1995.

Goldwater, Barry N. *The Conscience of a Conservative.* New York: Victor, 1960.

Perlstein, Rick. *Before the Storm: Barry Goldwater and the Unmaking of the American Consensus.* New York: Hill and Wang, 2001.

Gulf of Tonkin Incident (August 2 and 4, 1964)

Major event in the history of U.S. involvement in Vietnam that prompted the Gulf of Tonkin Resolution. On July 31, 1964, the U.S. Navy destroyer USS *Maddox* began a reconnaissance cruise in international waters off the coast of the Democratic Republic of Vietnam (DRV, North Vietnam). The destroyer carried extra radio gear and personnel to monitor North Vietnamese radio communications but not enough of either to give the ship the capabilities of a true electronic espionage vessel.

Around the time of the cruise, the United States also scheduled an unusually intense string of covert operations against the North Vietnamese coast. These were carried out by relatively small vessels (mostly Norwegian-built "Nasty" boats) that had Vietnamese crews but operated under American orders, were based in the vicinity of Da Nang, and were part of a program called Operation Plan 34A (OPLAN 34A). Two islands off the North Vietnamese coast were to be attacked on the night of July 30–31, and two points on the North Vietnamese mainland were to be shelled on the night of August 3–4. One island was to be shelled, and the crew of one fishing boat was to be seized and taken south for interrogation on August 5. One of the *Maddox*'s main missions was to learn about North Vietnamese coastal defenses, and it was apparently believed that more would be learned if those defenses were in an aroused state during the patrol.

On the evening of August 1 the *Maddox* approached within gun range of the island of Hon Me (one of the two islands shelled by OPLAN 34A vessels on the night of July 30–31), and the coastal defense forces became more aroused than the Americans had planned. On the afternoon of August 2 three North Vietnamese torpedo boats came out from the island and attacked the destroyer. The attack was unsuccessful, and the torpedo boats suffered varying degrees of damage and crew casualties from the *Maddox*'s guns and from strafing by four U.S. Navy aircraft from the carrier USS *Ticonderoga*, which reached the scene as the torpedo boats were retreating from the attack. The American belief that they actually sank one of the torpedo boats was mistaken, as was the Vietnamese belief that they had shot down one of the planes. President Lyndon Johnson was annoyed that the torpedo boats had not all been sunk but decided not to order any further retaliation, partly because he had reason to believe that the attack had been a result of confusion in the North Vietnamese chain of command rather than a deliberate decision by the government in Hanoi.

On August 3 the *Maddox* and another destroyer, USS *Turner Joy*, went back into the Gulf of Tonkin to resume the patrol, operating under orders more cautious than those with which the *Maddox* had gone into the Gulf of Tonkin on July 31. The new orders kept the destroyers farther from the North Vietnamese coast and completely out of the extreme northern section of the gulf. These limitations seriously reduced the ability of the destroyers to collect useful information.

Many sailors on the destroyers, including the patrol commander Captain John Herrick, thought that another attack by North Vietnamese torpedo boats was likely. For about two hours on the night of August 4 such an attack seemed to be in progress, but the situation was very confused. The *C. Turner Joy* was firing at objects on the radar screens that were invisible to the *Maddox*'s radar, while the *Maddox*'s sonar equipment was picking up sounds interpreted as the motors of North Vietnamese torpedoes, which could not be heard by the sonar equipment on the *Turner Joy*. Those who were aboard the destroyers that night are still divided on the issue. Some think that they were attacked by torpedo boats, while others think that what appeared on their radar screens was nothing but weather-generated anomalies, seagulls, foam on the crests of waves, or other natural disturbances. The overall weight of the evidence is with those who deny that an attack occurred.

In Washington, after some initial uncertainty it was decided that there had been a genuine attack. Intercepted North Vietnamese radio messages seemed to provide the clinching evidence. The texts of the messages have never been released; it seems likely that they were in fact descriptions of the combat between the *Maddox* and the three torpedo boats on August 2, being misinterpreted by the Americans as references to a more recent event. Years after the Vietnam War, former U.S. secretary of defense Robert McNamara traveled to Vietnam, where he met with the former North Vietnamese minister of defense, Vo Nguyen Giap, who assured McNamara that no second attack had occurred.

President Johnson, believing that an attack had occurred, ordered retaliatory air strikes (Operation PIERCE ARROW), which were carried out on the afternoon of August 5. He also asked for and quickly obtained a congressional resolution (the Gulf of Tonkin Resolution), passed almost unanimously on August 7, authorizing him to do whatever was necessary to deal with Communist aggression in Vietnam.

The Gulf of Tonkin Incident was politically very profitable for President Johnson in the short run. Public opinion polls showed not just overwhelming approval of the way he had handled the crisis but a dramatic improvement in the public's rating of his handling of the Vietnam War as a whole. In the long run, however, the cost to the president's credibility was considerable. It became plain that Congress and the public had been misled about the administration's intentions and about the relationship between the OPLAN 34A raids and the Gulf of Tonkin Incident. Eventually many people came to doubt that there had been any attack on the night of August 4 and suspected that the report of such an attack had been a deliberate lie rather than the honest mistake that it had been.

Edwin E. Moïse

References

Herring, George C. *America's Longest War: The United States and Vietnam, 1950–1975.* 4th ed. New York: McGraw-Hill, 2001.

Moïse, Edwin E. *Tonkin Gulf and the Escalation of the Vietnam War.* Chapel Hill: University of North Carolina Press, 1996.

Tucker, Spencer C. *Vietnam.* Lexington: University Press of Kentucky, 1999.

Gulf of Tonkin Resolution

Congressional resolution passed in response to the Gulf of Tonkin Incident of August 2 and August 4, 1964. During 1964, senior Lyndon Johnson administration officials became increasingly convinced that an acceptable conclusion of the war in the Republic of Vietnam (RVN, South Vietnam) would require some form of military attack on the Democratic Republic of Vietnam (DRV, North Vietnam) and began to consider obtaining a congressional resolution that would endorse U.S. military action. President Johnson, wary of the prospect of

President Lyndon Johnson signs the August 7, 1964, Gulf of Tonkin Resolution, which for all practical purposes gave him a free hand to commit U.S. military resources in Vietnam. (Lyndon B. Johnson Presidential Library)

a major war in Vietnam and cognizant of the problems that President Harry S. Truman had faced while waging the Korean War (1950–1953) without explicit congressional approval, was especially determined not to get into such a war without a prior commitment of congressional support. As Johnson put it, "I'm gonna get 'em on the takeoff so they'll be with me on the landing."

In May and June 1964 senior administration officials produced drafts of a possible resolution. They decided not to present these to Congress, however; there seemed too little chance of such a resolution being passed without a politically damaging debate.

On August 2 and again on August 4, it was reported that North Vietnamese torpedo boats had attacked U.S. Navy destroyers on the high seas (the Gulf of Tonkin Incident). A revised draft of the resolution was quickly presented to the Congress on August 5. The crucial passages read:

> Whereas naval units of the Communist regime in Vietnam, in violation of the principles of the Charter of the United Nations and of international law, have deliberately and repeatedly attacked United States naval vessels lawfully present in international waters, and have thereby created a serious threat to international peace; and
>
> Whereas these attacks are part of a deliberate and systematic campaign of aggression that the Communist regime in Vietnam has been waging against its neighbors and the nations joined with them in the collective defense of their freedom. . . .
>
> Congress approves and supports the determination of the President, as Commander in Chief, to take all necessary measures to repel any armed attack

against the forces of the United States and to prevent further aggression.

... [T]he United States is, therefore, prepared, as the President determines, to take all necessary steps, including the use of armed force, to assist any member or protocol state of the Southeast Asia Collective Defense Treaty requesting assistance in defense of its freedom.

The members of Congress were given the impression that the heart of the resolution, the aspect that they should consider voting for or against, was the passage about supporting the president in repelling armed attacks on U.S. forces. The congressional members were told that they should not worry about the implications of the next paragraph that authorized the president to do whatever he felt necessary to assist South Vietnam, because the administration had no intention of escalating American involvement in the war. Most members of Congress accepted these assurances, and the resolution passed on August 7, unanimously in the House of Representatives (416 to 0) and with only 2 dissenting votes, by Ernest Gruening (D-AK) and Wayne Morse (D-OR), in the Senate. In voting in favor of the measure, Congress gave Johnson carte blanche to wage war in Vietnam without a formal declaration of war. There was a very brief debate on the resolution in Congress, but few serious reservations surfaced.

After Johnson had sent U.S. combat forces to Vietnam and cited the Gulf of Tonkin Resolution as his authority, many who had voted for the resolution regretted their action, and some began to investigate the circumstances. They found that the first attack (on August 2, 1964) had not been so clearly unprovoked as they had been told, that there was serious reason to doubt that the second attack (on August 4) had ever happened, and that the administration had been working on preliminary drafts of such a resolution, which it wanted precisely because it was considering an escalation of the war long before the incidents had arisen. By 1968 the resulting disillusionment had become a serious liability for the administration.

When Senator Morse first proposed in 1966 that Congress repeal the Gulf of Tonkin Resolution, there was hardly any support. Sentiment gradually shifted, however, and the resolution was finally repealed by a vote in both houses of Congress at the end of 1970. Furthermore, in November 1973 Congress passed the War Powers Act, which very explicitly laid out the president's authority to wage war and the role that Congress should play in future conflicts.

Edwin E. Moïse

References

Herring, George C. *America's Longest War: The United States and Vietnam, 1950–1975.* 4th ed. New York: McGraw-Hill, 2001.

Moïse, Edwin E. *Tonkin Gulf and the Escalation of the Vietnam War.* Chapel Hill: University of North Carolina Press, 1996.

Tucker, Spencer C. *Vietnam.* Lexington: University Press of Kentucky, 1999.

H

Haig, Alexander Meigs, Jr. (1924–2010)

U.S. Army general, deputy assistant to the president for national security affairs (1970–1972), vice chief of staff of the U.S. Army (1972–1973), White House chief of staff (1973–1974), supreme allied commander of North Atlantic Treaty Organization (NATO) forces (1974–1979), and U.S. secretary of state (1981–1982). Born on December 2, 1924, in Bala-Cynwyd, Pennsylvania, Alexander Meigs Haig, Jr. graduated from the U.S. Military Academy, West Point, in 1947. After World War II he served on General Douglas MacArthur's personal staff in Japan and saw combat duty in the Korean War.

Haig studied at the Naval War College in Newport, Rhode Island, during 1955–1956 and was logistics staff officer at U.S. Army headquarters in Europe during 1958–1959. He received a master's degree in international relations from Georgetown University in 1961 and was assigned to the Pentagon. He served as deputy special assistant to the secretary and deputy secretary of defense during 1964–1965. Haig had the reputation of being a diligent administrator, well schooled in both politics and diplomacy.

From 1965 to 1967, Haig served in Vietnam with the 1st Infantry Division. As commander of a battalion of the 26th Infantry Regiment, he led a surprise clearing operation against the Communist-controlled village of Ben Suc; this operation became the subject of a best-selling book by journalist Jonathan Schell titled *The Village of Ben Suc*. Haig also won acclaim for his performance in commanding his battalion during a desperate but ultimately successful defense of a landing zone near the Cambodian border against a massive attack by Communist forces on April 1, 1967. After his Vietnam War service, he was stationed at West Point, where he became deputy commandant of cadets in 1968.

When Henry Kissinger reorganized the foreign affairs staff for newly elected president Richard M. Nixon in late 1968, Kissinger sought a capable military adviser with real experience in Vietnam and chose Haig. Colonel Haig became military assistant to the assistant to the president for national security affairs. Although the position was not well defined at first, his work included organizing Kissinger's staff for the National Security Council, acting as liaison between the Pentagon and the State Department, screening intelligence information, preparing security reports for the president, and running the National Security Council when Kissinger was absent. Haig was promoted to brigadier general in October 1969.

In early 1970 Haig went to Vietnam to make a personal assessment of the situation for Nixon and Kissinger and continued these visits every few months. In June 1970 Haig became deputy assistant to the president for national security affairs and thus gained direct access to President Nixon. Haig reportedly had a major role in planning and executing the secret bombing of Cambodia. In early 1972 he headed the advance party to the

U.S. Army general Alexander Haig as a lieutenant colonel commanded a battalion in Vietnam. He went on to serve in the administrations of Republican presidents Richard Nixon, Gerald Ford, and Ronald Reagan. He was U.S. secretary of state during 1981–1982. (Department of Defense)

People's Republic of China (PRC) that cleared the way for Nixon's historic February 1972 visit. Haig was promoted to major general in March 1972.

In September 1972 Nixon promoted Haig from two-star to four-star rank and to the post of U.S. Army vice chief of staff, bypassing 240 higher-ranking generals with greater seniority and prompting much criticism (Haig had been a lieutenant colonel as late as 1967). Some of these critics believed that Haig was simply a yes-man for the president and had been rewarded for this. In his new position, Haig continued to work with Kissinger on the secret peace negotiations concerning Vietnam and accompanied Kissinger on secret trips to Saigon and Paris. In 1973 Haig retired from the army to become White House chief of staff for President Nixon. After Nixon's August 1974

resignation, Haig engineered a smooth transition for President Gerald R. Ford.

In 1974 Haig resumed his military career when President Ford named him supreme commander of NATO operations in Europe, a post that Haig held until his second retirement from the army in 1979.

During the 1980 presidential election, Haig was a foreign policy and military adviser to Republican candidate Ronald Reagan. After Reagan won the election, Haig served as his first secretary of state (1981–1982). Haig advocated a tough stance against the Soviet Union and supported proposals to help Afghan rebels fight the Soviets in Afghanistan. In March 1981, when President Reagan was shot and seriously wounded, Haig appeared on national television in the chaos that followed, erroneously claiming that he was "in control" pending the return of the vice president. Haig's performance angered many, including those within the Reagan administration.

In 1982 Haig engaged in a spate of shuttle diplomacy, ostensibly designed to head off war between Great Britain and Argentina over the Falkland Islands. He appeared more supportive of the British, however, and his mismanagement of the crisis led to his resignation on June 25, 1982. Haig ran unsuccessfully for the 1988 Republican Party presidential nomination. He then formed his own consulting business. Haig died on February 20, 2010, at Johns Hopkins Hospital in Baltimore, Maryland.

Laura Matysek Wood

References

Haig, Alexander. *Caveat: Realism, Reagan, and Foreign Policy.* New York: Macmillan, 1984.

Haig, Alexander. *Inner Circles: How America Changed the World; A Memoir.* New York: Warner Books, 1992.

MacGarrigle, George L. *Combat Operations: Taking the Offensive, October 1966 to October 1967.* Washington, DC: Center of Military History, U.S. Army, 1998.

Morris, Roger. *Haig.* New York: Playboy, 1982.

Schell, Jonathan. *The Village of Ben Suc.* New York: Knopf, 1967.

Hamburger Hill, Battle of (May 11–20, 1969)

One of the bloodiest military engagements of the Vietnam War. The Battle of Ap Bia Mountain, also known as the Battle of Hamburger Hill, occurred during May 11–20, 1969, as part of Operation APACHE SNOW (May 10–June 7, 1969). The battle was fought against People's Army of Vietnam (PAVN, North Vietnamese Army) regulars who were entrenched and who, as they seldom did during the war, decided to stand against repeated U.S. frontal assaults. This created the bloody meat-grinder battle that led U.S. participants to call the location "Hamburger Hill." Coming near the time when the first American troop withdrawals were announced, the battle kindled controversy and a public debate over military objectives and tactics in Vietnam.

Dong Ap Bia, or Ap Bia Mountain, located in the A Shau Valley in the western I Corps Tactical Zone near the Laotian border southwest of Hue, is known to local Montagnards as "the mountain of the crouching beast." Not part of a larger chain, as are most other mountains on the western side of the A Shau Valley, Ap Bia stands alone some 3,175 feet above sea level. It sends several large ridges, fingers, and ravines out in all directions, covered by thick double-and-triple–canopy jungle. Hill 937 on the north and Hill 916 on the southeast are formed from these ridges.

Operation APACHE SNOW was designed to keep pressure on PAVN units and base camps in the A Shau Valley, a base area and terminus for replacements and supplies sent south by the Democratic Republic of Vietnam (DRV, North Vietnam) along the Ho Chi Minh Trail. The operation involved units from the 3rd Brigade, U.S. 101st Airborne Division (Airmobile); the U.S. 9th Marine Regiment; and the Army of the Republic of Vietnam (ARVN, South Vietnamese Army) 3rd Regiment of the 1st Infantry Division.

On the second day of the operation, Company B of the 3rd Battalion, 187th Infantry (3-187 Infantry), also known as "Rakassans," came under concentrated PAVN fire by machine guns and rocket-propelled grenades on Hill 937. The units they engaged were the 7th and 8th battalions of the PAVN 29th

Regiment, dug into heavily fortified bunker positions on the hill. After several assaults conducted over three days, the 3-187 Infantry was reinforced with two more 101st Airborne Division battalions (the 1-506 Infantry and 2-501 Infantry) and a battalion of the ARVN 3rd Regiment. On May 18, with the ARVN battalion posted to seal off the hill, a two-battalion assault nearly took the summit before a torrential rainstorm forced a withdrawal. Finally, on May 20, after 10 previous tries, a four-battalion assault drove the PAVN from their mountain fortress and into their Laotian sanctuaries.

Because the allied objective was to kill PAVN soldiers and disrupt operations in the valley, once the PAVN withdrew from the mountain, U.S. and ARVN forces abandoned it as well. And as in previous operations, as soon as U.S. and ARVN forces withdrew, PAVN troops moved right back into the area. Official U.S. casualty figures for the whole of Operation APACHE SNOW were 56 American and 5 South Vietnamese killed in action; enemy losses were estimated at 630. However, Samuel Zaffiri in *Hamburger Hill* (1988) gives American casualties as 70 dead and 372 wounded.

Fanned by media attention to the battle, which seemed to symbolize the frustration of winning battles without ever consummating the strategic victory, the debate questioned the cost in American lives of taking the hill only to abandon it for the Communists to reoccupy. The controversy led to the limiting of American military operations in the face of U.S. troop withdrawals and Vietnamization.

Arthur T. Frame

References

Stanton, Shelby L. *The Rise and Fall of an American Army: The U.S. Ground Forces in Vietnam, 1965–1975.* Novato, CA: Presidio, 1985.

Zaffiri, Samuel. *Hamburger Hill: The Brutal Battle for Dong Ap Bia, May 11–20, 1969.* Novato, CA: Presidio, 1988.

Ho Chi Minh (1890–1969)

Leading Vietnamese revolutionary and president of the Democratic Republic of Vietnam (DRV, North Vietnam) from 1945 until his death in 1969. Born Nguyen Sinh Cung in Nghe An Province on May 19, 1890, Ho Chi Minh was the son of Nguyen Sinh Sac, a mandarin and itinerant teacher. Ho received his formal education in Hue at the Quoc Hoc school. After graduation, he taught school in a number of southern Vietnamese towns, including Saigon. In 1911 Ho, now called Van Ba, hired on to a French ship as a galley helper and traveled to France and the United States and then back to Europe. While in the United States during 1912–1913, Ho supposedly was interested in the American concepts of political rights outlined in the Declaration of Independence and the Constitution. During his years abroad, he held a variety of jobs, working as a gardener, a waiter, and a photography assistant before settling on more permanent work in London as a dishwasher and an assistant pastry chef at the Carlton Hotel.

When World War I erupted, Ho moved from London to Paris, joining many Vietnamese nationals and changing his name to Nguyen Ai Quoc (Nguyen the Patriot). In France he accepted Marxist Leninism because of its anticolonial stance and position on national liberation. Ho argued that the true path to liberation for Vietnam rested in the writings of Lenin, and as a result Ho joined the French Socialist Party and founded the Association of Vietnamese Patriots. In 1920, after the Paris Peace Conference failed to address Indochinese independence, he helped

Ho Chi Minh was the most prominent Vietnamese revolutionary leader of the 1930s and 1940s and the president of the Democratic Republic of Vietnam from 1945 until his death in 1969. (Hulton Archive/Getty Images)

found the French Communist Party, claiming that anticolonial nationalism and class revolution were inseparable.

In 1923 and 1924 Ho traveled to Moscow to attend the Fourth and Fifth Comintern congresses and to receive formal theoretical and revolutionary training. While in Moscow he utilized his extensive foreign-language training, writing Marxist critiques of the Indochina problem in several languages.

In late 1924 Ho traveled to China, where he visited one of the most important Vietnamese nationalists of the modern period, Phan Boi Chau. Ho stayed in Canton for two years, organizing what would become the first Vietnamese Communist Party and writing his highly influential *Duong Cach Mang* (Revolutionary Path). In 1925 he founded the Viet Nam Thanh Nien Cach Menh Dong Chi Hoi (Vietnam Revolutionary Youth League), commonly known as the Thanh Nien. The Thanh Nien was an anticolonial organization that attempted to unite political and social issues for the ultimate liberation of Vietnam.

Ho's efforts within the Thanh Nien led to the founding of the Indochinese Communist Party in 1929, and Ho spent much of 1930 recruiting skilled organizers and strategists. He also managed to carry out a fusion of three Communist parties that had emerged in Vietnam. Ho attracted the attention of the British police in Hong Kong, and in June 1931 they arrested him. After release from a British prison, Ho returned to Moscow for more revolutionary training at Lenin University.

By the early 1940s, Nguyen Ai Quoc had changed his name to Ho Chi Minh (Ho the Bringer of Light or Ho the Enlightened One). With the Japanese invasion of Vietnam during World War II, he moved his revolutionary group to the caves of Pac Bo in the northernmost reaches of Vietnam. In Pac Bo at the Eighth Plenum of the Indochinese Communist Party in May 1941, Ho supervised the organization of the Viet Minh, a nationalist and Communist front organization created to mobilize the citizenry to meet party objectives.

During World War II, the Viet Minh entered into an alliance with the U.S. Office of Strategic Services (OSS), providing the allies with tactical and logistical support and helping to rescue downed American pilots. Some scholars have suggested that Ho's revolutionary army even received financial and military support from the OSS and that Ho himself was an official agent.

After the Japanese surrender in 1945, the Viet Minh seized power in Hanoi during the August Revolution. On September 2, 1945, with several Americans present, Ho declared Vietnamese independence from French colonial rule and announced the formation of the DRV. On March 2, 1946, he became president of the newly formed North Vietnam.

Not surprisingly, France and North Vietnam soon clashed, and a nine-year war began. Most of the Soviet-bloc countries had quickly recognized the North Vietnamese government, and it was therefore easy for the French to cast their colonial reconquest of Vietnam in Cold War terms. After years of bloody stalemate, in 1954 the French suffered a humiliating defeat at Dien Bien Phu and accepted the subsequent 1954 Geneva Accords that recognized the supremacy of Ho's Communists north of the 17th Parallel. The Geneva Accords called for nationwide elections in 1956 to reunify the country, but these elections never took place. Instead, the United States and southern Vietnamese nationals tried to build a non-Communist counterrevolutionary alternative south of the 17th Parallel.

The end result was the creation of the Republic of Vietnam (RVN, South Vietnam), with Ngo Dinh Diem as its president. Diem quickly went on the offensive, rounding up thousands of suspected Communists and sending them to prison. His anti-Communist sweeps devastated the party and led to a sharp decrease in the number of cadres operating in South Vietnam. Ho called these "the darkest days" for the revolutionary movement. He vowed to reunify the country and called the South Vietnamese government a historical aberration because "Vietnam is one country, and we are one people with four thousand years of history."

In 1960, after six years of trying to unify the country through political means, the Lao Dong, a national united Communist party under Ho's leadership, approved the use of armed violence to overthrow Diem and liberate Vietnam south of the 17th Parallel. In December 1960 the National Front for the Liberation of South Vietnam (National Liberation Front [NLF]) was established to unite former Viet Minh activists with elements of southern society who opposed the U.S.-backed Diem regime. The character and nature of the NLF and its relationship to the government in Hanoi remains one of the most controversial issues from the war. Some scholars have suggested that Ho and the Lao Dong Party (as the Communist Party was renamed in 1951) had little influence over the NLF and that the conflict in South Vietnam was essentially a civil war. Policy makers in Washington claimed that Ho himself had presided over the birth of the NLF and that the insurgency was an invasion by North Vietnam against South Vietnam. This provided the rationale for U.S. involvement in Vietnam. It appears that both explanations are wanting, since Ho's Communist party was a nationwide national organization with representation from all regions of Vietnam.

In March 1965 the United States intervened militarily in Vietnam, presenting Ho with the most difficult challenge of his life. He remained steadfast in his determination to see Vietnam reunified and refused to discuss any settlement with the United States that did not recognize this objective. In addition, Ho demanded that any settlement of the war must recognize the political and military supremacy of the NLF in South Vietnam. Because the second of these two goals was not compatible with Washington's rationale for fighting the war, Ho was clearly outlining the parameters of a struggle with no clear or easy solution.

Ho was a skillful leader who knew how to adapt revolutionary strategy to meet changing conditions. In 1965 he supervised the transition from total battlefield victory to victory through a protracted war strategy. He believed from his experience with the French that Westerners had little patience for a long and indecisive conflict. Supposedly Ho once remarked that "you can kill ten of our people for every one I kill of yours, but eventually you will grow tired and go home and I will win." From late 1965 until his death in 1969, Ho supervised the protracted war strategy that offered neither side a quick or decisive victory.

As the war dragged on, Ho used his considerable leadership gifts to mobilize the Vietnamese population. As preparations for the 1968 general offensive and uprising, known in the West as the Tet Offensive, were being made, Ho threw his enormous prestige behind the effort. He made his first public appearance in many months just weeks before the offensive to ensure universal support. Many scholars also credit Ho with ending several bitter inner-party disputes throughout the arduous conflict with the United States. He was especially skillful at managing the conflict between Le Duan, secretary-general of the Lao Dong Party, and his political rivals Truong Chinh, leader of the National Assembly, and Vo Nguyen Giap, commander in chief of the People's Army of Vietnam (PAVN, North Vietnamese Army).

Ho proved to be an able diplomat in the international arena as well. Beginning in 1956 the Soviets and the Chinese began a period of intense rivalry caused in part by Moscow's strategy of peaceful coexistence with the West and Beijing's adamant support of wars of national liberation. For years Ho skillfully managed to avoid taking sides in the Sino-Soviet dispute and had successfully played one against the other to secure increased aid. Eventually the Lao Dong Party moved closer to Moscow, and Ho accepted the Soviet-supported strategy of fighting while negotiating. During the last year of his life, Ho worked closely with the Vietnamese negotiators in Paris, outlining the nuanced differences in the Lao Dong Party's strategy.

Despite his indefatigable drive for Vietnamese liberation, Ho never lived to see his country reunified. He died on September 2, 1969, of a heart attack on the anniversary of his independence speech. His death inspired a tremendous emotional outpouring in Vietnam, adding significantly to the powerful imagery surrounding his name. Throughout the war, the Lao Dong Party cultivated the image of Ho as the protector of the Vietnamese people, and the label "Uncle Ho" was exploited to its fullest potential. Following the Communist victory in South Vietnam, the former South Vietnamese capital of Saigon was renamed Ho Chi Minh City in his honor. Today Ho's remains are enshrined in central Hanoi in a public mausoleum that attracts throngs of visitors each year.

Robert K. Brigham

References

Duiker, William J. *The Rise of Nationalism in Vietnam, 1900–1911*. Ithaca, NY: Cornell University Press, 1976.

Fenn, Charles. *Ho Chi Minh: A Biographical Introduction*. New York: Scribner, 1973.

Halberstam, David. *Ho*. Lanham, MD: Rowman and Littlefield, 2007.

Hemery, Daniel. *Ho Chi Minh: De l'Indochine au Vietnam*. Paris: Gallimard, 1990.

Herring, George C. *America's Longest War: The United States and Vietnam,*

1950–1975. 4th ed. New York: McGraw-Hill, 2001.

Ho Chi Minh. *Ho Chi Minh on Revolution: Selected Writings, 1920–1966*. New York: Signet Books, 1967.

Karnow, Stanley. *Vietnam: A History*. 2nd rev. and updated ed. New York: Penguin, 1997.

Lacouture, Jean. *Ho Chi Minh: A Political Biography*. New York: Vintage Books, 1968.

Sainteny, Jean. *Ho Chi Minh and His Vietnam: A Personal Memoir*. Chicago: Cowles, 1972.

Woodside, Alexander B. *Community and Revolution in Modern Vietnam*. Boston: Houghton Mifflin, 1976.

Young, Marilyn B. *The Vietnam Wars, 1945–1990*. New York: HarperCollins, 1991.

Ho Chi Minh Campaign (April 1975)

The Ho Chi Minh Campaign culminated in the April 1975 attack on Saigon, which gave the Democratic Republic of Vietnam (DRV, North Vietnam) the decisive victory over the Republic of Vietnam (RVN, South Vietnam) that North Vietnam had fought so long to achieve. Encouraged by the collapse of the Army of the Republic of Vietnam (ARVN, South Vietnamese Army) in early 1975 in Military Regions I and II, the Hanoi Politburo revised its timetable, deciding late in March that Saigon should be taken before the beginning of the 1975 rainy season rather than the following year. The plan was to achieve victory in what became known as the Ho Chi Minh Campaign before their dead leader's birthday (May 19).

In early April, People's Army of Vietnam (PAVN, North Vietnamese Army) units engaged ARVN forces around Saigon, blocking roads and shelling Bien Hoa Air Base. While cadres moved into the city to augment their already significant organization there, sappers positioned themselves to interrupt river transportation and attack Bien Hoa. At Xuan Loc, some 35 miles northeast of Saigon, a hard-fought battle began on April 8, the same day that a Republic of Vietnam Air Force (VNAF, South Vietnamese Air Force) pilot attacked the presidential palace and then defected.

The U.S. evacuation of Cambodia on April 12 further reinforced the North Vietnamese assessment that Washington would do nothing to prevent the collapse of the South Vietnamese government, although some members of the Saigon government could not bring themselves to believe that they would be abandoned. Even after the fall of Military Regions I and II, U.S. officials in Vietnam and visitors from Washington continued to act as if the Saigon government could successfully defend itself or, at worst, achieve some kind of negotiated settlement. Among South Vietnamese, however, opposition to President Nguyen Van Thieu was growing, and talk of a coup was widespread.

As PAVN forces cut Route 1 to the east and prepared to prevent reinforcement from the Mekong Delta by blocking Route 4 and from Vung Tau by interdicting Route 15 and the Long Tau River, the ARVN engaged in some maneuvering of its own. On April 21 President Thieu resigned in favor of Vice President Tran Van Huong, but all attempts by Washington to support the Saigon regime with increased aid failed in Congress.

Thieu's resignation did nothing to stall the PAVN offensive or buoy South Vietnamese morale. While some ARVN units fought on, leaders such as Thieu began sending personal goods and money out of the country. Banks and foreign embassies began closing, and a steady stream of foreign nationals,

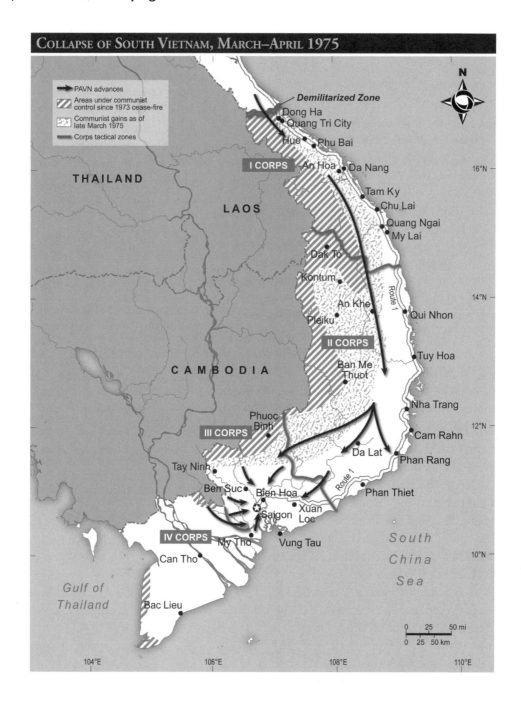

COLLAPSE OF SOUTH VIETNAM, MARCH–APRIL 1975

including many Americans, left the country, often with their Vietnamese employees.

Xuan Loc fell on April 21, and by April 25 ARVN forces around Saigon were under pressure from all sides. The PAVN attack on Saigon proper began on April 26

with artillery bombardments and a ground assault in the east, where troops had to move early to be in position to coordinate their final assault with units attacking from other directions. PAVN forces also occupied Nhon Trach, southeast of Saigon, enabling them to bring 130-millimeter artillery to bear on the Tan Son Nhut airport. On April 27 they cut Route 4, but ARVN forces fought back, counterattacking sappers who had seized bridges and putting up stiff resistance, particularly against PAVN units attacking from the east.

As an increasing number of ARVN military and civilian officials abandoned their posts, on April 28 President Huong resigned in favor of Duong Van Minh. That same day a flight of captured Cessna A-37 Dragonfly aircraft struck the Tan Son Nhut airfield, and the Communists pushed forward their attack, positioning units for the final assault and successfully attacking ARVN units in bases surrounding the city. U.S. ambassador Graham Martin delayed beginning a full evacuation, fearing its negative impact on morale. When the evacuation did begin on April 29, the final U.S. pullout was chaotic, a poorly organized swirl of vehicles and crowds trying to connect with helicopters, ships, and planes. In the confusion the Americans left many Vietnamese employees behind, and as few as a third of the individuals and families deemed to be at risk were evacuated or managed to escape.

Units around the Saigon perimeter came under heavy attack on April 29. While some PAVN units held outlying ARVN garrisons in check, other elements of General Van Tien Dung's large force moved toward the center of the city and key targets, including the presidential palace. Although some ARVN units continued to resist, they could not slow the PAVN advance. On April 30 President Minh ordered ARVN forces to cease fighting. The Ho Chi Minh Campaign had achieved its goal.

The Vietnam War ended just as students of revolutionary warfare theory had expected. Drawing upon the power developed in their North Vietnamese base area, the Communists combined five corps-sized regular army units with southern guerrillas and cadres in a final offensive that grew in strength as it piled victory upon victory against a demoralized opposition. PAVN forces could sustain their momentum in part because they did not have to detach a significant portion of their strength to administer conquered areas. That task could be left to local forces and the political infrastructure already in place before the final offensive began. Against such a strong opponent, the Saigon government proved incapable of continued resistance without active U.S. support.

John M. Gates

References

Dougan, Clark, and David Fulghum. *The Fall of the South*. The Vietnam Experience Series. Boston: Boston Publishing, 1984.

Hosmer, Stephen T., Konrad Kellen, and Brian M. Jenkins. *The Fall of South Vietnam: Statements by Vietnamese Military and Civilian Leaders*. New York: Crane, Russak, 1980.

Isaacs, Arnold R. *Without Honor: Defeat in Vietnam and Cambodia*. Baltimore: Johns Hopkins University Press, 1983.

Le Gro, William E. *Vietnam from Cease-Fire to Capitulation*. Washington, DC: U.S. Army Center of Military History, 1981.

Van Tien Dung. *Our Great Spring Victory*. New York: Monthly Review Press, 1977.

Ho Chi Minh Trail

A network of roads, paths, and waterways that stretched from the Democratic Republic of Vietnam (DRV, North Vietnam) through eastern Laos and Cambodia to the Republic of Vietnam (RVN, South Vietnam), forming the main supply route for troops and matériel that supported the North Vietnamese war against the South Vietnamese government. At its greatest extent, the Ho Chi Minh Trail

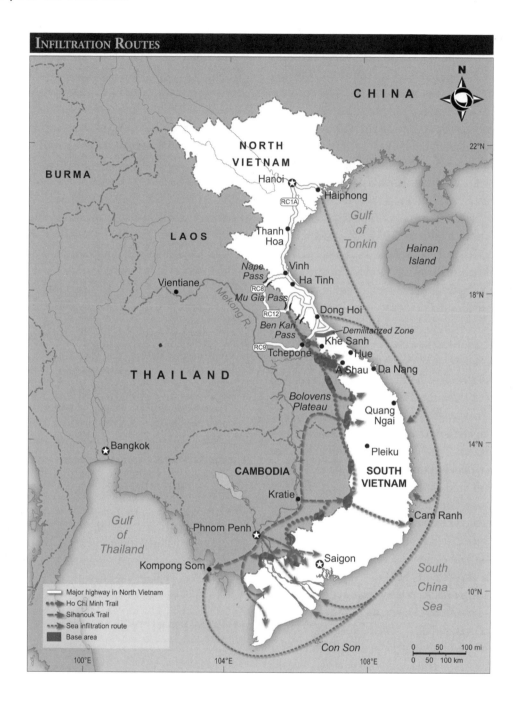

INFILTRATION ROUTES

consisted of some 12,700 miles of paths, trails, roads, and waterways that often traversed extraordinarily difficult terrain. Indeed, the trail represents one of history's great military engineering feats. The United States recognized the importance of this vital logistics link for the Communist forces in South Vietnam and waged a massive air interdiction campaign against it. This represented one of the central struggles of the Vietnam War.

On May 19, 1959, Ho Chi Minh's birthday, Major General Nguyen Van Vinh of

Hanoi's Central Military Committee instructed Major Vo Ban to open a supply route to South Vietnam. The Lao Dong Party's (Worker's Party or Communist Party) Central Committee had decided to support the Communist insurgency in South Vietnam, and men and matériel would have to be moved south to support this new phase of the struggle against the South Vietnamese government.

Assigned 500 troops for the task, Major Ban set to work building the necessary staging areas, depots, and command posts along the ancient system of footpaths and roads that connected North and South Vietnam. In August, Ban's Unit 559 (so named because it was formed during the fifth month of 1959) delivered the first supplies—20 boxes of rifles and ammunition—to Viet Cong (VC) insurgents in Thua Thien Province. By the end of the year, some 1,800 men had used the trail to infiltrate South Vietnam.

The need for secrecy led in 1960 to the development of a new route along the western side of the rugged Truong Son Range in Laos. The trail's segments gradually were widened during the year, and bicycles were introduced to transport supplies along the roads. With strengthened frames, each bicycle could handle loads averaging 220 to 330 pounds, with loads in excess of 700 pounds on occasion. The use of bicycles meant that three or four times the load of backpacking porters could move along the trail at 1.5 times the speed of porters on foot.

Hanoi continued to expand the trail during the next two years. Infiltration training centers were established at Son Tay and Xuan Mai, where soldiers underwent rigorous physical training and instruction in the use of camouflage. Once en route, infiltrators would average six miles a day along the trail. Major Ban spent 26 days on the trail at the end of 1962 observing conditions along the route. He came away impressed. He saw soldiers who were carrying loads that weighed more than 200 pounds. Not just soldiers but civilians living along the Truong Son Range helped transport supplies to South Vietnam, and although many civilians were themselves short of food, they continually offered sustenance to the soldiers.

By the winter of 1962–1963, North Vietnam had some 5,000 troops plus an engineering regiment assigned to the trail. The road complex now stretched for more than 600 miles, nearly all of it well hidden from aerial observation. Engineers had widened segments of the roads, enabling trucks to begin using portions of the route in the summer of 1962. Some 100 tons of supplies now moved weekly along the trail, transported by trucks, bicycles, elephants, and porters. An estimated 10,000 to 20,000 men had made the long journey to South Vietnam since the opening of the trail in 1959.

In October 1964, following a decision in Hanoi to expand the war in South Vietnam, the People's Army of Vietnam (PAVN, North Vietnamese Army) 95th Regiment completed its infiltration training and departed for Laos. This first large PAVN unit to move down the trail intact arrived in Kontum Province in South Vietnam's Central Highlands in December. Two additional regiments reached South Vietnam in January and February 1965.

The North Vietnamese in 1965 undertook a massive effort to improve the trail to handle the increased traffic. Engineers, assisted by North Korean, Russian, and Chinese advisers, widened footpaths into roads, strengthened bridges, and piled rocks in streams and rivers to create fords. Truck convoys, covering 50 to 75 miles during night, moved increasing amounts of matériel to South Vietnam.

Despite the beginning of heavy U.S. air attacks, the number of infiltrators increased from 12,000 in 1964 to 33,000, while truck traffic quadrupled, reaching 300 to 400 tons per week.

The tremendous expansion of the supply route led to a reorganization of the trail command. Unit 559's area of operation was redesignated a military zone under the authority of the Lao Dong Party's Central Committee. Brigadier General Phan Trong Tue took charge of the new zone, with the veteran Ban as his deputy. In December 1966 General Dong Sy Nguyen was assigned to replace Phan Trong Tue as the commander of Group 559 and the Ho Chi Minh Trail zone, a position he held until the war ended in 1975.

The war in South Vietnam during 1966 and 1967 saw heavy fighting between PAVN regular army units and U.S. forces that increased from 180,000 to 500,000 during the period. The trail ultimately became a sprawling network of hundreds of roads, paths, streams, rivers, passes, caves, and tunnels. It wound through bamboo thickets and heavy undergrowth in river valleys and under the layered canopies of tall trees in tropical rain forests at higher elevations.

Supplies were generally transported at night as trucks moved between stations 6–18 miles apart, with a PAVN officer at each station to ascertain if a convoy could reach the next station before daybreak. Trucks were hidden or camouflaged during daylight hours. Thirty to 60 PAVN soldiers manned each station, while PAVN personnel and civilian road repair crews, armed with tools and material to repair or maintain the trail, were positioned at vulnerable points between stations. Refueling facilities were located at every third to fifth station, all linked by field telephones. Convoys generally moved between three and seven shelter areas and returned to their starting point to familiarize drivers with the run and mechanics with particular trucks. This system lessened the likelihood of a large number of trucks piling up at bottlenecks and presenting a lucrative target.

By the end of 1966, according to U.S. intelligence estimates, the Ho Chi Minh Trail consisted of some 820 miles of well-hidden fair-weather roads. Supplies moved mainly during the dry season in southern Laos, which extended from November to April. It was becoming increasingly clear to U.S. planners that a major effort had to be undertaken to cut this essential supply route to South Vietnam.

In September 1966 Secretary of Defense Robert S. McNamara wrote to President Lyndon B. Johnson that the task of stopping the flow of troops and supplies from North Vietnam represented "one of our most serious unsolved problems." Attempts to use small ground units to disrupt the flow of supplies—Operation LEAPING LENA IN 1964, Operation PRAIRIE FIRE in 1965, and Operation SHINING BRASS in 1966—had proved ineffective. The U.S. Air Force had first attacked the trail in 1964 as part of Operation BARREL ROLL. Although air attacks had increased in 1965 with ROLLING THUNDER, operations against the trail remained secondary to the air war against North Vietnam. In any event, the bombing—including the introduction of Boeing B-52 Stratofortress strikes in December 1965—had not slowed the rate of infiltration.

A new study by the Jason Division of the Institute of Defense Analysis recommended the placement of an electronic barrier across the infiltration routes in Laos. McNamara warmed to this suggestion and ordered the construction of what became the McNamara Line (also known as Project Practice Nine, Project Dye Marker, and Project Muscle

Shoals). In December 1967 the electronic barrier, with its 20,000 sensors linked to computer arrays and mines, was placed into operation. The sensors were designed to detect motion and sound and were used to call in air strikes.

The appearance of the McNamara Line coincided with a shift in the air campaign from North Vietnam to Laos. On April 1, 1968, President Johnson announced a limitation on bombing North Vietnam. When the air war against North Vietnam ended in November, American air assets focused on interdiction. Operation COMMANDO HUNT formally began on November 15, 1968. Over the next five years, U.S. Air Force, Navy, and Marine Corps aircraft would drop more than three million tons of bombs on Laos in what historian Earl H. Tilford Jr. has described as the largest aerial interdiction campaign ever undertaken to that date.

The air campaign was directed in part against the trail itself. Mountainsides were bombed so that landslides would block key passes, cumulus clouds were seeded with silver iodide in an effort to extend the rainy season, and chemicals were used to defoliate the jungle. None of these tactics proved effective, however.

COMMANDO HUNT's main target was the truck traffic along the trail. Initially, propeller-driven fighter-bombers and jets had been used against the growing number of trucks that carried supplies to South Vietnam. As time passed, however, the offensive burden shifted to gunships. By the late 1960s, Lockheed AC-130 Spectres had replaced the earlier Douglas AC-47 Spookys and Fairchild AC-119K Stingers. Equipped with 20-millimeter (mm) Gatling guns and 40-mm Bofors guns (later computer-aimed 105-mm howitzers) that were combined with low-light television and infrared

and ignition detection systems, the AC-130s proved a formidable truck killer, at least until the North Vietnamese introduced surface-to-air missiles (SAMs) in the early 1970s.

The U.S. Air Force generated impressive numbers during COMMANDO HUNT. In 1969 the air campaign claimed 9,012 trucks destroyed. This number grew to 12,368 the following year. At the same time, however, the Central Intelligence Agency (CIA) estimated the total number of trucks in all of North Vietnam at only 6,000. In the end, none of the U.S. efforts to sever the trail or even sharply curtail the flow of matériel along it was successful. This failure meant that the war could not be won.

By late 1970 some 70,000 PAVN soldiers defended the trail in Laos. An estimated 8,000 men marched southward every month during the year, while more than 10,000 tons of war matériel moved monthly along the roads. Even the closure of the port of Sihanoukville in March 1970 (which since 1966 had been a major source of supplies, carried through Cambodia on the Sihanouk Trail to link up with the Ho Chi Minh Trail) failed to stem the tide of troops and matériel flowing south.

In 1971, following an abortive attempt by the United States to cut the Ho Chi Minh Trail at Tchepone in Laos (Operation LAM SON 719), the North Vietnamese seized Attopeu and Saravane in southern Laos, widening the trail to the west. It now included 14 major relay stations in Laos and 3 in South Vietnam. Each station, with attached transportation and engineering battalions, served as a petroleum-oil-lubricants (POL) storage facility, supply depot, truck park, and workshop. Soviet ZIL trucks, with a capacity of five to six tons, now traveled by day and night on all-weather roads. Protected by nature and sophisticated antiaircraft defenses, the PAVN thoroughly dominated a vast network of roads, trails, paths, and rivers stretching more than 12,700 miles in length.

On March 31, 1972, COMMANDO HUNT VII ended. It proved to be the last of the interdiction efforts waged by the U.S. Air Force against the Ho Chi Minh Trail. Following the Paris Peace Accords, the trail was extensively improved. By 1973 it had become a two-lane highway that ran from the mountain passes of North Vietnam to the Chu Pong Massif in South Vietnam. By 1974 the trail was a four-lane route from the Central Highlands to Tay Ninh Province, northwest of Saigon. The trail also boasted four oil pipelines. Reportedly from 1965 to 1975, the North Vietnamese government moved 1.777 million tons of supplies down the trail.

The North Vietnamese had won the battle of supply, a victory that spelled defeat for South Vietnam and its U.S. ally. There is a museum in Hanoi devoted exclusively to the Ho Chi Minh Trail and its important role in the Communist victory.

William M. Leary

References

Prados, John. *The Blood Road: The Ho Chi Minh Trail and the Vietnam War.* New York: Wiley, 1999.

Staaveren, Jacob Van. *The United States Air Force in Southeast Asia: Interdiction in Southern Laos, 1960–1968.* Washington, DC: Center for Air Force History, 1993.

Stevens, Richard Linn. *The Trail: A History of the Ho Chi Minh Trail and the Role of Nature in the War in Viet Nam.* New York: Garland, 1993.

Tilford, Earl H., Jr. *Crosswinds: The Air Force's Setup in Vietnam.* College Station: Texas A&M University Press, 1993.

Hue, Battle of (January 31– February 25, 1968)

Longest and bloodiest of all the Tet Offensive battles. The old imperial city of Hue, astride Highway 1 and situated about 6 miles from the coast and some 60 miles south of the demilitarized zone (DMZ), was a cultural and intellectual center of Vietnam. The city's Quoc Hoc school boasted among its alumni Ngo Dinh Diem, Ho Chi Minh, and Vo Nguyen Giap. The third-largest city in the Republic of Vietnam (RVN, South Vietnam) in 1968, Hue was a complex metropolis divided by the Perfume River. North of the river, the 2-square-mile Citadel formed the interior of the city, with the tightly packed district of Gia Hoi outside the Citadel's walls to the east. South of the river lay the

Refugees fleeing the fighting in Hue during the 1968 Tet Offensive manage to reach the south shore of the Perfume River despite the blown bridge. (National Archives)

hospital, the prison, the Catholic cathedral, many of the city's modern structures, and the newer residential districts.

The imposing Citadel was constructed in 1802. The fortress was surrounded by a zigzag moat and protected by an outer wall 30 feet high and 20 feet thick. The heart of the Citadel was the imposing Imperial Palace of Peace.

There were two key allied military installations in Hue: the headquarters of the Army of the Republic of Vietnam (ARVN, South Vietnamese Army) 1st Division at the northwest corner of the Citadel and the U.S. Military Assistance Command, Vietnam (MACV), compound on the south side of the river, near the city's eastern edge. On the morning of January 30, 1968, Brigadier General Ngo Quang Truong, commander of the ARVN 1st Division, put his headquarters on alert after receiving reports of the premature Tet Offensive attacks against the cities to the south. Truong's move was critical in preventing a complete Communist takeover of Hue.

Inside Hue, Communist supporters had been preparing for several months. Two days before the actual attack, elements of the Viet Cong (VC) 12th and Hue City Sapper battalions slipped into Hue and began their own preparations.

At 2:00 a.m. on January 31, ARVN patrols reported battalion-sized People's Army of Vietnam (PAVN, North Vietnamese Army) elements advancing on the city from the west. Aided by dense fog, these forces made their approach march unhindered. Less than two hours after the first reports, the 1st Division headquarters compound came under attack from 122-millimeter (mm) rocket fire.

The main attack on Hue was made by two regiments. The PAVN 6th Regiment, commanded by Lieutenant Colonel Nguyen

Trong Dan, attacked north of the river from the west. The 6th Regiment's objective was the Citadel. The PAVN 4th Regiment, commanded by Lieutenant Colonel Nguyen Van, approached Hue from the south and east. Initially delayed by an ARVN ambush, the 4th Regiment finally attacked the southern part of the city and the MACV compound. By dawn, Communist forces held much of Hue south of the river, all of Gia Hoi, and the southern half of the Citadel. At 8:00 a.m. they hoisted the VC flag on the huge flagpole in front of the Palace of Peace.

ARVN troops, however, still held the northern half of the Citadel, while inside the MACV compound approximately 200 Americans and a handful of Australian advisers continued to hold out. These two unexpected allied enclaves completely unhinged the Communist plans. Some eight miles south of Hue, the U.S. Marine Corps base at Phu Bai received the distress call from the MACV compound and dispatched a relief column. Unfortunately, this force, Company A, 1st Battalion, 1st Marines, commanded by Captain Gordon Batcheller, was far too small to accomplish the mission.

With additional augmentation, the marines eventually reached the MACV compound. They were then ordered to move across the river and link up with General Truong's ARVN forces. The marines still did not have sufficient combat power to accomplish that mission and were beaten back. Over the next few days, the 1st Marine Division continued to send units piecemeal into the action, all without achieving the desired effect of clearing the city.

When the Communists first stormed the city, they captured the jail and freed some 2,500 inmates, about 500 of whom joined the attacking forces. The PAVN troops also captured an ARVN depot that was well stocked with American-made weapons and ammunition. For most of the next three weeks the main Communist supply line into the city from the A Shau Valley, 30 miles to the west, remained open, ensuring that the attackers were well armed and well supplied. Eventually five PAVN reinforcing battalions joined the nine constituting the initial assault.

Believing that the situation in Hue required only local mopping-up action, the American high command underestimated the size and nature of the PAVN threat until well into the battle. MACV commander General William Westmoreland also continued to believe that the Communists would attempt to overrun Khe Sanh, and thus for several weeks he kept a tight rein on allied strategic reserve forces in that area. The nature of the urban fighting also considerably neutralized U.S. advantages in mobility, and the desire to minimize the damage to Hue itself hamstrung the allies' enormous firepower assets. As the fighting dragged on, however, on February 12 ARVN I Corps commander Lieutenant General Hoang Xuan Lam finally authorized allied forces to use whatever weapons necessary to dislodge the Communists.

In an attempt to cut the Communist supply lines into Hue, on February 2 the 2nd Battalion, 12th Cavalry, of the U.S. 1st Cavalry Division began an air assault into a landing zone six miles northwest of the city. Instead of cutting the supply lines, the Americans ran into a strong Communist blocking force. After three days of fighting, the 12th Cavalry was still four miles from the city. Meanwhile, another unit from the 1st Cavalry Division, the 5th Battalion, 7th Cavalry, approached from the west and attempted to link up with its sister battalion but was prevented from doing so until February 9.

PAVN blocking forces were much stronger than the allies had anticipated. In fact, the units opposing the 1st Cavalry Division consisted of elements of the PAVN 304th, 325C, and 324B divisions, all of which U.S. intelligence had placed at Khe Sanh massing to overrun the U.S. Marine Corps base there.

As Communist forces fighting inside Hue City came under increasing pressure, the local front headquarters recommended that Communist forces be withdrawn before they were destroyed. The PAVN high command in Hanoi, however, instructed them to hold on and to continue to fight in order to encourage and support the Communist offensive throughout the rest of South Vietnam. The high command also informed them that it was sending reinforcements to Hue. In view of the desperate situation and despite bad weather and total U.S. air supremacy, the Vietnam People's Air Force (VPAF, North Vietnamese Air Force) sent a number of Soviet-built twin-engined IL-14 transport aircraft down from Hanoi to drop ammunition and weapons by parachute to Communist forces attacking the ARVN 1st Division headquarters on the outskirts of the city. Between February 7 and February 12, a total of four IL-14 aircraft and their crews were lost while attempting to resupply Communist forces in Hue City.

By the second week in February, Westmoreland had committed six battalions to cutting off Hue. The 3rd Brigade, 1st Cavalry Division (reinforced to a strength of four battalions), attacked from the west and north, and two battalions of the 101st Airborne Division attacked from the south. The marines also continued to feed forces into the fight. By the time the south bank of the city was cleared on February 10, elements of the 1st Battalion, 1st Marines, and 1st and 2nd battalions, 5th Marines, were in the fight.

Late on February 11 the 1st Battalion, 5th Marines, crossed the river and joined the fight for the Citadel. ARVN forces, which now had close to 11 battalions in the city, had cleared about three-quarters of the Citadel, but Communist forces stubbornly held on to the southernmost section against the river. For another two weeks the bitter house-to-house fighting continued. In one of the few such instances in the Vietnam War, both sides used tear gas. Sometimes allied progress was as slow as 220 yards per day.

On February 21 the 1st Cavalry Division finally closed off the last Communist supply route into Hue. Three days later the ARVN 2nd Battalion, 3rd Regiment, overran the defenders on the south wall of the Citadel. On February 25, ARVN troops swept into the Imperial Palace, only to find that the few surviving Communist troops there had slipped away during the night. The Battle of Hue was for all practical purposes over, although Hue was not declared secure until March 2.

On February 26 the allies unearthed the first of the mass graves containing civilian victims of the Communist occupation. This systematic slaughter, which apparently was carried out by local VC cadres rather than PAVN regular troops, had begun as soon as the Communists had moved into Hue. Entire classes of people were purged, including foreigners, intellectuals, religious and political leaders, and other "cruel tyrants and reactionary elements." Searchers eventually found 2,810 bodies, while thousands more remained missing. Vietnamese scholar Douglas Pike has estimated that the Communists may have assassinated as many as 5,700 people.

Hue was a costly battle. Through February 26 the U.S. Army suffered 74 dead and 507 wounded, the U.S. Marine Corps lost 147 dead and 857 wounded, and ARVN losses totaled 384 dead and more than 1,830 wounded. The allies claimed PAVN and VC losses in excess of 5,000 dead, 89 captured, and countless more wounded. In addition to the civilians executed by the Communists, many others died or were hurt in the cross fire between the opposing forces. The intense fighting had destroyed upwards of half of the city, leaving 116,000 civilians homeless of a pre–Tet Offensive population of approximately 140,000. The experience did produce a sharp change in the attitude of the population there against the Communists, even from among Communist sympathizers.

David T. Zabecki

References

Braestrup, Peter. *Big Story: How the American Press and Television Reported and Interpreted the Crisis of Tet 1968 in Vietnam and Washington.* Novato, CA: Presidio, 1994.

Hammel, Eric. *Fire in the Streets: The Battle for Hue, Tet, 1968.* Chicago: Contemporary Books, 1991.

Hoang Ngoc Lung, Colonel. *The General Offensives of 1968–69.* Washington, DC: U.S. Army Center of Military History, 1981.

Ho Ban, ed. *Huong Tien Cong va Noi Day Tet Mau Than o Tri-Thien-Hue (nam 1968)* [The 1968 Tet Offensive and Uprisings in Tri-Thien Hue]. Hanoi: Military History Institute of Vietnam, 1988.

Laurence, John. *The Cat from Hue: A Vietnam War Story.* New York: PublicAffairs, 2001.

Oberdorfer, Don. *TET! The Turning Point in the Vietnam War.* Baltimore: Johns Hopkins University Press, 2001.

Palmer, Dave R. *Summons of the Trumpet: U.S.-Vietnam in Perspective.* San Rafael, CA: Presidio, 1995.

Pearson, Willard. *The War in the Northern Provinces, 1966–1968*. Washington, DC: Department of the Army, 1975.

Pike, Douglas. *The Viet-Cong Strategy of Terror*. Saigon: U.S. Mission South Vietnam, 1971.

Ta Hong, Vu Ngoc, and Nguyen Quoc Dung. *Lich Su Khong Quan Nhan Dan Viet Nam (1955–1977)* [History of the People's Air Force of Vietnam (1955–1977)]. Hanoi: People's Army Publishing House, 1993.

Willbanks, James H. *The Tet Offensive: A Concise History*. New York: Columbia University Press, 2007.

Ia Drang, Battle of (October 19–November 26, 1965)

Battle between U.S. and People's Army of Vietnam (PAVN, North Vietnamese Army) forces, significant because it prevented the PAVN from seizing control of the Central Highlands and cutting the Republic of Vietnam (RVN, South Vietnam) in two. The battle also demonstrated the effectiveness of air mobility against regular army units.

On October 19, 1965, PAVN troops attacked the Plei Me Special Forces camp southwest of Pleiku. Initially, troopers from the 1st Cavalry Division (Airmobile) helped Army of the Republic of Vietnam (ARVN, South Vietnamese Army) troops relieve Plei Me. On October 27 Military Assistance Command, Vietnam (MACV), commander General William Westmoreland ordered the 1st Cavalry Division to seek out and destroy the PAVN 32nd, 33rd, and 66th regiments commanded by Brigadier General Chu Huy Man. General Man also sought battle to learn how to fight the 1st Cavalry Division, whose base at An Khe blocked his route of advance to the coast.

The location of PAVN units was unclear until November 1, when the 1st Squadron, 9th Cavalry (1-9 Cavalry), commanded by Lieutenant Colonel John B. Stockton, located and captured a PAVN hospital area five miles west of Plei Me, killing or capturing 135 PAVN troops. Further reconnaissance indicated a PAVN presence in the Ia Drang Valley and on the Chu Pong Massif. The 1-9 Cavalry sprang a night ambush and developed contacts that were turned over to the infantry.

The heaviest contact developed on November 14 as Lieutenant Colonel Harold G. Moore's 1st Battalion, 7th Cavalry (1-7 Cavalry), assaulted landing zone (LZ) X-Ray on Chu Pong. Elephant grass, scrub trees, and tall anthills obstructed fields of fire. Moore made heavy contact with the PAVN 9th Battalion, 66th Regiment, before his whole understrength battalion could be landed. The American attack threw the PAVN 66th Regiment, which had just arrived in the area after a long trek down the Ho Chi Minh Trail, into total confusion. The 66th Regiment commander was away from his headquarters, leaving command of the regiment in the hands of Regiment Political Commissar La Ngoc Chau. The overall commander of all PAVN forces in the Ia Drang Valley was Colonel Nguyen Huu An, whose small forward headquarters arrived on the scene in the middle of the first day's fighting.

Under intense artillery fire and bombardment by the U.S. Air Force, Chau's 9th Battalion tried to outflank LZ X-Ray to the south, but Moore was able to get his companies in line just in time. One of Moore's platoons advanced too far and was cut off and almost destroyed, but it delayed Chau in locating the main American line. His line fully extended to the south, Moore called for help and received Company B, 2nd Battalion, 7th Cavalry, which he used as a reserve during the night.

At first light on November 15 Chau resumed the attack using his previously

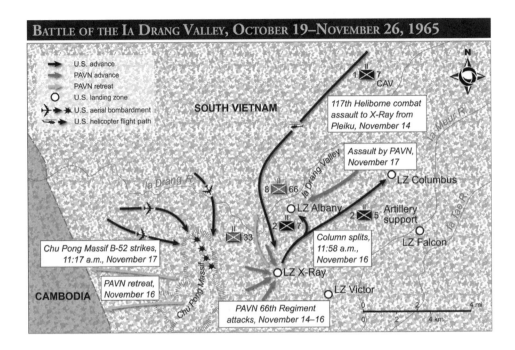

BATTLE OF THE IA DRANG VALLEY, OCTOBER 19–NOVEMBER 26, 1965

uncommitted 7th Battalion, and Lieutenant Colonel Robert Tully's 2nd Battalion, 5th Cavalry (2-5 Cavalry), marched in to give much-needed support. Chau's vicious attacks were all repulsed. The lost platoon's survivors were pulled to safety, and Boeing B-52 Stratofortresses began the first of six days of strikes on Chu Pong. Two additional batteries of artillery arrived at LZ Columbus to provide a total of 24 pieces in support. During the night, the PAVN 66th Regiment withdrew.

Early on November 16 Chau launched a last attack, which was easily repulsed. Lieutenant Colonel Robert McDade's 2nd Battalion, 7th Cavalry (2-7 Cavalry), arrived, and the 1st Cavalry Division troops located their dead and counted the dead of the PAVN 66th Regiment. By body count PAVN losses were 634, but U.S. estimates placed the number at 1,215 killed, more than 10 times the losses of the 1st Cavalry. During the day, Moore's battalion was lifted to Camp Holloway at Pleiku, but Tully's

2-5 Cavalry and McDade's 2-7 Cavalry remained to secure LZ X-Ray.

On November 17 continued B-52 sorties against the Chu Pong Massif made it necessary for Tully and McDade to move from LZ X-Ray and seek PAVN forces elsewhere. McDade's 2-7 Cavalry, with Company A of the 1-7 Cavalry attached, was ordered to march toward LZ Albany two miles away to try to regain contact with PAVN units. Tully's unit was ordered to march to the firebase at LZ Columbus.

Having little combat experience and not yet working together as a cohesive unit, McDade's men, who were strung out in a 500-yard column in high elephant grass and jungle, blundered into a PAVN ambush, and a savage battle ensued. The head of the column had just reached LZ Albany when McDade halted it and assembled his company commanders for a council.

The previous night Colonel Nguyen Huu An, not knowing that the U.S. troops planned to abandon LZ X-Ray the next morning, had ordered the 66th Regiment's 8th Battalion, which was some distance away and had not yet been engaged in the battle, to move to LZ X-Ray to attack the American units there. As he marched toward LZ X-Ray, 8th Battalion commander Le Xuan Phoi, who had no communications with either the 66th Regiment or Front Headquarters, learned of the presence of American forces in the area (McDade's 2-7 Cavalry). Phoi quickly deployed his battalion to attack McDade's men and requested assistance from nearby troops of the PAVN 1st Battalion, 33rd Regiment, who were in the area preparing to attack the U.S. artillery position at LZ Columbus. Phoi ordered his men to chop the American column into many pieces and to hug it as closely as possible in order to avoid U.S. artillery fire and air bombardment.

Bunched up at rest, McDade's men were easy targets for PAVN mortars and grenades. All unit cohesion was lost as the commanders were separated from their companies and the battle devolved into many individual combats. PAVN troops moved about killing the wounded. No artillery fire or air support was possible until McDade's men could mark their positions. After two hours of close combat, the survivors threw smoke grenades, and artillery fire and napalm rained down on the attacking PAVN troops, killing the commanders of both PAVN battalions.

By late afternoon, Company B of the 1st Battalion, 5th Cavalry (1-5 Cavalry), was ordered to help McDade's men. Marching from LZ Columbus, Company B of the 1-5 Cavalry fought its way into LZ Albany and collected the wounded into one of two perimeters for evacuation by helicopter. At dusk, Company B of the 2-7 Cavalry also reinforced McDade. PAVN troops withdrew during the predawn hours of November 18. PAVN losses were heavy, but McDade's unit lost 151 men killed, 121 wounded, and 4 missing in action.

When the Battle of Ia Drang ended on November 26, the 1st Cavalry Division had successfully spoiled the PAVN attack along Route 19 to the sea. The battle demonstrated the effectiveness of a new kind of warfare, that of air mobility. In the entire campaign U.S. losses were 305 killed, while PAVN killed were estimated at 3,561. Vietnamese postwar sources give much lower figures of PAVN losses: 559 killed and 669 wounded. These figures have been questioned by some PAVN veterans, and Vietnamese histories note that PAVN units involved in the battle suffered severe morale problems immediately following the battle. While acknowledging that its forces made many mistakes during the battle, PAVN commanders viewed the results of the battle, especially the heavy American casualties, as vindicating their new close-quarter battle tactics.

John L. Bell, Jr.

References

Dang Vu Hiep, General, with Le Hai Trieu and Ngo Vinh Binh. *Ky Uc Tay Nguyen* [Highland Memories]. Hanoi: People's Army Publishing House, 2002.

Kinnard, Harry W. O. "A Victory in the Ia Drang: The Triumph of a Concept." *Army* 17 (September 1967): 71–91.

Military History Institute of Vietnam. *Chien Thang Play Me: Ba Muoi Nam Sau Nhin Lai* [Plei Me Victory: Looking Back after Thirty Years]. Hanoi: People's Army Publishing House, 1995.

Moore, Harold G., and Joseph L. Galloway. *We Were Soldiers Once . . . and Young: Ia Drang—The Battle That Changed the War in Vietnam*. New York: Random House, 1992.

Pribbenow, Merle L. "The Fog of War: The Vietnamese View of the Ia Drang Battle." *Military Review* (January 2001): 93–97.

Stanton, Shelby L. *Anatomy of a Division: The 1st Cav in Vietnam.* Novato, CA: Presidio, 1987.

Tolson, John J. *Airmobility, 1961–1971.* Washington, DC: Department of the Army, 1973.

Indochina War (1946–1954)

Although there were other explosions of nationalist sentiment in the French Empire after World War II (most notably in Algeria in 1945 and Madagascar in 1947), that in Indochina was by far the most damaging. The Indochina War lasted eight years, from 1946 to 1954. The failure of the French government to realize that the days of colonialism were over collided with Vietnamese nationalist sentiment. The French fought the Indochina War not so much for economic reasons (by 1950 French military expenditures surpassed the total value of all French investments there) but rather for political and psychological reasons. Perhaps only with its empire could France be counted a great power. Colonial advocates also argued that if France let go of Indochina, the rest of its overseas possessions, including those in North Africa, would soon follow. This idea bore some similarity to the domino theory that was widely believed in the United States during the Vietnam War.

The Indochina War began in December 1946. Ho Chi Minh, leader of the Democratic Republic of Vietnam (DRV, North Vietnam), predicted how it would be fought. It would be, he said, the war of the tiger and the elephant. The tiger could not meet the elephant in an equal contest, so the tiger would lay in wait for the elephant, drop on his back from the jungle, and rip huge hunks of flesh with his claws. Eventually the elephant would bleed to death. The war played out very much along those lines.

Initially the war did not appear to proceed that way. After the defeat of Japan in World War II, French general Jacques-Philippe Leclerc arrived in Indochina with reinforcements. He used his small yet mobile force of about 40,000 men to dash through the country and secure southern Vietnam and Cambodia. The nationalist Viet Minh were quickly forced out into the countryside, and life returned to normal or almost so. There were those who dreaded the Viet Minh's retreat into the jungle. Leclerc was one; he was convinced that the Viet Minh represented a nationalist movement that France could not subdue militarily. Unlike most of his compatriots, he was aware of the great difficulties of jungle warfare and favored negotiations. In a secret report to Paris, Leclerc said that there would be no solution through force in Indochina.

Although the French Socialist Party showed interest in ending the war through peace talks, the steady drift of the coalition government to the Right and increasing bloodshed prevented this. French high commissioner to Indochina Admiral Georges Thierry d'Argenlieu and other French colonial administrators opposed meaningful concessions to the nationalists, and in the summer of 1946 Leclerc departed Indochina in frustration.

Leclerc was but the first in a succession of French military commanders. He was followed by generals Jean-Etienne Valluy, Roger Blaizot, Marcel Carpentier, Jean de Lattre de Tassigny, Raoul Salan, Henri Navarre, and Paul Henri Romuald Ély. This frequent change in commanders undoubtedly affected the overall efficiency and morale of the Expeditionary Force.

Most French leaders assumed that the conflict would be little more than a classic colonial reconquest, securing the population centers and then expanding outward in the classic oil slick

On November 20, 1953, a French paratrooper packs up his parachute upon landing as 2,200 French "paras" drop into the valley near Dien Bien Phu in northwestern Vietnam. (Staff/AFP/Getty Images)

(*tache d'huile*) method they had practiced so effectively in Morocco and Algeria. Meanwhile the Viet Minh, led by General Vo Nguyen Giap, steadily grew in strength and controlled more and more territory.

In May 1947 the French did make a stab at settling the war peacefully when Paul Mus traveled from Hanoi to meet with Ho Chi Minh in the latter's jungle headquarters. Mus was an Asian scholar sympathetic to the Vietnamese nationalist point of view and a personal adviser to Émile Bollaert, who had replaced d'Argenlieu as high commissioner. Mus told Ho that France would agree to a cease-fire on the condition that the Viet Minh lay down some of their arms, permit French troops freedom of movement in their zones, and turn over some deserters from the French Foreign Legion.

Ho rejected this offer, which was tantamount to surrender. In May, Bollaert declared that "France will remain in Indochina."

Despite its stated determination to hold on to Indochina, the French government never made the commitment in manpower necessary to have a chance to win. The war was essentially fought by the professional soldiers: officers and noncommissioned officers who led the French Expeditionary Corps. The French government never allowed draftees to be sent to Indochina. The small number of effectives available to French commanders left them very few options as far as strategy was concerned. Shortages of noncommissioned officers, a lack of trained intelligence officers and interpreters, and little interest in or knowledge of the mechanics of pacification all hampered the French military effort.

The French held much of Cochin China in large part because the powerful religious sects and Buddhists there opposed the Viet Minh. The French also controlled the Red River Delta in the north along with the capital, Hanoi. But the Viet Minh controlled much of the countryside, and the area they dominated grew as time went on. Initially the Viet Minh largely withdrew into the jungle to indoctrinate and train their troops. The French invested little attention and resources in pacification efforts, and their heavy-handedness alienated many Vietnamese. The French scenario had the Viet Minh eventually tiring of their cause and giving up. It never played out that way.

To increase available manpower, attract Vietnamese nationalist support, and quiet critics at home and in the United States, Paris sought to provide at least the facade of an indigenous Vietnamese regime as a competitor to the Viet Minh. After several years of negotiations, in March 1949 the French government concluded the Elysée Agreements with former emperor Bao Dai. These created the State of Vietnam, and Paris made a key concession that Vietnam was in fact one country.

The State of Vietnam allowed the French government to portray the war as a conflict between a free Vietnam and the Communists and thus not a colonial war at all. Washington, which supported France in Indochina because the United States needed French military support in Europe, claimed to be convinced.

The problem for Vietnamese nationalists was that the State of Vietnam never truly became established. The French continued to control all of its institutions, and its promised army never really materialized. France simply took the recruited soldiers and added them to its own Expeditionary Corps, in which they were commanded by French officers. In effect there were only two choices for the Vietnamese: either the Viet Minh or the French. The French therefore pushed Vietnamese nationalists into the Viet Minh camp.

In October 1947 the French mounted Operation LÉA. Involving some 15,000 men and conducted over a three-week period, it was devoted almost exclusively to the capture of Ho Chi Minh and the Viet Minh leadership and the destruction of their main battle units. LÉA involved 17 French battalions, and while it succeeded in taking Thai Nguyen and some other Viet Minh–controlled cities, it failed to both capture the Viet Minh leadership and destroy the main Communist units. It also showed the paucity of French resources in Indochina. The troops in LÉA were badly needed elsewhere, and their employment in the operation opened up much of the countryside to Viet Minh penetration. As time went on, the military situation continued to deteriorate for the French, despite the fact that by the end of 1949 Paris had expended $1.5 billion on the war.

The Indochina War changed dramatically in the autumn of 1949 when the Communists came to power in China. While that event and the recognition of the North Vietnamese government by the People's Republic of China (PRC) helped change Washington's attitude toward the war, in effect the war was lost for the French then and there. The long Chinese-Vietnam border allowed the Chinese to supply arms and equipment to the Viet Minh across their common border and provided sanctuaries in China in which the Viet Minh could train and replenish their troops. And there were plenty of arms available from the substantial stocks of weapons, including artillery, that the United States had previously supplied to the Chinese Nationalists.

The Korean War, which began in June 1950, also profoundly affected the U.S. attitude toward the war in Indochina. Korea and Vietnam came to be viewed as mutually dependent theaters in a common Western struggle against communism. Washington recognized the State of Vietnam and changed its policy of providing only indirect aid to the French effort in Indochina. In June 1950 President Harry S. Truman announced that the United States would provide direct military aid to French forces in Indochina and establish a military assistance and advisory group there. By the end of the Indochina War in 1954, the United States had provided a total of $2.5 billion in military aid to the French.

The French insisted that all U.S. military assistance be given directly to them rather than channeled through the State of Vietnam. Although a Vietnamese National Army was established in 1951, it remained effectively under French control, and France continued to dominate the State of Vietnam down to the 1954 Geneva Conference. Regardless, the Truman and Dwight D. Eisenhower administrations assured the American people that real authority in Vietnam had been handed over to the Vietnamese. With Paris refusing to concede real authority to the State of Vietnam, Vietnamese nationalists had no other recourse but the Viet Minh. In the end, Vietnamese nationalism was completely usurped by communism.

The Indochina War became an endless quagmire. By 1950 it was costing France 40–45 percent of its entire military budget and more than 10 percent of the national budget. That same year, Giap and the Viet Minh won control of Route Coloniale 4. Located in the far north, the highway paralleled the Chinese frontier and ran from the Gulf of Tonkin to Cao Bang. With the loss of this critical China frontier section, for all practical purposes the war was over for France. The Viet Minh now had ready

access to China. That the war was allowed to drag on past this point is proof of the dearth of political leadership in Paris.

In 1951 Giap, who believed that the circumstances were ripe for conventional large-unit warfare, went on the offensive in Operations HOANG HOA THAM and HA NAM NINH. His divisions were stopped cold by French forces led by General Jean de Lattre de Tassigny, probably the most capable of French commanders in the war. After these rebuffs, Giap simply shifted back to his phase-two strategy of engaging the French in circumstances of his own choosing.

In November 1951 de Lattre initiated a battle outside the important Red River Delta area. What became the Battle of Hoa Binh was a meat-grinder battle as de Lattre envisioned but for both sides. By the end of the battle in February 1952, the Viet Minh had paid a heavy price, but they had learned how to deal with French tactics and weapons and had penetrated the French defensive ring as never before.

Giap now undertook the conquest of the Thai Highlands in northwestern Vietnam. By the end of November 1952, Viet Minh units had penetrated to the Lao border. New French commander General Raoul Salan tried to halt this offensive by striking at Viet Minh supply lines. But Giap refused to take the bait, and Operation LORRAINE, which involved 30,000 French troops in special airborne, commando, and support formations, was soon in reverse. By December, Viet Minh units were still at the Lao border, and the French were back within their heavily fortified "de Lattre" defensive line of the Red River Delta.

The Viet Minh also made significant gains in central Vietnam. French control in the plateau area of the Central Highlands was narrowed to a few beachheads around Hue, Da Nang, and Nha Trang. The only areas where the French enjoyed real success were in Cochin China and in neighboring Cambodia.

In the spring of 1953 Giap assembled a powerful force to invade Laos. That country had an army of only 10,000 men supported by 3,000 French regulars. Giap employed four divisions totaling 40,000 men, and he had the assistance of 4,000 Communist Pathet Lao troops. Once more the French were compelled to disperse their slender resources. They were, however, successful in preventing the Communists from overrunning the Plain of Jars, and in late April the French halted the Viet Minh and inflicted heavy casualties on them. The onset of the rainy season forced the Viet Minh to fall back on their bases, and Laos was saved for another summer.

In July 1953 new French commander General Henri Navarre arrived in Indochina. Buoyed by promises of increased U.S. military aid, Navarre attempted a general counteroffensive. The press in both France and the United States gave much attention to the so-called Navarre Plan. Unknown to the public, however, was Navarre's own secret pessimistic assessment to his government that the war could not be won militarily and that the best that could be hoped for was a draw.

Using his increased resources (French forces now numbered about 517,000 men, while the Viet Minh had perhaps 120,000 men), Navarre vowed to go over to the offensive. He ordered the evacuation of a series of small posts, and this was accomplished successfully. At the same time, the State of Vietnam's army was given more responsibility, although this was a case of too little, too late.

Concurrently, Giap was gathering additional resources for a larger invasion of Laos. With five divisions he hoped to overrun all of Laos and perhaps Cambodia, then join up with Viet Minh units in the south for an assault on Saigon itself. In the meantime, some 60,000 guerrillas and five regular regiments would tie down the French in the north. In December 1953 and January 1954 the Viet Minh overran much of southern and central Laos.

Navarre's response was the establishment of an airhead in far northwestern Vietnam astride the main Viet Minh invasion route into Laos. Navarre envisioned this either as a blocking position or as bait to draw some enemy forces into a set-piece conventional battle, in which they would be destroyed by French artillery and airpower. The location that Navarre selected, the village of Dien Bien Phu, was in a large valley, and the French conceded the high ground around it to the Viet Minh. When he was asked later how he got into this position, Navarre said that at the time the French arrived there the Viet Minh did not have artillery, so there was no danger from the heights. It was an astonishing statement. Dien Bien Phu was also a considerable distance, some 200 miles by air, from Hanoi, and the French had only a very limited transport airlift capability (approximately 100 aircraft).

Giap took the bait, but he sent four divisions rather than the one that Navarre had envisioned to engage the French at Dien Bien Phu. The siege of the French fortress lasted from March 13 to May 7, 1954. The battle's outcome was largely decided by two key factors: the Viet Minh's ability to bring Chinese-supplied artillery to the heights by means of an extensive supply network of coolies (the "People's Porters," Giap called them) and the inadequacy of French air support. On May 7 the French garrison surrendered. Although there was some debate in Washington over possible U.S. military intervention (Operation VULTURE), President Dwight D.

Eisenhower rejected it because the British refused to go along.

The French defeat at Dien Bien Phu allowed political leaders in Paris to shift the blame to the generals and at last bring the war to an end. Attention now turned to a conference previously scheduled in Geneva to deal with a variety of Asian problems. New French premier Pierre Mendès-France imposed a 60-day timetable for an agreement, threatening to resign if one was not reached. The Geneva Accords were signed on the last day of the deadline.

The Vietnamese were pressured by China and the Soviet Union into an agreement that gave them less than they had won on the battlefield. Cambodia and Laos were declared independent, but the key provision was recognition of the unity of Vietnam. Pending unification, there were to be an armistice and a temporary dividing line at the 17th Parallel. The agreements also provided for the compulsory regroupment of troops and, if they desired, civilians. Nationwide elections were to be held in two years. Ultimately the Republic of Vietnam (RVN, South Vietnam), headed by Ngo Dinh Diem, refused to permit the elections, and the United States supported Diem in his stand. This led to a renewal of the war in an American phase.

In the Indochina War, the French and their allies sustained 172,708 casualties: 94,581 dead or missing and 78,127 wounded. These are broken down as 140,992 French Union casualties (75,867 dead or missing and 65,125 wounded), with allied Indochina states losing 31,716 (18,714 dead or missing and 13,002 wounded). Viet Minh losses were perhaps three times those of the French and their allies. Some 25,000 Vietnamese civilians also died.

For France, the struggle had been a distant one. Paris had not dared send draftees to Indochina, and the conflict had been fought largely by the professionals. The French government almost immediately transferred these men to Algeria, where another insurrection had broken out. The soldiers pledged that this time there would be no betrayal.

Spencer C. Tucker

References

Duiker, William J. *The Communist Road to Power in Vietnam.* 2nd ed. Boulder, CO: Westview, 1996.

Dunn, Peter M. *The First Vietnam War.* New York: St. Martin's, 1985.

Fall, Bernard B. *Hell in a Very Small Place: The Siege of Dien Bien Phu.* New York: Lippincott, 1966.

Fall, Bernard B. *Street without Joy: The French Debacle in Indochina.* Rev. ed. Mechanicsburg, PA: Stackpole Books, 1994.

Gras, Yves. *Histoire de la Guerre d'Indochine.* Paris: Éditions Denoël, 1992.

Hammer, Ellen J. *The Struggle for Indochina.* Stanford, CA: Stanford University Press, 1954.

Kelly, George A. *Lost Soldiers: The French Army and Empire in Crisis, 1947–1962.* Cambridge, MA: MIT Press, 1965.

Maneli, Mieczyslaw. *The War of the Vanquished.* New York: Harper and Row, 1969.

Porch, Douglas. *The French Foreign Legion: A Complete History of the Legendary Fighting Force.* New York: HarperCollins, 1991.

J

Johnson, Lyndon Baines (1908–1973)

Congressman, senator, vice president, and president (1963–1969) of the United States. Born in Stonewall in the Texas Hill country near Austin on August 27, 1908, Lyndon Baines Johnson became secretary to Texas congressman Richard Kleburg following graduation from Southwest Texas State Teachers College in 1930. President Franklin D. Roosevelt appointed Johnson Texas administrator of the National Youth Administration in 1935. Two years later he won election to the U.S. House of Representatives. He served very briefly in the U.S. Navy during World War II and in 1948 was elected to the U.S. Senate. In 1953 he became Senate minority leader and in 1955 became Senate majority leader.

As minority leader during the 1954 Dien Bien Phu crisis, Johnson opposed unilateral U.S. intervention. Later, despite opposition from other southerners in the Senate, he was instrumental in securing passage of the Civil Rights Acts of 1957 and 1960. He sought the Democratic nomination for the 1960 presidential election but lost to Massachusetts senator John F. Kennedy, who chose Johnson as his vice presidential running mate largely to help balance the ticket. Following Kennedy's assassination on November 22, 1963, Johnson took the oath of office aboard the presidential plane, Air Force One.

As president, Johnson tried to establish what he termed "the Great Society," an ambitious program of civil rights legislation and social welfare programs. Using his considerable legislative skill and the reverence attached to the memory of the slain Kennedy, Johnson won passage of the landmark Civil Rights Act of 1964. He declared a "War on Poverty" and secured passage of the Economic Opportunity Act. Soundly defeating Republican senator Barry Goldwater in the 1964 presidential race, Johnson used his popularity and the large Democratic majority in Congress to push through the Medicare Act of 1965, federal aid to education, increased funds for the War on Poverty, and enactment of consumer protection laws and environmental protection laws. In 1965 Johnson personally appeared before Congress to urge passage of the Voting Rights Act. The act became law that same year.

Johnson was less deft and less successful in foreign relations, however. In January 1964 Panamanians rioted against the U.S. presence there and demanded U.S. withdrawal. Skirmishes with U.S. soldiers resulted in the deaths of 4 U.S. soldiers and 20 Panamanians. The Panamanian government then broke relations with the United States for three months. In April 1965 Johnson ordered the landing of 20,000 U.S. troops in the Dominican Republic, fearing that Dominican internal strife posed a danger to Americans there and might result in a Communist takeover. During the June 1967 Six-Day War, Israeli jets attacked the U.S. intelligence ship USS *Liberty* off the Sinai coast, killing 10 crew members and wounding 100. The Six-Day War also produced strained relations with the

U.S. president Lyndon B. Johnson greets American troops in Vietnam in 1966. The Vietnam War shaped Johnson's entire presidency and overshadowed his considerable achievements in domestic policy. (National Archives)

Soviet Union, which supported the Arab states. Johnson made an effort to thaw the Cold War in a meeting to discuss nuclear weapons and other issues with Soviet premier Aleksei Kosygin in Glassboro, New Jersey, in June 1967, but Soviet military intervention in Czechoslovakia led to postponement of substantive follow-up negotiations.

It was the war in Vietnam, however, that consumed Johnson's energy and ultimately his presidency. Johnson, who fervently believed in containment and the domino theory, saw Vietnam as a test of national resolve. His foreign policy advisers (many of them retained from the Kennedy administration) shared his views. Moreover, Johnson had been in Congress when China became Communist in 1949, and he vividly recalled the domestic political turmoil that followed as Republicans attacked Democrats for "losing" China. He informed one biographer

that the fall of China to the Communists ended the effectiveness of the Harry S. Truman administration and was a factor in the rise of McCarthyism. Johnson would not, he vowed, "be the President who saw Southeast Asia go the way China went."

Soon after taking office, Johnson began escalating the war in Vietnam. In February 1964 he authorized Operation Plan (OPLAN) 34A, providing U.S. support for raids by forces of the Republic of Vietnam (RVN, South Vietnam) against the Democratic Republic of Vietnam (DRV, North Vietnam). In April he appointed General William C. Westmoreland as U.S. commander in Vietnam. In June, Johnson replaced Ambassador Henry Cabot Lodge with General Maxwell Taylor. Both Westmoreland and Taylor favored increased troop levels in Vietnam.

The Gulf of Tonkin Incident of August 1964 was a crucial event in the war's escalation. In retaliation for reported attacks on U.S. destroyers, President Johnson ordered bombing of North Vietnamese naval bases and oil depots. He also asked Congress to pass the Gulf of Tonkin Resolution, authorizing him to take "all necessary measures to repel any armed attacks against the forces of the United States and to prevent further aggression." The measure passed the House by a vote of 416 to 0 and the Senate by a vote of 88 to 2, with dissenting votes by Democratic senators Ernest Gruening of Alaska and Wayne Morse of Oregon. There was virtually no floor debate on the resolution.

In the years that followed, the Gulf of Tonkin Resolution was used to justify presidential war making in Vietnam. In February 1965 Johnson ordered retaliatory bombing of North Vietnam after Communist forces attacked U.S. military posts at Pleiku and Qui Nhon. When presidential adviser McGeorge Bundy, after a visit to Vietnam, warned Johnson that without increased U.S. action defeat appeared inevitable within a year, Johnson commenced Operation ROLLING THUNDER, regular (rather than reprisal) air strikes on North Vietnam. Along with intensified bombing came increased troop commitments. The same month that ROLLING THUNDER began, Westmoreland requested and received troop increases. In April 1965 Johnson approved Westmoreland's request to use U.S. forces for offensive operations anywhere in South Vietnam. An important turning point came in July 1965, when Johnson announced that U.S. forces there would be increased from 75,000 to 125,000 men, with additional troops to be provided as Westmoreland requested them. The war now became increasingly Americanized. Before the close of Johnson's presidency in January 1969, there were more than 500,000 U.S. troops in Vietnam.

Johnson frequently expressed desire for peace. In a speech at Johns Hopkins University on April 7, 1965, he offered to open discussions and suggested a Southeast Asia economic development plan that would include North Vietnam. On May 10 he called the first of several bombing halts, but when Hanoi did not respond, air strikes resumed. In 1966 an attempt by Polish diplomat Janusz Lewandowski to initiate discussions between the countries, code-named Operation MARIGOLD, failed after several months' effort. Speaking in San Antonio on September 29, 1967, Johnson offered to stop air and naval attacks on North Vietnam in exchange for a promise not to take advantage of the halt to infiltrate men and supplies into South Vietnam. Hanoi refused, insisting that discussions could not take place until the United States stopped bombing without conditions.

The war had a devastating impact on Johnson's Great Society program and the U.S. economy as a whole. The cost of the war forced steady cutbacks in programs and promoted inflation. Johnson agreed to a $6 billion budget reduction in nondefense spending in 1967 and the next year imposed a 10 percent tax surcharge. The U.S. international balance-of-payments deficit, not caused but rather aggravated by the war, and devaluation of the British pound in November 1967 contributed to a run on the U.S. dollar and a gold crisis in March 1968. The federal deficit grew from $8.7 billion in 1967 to $25.2 billion in 1968. By 1968, the Johnson administration suffered from a credibility gap resulting from public disillusion produced by falsely optimistic statements about the war.

Opposition to the Vietnam War soon developed at home. College students and faculty members began teach-ins against the war in 1964, and they were joined by others as the war continued. Democratic senator J. William Fulbright of Arkansas, chairman of the Senate Foreign Relations Committee, began hearings on the war in 1966. George F. Kennan, father of the containment doctrine, was among those who appeared before the committee to criticize the war. In October 1967, 100,000 war protestors gathered in Washington, D.C.

Passionate debate also swirled inside the Johnson administration. Undersecretary of State George W. Ball opposed the war early on, informing Johnson in a meeting on July 21, 1965, that it would be "long and protracted with heavy casualties." Ball continued to argue against escalation until he resigned in 1966. Presidential adviser Clark Clifford, in a letter dated May 17, 1965, cautioned Johnson to keep ground forces in Vietnam to a minimum and warned that the U.S. presence there could turn into a "quagmire." In a conference at the presidential retreat at Camp David, Maryland, on July 25, 1965, Clifford argued that the United States could lose 50,000 troops and spend hundreds of billions of dollars in a war that could not be won. By the spring of 1967, Secretary of Defense Robert S. McNamara, once a proponent of escalation, recommended restricting bombing and limiting troop levels. He soon resigned in protest. These war critics were opposed by General Westmoreland and the Joint Chiefs of Staff (JCS), who continued to press for a more intensive ground war involving additional troops and increased bombing.

It was during this period, in November 1967, that Johnson asked Clifford to arrange a meeting of a group of elder statesmen headed by Dean Acheson, subsequently dubbed the "Wise Men," to advise him on Vietnam policy. In their meeting with the president on November 21, they offered divided opinions that bolstered Johnson's determination to continue the war.

The January 1968 Tet Offensive caused Johnson to reevaluate the war. When General Westmoreland requested another 205,000 troops after Tet to take the offensive against Communist forces, the president asked Clifford—who had just replaced McNamara as secretary of defense—to head a task force examining the request. The task force offered a dramatic reassessment of Vietnam, recommending only a 20,000-man increase there and urging increased responsibility for the war effort by the South Vietnamese government and the Army of the Republic of Vietnam (ARVN, South Vietnamese Army). Johnson's acceptance of the task force's recommendations marked the first change in policy since escalation began in 1964.

Preliminaries to the 1968 presidential election demonstrated the additional political costs of the Vietnam War. In the March 13, 1968, New Hampshire primary election, Senator Eugene McCarthy of Minnesota, running on an antiwar platform, won 42 percent of the Democratic vote, which was regarded as a defeat for the president (who was not officially entered in the primary). Soon afterward Senator Robert F. Kennedy entered the nomination race as an antiwar candidate.

In a television address to the nation on March 31, Johnson announced a halt to naval and air attacks against North Vietnam except in the area just north of the demilitarized zone (DMZ). At the end of his speech he made the stunning announcement that he would neither seek nor accept the Democratic nomination for president.

North Vietnam expressed willingness to enter peace talks, which began in May 1968 in Paris with the United States represented by W. Averell Harriman. On October 31 Johnson ordered a complete cessation of air and naval attacks on North Vietnam. The Paris talks, which bogged down in disagreements about the shape of the negotiating tables, proved inconclusive through the end of Johnson's presidency. In the November presidential election, Richard Nixon narrowly defeated Vice President Hubert Humphrey in a decision that was seen as a referendum on "Johnson's War."

Johnson retired to his Texas ranch following Nixon's inauguration in January 1969. Vietnam continued to trouble him deeply. He told biographer Doris Kearns Goodwin that "I knew from the start that I was bound to be crucified either way I moved. If I left the woman I really loved—the Great Society—in order to get involved in that bitch of a war on the other side of the world, then I would lose everything at home. . . . But if I left that war and let the Communists take over South Vietnam, then I would be seen as a coward and my nation would be seen as an appeaser and we would both find it impossible to accomplish anything for anybody anywhere on the entire globe." He also stated that part of his rationale for escalating the war was to win over the support of hawks, especially Republicans, for his Great Society legislation. Johnson died of a heart attack at his ranch near Stonewall, Texas, on January 22, 1973.

Kenneth R. Stevens

References

Barrett, David M. *Uncertain Warriors: Lyndon Johnson and His Vietnam Advisers.* Lawrence: University Press of Kansas, 1993.

Berman, Larry. *Lyndon Johnson's War: The Road to Stalemate in Vietnam.* New York: Norton, 1989.

Berman, Larry. *Planning a Tragedy: The Americanization of the War in Vietnam.* New York: Norton, 1982.

Gardner, Lloyd C. *Pay Any Price: Lyndon Johnson and the Wars for Vietnam.* Chicago: Ivan R. Dee, 1995.

Goldman, Eric F. *The Tragedy of Lyndon Johnson.* New York: Knopf, 1969.

Goodwin, Doris Kearns. *Lyndon Johnson and the American Dream.* New York: Harper and Row, 1976.

Herring, George C. *LBJ and Vietnam: A Different Kind of War.* Austin: University of Texas Press, 1994.

Johnson, Lyndon B. *The Vantage Point: Perspectives of the Presidency, 1963–1969.* New York: Holt, Rinehart and Winston, 1971.

Schandler, Herbert Y. *The Unmaking of a President: Lyndon Johnson and Vietnam.* Princeton, NJ: Princeton University Press, 1977.

VanDeMark, Brian. *Into the Quagmire: Lyndon Johnson and the Escalation of the Vietnam War.* New York: Oxford University Press, 1991.

JUNCTION CITY, Operation (February 22–May 4, 1967)

Second corps-sized operation of the Vietnam War and one of the largest offensive operations conducted by allied forces. Lasting from February 22 to May 14, 1967, Operation JUNCTION CITY involved four Army of the Republic of Vietnam (ARVN, South Vietnamese Army) and 22 U.S. battalions, including elements of the U.S. 1st, 4th, 9th, and 25th Infantry divisions; the 11th Armored Cavalry Regiment; and the 196th Infantry and 173rd Airborne brigades.

JUNCTION CITY followed by one month Operation CEDAR FALLS, the first corps-sized operation of the war. Actually, JUNCTION CITY was planned first, in late 1966. At the last minute, Military Assistance Command, Vietnam (MACV), intelligence

U.S. infantrymen in the high grass of a clearing in War Zone C, 80 miles northeast of Saigon and near the Cambodian border on February 24, 1967, during Operation JUNCTION CITY. The soldiers are advancing on snipers who had fired on helicopters bringing in the troops. (AP/Wide World Photos)

located a Communist regional headquarters along the Saigon River in the area of the Iron Triangle. Major General Jonathan O. Seaman, commander of U.S. II Field Force, wanted to delay JUNCTION CITY and launch an immediate attack into the Iron Triangle, and this operation became CEDAR FALLS. Commander of the U.S. 1st Infantry Division Major General William E. DePuy opposed the delay, but MACV commander General William C. Westmoreland sided with Seaman. According to the revised schedule, JUNCTION CITY was to be launched immediately following CEDAR FALLS. It was delayed another month, however, to allow planners to correct some of the operational problems that surfaced during the first operation.

The primary objective of Operation JUNCTION CITY was the elimination of the elusive Viet Cong (VC) 9th Division,

commanded by Colonel Hoang Cam, a native of northern Vietnam who commanded a Viet Minh regiment at the Battle of Dien Bien Phu in 1954. The area of operations was War Zone C, a Communist-controlled sanctuary from which the VC 9th Division had long operated freely. War Zone C was a 50- by 30-mile flat, marshy area along the Cambodian border northwest of Saigon. The region was checkered with open areas of rice paddies and thick patches of heavy jungle. Dominating War Zone C was Nui Ba Den ("Black Virgin Mountain"). This 3,235-foot-high landmass rose straight up from the flat surrounding countryside. Honeycombed with caves, Nui Ba Den was long suspected of being the forward headquarters of the Central Office for South Vietnam (COSVN).

The JUNCTION CITY plan called for the 3rd Brigade, 4th Infantry Division, and the

196th Infantry Brigade to take up a western blocking position along the Cambodian border, roughly four to five miles east of Highway 22 and Highway 246. The 1st Infantry Division would block the east, along Highway 4. The 173rd Airborne Brigade and the 1st Brigade, 1st Infantry Division, would seal off the northern section. The 11th Armored Cavalry Regiment on the right and the 2nd Brigade, 25th Infantry Division, on the left would then sweep into this giant inverted horseshoe from the south.

Twenty days before the start of JUNCTION CITY the 25th Infantry Division launched Operation GADSDEN. Twelve days later, on February 14, the 1st Infantry Division launched Operation TUCSON. The objective of both operations was to position the western and eastern flank forces.

JUNCTION CITY commenced on February 22 with the north envelopment. The 173rd Airborne Brigade's 2nd Battalion, 503rd Infantry, parachuted into drop zones near Ca Tum, only seven miles from Cambodia. The unopposed drop was the only major U.S. combat jump of the war. Simultaneously, 249 helicopters inserted eight infantry battalions into the north side in one of the largest mass helicopter lifts of the war. The following day the southern forces positioned along Highway 247 started sweeping north into the horseshoe.

On February 28 units of the 173rd Airborne Brigade discovered the VC's Central Information Office, including an underground photographic laboratory complete with film. That same day near the eastern tip of the horseshoe, the 1st Division's 1st Battalion, 16th Infantry, engaged the PAVN's 2nd Battalion, 101st Regiment, at Prek Klok. Twelve days later, on March 10, the VC 272nd Regiment attacked the U.S. 168th Engineer Battalion, which was building a Special Forces base camp at Prek

Klok. The engineers were defended by the mechanized 2nd Battalion, 2nd Infantry, and the 2nd Battalion, 33rd Artillery, firing howitzers point-blank into the attackers.

On March 18 JUNCTION CITY entered its Phase II, which focused on clearing the eastern sector of War Zone C. The 173rd Airborne Brigade pulled out of the operation and was replaced by the 1st Brigade, 9th Infantry Division. During the course of the next two weeks, the three major engagements of Operation JUNCTION CITY followed in rapid succession.

During the night of March 19, the VC 273rd Regiment attacked and almost overran the 9th Infantry Division's Troop A, 3rd Squadron, 5th Cavalry, in its defensive perimeter at Ap Bau Bang. At one point the cavalry troopers were buttoned up inside their armored personnel carriers while artillery inside the perimeter fired antipersonnel beehive rounds directly at the vehicles to sweep off the attackers. While Troop A continued grimly to hold on, the 5th Cavalry's Troop B and Troop C fought their way into the beleaguered perimeter to assist their comrades. Throughout the night, U.S. Air Force planes carried out 87 close air support runs under flare illumination.

In the early morning hours of March 21 under the direct command of VC 9th Division commander Hoang Cam, two Communist regiments, the 273rd Regiment, 9th Division, and the PAVN 16th Regiment (also known as the 70th Guards Regiment) attacked the 4th Infantry Division's 3rd Battalion, 22nd Infantry, and 2nd Battalion, 77th Artillery, at Fire Support Base (FSB) Gold near Suoi Tre. As that battle wore on, a relief force from the 2nd Battalion, 12th Infantry, fought its way into FSB Gold. Fighting there continued into the daylight hours, when FSB Gold was finally relieved by elements of the 2nd Battalion, 34th

Armor Regiment. In his postwar memoirs General Hoang Cam, while still claiming victory, acknowledged that his forces suffered heavy losses during this battle.

The last big fight of JUNCTION CITY took place near Ap Gu at Landing Zone (LZ) George. The 1st Battalion, 26th Infantry, commanded by Lieutenant Colonel Alexander M. Haig, had occupied LZ George on March 26. Five days later the battalion was moving east from LZ George when Company B came under heavy attack and was pinned down. Haig had to commit his Company A to break Company B free. Near the end of the day both companies were able to withdraw to the defensive perimeter near the LZ, which had been reinforced by elements of the 1st Battalion, 16th Infantry. In the early morning hours of April 1, the VC 271st Regiment and the VC 1st Battalion, 70th Guards Regiment, attacked in force. A combination of artillery fire, helicopter gunships, and tactical air support finally drove them off.

Although Operation JUNCTION CITY was originally planned to have only two phases, Phase III kicked off on April 15. A floating brigade of one mechanized battalion from the 25th Infantry Division and an ARVN battalion made constant sweeps through War Zone C. Meanwhile, the 196th Infantry Brigade was sent north to the I Corps Tactical Zone. Units from the 9th Infantry Division temporarily moved into the 196th Infantry Brigade's former area of operations in the shadow of Nui Ba Den. For the most part, the Phase III sweeps turned up only empty countryside.

On the tactical level, Operation JUNCTION CITY was a success. Although Communist propaganda organs claimed that the U.S. and the ARVN lost 13,500 killed, 800 armored vehicles, and 119 artillery pieces, actual tallies were 282 killed and 1,576 wounded. Three tanks, 4 helicopters, 5 howitzers, and 21 armored personnel carriers were also lost. MACV claimed Communist forces dead at 2,728, with an undetermined number of wounded. The allies also seized 490 weapons, 850 tons of rations, 500,000 pages of documents, and more than 5,000 bunkers and other military structures.

Despite the tactical results, JUNCTION CITY, as with so many other American efforts in the war, failed to yield long-term strategic leverage. Although the three regiments of the VC 9th Division were temporarily shattered, they would be back in force less than a year later for the 1968 Tet Offensive. War Zone C was far from neutralized, but JUNCTION CITY made General Vo Nguyen Giap painfully aware that the major VC operating and supply bases in South Vietnam were vulnerable to the vastly superior U.S. mobility and firepower. As a result, the Communists moved their headquarters across the border into Cambodia, where North Vietnamese regular forces were already based. With the United States (for a wide variety of reasons) unwilling to expand large-scale offensive operations into Cambodia, American military planners were left with little choice but to pursue a defensive campaign with the objective of wearing down the VC and the PAVN through attrition.

David T. Zabecki

References

Hoang Cam and Nhat Tien. *Chang Duong Muoi Nghin Ngay* [The Ten Thousand-Day Journey]. Hanoi: People's Army Publishing House, 2001.

Rogers, Bernard W. *Cedar Falls Junction City: A Turning Point*. Vietnam Studies Series. Washington, DC: Department of the Army, 1974.

Stanton, Shelby L. *The Rise and Fall of an American Army: The U.S. Ground Forces in Vietnam, 1965–1975*. Novato, CA: Presidio, 1985.

K

Kennedy, John Fitzgerald (1917–1963)

U.S. congressman (1946–1952), senator (1953–1961), and president of the United States (1961–1963). John Fitzgerald Kennedy was born in Brookline, Massachusetts, on May 29, 1917, into a large and wealthy Irish Catholic family. His father, Joseph P. Kennedy, was a multimillionaire with presidential aspirations, and his mother, Rose Fitzgerald Kennedy, came from a prominent and politically active Boston family. After attending the elite Choate Preparatory School in Wallingford, Connecticut, Kennedy earned his bachelor's degree from Harvard University in 1940. He also spent six months of his junior year working in the U.S. London embassy while his father was U.S. ambassador to Great Britain. John Kennedy's observations during this time inspired his senior honors thesis on British foreign policies, which was published the year he graduated under the title *Why England Slept*. During World War II, Kennedy served four years in the U.S. Navy. He was awarded the Navy and Marine Corps Medal and the Purple Heart for action as commander of *PT-109*, which was rammed and sunk by a Japanese destroyer in the South Pacific.

Kennedy worked for a brief time as a newspaper correspondent before entering national politics at the age of 29, winning election as Democratic congressman from Massachusetts in 1946. In Congress, Kennedy backed social legislation that benefited his largely working-class constituents and criticized what he considered to be the Truman administration's "weak stand" against Communist China. Throughout his career, in fact, Kennedy was known for his strong anti-Communist sentiments.

Kennedy won election to the U.S. Senate in 1952. In 1953 he wed the New York socialite Jacqueline Bouvier. Kennedy had a relatively undistinguished Senate career. Never a well man, he suffered from several serious health problems, including a back operation in 1955 that nearly killed him. His illnesses limited his ability to become an activist senator. While he recuperated from his back surgery, Kennedy wrote—with the assistance of his wife—his second book, *Profiles in Courage*, that won the 1957 Pulitzer Prize for History.

Despite his fragile health and lackluster performance in the Senate, Kennedy nonetheless was reelected in 1958 after losing a close contest for the vice presidential nomination at the Democratic National Convention in 1956. He now set his sights on the presidency. In 1960 he won the Democratic nomination for president on the first ballot. As a northerner and a Roman Catholic, he recognized his weakness in the South and shrewdly chose Senator Lyndon Baines Johnson of Texas as his running mate. As a candidate Kennedy promised more aggressive defense policies, health care reform, and housing and civil rights programs. He also proposed his New Frontier agenda, designed to revitalize the flagging U.S. economy and to bring young people into

Democrat John F. Kennedy was elected president in November 1960. He escalated the U.S. military presence in South Vietnam but was reportedly contemplating a withdrawal of U.S. forces when he was assassinated in Dallas, Texas, on November 22, 1963. (John F. Kennedy Presidential Library)

government and humanitarian service. Kennedy also charged the Dwight D. Eisenhower administration with allowing the Soviet Union to secure superiority in ballistic missiles over the United States. Winning by the narrowest of margins, Kennedy became the nation's first Roman Catholic president. Only 42 years old, he was also the youngest man ever to be elected to that office.

In his inaugural address Kennedy spoke of the need for Americans to be active citizens and to sacrifice for the common good. His address, which in some respects was a rather bellicose call to arms, ended with the now-famous exhortation, "Ask not what your country can do for you, ask what you can do for your country." As president, Kennedy set out to fulfill his campaign

pledges. Once in office, he was forced to respond to the ever-more-urgent demands of civil rights advocates, although he did so rather reluctantly and tardily. By establishing both the Alliance for Progress and the Peace Corps, Kennedy delivered American idealism and goodwill to aid developing countries.

Despite Kennedy's idealism, no amount of enthusiasm could blunt the growing tension of the U.S.-Soviet Cold War rivalry. One of Kennedy's first attempts to stanch the perceived Communist threat was to authorize American-supported Cuban exiles to invade the Communist island in an attempt to overthrow Fidel Castro in April 1961. The Bay of Pigs Invasion, which turned into an embarrassing debacle for the president, had been planned by the Central Intelligence Agency (CIA) under the Eisenhower administration. Although Kennedy harbored reservations about the operation, he had nonetheless approved it. The failure heightened already-high Cold War tensions with the Soviets and ultimately set the stage for the Cuban Missile Crisis of 1962.

Cold War confrontation was not limited to Cuba. In the spring of 1961 the Soviet Union renewed its campaign to control West Berlin. Kennedy spent two days in Vienna in June 1961 discussing this hot-button issue with Soviet premier Nikita Khrushchev. In the months that followed, the crisis over Berlin intensified with construction of the Berlin Wall, which prevented East Germans from escaping to the West. Kennedy responded to the provocation by reinforcing troops in West Germany and announcing an increase in the nation's military strength. The Berlin Wall, unwittingly perhaps, eased tensions in Central Europe that had nearly resulted in a superpower conflagration.

With the focus directed away from Europe, the Soviets began to clandestinely install nuclear missiles in Cuba. On October 14, 1962, U.S. spy planes photographed the construction of missile-launching sites in Cuba. The placement of nuclear missiles only 90 miles from America's shores threatened to destabilize the Western Hemisphere and undermine the uneasy Cold War nuclear deterrent. Kennedy imposed a naval quarantine on Cuba that was designed to interdict any offensive weapons bound for the island. The world held its collective breath as the two Cold War superpowers appeared perched on the abyss of thermonuclear war, but after 13 harrowing days of fear and nuclear threat, the Soviet Union agreed to remove the missiles. In return the United States pledged not to preemptively invade Cuba and to remove its obsolete nuclear missiles from Turkey.

Both Kennedy and Khrushchev had been sobered by the Cuban Missile Crisis, realizing that the world had come as close as it ever had to a full-scale nuclear war. Cold War tensions were diminished when the Soviets, British, and Americans signed the Limited Nuclear Test Ban Treaty on August 5, 1963, forbidding atmospheric testing of nuclear weapons. In October 1963 the same three nations agreed to refrain from placing nuclear weapons in outer space. To avoid potential misunderstandings and miscalculations in a future crisis, a hotline was installed that directly linked the Oval Office with the Kremlin.

The situation in Southeast Asia proved intractable, however. Throughout much of the Kennedy administration, Vietnam yielded place to Laos, the immediate Indochina problem. Eisenhower had told Kennedy that Laos was the key to Southeast Asia, for if Laos fell, the Communists would bring "unbelievable pressure" on Thailand, Cambodia, and the Republic of Vietnam (RVN, South Vietnam). By the end of 1960, Washington had already provided the Laotian government

with $300 million in assistance, of which 85 percent was military.

Civil war in Laos flared anew. A military coup had overthrown the rightist government of Laos in August 1960, and civil war had broken out. Both the Democratic Republic of Vietnam (DRV, North Vietnam) and the Soviet Union actively intervened with troops and transport aircraft, but Kennedy decided not to send U.S. troops. In contrast to the Eisenhower administration, Kennedy was not averse to a neutralist solution. After much diplomatic activity, a 14-nation conference convened in Geneva in June 1961. During the next year, the conference hammered out a solution in the form of a tripartite coalition government, which proved short-lived. It was clear that the North Vietnamese government wanted to partition Laos in order to secure its vital Ho Chi Ming Trail network by which it supplied the Communist insurgents, known in South Vietnam as the Viet Cong (VC). The failure of the Communists to live up to the Geneva Accords concerning the neutralization of Laos greatly angered Kennedy and strongly influenced his policies regarding Vietnam, precluding an administration retreat there.

Kennedy continued the previous administration's policy of maintaining the South Vietnamese government. Indeed, well before he was president he had been a strong supporter of future South Vietnamese president Ngo Dinh Diem. In 1961 Kennedy sent Frederick Nolting to Saigon as the U.S. ambassador. Nolting had no Asian experience and deferred to Diem, meaning that there was no pressure on the South Vietnamese leader to institute meaningful reforms. Kennedy also escalated U.S. involvement, prompted by the long-standing U.S. commitment to battle communism as enunciated in the Containment Doctrine. Many in Washington professed to seeing South Vietnam as part of a larger fabric of Communist expansion. While Kennedy and many of his advisers tended to regard the fighting in Vietnam as a civil war, this position was not shared by Secretary of State Dean Rusk, who held to the belief in "aggression from the North" in Vietnam. The so-called domino theory also held sway. This was the belief that if South Vietnam fell to the Communists, then the rest of Southeast Asia would surely follow. There was also the argument that U.S. prestige was on trial. If the United States failed in Vietnam, other nations would lose confidence in Washington's willingness to project power. Also at stake was the matter of whether the West could respond to what was regarded as a new Communist strategy of wars of national liberation.

Domestic political considerations also played a role. Kennedy was sensitive to Republican charges that the Democrats had "lost" China, and he had suffered rebuffs in the failure of the Bay of Pigs Invasion and in the erection of the Berlin Wall. Another "retreat" before communism could have serious political repercussions.

In May 1961 Kennedy dispatched Vice President Johnson to Saigon, and less than a week after his return Kennedy agreed to an increase in the size of the Army of the Republic of Vietnam (ARVN, South Vietnamese Army) from 170,000 to 270,000 men. The ARVN, however, continued to be indifferently led, inadequately equipped, and ineffective in combat. Kennedy then sent two fact-finding missions to Vietnam. Economist Dr. Eugene Staley led the first in June and July 1961. His findings stressed that military action alone would not work, and he called for substantial social and political reform. He also pointed out the necessity for greater security and called for the construction of a network of strategic hamlets to protect the peasants. This belated South Vietnamese

effort at counterinsurgency, run by Diem's brother Ngo Dinh Nhu, was plagued by inefficiency and corruption and proved to be a failure.

In October 1961 Kennedy's chief military adviser General Maxwell D. Taylor and his special assistant for national security affairs Walt W. Rostow led another fact-finding mission to Vietnam. They saw the situation primarily in military terms and, among other recommendations, urged a large increase in airplanes, helicopters, and support personnel. They even recommended the deployment of 8,000 American combat troops under the guise of a flood-control team. Undersecretary of State George W. Ball argued against any escalation in the U.S. role. He met privately with Kennedy to express his opposition to the Taylor-Rostow proposals and predicted that if the United States accepted these recommendations, in five years it would have 300,000 men in Vietnam. Kennedy responded, "George, you're just crazier than hell. That isn't going to happen."

Kennedy accepted the Taylor-Rostow recommendations except for the introduction of U.S. troops, which Diem, prescient in this at least, opposed as a potential propaganda bonanza for the Communists. To coordinate this increased aid, however, in February 1962 Washington opened a new military headquarters in Saigon. Known as the Military Assistance Command, Vietnam (MACV), it was headed by General Paul D. Harkins.

U.S. helicopter pilots were soon at work supporting ARVN troops in the field, and by the end of 1962 the number of American military personnel in South Vietnam had quadrupled to 11,326. The U.S. military infusion may have helped prevent an outright VC victory in 1962, but the advantage was only temporary. The North Vietnamese government was also escalating its support in the south, and increasingly large numbers of troops, along with weapons and ammunition, were arriving in South Vietnam.

The war was not the only thing going badly for the Diem government. Buddhist displeasure with Diem's government, which was heavily staffed with Catholics, led to demonstrations throughout the country and to the self-immolation of Buddhist monks. Diem's brother Nhu, who directed the secret police, greatly embarrassed the Kennedy administration with his raids on Buddhist pagodas and the arrest of some 1,400 people. Diem saw only the Communist threat and was quite oblivious to the fact that his regime's oppression was feeding the insurgency. His response was more oppression. Increasing numbers of South Vietnamese saw Diem as isolated and out of touch with the people.

Henry Cabot Lodge replaced Nolting in August 1963 and came to the conclusion that the war could not be won with Diem. The CIA had already reported that an influential faction of South Vietnamese generals wanted to overthrow Diem. Washington was initially opposed to a coup and favored a purge of Diem's close advisers, but Diem refused to part with his brother and other loyal supporters, and the Kennedy administration then assured the generals that it would not intervene. Meanwhile, further outrages against the Buddhists led the Kennedy administration on October 2, 1963, to suspend economic subsidies and cut off financial support of Nhu's Special Forces. This was a further encouragement to the plotters, who struck early on November 1, 1963. The next day both Diem and Nhu, who Washington had assumed would be given safe passage out of the country, were murdered.

Diem's death did not bring political stability, for Washington never could find a worthy successor to him. The United States, which could not win the war with Diem,

apparently could not win the war without him either.

Kennedy's position on the war was by now ambiguous. In the spring of 1963 he told close advisers that he planned to use optimistic reports from Harkins and Taylor to justify a complete withdrawal of U.S. forces, something that he intended to keep secret until after the 1964 presidential elections. Kennedy's last statement on Vietnam, made in Fort Worth, Texas, on November 22, 1963, reveals the dilemma he faced: "Without the United States, South Vietnam would collapse overnight." While there is simply no way of knowing what Kennedy would have done about Vietnam had he lived, his statements about withdrawal were made when the United States was seen to be winning the war.

In an effort to solidify political support in Texas, in November 1963 Kennedy embarked on a whirlwind tour of the state with his wife and vice president. On November 22, 1963, in Dallas, Texas, Kennedy, who was riding in an open car, was instantly killed by an assassin's bullet. In the hours immediately after the murder, Lee Harvey Oswald was arrested for the assassination of the president. Two days later as the president's body lay in state at the U.S. Capitol, Jack Ruby fatally shot Oswald in the basement of the Dallas police station as millions of Americans watched on television. In a great national outpouring of grief, Kennedy was laid to rest in Arlington National Cemetery on November 25, 1963.

Lacie A. Ballinger and Spencer C. Tucker

References

Beschloss, Michael R. *The Crisis Years: Kennedy and Khrushchev, 1960–1963.* New York: HarperCollins, 1991.

Bradlee, Benjamin C. *Conversations with Kennedy.* New York: Norton, 1975.

Dallek, Robert. *An Unfinished Life: John F. Kennedy, 1917–1963*. Boston: Little, Brown, 2003.

Freedman, Lawrence. *Kennedy's Wars: Berlin, Cuba, Laos, and Vietnam*. New York: Oxford University Press, 2000.

Schlesinger, Arthur M. *A Thousand Days: John F. Kennedy in the White House*. New York: Houghton Mifflin, 1965.

Sidey, Hugh. *John F. Kennedy, President*. New York: Atheneum, 1964.

Kennedy, Robert Francis (1925–1968)

U.S. attorney general, 1961–1964; U.S. senator, 1965–1968; and presidential candidate, 1968. Born in Brookline, Massachusetts, on November 20, 1925, Robert Francis Kennedy enlisted in the Naval Reserve and attended the V-12 training program at Harvard University. After a period of active duty during which he served on a destroyer, he received his honorable discharge in May 1946 and returned to Harvard, where he graduated in 1948. In 1951 he received a law degree from the University of Virginia and was admitted to the bar. The following year he managed his brother John F. Kennedy's successful senatorial campaign. In September 1951 Robert Kennedy covered the proceedings surrounding the U.S.-Japan Peace Treaty in San Francisco for the *Boston Post*.

As legal counsel to several Senate committees in the 1950s, Kennedy served on Republican senator Joseph McCarthy's Senate Subcommittee on Investigations. In 1957, as head counsel and staff director on the committee investigating racketeering in U.S. labor unions, Kennedy engaged in a high-profile confrontation with Teamster boss James (Jimmy) Hoffa, which earned Kennedy national notoriety. He also played a peripheral role in the famous Army-McCarthy Hearings of 1954, although he allegedly professed a continued fondness for his former mentor.

In 1960 Kennedy managed his brother's successful campaign for the presidency. The president-elect soon selected his brother as attorney general of the United States. Not surprisingly, the move resulted in charges of nepotism among Kennedy's detractors. At the Justice Department, Kennedy made civil rights and organized crime his top priorities. Indeed, he placed the full weight of the Justice Department behind the growing civil rights effort, while also keeping close tabs on civil rights leader Martin Luther King Jr. But Kennedy's influence extended beyond the Justice Department. As his brother's closest adviser, he became increasingly involved in foreign policy and national security issues and played a significant role in the October 1962 Cuban Missile Crisis. He also supported U.S. initiatives in Southeast Asia, including those in Indochina.

Following his brother's assassination in November 1963, Kennedy stayed on as attorney general under President Lyndon B. Johnson but in 1964 resigned to run for the U.S. Senate from New York. Indeed, Johnson and Kennedy had little in common and little use for one another. In the Senate, Kennedy continued to support U.S. efforts in Vietnam, at least initially. He did lament the toll that the war took upon his brother's Alliance for Progress and Johnson's Great Society programs and criticized the 1965 U.S. intervention in the Dominican Republic. Despite his growing apprehension toward the Vietnam War, especially the massive bombing of the Democratic Republic of Vietnam (DRV, North Vietnam), Kennedy refrained from openly opposing administration policy. He was also acutely aware of the appearance of opportunism and the public perception of his political motives. But as racial strife and urban violence convulsed the country along with mounting antiwar sentiment and massive protests, Kennedy found it increasingly difficult to support the war or to refrain from criticizing the Johnson administration.

The presidential campaign of 1968 opened the door for Kennedy, but he held back, refusing at first to jump into the fray. After antiwar senator Eugene McCarthy's unexpectedly strong performance in the New Hampshire primary, which essentially was a repudiation of Johnson, Kennedy entered the race. In March 1968, when President Johnson announced that he would not seek reelection, Vice President Hubert Humphrey became the administration's presidential candidate.

In addition to his stated desire to end the fighting in Southeast Asia, Kennedy also sought to bridge the many rifts within American society. He quickly emerged as a serious contender for the presidency and became the darling of many in the antiwar Left. On June 4, 1968, he won the all-important California primary, thereby becoming his party's front-runner. In the early morning hours of June 5 after addressing his supporters at the Ambassador Hotel in Los Angeles, he was shot by Sirhan Sirhan. Kennedy died the following day at the age of 42. Kennedy's assassination, less than five years after that of his brother and only two months after that of King, devastated the nation and added sad punctuation to the divisive era.

David Coffey

References

Palermo, Joseph A. *In His Own Right: The Political Odyssey of Senator John F. Kennedy.* New York: Columbia University Press, 2001.

Schlesinger, Arthur M., Jr. *Robert Kennedy and His Times.* Boston: Houghton Mifflin, 1978.

Kent State University Shootings (May 4, 1970)

Site of an incident on May 4, 1970, involving members of the Ohio National Guard and antiwar demonstrators that left four students dead and nine wounded. The incident at Kent State University in Ohio was perhaps the climax of both protests against the war in Vietnam and student unrest on campuses across the nation.

The protests at Kent State were part of a widespread spontaneous reaction to the announcement by President Richard M. Nixon of the U.S. incursion into Cambodia, which had begun only days earlier. Other universities, Princeton University among them, voted at this time to strike in protest against the war. A strike center was established at Brandeis University, and by May 4 nearly 100 campuses were on strike or planning to do so.

At Kent State, demonstrations began on May 1. Whether actually political in motivation or just an example of the rites of spring, property was damaged, and the mayor of Kent called for the National Guard. On May 2 a large rally took place on campus. After the rally, although not necessarily because of it, the Reserve Officers' Training Corps (ROTC) building on campus was set alight and burned down. The following day, a Sunday, the Ohio National Guard took up positions on campus. That evening students gathered on the Commons were tear-gassed and dispersed.

On May 4 a rally was scheduled for noon. The National Guard attempted to disperse a crowd of perhaps 2,000 people. After some unsuccessful efforts, the National Guard suddenly began firing from the top of a small rise called Blanket Hill at students gathered in a parking lot below. The firing,

A Kent State University student lies on the ground after National Guardsmen fired into a crowd of demonstrators on May 4, 1970, in Kent, Ohio. Four students were killed and nine were wounded when the Guard opened fire during a campus protest against the U.S. "incursion" into Cambodia. (AP/Wide World Photos)

which began at 12:25 p.m., lasted for 13 seconds. It was estimated that 61 rounds were fired. Four people were killed: Allison Krause, Jeffrey Miller, Sandra Scheuer, and William Schroeder. Only Krause and Miller had been active participants in the rally. The university was closed by court order later that day, but the National Guard remained on duty until May 8.

As a result of what had transpired, hundreds more campuses went on strike or experienced demonstrations against the war and the killings at Kent State. Estimates vary, but it is likely that at least 500 campuses either went on strike or experienced serious disruption after the Kent State

shootings. The nature of the strikes and demonstrations varied from campus to campus, but a few common denominators were evident. In addition to events held on campuses to protest the war and the incident at Kent State, students often attempted to influence public opinion in nearby communities. Plans were also made to take an active role in the congressional campaign that autumn (the Movement for a New Congress, or the Princeton Plan), the idea being to elect as many peace candidates as possible. Finally, some students formed committees to support the Nixon administration. A few students traveled from campus to campus to encourage strikes, but strike movements were almost always spontaneous reactions to events and were locally organized.

Ten days after the shootings at Kent State, 2 students were killed and 12 wounded when police opened fire on a women's dormitory at Jackson State College in Mississippi in the aftermath of another student antiwar rally. Although many saw the Jackson State incident as another sign of disturbing trends, reaction to that event was relatively muted, and it has never been given the same attention as the Kent State incident. Some have argued that race played a role in that, as Jackson State was historically African American, and the students killed were black.

The President's Commission on Campus Unrest (also known as the Scranton Commission) issued its report on the Kent State shootings in September 1970. Although criticizing violent protest, the report condemned the actions of the National Guard as "unnecessary, unwarranted, and inexcusable." The report also called on President Nixon to provide "compassionate, reconciling moral leadership . . . [to] bring the country together again."

Although protests against the war in Vietnam continued with some impressive events in the early 1970s, campus-based protest lost most of its momentum after the Kent State shootings. The Movement for a New Congress had little effect on the autumn campaigns. Other initiatives produced in reaction to the Cambodia Incursion and the Kent State shootings had a similar lack of impact. The Kent State shootings marked the end of an era.

Michael Richards

References

Anderson, Maggie, and Alex Gildzen, eds. *A Gathering of Poets*. Kent, OH: Kent State University Press, 1992.

Bills, Scott L., ed. *Kent State/May 4: Echoes through a Decade*. Kent, OH: Kent State University Press, 1982.

Gordon, William A. *The Fourth of May: Killings and Coverups at Kent State*. Buffalo, NY: Prometheus Books, 1990.

Morgan, Edward P. *The 60s Experience: Hard Lessons about Modern America*. Philadelphia: Temple University Press, 1991.

Zaroulis, N. C., and Gerald Sullivan. *Who Spoke Up? American Protest against the War in Vietnam, 1963–1975*. Garden City, NY: Doubleday, 1984.

Khe Sanh, Battle of (April–October 1967 and January–March 1968)

There were two distinct phases in the Battle of Khe Sanh. The first phase in the battle for the Khe Sanh base occurred in 1967 and evolved from U.S. and People's Army of Vietnam (PAVN, North Vietnamese Army) engagements in the northern region of the Republic of Vietnam (RVN, South Vietnam). As part of his overall strategy, Military Assistance Command, Vietnam (MACV), commander General William Westmoreland ordered the construction of interconnected bases along the supposedly demilitarized zone (DMZ) between the Democratic Republic of Vietnam (DRV, North Vietnam) and South Vietnam to act as an infiltration barrier, later using sensors and motion detectors to alert these bases to Communist troop movements. The outposts were designed not to stop PAVN infiltration but instead to funnel the troop movements to areas where bombers could easily strike them.

One such outpost was Khe Sanh, a base camp on high ground surrounded by dense tree-canopied heights of up to 3,000 feet. It was some 6 miles from Laos to the west

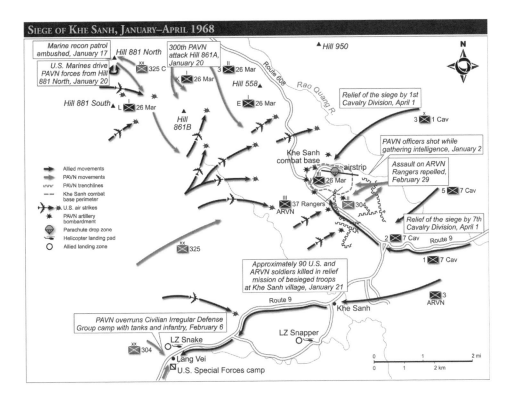

SIEGE OF KHE SANH, JANUARY–APRIL 1968

Marine recon patrol ambushed, January 17

Hill 881 North

U.S. Marines drive PAVN forces from Hill 881 North, January 20

300th PAVN attack Hill 861A, January 20

325 C

▲ Hill 950

N

Hill 881 South ▲

L 26 Mar

325 C

K 26 Mar

3 26 Mar

Hill 558 ▲

E 26 Mar

Route 608

Rao Quang R.

Relief of the siege by 1st Cavalry Division, April 1

3 1 Cav

Hill 861B

Khe Sanh combat base

airstrip

26 Mar

PAVN officers shot while gathering intelligence, January 2

Assault on ARVN Rangers repelled, February 29

5 7 Cav

37 Rangers ARVN

304

Relief of the siege by 7th Cavalry Division, April 1

2 7 Cav

Route 9

1 7 Cav

Allied movements
PAVN movements
PAVN trenchlines
Khe Sanh combat base perimeter
U.S. air strikes
PAVN artillery bombardment
Parachute drop zone
Helicopter landing pad
Allied landing zone

325

Approximately 90 U.S. and ARVN soldiers killed in relief mission of besieged troops at Khe Sanh village, January 21

Route 9

Khe Sanh

3 ARVN

PAVN overruns Civilian Irregular Defense Group camp with tanks and infantry, February 6

LZ Snake

LZ Snapper

304

Lang Vei
U.S. Special Forces camp

0   1   2 mi
0   1   2 km

and 14 miles from the DMZ to the north. The village of Khe Sanh, inhabited by Vietnamese and Montagnards, was surrounded by smaller villages and French coffee plantations in a majestic landscape of emerald-green jungles, piercing mountains, and mist-shrouded waterfalls. Westmoreland hoped that Khe Sanh could be used as a patrol base for arresting PAVN infiltration from Laos along Route 9, a long-range patrol base for operations in Laos, an airstrip for reconnaissance planes scanning the Ho Chi Minh Trail, an anchor for defenses south of the DMZ in the west, and a stepping-off point for ground operations against the Ho Chi Minh Trail.

In August 1962 MACV had ordered U.S. Special Operations Forces (SOF) and allied troops to establish the camp near the village of Khe Sanh. The Special Operations troops from the Study and Observation Group (SOG) used it to launch extended long-range reconnaissance operations into Laos to observe PAVN infiltration. If they located a large enemy concentration, they would call in air strikes.

In April 1966 a single marine battalion temporarily occupied the base. Six months later General Westmoreland directed the U.S. Marine Corps, over its objections, to build a single-battalion base immediately above the SOG base. In October one battalion of marines occupied the base. By the spring of 1967, the battalion had been reinforced to regimental strength by the III Marine Amphibious Force.

Soon afterward SOG patrols observed marked increases in traffic on the Ho Chi Minh Trail, as did observation posts along the DMZ. Westmoreland believed that the Communists were planning a siege at Khe Sanh reminiscent of that at Dien Bien Phu in 1954. In September he directed Seabees to upgrade the Khe Sanh landing strip to accommodate Lockheed C-130 Hercules aircraft. Moreover, 175-millimeter (mm) guns with a 20-mile range were placed in a more secure area at Camp Carroll, 12 miles distant.

In the spring of 1967, as part of the PAVN plan to open up a new battlefront along South Vietnam's northern border to draw U.S. forces away from the heavily populated lowlands to the south and to inflict heavy U.S. losses by luring American units into terrain favorable to PAVN forces, the PAVN sent a reinforced regiment (95C Regiment, 325C Division, plus a battalion from the division's 18C Regiment) south to the Khe Sanh area to attack U.S. forces there.

In April 1967 a marine patrol was ambushed near one of the surrounding hills west of Khe Sanh. A large rescue patrol suffered heavy casualties when many of its M16 rifles jammed. This incident led to congressional hearings and army modifications that improved M16 reliability.

From April 24 to May 12, 1967, the 3rd Marines initiated several major assaults on three Communist-occupied hills surrounding Khe Sanh. These so-called Hill Fights produced fierce hand-to-hand fighting that left 160 marines dead and 700 wounded, but the Americans destroyed one entire PAVN regiment and a large artillery emplacement in progress. At the end of this period the 3rd Marines were replaced by the 26th Marines, which left its 1st Battalion at Khe Sanh. The above operations were part of Operations CROCKETT (April–July 1967) and ARDMORE (July–October 1967). Both were supported by Operation NIAGARA, a massive bombing campaign (SLAM, for Seek, Locate, Annihilate, and Monitor) planned by U.S. Seventh Air Force commander General William Momyer.

These 1967 engagements convinced Westmoreland that with adequate bombing and aerial resupply, U.S. outposts could survive even when outnumbered, a notion that he sold to the Lyndon B. Johnson administration. Thus, U.S. military planning called for maintaining and enlarging DMZ outposts, especially Khe Sanh. This led to the 1968 Battle of Khe Sanh.

Between October and December 1967 PAVN commander General Vo Nguyen Giap greatly built up PAVN strength near Khe Sanh. U.S. marines, reluctant to garrison the base in the first place, were now ordered to fortify their defensive positions.

At 8:30 p.m. on January 2, 1968, a marine reconnaissance patrol spotted six shadowy figures on a slope near the base's outer defenses. The marines opened fire and killed five PAVN officers who were apparently on a reconnaissance mission. The incident convinced General Westmoreland that several thousand enemy soldiers were near Khe Sanh and that Giap hoped to repeat his Dien Bien Phu victory at Khe Sanh. Westmoreland, who was clearly using the marines as bait to draw out the PAVN units, saw this as an opportunity for a decisive engagement.

Indeed, two regiments of the PAVN 325C Division that had fought at Dien Bien Phu had crossed into South Vietnam from Laos and were then located northwest of Khe Sanh. Two regiments of the 320th Division had crossed the DMZ and were 20 miles northeast. They were supported by an armored regiment, two artillery regiments, and the 304th Division in Laos. PAVN forces totaled between 20,000 and 30,000 men, many of whom were actually support or reserve forces.

Route 9, the only road to Khe Sanh, had been cut by Communist forces months earlier, so Westmoreland poured in supplies and reinforcements by air. Included on the flights were numerous reporters anxious for a big story. By mid-January, 6,000 marines defended the main plateau and four surrounding hills named for their height: Hill 950, Hill 881, Hill 861, and Hill 558. Approximately 3,000 marines defended the Khe Sanh base itself, and the same number were split among the hill positions. Infantry at each garrison were supported by 105-mm howitzers and mortars.

At 5:30 a.m. on January 20, Captain William Dabney and 185 men of Company I launched a patrol from Hill 881 South to Hill 881 North. Although such patrols were common practice, Dabney sensed that he would make contact that day and requested additional support. Colonel David Lownds, commander of the 26th Marines, deployed 200 additional men to support the patrol. Dabney divided his group, sending one platoon up one ridge and another two platoons up the other. As they ascended, the marines were preceded by a rolling artillery barrage. Dabney hoped that the Communist troops would respond and give away their positions. Instead, the PAVN veterans waited until a platoon led by Lieutenant Thomas Brindley came within close range and opened up with automatic rifles, machine guns, and rocket-propelled grenades. The point man was killed immediately, and several other platoon members were hit.

Dabney sent a second platoon to flank the PAVN position, while Brindley called in artillery directly on his position. The second unit was hit as it advanced, and a massive firefight followed. Brindley ordered his men to make a dash for the PAVN position. Even though Brindley was killed and dozens of his men were wounded, with the support of fighter-bombers dropping napalm the marines took the position.

Lownds concluded early the same morning that a larger attack would ensue, and he ordered Dabney to withdraw. Already the marines had lost 7 killed and 35 wounded.

By nightfall Dabney's men were back on Hill 881 South, and the Khe Sanh combat base was on maximum alert. (Years later Dabney was awarded the Navy Cross for his heroic leadership.)

That night the marines received information from an apparent Communist deserter that a major attack was planned on Hill 881 South and Hill 861 at 12:30 a.m. on January 21. The marines brought up several special weapons, including two Ontos assault vehicles capable of firing fléchette rounds, each with thousands of steel darts. They also set out several layers of razor-sharp concertina wire, hundreds of Claymore mines, and trip flares.

PAVN forces attacked Hill 861 on schedule using bangalore torpedoes to break through marine defenses. The marines' initial position was overrun, but at 5:00 a.m., supported by mortars, they counterattacked with success. At 5:30 a.m. PAVN forces commenced an intense rocket and artillery attack against Khe Sanh proper. The main ammunition dump took a direct hit, resulting in a succession of explosions that left the defenders with barely enough ordnance to return fire. Artillery officer Major Roger Campbell measured craters caused by enemy shells to target the distance and direction of the PAVN guns. Despite heavy damage to the landing strip, that afternoon six C-130 planes arrived. Their 24 tons of cargo was mostly artillery shells, but Colonel Lownds estimated that he would need 160 tons of supplies per day to hold out.

At 6:30 a.m. the PAVN attacked the village of Khe Sanh. Allied troops utilized air and artillery support to repel the attack, but thousands of local villagers fled their homes to seek refuge with the marines. The marines did not allow them into their lines for fear of sabotage. Nearly 3,000 tried to escape down Route 9 to Dong Ha, but only 1,432 arrived. Despite setbacks, marine defenses remained strong.

The ammunition dump explosion did produce wild headlines that fed public concerns about U.S. involvement in Vietnam. President Johnson became so concerned that he had hourly reports sent to him and a map room set up in the White House basement with a large board replica of Khe Sanh.

Westmoreland controlled air operations, personally picking targets based on advice from General Momyer. For several days after the first attacks, Boeing B-52 Stratofortresses bombed targets every three hours. By March 31 they had dropped between 60,000 and 75,000 tons of bombs. In addition, U.S. fighter-bombers flew an average of 300 sorties daily. B-52s also struck PAVN command center caves in Laos. On occasion the B-52s dropped bombs within 1,000 yards of the Khe Sanh perimeter even though the marines were unable to see the high-flying bombers.

Still, regular PAVN rocket attacks continued, making life on the plateau both difficult and dangerous. Hygiene and psychological strains were also a problem. Sniper duels were commonplace and became macabre games of life and death. Despite tensions, morale at Khe Sanh remained high throughout the siege.

Between January 21 and February 5, PAVN forces mounted several small attacks against new marine positions on Hill 861A near a quarry just outside the perimeter. On February 5 PAVN troops overran a portion of Hill 861, killing seven marines. The marines retook the position using tear gas and air and artillery support. Mortar crews on Hill 881 South fired 1,100 rounds into PAVN positions. The fighting ended in hand-to-hand combat.

Early on February 7 PAVN forces overran the Lang Vei Special Forces Camp about five miles southwest of Khe Sanh and only a mile from Laos. Early on February 8 three PAVN companies struck a platoon of about 50 members of A Company, 1st Battalion, 9th Marines, holding little Hill 64 just outside the combat base. The assaulting troops knocked out the marine bunkers with satchel charges and rocket-propelled grenades. When Marine reinforcements arrived at about 9:00 a.m., they found 21 marines dead, 26 badly wounded, and 4 missing in action. Only 1 of the defenders was unscathed.

On February 25 a 29-man marine patrol looking for a Communist mortar position stumbled on a PAVN bunker and was overwhelmed. Unable to rescue the marines, Lownds ordered the men to escape the best way they could. Only 3 got away. Corporal Roland Ball, a Sioux Native American, carried out the body of his commanding officer, Lieutenant Dan Jacques. Dead marines lay on the field unburied for another month until the siege ended.

On March 6 Communist forces began their withdrawal. By March 9 only a few thousand rear-guard units remained. Operation SCOTLAND, the final part of the siege at Khe Sanh, ended on April 1, officially terminating the battle. The same day, allied units began Operation PEGASUS to reopen Route 9. On April 8 they linked up with Khe Sanh. The next day was the first since January 21 that no PAVN shells struck the marine base. Two months later, on June 26, 1968, U.S. forces abandoned the Khe Sanh base.

The official casualty count for the second phase of the Battle of Khe Sanh was 205 marines killed in action and more than 1,600 wounded; however, base chaplain Ray W. Stubbe placed the death toll closer to 475. This does not include Americans killed in collateral actions, Army of the Republic of Vietnam (ARVN, South Vietnamese Army) Ranger casualties on the southwest perimeter, 1,000 to 1,500 Montagnards who died during the fighting, or the 97 U.S. and

33 ARVN troops killed in the relief operation. MACV estimated PAVN losses at 10,000 to 15,000 men. Most of these casualties occurred as a result of U.S. B-52 ARC LIGHT bombing raids and other aerial and artillery support. The official body count was 1,602. PAVN sources list a total of 2,270 PAVN troops killed during the siege of Khe Sanh, although it is not clear whether this total includes soldiers missing in action.

The siege of Khe Sanh in particular and the Tet Offensive in general disheartened the American public, which began to question the cost and worth of the Vietnam War to America. Indeed, Khe Sanh and the Tet Offensive marked the beginning of the end for America's involvement in Southeast Asia.

Who won the second phase of the Battle of Khe Sanh? U.S. Marine Corps historian Jack Shulimson observed that is not clear if North Vietnamese forces actually intended to seize Khe Sanh or merely used the assault as a way to draw American forces away from cities. General Giap claimed victory for the PAVN. According to him, the Communists never intended to overrun the marine base.

Communist documents and histories that have become available since the war ended do not entirely support General Giap's claim. These records state that the 1968 attacks on Khe Sanh and the rest of northern Quang Tri Province had two objectives: to draw U.S. and South Vietnamese forces away from the populated areas of South Vietnam and to inflict massive casualties on opposing forces (specific goals set were to kill 20,000–30,000 "enemy," primarily American, soldiers and to "totally annihilate five to seven U.S. battalions"). These documents also reveal that while the primary PAVN plan was to lure U.S. forces out of their dug-in fortified positions and into the open so that they could be killed in large numbers, there was a provision in the plan to "attack and liberate [overrun] Khe Sanh" if that was possible.

If the siege of Khe Sanh was meant to be only a Communist ruse, then it was a successful one. Significant U.S. military assets were diverted to this isolated area of South Vietnam, permitting Communist forces to attack many key cities in South Vietnam during the Tet Offensive.

Looking back after the war while congratulating itself for important successes in the Khe Sanh campaign, the PAVN also admitted to a number of failures and "shortcomings." In an internal battle study conducted 20 years after the Battle of Khe Sanh, PAVN historians concluded that "we did not draw U.S. relief forces out to the Route 9–Khe Sanh area as quickly as we should have" and that the PAVN had failed to reach its goals for killing U.S. troops and "annihilating" entire U.S. battalions. The battle study faulted the PAVN high command and the Khe Sanh Campaign Headquarters for their incorrect analysis of the probable U.S. reaction to the attack, for overestimating the PAVN's own capabilities, for inadequate preparations, for failing to mass adequate forces to mount "annihilation attacks," and for their "failure to direct the campaign with clarity."

For the Americans, the Battle of Khe Sanh was meant to be the best opportunity to implement the strategy of attrition, to destroy Communist military forces at a rate above which they could be replaced. In the battle U.S. forces achieved one of their most satisfying victories. Colonel Lownds was convinced that they destroyed two entire PAVN divisions. Thus, if Khe Sanh was intended as another Dien Bien Phu, it had failed.

William P. Head and Peter W. Brush

References

Head, William, and Lawrence Grinter, eds. *Looking Back on the Vietnam War: A 1990s Perspective on the Decisions, Combat, and Legacies*. Westport, CT: Greenwood, 1993.

Military History Institute of Vietnam. *Chien Dich Tien Cong Duong So 9–Khe Sanh, Xuan He 1968* [The Route 9–Khe Sanh Offensive Campaign, Spring–Summer 1968]. Hanoi: Ministry of Defense, 1987.

Momyer, William W. *Airpower in Three Wars: World War II, Korea and Vietnam*. Washington, DC: U.S. Government Printing Office, 1978.

Murphy, Edward F. *The Hill Fights: The First Battle of Khe Sanh*. New York: Random House, 2003.

Nalty, Bernard C. *Air Power and the Fight for Khe Sanh*. Washington, DC: Office of Air Force History, U.S. Air Force, 1973.

Nguyen Viet Phuong, Le Van Bien, and Tu Quy. *Cong Tac Hau Can Chien Dich Duong 9 Khe Sanh Xuan He 1968 (Mat)* [Rear Services Operations during the Route 9–Khe Sanh Campaign, Spring–Summer 1968 (Secret)]. Hanoi: General Department of Rear Services, 1988.

Pham Gia Duc. *Su Doan 325, 1954–1975*, Tap II [325th Division, 1954–1975, Vol. 2]. Hanoi: People's Army Publishing House, 1986.

Pisor, Robert. *The End of the Line: The Siege of Khe Sanh*. New York: Norton, 1982.

Prados, John, and Ray W. Stubbe. *Valley of Decision: The Siege of Khe Sanh*. Boston: Houghton Mifflin, 1991.

Shulimson, Jack, Leonard A. Blasiol, Charles R. Smith, and David A. Dawson. *U.S. Marines in Vietnam: The Defining Year, 1968*. Washington, DC: History and Museums Division, Headquarters, U.S. Marine Corps, 1997.

Kissinger, Henry Alfred (1923–)

Academic, foreign policy consultant, national security advisor to presidents Richard Nixon and Gerald Ford (1969–1975), and secretary of state (1973–1977). Henry Alfred Kissinger was born in Fuerth, Germany, on May 27, 1923. His family immigrated to New York in 1938 to escape the Nazi regime. After becoming a U.S. citizen, Kissinger was drafted into the U.S. Army in 1943. He returned to his birthplace as a member of the 84th Infantry Division. After discharge, he completed his undergraduate education at Harvard University in 1950 and entered the graduate program in government, completing a PhD there in 1954. Kissinger's doctoral dissertation on Metternich, Castlereagh, and the Congress of Vienna, a study of how statesmen sought to preserve world order by maintaining a geopolitical balance of power, became a theme that has occupied him ever since.

In 1955 Kissinger headed a Council on Foreign Relations study group on weapons and foreign policy, and the next year he directed a Rockefeller Fund project to examine the critical issues facing the United States. In reports for the two panels, he suggested that limited nuclear war was preferable to all-out nuclear war or surrender and recommended the construction of home bomb shelters. In 1957 Kissinger accepted a joint appointment as lecturer in the Government Department at Harvard and associate director of the university's Center for International Affairs. He continued at Harvard until 1968 while also acting as an independent foreign policy consultant. A skilled politician in his own right, Kissinger used his Harvard credentials and growing name recognition to form relationships with influential Republicans, including New York governor Nelson A. Rockefeller and former vice president Richard M. Nixon.

When Nixon was elected president in 1968, he named Kissinger as his national security advisor. Kissinger retained this

Henry Alfred Kissinger, U.S. national security adviser (1969–1975) and secretary of state (1973–1977). (Library of Congress)

post until 1975, and from 1973 to 1975 he was the only person ever to hold the posts of national security advisor and secretary of state concurrently. The two men shared a suspicion of the traditional, bureaucratic diplomacy found in the State Department, which they considered uncreative and slow moving. Nixon intended to keep control of foreign relations in the White House, with Kissinger as a more important adviser than Secretary of State William P. Rogers. Nixon and Kissinger also agreed that foreign policy should be based on realism rather than wishful idealism or moralism. Self-interest required that foreign policy should rely on strength and the willingness to use force and that other nations understand this.

In developing their realist policies, Kissinger and Nixon perceived a shift from the bipolar balance of power between the United States and the Soviet Union to a more multipolar world that also included the People's Republic of China (PRC). Working together although often not harmoniously, Nixon and Kissinger eventually brought an end to U.S. participation in the Vietnam War, reached a détente with the Soviet Union that culminated in the Strategic Arms Limitation Talks (SALT) agreement, established diplomatic relations with the PRC, and helped achieve stability in the Middle East following the October 1973 Yom Kippur (Ramadan) War. In engaging both the Chinese and Soviets concurrently, Kissinger and Nixon hoped to take advantage of the Sino-Soviet split and perhaps play one power off the other. They certainly hoped to shape policy in Vietnam by engaging both the Chinese and Soviets in meaningful diplomacy, as both nations considered the Democratic Republic of Vietnam (DRV, North Vietnam) as a client state.

The war in Vietnam was probably the most difficult issue Kissinger faced. His concern about the conflict predated his service in the Nixon administration. During Lyndon Johnson's presidency, Kissinger visited Vietnam in October 1965 and July 1966 as a government consultant. He concluded that U.S. military victory was unlikely, and in 1967, using French contacts, he acted as an intermediary between the North Vietnamese government and the Johnson administration in a fruitless effort to start negotiations. In a critique of the Vietnam War written before he became national security advisor but published in the January 1969 issue of *Foreign Affairs*, Kissinger argued that the United States could not win the war "within a period or with force levels politically acceptable to the American people" but could not precipitately withdraw without damaging its "credibility."

Soon after taking office in 1969, Kissinger ordered a study of the Vietnam problem from the RAND Corporation. The resulting National Security Study Memorandum 1 (NSSM-1), headed by Daniel Ellsberg, collected responses from government departments and agencies to 78 queries about the war. The responses demonstrated the differences that had developed within the government over the prospect of a satisfactory end to the war, with the Central Intelligence Agency (CIA) and the State Department generally more pessimistic than the military.

Peace talks between the United States and North Vietnam—initiated on March 31, 1968, when Lyndon Johnson announced that he would not seek another presidential term—had stalled by the time Nixon took office. Before his inauguration Nixon, with Kissinger's encouragement, sent a message to the North Vietnamese government indicating the new administration's desire for serious discussions. The North Vietnamese reply of December 31, 1968, insisted on two points: unilateral withdrawal of U.S. forces and removal of the government of the Republic of Vietnam (RVN, South Vietnam). These demands, which Nixon and Kissinger found unacceptable, were repeated in the first substantive private meeting between U.S. and North Vietnamese officials on March 22, 1969, and remained constant until nearly the end of negotiations in 1973.

Negotiations were further hindered by events in Cambodia. In March 1969 Nixon ordered the secret bombing of Cambodia (Operation MENU), which continued until May 1970. When news of this was leaked to the *New York Times* in May 1969, Nixon—with Kissinger's knowledge—initiated wiretaps on a number of government officials and reporters.

In a press conference on May 14, 1969, Nixon unveiled his Vietnam policy, known as Vietnamization. He proposed simultaneous mutual withdrawal of U.S. and North Vietnamese forces, supervised free elections in South Vietnam with participation by the National Front for the Liberation of South Vietnam (National Liberation Front [NLF]), and a cease-fire. The following month on June 8 during a meeting with South Vietnamese president Nguyen Van Thieu at Midway Island, Nixon announced U.S. troop withdrawals. Kissinger questioned Vietnamization in a memorandum to the president, arguing that unilateral troop withdrawals would encourage North Vietnamese intransigence in negotiations, demoralize troops remaining in Vietnam, and result in further demands for troop reductions in the United States.

Kissinger began intermittent secret peace talks with North Vietnamese representatives in Paris in August 1969. The negotiations deadlocked on North Vietnam's insistence that the United States unilaterally withdraw its forces and that the Thieu government in Saigon be removed.

On May 1, 1970, U.S. and South Vietnamese troops invaded Cambodia. Antiwar demonstrations erupted in the United States and climaxed when Ohio National Guardsmen fired on protesters at Kent State University in Ohio on May 4, killing four students. Several of Kissinger's longtime aides resigned over the Cambodian Incursion.

In the aftermath of the Cambodian invasion, Nixon and Kissinger developed a proposal to restart negotiations with North Vietnam. In a press conference on October 7, 1970, Nixon suggested a cease-fire in place (meaning that North Vietnamese troops then in South Vietnam would remain there). In a session in Paris on May 31, 1971, Kissinger spelled out the offer in detail, agreeing to unilateral withdrawal of U.S. troops according to a timetable, with an understanding that there would be no further infiltration of "outside forces" into Vietnam; there would be a cease-fire in place throughout Indochina, guarantees for the neutrality and territorial integrity of Laos and Cambodia, release of prisoners of war, and an agreement to leave the political future of South Vietnam up to its people. Although these provisions signaled significant concessions from the United States, North Vietnam rejected them, probably because it thought that it could yet win greater concessions regarding the political settlement in South Vietnam.

The Nixon administration's simultaneous overtures to China and the Soviet Union likely had some impact on the Vietnam negotiations. In July 1971, following a series of preliminary contacts, Kissinger secretly traveled to Beijing, where he and Chinese leader Zhou Enlai arranged for an official presidential visit to China. The historic summit, which took place in February 1972, reversed a policy of nearly 25 years during which the United States denied the legitimacy of the PRC. Following Nixon's trip, China moderated its protests against American action in Vietnam. In August 1972, following Nixon's May summit meeting with Soviet premier Leonid Brezhnev in Moscow, the Hanoi Politburo authorized a negotiated settlement with the United States.

In a meeting with Kissinger on October 8, 1972, North Vietnamese representative Le Duc Tho proposed an accord settling military questions—a cease-fire, withdrawal of U.S. forces, acceptance of continuing U.S. aid to South Vietnam, and return of prisoners of war—while leaving political matters, namely the future of the South Vietnamese government, to an "Administration of National Concord" representing the Saigon government and South Vietnamese Communists. These terms were agreed to on October 11, with details to be worked out later. On his return to the United States, Kissinger announced in a press conference on October 26 that "We

believe that peace is at hand." On November 7 Richard Nixon easily won reelection as president over Democratic challenger George McGovern.

Peace was not at hand, however. President Thieu refused to accede to the terms. Discussions with North Vietnam bogged down in disagreements about changes demanded by Thieu, details of prisoner exchanges, withdrawals, and other matters. Talks broke off on December 13.

This interruption led to one of the most controversial acts of Nixon's presidency. Although Kissinger urged Nixon to sign the agreement without Thieu, Nixon refused. Blaming Hanoi for the impasses, Nixon initiated Operation LINEBACKER II, the so-called Christmas Bombings of North Vietnam, on December 18, 1973. For the first time in the war, the United States employed Boeing B-52 Stratofortresses over Hanoi and Haiphong. The raids proved costly for the United States as well as North Vietnam, and they met with outrage in the United States and throughout the world. Nixon halted them on December 30 after Hanoi, having exhausted its supply of surface-to-air missiles, indicated its willingness to return to negotiations.

Kissinger and Le Duc Tho reached a final agreement on January 9, 1973. The terms were substantially the same as those reached the previous October and close to those discussed in 1969 except for provisions regarding the continuance of the South Vietnamese government. President Nixon announced the agreement on inauguration day, January 20, 1973.

Ending U.S. involvement in the war in Vietnam was the capstone of Kissinger's diplomacy and earned him wide acclaim. In December 1972 *Time* magazine named Nixon and Kissinger "Men of the Year," and a 1973 Gallup Poll rated Kissinger first in a list of most-admired Americans. In September 1973 Kissinger replaced William P. Rogers as secretary of state, a position that Kissinger retained through the end of the Gerald Ford administration in 1977. In October, Kissinger and Le Duc Tho were jointly awarded the Nobel Peace Prize for their Vietnam settlement. The North Vietnamese representative rejected the prize and his share of the $130,000 award. Kissinger accepted but donated the prize money to a scholarship fund for children of military personnel killed in Vietnam.

In fact, Kissinger had achieved only what became known as a "decent interval" between removal of U.S. forces and a Communist takeover. Within a few months of the peace accord the Watergate Scandal began to unravel Nixon's presidency, and the Vietnam peace accords came apart. Nixon resigned on August 9, 1974; Saigon fell to the Communists on April 30, 1975.

Kissinger has remained active as a presidential adviser, consultant, commentator, and speaker on international affairs. For many, however, Kissinger remains a deeply polarizing figure. Among the Left he has been vilified, and some have called for his trial for war crimes in association with his Indochina policies. For much of the 1980s and 1990s, Republicans and neoconservatives paid him little attention because they disagreed with his policies of détente with the Soviets and Chinese. In the new century, however, Kissinger has enjoyed renewed visibility, at least among Republicans. He reportedly met frequently with President George W. Bush about the Iraq War, especially after the insurgency became critical, telling the president that a complete defeat of the insurgents was the only acceptable exit strategy. From 2001 to 2005 Kissinger also served as the chancellor of the College of William and Mary.

Kenneth R. Stevens

References

Herring, George C., ed. *The Secret Diplomacy of the Vietnam War: The Negotiating Volumes of the Pentagon Papers*. Austin: University of Texas Press, 1983.

Hersh, Seymour. *The Price of Power: Kissinger in the Nixon White House*. New York: Summit, 1983.

Isaacson, Walter. *Kissinger: A Biography*. New York: Simon and Schuster, 1992.

Kalb, Marvin, and Bernard Kalb. *Kissinger*. Boston: Little, Brown, 1974.

Kissinger, Henry. *White House Years*. Boston: Little, Brown, 1979.

Kissinger, Henry. *Years of Upheaval*. Boston: Little, Brown, 1982.

Morris, Roger. *Uncertain Greatness: Henry Kissinger and American Foreign Policy*. New York: Harper and Row, 1977.

Schulzinger, Robert. *Henry Kissinger: Doctor of Diplomacy*. New York: Columbia University Press, 1989.

Stoessinger, John. *Henry Kissinger: The Anguish of Power*. New York: Norton, 1976.

Komer, Robert W. (1922–2000)

Deputy to the commander, U.S. Military Assistance Command, Vietnam (MACV), for Civil Operations and Revolutionary Development Support (CORDS) during 1967–1968. Born on February 23, 1922, in Chicago, Robert W. Komer graduated from Harvard in 1942 and, following World War II army duty, received an MBA at Harvard in 1947. He worked for the Central Intelligence Agency (CIA) as an analyst during 1947–1960 and then moved to the National Security Council (NSC) as a senior staff member during 1961–1965.

As a deputy special assistant to the president for national security affairs (1965–1966) and special assistant (1966–1967), Komer became increasingly involved with

Robert Komer, deputy to the commander, U.S. Military Assistance Command, Vietnam, for Civil Operations and Revolutionary Development Support (CORDS) meets with President Lyndon B. Johnson, November 16, 1967. (Lyndon B. Johnson Presidential Library)

the pacification program in Vietnam. In February 1966 President Lyndon Johnson appointed him Washington coordinator for pacification activities.

Komer's office became useful to young army officers trying to overcome institutional resistance to results of the Program for the Pacification and Long-Term Development of South Vietnam (PROVN) study, which had concluded that the attrition strategy and search-and-destroy tactics being employed by General William Westmoreland were not working and could not work. The key to success, the study held, was concentration on population security and pacification. Komer was sympathetic to that viewpoint and helped advance such ideas.

Meanwhile, reporting on a June 1966 trip to Vietnam, Komer told President Johnson that the pacification effort was lagging: "Until we can get rolling on pacification in

its widest sense—securing the villages, flushing out the local VC [Viet Cong] (not just the main force) and giving the peasant both security and hope for a better future," he wrote, "we cannot assure a victory."

Soon Komer drafted a proposal that responsibility for support of pacification be assigned to the U.S. military establishment in the Republic of Vietnam (RVN, South Vietnam), with a civilian deputy running it. He had in effect written his own job description, although it took Secretary of Defense Robert McNamara's backing for the idea to gain acceptance. In March 1967 the decision was announced to put the CORDS program under Westmoreland, with Komer as his deputy. In May 1967 Komer, given the personal rank of ambassador, headed for Vietnam to undertake his new duties.

Ambassador Ellsworth Bunker recalled in his oral history that Komer was both very able and very abrasive, thereby staking out the spectrum of viewpoints on Komer's contribution, adding that he could be too pushy. In fact, Komer maintained that it was necessary to prod people aggressively if anything was going to be accomplished. He also took pride in his own incorrigible optimism.

Once on the job Komer had been given his way by General Westmoreland who, according to William Colby in *Lost Victory*, did so with some relief that Westmoreland could let Komer do it while the general continued to conduct the military war that he saw as his primary responsibility. Colby credited Komer with an overdue effort to build up the territorial forces and with pulling together disparate elements of the American advisory effort at the province level.

Komer's overall influence on the pacification program remains uncertain. McNamara accords him a single mention, indeed a single sentence, in his memoirs, hardly an indication of substantial impact. The record shows that it was only after the Communists suffered disastrous losses during the 1968 Tet Offensive, after General Creighton Abrams assumed command of MACV and William Colby took over as deputy for CORDS, and after President Nguyen Van Thieu personally launched and pushed the Accelerated Pacification Campaign in November 1968, that pacification really began to show results.

Komer meanwhile had become ambassador to Turkey, an appointment that proved short-lived when the White House changed parties soon after he was nominated. He then spent a number of years at the RAND Corporation (1969–1977) and as a Pentagon official working on North Atlantic Treaty Organization (NATO) affairs (1977–1979) and as undersecretary of defense for policy (1979–1981). Komer died of a stroke in Arlington, Virginia, on April 9, 2000.

Lewis Sorley

References

Clarke, Jeffrey J. *Advice and Support: The Final Years; The U.S. Army in Vietnam.* Washington, DC: U.S. Government Printing Office, 1988.

Komer, Robert W. *Bureaucracy at War: U.S. Performance in the Vietnam Conflict.* Boulder, CO: Westview, 1986.

Scoville, Thomas W. *Reorganizing for Pacification Support.* Washington, DC: U.S. Army Center of Military History, 1982.

L

Laird, Melvin Robert (1922–)

Republican politician and U.S. secretary of defense (1969–1973). Born in Omaha, Nebraska, on September 1, 1922, Melvin Robert ("Bom") Laird graduated from Carleton College in 1942 and served in the U.S. Navy during World War II. After the war, he won election to the Wisconsin State Senate as a Republican and served there until his 1952 election to the U.S. House of Representatives from Wisconsin's 7th Congressional District, a seat he held continuously until President Richard Nixon named him his first secretary of defense in 1969.

As secretary of defense, Laird faced daunting problems in formulating policy, budgets, and force structure during a period of declining resources and shrinking manpower committed to defense. He gave the service secretaries and the Joint Chiefs of Staff (JCS) more of a role in these matters than had his predecessor, a welcome development from their standpoint. As a former congressman, he also proved effective in dealing with Congress.

Sensitive to declining congressional support for the war in Vietnam, Laird pushed hard for rapid withdrawal of American ground forces. This put him frequently at odds with National Security Advisor Henry Kissinger on such issues as the 1970 cross-border incursion into Cambodia. Indeed, a later analysis found that Laird had been bypassed on the planning for that operation, an extreme example of the Byzantine workings of the Nixon White House. Laird frequently attempted to change or countermand White House instructions.

Nixon noted in his memoirs that "it was largely on the basis of Laird's enthusiastic advocacy that we undertook the policy of Vietnamization." Although this program of handing off more responsibility for the war to forces of the Republic of Vietnam (RVN, South Vietnam) had actually begun in the Lyndon Johnson administration, Laird was committed to making it work, so much so that in his book *Lost Victory*, William Colby, who headed American support for pacification in South Vietnam, called Laird "the unsung hero of the whole war effort."

Laird was also supportive of Military Assistance Command, Vietnam (MACV), commander General Creighton Abrams and greatly admired his stoicism in fighting on even as his forces were progressively being taken from him. It was Laird who insisted that Abrams be named army chief of staff when he returned from Vietnam. Then the two men devised and promulgated a total-force policy that sought to ensure that reserve forces would be utilized in any future conflicts.

In his final report as secretary of defense, Laird stated his view that "as a consequence of the success of the military aspects of Vietnamization, the South Vietnamese people today . . . are fully capable of providing for their own in-country security against the North Vietnamese." However dubious that view was at the time, Laird had accomplished his major objective of withdrawing U.S. forces from Vietnam.

Laird had stated at the outset that he intended to serve only four years as defense secretary. Leaving that post in January 1973, he later served briefly as counselor to the president for domestic affairs before returning to the private sector in February 1974. He later had a long association with *Reader's Digest* as senior counselor for national and international affairs. In January 2006 Laird participated in a White House meeting that gathered current and past secretaries of defense and state to discuss the George W. Bush administration's foreign and military policies, including the vexing war in Iraq.

Lewis Sorley

References

Kissinger, Henry. *White House Years*. Boston: Little, Brown, 1979.

Nixon, Richard M. *RN: The Memoirs of Richard Nixon*. New York: Grosset and Dunlap, 1978.

Van Atta, Dale. *With Honor: Melvin Laird in War, Peace, and Politics*. Madison: University of Wisconsin Press, 2008.

LAM SON 719, Operation (February 8–March 24, 1971)

Army of the Republic of Vietnam (ARVN, South Vietnamese Army) campaign to curtail southbound Communist supply shipments on the Ho Chi Minh Trail network. The operation occurred during February 8–March 24, 1971. In 1971, with Vietnamization under way and the withdrawal of American forces proceeding, troops and supplies continued to flow down the Ho Chi Minh Trail from the Democratic Republic of Vietnam (DRV, North Vietnam) and into the Republic of Vietnam (RVN, South Vietnam), U.S. Air Force claims of having destroyed legions of trucks in its commando hunt campaigns notwithstanding.

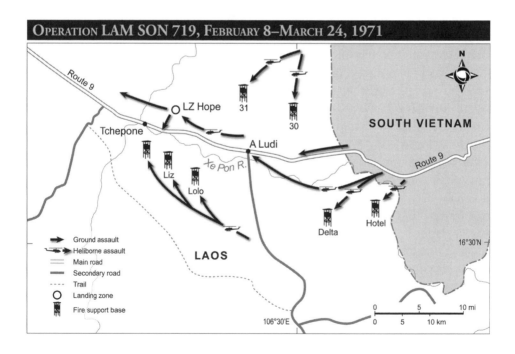

OPERATION LAM SON 719, FEBRUARY 8–MARCH 24, 1971

Operation LAM SON 719 had two objectives. The first was to capture Tchepone in Laos, a key transshipment point on Route 9 some 25 miles west of Khe Sanh. As a part of this effort, the ARVN was to destroy supplies in nearby Base Area 604 and in Base Area 611 south of Route 9, an area adjacent to the South Vietnamese border. The second, and more optimistic, objective was to sever the Ho Chi Minh Trail, the long logistical corridor running through eastern Laos with several hundred miles of paved roads and thousands of miles of dirt roads, tracks, pathways, and waterways down which supplies could be funneled to South Vietnam. This logistical network was vital to North Vietnam's ongoing war inside South Vietnam.

The Cooper-Church Amendment, passed by the U.S. Congress on December 29, 1970, forbade the use of American ground forces in Laos. However, U.S. forces played a key part in LAM SON 719. American helicopters ferried ARVN troops into Laos, and U.S. fighter-bombers and Boeing B-52 Stratofortresses were available to provide air cover. On the ground in South Vietnam, the 1st Brigade of the 5th Infantry Division led the way back into Khe Sanh as a part of Operation DEWEY CANYON II. From Khe Sanh and from surrounding fire-support bases inside South Vietnam, some 9,000 U.S. troops gave logistical support to the ARVN and provided artillery fire into Laos. From Khe Sanh and other fire-support bases, some 2,600 helicopters carried ARVN troops into and, later, out of Laos. The ARVN plan had the full support of U.S. president Richard Nixon, who fully expected it to show the success of Vietnamization, the turning over of the war to the South Vietnamese.

On February 8, 1971, a task force of 15,000 ARVN troops invaded Laos. The main thrust was along Route 9, a single-lane dirt road leading from the Lao-Vietnamese border westward to Tchepone. At first the troops moved easily through the low hills that, within miles, turned more rugged and then changed to jungle as the road wound toward Tchepone. In imitation of the Americans, the ARVN built fire-support bases to serve as base camps and placed 105-millimeter (mm) and 155-mm howitzers in them to provide artillery support. The camps were also supposed to serve as bases from which patrols and raids could be mounted into the surrounding countryside.

LAM SON 719 was a major test of Vietnamization. Because of the Cooper-Church Amendment, the ARVN was on its own. There were no U.S. advisers with the South Vietnamese and no American forward air controllers. The ARVN had only a few English-speaking soldiers who could serve in that capacity, and they were not very proficient.

Intelligence estimates indicated that 11,000 to 12,000 People's Army of Vietnam (PAVN, North Vietnamese Army) troops would be present. About half of those were thought to be workers assigned to running daily activities along the Ho Chi Minh Trail, including managing the truck depots, cooking food for the troops and truck drivers, attending infirmaries, and repairing roads. The other half were security forces used to patrol the trail and to man the 1,400–2,000 heavy machine guns and anti-aircraft artillery (AAA) in the area.

In one of the greater intelligence miscalculations of the war, it was thought that it would take up to a month for the PAVN to move one division from the panhandle of North Vietnam into the LAM SON 719 area of operations. In fact, within two weeks as many as five PAVN divisions, including the fabled 304th, 308th, and 320th Divisions, were engaging the ARVN.

Postwar Vietnamese sources reveal that the North Vietnamese Politburo concluded as early as the summer of 1970, shortly after the U.S.–South Vietnamese Cambodian Incursion in May 1970, that the next U.S. move would be an attack aimed at cutting the PAVN supply route along Ho Chi Minh Trail, although they were not sure precisely where along the trail such an attack would be made. To defend against such an attack, which the PAVN anticipated would occur in the autumn of 1970, the PAVN formed 70B Corps, which included the 304th, 308th, and 320th Divisions along with supporting artillery, armor, engineer, and antiaircraft units. The provisional corps and its subordinate units conducted extensive reconnaissance, planning, and logistics preparations to prepare for the anticipated attack. Even though the ARVN operation began several months later than the PAVN anticipated that it would, these advance preparations made it possible for PAVN forces to quickly move into position to block the ARVN operation.

Famed Communist spy and *Time* magazine correspondent Pham Xuan An claimed to have provided the PAVN high command with advance warning of the LAM SON 719 operation. However, it is not clear just how important this intelligence was to the outcome of the battle.

By the third week of LAM SON 719, the ARVN advance had stalled at A Luoi, a fire-support base 12 miles inside Laos. ARVN armor was bottled up along Route 9, and other ARVN units had holed up inside A Luoi and other fire-support bases in the area. PAVN forces attacked these bases, first pounding them with 122-mm and 130-mm artillery, Soviet-built guns with range superior to the 105-mm and 155-mm howitzers used by the ARVN. After the artillery had softened the ARVN positions, PAVN infantry, supported by PT-76 light tanks and, for the first time, heavier T-34 and T-54 tanks, attacked the fire-support bases. One after another, the bases fell to the counterattacking PAVN.

Conventional wisdom held that U.S. airpower would be the pivotal, if not the deciding, factor. This was another miscalculation. As the PAVN counterattack commenced, the weather deteriorated. Low clouds prevented the use of American fighter-bomber jets. B-52s, which could bomb through the cloud cover, were useful against large-area targets, but PAVN leaders knew that the big bombers would not be employed against targets closer than about 1.8 miles from friendly forces except in the most dire circumstances. Accordingly, the PAVN adopted General Vo Nguyen Giap's dictum of "clinging to the cartridge belts" of the ARVN and, by staying close to them, negated the effective use of B-52s.

When the weather cleared, there was North Vietnamese antiaircraft fire with which to contend. As they did in North Vietnam, the PAVN relied on AAA and heavy machine guns to deny the Americans effective use of the air. Heavy machine guns, supplemented by 23-mm and 37-mm AAA guns, covered virtually every potential helicopter landing zone. The 23-mm and 37-mm guns blanketed the area, and SA-2 surface-to-air missile (SAM) sites were placed in Ban Raving Pass. These threatened B-52s bombing within 17 miles of the pass and fighter-bombers flying above 1,500 feet in the same area. During LAM SON 719, the U.S. Air Force directed 1,285 sorties against AAA guns, reportedly destroying 70 of them. In support of LAM SON 719, B-52s flew 1,358 sorties and dropped 32,000 tons of bombs, with most missions directed against suspected supply dumps in Base Area 604, well away from Ban Raving Pass.

Despite increasingly heavy opposition from the PAVN, President Nguyen Van

Thieu ordered the commander of Operation LAM SON 719, General Hoang Xuan Lam, to launch an airborne assault on Tchepone. By March 1 Tchepone had been abandoned by the PAVN and had little military value. But its psychological and political value seemed significant to Thieu. On March 6, 120 U.S. Army Bell UH-1 Iroquois ("Huey") helicopters, protected by Bell AH-1G Cobra helicopter gunships and U.S. Air Force fighter-bombers, lifted two ARVN battalions from the U.S. Marine Corps base at Khe Sanh into Tchepone. Only one helicopter was lost to AAA en route. Two days later another two ARVN battalions reached Tchepone on foot. The South Vietnamese troops spent the next two weeks ferreting out PAVN supply caches around the village.

The capture of Tchepone achieved one of LAM SON 719's primary objectives. President Thieu then ordered General Lam to begin withdrawing the ARVN from Laos. Retreats are, however, among the most difficult of operational maneuvers. Even fine armies have disintegrated during withdrawals, especially if harried by enemy forces. By 1971 the best ARVN units were as good as many PAVN units, but they were not well enough trained, led, or disciplined to conduct an orderly retreat in the face of vigorous attack.

The PAVN intensified its attacks on the withdrawing ARVN. Again, poor weather hampered effective air operations. But when the weather cleared, devastating AAA fire and the inability of U.S. Air Force pilots to coordinate their attacks with ground units diminished the effectiveness of airpower. The retreat turned into a rout.

Meanwhile, almost 60,000 PAVN troops, including three armored battalions, five artillery regiments, and four antiaircraft regiments, hammered home their attacks on a massively outnumbered and increasingly demoralized South Vietnamese force. In large part due to the selflessness and bravery of U.S. Army helicopter pilots, about half of the original ARVN force of 15,000 troops managed to make its way to safety. At least 5,000 ARVN troops were killed or wounded, and more than 2,500 were unaccounted for and listed as missing. Additionally, 253 Americans were killed and another 1,149 wounded during LAM SON 719, although no Americans fought on the ground inside Laos. Many American troops were killed or wounded when the PAVN counterattack spilled into South Vietnam and when Khe Sanh came under a fierce artillery attack on March 15.

In operations over Laos, at least 108 U.S. Army helicopters were destroyed and another 618 were damaged, many so badly that they were scrapped. Seven U.S. Air Force fixed-wing aircraft were also shot down.

Despite the outcome and the losses, the allies declared victory. President Richard M. Nixon, in a televised address to the nation on April 7, 1971, stated that "Tonight I can report Vietnamization has succeeded." President Thieu dubbed LAM SON 719 "the biggest victory ever." In North Vietnam, however, Radio Hanoi proclaimed that "The Route 9–Southern Laos Victory" (as they called it) was "the heaviest defeat ever for Nixon and Company." In retrospect, North Vietnam's claim seems the correct one. The ARVN had suffered grievous losses, particularly among its junior officers.

Earl H. Tilford, Jr.

References

Berman, Larry. *Perfect Spy: The Incredible Double Life of Pham Xuan An*, Time *Magazine Reporter and Vietnamese Communist Agent*. New York: HarperCollins, 2007.

Fulghum, David, and Terrence Maitland. *South Vietnam on Trial, Mid-1970 to 1972.* The Vietnam Experience Series. Boston: Boston Publishing, 1984.

Ho De, Tran Hanh, and Hung Dat. *Chien Dich Phan Cong Duong So 9–Nam Lao, Nam 1971* [The Route 9–Southern Laos Counter-offensive Campaign, 1971]. Hanoi: Military History Institute of Vietnam, 1987.

Military History Institute of Vietnam. *Victory in Vietnam: The Official History of the People's Army of Vietnam, 1954–1975.* Lawrence: University Press of Kansas, 2002.

Nolan, Keith William. *Into Laos: The Story of Dewey Canyon II/Lam Son 719, Vietnam 1971.* Novato, CA: Presidio, 1986.

Palmer, Dave R. *Summons of the Trumpet: U.S.-Vietnam in Perspective.* San Rafael, CA: Presidio, 1995.

Laos

Landlocked Southeast Asian nation with a 1968 population of 2.73 million people. Laos is bordered by China and Burma (Myanmar) to the northwest, Vietnam to the east, Cambodia to the south, and Thailand to the west. Laos covers approximately 91,429 square miles. The northern part of the country is very mountainous, with steep river valleys leading to the Mekong River, which in this region is tumultuous and unnavigable except by small craft. The Plain of Jars is a distinctive rolling plain. The center is notable for its karst formations stretching from the Mekong Valley to the Annamite Mountains to the east. The topography of the south is more even and uniform, with broad river valleys suitable for rice cultivation and the high Bolovens Plateau. The Mekong flows into Cambodia over a series of waterfalls known as the Khong Falls.

In 1968, as now, the Lao economy was primarily agricultural. The country was inhabited by lowland rice cultivators, mostly Lao, and by highlanders from dozens of tribes who grew rice in forest clearings, raised a variety of other crops, and tended animals. Although the Lao are Theravada

Laotian students demonstrate their support for signed cease-fire in Vientiane, February 22, 1973. They carry banners reading "let this ceasefire be permanent." (AP/Wide World Photos)

Buddhists, the highlanders are mainly animists. In the towns there are minority Chinese, Vietnamese, and Indian populations who are mainly traders and shopkeepers. Some 85 percent of the Laotian population still reside in rural areas. The original inhabitants of Laos were Austroasiatic peoples who lived by hunting and gathering before the advent of agriculture. Trade developed at an early date, and the Laotians were skilled canoe navigators.

The first political entities identified in what is today Laos were princely fiefdoms exercising power over their neighbors by expanding and contracting spheres of influence known as mandalas. From the first century CE through the thirteenth century, Laos was influenced by the Chams, the Khmers, the Yunnanese, the Thais, and the Mongols. It was as a result of Mongol interference at Luang Prabang that the first kingdom to encompass all the territory of present-day Laos, known as the Kingdom of Lan Xang, was founded in 1353 by the warrior king Fa Ngum.

After fending off invasions from Vietnam (1478–1479), Siam (1536), and Burma (1571–1621), Fa Ngum's successors fell to squabbling, and their kingdom split in 1690 into Luang Prabang, Vientiane, and Champassak. Siam assumed ever-greater ascendancy over Laos, defeating the Vientiane kingdom and razing the capital in 1828. The court at Bangkok established outposts on the left bank of the Mekong all the way up to the Annamite Cordillera and treated the kings of Luang Prabang and Champassak as vassals. Siamese military expeditions were actively involved in suppressing bands of pillagers, known as Haws, from Yunnan.

When the French signed a protectorate agreement in 1884 with the Vietnamese court at Hue, which had been worried about Siamese expansion, they saw themselves as being entitled to establish a presence on the left bank of the Mekong in the name of the Vietnamese emperor by right of historic claims and proceeded to expel the Siamese garrisons. However, instead of claiming the left bank, the French established direct rule over southern Laos and signed a protectorate treaty with the king of Luang Prabang. French rule in Laos was consolidated by the treaty of October 3, 1893, signed with the king of Siam.

The French ruled Laos with a generally light hand. They established hospitals, schools, and a unified civil service. They also levied taxes and imposed work on public road construction projects, which led to sporadic revolts in the provinces. Vientiane remained a sleepy town on the bank of the Mekong, and the French restored a number of ancient monuments, including Buddhist temples.

Laos was hardly affected by World War II until March 9, 1945, when the Japanese suddenly ousted the French administration and made a brief but brutal appearance. In the wake of the Japanese surrender in August 1945, a group of nationalist-minded Laotians led by Prince Phetsarath, the viceroy of the kingdom of Luang Prabang, took the opportunity to seize power and form an independent government, ignoring the king's proclamation that the French protectorate had been restored.

The advocates of independence, known as the Lao Issara, received support from the Viet Minh in neighboring Vietnam and prepared to oppose the return of the French. The French received significant support, however, from some of the highlanders, particularly the Hmongs, and with the approval of the king and Prince Boun Oum na Champassak, the most influential figure in the south, succeeded in reimposing their presence in Laos by mid-1946. The Lao Issara fled across the river to Thailand, where they continued to agitate for opposition to France.

The French progressively granted the attributes of independence to the royal government in Vientiane and in 1947 unified the country under the rule of the king of Luang Prabang, who became the king of Laos. A three-headed white elephant on a red background became the kingdom's flag. Elections were held, a constitution was promulgated, and political parties flourished. Complete independence, including foreign affairs and defense, was granted by France in October 1953. Laos also took part in the 1954 Geneva Conference that ended the Indochina War.

The major problem facing the royal government was the reintegration of the Pathet Lao rebels, some of them ex–Lao Issara, who had fought alongside the Viet Minh during the war. By the terms of the cease-fire agreement, the Pathet Lao had been awarded two northern provinces in which to regroup while the Viet Minh regular units withdrew from Laos into the Democratic Republic of Vietnam (DRV, North Vietnam). Difficulties soon arose in the operations of the joint armistice commission and the International Commission for Supervision and Control (ICSC) that consisted of representatives from India, Canada, and Poland. Higher-level negotiations between the royal government and the Pathet Lao led to the formation of a coalition government in 1957, a move supported by the powers that had been represented at Geneva. The United States, however, deeply suspicious of the Communist ties of the Pathet Lao and worried that Congress would cut off aid to Laos for having Communists in its government, maneuvered behind the scenes to bring down the coalition in 1958, when partial elections revealed the popular strength of the party formed by the Pathet Lao, the Neo Lao Hak Sat (NLHS).

The Pathet Lao, for their part, had not given up their arms and now, having rejected integration into the royal army on their own terms, resumed military action against the U.S.-backed royal army in the two northern provinces. A series of attacks against royal army outposts in Sam Neua during the monsoon season of 1959 produced an international crisis in which the royal government charged that North Vietnam was aiding the insurgents and appealed for help to the United Nations (UN). The NLHS deputies to the National Assembly in Vientiane were imprisoned on charges of sedition but were never tried. Postwar Vietnamese historical documents now admit that the Royal Lao Government's charges were true. The Vietnamese provided logistical and training support, advisers, and Vietnamese "volunteer army" units to support the Pathet Lao for two months during the late summer of 1959 before pulling their forces back to avoid giving their opponents an excuse to further complicate the situation.

The United States stepped up aid to the royal army, which was channeled through a clandestine military aid mission, the Programs Evaluation Office (PEO). Following the establishment of a rightist government, excluding the NLHS, and the escape from prison of the NLHS deputies, on August 9, 1960, a young army captain, Kong Le, staged a coup d'état in Vientiane and demanded the resignation of the government and an end to the civil war.

A new government was formed that vowed to end the fighting and renew negotiations for a peaceful settlement with the Pathet Lao. Not surprisingly, this initiative met with the overt hostility of Thailand, which instituted a blockade of Vientiane, and the more camouflaged opposition of the United States, which maintained its aid to the Laotian army outside Vientiane in view of the threat posed by the Pathet Lao.

Attempts to find grounds for compromise proved unavailing, and even the king, Savang Vatthana, was completely ineffectual in steering the country away from disaster. Rightist forces under General Phoumi Nosavan, with U.S. arms, attacked Vientiane in mid-December 1960 and after three days of artillery and tank shelling drove Kong Le's paratroop battalion out. However, Kong Le had received arms, ammunition, and a small Vietnamese advisory group led by General Chu Huy Man that included a small artillery unit equipped with 105-millimeter (mm) howitzers and 120-mm mortars flown into Vientiane by Soviet aircraft from Hanoi. As Kong Le's troops retreated northward along the road toward Luang Prabang, Soviet aircraft continued to drop supplies. After the leftist troops captured the Plain of Jars on January 1, 1961, they were supplied by Soviet aircraft flying into the airfield there. The entry of the Soviet Union into the Laos crisis led to U.S. protests to Moscow. Furthermore, North Vietnamese troops were now openly involved as "volunteers" fighting on the side of the Pathet Lao–Kong Le alliance.

Prime minister Prince Souvanna Phouma, who had fled to Phnom Penh before the battle, proclaimed the continued legitimacy of his government and began a campaign to drum up international support for a neutral Laos. The new administration of President John F. Kennedy had decided not to intervene with U.S. troops and was not averse to any plan to neutralize Laos, a solution propounded in January by the U.S. ambassador in Vientiane, Winthrop Brown. Kennedy asked roving ambassador W. Averell Harriman to meet with Souvanna Phouma in New Delhi and see whether a non-Communist outcome to the crisis could be salvaged. The two men got on well at their first

meeting. From that point on the Kennedy administration worked for a new international conference on Laos of the Geneva type, a plan that had already been suggested by Prince Norodom Sihanouk of Cambodia. After much diplomatic activity on all sides, a 14-nation conference convened in Geneva in June 1961 and during the next year worked on a solution by coalition government.

In the spring of 1961 the Vietnamese exploited the unsettled situation to seize a large area along the Vietnamese border in central and southern Laos through which they could build roads (the famed Ho Chi Minh Trail) in order to send troops and supplies to the Vietnamese Communist insurgency in the Republic of Vietnam (RVN, South Vietnam). Vietnamese regular army military units maintained control of this area from this time to the end of the war in 1975.

Several factors favored the tripartite coalition that emerged in June 1962. One was the growing disinterest of Soviet premier Nikita S. Khrushchev in the Laos affair. His actions had been dictated by Moscow's rivalry with Beijing, but by 1962 the Sino-Soviet split had grown so wide that he no longer had any leverage to compete with Beijing's radical line. He admitted as much in his June 1961 meeting with Kennedy in Vienna, where the two leaders agreed that a neutral Laos without involvement of either power was in their mutual interest. The North Vietnamese, while receiving pledges of militant solidarity from Beijing, were finding their campaign to seize South Vietnam much more difficult than they had expected. Since they now controlled the section of Laos needed for them to send assistance to the insurgency in South Vietnam, their interest in the revolution in Laos accordingly diminished, at least temporarily.

The North Vietnamese government did not, however, withdraw its troops from

Laos as outlined under the 1962 Geneva Agreement, leaving them instead to revive the effort at a later date. After 1963 the second coalition existed in name only. Ignoring the cease-fire, both sides resumed military operations. The North Vietnamese and Pathet Lao subverted a section of Kong Le's army, compelling Kong Le to withdraw from the Plain of Jars and ally himself with the rightists once again. Among the most effective forces against the renewed North Vietnamese–Pathet Lao offensive became the irregular Meo (Hmong) troops of General Vang Pao. These troops stayed in the field, thanks to a large-scale resupply effort mounted by the U.S. Central Intelligence Agency (CIA). Another important factor in keeping the Communists at bay was bombing by the U.S. Air Force and the U.S. Navy during 1964–1973. The war seesawed back and forth, with the Hmongs capturing the Plain of Jars only to have to abandon it again.

By 1973 Laos was in effect divided, with the Communists holding the entire east from China to the Cambodian border. This was the area through which the Ho Chi Minh Trail, built and maintained at great cost by the North Vietnamese beginning in 1959, passed. The trail was defended by regular People's Army of Vietnam (PAVN, North Vietnamese Army) units in complete mockery of Lao sovereignty and the royal government, with which Hanoi nevertheless maintained diplomatic relations. The lowlands along the Mekong, on the other hand, were held by the royal government. The mountainous area between Vientiane and the Plain of Jars was held by the Hmongs.

Under an agreement signed in Vientiane on February 21, 1973, a new cease-fire was declared that was to take effect on the following day and gave the Pathet Lao equal status with the royal government for the first time. The U.S. bombing, which had dropped almost 2.1 million tons of ordnance on Laos (more than the total tonnage dropped by the United States in the European and Pacific theaters in World War II), came to a halt at noon on February 22.

The new coalition government took office on April 5, 1974, and each ministry had a minister from one side and a vice minister from the opposite side. Although the 1973 cease-fire left some 300 U.S. personnel unaccounted for in Laos, no U.S. prisoners of war (POWs) were returned by the Pathet Lao, with the exception of 8 who had been held in North Vietnam and were released in Hanoi.

On April 27, 1975, North Vietnamese–Pathet Lao forces launched a strong attack against General Vang Pao's Hmong troops at the strategic road junction of Sala Phou Khoun and drove southward toward Vientiane. Wishing to avoid a resumption of the war, Souvanna Phouma ordered Vang Pao to defend himself as best he could but without the benefit of air strikes by the small Royal Laotian Air Force. Feeling himself abandoned, Vang Pao had a last stormy meeting in Vientiane with the prime minister and then appealed to the CIA for evacuation of his troops and their families to safe haven in Thailand. On May 10 Vang Pao and 12 Hmong leaders signed a treaty reminding the United States of past pledges and agreeing to leave Laos and never return. The CIA refused an airlift, the only possible exit by that stage, although it did evacuate Vang Pao and his wives on May 14 as the North Vietnamese Pathet Lao closed in on his base at Long Chieng, which they captured without a fight and where they found the personnel files of Vang Pao's Hmong soldiers intact.

Meanwhile, a campaign of intimidation against the non–Pathet Lao members of the coalition government gathered momentum in Vientiane. Key ministers, including the defense minister, fled across the Mekong. Demonstrators occupied the compound of the U.S. aid mission, forcing termination of the large aid program and the evacuation of its U.S. employees. Orchestrated demonstrations and the takeover of government offices led to the entry of the Pathet Lao into the other major towns of Laos, without their being damaged by fighting. The Pathet Lao seizure of power was completed on August 23, 1975. Military units belonging to the royal army were said to have requested Pathet Lao "advisers," thereby facilitating the integration of the army. Officers and high-ranking government officials who remained in Vientiane, hoping for the best, were sent to attend "seminars" at camps in Sam Neua, where many of them died.

At the beginning of December 1975 the Pathet Lao did away with the last facade of the coalition government and abolished the 600-year-old monarchy. A republic, the Lao People's Democratic Republic (LPDR), was proclaimed. Political parties were prohibited. King Savang Vatthana was named an adviser to the new president, but the king in fact played no role after his abdication. He died in a seminar camp in 1978 along with the queen and their eldest son.

The December 1975 events also saw the emergence of the Lao People's Revolutionary Party (LPRP), the Communist party behind the Pathet Lao front. The LPRP acknowledged its lineage from the Indochinese Communist Party (ICP), founded by Ho Chi Minh in 1930, that had been divided into three national parties for Vietnam, Laos, and Cambodia in 1951. The LPRP declared itself a Marxist-Leninist party and, as the sole ruling party in the LPDR, began elaborating policies.

For the first decade these policies were centered on state control of every aspect of life, although efforts to collectivize agriculture amounted to little more than rhetoric. A constitution was not elaborated until 1991. Meanwhile, the party's propaganda organs extolled the heroic deeds of the victorious "people's army" against the superior forces of the United States. Surprisingly, through all of this the U.S. embassy in Vientiane, manned by a skeleton staff since the departure of the last ambassador to the royal government in May 1975, was untouched, and the United States maintained diplomatic relations with the LPDR.

The LPRP counted 60,000 members by March 1996, when the party held its Sixth Congress. Party leadership continued to be dominated by the veteran leaders of the 30-year struggle against the French and the Americans. Eight of the 9 Politburo members named in 1996 were military officers. The 49-member Central Committee, however, included several younger figures more in keeping with economic reforms enacted between 1986 and 1996. Overall, the degree of stability of leadership that the party has exercised during its three decades of being the only legal political party in the country has been remarkable.

The lingering effect of the war also manifested itself in two of the major issues between the LPDR and the United States. These were the issue of POWs and those missing in action and the LPDR's demand for U.S. humanitarian aid to help cope with the hundreds of thousands of unexploded bombs that were left scattered about the countryside and continued to cause injuries and death for civilians, particularly in the north, more than two decades after the end of hostilities.

By the mid- to late 1990s, the LPDR had begun to open its economy and move somewhat haltingly toward a more market-oriented system. In recognition of this, the

United States in 2005 normalized trade relations with Laos, ending years of punitive import duties on Laotian goods. Normalized relations between Vietnam and the United States, which occurred in the 1990s, also helped repair U.S.-Laotian ties. Nevertheless, Laos remains a one-party state, and the LPDR is the only legal political entity, which governs via an all-powerful 9-member Politburo. Since 1992 Laos has had an 85-seat national assembly, but only LPDR members can be elected to it, and it is a body that largely rubber-stamps LPDR policies.

Faced with the problems of economic opening coupled with political repression, lack of government funding for development projects, and leftovers from the war, Laos continues to be an impoverished nation with an economy more akin to the nineteenth century than the twenty-first century. Laos has practically no modern infrastructure and has only one railway, which links Vientiane with Thailand. There are few paved roads, and the existing road network that connects the nation's many remote villages is antiquated and frequently impassable. Communication networks are sparse and marginally reliable at best, which is a large disadvantage in a modern era of instantaneous communications. It will likely be some time before Laos frees itself from the ranks of the world's least-developed countries and catches up with the other non-Communist Southeast Asian countries.

Arthur J. Dommen

References

Cordell, Helen, comp. *Laos*. World Bibliographical Series, Vol. 133. Santa Barbara, CA: ABC-CLIO, 1991.

Lewis, Judy, ed. *Minority Cultures of Laos: Kammu, Lua', Lahu, Hmong, and Iu-Mien.* Rancho Cordova, CA: Folsom Cordova Unified School District, 1992.

Military History Institute of Vietnam. *Lich Su Quan Tinh Nguyen Va Cac Doan Chuyen Gia Quan Su Viet Nam Tai Lao (1945–1975)* [History of the Vietnamese Volunteer Army Forces and Vietnamese Military Advisory Units in Laos (1945–1975)]. Hanoi: People's Army Publishing House, 1999.

Military History Institute of Vietnam. *Victory in Vietnam: The Official History of the People's Army of Vietnam, 1954–1975.* Lawrence: University Press of Kansas, 2002.

Savada, Andrea Matles, ed. *Laos: A Country Study.* Washington, DC: Federal Research Division, Library of Congress, 1995.

Stuart-Fox, Martin, and Mary Kooyman. *Historical Dictionary of Laos.* Asian Historical Dictionaries No. 6. Metuchen, NJ: Scarecrow, 1992.

Zasloff, Joseph J., and Leonard Unger, eds. *Laos: Beyond the Revolution.* London: Macmillan, 1991.

Le Duan (1907–1986)

Secretary-general of the Communist Party of Vietnam and de facto leader of the Democratic Republic of Vietnam (DRV, North Vietnam) following the 1969 death of Ho Chi Minh. Born Le Van Nhuan on April 7, 1907, in Trieu Phong District, Quang Tri Province, Le Duan developed an early and active devotion to revolutionary politics. During the 1920s, he worked as a clerk for French Railways in Hanoi and during that time cultivated his Marxist interests. He first joined the Vietnam Revolutionary Youth League and then in 1930 became a charter member of the Indochinese Communist Party. He was elected to membership in the Communist Party Central Committee in 1939. An ardent opponent of French rule, Le Duan was twice imprisoned, from 1931 to 1936 and again from 1940 to 1945, on charges of political subversion.

In the years following World War II, Le Duan emerged as a trusted lieutenant of Ho Chi Minh and a key figure in the Viet Minh challenge to continued French rule. A capable strategist and tactician, Le Duan directed Viet Minh efforts in Cochin China from 1946 until 1952, when he was sent to North Vietnam to work at party headquarters. Le Duan was elected to membership in the Communist Party Politburo in 1951.

Although the 1954 Viet Minh victory at Dien Bien Phu brought an end to French rule in Vietnam, the brokered agreement at the 1954 Geneva Conference left the country divided. Le Duan, who clung to the nationalist ideal of a united (as well as an independent) Vietnam, openly opposed the agreement. He nonetheless worked with Ho Chi Minh to secure Communist control in North Viet.

Le Duan's long service resulted in his continued upward advance within the party. In 1954 he was sent to the Republic of Vietnam (RVN, South Vietnam), where he again served as secretary of the Lao Dong (Workers' Party, or the Communist Party) Central Committee for the Southern Region until 1957. In 1956 Le Duan wrote the "Tenets of the Revolution in South Vietnam," which became the foundation of the Communist struggle in South Vietnam. In 1957 Le Duan was recalled to North Vietnam, where he was entrusted with the leadership of the party following the removal of Truong Chinh as party secretary-general as the result of the disastrous Land Reform Program in North Vietnam. In 1959 Le Duan was elected as party first secretary, a position he held for the next decade. A member of the Lao Dong Politburo as well as the Central Committee and Secretariat, he moved to the top echelon of the North Vietnamese power structure.

In 1958 Le Duan secretly revisited South Vietnam to observe the situation there. He returned with recommendations for a dramatic escalation. Hanoi-supported Viet Cong (VC) guerrillas operating against the U.S.-backed government of Ngo Dinh Diem faced total destruction, Le Duan warned, unless the effort was prosecuted vigorously. Over the course of the next three years, largely under Le Duan's direction, the VC launched a sweeping program of assassinations and urban terrorism while stepping up more conventional forms of military confrontation.

Le Duan continued to play an important role in Hanoi's prosecution of the conflict. A consistent advocate of the offensive, he supported the infusion of People's Army of Vietnam (PAVN, North Vietnamese Army) forces to South Vietnam as well as stronger support for the VC. In 1965, as U.S. involvement in the war increased, he advocated the move to conventional warfare, joining other North Vietnamese leaders in shunning Chinese advice to de-escalate. He maintained that only through conventional offensive warfare, as practiced against the French, could Vietnam expel the foreign invaders. Le Duan reportedly had frequent clashes with North Vietnam's military commander General Vo Nguyen Giap and other party leaders over war strategy and political ideology, culminating in a dispute during the summer of 1967 over the plan for the 1968 Tet Offensive. At around the same time Le Duan also presided over what was called the Anti-Party Affair, a purge of senior party and military figures including a number of General Giap's closest supporters.

With Ho Chi Minh's death in September 1969, Le Duan became the undisputed leader of the party and the North Vietnamese government. He continued to press the war and maintained a hard line during cease-fire negotiations with the United States. He viewed a continued division of Vietnam as unacceptable; the conflict would be pressed until the invaders withdrew and unity was achieved. Under the leadership of Le Duan, Vo Nguyen Giap, and Prime Minister Pham Van Dong, Communist forces cemented their victory over South Vietnam with the capture of Saigon in 1975.

As the leader of a united Vietnam, Le Duan faced the mammoth task of rebuilding a country ravaged by 35 years of almost continuous war. Reconciling opposing ideologies, restoring the economy, and feeding the people of Vietnam all posed major obstacles, with which he dealt with varying degrees of success. A devoted Marxist, he maintained close ties with the Soviet Union, a relationship that he solidified with the signing of the Friendship Treaty in 1978. Le Duan died in Hanoi on July 10, 1986.

David Coffey

References

Burgess, Patricia, ed. *The Annual Obituary, 1986*. Chicago: St. James, 1989.

Duiker, William J. *The Communist Road to Power in Vietnam*. 2nd ed. Boulder, CO: Westview, 1996.

Karnow, Stanley. *Vietnam: A History*. 2nd rev. and updated ed. New York: Penguin, 1997.

Lien-Hang T, Nguyen. *Hanoi's War: An International History of the War for Peace in Vietnam*. Chapel Hill: The University of North Carolina Press, 2012.

Military History Institute of Vietnam. *Victory in Vietnam: The Official History of the People's Army of Vietnam, 1954–1975*. Lawrence: University Press of Kansas, 2002.

Pribbenow, Merle. "General Vo Nguyen Giap and the Mysterious Evolution of the Plan for the 1968 Tet Offensive." *Journal of Vietnam Studies* 3(2) (Summer 2008): 1–33.

Quinn-Judge, Sophie. "The Ideological Debate in the DRV and the Significance of
the Anti-Party Affair, 1967–1968." *Cold War History* 5(4) (November 2006): 479–500.

Who's Who in the World, 1984–1985. Chicago: Marquis Who's Who, 1989.

LINEBACKER I, Operation (May 10–October 23, 1972)

U.S. airpower response to the 1972 Nguyen Hue Offensive (Spring Offensive) carried out by the Democratic Republic of Vietnam (DRV, North Vietnam). Operation LINEBACKER I is notable for three reasons. First, it remains a classic aerial interdiction operation. Second, it was arguably the most effective use of airpower in the Vietnam War. And third, it was the first modern air campaign in which precision-guided munitions (laser-guided bombs, LGBs) and electro-optically guided bombs (EOGBs) played a key role.

What made LINEBACKER I effective was the use of conventional airpower against North Vietnam to stop a conventional invasion by 14 divisions of the People's Army of Vietnam (PAVN, North Vietnamese Army). By the spring of 1972, the war involved two modern and relatively well-equipped armies, the PAVN and the Army of the Republic of Vietnam (ARVN, South Vietnamese Army), locked in combat. U.S. airpower provided close air support for the ARVN while simultaneously attacking the transportation system, military installations, and other vital military targets inside North Vietnam.

LINEBACKER I had three operational objectives: to destroy military supplies inside North Vietnam, to isolate North Vietnam from outside sources of supply, and to interdict the flow of supplies and troops to the battlefields of South Vietnam. The targets were basically the same as those attacked during

Rows of B-52D Stratofortress aircraft at Anderson Air Force Base in Guam on December 15, 1972. B-52s of the Strategic Air Command fleet were employed largely over South Vietnam in ARC LIGHT missions but were used effectively over North Vietnam during Operations LINEBACKER I and II. (Department of Defense)

Operation ROLLING THUNDER: highways, railroads, bridges, warehouses, petroleum storage facilities, barracks, and power-generating plants. Operationally, two things were different. First, military commanders were given more latitude to select targets and to determine the best combination of tactics and weapons. Second, technological advances such as LGBs, EOGBs, and the introduction of the long-range electronic navigation (LORAN) bombing system made it possible to attack a greater variety of targets with the kind of precision that minimized collateral damage and civilian casualties.

Operation LINEBACKER I commenced on May 10, 1972, when 32 U.S. Air Force McDonnell Douglas F-4 Phantoms attacked

Long Bien Bridge (formerly Paul Doumer Bridge) and the Yen Vien railroad yard in Hanoi. The Phantoms successfully dropped 29 LGBs on the bridge and 84 conventional bombs on the railroad marshaling yard. Two days earlier, U.S. Navy Grumman A-6 Intruder and Ling-Temco-Vought A-7 Corsair II fighter-bombers had sown 2,000-pound mines at the entrance to Haiphong Harbor, initiating the isolation of North Vietnam from outside sources of supply.

During the next few days, LGBs and EOGBs were used to destroy bridges and tunnels along the northwest and northeast highways and railroads leading from Hanoi to the Chinese border. Because the bridges spanned gorges in the rugged Annamite

Mountains, they were not as easily repaired as those that crossed the sandy streams of North Vietnam's southern panhandle. Supplies, stacked up while North Vietnamese workers tried to repair the bridges and tunnels, were susceptible to attack by fighter-bombers using conventional munitions. By the end of June, more than 400 bridges and tunnels had been destroyed, including the infamous Thanh Hoa and Long Bien bridges.

Once the bridges were down and the railroads and highways had been interdicted, LINEBACKER I focused on petroleum-storage facilities, power-generating plants, military barracks, training camps, and air-defense facilities. Again, precision-guided munitions made it possible to attack targets proscribed during ROLLING THUNDER because of their proximity to civilian structures. For instance, on May 26 a flight of four F-4s used LGBs to destroy the three main buildings of the Son Tay warehouse complex, located in the middle of a residential area. All bombs hit their targets without causing collateral damage to the surrounding dwellings. Furthermore, because truck-repair facilities, often no larger than a neighborhood service station in the United States, were located in the middle of housing areas, these had been off-limits during ROLLING THUNDER. During LINEBACKER I, however, LGBs destroyed many such repair facilities.

By September, it was evident that LINEBACKER I was having an effect. Imports into North Vietnam dropped to half what they had been in May. The PAVN offensive inside South Vietnam stalled, and the ARVN regained much of the territory lost in the initial onslaughts of April and May. American airpower continued to pummel PAVN units inside South Vietnam while LINEBACKER missions pounded North Vietnam.

Although LINEBACKER I was a classic interdiction campaign, it was one with a strategic effect. There were two strategic objectives. The first was to prevent North Vietnam from using military force to win the war. By June it was clear the offensive would not succeed. Second, the bombing was intended to force North Vietnam to negotiate seriously so that an acceptable peace agreement could be obtained by the end of the year. Peace talks, which had been suspended on May 2, 1972, resumed 10 days later, just as the first LINEBACKER strikes hit North Vietnam. But the North Vietnamese did not negotiate seriously until September, when some 27,500 tons of bombs fell on their country. Between October 8 and 23, a peace agreement acceptable to Washington and Hanoi took shape. And on October 23, 1972, President Richard Nixon ordered a halt to bombing north of 20 degrees latitude, but South Vietnamese president Nguyen Van Thieu balked at the peace terms.

Still, LINEBACKER I had achieved its stated objectives. From March 31 to October 23, 1972, some 155,548 tons of bombs fell on North Vietnam. LINEBACKER I had indeed succeeded where ROLLING THUNDER had failed. There were four reasons for its success. First, President Nixon used airpower more decisively than his predecessor. President Lyndon Johnson had worried about Chinese or Soviet intervention; he had also fretted about the domestic political reaction to bombing and was constantly searching for political consensus among his advisers. By 1972 Henry Kissinger's diplomacy had exploited the Sino-Soviet split, and intervention was no longer a major concern. Furthermore, Nixon's primary political concern was with the Republican Right, which trusted him and wanted an end to the war. He was comparatively unconcerned with the political Left. Second, the nature of the war had changed. The 14 PAVN divisions attacking South Vietnam included hundreds of tanks and trucks that needed fuel. PAVN troops needed food as well as medical supplies to treat the considerable casualties they were sustaining. Their tank and artillery tubes required ammunition. This force required about 1,000 tons of supplies a day to sustain its offensive. Third, Nixon provided the military more latitude in deciding what targets should be struck and when. Finally, the employment of LGBs, EOGBs, and LORAN bombing techniques made precision strikes possible and helped limit collateral damage. These factors combined to make LINEBACKER I the most effective use of airpower in the Vietnam War. It remains the classic air interdiction campaign.

Earl H. Tilford, Jr.

References

Clodfelter, Mark. *The Limits of Air Power: The American Bombing of North Vietnam.* New York: Free Press, 1989.

Frankum, Ronald B., Jr. *Like Rolling Thunder: The Air War in Vietnam, 1964–1975.* New York: Rowman and Littlefield, 2005.

Momyer, William W. *Airpower in Three Wars: World War II, Korea and Vietnam.* Washington, DC: U.S. Government Printing Office, 1978.

Morrocco, John. *Rain of Fire: Air War, 1969–1973.* The Vietnam Experience Series. Boston: Boston Publishing, 1985.

Sharp, Ulysses S. Grant. *Strategy for Defeat: Vietnam in Retrospect.* San Rafael, CA: Presidio, 1978.

Tilford, Earl H., Jr. *Crosswinds: The Air Force's Setup in Vietnam.* College Station: Texas A&M University Press, 1993.

LINEBACKER II, Operation (December 18–29, 1972)

U.S. bombing campaign over the Democratic Republic of Vietnam (DRV, North Vietnam). On December 13, 1972, the Paris negotiations, which had resumed in early November, broke down. Nguyen Van Thieu, president of the Republic of Vietnam (RVN, South Vietnam), had rejected the original terms agreed to in Paris, and the North Vietnamese government refused to make significant changes in a document already signed and, indeed, published the peace terms. When negotiations resumed and reached an impasse, President Richard M. Nixon blamed North Vietnam and issued an ultimatum that North Vietnamese representatives return to the conference table within 72 hours "or else." Hanoi rejected Nixon's demand. Nixon proved better than his word when he turned to airpower to enforce his ultimatum.

Plans already existed for a winter phase of the original LINEBACKER campaign. The wintry skies over North Vietnam were overcast with a drizzle reminiscent of Germany or England at the same time of year. Such weather precluded operations focused on the use of laser-guided bombs (LGBs) or electro-optically guided bombs (EOGBs). The only planes in the U.S. military inventory capable of all-weather bombing operations were the U.S. Air Force's Boeing B-52 Stratofortresses and General Dynamics F-111 Aardvark fighter-bombers and the U.S. Navy's Grumman A-6 Intruders.

Although A-6s and F-111s were capable of bombing almost any target with relative precision, there simply were not enough of them to continue the bombing of North Vietnam at the desired intensity. Targets suitable for B-52 attacks were those generally defined as area targets: airfields, petroleum-storage facilities, warehouse complexes, and railroad marshaling yards. A comprehensive list of those kinds of targets had been drawn up in August.

On December 14 Nixon ordered mines resown in Haiphong Harbor. Meanwhile, the evacuation of Hanoi and Haiphong proceeded in anticipation of what was to come. On December 18 Operation LINEBACKER II, originally conceived as a three-day maximum-effort strategic bombing campaign, commenced. By that time more than half of the Strategic Air Command (SAC) B-52 force was in the theater with 150 bombers at Andersen Air Force Base, Guam, and 60 B-52s based at U-Tapao Royal Thai Air Force Base, Thailand.

Flying in three-ship cells, each designated by a different color (e.g., red, blue, brown, cobalt, etc.), the B-52s carried the brunt of what airmen dubbed the "Eleven-Day War" and peace activists called the "Christmas Bombings." On December 18 just after dark at 7:45 p.m., the first wave of 48 B-52s struck the Kinh No storage complex, the Yen Vien rail yard, and three airfields around Hanoi. An SA-2 surface-to-air missile (SAM) claimed one B-52 over Yen Vien. At midnight, 30 Guam-based B-52s bombed additional targets around Hanoi. A second B-52 was severely damaged by a SAM but limped back to Thailand before crashing. The third wave struck just before dawn, and a third B-52 went down. A total of 129 B-52 sorties had taken off, and 3 bombers had been lost. The 3 percent loss rate, while regrettable, was also predictable and acceptable.

The second night was a rerun of the first. Ninety-three B-52s struck the Thai Nguyen thermal power plant and the Yen Vien rail yard. Although SAMs damaged 2 bombers, there were no losses. The old saying "If it ain't broke don't fix it" seemed to apply. On the night of December 21, the same basic attack plan was used when three waves of 33 B-52s each returned to the Yen Vien rail yard and the Thai Nguyen thermal power plant while oil-storage areas at Kinh No and other storage facilities around

Hanoi were also struck. This time 6 B-52s were lost, and 1 B-52 was heavily damaged.

Although a 6 percent loss rate was acceptable for World War II B-17 missions over Germany, such a loss rate could not be sustained for long given the relatively small number of B-52s in the SAC inventory. The fault, however, lay squarely with the U.S. Air Force and SAC. Years of jungle-bashing missions in the relatively safe skies over South Vietnam, Laos, and Cambodia had lulled SAC planners into a false sense of security. The result was mission planning more suitable to raids on Schweinfurt or Dresden, Germany, nearly 30 years earlier. Furthermore, whereas LINEBACKER I had been a truly modern air campaign, LINEBACKER II was a throwback to the long bomber streams of B-17s and B-29s that ambled over their targets during World War II. The B-52 bomber streams during those first three nights were up to 70 miles long. The three-plane cells lumbered along toward their targets at more or less the same altitude, speed, and heading. The turn points were uniform and predictable, and the losses were inevitable.

SAC now was forced to revamp its planning. The result was a switch in both force packaging and strategy. Over the next two nights the number of bombers scheduled dropped from the 100-plus raids of the first three nights to 33 raids. On the night of December 21 the air defense support system took top priority as B-52s bombed SAM storage facilities. But because 2 more B-52s were lost on December 21, missions in the immediate vicinity of Hanoi were curtailed. On the following night, B-52s pounded petroleum-storage areas and rail yards around the port of Haiphong. There were no losses. One B-52 was shot down on raids over each of the next two nights before bombing was suspended for a 36-hour period to mark

Christmas. At that point, 11 B-52s had been shot down.

By Christmas, most of the legitimate targets in North Vietnam had been reduced to rubble. In fact, it was LINEBACKER I that had devastated North Vietnam. The so-called Christmas Bombings mostly just rearranged the rubble. The differences in the two campaigns, however, were in their objectives and in their intensity. During LINEBACKER I, the primary objective was to stop a massive, conventional invasion. LINEBACKER I was an interdiction campaign that had the strategic effect of compelling North Vietnam to negotiate seriously for the first time in the war. LINE-BACKER II, on the other hand, was a strategic bombing campaign aimed at the will of the North Vietnamese leadership. The campaign's sole objective was to force the Hanoi government to quickly come to an agreement on a cease-fire. The fact that most of the targets constituted parts of the transportation system was simply because these targets, along with airfields and storage complexes, were suitable for area bombing. Furthermore, other than the Thai Nguyen steelworks, North Vietnam had no war-making industries.

Most of the destruction wrought on North Vietnam during LINEBACKER I had been inflicted by fighter-bombers, and while the bombing was substantial, it had taken place over a period of several months. North Vietnam had plenty of time to adjust and to get used to the bombing. LINEBACKER II was much more focused and intensive, meaning that more bombs fell on North Vietnam in a shorter period of time. The attacks by the B-52s were therefore psychologically more devastating if for no other reason than that a three-plane cell of B-52s could drop more than 300 bombs into an area the size of a railroad marshaling yard or an airfield in less than a minute. Although the effect could be mind-numbing, by Christmas the Hanoi leadership had given no indication that it was ready to negotiate seriously.

The bombing resumed at dawn the day after Christmas. The objective at that point was to make the Politburo feel desperate by rendering North Vietnam defenseless. The Hanoi leadership would certainly notice that virtually every military target had been obliterated and that only the dike system and neighborhoods remained unscathed. Whether or not these would have been attacked is open to conjecture, but with no defenses the risk was not worth taking.

At dawn on December 26, "Ironhand" Republic F-105 Thunderchief and McDonnell Douglas F-4 Phantom fighter-bombers, planes specially modified to attack SAM sites and their guidance radars, pummeled North Vietnam's air defense system. During the day, although the weather was overcast, 16 U.S. Air Force F-4 Phantoms used the long-range electronic navigation (LORAN) bombing technique to blast the main SAM assembly area in Hanoi. When the remaining operational SAM sites fired the missiles they had on hand, there would be no resupply. At dusk, U.S. Air Force General Dynamics F-111 Aardvark swing-wing fighter-bombers swooped in low over the major airfields to crater the runways so that MiG interceptors could not take off. By dark, North Vietnam lay almost defenseless before the most concerted B-52 attack in history.

That night's B-52 assault was overwhelming. Instead of bombing throughout the night, 120 B-52s struck 10 different targets in a 15-minute period. Surviving SAM sites still had missiles, and 2 B-52s were lost. But the 1.66 percent loss rate was acceptable, especially since those seasoned in the art of aerial warfare knew that the endgame was at hand.

The bombing on the night after Christmas got the Politburo's attention. Hanoi cabled Washington asking if January 8, 1973, would be an acceptable date to reopen negotiations. Nixon replied that negotiations must begin on January 2 and that there would a time limit for reaching an acceptable agreement. Until Hanoi acknowledged and accepted these terms, the bombing would continue.

On December 27, 60 B-52s struck airfields and warehouses around Hanoi and Vinh. A number of B-52s bombed the Lang Dang rail yard near the Chinese border. SAMs knocked down 2 more B-52s, but returning pilots noted that missile firings were more random and that the entire North Vietnamese defense effort seemed uncoordinated and sporadic. No more B-52s were lost during LINEBACKER II. Sixty B-52 sorties were flown during each of the next two nights. Virtually no SAM firings were recorded, and B-52 crews were confident that they could fly over North Vietnam with impunity. On December 28 Hanoi agreed to all of President Nixon's provisions for reopening negotiations. The next day Nixon limited the bombing to targets south of the 20th Parallel, and LINEBACKER II came to an end.

Even though Operation LINEBACKER II ended, the bombing did not. B-52s and fighter-bombers continued to pound North Vietnamese troops, supply lines, roads, bridges, and other military facilities in North Vietnam's southern panhandle. People's Army of Vietnam (PAVN, North Vietnamese Army) troops inside South Vietnam were bombed up until the cease-fire agreement was signed. This continued bombing was meant to encourage the North Vietnamese to negotiate quickly, seriously, and in good faith.

For airmen, the "Eleven-Day War" took on special meaning. Airpower enthusiasts claimed that if given the opportunity, bombing on the scale of LINEBACKER II could have ended the war just as quickly at any time. It became an article of faith within the U.S. Air Force that LINEBACKER II had forced the enemy to capitulate.

Likewise, antiwar activists held that the raids constituted another Dresden, referencing the destruction of that German city by Allied bombers in February 1945. Gloria Emerson, in her book *Winners and Losers*, quoted an unnamed Vietnamese official who claimed that 100,000 tons of bombs had fallen on Hanoi alone during the 11-day campaign. Both interpretations, although overly simplistic, took on mythological proportions among their proponents, and both were wrong.

During LINEBACKER II, 739 B-52 sorties struck North Vietnam, dropping 15,237 tons of bombs. U.S. Air Force and U.S. Navy fighter-bombers added another 5,000 tons. The North Vietnamese launched virtually every SAM in their inventory to shoot down 15 B-52s, 9 fighter-bombers, 1 U.S. Navy R-5A reconnaissance plane, and a U.S. Air Force CH-53 Sea Stallion "Jolly Green Giant" rescue helicopter.

Damage inflicted on targets inside North Vietnam was significant, but the country was far from devastated. Although spent SAMs falling back to earth, crashing B-52s, and an occasional stray bomb caused some damage to neighborhoods in Hanoi, Haiphong, Vinh, and elsewhere, most were left virtually unscathed. According to Hanoi's own figures, 1,312 people perished in the capital, and 300 more were killed in Haiphong. This is hardly comparable to the 100,000 people who perished in Dresden on the night of February 13–14, 1945. What LINEBACKER II did was to have a psychological effect on Hanoi's leaders. With their air defense in shambles and virtually all the military targets left in rubble, they did not need to take the risk that the neighborhoods and dike system might be next. Accordingly, peace talks moved ahead expeditiously until January 23, 1973, when the United States, North Vietnam, South Vietnam, and the Viet Cong (VC) signed a cease-fire agreement, little different from its predecessor, that took effect five days later.

Earl H. Tilford, Jr.

References

Clodfelter, Mark. *The Limits of Air Power: The American Bombing of North Vietnam.* New York: Free Press, 1989.

Eschmann, Karl J. *Linebacker: The Untold Story of the Air Raids over North Vietnam.* New York: Ivy Books, 1989.

Michel, Marshall L., III. *The Eleven Days of Christmas: America's Last Vietnam Battle.* San Francisco: Encounter Books, 2002.

Momyer, William W. *Airpower in Three Wars: World War II, Korea and Vietnam.* Washington, DC: U.S. Government Printing Office, 1978.

Morrocco, John. *Rain of Fire: Air War, 1969–1973.* The Vietnam Experience Series. Boston: Boston Publishing, 1985.

Tilford, Earl H., Jr. *Crosswinds: The Air Force's Setup in Vietnam.* College Station: Texas A&M University Press, 1993.

Lon Nol (1913–1985)

Cambodian Army officer; prime minister (1966–1967, 1969–1972); and after the overthrow of Prince Norodom Sihanouk, president of the short-lived Khmer Republic (1972–1975) prior to the takeover by the Khmer Rouge. Born in Prey Veng Province, Cambodia, on November 13, 1913, Lon Nol was the grandson of a Khmer Krom (ethnic Cambodian resident of Vietnam) official from Tay Ninh and the son of a district chief in the Cambodian civil service. Lon Nol was educated at the Lycée Chasseloup Laubat in Saigon from 1928 to 1934. Starting as a magistrate, he rose through the ranks to become a deputy governor in 1945. He held important posts, notably in the armed forces, throughout the Sihanouk period.

Lon Nol was sufficiently popular with the Cambodian elite that at a National Congress convoked by Sihanouk in August 1969, Lon Nol received the highest number of votes (115) among 10 possible candidates to head a "national salvation" government to deal with mounting economic and foreign problems. Prince Sisowath Sirik Matak received the second-highest number of votes (99). These were the two men who were to emerge within months as Cambodia's leaders. However, they were extraordinarily reluctant leaders. Both declined the offer by the Cambodian National Assembly to form the new government, and it was only on Sihanouk's virtual order that Lon Nol finally agreed to become prime minister.

Lon Nol has often been accused of plotting Sihanouk's overthrow, but during most of the crucial period preceding the National Assembly's vote of no confidence on Sihanouk, Lon Nol was not even in Cambodia. From October 30, 1969, to February 18, 1970, he was undergoing medical treatment in France, having left Sirik Matak in charge in Phnom Penh. Whatever ambitions Lon Nol may have harbored at that point, his actions were hardly those of a coup plotter.

Lon Nol met with Sihanouk when the latter arrived in Europe on one of his regular annual foreign tours at the beginning of January 1970 and reportedly persuaded the prince to sanction tougher measures against the Democratic Republic of Vietnam (DRV, North Vietnam) and the Viet Cong (VC) in their operations inside Cambodia, notably

General Lon Nol, the president of Cambodia's new Salvation Government, addressing a rally in Phnom Penh, April 11, 1970. He took over from Norodom Sihanouk in a bloodless coup. (AP/Wide World Photos)

denying them the requisitioning of rice and other supplies and the use of base camps opposite the border of the Republic of Vietnam (RVN, South Vietnam) to support offensives against the Saigon government. In February 1970 the small Cambodian Army began artillery bombardments against People's Army of Vietnam (PAVN, North Vietnamese Army) and VC positions on Cambodian soil, and in one of his first moves on returning to Phnom Penh, Lon Nol called in all outstanding 500-riel notes, thereby creating chaos with the Communist Vietnamese rice-purchasing operations.

On March 8, 1970, the first of a series of anti-Vietnamese demonstrations occurred in Svay Rieng, a province containing large North Vietnamese base areas. Four days later Lon Nol sent Sihanouk a telegram through the Cambodian embassy in Paris demanding that Cambodia's military forces

be increased to 100,000 men. Sihanouk was outraged by publication of the message and shouted threats of execution against his ministers, which were reported back to Phnom Penh, so frightening Lon Nol that he decided to join with Sirik Matak in ousting Sihanouk. However, on the night before the decisive vote in the National Assembly, Lon Nol reportedly had to be persuaded at gunpoint by Sirik Matak to sign a document authorizing the ouster. The next day, March 18, after a debate in which Sihanouk's conduct was criticized by all speakers, Sihanouk was voted out.

Cheng Heng, chairman of the National Assembly, became head of state pending election of a new head of state under the constitution. Lon Nol and Sirik Matak remained as prime minister and deputy prime minister, respectively. The deputies' anger against Sihanouk had been further stoked by news of an abortive attempt by the head of the national police, Colonel Oum Manorine, a half brother of Sihanouk's wife, Monique, to arrest Lon Nol.

Faced with the determination of PAVN and VC forces to hang on to their valuable Cambodian sanctuaries and sources of supply in addition to the growing threat posed by an indigenous Khmer Communist movement headed by Pol Pot, whose forces increasingly took over the fighting from the Vietnamese, the government in Phnom Penh blundered from one failure to another. Its rapid loss of control of most of the provinces was not helped by massive military maneuvers along the main roads, and Phnom Penh itself became a beleaguered city crowded with refugees. The country's economy, already seriously strained, collapsed. A pogrom against Vietnamese residents resulted in many thousands of civilian deaths. The Chinese merchant class fled. Some foreign journalists disappeared a few miles outside the capital, and it was later discovered that they had been executed by the xenophobic guerrillas.

In this crisis Lon Nol showed a definite and surprising lack of leadership. Despite the fact that in March 1972 he announced that he was taking over from Cheng Heng as head of state in a new Khmer Republic to be approved by popular referendum, Lon Nol relied increasingly on mystical solutions. Always a superstitious man, he called the Vietnamese *thmil*, the Khmer word for the evil spirits that lurked in the forests. He consulted astrologers with increasing frequency. Resisting suggestions that he step down to pave the way for a negotiated armistice with Sihanouk in Beijing, he stayed on doggedly. But Lon Nol faced real health problems, and a few weeks before the Khmer Rouge entered Phnom Penh in 1975, he departed for Hawaii to receive medical treatment. He then moved to California and died there in Fullerton on November 17, 1985.

Arthur J. Dommen

References

Chandler, David P. *The Tragedy of Cambodian History: Politics, War, and Revolution since 1945*. New Haven, CT: Yale University Press, 1991.

Hamel, Bernard. *Sihanouk et le Drame Cambodgien*. Paris: Editions L'Harmattan, 1993.

Kirk, Donald. *Wider War: The Struggle for Cambodia, Thailand, and Laos*. New York: Praeger, 1971.

M

MARKET TIME, Operation (1965–1972)

Long-term allied naval operation to conduct surveillance of the 1,200-mile coastline of the Republic of Vietnam (RVN, South Vietnam) and halt seaborne infiltration of supplies to Communist forces. Initially the U.S. Seventh Fleet had charge of the American operation, which was designated the Vietnam Patrol Force, or Task Force 71. Weeks later, naval leaders code-named the operation MARKET TIME. On July 31, 1965, operational command transferred from the Seventh Fleet to the Naval Advisory Group, and the Vietnam Patrol Force became the Coastal Surveillance Force, or Task Force 115. On April 1, 1966, the newly created Naval Forces, Vietnam (NAVFORV), assumed command of Operation MARKET TIME.

In order to ensure the success of the Coastal Surveillance Force, NAVFORV created a three-pronged patrol system consisting of outer and inner ship barriers and an air barrier, which comprised the farthest outer barrier. Using Dixie Station (located in the South China Sea, southeast of Cam Ranh Bay) for Task Force 77 strikes against Cambodia, Laos, and South Vietnam, propeller-driven Douglas A-1 Skyraiders operated for a short time in 1965 but soon were replaced by Lockheed P-3 Orions. Other aircraft of Operation MARKET TIME included Lockheed P-2 Neptunes and Martin P-5 Marlins. The P-2s and P-3s operated from several bases, including Cam

Ranh Bay, Tan Son Nhut, U-Tapao in Thailand, and Sangley Point in the Philippines. The P-5s, before their withdrawal in 1967, operated out of Sangley Point and had seaplane tenders at Cam Ranh Bay, Poulo Condore, and the Cham Islands. Air surveillance duties included identifying suspicious vessels, photographing them, and then reporting them to one of five Coastal Surveillance Centers located along the South Vietnamese coastline to disseminate and pass on information to other aircraft and surface ships for further investigation.

The outer ship barrier operated within 40 miles of the South Vietnamese coast, stretching from the 17th Parallel to the Cambodian border in the Gulf of Thailand. Ships included high-endurance Coast Guard cutters, destroyer escorts, radar picket escort ships, ocean and coastal minesweepers, and patrol gunboats. Their mission was the interdiction of seaborne supplies carried by trawler-type vessels. Throughout the history of the operation, MARKET TIME forces neutralized more than 50 infiltrating vessels.

The inner ship barrier operated in the shallow waters along the South Vietnamese coastline, where Communists, using wooden junks to transport men and supplies, could easily intermingle with thousands of innocent junks and sampans. Thus, the South Vietnamese government authorized American MARKET TIME forces to stop, search, and seize any vessel involved in fishing or trade within a 12-mile limit.

U.S. naval leaders realized that the South Vietnamese Junk Force needed to be phased into the Republic of Vietnam Navy (VNN, South Vietnamese Navy) in order to investigate junk traffic sailing close to shore. In July 1965 the Junk Force integrated into the VNN. Yet U.S. Navy leaders believed that without American supervision, the Junk Force would be ineffective. To augment the junks, the U.S. Navy adopted the fast patrol craft, or Swift Boats, originally used by oil companies in the Gulf of Mexico to transport crews to and from offshore rigs.

Additional duties of MARKET TIME forces included fire support for ground troops. And in 1968, elements of Task Force 115 became MARKET TIME Raiders, which operated with the newly created Southeast Asia Lake Ocean River Delta Strategy (SEALORDS) forces to conduct river raiding operations. As the American withdrawal began, under Vietnamization MARKET TIME forces slowly shifted matériel to the VNN, while U.S. sailors transferred to other duties.

Postwar Vietnamese histories attest to the effectiveness of the U.S. Navy's Operation MARKET TIME. During the two-year period from the end of 1962 to the end of 1964, North Vietnamese vessels disguised as fishing boats delivered more than 4,000 tons of weapons and ammunition to Communist forces in South Vietnam, while during the next seven years, from early 1965 to early 1972, less than 500 tons of supplies successfully made it through MARKET TIME's maritime gauntlet.

R. Blake Dunnavent

References

Cutler, Thomas J. *Brown Water, Black Berets: Coastal and Riverine Warfare in Vietnam.* Annapolis, MD: Naval Institute Press, 1988.

Marolda, Edward J. *By Sea, Air, and Land: An Illustrated History of the U.S. Navy and the War in Southeast Asia.* Washington, DC: Naval Historical Center, Department of the Navy, 1994.

Schreadley, R. L. *From the Rivers to the Sea: The United States Navy in Vietnam.* Annapolis, MD: Naval Institute Press, 1992.

Vietnamese People's Navy Political Department. *35 Nam Duong Ho Chi Minh Tren Bien va Thanh Lap Lu Doan 125 Hai Quan* [The 35th Anniversary of the Ho Chi Minh Trail at Sea and of the Formation of the 125th Naval Brigade]. Hanoi: People's Army Publishing House, 1996.

Wunderlin, Clarence E., Jr. "Paradox of Power: Infiltration, Coastal Surveillance, and the United States Navy in Vietnam, 1965–1968." *Journal of Military History* 53 (July 1989): 275–290.

McCarthy, Eugene Joseph (1916–2005)

U.S. senator, Democratic candidate for president in 1968, and leading critic of American involvement in Vietnam. Convinced that many Americans shared his frustration over Vietnam, McCarthy attempted to merge the antiwar movement with politics, and his early success helped bring down President Lyndon B. Johnson's presidency. Born in Watkins, Minnesota, on March 29, 1916, Eugene McCarthy graduated from St. John's University (Minnesota) in 1935 and earned a master's degree from the University of Minnesota in 1939. He worked as a high school teacher and college professor at St. John's University and the College of St. Thomas (Minnesota) and was a civilian technical assistant in the War Department's Military Intelligence Division for a time during World War II. In 1948 he was elected to the U.S. House of Representatives as a Democrat. He was elected to the U.S. Senate in 1958.

A member of the Senate Foreign Relations Committee, McCarthy voted for the 1964 Gulf of Tonkin Resolution, but he considered it a vote for a holding action rather than a vote for an open-ended war. In McCarthy's view, the Vietnam War escalated in 1966 into a war of conquest. His opposition began to be evident in that year. He believed that the Johnson administration was moving from a policy of nation building in the Republic of Vietnam (RVN, South Vietnam) to an effort to save all of Southeast Asia from communism. McCarthy was also disturbed by the U.S. bombing of the Democratic Republic of Vietnam (DRV, North Vietnam).

On November 30, 1967, McCarthy announced his bid for the 1968 presidential nomination as a candidate committed to bringing about a negotiated settlement of the war. He believed that the American people should be given the "opportunity to make an intellectual and moral determination on the war in Vietnam." Large numbers of idealistic antiwar students flocked to his campaign, as they had to his earlier speaking engagements on major college campuses. McCarthy's surprisingly strong showing in the March 12, 1968, New Hampshire Democratic primary (although later shown to be primarily an anti-Johnson vote rather than a vote for McCarthy's program per se) prompted Senator Robert F. Kennedy (D-NY) to join the presidential race. By month's end, President Johnson announced that he would not seek reelection. At the same time, Johnson announced a partial bombing halt and authorized presidential emissary W. Averell Harriman to open negotiations with North Vietnam.

Kennedy's campaign soon eclipsed that of McCarthy, although McCarthy remained in the race. Kennedy's assassination in June 1968 again changed the dynamics of the presidential race. At the violence-marred August 1968 Democratic National Convention in Chicago, Vice President Hubert Humphrey received the nomination, ending McCarthy's idealistic antiwar political crusade.

In 1969 McCarthy resigned from the Foreign Relations Committee, and he left the Senate on completion of his second term in 1970. After his retirement from the Senate, his involvement in politics consisted primarily of writing and making speeches. He also worked in the publishing industry and authored a syndicated newspaper column for a number of years. In 1976 and again in 1988 he made unsuccessful bids for the presidency as an independent candidate. McCarthy died on December 10, 2005, in Washington, D.C.

James E. Southerland

References

Eisele, Albert. *Almost to the Presidency: A Biography of Two American Politicians.* Blue Earth, MN: Piper, 1972.

Herzog, Arthur. *McCarthy for President.* New York: Viking, 1969.

McCarthy, Eugene. *The Year of the People.* New York: Doubleday, 1969.

White, Theodore H. *The Making of the President, 1968.* New York: Atheneum, 1969.

McNamara, Robert Strange (1916–2009)

Businessman, auto executive, secretary of defense (1961–1968), and president of the World Bank (1968–1982). Born on June 9, 1916, in San Francisco, Robert Strange McNamara studied economics at the University of California at Berkeley. He next earned a master's degree in business administration at Harvard University and then soon joined

As secretary of defense during 1961–1968, Robert S. McNamara was one of the chief architects of U.S. policy in Vietnam under presidents John F. Kennedy and Lyndon B. Johnson. He began to have doubts about the war only late in his tenure but did not voice them publicly, much to the anger of many. McNamara spent his retirement writing about the lessons to be learned from the conflict. (Yoichi R. Okamoto/Lyndon B. Johnson Presidential Library)

the faculty. During World War II, he was a U.S. Army Air Force statistical control officer. Following the war he went to work for the Ford Motor Company, where he rose to president in 1960 at the age of 44. A few weeks later, President John F. Kennedy appointed him secretary of defense.

McNamara came to the job determined to take control of the Pentagon bureaucracy. Among his early initiatives were the installation of a programming-planning-budgeting system, the introduction of systems analysis into the department's decision-making process, and the revitalization of conventional forces, neglected under the prior administration's defense policy based on massive retaliation. The Kennedy administration's new approach became known as flexible response. McNamara also evinced a continuing concern for the control of nuclear weapons, a subject that continued high on his personal agenda even after he had left his Pentagon post. McNamara embraced the fiasco that became the Bay of Pigs Invasion in April 1961, but in October 1962 during the Cuban Missile Crisis, he favored the moderate position of a naval quarantine around Cuba, advice that President Kennedy followed.

Within a year of heading the Pentagon, McNamara had also gone on record as supporting the recommendations of General Maxwell Taylor and Walt Rostow that the United States should commit itself to preventing the fall of the Republic of Vietnam (RVN, South Vietnam) to communism, although he later wrote that within days he realized that "the complexity of the situation and the uncertainties of our ability to deal with it by military means became apparent" and that supporting further American involvement "had been a bad idea."

During successive levels of increasing U.S. commitment, including the deployment of increasingly more ground combat forces to Vietnam, McNamara supported meeting the field commander's requirements, at the same time insisting on a "graduated response" to "aggression" by the Democratic Republic of Vietnam (DRV, North Vietnam), particularly with regard to the air war against North Vietnam. By the end of 1965, however, McNamara had begun to doubt the possibility of achieving a military solution in Vietnam, a view he expressed to President Lyndon B.

Johnson. Nevertheless, a month later McNamara recommended adding 200,000 men to forces in Vietnam and expanding air operations. At the same time, he suggested that the odds were even that the result would be "a military standoff at a much higher level."

In the autumn of that same year, McNamara advised Johnson that he saw no palatable way to end the war quickly, and by May 1967 McNamara had advised the president in writing that the United States should alter its objectives in Vietnam and the means to achieve them. McNamara refused to support General William Westmoreland's most recent request for 200,000 more troops and argued instead that his approach "could lead to a major national disaster." But then in July 1967, back from a trip to Vietnam, McNamara told the president that there was not a stalemate in the war, and indeed, according to Tom Johnson's notes of the meeting, "he felt that if we follow the same program we will win the war and end the fighting." Faced with this pervasive inconsistency on the part of his war minister, Johnson soon decided to replace him. Later McNamara would recall the "loose assumptions, unasked questions, and thin analyses underlying our military strategy in Vietnam" and admit that he "misunderstood the nature of the conflict."

In their book *The Economics of Defense in the Nuclear Age*, Charles J. Hitch, who had been McNamara's comptroller in the Defense Department, and Roland N. McKean observed that "there are excellent reasons for making most decisions at lower levels. Officials on the spot have far better technical information; they can act more quickly; giving them authority will utilize and develop the reservoir of ingenuity and initiative in the whole organization." McNamara meanwhile brought an unprecedented degree of centralization to the management of the Defense Department, even though, as Hitch

and McKean also observed, "if large numbers of detailed decisions are attempted at a high level ... the higher levels will become swamped in detail, decisions will be delayed, the organization will become muscle-bound, and the higher levels will have neither time nor energy for their essential functions of policymaking."

The accuracy of this analysis became clear when McNamara, in his book *In Retrospect*, offered the observation that he was just too busy to deal with the Vietnam War, that "an orderly, rational approach was precluded by the 'crowding out' which resulted from the fact that Vietnam was but one of a multitude of problems we confronted."

Under McNamara, there were huge gaps between the rhetoric and the reality. As late as 1971, for example, more than three years after McNamara had left the Pentagon, Alain C. Enthoven and K. Wayne Smith argued in *How Much Is Enough?* that one of the strengths of McNamara's regime was that he "insisted on integrating and balancing the nation's foreign policy, military strategy, force requirements, and defense budget." Instead, he had so ineptly managed the requirements of the war in Vietnam and competing commitments elsewhere that the U.S. Army in Europe was virtually destroyed to make up for Vietnam War shortfalls, while reserve forces were similarly ravaged. By the time McNamara was through, wrote General Bruce Palmer, Jr. in *The 25-Year War*, "the proud, combat-ready Seventh Army ceased to be a field army and became a large training and replacement depot for Vietnam." The result was that it "became singularly unready, incapable of fulfilling its NATO mission."

McNamara left office at the end of February 1968, in the midst of the debate over Vietnam policy precipitated by the Tet Offensive, to become president of the

World Bank, a post he held until 1982. His 1995 book *In Retrospect: The Tragedy and Lessons of Vietnam* reignited Vietnam War passions but did little to rebuild his reputation. McNamara died in Washington, D.C., on July 6, 2009.

Lewis Sorley

References

Enthoven, Alain C., and K. Wayne Smith. *How Much Is Enough? Shaping the Defense Program, 1961–69*. New York: Harper and Row, 1971.

Hitch, Charles J. *Decision Making for Defense*. Berkeley: University of California Press, 1965.

Hitch, Charles J., and Roland M. McKean. *The Economics of Defense in the Nuclear Age*. Santa Monica, CA: RAND Corporation, 1960.

McNamara, Robert S., with Brian VanDeMark. *In Retrospect: The Tragedy and Lessons of Vietnam*. New York: Vintage Books, 1995.

Palmer, General Bruce. *The 25-Year War: America's Military Role in Vietnam*. Lexington: University Press of Kentucky, 1984.

Palmer, Gregory. *The McNamara Strategy and the Vietnam War: Program Budgeting in the Pentagon, 1960–1968*. Westport, CT: Greenwood, 1978.

Shapley, Deborah. *Promise and Power: The Life and Times of Robert McNamara*. Boston: Little, Brown, 1993.

MENU, Operation (March 18, 1969–May 26, 1970)

Code name for the secret U.S. bombing of Cambodia. Operation MENU had three objectives. Tactically, its first objective was the destruction of supplies and the disruption of People's Army of Vietnam (PAVN, North Vietnamese Army) and Viet Cong (VC) base camps in the border area between Cambodia and the Republic of Vietnam (RVN, South Vietnam). The U.S. intelligence community believed, correctly as postwar Communist sources have revealed, that the Central Office for South Vietnam (COSVN), thought to be a massive Communist headquarters, was also located in that region. Its destruction was the second objective. At the strategic level, U.S. president Richard M. Nixon's plan for disengagement would have been imperiled had the Communists launched another attack on the scale of the 1968 Tet Offensive before Vietnamization and the withdrawal of American troops were complete, or nearly so. Thus, the third objective was to prevent such an attack.

Bombing in the border region was nothing new, even in 1969. The boundary between South Vietnam and Cambodia was ambiguous and ill defined. But since Cambodia had declared its neutrality, bombing targets inside that country was inappropriate if not illegal. From 1965 on, whenever bombs were dropped on base areas or supply caches in extreme western South Vietnam, the mission reports always indicated that the bombs fell on Vietnam's side of the border.

Between October 1967 and March 1969, the buildup of PAVN forces and supplies in the border region increased as Hanoi stepped up the infiltration of troops down the Ho Chi Minh Trail. Supplies were brought by ship into the harbor at Sihanoukville and hauled over Friendship Highway, a road built with U.S. foreign aid funds, to the sanctuaries along the border.

The first Boeing B-52 Stratofortress missions into Cambodia were flown on March 18, 1969. The target was Base Area 353, a network of supply caches and staging points just west of the border. The Pentagon assigned the code name BREAKFAST to this mission. Additional missions to other base areas were code-named SUPPER, LUNCH, DESSERT, and SNACK. The series was dubbed Operation MENU.

Only a handful of people knew the truth about the bombing. The president, White House chief of staff Brigadier General Alexander Haig, National Security Advisor Henry A. Kissinger, key members of Congress, and a select few military and civilian defense officials were among those who knew that the targets were actually in Cambodia. As for the aircrews actually flying the B-52s, only the pilots and navigators, not the rest of the crew members, were informed that their targets were actually in Cambodia. Secretary of the U.S. Air Force Dr. Robert Seamans and U.S. Air Force chief of staff General John D. Ryan were not advised.

U.S. Air Force colonel Ray B. Sitton, who had a background in the Strategic Air Command (SAC), worked out a system that used ARC LIGHT (B-52) strikes in South Vietnam as a cover for the secret bombing. Radar bomb navigators in the B-52s controlled the heading input for the plane in the final moments before the bombs were dropped. The rest of the flight crew would be unaware of the change in heading. Because the actual targets in Cambodia were, at most, only a few miles from the targets originally briefed to the aircrews, the crew members would not know the difference. After the routine mission briefings, radar navigators were told that when they neared their drop points, new sets of coordinates would be secretly forwarded to them by U.S. Air Force radar operators inside South Vietnam. The bombs would be dropped on the new coordinates rather than the designated targets. Post-strike reports would indicate that the original targets had been struck. A top-secret back-channel communications network that was used to pass sensitive intelligence information would then transmit the actual target information to the handful of civilian and military officials cleared for MENU bombing intelligence.

The secrecy began unraveling just before the bombing came to an end. On May 2, 1970, the *New York Times* ran a brief article on the bombing. By that time, 3,630 B-52 sorties had dropped close to 100,000 tons of bombs inside Cambodia.

The need for secrecy passed after General Lon Nol deposed Prince Norodom Sihanouk on March 18, 1970. Two days later, a Cambodian commander asked South Vietnamese spotter planes and artillery to help repulse a VC attack on his outpost. Army of the Republic of Vietnam (ARVN, South Vietnamese Army) operations inside Cambodia began in earnest a week later. On April 29, U.S. aircraft supported 6,000 ARVN troops when they launched an attack into the Parrot's Beak area of Cambodia.

Covert MENU bombing continued until May 26, 1970. After that, until a congressionally mandated end to all U.S. air strikes took effect on August 15, 1973, bombing in Cambodia, although still classified, was no longer covert. Even after May, missions into the base areas struck during the secret bombing were still referred to as "MENU Bombing" by SAC, but the veil of deception was lifted. The covert passing of coordinates to radar bomb navigators stopped, as did the double reporting.

The extent of the secret bombing of Cambodia was revealed by retired U.S. Air Force major Hal Knight Jr., a former Combat Skyspot radar site operator, in a January 1973 letter to Senator William Proxmire. As a result of this letter, in July and August 1973 the Senate Armed Services Committee held hearings on the MENU bombing. By exposing the extent of the secrecy, the hearings further damaged the credibility of the Nixon administration, already under increasing pressure from unfolding revelations that became the Watergate Scandal.

Between March 1969 and August 1973, some 500,000 tons of bombs fell on

Cambodia. The MENU bombing accounted for about 100,000 tons of bombs. The extent to which the bombing disrupted Communist military operations can only be speculated. Undoubtedly supply caches were hit and some base camps were destroyed, but COSVN's operations were never seriously disrupted. On the other hand, Vietnamization continued, and the withdrawal of American ground forces was nearly complete before North Vietnam launched its Easter Offensive on March 31, 1972.

Earl H. Tilford, Jr.

References

Berger, Carl, ed. *The United States Air Force in Southeast Asia, 1961–1973: An Illustrated Account.* Washington, DC: Office of Air Force History, 1977.

Littauer, Raphael, and Norman Thomas Uphoff. *The Air War in Indochina.* Rev. ed. Boston: Beacon, 1971.

Nalty, Bernard C. *Air War over South Vietnam, 1968–1975.* Washington DC: Air Force History and Museums Program, 2000.

Shawcross, William. *Sideshow: Kissinger, Nixon and the Destruction of Cambodia.* New York: Simon and Schuster, 1979.

My Lai Massacre (March 16, 1968)

Most notorious U.S. military atrocity of the Vietnam War. On March 16, 1968, between 347 and 504 Vietnamese civilians were massacred by U.S. soldiers of Company C, 1st Battalion, 20th Infantry, 11th Infantry Brigade (Light) of the 23rd Infantry (American) Division. Equally infamous was the cover-up of the incident perpetrated by the brigade and division staffs.

My Lai 4 was a cluster of hamlets, part of Son My village of Son Tinh District in the coastal lowlands of Quang Ngai Province,

I Corps Tactical Zone, in the Republic of Vietnam (RVN, South Vietnam). The broad range in numbers of civilian deaths was the result of varying reports on the massacre, including the testimony of participants and observers. The high figure of 504 is that of the government of the Socialist Republic of Vietnam. In some instances, reports included the related massacre in the nearby hamlet of My Khe 4 by Company B, 4th Battalion, 3rd Infantry. Because of false reporting and the subsequent cover-up, actual casualty figures are difficult to substantiate.

While the American Division's primary operation was the yearlong WHEELER/WALLOWA (November 1967–November 1968), numerous side operations were also conducted. The operation in the hamlets of Son My village, nicknamed "Pinkville" by the division's soldiers because of the concentration of Communist sympathizers and Viet Cong (VC) activity in the area, was one of those side operations. It was to be a classic search-and-destroy sweep intended to snare some of the estimated 250 VC operating in the area as part of the VC 48th Local Force Battalion. Prior to the operation, sweeps such as this were characterized by only lightly scattered direct VC contact but a high rate of friendly losses to snipers, mines, and booby-trap incidents. The My Lai operation was no different.

Charlie Company, 1st Battalion, 20th Infantry, was organized as part of an ad hoc battalion known as Task Force Barker (named for its commander, Lieutenant Colonel Frank A. Barker Jr.), reinforcing the 11th Infantry Brigade. The American Division was itself initially an ad hoc organization of separate infantry brigades put together during the U.S. military buildup and, by many accounts, suffered from poor training and weak leadership. Major General Samuel H. Koster commanded the division. Some elements of the 11th Infantry Brigade,

Former residents of My Lai hamlet who were killed by U.S. soldiers. During the most notorious publicly acknowledged military atrocity of the Vietnam War, between 200 and 500 Vietnamese civilians were massacred by U.S. soldiers at My Lai hamlet on March 16, 1968. A cover-up kept the massacre a secret for a year, after which 14 soldiers were charged with the crime. Only one, Lt. William L. Calley, was found guilty and sentenced to prison, and he served little more than a year. (Ronald S. Haeberle/Time & Life Pictures/Getty Images)

commanded at the time by Colonel Oran K. Henderson, have been described as little more than "organized bands of thugs" and had been ordained the "Butcher Brigade" by its soldiers in the field.

The airmobile assault into My Lai was timed to arrive shortly after the local women had departed for market. The soldiers had been briefed to expect an engagement with elements of the VC 48th Local Force Battalion, one of the most successful units in the area. Instead they found only women, children, and mostly old men still cooking breakfast. The soldiers of Charlie Company, commanded by Captain Ernest Medina, ran wild, particularly the men of the 1st Platoon, commanded by 1st Lieutenant William Laws Calley Jr. They indiscriminately shot people as they ran from their huts and then systematically rounded up survivors, allegedly led them to a nearby ditch, and executed them. More villagers were killed as huts and bunkers were destroyed by fire and explosives as the unit continued its sweep of the hamlet. The killing was brought to a halt some time later when Warrant Officer Hugh Thompson, an aero-scout pilot supporting the operation, landed his helicopter between the Americans and some fleeing Vietnamese and confronted the soldiers.

The massacre was brought to light a year later, thanks to the efforts of former soldier Ronald Ridenhour, who had served in the 11th Infantry Brigade in Vietnam and had learned of the events by talking to members of Charlie Company, who had participated in it. On his return to the United States, in March 1969 (a full year after the event) Ridenhour sent letters detailing it to President Richard M. Nixon, officials in the Defense Department and the State Department, and members of Congress. Most of those who received the letter chose to ignore it, with the exception of Congressman Morris Udall (D-AZ). Independent investigative journalist Seymour Hersh interviewed Calley and broke the story on November 12, 1969. Within a week *Time, Life*, and *Newsweek* magazines all covered the story. The Cleveland *Plain Dealer* newspaper also published photographs of the villagers killed at My Lai.

The U.S. Army Criminal Investigation Division and an army board of inquiry, headed by Lieutenant General William Peers, then investigated the incident. Although the findings and recommendations of the board of inquiry did not attempt to ascribe causes for the massacre, many others have cited the frustrations of soldiers too long faced with unanswerable losses of comrades to snipers, mines, and booby traps; the lack of experience of junior leaders and poor leadership from the division commander on down the ranks; and the confusion of the war's measurement of success by the statistical yardstick of body count, which became objectives in place of the occupation of the enemy's terrain.

The Peers Inquiry report produced a list of 30 persons, mostly officers (including Koster), who knew of the atrocities; however, only 14 were charged with crimes. All eventually had their charges dismissed or were acquitted by courts-martial except for the most junior officer, Lieutenant Calley, whose platoon allegedly killed some 200 innocents. Calley was found guilty of murdering 22 civilians and sentenced to life imprisonment. The sentence was reduced to 20 years by the Court of Military Appeals and then later reduced to 10 years by the secretary of the U.S. Army. Proclaimed by much of the public as a "scapegoat," Calley was paroled by President Nixon in November 1974 after he had served about a third of his 10-year sentence.

On March 6, 1998, the army belatedly recognized Thompson, his former gunner Lawrence Colburn, and his crew chief Glenn Andreatta (who was killed in April 1968) with the Soldier's Medal for Gallantry.

Arthur T. Frame

References

Angers, Trent. *The Forgotten Hero of My Lai: The Hugh Thompson Story.* Lafayette, LA: Acadian House Publishing, 1999.

Belknap, Michael R. *The Vietnam War on Trial: The My Lai Massacre and the Court-Martial of Lieutenant Calley.* Lawrence: University Press of Kansas, 2002.

Bilton, Michael, and Kevin Sim. *Four Hours in My Lai.* New York: Penguin, 1992.

Goldstein, Joseph, Burke Marshall, and Jack Schwartz. *The My Lai Massacre and Its Cover-Up: Beyond the Reach of the Law?* New York: Free Press, 1976.

Hersh, Seymour M. *Cover-Up: The Army's Secret Investigation of the Massacre at My Lai 4.* New York: Random House, 1972.

Hersh, Seymour M. *My Lai 4: A Report on the Massacre and Its Aftermath.* New York: Random House, 1970.

Peers, William R. *The My Lai Inquiry.* New York: Norton, 1979.

N

Ngo Dinh Diem (1901–1963)

President of the Republic of Vietnam (RVN, South Vietnam) from October 1955 to November 1963. Ngo Dinh Diem was born in Quang Binh Province on January 3, 1901. His father, Ngo Dinh Kha, an official in the imperial court at Hue, rose to the rank of counselor to Emperor Thanh Thai. Seventeenth-century Portuguese missionaries converted the Ngo Dinh clan to Catholicism. When the French deposed the emperor in 1907, Ngo Dinh Kha protested by refusing to sign the French-supported court resolution against Thanh Thai and returned to his village of Phu Cam to teach and farm.

Ngo Dinh Diem was one of nine children and the third of six sons. He attended his father's private school and French Catholic schools in Hue. As a teenager he considered becoming a priest like his older brother Ngo Dinh Thuc, who later became archbishop of Hue. Instead, Diem entered the School of Law and Public Administration in Hanoi, graduating four years later at the top of his class. His first assignment was to the bureaucracy in Annam. At age 25 he became a provincial governor.

Diem was very popular, personally riding on horseback throughout the province to carry out land reforms and ensure justice for even the poorest peasants. In 1929 he uncovered a Communist-led uprising and crushed it. This event deeply affected Diem, who now became an ardent anti-Communist.

In 1932 the 18-year-old Bao Dai returned from France to take the throne as emperor. Early in 1933 upon French advice, he appointed Diem as interior minister and chief of the newly formed Commission for Administrative Reforms. Diem soon discovered that the positions were powerless. After only three months he resigned, and French authorities stripped him of his decorations and rank and threatened to arrest him.

For the next 10 years Diem lived in seclusion in Hue with his mother and younger brother, Ngo Dinh Can. Diem met regularly with nationalist comrades even though the French closely watched him. French authorities even dismissed his older brother, Ngo Dinh Khoi, as governor of Quang Nam Province. In early 1942, not long after the Japanese took over in Vietnam, Diem tried to persuade them to grant independence. Instead, the Japanese operated through the Vichy French colonial bureaucracy.

In September 1945, with the Japanese surrender and fearing that Bao Dai's puppet government might side with the powerful Viet Minh forces of Ho Chi Minh and Vo Nguyen Giap, Diem set out for Hanoi to convince the emperor otherwise. On the way Diem was kidnapped by Viet Minh agents and taken to a remote village near the Chinese border, where he contracted malaria. When he recovered, he discovered that the Viet Minh had shot and killed his brother Ngo Dinh Khoi.

After six months Diem was taken to Hanoi, where he met Ho Chi Minh, who asked him to join the Communists. Diem

When the Geneva Accords temporarily divided Vietnam in two in 1954, Ngo Dinh Diem, a fiercely anti-Communist Catholic in a traditionally Buddhist nation, became prime minister of South Vietnam. Although Lyndon Johnson had private reservations about Diem, he publicly called Diem the "Winston Churchill of Southeast Asia." Diem was president of the Republic of Vietnam (RVN) from June 1954 until his assassination in November 1963. (Hulton Archive/Getty Images)

where he spent two years at Maryknoll seminaries in New Jersey and New York as a novice, performing menial jobs and meditating. While in the United States, he met prominent individuals such as Francis Cardinal Spellman, U.S. Supreme Court justice William O. Douglas, and Senator John F. Kennedy. Diem effectively argued his case, declaring that he opposed both the French and Communists and represented the only real nationalist course. As a result of his devout Catholicism, he and Spellman became close friends, and the cardinal soon became Diem's greatest American promoter.

In May 1953, frustrated by the Dwight D. Eisenhower administration's support of the French, Diem went to a Benedictine monastery in Belgium. From there he regularly traveled to Paris, where he met with the large community of Vietnamese exiles, including his youngest brother, Ngo Dinh Luyen, a prominent engineer. Through Luyen, Diem finally began to gain supporters and real political power.

In 1954 delegates at the Geneva Conference settled the first Indochina War, restoring Indochina as three nations: Cambodia, Laos, and Vietnam. Vietnam was temporarily divided at the 17th Parallel, with national elections set for 1956. At this time Bao Dai was in Cannes, France, fearful that his future as emperor was in jeopardy. Diem needed Bao Dai to legitimate his rise to power, and Bao Dai needed the support of Diem's powerful allies, including his brother Ngo Dinh Nhu, who had set up the influential Front for National Salvation in Saigon as an alternative to Ho Chi Minh. Because of Diem's time in the United States and meetings with American leaders, Bao Dai believed that the U.S. government backed Diem.

On June 18, 1954, Bao Dai summoned Diem to his chateau in Cannes and appointed him prime minister. With growing American

refused even though he expected that this would cost him his life. Instead, Ho released him. Communist leaders later realized that this had been a mistake and sentenced Diem to death in absentia. Over the next four years Diem traveled in Vietnam trying to gain political support. An attempt on his life in 1950 convinced him to leave the country.

In 1950 Diem went to the Vatican and had an audience with Pope Pius XII. The next year Diem traveled to the United States, support, Diem returned to Saigon on June 26 and then on July 7 officially formed his new government, technically for all of Vietnam.

Fearing that the Communists would overrun this fledgling Asian "domino," President Eisenhower and Secretary of State John Foster Dulles began sending aid to the new regime. Unfortunately, Diem's power base was largely limited to minority Catholics, rich and powerful Vietnamese, and foreigners. But his earlier trip to the United States meant that Diem was the only non-Communist Vietnamese whom U.S. officials knew. Washington dispatched Colonel Edward Lansdale, the successful architect of the Philippine anti-Communist counterinsurgency, to counsel Diem.

After the 1954 Geneva Accords, the United States pressured France to withdraw all its remaining forces from Vietnam, the last leaving on April 28, 1956. In early 1955 Diem moved to consolidate his power. Employing five loyal army battalions, Diem moved against his opponents, culminating the action on May 6, 1955, when his forces defeated those of the Binh Xuyen in Saigon. Diem also moved against the political cadres of the Viet Minh, allowed in South Vietnam by the Geneva Convention. In 1955 he ignored an effort by Bao Dai (then in France) to remove him from office; instead, Diem called an October election for the people to choose between them. Clearly Diem would have won any honest election, but he ignored appeals of U.S. officials for such and managed the results so that the announced vote in his favor was 98.2 percent. On October 26, 1955, using the referendum as justification, Diem proclaimed the new government of South Vietnam with himself as president. Washington, prompted by Lansdale, officially recognized him in this position and withdrew its support for Bao Dai.

During Eisenhower's last six years as U.S. president, material aid from Washington to South Vietnam totaled $1.8 billion. In an effort to bolster Diem's image, Eisenhower arranged state visits to South Vietnam by Dulles in 1955 and Vice President Richard Nixon in 1956. In 1957 Diem traveled to the United States and spoke to a joint session of Congress.

By 1960 the situation in South Vietnam had deteriorated. The Viet Minh had resumed guerrilla activities, and in spite of massive U.S. aid to fight communism, Diem used 8 of every 10 aid dollars for internal security. Worse, he estranged himself from the peasants. Little was done to carry out land reform, and by 1961, 75 percent of the land in South Vietnam was owned by 15 percent of the population. Diem also isolated himself in Saigon, choosing to rely only on his family members for advice and making loyalty to him rather than ability the test for appointments to political office or military command.

When John F. Kennedy became president in 1961, he reexamined U.S. policy in Vietnam and demanded that Diem institute domestic reforms. But seeing no alternative to Diem, Kennedy also sent 400 Special Operations military advisers to Vietnam to bolster America's sagging ally. He also dispatched Vice President Lyndon Johnson to Vietnam on a fact-finding mission. Although Johnson had private reservations, he publicly called Diem the "Winston Churchill of Southeast Asia." Less than a week after Johnson returned, Kennedy agreed to increase the size of the Army of the Republic of Vietnam (ARVN, South Vietnamese Army) from 170,000 to 270,000 men. ARVN forces as a rule did not perform well, and by October 1963 U.S. forces in Vietnam had increased to 16,732 men.

Concurrently, despite constant pleading by Lansdale, Diem's oppression of the Buddhist majority and his political opponents grew. To U.S. officials, it seemed that internal opposition to Diem rivaled opposition to the Communists. Diem threw hundreds of political adversaries, real or imagined, into hellish prison camps. Hundreds were tortured and assassinated. His family and friends (mostly Catholics) held all the senior government positions. Most influential were his brother Nhu and his wife, Madame Nhu. Diem himself was celibate. His oldest brother, Archbishop Thuc, controlled Catholic property in South Vietnam that included 370,000 acres of nontaxable farmland exempt from redistribution.

Nhu was particularly embarrassing. He set up the Personalist Labor Party, which used totalitarian techniques such as self-criticism sessions, storm troops, and mass rallies. He was also the leading advocate of the Agroville and Strategic Hamlet programs that forcibly resettled whole villages into armed compounds to "protect" them from the Viet Cong (VC). The rampant corruption in the program soon alienated the majority of peasants from the regime.

Madame Nhu used her position as state host to enrich herself and influence her brother-in-law to violent acts against the Buddhist majority. She also undertook morality campaigns, persuading Diem to outlaw divorce, dancing, beauty contests, gambling, fortune-telling, boxing, kung fu, cockfighting, prostitution, contraception, and adultery. The harsh punishments that accompanied these excessive rules eventually antagonized large sections of the South Vietnamese population.

In the summer of 1963 Buddhist protests and rallies became more frequent and intense. On June 11 the elderly Buddhist monk Thich Quang Duc publicly burned himself alive. By November, six more monks had followed suit. Madame Nhu exacerbated the crisis by calling these self-immolations "barbecues."

In late August 1963 Henry Cabot Lodge replaced Frederick Nolting as U.S. ambassador. On August 24 Lodge reported to Washington that an influential faction of South Vietnamese generals wanted to overthrow Diem. With the president and most senior officials out of Washington, Acting Secretary of State George Ball, Acting Secretary of Defense Roswell Gilpatrick, and General Maxwell Taylor formulated a reply. After a phone consultation with Kennedy and Secretary of State Dean Rusk, they cabled Lodge and informed him that while they wanted to afford Diem a reasonable time to remove the Nhus, the United States was "prepared to accept the obvious implications that we can no longer support Diem . . . [and] to tell the appropriate military commanders we will give them direct support in any interim period of breakdown of the central government mechanism."

Lodge immediately met with senior U.S. officials in Vietnam and then cabled Washington that Diem would never replace Nhu and that to ask him to do so would only alert Nhu and lead to a bloodbath, because Nhu had loyal troops in Saigon. Lodge recommended going straight to the generals, bypassing Diem, and leaving it up to them if they wanted to keep Diem. Ball and Roger Hilsman agreed. Kennedy later affirmed their instructions. On August 25 Lodge immediately called another meeting. He decided to distance the United States from the proposed coup and expressed support for the generals through lower-ranking Central Intelligence Agency (CIA) officers, specifically Lieutenant Colonel Lucien Conein, the former World War II Office of Strategic Services (OSS) agent who had a long-standing friendship with many of the conspiring generals.

By September 1963 most U.S. administration officials began to have second thoughts, especially General Taylor. At his urging, Kennedy called a meeting of the National Security Council. It was hopelessly divided, with the State Department favoring the coup and Taylor, Secretary of Defense Robert McNamara, and especially Johnson vehemently opposed. Kennedy, although coy about the matter, never acted to prevent the coup or to restrain Lodge.

On October 2 Kennedy suspended economic subsidies for South Vietnamese commercial imports, froze loans for Saigon waterworks and electrical power plant projects, and cut off financial support of Nhu's Vietnamese Special Forces units. Just over an hour after midnight on November 1, 1963 (All Soul's Day for Catholics), the generals, led by major generals Duong Van "Big" Minh, military governor of Saigon Ton That Dinh, and Tran Van Don, began their coup.

Upon learning of the coup, Diem phoned Lodge to ask "what is the attitude of the U.S.?" Lodge feigned ignorance and replied, "I do not feel well enough informed to be able to tell you." He assured Diem that he would do anything possible to guarantee Diem's personal safety. Diem and Nhu fled the presidential palace through a tunnel and took refuge in Cho Lon, the Chinese section of Saigon. At about 6:00 a.m. the next morning, the two men agreed to surrender.

The generals leading the coup guaranteed them safe passage out of the country. While negotiations for their flight dragged on, they were discovered by troops commanded by a longtime foe. The brothers were ordered into the rear of an armored personnel carrier and shot to death. Nhu's body was repeatedly stabbed. Madame Nhu was in Los Angeles, California, at the time.

Washington never did find a viable alternative to Ngo Dinh Diem. Certainly no subsequent leader of South Vietnam had his air of legitimacy. As a result, U.S. leaders, who had seen Diem as an alternative to Ho Chi Minh and an agent to stop the spread of communism, soon found themselves taking direct control of the war in Vietnam.

William P. Head

References

Catton, Philip E. *Diem's Final Failure: Prelude to America's War in Vietnam.* Lawrence: University Press of Kansas, 2002.

Jacobs, Seth. *Cold War Mandarin: Ngo Dinh Diem and the Origins of America's War in Vietnam, 1950–1963.* Lanham, MD: Rowman and Littlefield, 2006.

Karnow, Stanley. *Vietnam: A History.* 2nd rev. and updated ed. New York: Penguin, 1997.

Moyar, Mark. *Triumph Forsaken: The Vietnam War, 1954–1965.* New York: Cambridge University Press, 2006.

U.S. Senate Committee on Foreign Relations. *U.S. Involvement in the Overthrow of Diem, 1963.* Washington, DC: U.S. Government Printing Office, 1972.

Warner, Denis. *The Last Confucian.* London: Angus and Robertson, 1964.

Nguyen Van Thieu (1923–2001)

Army of the Republic of Vietnam (ARVN, South Vietnamese Army) general and president of the Republic of Vietnam (RVN, South Vietnam) from 1967 to 1975. Born near Phan Rang on April 5, 1923, Nguyen Van Thieu joined the Viet Minh in 1945 but became disillusioned with their ruthless disregard for life. He then fought for the State of Vietnam side aligned with the French, entering the National Military Academy and graduating from there in 1949. He also attended infantry school in France and the

Nguyen Van Thieu takes the oath as the elected president of the Republic of Vietnam in Saigon on October 30, 1967. At right is Premier Nguyen Cao Ky, who stepped down to become the vice president. (AP/Wide World Photos)

staff college in Hanoi (1952). As a battalion commander in 1954, he drove the Viet Minh out of his native village. In 1955 he commanded the Military Academy in Da Lat in South Vietnam.

In 1957 Colonel Thieu graduated from the Command and General Staff College at Ft. Leavenworth, Kansas. In 1962 he joined the secret Can Lao Party organized by Ngo Dinh Diem's brother Ngo Dinh Nhu. After commanding the ARVN's 1st Infantry Division for two years, Thieu assumed command of the 5th Infantry Division in 1963, leading one of his regiments against the presidential bodyguard in the coup that brought down Diem in November 1963. Promoted to major general, Thieu commanded IV Corps.

While serving on the Armed Forces Council in 1964, Thieu cooperated with the coup by Air Vice Marshal Nguyen Cao Ky, who led a faction of the generals referred to as the Young Turks against General Nguyen Khanh. Thieu served as deputy premier in the short-lived government of Dr. Phan Huy Quat until June 12, 1965, when Thieu became chief of state in Prime Minister Ky's new government. Together Ky and Thieu in 1966 made plans to strengthen the armed forces, met with President Lyndon B. Johnson in Honolulu and Manila, successfully quashed a coup attempt by General Nguyen Chanh Thi, gained Buddhist support, and promised a constitution.

Despite their temporary cooperation, the two leaders became bitter political rivals.

Although Thieu had declined the premier's post in 1965, his determination to challenge Ky for the highest office in the 1967 elections led the Armed Forces Council to force Ky and Thieu onto a joint ticket, giving the presidential nomination to Thieu and the vice presidential nomination to Ky purely on the basis of military seniority. The Thieu-Ky ticket won the election with 34.8 percent of the vote against 10 other tickets.

During the 1968 Tet Offensive, Thieu had gone to his wife's home in the Mekong Delta town of My Tho. Thus, it was Ky who handled the counterattack in the capital. As a result the Americans pressed Thieu to give more responsibility to Ky, which led to renewed bickering between them. Thieu took advantage of the Tet Offensive to push through a general mobilization, which doubled the size of the armed forces. Fighting charges of widespread official corruption, Thieu launched an anticorruption campaign that led to the replacement of four province chiefs, two corps commanders, and others, but the prospect of negotiations with the Democratic Republic of Vietnam (DRV, North Vietnam) in Paris made him more reluctant to broaden the base of his government. His initial refusal to attend the Paris peace talks when they began was an attempt to ensure direct negotiations between North Vietnam and South Vietnam and also an effort to help Republican Party nominee Richard Nixon in his race for the presidency against Democratic Party contender Hubert Humphrey, who had threatened Thieu with an aid cutoff if he did not implement significant reform.

President Thieu distributed land to some 50,000 families and by 1968 had secured legislation that froze rents and forbade landlords from evicting tenants. He also began the restoration of elected village chiefs so that, by 1969, 95 percent of villages under South Vietnamese control had elected chiefs and councils. Village chiefs were given a role in national defense and control over Popular Forces and police; they also received some government financial support.

In 1969, after the United States initiated the Vietnamization program to turn over combat responsibilities to the ARVN and gradually withdraw U.S. troops, Thieu was faced with the challenge of replacing the departing American units. In 1970 he mobilized large numbers of high school and college students for the war effort, but this resulted in considerable opposition, which in turn led to government arrests and trials.

On March 26, 1971, Thieu presented land to 20,000 people in an impressive ceremony following the passage of the Land-to-Tiller Act, which reduced tenancy to only 7 percent. With the U.S. Congress considering measures to end American involvement in Vietnam, in 1971 Thieu engineered an election law to disqualify his major opponents, Ky and General Duong Van Minh. Although the Vietnamese Supreme Court said that Ky, who had charged Thieu's government with corruption, could run, he chose not to do so. Thieu's election made one-person rule a reality and did serious damage to his government's image.

During February–March 1971, Operation LAM SON 719, an ARVN attempt at a preemptive strike into Laos to disrupt the People's Army of Vietnam (PAVN, North Vietnamese Army) buildup for a major invasion of South Vietnam, Thieu disappointed General Creighton Abrams, commander of the U.S. Military Assistance Command, Vietnam (MACV), by withdrawing his forces prematurely. The ARVN did not perform well and paid a heavy price in casualties in this operation, especially among junior officers. However, PAVN units suffered heavy losses to U.S. airpower in this operation and also in the subsequent 1972 spring conventional invasion of South Vietnam, which Thieu's forces defeated with the assistance of U.S. airpower.

As a result of the Paris peace talks, U.S. national security advisor Henry A. Kissinger brought a draft agreement to Saigon in October 1971. President Thieu refused to sign, insisting on 26 changes and accusing the United States of betraying the South Vietnamese government. His chief objection was that the agreement did not require North Vietnamese troops to withdraw from South Vietnam.

Kissinger was furious with Thieu for torpedoing the agreement and urged President Nixon to proceed alone, but following the LINEBACKER II bombing campaign against North Vietnam in December 1972, Kissinger secured a new agreement with North Vietnam: the Paris Peace Accords of January 23, 1973. There was little substantive difference between the new agreement and the previous October draft agreement, and the new agreement allowed approximately 145,000 PAVN troops to remain in South Vietnam. Thieu, whose government was the beneficiary of a massive last-minute airlift of U.S. military supplies (Operation ENHANCE PLUS), was threatened with a total cutoff of U.S. aid if he refused to sign, and he finally acquiesced to heavy U.S. pressure to sign the agreement.

General Tran Van Tra, a key PAVN commander in South Vietnam, wrote in *Concluding the Thirty Year War* that it was ironic that after the cease-fire there was "not a day on which the guns fell silent" on South Vietnamese battlefields, and yet he conceded that "the puppet administration" had become "stronger politically, militarily and economically." He also pointed out that PAVN and National Front for the Liberation of South Vietnam (National Liberation Front [NLF]) units were in disarray from their 1972 Easter Offensive as well as from fighting in Laos and Cambodia. This permitted Thieu's forces to recapture some areas, to abolish hamlet and village elections in an effort to keep them in government hands, and to bar neutralist protest activities against the government. The latter was a violation of Article 11 of the Paris Peace Accords, but the Communists were violating Article 20 with regard to the neutrality of Laos and Cambodia and during the first year of the agreement sent more than 100,000 troops down from North Vietnam to build up their base areas from Quang Tri Province southward to the Mekong Delta.

To no one's surprise, the Third Indochina War was under way as soon as the dry season came in January 1974. While Thieu's forces drove the PAVN back in some areas, even pursuing them into Svay Rieng, the Parrot's Beak region of Cambodia, the ARVN steadily lost ground in other areas, particularly the Central Highlands. This proved to be the last ARVN offensive. By the summer, the ARVN was losing 500 men a week to the rejuvenated PAVN and NLF forces and also had been forced to impose rigid supply controls because of severe shortages.

Thieu was shocked when the Watergate Scandal forced President Nixon to resign in August 1974. This called into question the promises that the United States would respond militarily if the South Vietnamese government was threatened. Nixon had convinced Congress to authorize $1 billion in military aid to South Vietnam for the 1974–1975 fiscal year, but Congress appropriated only $700 million. After deductions for administrative costs, shipping, and other expenses, less than $500 million remained to purchase weapons, equipment, and fuel. Ammunition was now rationed, 224 aircraft and 21 riverine units were placed in storage, and only 55 percent of available transport could be fueled.

Saigon was in turmoil, and the People's Anti-Corruption Movement led by a Catholic priest developed into a massive antigovernment crusade. The problem was real, but Thieu tried to sidestep it and place all blame on the Communists.

When PAVN forces unleashed their offensive in the Central Highlands and the Gerald R. Ford administration did not respond in accordance with the terms of the Paris Peace Accords, Thieu made the fateful surprise decision to abandon the northern half of the country. To make matters worse, the government made no public announcement and had no plan for its effective execution. Government supporters in Military Regions I and II believed that they had been abandoned, first by the Americans and then by their own government and army. Although the ARVN put up a good fight at Xuan Loc, it lost the battle, and four PAVN corps converged on the capital of Saigon.

On April 21, 1975, President Thieu resigned in a tearful address to the nation. He took no responsibility for the debacle and blamed the United States. Five days later he left Vietnam, flying to Taiwan and then on to Great Britain. He later settled in the United States in Foxboro, Massachusetts, a suburb of Boston. He died there on September 29, 2001.

Claude R. Sasso

References

Berman, Larry. *No Peace, No Honor: Nixon, Kissinger, and Betrayal in Vietnam*. New York: Free Press, 2001.

Bui Diem, with David Chanoff. *In the Jaws of History*. Boston: Houghton Mifflin, 1987.

Bunker, Ellsworth. *The Bunker Papers: Reports to the President from Vietnam, 1967–1973*. 3 vols. Edited by Douglas

Pike. Berkeley, CA: Institute for East Asian Studies, 1990.

Westmoreland, William C. *A Soldier Reports*. New York: Doubleday, 1976.

Nixon, Richard Milhous (1913–1994)

U.S. congressman (1947–1950), U.S. senator (1950–1952), vice president (1953–1961), and 37th president of the United States (1969–1974). Born in Yorba Linda, California, on January 9, 1913, Richard Milhous Nixon attended Whittier College

Richard M. Nixon became president in 1969 and directed the protracted withdrawal of U.S. troops from Vietnam and the shift of responsibility for the war to the South Vietnamese forces. He was forced to resign from office in August 1974 as a result of the Watergate Scandal. (National Archives)

and Duke University Law School. He served in the Pacific during World War II as a U.S. Navy lieutenant (junior grade) and in 1946 won the first of two terms in the House of Representatives.

A Republican, in Congress Nixon concentrated zealously on the issue of anticommunism and won election to the Senate in 1950 in a race that was tinged with heavy-handed anti-Communist smear tactics. In 1952 Dwight Eisenhower chose Nixon as his vice presidential running mate. The successful campaign was marred only by Nixon's need to publicly defend himself against charges of profiting from a secret fund of monies raised by his California friends. Nixon took office in January 1953.

In October 1953 Nixon visited French Indochina as part of his first overseas trip as vice president. He visited Saigon, Hanoi, Vientiane, and Phnom Penh, coming away convinced that the French troubles in the region stemmed from France's failure to win the hearts and minds of the Indochinese peoples. Nixon was privately concerned that the Eisenhower administration was not doing enough to prevent the spread of communism in Southeast Asia. Nixon was one of the earliest supporters of a Southeast Asia Treaty Organization (SEATO), with the United States at its head.

When in April 1954 the French found themselves trapped at Dien Bien Phu, Nixon argued strongly that the United States should intervene militarily. At a National Security Council meeting, he spoke in favor of a proposal put forth by Admiral Arthur Radford, then chairman of the Joint Chiefs of Staff (JCS), to bomb and destroy Viet Minh positions with three small tactical atomic bombs. Code-named Operation VULTURE, the plan was rejected by Eisenhower. Continuing to argue the point, Nixon suggested that the United States send more technicians and supplies to Vietnam, and he told an audience of newspaper reporters that the executive branch "has to take the politically unpopular position" of stopping the Communists and said that "I personally would support such a decision." Despite Nixon's vigor, Eisenhower refused to intervene. The situation only cemented in Nixon's mind the need to halt what he viewed to be Communist aggression in the region, a belief made even more secure in June 1956 when he met with President Ngo Dinh Diem of the Republic of Vietnam (RVN, South Vietnam) and came away with the feeling that despite Diem's excesses, the South Vietnamese leader was capable of establishing order in his nation.

After his devastating loss to John F. Kennedy in the 1960 presidential election and a subsequent failure in California's 1962 gubernatorial race, Nixon appeared to be finished politically. But in 1968 he emerged as the unlikely Republican candidate for president. The war in Vietnam held the potential for being the major issue in the 1968 presidential campaign. Nixon had nothing to gain from meeting the issue head-on, and he refused to do so.

Concentrating his efforts on denouncing President Lyndon B. Johnson's record on law and order, Nixon was reported to have a secret plan to end the war, a plan that he later admitted to an interviewer never existed. The tactic worked; even Johnson's decision to stop the bombing of the Democratic Republic of Vietnam (DRV, North Vietnam) less than a week before the election could not turn the tide against Nixon.

The entirety of the Nixon presidency must be seen through the prism of Vietnam; this is unquestionably how he saw it. On many occasions Nixon wrote or stated that ending the Vietnam War was his "first priority"; détente with the People's Republic of

China (PRC) and the Soviet Union would follow. Yet he did not seriously entertain an escalation of the conventional war in 1969. Indeed, faced with mounting domestic opposition to the war, Nixon accelerated the policy of turning over more of the war to the South Vietnamese (the policy of Vietnamization) that had begun at the end of the Johnson administration. To protect withdrawals of American troops and buy time for Vietnamization, Nixon authorized a widening of the war into Cambodia and Laos. He hoped thereby to force the North Vietnamese to entertain serious negotiations.

Nixon's plan was immediately put to the test in February 1969 when Hanoi launched its spring offensive. General Creighton Abrams asked Nixon, as he had asked Johnson many times before, to bomb North Vietnamese supply lines in Cambodia. Unlike Johnson, Nixon supported the plan from the start. Nixon viewed Southeast Asia as he had visited it as vice president not as four separate countries but as one theater of war. He had come to believe that the key to winning the war was in the destruction of the North Vietnamese supply lines that ran through Laos and Cambodia, the Ho Chi Minh and Sihanouk trails.

Nixon gave the approval for Operation MENU, a plan for bombing suspected Communist sanctuaries in Cambodia. To skirt what would be certain worldwide condemnation for bombing a technically neutral nation, Nixon ordered that the bombings be kept secret. The MENU bombings succeeded only in driving the North Vietnamese deeper into Cambodia and fomenting wider antiwar protests at home. The bombings also began the chain of abuses of power known collectively as the Watergate Scandal that involved Secretary of State Henry Kissinger ordering the tapping of the phones of several White House aides in an effort to find out who leaked the story about the bombing to the *New York Times*.

Nixon combined the secret bombings with attempts to show the world that American commitment to the war was winding down. In June he ordered an immediate withdrawal of 25,000 troops from Vietnam. The next month he let it be known that once the American withdrawal was complete, he did not expect to recommit troops to the region any time soon. This was part of what became known as the Nixon Doctrine: unless directly attacked, the United States should not commit its troops to the defense of a Third World country.

Hoping that these moves would show his good faith, Nixon secretly gave the North Vietnamese a November 1 deadline to show some significant steps toward peace. However, Nixon's moves did not satisfy the antiwar movement at home. The large-scale demonstrations known as the Moratorium to End the War in Vietnam, which took place on October 15 and November 15, 1969, were a huge success. As a result, Nixon was forced to let his deadline go by unchallenged.

In an effort to regain the initiative, on November 2 Nixon spoke directly to his supporters in the middle class—those whom he dubbed the "great, silent majority of my fellow Americans"—and begged them to help him control dissent in the nation, asking that they recognize that "North Vietnam cannot defeat or humiliate the United States. Only Americans can do that." By the end of the year, Nixon had promised a further withdrawal of 50,000 troops by April 15, 1970.

However, Nixon's response to events threatened to widen the scope of the war just as his withdrawals were becoming significant. He argued that it was the advent of the North Vietnamese attack on Cambodia, begun in the wake of the overthrow of the Norodom Sihanouk government on March 11, 1970, that convinced him that he must take further military action there. Other observers note the failure of the MENU bombings as the cause. Either way, the March 26 decision to send American troops into Cambodia to search out and destroy Communist sanctuaries along the border was consistent with Nixon's desire to support his withdrawals by cutting off North Vietnam's western route of supplies.

This decision was the most fateful of Nixon's presidency. Nixon had tried to soften the blow by announcing on April 20 the withdrawal of 150,000 more American troops before the end of 1971. However, his April 30 announcement of what had become known as the Cambodian Incursion led to a firestorm of protest on college campuses, culminating in the deaths of student protesters and others not involved in the demonstrations at Kent State University and Jackson State University. The Cambodian Incursion proved little except that the Army of the Republic of Vietnam (ARVN, South Vietnamese Army) was not yet ready to fight on its own.

In an attempt to rectify that situation as well as take one more step toward cutting the supply lines to the west, in January 1971 Nixon sanctioned an offensive into Laos (Operation LAM SON 719) using only ARVN troops on the ground. The initiative began on February 8, but within six weeks ARVN troops were forced to withdraw, leaving the Ho Chi Minh Trail virtually intact. The Laotian fiasco only stiffened Nixon's resolve and may have contributed to the harshness of his response to the June 13, 1971, release of the Pentagon Papers in the *New York Times*. Yet despite the criticism that followed in the press, Nixon would not be rushed. Convinced that his February 1972 rapprochement with China would frighten their North Vietnamese clients back to the peace table, Nixon continued to withdraw troops and wait.

For the fourth straight year, however, Hanoi did not bow to Nixon's tactics. The North Vietnamese government spurned Nixon's request for further talks and on Good Friday, March 30, 1972, launched what was to that point the largest offensive of the war. Furious, Nixon ordered the resumption of the bombing of North Vietnam. On April 1 he authorized bombing within 25 miles north of the demilitarized zone (DMZ), and two weeks later he expanded the bombing zone up to the 20th Parallel. The bombing campaign against North Vietnam continued to expand and was officially dubbed Operation LINEBACKER the following month. On May 8 Nixon ordered the mining of Haiphong Harbor, telling the American people that the only way to stop the war was to "keep the weapons of war out of the hands of the international outlaws of North Vietnam." Nixon had become certain that only a massive show of force would convince North Vietnam to negotiate. Kissinger and Le Duc Tho resumed their peace talks within a month of the start of the renewed bombing of North Vietnam; by late autumn the talks were in earnest.

It was soon clear that the only party who would not agree to a truce was South Vietnamese president Nguyen Van Thieu. In an effort to gain his support, Nixon sent secret correspondence to Thieu promising that if the North Vietnamese broke the truce, the United States would recommit troops to South Vietnam. But when North Vietnam balked at changes in a document already agreed to, Nixon had finally had enough. At Camp David he told JCS chairman Admiral Thomas Moorer that "I don't want any more of this crap about the fact that we couldn't hit this target or that one. This is your chance to use military power effectively to win the war, and if you don't, I'll consider you responsible."

On December 17 Nixon ordered renewed saturation bombing of North Vietnam. Operation LINEBACKER II, also known as the Christmas Bombings, dropped some 36,000 tons of bombs in an 11-day period, concentrating on the Hanoi-Haiphong area. On December 26 Hanoi sent signals about wanting to resume negotiations. On January 9, 1973, in Paris, Secretary of State William Rogers initialed the peace agreement.

Nixon understood that the peace agreement was a particularly weak one, writing later that the only way he had been able to get North Vietnam to buy into the deal was to allow them to keep a military presence in South Vietnam. As a result, Nixon never believed that the truce meant that the United States was to stop sending monies and supplies to South Vietnam, which he continued to do until the June 30, 1973, Cooper-Church Amendment precluded him from doing so. Nevertheless, Nixon's memoranda make it clear that he fully expected to uphold his secret pledge to Thieu and to push Congress to recommit troops when North Vietnam violated the peace. However, the November 7, 1973, passage of the War Powers Act would have precluded Nixon from doing this.

Meanwhile, Nixon's foreign policies were quite successful vis-à-vis the Chinese and Soviets. He had managed to open relations with China, which had been on ice for nearly a quarter of a century. He also engaged the Kremlin in détente, which included improved relations with the Soviet Union, increased educational and cultural exchanges and, most critically, arms limitation agreements (the Strategic Arms Limitation Treaty, or SALT I, and the Anti-Ballistic Missile Treaty). On the home front, Nixon battled escalating inflation, stagnating growth, and rising unemployment, all made significantly worse during 1973–1974 when Arab nations instituted an oil embargo against the United States and other Western nations for their support of Israel in the October 1973 Yom Kippur (Ramadan) War. Meanwhile, the fallout from the Watergate Scandal began to engulf the White House and Nixon himself, who had been complicit in the cover-up of the affair. After a debilitating fight with Congress and the courts, which sought unfettered access to Nixon's tapes that would prove his undoing, Nixon resigned on August 9, 1974. He is the only U.S. president to have resigned his office.

Nixon later said that he believed that his policies had won what could have been a lasting peace had Congress not weakened his hand or that of his successor, Gerald R. Ford, in terms of enforcing that settlement. In a 1985 defense of his Vietnam policies titled *No More Vietnams*, Nixon argued that "when we signed the Paris peace agreements in 1973, we had won the war. We then proceeded to lose the peace. . . . In the end, Vietnam was lost on the political front in the United States, not on the battlefront in Southeast Asia." Nixon was also convinced that his numerous escalations of the war, far from being a useless waste of life, shortened that conflict. He would later tell a British audience that his only regret about expanding the war into Cambodia was not having done it sooner.

Most contemporary observers believe that Nixon relegated domestic policies to a secondary role, concentrating instead on the war and his other foreign policy initiatives. This is only partially true. For example, Nixon and his staff developed innovative proposals for welfare reform and for new financial relationships between state and local governments. However, these initiatives were defeated by a Congress that had become increasingly alienated from his administration largely because of Nixon's heavy-handed conduct of the war.

It was in foreign affairs that Nixon made his greatest mark, again largely because of the war in Vietnam. The success of his overtures to China and the Soviet Union was based largely upon his success in playing each of these nations against the other as well as against North Vietnam. Nixon called this "linkage diplomacy." As a condition of doing business, Nixon required that both China and the Soviet Union lessen their overt commitment to North Vietnam. Although both states continued to publicly support Ho Chi Minh, the amount of military and financial aid they gave to North Vietnam decreased dramatically after 1972.

Following his resignation, there were many reports that Nixon would reenter the political arena, but he preferred to play the role of elder statesman, writing eight books between 1978 and 1994. His *No More Vietnams* (1985) was a thoughtful defense of his administration's policies as well as an acerbic critique of Congress's refusal to fund the requests of the Ford administration for further aid to South Vietnam in 1975.

Nixon's successors in the White House kept him informed on major foreign policy initiatives. Ronald Reagan and George Bush even solicited his advice on a number of issues. Nixon died in New York City on April 22, 1994, following a stroke.

John Robert Greene

References

Ambrose, Stephen E. *Nixon*. 3 vols. New York: Simon and Schuster, 1987, 1989, 1991.

Greene, John Robert. *The Limits of Power: The Nixon and Ford Administrations*. Bloomington: Indiana University Press, 1992.

Litwak, Robert S. *Détente and the Nixon Doctrine: American Foreign Policy and the Pursuit of Stability, 1969–1976*. Cambridge: Cambridge University Press, 1984.

Nixon, Richard. *No More Vietnams*. New York: Avon Books, 1985.

Willbanks, James H. *Abandoning Vietnam: How America Left and South Vietnam Lost Its War*. Lawrence: University Press of Kansas, 2004.

P

Paris Peace Accords (January 17, 1973)

The "Agreement on Ending the War and Restoring Peace in Vietnam," signed in Paris on January 27, 1973, ended direct U.S. military involvement in the conflict but failed to end the war itself. The signing ceremony revealed the hostility that still existed between the warring sides. The foreign ministers of the two South Vietnamese opponents, the Republic of Vietnam (RVN, South Vietnam) and the Provisional Revolutionary Government (PRG, Communists), would not even put their signatures on the same copy of the document but instead signed on separate pages, while representatives of the United States and the Democratic Republic of Vietnam (DRV, North Vietnam) signed yet a third copy.

The agreement opened by declaring that "the United States and all other countries respect the independence, sovereignty, unity and territorial integrity of Vietnam as recognized by the 1954 Geneva Agreements on Vietnam." This was meaningful because it reflected the position that the Communist side had argued for years: that Vietnam was one country, not two, and thus their revolution was not "foreign aggression," as Saigon and the United States had maintained but instead was a legitimate struggle to regain national independence and unity.

The agreement's other provisions called for the following:

- A cease-fire, to take effect on January 27 at midnight, Greenwich mean time (8:00 a.m. the next day, Saigon time). Following the cease-fire, Vietnamese forces would remain in place; resupply of weapons, munitions, and war matériel would be permitted but only to replace items destroyed or used up during the truce.
- Withdrawal of all U.S. and other foreign troops within 60 days, with the release of all U.S. prisoners of war (POWs) "carried out simultaneously" with the troop withdrawal. The signers also promised to assist in accounting for missing personnel and to help find, identify, and repatriate the remains of those who had died.
- Negotiations between South Vietnamese parties for a settlement that would "end hatred and enmity" and allow the South Vietnamese people to freely decide their political future. A National Council of National Reconciliation and Concord, with members representing both South Vietnamese sides and a neutral "third force," would oversee the negotiations and organize elections for a new government. Following a settlement in South Vietnam, reunification of the two Vietnams was to be "carried out step by step through peaceful means."

Other clauses covered such matters as establishing an international observer force and respect for the neutrality of Laos and Cambodia.

The withdrawal of U.S. forces was completed as promised. Some 23,000 American

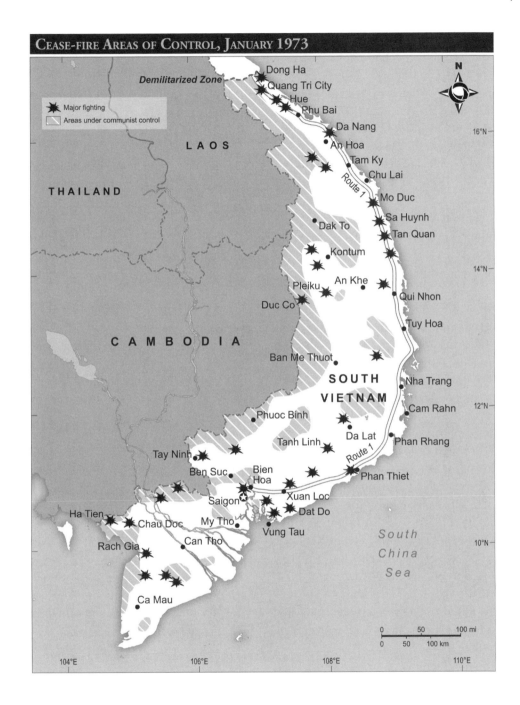

CEASE-FIRE AREAS OF CONTROL, JANUARY 1973

troops, the last of a force that had once numbered more than 500,000 men, left during the 60 days following the truce. On the final day the U.S. command issued its last general order: "Headquarters Military Assistance Command Vietnam is inactivated this date and its mission and functions reassigned." At 6:00 p.m. the last troops boarded a U.S. Air Force transport and flew out of the country. Only the truce observers, a detachment of U.S. Marine Corps embassy guards, a small team of missing in action

(MIA) negotiators, and 50 military person-nel assigned to the Defense Attaché Office now remained in South Vietnam.

The North Vietnamese government mean-while released 591 American POWs. Although the POW issue remained contentious for many years afterward, the Hanoi leadership never wavered from its insistence that it had turned over all the POWs in its hands at the time of the agreement.

Aside from ending U.S. military involve-ment, the agreement achieved none of its other objectives. No political settlement was reached, the national reconciliation council was never created, and no election was held. Nor did the fighting stop or even slow down. Only the United States, among the four sig-natories, observed the cease-fire. For the Vietnamese, the war continued as before.

The failure of the truce was ordained even before it was supposed to take effect. The agreement called for a "cease-fire in place" but made no provision for establishing, even in rough terms, where the forces of each side belonged. Consequently, there was an irresistible temptation for both sides to try to seize as much territory as possible in the final hours. The Communist side, which was not tied down, as was Saigon's army, by the need to keep large forces deployed to protect major towns and com-munications routes, struck more aggres-sively. In the 36 hours before the cease-fire was to begin, Communist forces penetrated more than 400 towns and villages and cut every major highway in the country.

Although not technically violating the agreement, the attacks drastically altered the true battle lines that the truce was intended to preserve. Had South Vietnamese troops actually frozen in place at the cease-fire hour, South Vietnam's enemy would have been left occupying hundreds of posi-tions that were normally under Saigon's control. There was no possibility that President Nguyen Van Thieu and his gener-als would accept that situation, and they did not. Thieu ordered his forces to keep fighting, even if offensive operations contin-ued after the cease-fire hour.

In about two weeks South Vietnamese troops recaptured most of the territory seized in fighting before the cease-fire. Had they paused at that point with more or less normal battle lines reestablished, the cease-fire might have taken hold. Instead, they remained on the offensive.

As fighting continued, both sides took the position that military operations, including attacks anywhere in the enemy's zone, were justified by the other side's prior violations of the cease-fire. Because there had never been any agreement on where either side's forces belonged in the first place (in fact, neither ever conceded that its enemy had a right to any territory at all), there was no way to restore the lines that were supposed to have been frozen by the truce. Instead, there was only an endless chain of retalia-tions in which over time even the idea of peace gradually disappeared. Casualties told the story: 51,000 South Vietnamese sol-diers were killed in 1973 and 1974, the high-est two-year toll of the entire war. Two years after it was signed, the agreement was all but forgotten "like a dictionary," said one member of the international observer force, "for a language that nobody speaks."

Arnold R. Isaacs

References

Dillard, Walter Scott. *Sixty Days to Peace: Implementing the Paris Peace Accords, Vietnam 1973*. Washington, DC: National Defense University, 1982.

Isaacs, Arnold R. *Without Honor: Defeat in Vietnam and Cambodia*. Baltimore: Johns Hopkins University Press, 1983.

Le Gro, William E. *Vietnam from Cease-Fire to Capitulation*. Washington, DC: U.S. Army Center of Military History, 1981.

Porter, D. Gareth. *A Peace Denied: The United States, Vietnam, and the Paris Agreement*. Bloomington: Indiana University Press, 1975.

Pentagon Papers and Trial (1971)

The Pentagon Papers encompassed a formerly top-secret U.S. Defense Department study of the course of American Vietnam policy. The trial resulted from the unauthorized publication of the study in 1971. By 1967, Secretary of Defense Robert McNamara was questioning the course of the Vietnam War, and he created a task force within the Defense Department to investigate the history of U.S. policy in Vietnam. The task force conducted no interviews; its work was based on written materials, mostly files from the Defense Department, the State Department, the Central Intelligence Agency (CIA), and to some extent the White House.

The end product was a history accompanied by the original texts of many of the documents on which it had been based. Formally titled *United States–Vietnam Relations, 1945–1967*, it is commonly referred to as the Pentagon Papers. The narrative and documents totaled well over 7,000 pages arranged in 47 volumes. There were only 15 copies: 7 for distribution within the Department of Defense and 8 elsewhere.

Dr. Daniel Ellsberg, an economist and researcher with the RAND Corporation

Daniel Ellsberg, who helped compile the Defense Department's record of U.S. involvement in Vietnam and was at the center of the Pentagon Papers scandal, testifies before a House panel investigating the leak in July 1971. (AP/Wide World Photos)

(a renowned think tank that had been given 2 of the 15 copies), was one of the study's authors. After the project was completed, he examined the entire manuscript carefully. He had already developed doubts about U.S. Vietnam policy; reading the Pentagon Papers convinced him that the American involvement there had been fundamentally immoral and should be ended immediately.

Ellsberg believed that the evidence that had led to his beliefs about the war should be made available to Congress and the public, and late in 1969 he began photocopying large sections of the Pentagon Papers. After failing to persuade several U.S. senators to make the material public, in March 1971 he delivered it to reporter Neil Sheehan of the *New York Times*.

Sheehan and others at the *New York Times*, working in extreme secrecy, produced a series of articles intended for publication on 10 consecutive days. Each daily installment was made up of a long article plus the original text of some of the most important supporting documents. The articles were not abridged versions of the corresponding sections of the narrative that had been written by persons within the Department of Defense; they were written by reporters of the *New York Times*, using information from both the narrative and the documents in the Defense Department version. The first installment was published on Sunday, June 13, 1971.

On June 14 U.S. attorney general John Mitchell informed the *New York Times* that "publication of this information is directly prohibited by the provisions of the Espionage Law." He asked that the newspaper cease publication immediately and return the documents to the Department of Defense. The *New York Times* refused.

On June 15 the Justice Department sought an injunction forbidding the publication of further installments. Judge Murray I. Gurfein of the Southern District of New York issued a restraining order preventing publication for four days to allow time for the case to be argued. This was the first occasion that a U.S. court had restrained a newspaper in advance from publishing a specific article.

Ellsberg immediately gave a substantial portion of the Pentagon Papers to the *Washington Post*, which began publishing articles based on this material on June 18. The Justice Department filed suit against the *Washington Post* the same day.

The Justice Department had obtained the initial restraining order without first proving to Judge Gurfein's satisfaction that such restraint was either necessary or legal. All of the courts that became involved in the case agreed that such an order could not remain in effect for the length of time usually required for the U.S. court system to decide a matter of such importance. The district courts in New York and Washington, D.C., took only a few days to hand down decisions in favor of the newspapers, citing principles of freedom of the press and a lack of evidence that publication of the Pentagon Papers posed a serious danger to the nation.

The government appealed, and both cases reached the U.S. Supreme Court on June 24. Four justices voted to reject the government's appeal without a hearing and to allow the newspapers to proceed with publication forthwith. The majority, however, voted to combine the two cases and hear them on June 26.

The two newspapers had refused, as a matter of principle, to reveal what information they intended to publish or even what portions of the Pentagon Papers that Ellsberg had given them. The four volumes of the original study dealing with efforts made through various intermediaries to negotiate an end to the war, the disclosure of which, the government warned, might impede future negotiations, had never been given to either newspaper because Ellsberg shared the government's view of that risk. Of the material that Ellsberg did furnish, the *New York Times* exercised some restraint in its disclosure, avoiding the publication of information about which the newspaper believed there might be legitimate national security concerns. The *Washington Post* exercised greater restraint, avoiding the publication of texts from any of the source documents in the Pentagon Papers. Had the newspapers been less secretive, court proceedings might have centered on the articles scheduled for publication rather than on the whole text of the Pentagon Papers, and the argument that publication would imperil national security might have been strengthened.

On June 26 the Supreme Court heard arguments. By that time, the Justice Department had shifted the legal basis of its case from the Espionage Act to the inherent powers of the presidency. Solicitor General Erwin Griswold argued that the president's responsibility for the conduct of foreign policy and his role as commander in chief of the armed forces required that he have the ability to forbid the publication of military secrets.

On June 30 the Supreme Court found for the newspapers in a vote of 6 to 3. Justices Hugo Black, William J. Brennan, William O. Douglas, Thurgood Marshall, Potter Stewart, and Raymond White were able to agree on a very short statement, the core of which was that given the constitutional protection of freedom of the press, a request by the government for prior restraint of publication "carries a heavy burden of showing justification," and the government had not met that burden.

Each of the six justices, however, wrote a separate concurring opinion. Black and Douglas each joined in the others' opinions, and Stewart and White did likewise. No common thread unites all six concurring opinions. Important elements found in various aspects of them included assertions that Congress had passed no law, and indeed had repeatedly rejected proposed laws, under which the government could enjoin publication of government secrets by the press; that the government had failed to prove that publication of the Pentagon Papers would cause such dire harm as to justify making an exception to the general principles of the First Amendment; and that the government's claims for the inherent powers of the presidency could not be accepted.

Those who dissented—Chief Justice Warren Burger and Justices Harry Blackmun and John Marshall Harlan—were more nearly in agreement with one another. In the realm of foreign affairs, they were willing to grant the executive branch almost unfettered authority to decide which government secrets the press should be forbidden to publish. They did not claim that the government had proved that publication of the Pentagon Papers would cause such dire harm to the nation as would justify an exception to the First Amendment; they did not believe that the government should have been required to provide such proof. They argued that only the executive branch was qualified to decide whether publication threatened the national security and that the courts should enforce the judgment of the executive branch on the press without asking for any detailed explanation of the basis for that judgment.

The Supreme Court had rejected prior restraint of publication in this case. The key to the outcome had rested with Stewart and White, the two justices who had not been willing to find for the newspapers on June 25 without a hearing but who did find for them on June 30. They suggested that the government protect its secrets through the deterrent effect of criminal prosecution rather than prior restraint of publication. The Justice Department did not attempt criminal action against the newspapers but did indict Ellsberg for conspiracy, theft of government property, and violation of the Espionage Act.

The trial of Ellsberg and an alleged coconspirator, Anthony Russo, began on January 3, 1973, in Los Angeles. Its verdict might have clarified some of the issues that had been left unresolved by the 1971 decision, but on May 11 the judge dismissed the charges, citing a pattern of government misconduct including the fact that White House "plumbers," a team selected to plug information leaks, in search of evidence against Ellsberg had burglarized the office of Ellsberg's psychiatrist. These same so-called plumbers would later be involved in other illegal activities, including the break-in at the Watergate Complex in June 1972 that would set in motion the Watergate Scandal, which would force President Richard Nixon to resign in August 1974. Thus, in a significant sense the Watergate Scandal had as its origins the Vietnam War and the Pentagon Papers.

Before the end of 1971, two sets of selections from the Pentagon Papers that were much more complete than any newspaper could have published appeared in book form, one published by the U.S. Government Printing Office after formal declassification and the other released by Senator Mike Gravel of Alaska and published by Beacon Press. Between them, these publications contained essentially all of the narrative history except for the sections dealing with negotiations to end the war; those sections were published only in 1983. Many of the source documents that had been appendices to the original Pentagon Papers were included in various versions published in 1971, but many others remained unreleased.

Edwin E. Moïse

References

Herring, George C., ed. *The Secret Diplomacy of the Vietnam War: The Negotiating Volumes of the Pentagon Papers*. Austin: University of Texas Press, 1983.

The Pentagon Papers: The Defense Department History of United States Decisionmaking on Vietnam. 5 vols. Boston: Beacon, 1971–1972.

Schrag, Peter. *Test of Loyalty: Daniel Ellsberg and the Rituals of Secret Government*. New York: Simon and Schuster, 1974.

Sheehan, Neil, et al. *The Pentagon Papers: As Published by the New York Times*. New York: Bantam, 1971.

Ungar, Sanford J. *The Papers & the Papers: An Account of the Legal and Political Battle over the Pentagon Papers*. 1972; reprint, New York: Columbia University Press, 1988.

United States Department of Defense. *United States–Vietnam Relations, 1945–1967: Study Prepared by the Department of Defense*. 12 vols. Washington, DC: U.S. Government Printing Office, 1971.

Pham Van Dong (1906–2000)

One of the three most influential leaders of the Democratic Republic of Vietnam (DRV, North Vietnam) and, until the late 1980s, its most public figure. Born in Quang Ngai Province on March 1, 1906, to an educated mandarin family, Pham Van Dong attended the Lycée Nationale in Hue, where his classmates included Vo Nguyen Giap and Ngo Dinh Diem. During Dong's student years, he was actively involved in Vietnamese

Pham Van Dong, Vietnamese diplomat and bureaucrat, served as premier of the Democratic Republic of Vietnam (North Vietnam) after independence from the French in 1954 and headed the government of a reunified Vietnam from 1976 to 1987. A close associate of Ho Chi Minh, he was one of the founders of the Viet Minh in 1941. (Hulton Archive/Getty Images)

techniques and politics. This was soon interrupted by the defeat of the French by Germany, whereupon Ho instructed Dong and Giap and other Vietnamese Communists in China to return to Vietnam and set up an organization to fight for independence.

They soon formed the Viet Minh and organized camps in the mountains along the Vietnamese-Chinese border. From this base the Viet Minh conducted training and propaganda as well as minor ambushes and assassinations. The French and Japanese saw the Viet Minh as only a minor annoyance.

Dong played a leading role in the Viet Minh's fight against the French during the Indochina War (1946–1954). He also headed the Viet Minh delegation to the 1954 Geneva Conference. Dong initially took a hard line by demanding that the Vietnamese be allowed to settle their own differences. When the French rejected this demand, the conference ground to a halt. From this point on, Zhou Enlai, who headed the People's Republic of China (PRC) delegation, Soviet foreign minister Vyacheslav Molotov, and French premier Pierre Mendès-France took over the negotiations. Dong's role declined to that of accepting or denying proposals.

Dong sought during the Geneva Conference to maintain the momentum gained by the Viet Minh on the battlefield, but he was largely unsuccessful. He wanted the demarcation line drawn at the 13th Parallel and also wanted a six-month cease-fire. Dong came away from the conference believing that Zhou had sold out the Viet Minh, as the division was moved to the 17th Parallel and the cease-fire was set at two years. As a result, the Viet Minh ended up with less than they had won on the battlefield.

Dong served as the prime minister of North Vietnam and after Vietnam's unification of the Socialist Republic of Vietnam (SRV) for 36 years, from 1950 to 1986.

nationalist organizations, leading to his belief that the French should be expelled from Vietnam. In 1930 French authorities arrested him for sedition. He then served eight years on the prison island of Poulo Condore, where he kept up his morale by studying languages, literature, and science.

After the French government outlawed the Indochinese Communist Party on September 26, 1939, its Central Committee ordered Dong and Giap to China, there to be trained in guerrilla warfare. In June 1940 in Kuming they met Ho Chi Minh. Ho instructed Dong and Giap to go to Yenan and learn military

Throughout the period of U.S. involvement in Vietnam, he maintained a consistent attitude toward the American presence and negotiations, refusing any discussions until the U.S. bombing of North Vietnam ended. He also required that any settlement include the creation of a neutral coalition government in Saigon with Viet Cong (VC) representatives. Dong's negative attitude toward negotiations with the Americans had everything to do with his experience with the French and the failure of the Geneva Accords.

After the death of Ho on September 2, 1969, Dong became the most public figure in North Vietnam. He skillfully used the American press to encourage antiwar protestors in the United States by issuing statements that the Vietnamese appreciated their support. In other statements he claimed that the Vietnamese believed that the only viable alternative for President Richard Nixon was the honorable exit they were offering to him.

Dong played a key role in the secret peace negotiations in Paris between Henry Kissinger and Le Duc Tho that began in February 1970. Dong's influence was evident in Tho's initial demands for nothing less than a simultaneous armistice and a coalition government, to include the removal of President Nguyen Van Thieu. Negotiations were deadlocked until August 1972, when Dong came to believe that temporary compromise on the matter of Thieu would allow for a settlement. On August 1 Tho no longer demanded that military and political issues be resolved at one time. He also hinted that the North Vietnamese government would no longer require Thieu's withdrawal.

The resolution of final problems in the talks was delayed when Dong, in an October 18 interview with Arnaud de Borchgrave, made reference to the National Council of National Reconciliation and Concord as a "coalition of transition." This again raised the specter of a coalition government and temporarily halted the agreement until things could be worked out. The final agreement was signed on January 27, 1973.

Dong continued in office after the capitulation of the Republic of Vietnam (RVN, South Vietnam) on April 30, 1975. He remained as chairman of the Council of Ministers of the SRV and as a member of the Vietnamese Communist Party (VCP) Politburo until a series of economic setbacks and a VCP struggle for power following the death of VCP secretary-general Le Duan forced Dong's resignation in December 1986. He then became adviser for the Central Committee of the VCP, although without actual power, until 1997. As such, Dong consistently pushed the VCP to rid itself of corruption. Many North Vietnamese regarded Dong as one of their few incorruptible leaders although never, despite his many years as prime minister, a skillful administrator. He died in Hanoi on April 29, 2000.

Michael R. Nichols

References

Bain, Chester A. *Vietnam: The Roots of Conflict*. Englewood Cliffs, NJ: Prentice Hall, 1967.

Davidson, Phillip A. *Vietnam at War: The History, 1946–1975*. Novato, CA: Presidio, 1988.

Duncanson, Dennis J. *Government and Revolution in Vietnam*. New York: Oxford University Press, 1968.

Fishel, Wesley R., ed. *Vietnam: Anatomy of a Conflict*. Itasca, IL: Peacock, 1968.

Karnow, Stanley. *Vietnam: A History*. 2nd rev. and updated ed. New York: Penguin, 1997.

Phoenix Program (1968–1972)

Program to identify and eliminate the Viet Cong infrastructure (VCI) in the Republic of Vietnam (RVN, South Vietnam). The VCI represented the political and administrative arm of the insurgency in South Vietnam and logistically supported Viet Cong (VC) operations, recruited new members, and directed terrorist activities against allied forces.

Initially the South Vietnamese intelligence apparatus and elimination forces proved inadequate at gathering intelligence. In May 1967 Robert Komer, whom President Lyndon Johnson chose to oversee pacification efforts in South Vietnam, arrived in Vietnam to head U.S. Civil Operations and Revolutionary Development Support (CORDS). This organization combined U.S. and Vietnamese civilian and military intelligence and pacification programs and was placed within the Military Assistance Command, Vietnam (MACV), chain of command.

Supervised by CORDS and financially supported by and directed by the Central Intelligence Agency (CIA), a new program, Intelligence Coordination and Exploitation (ICEX), began building district intelligence and operations coordinating centers (DIOCCs) to collect, disseminate, and forward information to field units. Additional centers were also built at the province level.

In early 1968 questions were raised regarding whether the CIA had violated the sovereignty of South Vietnam. To justify the legality of ICEX, William Colby, chief of the CIA's Far East Division, sought and obtained a decree signed by President Nguyen Van Thieu formally establishing Phuong Hoang (Phoenix), a name chosen because of its symbolic meaning, to assume ICEX operations. The ICEX became the deadliest weapon against the VCI. With renewed fervor, American and South Vietnamese personnel began collecting and analyzing data while concurrently arresting and neutralizing targeted individuals.

The DIOCCs circulated to every district and province in South Vietnam blacklists of known VCI operatives so that Phoenix forces could arrest and interrogate these individuals. The blacklists consisted of four rankings from A to D, with "A" being the most wanted. District and province intelligence centers distributed these lists to Phoenix field forces, which would then apprehend or neutralize the individuals. These forces included Vietnamese units such as the National Police, the National Police Field Force, Provincial Reconnaissance Units, and U.S. Navy Sea Air Land teams (SEALs). If not neutralized (killed) by these units, the targeted individual was transported to a provincial interrogation center (PIC). After PIC personnel, consisting of CIA advisers and their Vietnamese counterparts, gathered sufficient intelligence, they sent the information up the chain of command for analysis by DIOCC and CORDS officials.

With the advent of Vietnamization and the withdrawal of American personnel, the Phoenix Program suffered. Also, public pressure generated by news reports led to congressional interest in the program. Reporters described Phoenix as nothing more than an assassination program. This culminated in Phoenix being one of the programs to come under congressional investigation, and in 1971 William Colby, then deputy to the MACV commander for CORDS (and future director of the CIA), appeared before a House Committee to explain it.

Another factor in the program's demise was the 1972 Easter Offensive. This People's Army of Vietnam (PAVN, North Vietnamese Army) invasion of South Vietnam forced the South Vietnamese government to focus its military strength against conventional rather than unconventional forces. Thus, in the spring of 1972 the National Police assumed responsibility for Phoenix, and by December 1972 the United States ended its role in the program.

Despite the media's negative reports, top-ranking CIA officials as well as leaders of the VC and the Democratic Republic of Vietnam (DRV, North Vietnam) agree that the Phoenix Program was a success. According to available sources, from 1968 to 1972, captured VC numbered around 34,000; of these 22,000 rallied to the South Vietnamese government, while those killed numbered some 26,000.

Proof of Phuong Hoang's success could be seen in Quang Tri Province during the 1972 Easter Offensive. For the first time there were front lines, behind which civilians and troops could move freely at night. Most bridges in rear areas did not have to be guarded as they had been in the past. And when Communist forces took northern Quang Tri Province, they were unable to find trustworthy sympathizers at the village level.

R. Blake Dunnavent

References

Andradé, Dale. *Ashes to Ashes: The Phoenix Program and the Vietnam War.* Lanham, MD: Lexington Books, 1990.

Colby, William, with James McCargar. *Lost Victory: A Firsthand Account of America's Sixteen-Year Involvement in Vietnam.* Chicago: Contemporary Books, 1989.

DeForest, Orrin, and David Chanoff. *Slow Burn: The Rise and Bitter Fall of American Intelligence in Vietnam.* New York: Simon and Schuster, 1990.

Herrington, Stuart A. *Silence Was a Weapon: The Vietnam War in the Villages; A Personal Perspective.* Novato, CA: Presidio, 1982.

Moyar, Mark. *Phoenix and the Birds of Prey: The CIA's Secret Campaign to Destroy the Viet Cong.* Annapolis, MD: Naval Institute Press, 1997.

Prisoners of War, Allied

In accordance with the 1973 Paris Peace Accords, a total of 565 American military and 26 civilian prisoners of war (POWs) were released by the Democratic Republic of Vietnam (DRV, North Vietnam) in February and March 1973, and 2 military persons and 2 civilians held in the People's Republic of China (PRC) were freed at the same time. The civilians included contract pilots; Central Intelligence Agency (CIA), State Department, and Voice of America personnel; agricultural specialists; missionaries; and other nonmilitary personnel. Six foreign nationals—2 Canadians, 2 South Koreans, and 2 Filipinos—also departed.

At various points during the Vietnam War, Hanoi had turned over a total of 12 POWs to visiting peace delegations, and early in the war the Viet Cong (VC) released a few prisoners. A small number of Americans escaped from the VC control or from Communist forces in Laos. Although many pilots shot down over hostile territory evaded capture until being rescued, no one actually brought into the prison system successfully escaped from North Vietnam. Only a few civilians captured after the 1973 cease-fire agreement and convicted U.S. Marine Corps defector Robert Garwood came home after the 1973 release.

Estimates of POWs who died in captivity vary. The North Vietnamese listed 55 deaths. One American source cited 54 military and at least 13 American and foreign civilians; another source gives the number as 72 Americans. For POWs so injured and mistreated, the casualty rate was amazingly low in the North Vietnamese camps. The returned POWs cited 8 known deaths of military personnel in the Hanoi system: 2 considered outright murder, 3 from a combination of brutality and neglect, and 3 from appallingly substandard medical care. The largest number of deaths of military personnel and civilians occurred in the jungle camps in the Republic of Vietnam (RVN, South Vietnam).

Justifiably proud of their communication network, command structure, and memory bank, which attempted to register every individual in the system, the POWs recorded at least 766 verified captives at one point or another. But accountability for those outside the North Vietnamese prison system was less certain. Of the hundreds who disappeared in Laos, only 10 came home in 1973, and no one knows the fate of the many captives of local VC units. At the time of release, more than 2,500 men were still listed as missing in action (MIA). Many of those most likely died when shot down, but their deaths were not confirmed. Others known to be alive on the ground and even in the prison system mysteriously disappeared.

All but 71 of the military personnel who returned in early 1973 were officers, primarily U.S. Air Force or U.S. Navy aviators shot down during combat missions. With the exception of a handful of U.S. Air Force personnel, the enlisted men consisted of army and marine personnel captured in South Vietnam. The fliers had received survival and captivity training; for the most part those captured in South Vietnam had not. The first pilot captured by the North Vietnamese was U.S. Navy lieutenant (junior grade) Everett Alvarez, shot down on August 5, 1964, in the first bombing raid on North Vietnam following the Gulf of Tonkin Incident. But the longest-held POW was U.S. Army Special Forces captain Floyd James Thompson, whose light reconnaissance plane was shot down by small-arms fire on March 26, 1964. He spent five years in solitary confinement, three with the VC

in South Vietnam and two more after being moved to North Vietnam. Thompson suffered a broken back in the crash, numerous illnesses, and a heart attack during his almost nine years of captivity, becoming the longest-held American POW in history.

Most of the POWs were aviators shot down during the ROLLING THUNDER bombing campaign of North Vietnam from February 1965 through November 1968; the year 1967 produced the most captives. The Tet Offensive in the first half of 1968 generated the most captives on the ground; almost half the U.S. Army and U.S. Marine Corps POWs were captured in that year. Eighteen of the 26 civilian POWs released in 1973 were captured during a one-week period, the first week of February 1968. With the end of ROLLING THUNDER, the number of captives dropped off dramatically from late 1968 through early 1972, virtually all of them taken in South Vietnam or in Laos. The LINEBACKER I bombings led to an upsurge of captives in the spring of 1972, and during LINEBACKER II 44 aviators were shot down in December 1972 alone. Only one pilot was added in 1973, captured on January 27, the day that the peace accords were signed. The 131 POWs captured in 1972 and 1973 experienced a short and very different captivity from those held in the earlier years.

Among the military POWs, one commentator surveying the 356 aviators held in 1970 recorded that the average flier was approximately 32 years old, a U.S. Air Force captain or U.S. Navy lieutenant, and married with two children. The POWs were for the most part career officers, skilled pilots of high-performance aircraft, highly disciplined, intensely competitive, and college graduates.

American POWs were held in 11 different prisons in North Vietnam, 4 in Hanoi, 6 others within 50 miles of the city (more or less up and down the Red River), and 1 on the Chinese border. The most famous of these was North Vietnam's main penitentiary, Hoa Lo Prison in downtown Hanoi, which the POWs dubbed the "Hanoi Hilton." They gave the other prisons names as well: Briar Patch, Faith, Hope (Son Tay), Skidrow, D-1, Rockpile, Plantation, the Zoo, Alcatraz, and Dogpatch.

From the first captive on, a test of wills existed between the Hanoi camp authority and the American military personnel over the U.S. Code of Conduct, which had been adopted in 1955 in response to the allegedly disgraceful performance of some American POWs during the Korean War. The Vietnam War POWs were determined to maintain a record of honor that would reflect well upon themselves personally, the U.S. military, and the nation. The camp authority employed every means at its disposal, including isolation, torture, and psychological abuse, to break POW discipline. Senior commanders such as U.S. Air Force lieutenant colonel Robinson Risner, U.S. Navy commander James Stockdale, U.S. Navy lieutenant commander Jeremiah Denton, and many others emerged as the leaders in the POW resistance campaign. And tough resisters such as George Day, George Coker, John Dramesi, George McKnight, and Lance Sijan, to name but a few, played significant roles in the effort. Stockdale, Day, and Sijan (the latter posthumously) received the Medal of Honor for their heroism and leadership as POWs. U.S. Army captain Rocque Versace, who was executed in captivity as a prisoner of the VC in South Vietnam, also received the Medal of Honor.

The POW experience broke down roughly into several periods. From 1965 through 1969, POWs were isolated, kept in stocks, bounced from one camp to another, malnourished, and brutally tortured to break their morale, discipline, and commitment to the U.S. Code of Conduct. Following the death of Ho Chi Minh in September 1969, the torture ended, and conditions improved in the camps. After the Son Tay Raid in November 1970, the North Vietnamese closed the outlying camps and consolidated all of the POWs in Hanoi. Compound living began in what the prisoners called Camp Unity. In February 1971 U.S. Air Force colonel John Flynn, the highest-ranking POW, who had spent most of his captivity isolated from the others, assumed command and organized the military community into the 4th Allied POW Wing. A few Thais and South Vietnamese POWs, who had distinguished themselves in working with the Americans, were included in the wing.

From this point on, the greatest attention was given to how the POWs would return home. Amnesty was tendered to those who had cooperated with the enemy if they would now adhere to the Code of Conduct. All but a few accepted the offer. During the final two years, the POWs' story was collected, shaped, and honed.

With the end of the war, the POWs returned home in Operation HOMECOMING to great fanfare as the only heroes of a frustrating war. Much to the dismay of senior POW officers, the Defense Department decided that POWs who had collaborated would not be prosecuted. Only Robert Garwood, when he returned to the United States in 1979, faced court-martial. Although many divorces resulted from their captivity, the Vietnam War POWs adjusted relatively well. Ten years later only about 30 had been treated for psychological or mental problems, although two had committed suicide and three died of other causes. Almost half were still in the military.

The POW story is recorded in the more than 50 individual and collective participant narratives.

Joe P. Dunn

References

Doyle, Robert C. *Voices from Captivity: Interpreting the American POW Narrative.* Lawrence: University Press of Kansas, 1994.

Dunn, Joe P. "The Vietnam War and the POWs/MIAs." In *Teaching the Vietnam War: Resources and Assessments*, 68–93. Los Angeles: Center for the Study of Armament and Disarmament, California State University–Los Angeles, 1990.

Howes, Craig. *Voices of the Vietnam POWs: Witnesses to Their Fight.* New York: Oxford University Press, 1993.

Hubbell, John G., Andrew Jones, and Kenneth Y. Tomlinson. *P.O.W.: A Definitive History of the American Prisoner-of-War Experience in Vietnam, 1964–1973.* New York: Reader's Digest, 1976.

Philpott, Tom. *Glory Denied: The Saga of Jim Thompson, America's Longest-Held Prisoner of War.* New York: Norton, 2001.

Rowan, Stephan A. *They Wouldn't Let Us Die: The Prisoners of War Tell Their Story.* Middle Village, NY: Jonathan David, 1973.

R

RANCH HAND, Operation
(January 12, 1962–January 7, 1971)

Code name for U.S. missions during the Vietnam War involving the aerial spraying of herbicides. RANCH HAND operations evolved from two primary objectives: to deny Communist forces the use of thick jungle cover through defoliation and to deny them access to food crops in the Republic of Vietnam (RVN, South Vietnam). In 1961, in the face of increasing pressure from the Viet Cong (VC), South Vietnamese president Ngo Dinh Diem intensified his requests for U.S. assistance. On November 30, 1961, President John F. Kennedy approved the use of herbicides in Vietnam.

Political and other events leading to that decision signaled its importance. While the agricultural use of herbicides in the United States was climbing, with annual spraying occurring on more than 53 million acres, the use by the military had steadily declined for a decade despite the fact that the small Special Aerial Spray Flight (SASF) was upgrading its aircraft from the Douglas C-47 to the Chase Fairchild C-123 Provider. After an extremely effective defoliation experiment at Camp Drum, New York, in 1959 and following a visit to Vietnam by Vice President Lyndon Johnson in May 1961, a joint U.S.–South Vietnamese counterinsurgency center was established. Its principal task was to evaluate the use of herbicides against guerrilla food sources and the thick jungle foliage that shielded VC activities. Dr. James Brown,

deputy chief of the U.S. Army's Chemical Warfare Center, supervised the tests.

Difficulties abounded. Little was known about the multitude of vegetation found in South Vietnam, and the only airplane available for testing was the old C-47, although some tests included other delivery systems such as the Sikorsky H-34 Choctaw helicopter and a ground-based turbine sprayer. However, the success of these tests led Brown to recommend, through General Maxwell Taylor and Walt W. Rostow, that the SASF from Langley Air Force Base, Virginia, be deployed to Vietnam. Expecting President Kennedy's approval, on November 28, 1961, six C-123s, under Operation FARM GATE and equipped with newly installed MC-1 spray tanks capable of holding 1,000 gallons of herbicide, departed their home station on the first leg of a deployment to South Vietnam.

Following a month's delay in the Philippines, on January 7, 1962, three C-123s arrived at Tan Son Nhut Airport outside Saigon; their crews expected to remain there on temporary duty (TDY) status for less than 90 days. They began operational missions on January 12. Initially their assignment was to clear foliage along a major roadway north of Saigon; later, mangrove forests near the coast and rice-growing areas in the Mekong Delta were added as approved targets.

Although the aircrews were using Agent Purple and Agent Blue (military code names for specific herbicides), the results were somewhat less successful than expected. As a result of further testing in Florida, the number of

U.S. Air Force UC-123 Providers spray the defoliant chemical Agent Orange over dense vegetation in South Vietnam in 1966. (AP/Wide World Photos)

nozzles on each wing boom was decreased from 42 to 35. This was done to increase the droplet size of the herbicide to between 300 and 350 micrometers, which was expected to minimize drift.

Another concern was the extremely dangerous mission profile. To ensure accurate delivery of the herbicide, the aircrews needed to fly very low, about 150 feet above the ground, in a straight and level flight path and at a relatively slow airspeed of about 130 miles per hour. In this environment the aircraft were vulnerable to everything from small-arms fire to antiaircraft artillery, especially after 1963. Although tactics changed somewhat throughout the war, the basic herbicide delivery parameters kept the crews constantly at risk.

In the early years of the war, the small detachment, still composed primarily of TDY aircrews, gradually expanded its operations. Defoliation missions for the three aircraft increased from 60 in 1962 to 107 in 1963 and then to 273 in 1964. Significantly, the difficulty of the aerial tactics increased as

operations were expanded from the relatively flat areas surrounding lines of communication in the south to the rugged topography of the mountain passes in the more northern provinces.

In October 1964 following the Gulf of Tonkin Incident, tactics were further complicated. Previously crop-destruction missions were flown by South Vietnamese helicopter pilots. On October 3 RANCH HAND aircrews, initially with South Vietnamese observers, flew against crop targets in War Zone D north of Saigon. Because crops were planted in tightly defined areas, such as in valleys or small openings in the jungle, delivery tactics in these controlled target areas necessitated the use of more dangerous maneuvering and even dive-bombing approaches to the target box. With this range of tactics and the addition of a fourth aircraft in December 1964, the unit had established its value in the war effort.

As a prologue to future growth, 1965 was an important year. To meet the need for more experienced aircrews, TDY personnel were replaced with aircrews assigned for a full year's rotation. In November three additional aircraft (by then known as the UC-123B) were added to the inventory. Furthermore, while Agent Blue continued to be used against crops, the less costly and more effective Agent Orange was added for jungle-defoliation missions. Finally, 1965 saw a detachment of aircraft deployed to Da Nang Air Base for operations against the Ho Chi Minh Trail.

This pattern of exponential growth continued. In 1966 the unit had 14 authorized aircraft, and in 1968 the number was 25; in 1969, 33 of the improved C-123K model aircraft were authorized. With this growth came, in October 1966, a change in name from the 309th Spray Flight to the 12th Air Commando Squadron. Nearly concurrently, the unit moved to Bien Hoa Air Base to increase the logistical efficiency of the operations.

With the expansion to squadron status, RANCH HAND aircrews assumed a number of collateral duties, including flying airlift missions during the 1968 Tet Offensive and flying classified missions in Laos and Thailand. Still, the squadron's primary workload increased. In 1965 RANCH HAND aircrews flew only 897 missions covering 253 square miles of jungle; in 1968, the squadron's busiest year, 5,745 herbicide sorties were flown in addition to 4,000 collateral sorties.

The contraction of RANCH HAND operations occurred quickly. In 1969 the results of a five-year study at the National Cancer Institute reached the Department of Defense and confirmed a series of earlier preliminary studies indicating that serious health problems might occur with exposure to herbicides. Public disapproval also erupted when the Cambodian government made an unsubstantiated claim that 170,000 acres of its land had been intentionally sprayed with herbicides. These concerns along with a drastic decrease in funding from a requested $27 million to $3 million under Vietnamization caused a rapid decline in the number of operational sorties flown.

In mid-1970 the 12th Air Commando Squadron was reduced to eight aircraft, reassigned to Phan Rang Air Base as a flight unit, and restricted from using Agent Orange, replacing that herbicide with the less effective Agent White. On January 7, 1971, after nine years of operations, RANCH HAND aircrews flew the last three herbicide missions of the war.

Charles J. Gaspar

References

Buckingham, William. "Operation Ranch Hand." *Air University Review* 34 (1983): 42–53.

Cecil, Paul F. *Herbicidal Warfare: The Ranch Hand Project in Vietnam.* New York: Praeger, 1986.

Wolfe, William. "Health Status of Air Force Veterans Occupationally Exposed to Herbicides in Vietnam." *JAMA* 264 (October 10, 1990): 1824–1832.

ROLLING THUNDER, Operation (March 2, 1965–October 31, 1968)

Prolonged U.S. bombing campaign against the Democratic Republic of Vietnam (DRV, North Vietnam). Operation ROLLING THUNDER became the longest bombing campaign ever conducted by the U.S. Air Force (USAF). The bombing cost North Vietnam more than half its bridges, virtually all of its large petroleum-storage facilities, and nearly two-thirds of its power-generating plants. ROLLING THUNDER also killed an estimated 52,000 North Vietnamese citizens. North Vietnamese air defenses cost the United States nearly 1,000 aircraft, hundreds of prisoners of war (POWs), and hundreds of airmen

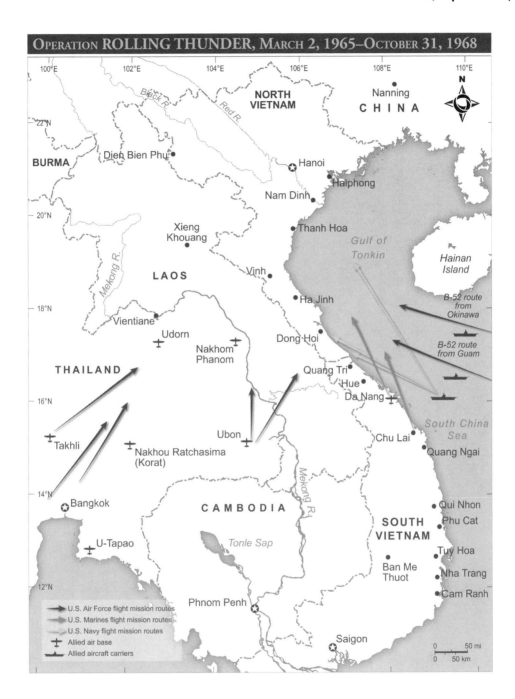

OPERATION ROLLING THUNDER, MARCH 2, 1965–OCTOBER 31, 1968

killed or missing in action. Although the USAF, the U.S. Navy, and the U.S. Marine Corps flew almost one million sorties (one plane, one mission) to drop nearly 750,000 tons of bombs, ROLLING THUNDER failed to achieve its major political and military objectives. In the overwhelming judgment of history, ROLLING THUNDER stands as the classic example of airpower failure.

Preparations for an extended bombing campaign against North Vietnam began in early 1964. Over the course of the year, competing plans emerged. The USAF, led by chief of staff General Curtis E. LeMay, advocated an all-out assault wrapped around 94 targets. The USAF's air campaign was designed to bomb North Vietnam "back to the Stone Age" by destroying its industrial base and war-making capability. The U.S. State Department advocated an escalating campaign that would increase in intensity with the number of targets, expanding over time until the Hanoi regime stopped supporting the Viet Cong (VC) and agreed to allow the Republic of Vietnam (RVN, South Vietnam) to develop as an independent non-Communist state. The U.S. Navy, because its planes did not have the range to strike targets deep inside North Vietnam, proposed an interdiction campaign south of 20 degrees north latitude, concentrating on roads, bridges, and railroads in the southern panhandle.

President Lyndon B. Johnson and his advisers turned to airpower in 1965 out of frustration. The war was going poorly in South Vietnam. The political situation in South Vietnam remained unstable, and VC guerrillas, with growing support from the North Vietnamese government, seemed very close to achieving victory. Based on their perceptions of the accomplishments of airpower in World War II and in the Korean War, USAF and U.S. Navy airpower advocates promised what airpower enthusiasts have always promised: quick victory at an acceptable cost by striking at an enemy's vital centers. They argued that by holding hostage the small industrial base of North Vietnam, Hanoi would be faced with the choice of either abandoning its efforts inside South Vietnam or risking economic ruin.

In the early nineteenth century, Prussian military theorist Carl von Clausewitz wrote that "The first, supreme, the most far-reaching act of judgment that the statesman and commander have to make is to establish . . . the kind of war on which they are embarking; neither mistaking it for, nor trying to turn it into, something that is alien to its nature." The war in Vietnam was not World War II or the Korean War, a fact that seemingly escaped airpower leaders. Furthermore, President Johnson's objectives were both limited and negative. The limited objective was to secure the right of South Vietnam to exist as a free and independent state. North Vietnam did not have to be destroyed to achieve this objective and instead only had to be persuaded to desist from supporting the insurgents. The negative objective was to avoid military action that might risk Chinese or Soviet intervention.

Such limited and negative objectives were not readily amenable to what airpower—at least theoretically—can deliver: decisive victory through vigorous offensive action. Although airpower had never been decisive in warfare, the USAF was structured and equipped to deliver that kind of victory in total nuclear war with the Soviets. The USAF, and to a lesser extent the U.S. Navy, were not structured, equipped, or doctrinally inclined to engage in limited warfare. Unfortunately, their leaders probably did not realize that they did not know how to fight this kind of war.

Following two retaliatory air strikes against North Vietnam in February 1965 (Operations FLAMING DART I and II), on March 2, 1965, the first ROLLING THUNDER mission took place when 100 USAF and Republic of Vietnam Air Force (VNAF, South Vietnamese Air Force) sorties struck the Xom Bang ammunition depot 35 miles north of the demilitarized zone (DMZ). Twelve days passed before the second ROLLING THUNDER missions were flown, when USAF and U.S. Navy planes struck an ammunition dump 100 miles southeast of Hanoi. ROLLING THUNDER was under way, and before it ended three years and nine months later, nearly 900 American planes would be shot down trying to accomplish its three objectives.

The first objective was strategic persuasion. Emanating from deterrence theory, the concept behind strategic persuasion was to employ airpower in ever-intensifying degrees in an effort to persuade North Vietnam to stop supporting the VC and enter negotiations to end the war. When ROLLING THUNDER began, strategic persuasion was its primary objective. Military planners and civilian officials alike seemed convinced that when faced with vigorous demonstrations of American power, Hanoi would back down.

By July, no one in Hanoi had blinked. But in Saigon, General William C. Westmoreland, commander of Military Assistance Command, Vietnam (MACV), had asked Secretary of Defense Robert McNamara to pass along his request for 44 combat maneuver battalions to take the war to the VC. This was the beginning of a massive buildup of ground forces, and ROLLING THUNDER switched from strategic persuasion to interdiction. For the next three years and five months, ROLLING THUNDER was primarily an effort at reducing the flow of troops and supplies moving from North Vietnam to the battlefields of South Vietnam.

The third objective was to boost the morale of South Vietnamese political and military elites by demonstrating U.S. resolve. After the assassination of President Ngo Dinh Diem in the military coup of November 1963, the political situation in Saigon had been unsettled. A large portion of the ARVN spent a disproportionate amount of time on coup alert, either protecting a given regime or preparing to overthrow it. Meanwhile, the VC were growing stronger in the countryside.

The air war against North Vietnam was meant as a demonstration of U.S. resolve to stay the course.

Targets in ROLLING THUNDER included ammunition depots and storage areas; highways and railroads; bridges and marshaling yards; warehouses; facilities for storage of petroleum, oil, and lubricant, or POL (North Vietnam had no refineries); airfields; army barracks; and power-generating plants. North Vietnam possessed three important industrial works: the Thai Nguyen Steel Works, an ammunition plant, and a cement factory. They were all eventually destroyed. The target list grew from the original 94 devised by the Joint Chiefs of Staff (JCS) in 1964 to nearly 400 targets by late 1967.

ROLLING THUNDER went through five phases. In Phase One, from March through June 1965, a variety of targets, including ammunition depots, radar sites, and barracks, were struck as Washington tried to convince North Vietnamese leaders of the seriousness of its intentions. Hanoi responded by increasing its support for the VC, who had begun attacking American air bases in South Vietnam. When U.S. troops began arriving in substantial numbers to protect those bases, the focus of ROLLING THUNDER switched from strategic persuasion to interdiction. Although the bombing retained the objective of persuading North Vietnam to withdraw its support from the VC and negotiate an end to the conflict, after July 1965 ROLLING THUNDER remained basically an interdiction campaign.

During Phase Two, from July 1965 to the end of June 1966, despite several bombing halts to accommodate bad weather and to allow for unsuccessful diplomatic efforts aimed at starting negotiations, the bombing focused on roads, bridges, and railroads. There were two kinds of targets: numbered and unnumbered. The former included such targets as the Ham Rong (Dragon Jaw) Bridge in Thanh Hoa Province and the Thai Nguyen Steel Works, which had designated target numbers. Those targets were difficult to strike, not only because they were well defended but also because the targeting process for attacking a numbered target was cumbersome and time consuming. Clearance procedures that extended from Saigon through Honolulu to the Pentagon, the State Department, and into the White House were not unusual. More than 75 percent of the interdiction effort in 1965 and 1966 concentrated on trucks, railroad rolling stock, locomotives, and boats moving along the rivers and down the coast of North Vietnam. In 1965 and 1966, according to Pentagon estimates, attacks on these fleeting targets accounted for a claimed 4,600 trucks destroyed and another 4,600 damaged. Some 4,700 boats were reportedly sunk and 8,700 damaged, while 800 railroad cars and 16 locomotives were claimed destroyed and another 800 railroad cars damaged.

The attacks were costly. In the first 20 months of ROLLING THUNDER, more than 300 planes were shot down, and the General Accounting Office estimated that it cost the United States $6.60 to inflict $1.00 worth of damage in North Vietnam. The price for bombing North Vietnam was going to go up. Meanwhile, between 150,000 and 200,000 North Vietnamese were pressed into various forms of active and passive antiaircraft defenses, ranging from managing air raid shelters to manning antiaircraft guns or firing away at planes with rifles and submachine guns. Another 500,000 North Vietnamese worked at repairing roads, railroad beds, and bridges. Accordingly, the flow of troops and supplies moving from north to south doubled during the first year of ROLLING THUNDER.

In January 1966 U.S. Pacific commander in chief Admiral Ulysses S. Grant Sharp told the JCS that the destruction of North Vietnam's POL facilities would make it difficult for them to support the war in South Vietnam. The VC and People's Army of Vietnam (PAVN, North Vietnamese Army) units in South Vietnam were likely to "wither on the vine." At the end of June 1966, Phase Three of ROLLING THUNDER got under way.

The concerted attack on North Vietnam's POL facilities lasted through the summer and into early autumn. In that time, estimates were that 70 percent of North Vietnam's POL storage capacity had been destroyed. The remaining 30 percent had been dispersed, that is, put into caches of 100 or more 55-gallon drums and placed in the middle of villages near pagodas, churches, schools, or dikes, areas that U.S. bombers were not likely to strike. Despite the bombing of petroleum-storage facilities, the movement of troops and supplies continued, and the ground war inside South Vietnam intensified.

Phase Four began in October 1966 with a shift to industrial targets and electric power–generating capabilities. Targets in and around Hanoi, previously kept off-limits for fear of inflicting collateral damage on nonmilitary structures and causing civilian casualties, were struck. The Thai Nguyen Steel Works, North Vietnam's only cement plant, power-generating plants, and transformers were bombed. After May 1967, sporadic attacks on what remained of the industrial infrastructure, the transportation system, and the fleeting targets continued. But one thing was becoming increasingly evident: the bombing was not having the desired effect. Meanwhile, by mid-1967 more than 600 aircraft had been shot down, and in the United States the antiwar movement increasingly focused on the bombing as a cruel and unusual technology unleashed on a peaceful and peace-loving people.

The 1968 Tet Offensive, which began in late January and lasted through February and into March, ushered in the final phase of ROLLING THUNDER. On March 31 President Johnson, in an effort to get peace negotiations started, limited the bombing of North Vietnam to areas in the southern panhandle below 19 degrees north latitude. Seven months later on October 31, 1968, to boost the prospects for the Democratic Party's nominee for the presidency in the November elections, Johnson ended ROLLING THUNDER.

For the most part, ROLLING THUNDER was over. Escorted reconnaissance flights were flown, and from time to time attacks on North Vietnam were undertaken. Officially these were called ROLLING THUNDER missions, but they were rare, sometimes covert, and always militarily inconsequential.

During ROLLING THUNDER, more than 643,000 tons of bombs fell on North Vietnam. The bombing destroyed 65 percent of North Vietnam's POL storage capacity and an estimated 60 percent of its power-generating capability. At one time or another, half of its major bridges were down. Nearly 10,000 trucks, 2,000 railroad cars, and 20 locomotives were destroyed. Of the 990 USAF, U.S. Navy, and U.S. Marine Corps aircraft lost over North Vietnam during the war, most were shot down flying ROLLING THUNDER missions. USAF pilots flying Republic F-105 Thunderchiefs, the primary fighter-bombers involved in ROLLING THUNDER, stood a 50 percent chance of surviving a one-year tour. In some squadrons, attrition rates reached 75 percent.

Although the bombing intensified in 1967, its effect was not apparent on the battlefields of South Vietnam. According to MACV's own estimates, the flow of troops and supplies moving from North Vietnam into South Vietnam doubled each year of ROLLING THUNDER. North Vietnam responded to the bombing of its roads, bridges, and railroads by building redundancy into its transportation system so that by 1968 it was capable of handling three times as much traffic through the panhandle as it could in 1965.

Other than perhaps boosting the morale of a few ARVN generals and South Vietnamese politicians, ROLLING THUNDER failed to achieve its objectives. Its primary failure was one of strategy. Conventional airpower employed against North Vietnam had very little impact on the unconventional war in South Vietnam. Although after 1965 increasing numbers of PAVN troops were entering the war in South Vietnam, until 1968 the conflict was basically an unconventional and guerrilla war. Airpower leaders, especially USAF generals, blinded by their perceptions of airpower gained in World War II and the Korean War, were unable to devise a strategy appropriate to the Vietnam War. At best, their concept of guerrilla war was the kind of partisan warfare carried out by Tito in Yugoslavia during World War II. They had little or no understanding of people's war as articulated by Mao Zedong or Ho Chi Minh.

There are three more specific reasons for the failure of ROLLING THUNDER. First, North Vietnam was a preindustrial agricultural country. It was not vulnerable to the kind of bombing that played a role in defeating industrial powers such as Nazi Germany and imperial Japan. North Vietnam had no war-making industries. Its primitive economy could not be held hostage to an emerging industrial base. Besides, its leadership held that reunification was more important than industrialization.

Second, for all its sound and fury, the potential effectiveness of the bombing was hampered by politically conceived constraints. Although airpower enthusiasts in the USAF and the U.S. Navy make too much of this point, there is something to it. President Johnson exercised far more control than was prudent or necessary, partly out of fear of prompting Chinese or Soviet intervention and partly out of his inherent distrust of generals.

Third, the North Vietnamese were a very determined foe. Hanoi remained constant in its war aims, which were both total and limited. Against South Vietnam, Hanoi had the total war aim of overthrowing the South Vietnamese government and reunifying the country under a single Communist system. As an expedient, Hanoi might be willing to delay realization of that objective, but despite setbacks on the battlefield in 1965, in 1968, and again in 1972, the North Vietnamese leadership remained true to that total objective until final victory in 1975. The destruction of three factories, half their bridges, and 60 percent of their power-generating capability failed to dissuade them. Against the United States, war aims of the North Vietnamese leadership were limited. Hanoi had only to compel the United States to withdraw both its troops from South Vietnam and its support for the South Vietnamese government. To accomplish this, the North Vietnamese leadership had to make the war more costly for the Americans than it was worth. The defeat inflicted on the U.S. air components during ROLLING THUNDER helped realize that objective. In July 1969, under the rubric of Vietnamization, the withdrawal of American forces began. By 1972 the return of American POWs was a primary U.S. war objective. Most of those POWs were airmen shot down during ROLLING THUNDER.

In retrospect, ROLLING THUNDER has become the classic example of an airpower failure. The USAF generals and U.S. Navy admirals who planned and executed ROLLING THUNDER were victims of their own historical experiences. Most were former bomber pilots who believed too much in the efficacy of strategic bombing. They had neither the training, the experience, nor the inclination for fighting an unconventional war against a preindustrial agrarian foe. In the minds of airpower leaders, the very concept of limited war was an oxymoron. Furthermore, USAF doctrine and most of its equipment were not suited to the kind of war that developed in Vietnam.

But most of all, the failure of ROLLING THUNDER was a result of the inability of airpower leaders, especially those in the USAF, to devise a strategy appropriate to the war at hand.

Earl H. Tilford, Jr.

References

Cable, Larry. *Unholy Grail: The U.S. and the Wars in Vietnam, 1965–68.* London: Routledge, 1991.

Clausewitz, Carl von. *On War.* Edited and translated by Michael Howard and Peter Paret. Princeton, NJ: Princeton University Press, 1976.

Clodfelter, Mark. *The Limits of Air Power: The American Bombing of North Vietnam.* New York: Free Press, 1989.

Frankum, Ronald B., Jr. *Like Rolling Thunder: The Air War in Vietnam, 1964–1975.* New York: Rowman and Littlefield, 2005.

Littauer, Raphael, and Norman Thomas Uphoff. *The Air War in Indochina.* Rev. ed. Boston: Beacon, 1971.

Thompson, James Clay. *Rolling Thunder: Understanding Policy and Program Failure.* Chapel Hill: University of North Carolina Press, 1979.

Tilford, Earl H., Jr. *Crosswinds: The Air Force's Setup in Vietnam.* College Station: Texas A&M University Press, 1993.

Rusk, David Dean (1909–1994)

Diplomat and U.S. secretary of state (1961–1969). David Dean Rusk was born in rural Cherokee County, Georgia, on February 9, 1909. He worked his way through Davidson College in North Carolina, graduating in 1931. That same year he entered Oxford University on a Rhodes Scholarship and earned a BS in 1934 and an MA the following year. Returning to the United States, he taught at Mills College in Oakland, California, and attended the University of California Law School. In 1940 he entered the Army Reserve as a captain. On active duty in Washington, D.C., he worked in military intelligence. In 1943 he was transferred to the Far East and served in China and Burma, where he became deputy chief of staff to General Joseph Stilwell. Discharged in 1946 with the rank of colonel, Rusk joined the State Department in 1947.

In the State Department, Rusk held a variety of important posts and worked on such issues as the establishment of the 1947 Marshall Plan, the creation of the State of Israel in 1948, and the founding of the North Atlantic Treaty Organization (NATO) in 1949. In 1950 he became assistant secretary of state for Far Eastern affairs and as such was heavily involved in the formulation of Korean War policy. He strongly supported the policy of containment in Asia and encouraged the decision to remove General Douglas MacArthur from the United Nations Command (UNC) in April 1951. In 1952 Rusk left the State Department to assume the presidency of the Rockefeller Foundation.

In 1960 President-elect John F. Kennedy chose Rusk as his secretary of state over

Dean Rusk was secretary of state in the administrations of presidents John F. Kennedy and Lyndon B. Johnson and a strong supporter of U.S. involvement in Vietnam. (Yoichi R. Okamoto/Lyndon B. Johnson Presidential Library)

such notables as Chester Bowles and Adlai Stevenson, who then became Rusk's subordinates. Upon assuming office, Rusk immediately confronted myriad international problems, the most serious being Communist threats in Cuba, Southeast Asia, and Berlin. A staunch anti-Communist, he largely worked behind the scenes in the Kennedy administration, offering advice only when it was solicited. Rusk urged moderation during the Berlin Crises and the Cuban Missile Crisis, but he believed that Communist aggression had to be met with determination and feared that China would intervene in Vietnam, as it had in Korea. He had little faith in Ngo Dinh Diem and urged a stronger American commitment in the Republic of Vietnam (RVN, South Vietnam). Along with Secretary of Defense Robert McNamara, Rusk usually deferred to the Pentagon position on Southeast Asia.

When Lyndon Johnson assumed the presidency after Kennedy's assassination in November 1963, Rusk continued as secretary of state. Under Johnson, Rusk took a much more active role. He quickly became one of Johnson's most trusted advisers. As antiwar sentiment intensified, many of Johnson's advisers, including secretaries of defense Robert McNamara and Clark Clifford, began to mirror the public's exasperation. Rusk steadfastly supported Johnson's position, however. Rusk backed Pentagon calls for larger troop commitments to Southeast Asia and the bombing of the Democratic Republic of Vietnam (DRV, North Vietnam). He urged Johnson to stay the course, despite mounting pressure to end U.S. involvement in the war. Rusk did not, as is often suggested, oppose negotiations with Hanoi. He constantly warned against the appearance of weakness in the face of Communist aggression but in 1967 suggested that Johnson pursue negotiations. Rusk left office in 1969 when the Republican administration of Richard Nixon took office.

Throughout his career Rusk displayed marked ability and an intense loyalty to his superiors. Although admirable, his loyalty proved damaging; with the exception of Johnson, no other political figure became more closely associated with America's failure in Vietnam than Rusk. He was also an outsider. A southerner among Ivy League easterners, he never fell in with the so-called Wise Men. Rusk also found himself an outcast. Shunned by more prestigious academic institutions after he left the State Department, he eventually accepted a position at the University of Georgia, where he taught international law until his retirement in 1984. His memoir, *As I Saw It*, was published in 1990 to much less hoopla than McNamara's subsequent effort. Rusk died at his home in Athens, Georgia, on December 20, 1994.

David Coffey

References

Current Biography Yearbook, 1961. New York: H. W. Wilson, 1961.

Current Biography Yearbook, 1995. New York: H. W. Wilson, 1995.

Halberstam, David. *The Best and the Brightest.* New York: Random House, 1972.

Isaacson, Walter, and Evan Thomas. *The Wise Men: Six Friends and the World They Made.* New York: Simon and Schuster, 1986.

Karnow, Stanley. *Vietnam: A History.* 2nd rev. and updated ed. New York: Penguin, 1997.

Rusk, Dean. *As I Saw It.* Edited by Daniel S. Papp. New York: Norton, 1990.

S

Search and Destroy

U.S. military tactical procedure of attrition used in Vietnam between 1965 and 1968. Developed by Military Assistance Command, Vietnam (MACV), commander General William Westmoreland and his deputy chief of staff for operations (G-3) Brigadier General William DePuy, search and destroy emerged not from the conclusions of study committees, think-tank reports, or tactical doctrine developed at the U.S. Army Command and General Staff College. As with many U.S. tactics, the development of search and destroy depended on military capabilities at the given time. It was an ad hoc approach that grew out of discussions between Westmoreland and DePuy. Charles MacDonald, spokesman at the U.S. Army Center of Military History, revealed that Westmoreland turned to his trusted associate and said, "Bill, what should we call this?" DePuy responded, "How about search-and-destroy?"

Although Westmoreland would later deny that search and destroy was even a specific tactical procedure, it was certainly the dominant approach followed by American fighting units of all sizes in Vietnam. Search and destroy relied on the assumption that American firepower and technology were so superior and could cause such severe casualties that neither the Viet Cong (VC) nor the People's Army of Vietnam (PAVN, North Vietnamese Army) would be able to withstand the punishment that U.S. forces could visit upon them.

Search and destroy was to be an aggressive military tool. Ground forces, transported by U.S. Army aviation helicopter units and supported by artillery, would locate enemy forces and destroy them and, on occasion, their base areas. The tactic emphasized attacking the Communist forces rather than acquiring territory. Troopers struck into areas of supposed Communist strength to find, fix, and finish their enemy. Mission accomplished, they withdrew to their home base until ordered out on the next such operation. Westmoreland believed that the Communists, unable to stand against such forays, would seek peace.

Not everyone agreed with this approach. U.S. Air Force chief of staff General John P. McConnell and U.S. Marine Corps commandant General David M. Greene opposed it. U.S. Army general James Gavin called for U.S. military aid to Vietnam to be restricted to sending forces to certain enclaves, providing those locations with protection, and freeing troops of the Army of the Republic of Vietnam (ARVN, South Vietnamese Army) to carry the brunt of the fight. Major General Edward Lansdale argued that the main American commitment should be directed toward countrywide pacification and counterinsurgency rather than employing combat maneuver battalions.

Westmoreland wanted no static defensive posture, was unwilling to confine his command to a defensive role, and rejected the enclave strategy. An early indication of his desire to expand in-country operations came in June 1965 when he ordered the

U.S. Army Bell UH-1D helicopters airlift members of the 2nd Battalion, 14th Infantry Regiment from the Filhol Rubber Plantation area to a new staging area, during Operation WAHIAWA, a search and destroy mission conducted by the 25th Infantry Division, northeast of Cu Chi, South Vietnam, May 16, 1966. (National Archives)

173rd Airborne Brigade deployed to Phuoc Long Province north of Saigon to be ready to intervene in support of ARVN forces in the Battle of Dong Xoai; the 173rd Airborne Brigade had only arrived in Vietnam on May 7. On June 26 the Pentagon gave Westmoreland authority to assign U.S. troops to field action. Two days later on June 28, 3,000 soldiers of the 173rd Airborne Brigade moved into a VC stronghold, War Zone D, 20 miles northwest of Saigon.

Perhaps Westmoreland believed that he had no choice. Previous military preparation had equipped and prepared the army only to fight in Europe to contain a Soviet strike through the Hof Corridor or the Fulda Gap in Germany on its way to the Rhine. Suddenly faced with Vietnam, planners sent military forces intact to Southeast Asia. Surely they could easily handle a fight with irregular guerrilla forces.

Westmoreland has been soundly criticized for adopting this tactic of attrition. It grew from his own experience in World War II and the Korean War and the erroneous assumption that American soldiers and firepower could inflict devastating losses on Communist forces in Vietnam while keeping U.S. casualties to an acceptable level. Westmoreland's hopes were doomed by wartime reality. The level of attrition that he was able to bring to bear on the Communists was neutralized by the fact that more than 200,000 North Vietnamese males, replacements for PAVN losses in battle, reached draft age every year. Westmoreland's army never came close to inflicting that many casualties in any 12-month period. A bigger problem with Westmoreland's tactics was the fact that the Communists rather than U.S. forces generally initiated hostilities. The Communists chose locations for battle that were favorable to them and often ended combat when they saw fit, leaving the site of an attack along safe avenues of retreat.

Lieutenant General Dave Richard Palmer roundly criticized Westmoreland's war of attrition as an indication of his failure to conceive of an alternative, as irrefutable proof of the absence of any strategy, and as an approach demonstrating that the U.S. Army was strategically bankrupt in Vietnam. Others also criticized the strategy, but Westmoreland stubbornly relied on search and destroy throughout his tenure as commander of the U.S. Military Assistance Command, Vietnam (MACV). Following the 1968 Tet Offensive, however, MACV public affairs officers did not often use the term "search and destroy," replacing it with the phrase "reconnaissance in force." An observer would have been hard-pressed, however, to note any actual change in American approaches to locating Communist forces.

Cecil B. Currey

References

Palmer, Dave Richard. *Readings in Current Military History*. West Point, NY: Department of Military Art and Engineering, U.S. Military Academy, 1969.

Shaplen, Robert. *The Road from War: Vietnam, 1965–1970*. New York: Harper and Row, 1970.

Sorley, Lewis. *Westmoreland: The General Who Lost Vietnam*. New York: Houghton Mifflin Harcourt, 2011.

Sihanouk, Norodom (1922–2012)

The leading figure of modern Cambodia, at various times prince, king (1941–1955, 1993–2004), prime minister (1955–1960), head of state (1960–1993), palace prisoner, and guerrilla figurehead who throughout tried in vain to keep his country out of the Vietnam War. Born in Phnom Penh on October 31, 1922, the son of Prince Norodom Suramarit and Princess Sisowath Kossamak of a line going back to the emperors of Angkor, Norodom Sihanouk was educated at the École François Baudoin in Phnom Penh and the Lycée Chasseloup Laubat in Saigon, where he excelled at music, literature, and drama. When King Monivong, his maternal grandfather, died on April 23, 1941, the French, who then exercised a protectorate over Cambodia, picked Sihanouk to succeed him in preference to Monivong's son, Prince Sisowath Monireth.

Norodom Sihanouk was the king of Cambodia, who rejected U.S. aid during the U.S. involvement in Vietnam but was removed by General Lon Nol in 1970. He subsequently supported the communist Khmer Rouge government, only to be arrested and imprisoned by them. In October 2004, Sihanouk abdicated the throne because of his advanced age and increasing health problems. (AP/Wide World Photos)

In the first of many gestures designed to show his independent will, Sihanouk expressed his support for the Japanese when they temporarily interned the French administration in Indochina on March 9, 1945, and proclaimed the end of the French protectorate. Sihanouk assumed the additional position of prime minister, but his power was overshadowed by an ambitious politician, Son Ngoc Thanh, whom the Japanese imposed as foreign minister. Sihanouk was obliged to accept the return of the French following Japan's surrender in August 1945 but distanced himself from a modus vivendi signed in January 1946 by his uncle, Prince Monireth.

Cambodian elections held under a French-inspired constitution in 1946 and 1947 resulted in big wins for the Democratic Party, the only one with a grassroots organization. Sihanouk viewed this as a challenge by rivals, and within five years, motivated by an unshakable belief that he knew what was best for Cambodia, he managed to eliminate the Democrats and secure a firm grip on Cambodia's political evolution that he was not to give up until 1970.

In 1953 Sihanouk embarked upon what he called a "royal crusade for independence" involving exchanges with Paris, travels abroad (including to the United States, where he was unimpressed by his reception by the Dwight Eisenhower administration), and even a well-publicized period of exile that ended finally in an agreement that consecrated Cambodia's juridical independence on November 9, 1953. Sihanouk also formed a liaison at this time with a métis beauty contestant, Monique Izzi, who later became his wife and queen.

The instrument of Sihanouk's political power in a Cambodia whose independence and sovereignty had been reinforced by the favorable armistice terms negotiated by the Cambodian delegation at the 1954 Geneva Conference on Indochina was the Sangkum

Reastr Niyum (People's Socialist Community). Sihanouk's founding of the Sangkum Reastr Niyum followed by a month his dramatic announcement on March 2, 1955, that he was abdicating the throne. Persuading his father to succeed him, Sihanouk took the title "Samdech Upayuvareach" (the prince who has been king). Also in April he attended the Afro-Asian Conference in Bandung, which increased his feeling of self-importance and convinced him that Cambodia's foreign policy should henceforth be non-aligned. For his own diversion he played the saxophone, produced films with pseudohistorical themes, and fathered countless children.

But Sihanouk's efforts to keep Cambodia at peace proved only temporarily successful. First he experienced increasing difficulties with his two powerful neighbors, Thailand and the Republic of Vietnam (RVN, South Vietnam). Their pro-Western regimes gave sanctuary to armed dissidents, who under the name of Khmer Serei (Free Khmer or Free Cambodians) broadcast anti-Sihanouk propaganda to Cambodia. A more serious threat to Sihanouk's control, however, was the growing use of Cambodia's eastern border provinces by Viet Cong (VC) and North Vietnamese forces fighting the Saigon government. Such use of Cambodian territory was carefully camouflaged by Hanoi and the National Front for the Liberation of South Vietnam (National Liberation Front [NLF]), which went to great lengths to maintain correct relations with Sihanouk's government, supporting its stands on foreign affairs, for example, in their radio broadcasts.

When his father died in 1960, Sihanouk chose to leave the throne vacant and took the title "head of state" as a way of letting people know who was in charge. By the mid-1960s, he was again having difficulties controlling Cambodia's destiny. The situation on the border was now marked by repeated bombings of Cambodian villages by South Vietnamese and U.S. planes. In late 1963 Sihanouk ended the small U.S. economic and military aid programs in Cambodia, and in April 1965 he severed diplomatic relations entirely. Trying to counterbalance the influence of Hanoi, whose demands on Cambodia now included the furnishing of rice and other goods for its soldiers, Sihanouk steered ever closer to China. But here too there was no salvation in sight, as the Cultural Revolution absorbed China's attention, and his old friend Zhou Enlai had little influence left. Moreover, Sihanouk suspected China of being involved in the only insurgency within Cambodia's borders, an agrarian-based movement that instigated a popular uprising against the army in the western region of Samlaut in 1967 and whose leaders Sihanouk habitually derided as "Khmer Rouge."

In 1969 Sihanouk renewed diplomatic relations with the United States and named a national salvation government headed by General Lon Nol to try to deal with the mounting insecurity in the countryside and to reverse his previous Socialist economic policies, which were unpopular with the emerging middle class. The situation continued to deteriorate, and at the beginning of March 1970 demonstrations took place in Phnom Penh against the VC and North Vietnamese presence in Cambodia. On March 18, taking advantage of Sihanouk's absence abroad, the National Assembly unanimously voted to depose him as head of state.

Sihanouk arrived in Beijing hours later and issued a call for armed resistance to the leaders in Phnom Penh. It was the decisive moment in his career. Assured of the support of the People's Republic of China (PRC) and the Democratic Republic of Vietnam (DRV, North Vietnam), Sihanouk refused to accept the Phnom Penh decision and proceeded to establish a broad political front and a military command, even though this meant accepting the preponderant influence of the Khmer Rouge, the only Cambodian group with the organization and the means to wage a guerrilla war against the Phnom Penh government and its U.S. backers. Sihanouk continued to reside in Beijing, with the exception of one hurried visit to guerrilla bases in Cambodia in 1973, until after the Khmer Rouge capture of Phnom Penh in April 1975.

Sihanouk was returned to the royal palace in Phnom Penh by the Khmer Rouge as their virtual prisoner. In the egalitarian society they were trying to create by radical policies, they had no use for someone who represented in their eyes both the feudalism and the nexus of connections to Western democracies of the past. They used him only as a tool to preserve their seat at the United Nations (UN). Sihanouk has written movingly of his detestation for the Khmer Rouge. The leader of the Khmer Rouge was Pol Pot, who was responsible for the execution of several of Sihanouk's children and the systematic murder of hundreds of thousands of Cambodians. Khmer Rouge xenophobia extended to the newly reunified Vietnam, and Sihanouk's cozy relations with Hanoi also became a thing of the past.

A Chinese plane spirited Sihanouk to safety just before invading Vietnamese troops entered Phnom Penh in early January 1979. But he was once more an exile and was far from his beloved Kampuchea, as it was now known. He divided his time between China and North Korea, where his great friend Kim Il Sung ruled unopposed. Once again Sihanouk assumed the role of figurehead leader of a resistance movement, this time a coalition of two small non-Communist groups and the Khmer Rouge, who were still supported by China, in a drawn-out struggle against the Vietnamese-installed People's Republic of Kampuchea president

Heng Samrin and Prime Minister Hun Sen. Once again Sihanouk ensured that Cambodia's UN seat was preserved for his side.

This situation was to last for a decade, until the withdrawal of Vietnamese troops from Cambodia and an internationally brokered peace agreement under UN peacekeeping safeguards allowed Sihanouk to return in triumph to the refurbished royal palace in Phnom Penh in November 1991. Expressing annoyance at UN interference in Cambodia's affairs, Sihanouk immediately declared that the policies of Hun Sen's government had been correct and likened them to those of the Sangkum instead of presiding impartially over a four-sided Supreme National Council, as called for in the peace plan. In an astute move, he adopted the title "Samdech Euv" (Father Prince) and embraced Hun Sen as his adopted son. Elections to the National Assembly in May 1993 gave Sihanouk's followers, who had capitalized on his popularity in the countryside, a majority; however, they were forced to share power with the former Phnom Penh government in a two-sided arrangement in which his son, Prince Norodom Ranariddh, became first prime minister.

Sihanouk, never forgiving those who had deposed him, declared himself to have been retroactively head of state since March 18, 1970. No one in Phnom Penh dared contest his right to be head of state. A new constitution tailored to the requirements of the situation made him king once more, although Sihanouk himself modestly proclaimed that he would reign but not rule in a parliamentary democracy in which he would remain above politics.

Sihanouk was once again at center stage. The only factors that detracted from his triumph were his poor health and the Khmer Rouge. Cancer of the bone marrow forced him to spend months at a time in Beijing undergoing radiation treatment by Chinese doctors. Meanwhile, the Khmer Rouge, having boycotted the elections, renewed their insurgency while avoiding criticizing Sihanouk. With the future thus mortgaged and with a successor to the throne still undecided, Sihanouk could still feel some uncertainty about whether he would go down in history as his country's benefactor or as a publicity-hungry manipulator willing to deal with anyone and everyone as circumstances dictated.

On July 5, 1997, Second Premier Hun Sen seized power in Cambodia and ousted First Premier Ranariddh, Sihanouk's son, who then fled abroad. In the coup a number of prominent Ranariddh supporters were also slain. After trying without success to mediate a solution, in October 1997 Sihanouk left Cambodia, saying that he did not know when and if he would ever return. He retained the throne, however, until October 7, 2004, when he abdicated in favor of his son Nordom Sihamoni, who was crowned king on October 29. Sihanouk died on October 15, 2012, in Beijing. He was 89.

Arthur J. Dommen

References

Chandler, David P. *The Tragedy of Cambodian History: Politics, War, and Revolution since 1945*. New Haven, CT: Yale University Press, 1991.

Hamel, Bernard. *Sihanouk et le Drame Cambodgien*. Paris: Editions L'Harmattan, 1993.

Osborne, Milton. *Sihanouk: Prince of Light, Prince of Darkness*. Honolulu: University of Hawaii Press, 1994.

STEEL TIGER, Operation (April 3, 1965–December 11, 1968)

U.S. air interdiction campaign over the Ho Chi Minh Trail, particularly in the northern panhandle of Laos. Operation STEEL TIGER represented yet another unsuccessful use of limited airpower in the Vietnam War. Although air planners hoped that STEEL TIGER would complement the larger ROLLING THUNDER campaign, the political dangers of bombing Laos haunted the Lyndon B. Johnson administration. Concern over possible Chinese or Soviet intervention coupled with the potential wrath of the world community that had guaranteed Laotian neutrality in 1962 drove Washington to restrict U.S. Navy and U.S. Air Force target lists. In fact, civilians in Washington selected the targets. This information was then sent on to air planners in Saigon for implementation. The U.S. Air Force commenced Operation STEEL TIGER on April 3, 1965, using Republic F-105 Thunderchiefs, Lockheed AC-130 Spectre gunships, and numerous other aircraft stationed in the Republic of Vietnam (RVN, South Vietnam) and Thailand, while the U.S. Navy flew strike missions from aircraft carriers stationed in the South China Sea.

As with most limited uses of airpower, STEEL TIGER did not stop the flow from the Democratic Republic of Vietnam (DRV, North Vietnam) of men and materials to South Vietnam. The Ho Chi Minh Trail was an elaborate network of intertwined truck tracks and footpaths through deep jungle terrain. Visibility from the air was poor, and damage assessments were largely inaccurate. If U.S. airmen bombed a critical choke point, the North Vietnamese either repaired it quickly or transferred the movement of supplies to bicycles. During the monsoon season, most of the traffic on the trail was by foot, which complicated air operations even further.

The development of target lists in Washington led to an additional problem: the command and control of air operations over the Laotian panhandle became hopelessly muddled. Although the U.S. Navy played a large role in STEEL TIGER, both U.S. Navy and U.S. Air Force planners were loath to compromise their autonomy by fully cooperating with each other. Navy pilots less than affectionately referred to STEEL TIGER missions as "truck busting." Although many trucks were destroyed along the trail, a simple cost-benefit analysis showed that the insurgents in South Vietnam, while receiving fewer supplies than before, were still getting enough to prosecute the war.

On December 11, 1968, STEEL TIGER merged with Operation TIGER HOUND, which had focused on interdicting Communist supply routes in the southern Laotian panhandle. The newly christened Operation COMMANDO HUNT was intended to interdict supplies from North Vietnam all along the Ho Chi Minh Trail.

Lincoln Hill

References

Berent, Mark. *Steel Tiger.* New York: Putnam, 1990.

Berger, Carl, ed. *The United States Air Force in Southeast Asia, 1961–1973: An Illustrated Account.* Washington, DC: Office of Air Force History, 1977.

Gurney, Gene. *Vietnam: The War in the Air.* New York: Crown, 1985.

Strategic Hamlet Program (1961–1964)

The most ambitious and well-known effort by President Ngo Dinh Diem of the Republic of Vietnam (RVN, South Vietnam) to pacify the countryside and neutralize the Viet Cong (VC) insurgents. The Strategic Hamlet Program sought to provide security and a better life for the rural populace by settling them in protected hamlets, where

Women and children of the Da Ban strategic hamlet in the Republic of Vietnam pose for a military photographer in 1963. The strategic hamlet program was designed to provide security for the rural populace in South Vietnam by settling them in protected villages where the government could carry out political and economic programs. (National Archives)

government cadres could carry out economic and political programs. Following in the wake of a similar effort, the Agroville Campaign, the Strategic Hamlet Program was inaugurated in 1961 and officially ended early in 1964, but it began to wane even before Diem was overthrown in November 1963.

The concept of the Strategic Hamlet Program derived from British counterinsurgency expert Sir Robert Thompson's experiences in quashing the Malayan Emergency in the 1950s. Between 1961 and 1965, Thompson served as head of the British Advisory Mission and advised the Diem government on counterinsurgency or pacification programs. Thompson's notion was to organize villagers to provide for their own defense. In Malaya the failure of the Chinese insurgents, who

were ethnically different from the villagers, to penetrate the population meant that little more was required than to organize a home guard, a local security force supported by local police. The government could then relocate the Chinese squatters. The situation in Vietnam was more complex, however. The VC were well established in all areas of the country and were of the same ethnicity as the villagers. Therefore, the insurgents were not easily identified and segregated from the rest of the people.

Thompson's notion was to bring security to where the people already lived. Relocation was to be minimal. Thompson estimated at the start of the program that only 5 percent of the hamlets, those in VC-controlled areas, would have to be moved to new sites. The strategic hamlets were intended to physically and politically isolate the insurgents from the people, their recruiting base.

American civilians, notably Roger Hilsman and Walt Rostow in the State Department as well as embassy personnel in Saigon, favored the program, but American military leaders criticized the concept of strategic hamlets, believing that it tied military forces into a defensive posture. Lieutenant General Lionel McGarr, head of the U.S. Military Assistance and Advisory Group (MAAG), thought that this role was more appropriate for police than for regular forces. He urged military clearing operations instead of tying down forces in static positions.

Diem undertook the Strategic Hamlet Program on his own without first informing the Americans, merely presenting them with a fait accompli. But Diem had his own reasons for embarking on the program. He saw it as a way to secure assistance from the United States while managing the program himself. Aware of the danger of being perceived by the Vietnamese as an American puppet, he wanted to control the program in order to fend off critics, retain independence, and resist Washington's pressure for political reforms.

Diem and his brother, Ngo Dinh Nhu, who carried out the program, significantly changed Thompson's original concept. Thompson proposed surrounding existing hamlets with security forces, but Diem and Nhu decided that security should begin within the hamlets and embarked on an ambitious plan to build fortified hamlets, which in practice involved relocating villagers. Nhu established three goals. First, the government would link the people in fortified hamlets in a communications network, allowing them to summon local defense and reaction forces in case of emergency. Second, the program would unite the people and bind them to the government. Third, the government would work to improve living standards.

Nhu wanted half of South Vietnam's 14,000 hamlets to be completed by early 1963 and another 5,000 completed by early 1964. The remainder would be swept along by example. To meet these ambitious quotas, Nhu exerted severe pressure on province chiefs, despite their lack of authority over local officials. Nhu's plans led to overexpansion, creating far more hamlets than Saigon's forces could protect or its cadres could administer. Under pressure from Saigon to show results, province officials often appeased Nhu with meaningless data. In 1962 the government designated 2,600 settlements in the I, II, and III Corps tactical zones as "completed," but American officials ruefully concluded that the definition of "completed" varied greatly from hamlet to hamlet in terms of quality of defenses and percentage of the population under government control.

Pressure to meet unrealistic goals encouraged a focus on the superficial aspects of the program, such as erecting fences, that often sufficed to officially reclassify an existing settlement as a strategic hamlet. The program imposed onerous burdens on the people, such as controls on their movement and demands for guard duty. According to the U.S. embassy, most villagers viewed the program as a security measure, not as an element of revolution.

In May 1963 General Paul Harkins, head of U.S. Military Assistance Command, Vietnam (MACV), criticized the program's execution as superficial because it left Communist-controlled hamlets and salients in government areas. He urged Diem to expand the program more logically to consolidate his hold on the countryside.

The Communists initially limited their opposition to disseminating propaganda that compared the strategic hamlets to prisons and inserting agents to collect taxes, recruit, and stir up resentment toward the government. By the summer of 1963, they shifted tactics, directly attacking hamlets and severing links between them and nearby reaction forces. The hamlets were vulnerable because there were too many that were poorly built and weakly defended. The Communists' new approach bore results, and the number of government-run strategic hamlets drastically fell. By July 1964, for example, only 30 of the 219 strategic hamlets in Long An Province remained under government control.

After the Strategic Hamlet Program had ended, Thompson criticized its implementation on three grounds. First, using the Can Lao Party, Nhu attempted to control the program from the top down instead of winning political and popular support at the bottom. Second, by emphasizing the Republican Youth, he created divisions between the youths and the village elders, the traditional leaders. Third, Nhu failed to understand the extent of VC penetration and was unprepared to take the harsh measures necessary to eliminate it within the hamlets.

Faulty execution compromised a promising pacification program. Not only did the Strategic Hamlet Program fail to halt the insurgency, but it manifested the arbitrary and repressive aspect of Diem's rule. The program was also plagued by corruption. The inadequacy of the Strategic Hamlet Program served as a metaphor for the regime's failure to stem the insurgency, to gain and hold the support of the people, and to win the confidence of the John F. Kennedy administration, which acquiesced in Diem's overthrow.

The failure of the Strategic Hamlet Program had a larger significance: pacification would be supplanted as a strategy for fighting the war. Two successor pacification efforts in 1964, the Chien Thang Program and Operation HOP TAC, were also poorly executed and failed to reverse Saigon's declining fortunes in the countryside. In late 1964 the emboldened Communists began to infiltrate conventional People's Army of Vietnam (PAVN, North Vietnamese Army) units into South Vietnam to administer the coup de grâce. It was a situation beyond the scope of pacification to remedy, forcing Washington to intervene with a bombing campaign and ground troops.

Richard A. Hunt

References

Colby, William, with James McCargar. *Lost Victory: A Firsthand Account of America's Sixteen-Year Involvement in Vietnam.* Chicago: Contemporary Books, 1989.

Hunt, Richard A. *Pacification: The American Struggle for Vietnam's Hearts and Minds.* Boulder, CO: Westview, 1995.

Osborne, Milton. *Strategic Hamlets in Vietnam.* Data Paper 55. Ithaca, NY: Cornell University Southeast Asia Program, April 1965.

Thompson, Sir Robert. *Defeating Communist Insurgency.* New York: Praeger, 1966.

T

Taylor, Maxwell Davenport (1901–1987)

U.S. Army general, military representative of the president during 1961–1962, chairman of the Joint Chiefs of Staff (JCS) during 1962–1964, ambassador to Vietnam during 1964–1965, and presidential consultant on Vietnam during 1965–1968. Born in Keytesville, Missouri, on August 26, 1901, Maxwell Davenport Taylor graduated from the United States Military Academy, West Point, in 1922. Commissioned in the engineers, in 1926 he transferred to the field artillery. A talented linguist, he taught French and Spanish for five years at West Point; graduated from the Command and General Staff College, Fort Leavenworth, Kansas, in 1935; and then was assigned to Tokyo as an assistant military attaché to learn Japanese. In late 1937 he was briefly assistant military attaché in Beijing.

During 1939–1940, Taylor attended the Army War College. He was then assigned to the staff of U.S. Army chief of staff General George C. Marshall and was promoted to lieutenant colonel. In July 1942 Taylor became chief of staff of the 82nd Airborne Division as a colonel, and in December he was promoted to brigadier general as the divisional artillery commander.

During World War II, Taylor joined the division in Sicily after the Allied invasion, and on September 7, 1943, he volunteered for a clandestine mission behind enemy lines to Rome to determine if an airborne operation there was feasible. Meeting with Italian officials, he decided that the Germans had secured the facilities that would be needed for the airborne operation to succeed. On his recommendation, the mission was cancelled. Taylor was then senior representative on the commission that convinced the new Italian government to declare war on Germany.

Taylor returned to the 82nd Airborne Division. In March 1944 in the United Kingdom, he took command of the 101st Airborne Division. Promoted to major general in March 1944, he jumped with the division behind Utah Beach during the Normandy Invasion. Rotated back to Britain after more than a month of combat, Taylor and his division next participated in Operation MARKET GARDEN in September. Taylor was wounded and was out of action for two weeks. He was in Washington on temporary assignment when the Battle of the Ardennes (Battle of the Bulge) began. The divisional artillery commander, Brigadier General Anthony McAuliffe, was the acting commander of the 101st Airborne Division when it was sent to defend Bastogne. Taylor reached Bastogne with the relieving 4th Armored Division and resumed command. The division then mopped up pockets of resistance in the Ruhr before resuming the advance east.

In September 1945 Taylor became superintendent of West Point, where he initiated necessary curriculum changes. Between 1949 and 1951, he headed the Berlin Command. In 1951 he was promoted to lieutenant general and became U.S. Army deputy chief of staff for operations and training.

U.S. Army general Maxwell D. Taylor was chair of the Joint Chiefs of Staff during 1962–1964 and U.S. ambassador to the Republic of Vietnam during 1964–1965, when he advocated an enhanced counterinsurgency program and the bombing of North Vietnam. (National Archives)

In February 1953 Taylor, as a full general, took command of the Eighth Army in Korea at a time when an armistice was imminent. He then served as commanding general, Army Forces Far East, in 1954 and commander in chief, Far East Command, in 1955.

Taylor was U.S. Army chief of staff from 1955 to 1959. Taking issue with the doctrine of massive nuclear retaliation supported by JCS chairman Admiral Arthur W. Radford, Taylor favored a larger military capable of flexible response. When Radford's view prevailed and the 1960 budget called for 55,000 fewer men than he had advocated, Taylor resigned in July 1959.

Taylor then wrote *The Uncertain Trumpet* (1960), urging a reappraisal of military policy. He advocated a buildup of conventional forces and the doctrine of flexible response. Taylor had been warning for years that brush-fire wars, not nuclear conflicts, presented the greatest military challenge to the United States.

In April 1961 President John F. Kennedy called on Taylor to study the role of the Central Intelligence Agency (CIA) in the Bay of Pigs fiasco. In July he took on the newly established post of military representative of the president. Serving as Kennedy's chief military adviser, Taylor also had the responsibility of apprising the president on the adequacy of U.S. intelligence operations. The position made him the president's senior military representative at home and abroad.

In October 1961 Kennedy sent Taylor and Walt Rostow on a fact-finding mission to Vietnam. Taylor recognized a "double crisis of confidence" there: doubts about American determination to hold Southeast Asia and doubts that the methods of Ngo Dinh Diem, president of the Republic of Vietnam (RVN, South Vietnam), could defeat the Communists. Taylor advocated sending additional military aid and advisers while at the same time urging South Vietnamese reforms. He strongly recommended the commitment of 8,000 U.S. ground combat troops under the cover of a flood-control team to overcome Diem's sensitivity on the issue of foreign combat troops. Taylor also wanted intensive training of local self-defense forces and a large increase in helicopters, fighter-bombers, reconnaissance aircraft, and support personnel. Kennedy approved the recommendations, with the exception of sending ground combat troops. This report, flawed by its de-emphasis of political problems and underestimation of the Communists, marked the zenith of Taylor's influence.

In October 1962, in an unprecedented move, Kennedy recalled Taylor from retirement to serve in the nation's highest military position, chairman of the JCS. Taylor and Secretary of Defense Robert McNamara were in general agreement on strategy and shared similar management styles that favored clear-cut decisions and emphasis on detail. The two made three trips to Vietnam together. Perhaps the most important came in September 1963, when they noted great military progress and expressed confidence that it would continue. Two of their conclusions remain disturbing. The first, that "the security of South Vietnam remains vital to United States security," inhibited discussion of disengagement. The second, advocacy of a training program for the Vietnamese that would allow the United States to withdraw the bulk of its personnel by the end of 1965, showed stunning naïveté about Vietnamese political and military potential.

Taylor was critical of the November 1963 coup against Diem, faulting the State Department and the CIA. In January 1964 Taylor informed McNamara that the JCS favored the elimination of many military restrictions and sought "bolder actions." Taylor advocated both an intensified counterinsurgency program and selected air and naval strikes against the Democratic Republic of Vietnam (DRV, North Vietnam). He saw bombing as a deterrent to Hanoi's "aggression," a morale booster in South Vietnam, and a means to bring North Vietnam to the negotiating table. He continued to stress this two-part program in years to come.

Taylor undertook his most controversial role in July 1964 when he succeeded Henry Cabot Lodge as U.S. ambassador to South Vietnam. When Taylor arrived in Saigon, he was seemingly in a powerful position, in control of American military forces. He and Military Assistance Command, Vietnam

(MACV), commander General William Westmoreland began to Americanize the war. Taylor had little patience for the political complexities of South Vietnam, and he could not understand its leaders. By December, relations between the ambassador and Prime Minister Nguyen Khanh became so strained that Taylor demanded that Khanh resign, while Khanh threatened to ask Washington for Taylor's recall.

In early 1965 Taylor foresaw the probability of a U.S. troop commitment, which, according to journalist Stanley Karnow, "rattled him." Taylor now embraced the notion that the United States should avoid Asian land wars and told President Lyndon Johnson that the Vietnamese lacked motivation rather than manpower. In February, Westmoreland requested two marine battalions to protect the air base at Da Nang. Taylor differed with Westmoreland over the introduction of U.S. combat troops and in March returned to Washington to voice his objections to what he saw as a first installment in an inevitably increasing American commitment. Taylor believed that a major U.S. commitment would take too much of the burden from the Army of the Republic of Vietnam (ARVN, South Vietnamese Army) and encourage it to let the United States fight the war.

Taylor did not oppose the introduction of U.S. troops per se, but he did advocate their restrained use. He supported an enclave strategy that would secure major cities, towns, and U.S. military bases, mainly along the coast, by aggressive patrolling rather than Westmoreland's search-and-destroy strategy. Taylor also opposed the immediate dispatch of additional U.S. troops.

During the April 1965 Honolulu Conference, Taylor had a brief argument on the troop issue with McNamara and Westmoreland. This conference saw a major shift in U.S. policy from counterinsurgency to large-scale ground war. It also represented a first step from Taylor's enclave strategy to Westmoreland's big-unit search-and-destroy strategy. Taylor's defeat on this issue ended the fiction of an all-powerful ambassador and was, according to journalist David Halberstam, the "last time that Max Taylor was a major player, his farewell in fact."

Returning to Washington in July 1965, Taylor was haunted by a sense of failure. Johnson thought that Taylor's intransigence had created unnecessary friction with South Vietnamese leaders, some of whom saw Taylor as too outspoken—more soldier than statesman—to function as a diplomat. He nonetheless retained an important advisory role and joined the group of Johnson's senior policy consultants known as the Wise Men. Taylor's memoir, *Swords and Ploughshares* (1972), received mixed reviews. As late as 1973 he still hoped for an acceptable outcome to the war.

Taylor, one of the major American military figures of the twentieth century, died in Washington, D.C., on April 19, 1987.

Paul S. Daum and Elizabeth W. Daum

References

Cooper, Chester L. *The Lost Crusade: America in Vietnam*. Rev. and updated ed. New York: Dodd, Mead, 1973.

Halberstam, David. *The Best and the Brightest*. New York: Random House, 1972.

Isaacson, Walter, and Evan Thomas. *The Wise Men: Six Friends and the World They Made*. New York: Simon and Schuster, 1986.

Karnow, Stanley. *Vietnam: A History*. 2nd rev. and updated ed. New York: Penguin, 1997.

Kinnard, Douglas. *The Certain Triumph: Maxwell Taylor and the American Experience in Vietnam*. New York: Brassey's, 1991.

Taylor, John M. *General Maxwell Taylor: The Sword and the Pen*. New York: Doubleday, 1989.

Taylor, General Maxwell D. *Responsibility and Response*. New York: Harper and Row, 1967.

Taylor, General Maxwell D. *Swords and Plowshares*. New York: Norton, 1972.

Taylor, General Maxwell D. *The Uncertain Trumpet*. New York: Harper, 1960.

Tran Van Don. *Our Endless War: Inside Vietnam*. Novato, CA: Presidio, 1978.

Young, Marilyn B. *The Vietnam Wars, 1945–1990*. New York: HarperCollins, 1991.

Zaffiri, Samuel. *Westmoreland: A Biography of General William C. Westmoreland*. New York: William Morrow, 1994.

Tet Offensive, Overall Strategy (January 30–March 31, 1968)

Decisive turning point of the Vietnam War. On July 6, 1967, the top leadership of the Democratic Republic of Vietnam (DRV, North Vietnam) gathered in Hanoi for the state funeral of Senior General Nguyen Chi Thanh, who had been the Communist military commander in the Republic of Vietnam (RVN, South Vietnam) and a member of the Vietnamese Communist Party's Politburo. After the funeral, members of the Politburo met to consider plans to bring the Vietnam War to a speedy and successful conclusion.

Militarily, the war had not been going well for the Viet Cong (VC) and the People's Army of Vietnam (PAVN, North Vietnamese Army), who were unable to compete with U.S. military firepower and mobility. Thanh had been in favor of scaling back operations in South Vietnam and conducting an even more protracted war to wear the Americans down. Defense minister General Vo Nguyen Giap apparently supported this strategy, but the North Vietnamese leadership was determined to try to end the war in one master stroke. In essence, they sought to repeat the

Heavy black smoke rises from fires in Saigon during the Tet Offensive in early 1968. The heaviest fighting in Saigon occurred in the Cholon district. (National Archives)

triumph over the French at Dien Bien Phu in 1954. The plan has been attributed to Giap, but information has surfaced that indicates that he did not take part in drafting the plan and was in fact in Eastern Europe for "medical treatment" during the time the plan was drafted and implemented. The plan borrowed from Chinese Communist doctrine and was based on the concept of the general offensive. Accompanying the general offensive, in something of a one-two punch, would be the general uprising during which the people of South Vietnam would rally to the Communist cause and overthrow the Saigon government. The general uprising was a distinctly Vietnamese element of revolutionary dogma.

The success of the plan depended on three key assumptions: the Army of the Republic of Vietnam (ARVN, South Vietnamese Army) would not fight and would in fact collapse under the impact of the General Offensive, the people of South Vietnam would follow through with the general uprising, and American will to continue would crack in the face of the overwhelming shock.

The general offensive was set for Tet 1968, the beginning of the Lunar New Year and the most important holiday in the Vietnamese year. The plans, however, were a tightly held secret, and the exact timing and objectives of the attack were withheld from field commanders until the last possible moment. The Communist military buildup and staging for the Tet Offensive were a masterpiece of deception. Beginning in the autumn of 1967, VC and PAVN forces mounted a series of bloody but seemingly pointless battles in the border regions and the northern part of South Vietnam near the demilitarized zone (DMZ).

The battles at Loc Ninh and Dak To were part of the Communist peripheral campaign, designed to draw U.S. combat units out of the urban areas and toward the borders. The operations also were designed to give Communist forces experience in larger-scale conventional attack formations. In January 1968 several PAVN divisions began to converge on the isolated U.S. Marine Corps outpost at Khe Sanh in the northern I Corps Tactical Zone, near the DMZ.

Khe Sanh was a classic deception, and the North Vietnamese depended on the Americans misreading history and seeing another Dien Bien Phu in the making, although they were not averse to taking the base there if this proved feasible. From January 21, 1968, until the point at which the countrywide attacks erupted during Tet, the attention of most of the U.S. military and the national command structure was riveted on Khe Sanh. The battle became an obsession for President Lyndon Johnson, who had a scale terrain model of the U.S. Marine Corps base built for the White House Situation Room.

Meanwhile, the Communists used the Christmas 1967 cease-fire to move their forces into position, while senior commanders gathered reconnaissance on their assigned objectives. In November 1967 troops of the 101st Airborne Division had captured a Communist document calling for the general offensive/general uprising, but U.S. intelligence analysts dismissed it as mere propaganda. Such a bold stroke seemed too fantastic, because U.S. intelligence did not believe that the Communists had the capability to attempt it.

One senior U.S. commander was not thrown off by the peripheral campaign. Lieutenant General Frederick C. Weyand, commander of U.S. II Field Force headquartered in Long Binh some 15 miles east of Saigon, did not like the pattern of increased Communist radio traffic around the capital, combined with a strangely low number of contacts made by his units in the border regions. On January 10, 1968, Weyand convinced General William Westmoreland to let him pull more U.S. combat battalions back in around Saigon. As a result, there were 27 battalions (instead of the planned 14) in the Saigon area when the attack came. Weyand's foresight would be critical for the allies.

The countrywide Communist attacks were set to commence on January 31, but the secrecy of their buildup cost them in terms of coordination. At 12:15 on the morning of January 30 Da Nang, Pleiku, Nha Trang, and nine other cities in central South Vietnam came under attack. Commanders in VC Region 5 had started 24 hours too early. This was apparently because they were following the lunar calendar in effect in South Vietnam rather than a new lunar calendar proclaimed by the North Vietnamese leadership for all of Vietnam.

As a result of this premature attack, the Tet holiday cease-fire was canceled, ARVN troops were called back to their units, and U.S. forces went on alert and moved to blocking positions in key areas. Communist forces had largely lost the element of surprise.

At 1:30 a.m. on January 31 the Presidential Palace in Saigon came under attack. By 3:40 a.m. the city of Hue was under attack, and the Tet Offensive was in full swing. Before the day was over, 5 of 6 autonomous cities, 36 of 44 provincial capitals, and 64 of 245 district capitals were under attack.

With the exception of Khe Sanh, the ancient capital of Hue, and the area around Saigon, the fighting was over in a few days. Hue was retaken on February 25, and the Cholon area of Saigon was finally cleared on March 7. By March 20, PAVN units around Khe Sanh began to melt away in the face of overwhelming American firepower.

Militarily, the Tet Offensive was a tactical disaster for the Communists. By the end of March 1968, they had not achieved a single one of their objectives. More than 58,000 VC and PAVN troops died in the offensive, with the Americans suffering 3,895 dead and the ARVN suffering 4,954 dead. Non-U.S. allies lost 214 killed. More than 14,300 South Vietnamese civilians also died.

Communist forces had achieved significant surprise both in the timing and scale of their offensive, but they were unable to exploit it; they had violated the principle of mass. By attacking everywhere, they had superior strength nowhere. Across the country the attack had been launched piecemeal and was repulsed piecemeal. The North Vietnamese leadership had also been wrong in two of its three key assumptions. The people of South Vietnam did not rally to the Communist cause, and the general uprising never took place even in Hue, where Communist forces held the city for the longest time. Nor did the ARVN fold. This required significant stiffening in certain areas, but on the whole the ARVN fought and fought well.

The biggest loser in the Tet Offensive was the VC. Although a large portion of the PAVN conducted the feint at Khe Sanh, VC guerrilla forces had led the major attacks in the south and suffered the heaviest casualties. The guerrilla infrastructure developed over so many years was wiped out. After Tet 1968, the war was run entirely by North Vietnam. The VC were never again a significant force on the battlefield. When Saigon fell in 1975, it was to four PAVN corps.

The North Vietnamese leadership had been absolutely correct in their third major assumption, however. Their primary enemy did not have the will. With one hand the United States delivered the Communists a crushing tactical defeat and then with the other hand proceeded to give them a strategic victory. Thus, the Tet Offensive is one of the most paradoxical of history's decisive battles.

The Americans and the South Vietnamese government and military had been caught by surprise by both the timing and the intensity of the Communist offensive but had still won overwhelmingly. Communist forces, and especially the VC, were badly hurt. As a follow-up, U.S. military planners immediately began to formulate plans to finish off the Communist forces in South Vietnam. Westmoreland and Joint Chiefs of Staff (JCS) chairman General Earle Wheeler were preparing to request an additional 206,000 troops to finish the job when a disgruntled staff member in the Johnson White House leaked the plan to the press. The story broke in the *New York Times* on March 10, 1968. With the fresh images of the besieged U.S. embassy in Saigon still in their minds, the press and the public immediately concluded that the extra troops were needed to recover from a massive defeat.

The Tet Offensive was the psychological turning point of the war. U.S. military historian Brigadier General S. L. A. Marshall probably summed up the Tet Offensive best: "a potential major victory turned into a disastrous defeat through mistaken estimates, loss of nerve, and a tidal wave of defeatism."

Two decades after the war while reviewing the results of the 1968 Tet Offensive in light of history, senior PAVN generals who had participated in it concluded that there had in fact been no general uprising at Tet 1968 and that rather than calling the 1968 Tet attack a "general offensive–general uprising," it could be more accurately described as a "strategic raid."

David T. Zabecki

References

Braestrup, Peter. *Big Story: How the American Press and Television Reported and Interpreted the Crisis of Tet 1968 in Vietnam and Washington.* Novato, CA: Presidio, 1994.

Currey, Cecil B. *Victory at Any Cost: The Genius of Viet Nam's General Vo Nguyen Giap.* Washington, DC: Brassey's, 1997.

Military History Institute of Vietnam. *Tap Chi Lich Su Quan Su: So Dac Biet 20 Nam Tet Mau Than* [Military History Magazine: 20th Anniversary of the 1968 Tet Offensive Special Issue], Issue 2, 1988.

Oberdorfer, Don. *TET! The Turning Point in the Vietnam War.* Baltimore: Johns Hopkins University Press, 2001.

Palmer, General Bruce, Jr. *The 25-Year War: America's Military Role in Vietnam.* Lexington: University Press of Kentucky, 1984.

Palmer, Dave R. *Summons of the Trumpet: U.S.-Vietnam in Perspective.* San Rafael, CA: Presidio, 1995.

Pribbenow, Merle L. "General Vo Nguyen Giap and the Mysterious Evolution of the

Plan for the 1968 Tet Offensive." *Journal of Vietnamese Studies* (Summer 2008): 1–33.

Summers, Harry G. *On Strategy: The Vietnam War in Context*. Carlisle Barracks, PA: U.S. Army War College, Strategic Studies Institute, 1981.

Willbanks, James H. *The Tet Offensive: A Concise History*. New York: Columbia University Press, 2007.

Young, Stephen. "How North Vietnam Won the War." Interview with former Colonel Bui Tin. *Wall Street Journal*, August 3, 1995.

Zabecki, David T. "Battle for Saigon." *Vietnam* (Summer 1989): 19–25.

U

Union of Soviet Socialist Republics

Large ethnically diverse Eurasian nation officially founded in 1922 and dissolved in 1991. A Communist nation, the Union of Soviet Socialist Republics (USSR, Soviet Union) was composed of 15 constituent or union republics (Armenia, Azerbaijan, Belorussia, Estonia, Georgia, Kazakhstan, Kirghizia, Latvia, Lithuania, Moldavia, Russia, Tadzhikstan, Turkmenistan, Ukraine, and Uzbekistan). Many of the republics became independent nations in the early 1990s. The Soviet Union's landmass of 8.65 million square miles made it about 2.5 times as large as the United States.

The successor state to the Soviet Union is now the Russian Federation, covering approximately 6.5 million square miles. The Soviet Union bordered 12 nations (6 in Europe and 6 in Asia). Its 1968 population was 128.9 million.

The Soviet Union was born out of the 1917 Bolshevik Revolution, which began during World War I. A civil war ensued that was largely settled by 1922 with the ascension of the Bolsheviks, who sought to impose a Marxist political-economic system in Russia. Almost immediately tensions arose between the new Soviet government and the democratic capitalist regimes of the West. The United States would not establish diplomatic relations with Moscow until 1933, and relations between the two countries remained aloof until 1941, when the countries formed an uneasy alliance against the Axis powers in World War II. Tensions surfaced anew toward the end of the war, and by the mid-1940s mutual distrust provided the foundation for the Cold War, which would not recede until the late 1980s.

Although the Soviet Union had incurred horrific destruction during World War II, it nevertheless emerged from the conflict as the most significant world power besides the United States, another factor in the development of the Cold War. By the mid-1950s, the Soviet Union, with its significant industrial output, large standing army well equipped with modern weapons, and a potent nuclear arsenal, posed a significant challenge to the United States and the West.

The history of relations between the Soviet Union and the Democratic Republic of Vietnam (DRV, North Vietnam) until well into the decisive 1960s has been characterized by Douglas Pike in *Vietnam and the Soviet Union* as "nominal and cursory, having neither much intercourse and emotional attachment for either party." Then during the Vietnam War and for a decade afterward until the mid-1980s, relations were very close. The Soviet Union fully supported the North Vietnamese war effort militarily, economically, and diplomatically. While Mikhail Gorbachev was in power from 1985 to 1991, however, relations between the Soviet Union and the DRV/Socialist Republic of Vietnam (SRV) steadily deteriorated until there was little discourse between the two on any front.

The Bolshevik Revolution was profoundly meaningful for Vietnamese revolutionaries, although early Bolshevik leaders had little knowledge of Southeast Asia. Ho Chi Minh attended the fifth Comintern Congress in Moscow in 1924, which denounced Western imperialism and colonialism, including French control of Indochina. He also visited Moscow frequently between 1924 and 1941. Although there existed extensive sentimental and psychological ties, there were few specific political and diplomatic connections. Ho considered the Comintern of limited usefulness.

The Joseph Stalin years (1929–1953) were ones of complete indifference on the part of the Soviet Union. Stalin regarded anticolonial activity as sometimes useful but always undependable, believing that something would invariably go wrong. Furthermore, throughout the whole period he and his government were preoccupied with internal Soviet and European problems, namely the survival of Stalin, his system, and the Soviet Union. Vietnam was hardly a concern. During World War II, Ho received no Soviet assistance in his struggle against the Japanese, and Soviet reaction to Ho's declaration of independence in August 1945 was guarded. In fact, the Soviet Union did not recognize the North Vietnamese government until January 1950, 13 days after the People's Republic of China (PRC) had done so.

Because the Soviet Union sought good relations with France, political support for the Viet Minh throughout the Indochina War (1946–1954) remained restrained. In addition, Stalin never trusted Ho, regarding him as too independent. Yet behind the scenes the Soviet Union funneled large and increasing amounts of military aid to the Viet Minh through the PRC that amounted to some $1 billion. That aid was an important factor in the Viet Minh's victory against the French. Vietnam's Communist leaders hoped that this benign neglect by the Soviet

Union would change after Stalin's death in March 1953.

After Stalin's death, the new Soviet leaders wanted to relax tensions with the West. As part of this new foreign policy, Moscow supported an international peace conference in Geneva in 1954 to settle the Indochina War. During the conference, the Soviet delegation, led by Foreign Minister Vyacheslav Molotov, forced the Viet Minh to compromise by accepting terms less favorable than its military achievements might otherwise have dictated, which may have had something to do with French rejection of the European Defense Community (EDC). Consequently, after the Geneva Conference relations were cool between the North Vietnamese government and the Soviet Union.

When Nikita Khrushchev achieved complete power by 1956, North Vietnamese leaders held great hopes. Khrushchev shifted Soviet interests from European to a global scope that included Asia. He saw potential advantages in Vietnam and in its renewed war and stepped up military and economic aid, thus deepening relations. Soviet economic aid propelled rapid economic development in North Vietnam. Yet as the war intensified, Khrushchev became more cautious. Originally his goal was to oust the West from Asia, but the increasing Sino-Soviet dispute complicated efforts. Khrushchev feared that a quick and total victory by the Communists in Vietnam would only help China and precipitate an unnecessary confrontation with the United States. By the end of his rule in 1964, Khrushchev had completely soured on Vietnam, regarding the war as too risky and the North Vietnamese leaders as crafty and manipulative. All that prevented a total Soviet disengagement was the coup that ousted Khrushchev in October 1964.

The Vietnam War was the central event in Vietnamese-Soviet relations. The conflict dictated day-to-day events and locked the two in an association. Soviet premier Aleksei Kosygin's visit to Hanoi in February 1965 initiated fuller and closer relations. Soviet and Vietnamese leaders signed economic and military treaties in which the Soviet Union pledged full support for the North Vietnamese war effort. The Soviets and the North Vietnamese leadership planned military strategy and entered into discussions to determine North Vietnam's needs to implement such a strategy. The Soviet Union would supply North Vietnam with all the necessary war matériel, including air defenses for North Vietnam and offensive weapons to be employed in the Republic of Vietnam (RVN, South Vietnam).

The Soviet Union also conducted a propaganda war against the United States in world forums, such as the United Nations (UN), and at times threatened to send Soviet and East European "volunteers" to Vietnam. The Soviet Union hoped to use the war to seek an ideological advantage over China, as the dispute between the two Communist powers became increasingly bitter. Yet it became clear that the Soviet Union would not directly intervene in the war, and its policies remained ambiguous and cautious. But as the war intensified, so did Soviet aid, until it amounted to some 80 percent of all supplies reaching North Vietnam.

After the 1968 Tet Offensive, the Soviets believed for the first time that a total victory was possible. Yet as the war continued, the Soviet spirit waned; its leaders and people became increasingly weary of the war. They believed that little more was to be gained from a war that was proving very expensive for the Soviet Union. Therefore, the Soviets fully endorsed the peace talks that began in Paris in 1968. When the talks deadlocked in 1972, the Soviet Union pressured North Vietnam to accept a compromise settlement with South Vietnam and the United States in January 1973. The success of the 1975 Communist military offensive came as a great surprise to both the North Vietnamese and the Soviet leadership, however.

The Vietnam War proved a great propaganda victory for the Soviet Union, which supported North Vietnam fully and yet avoided a confrontation with the United States. The war served Soviet interests well by keeping the United States fully occupied in an area not of crucial importance to the Soviet Union. Historians are in disagreement, however, regarding Soviet influence over North Vietnamese decision making during the war.

Economic relations between the two countries were largely a one-way street. The Soviet Union poured billions of rubles into Vietnam, but few rubles returned to the Soviet Union. A formal economic treaty was first signed in 1955 and was then renewed yearly. Economic aid consisted of food, oil, and other basic necessities; the expansion and modernization of industries and farming; services such as sending Soviet economic and military advisers to Vietnam and the sending of Vietnamese to the Soviet Union for education and training; and, of course, military aid. During the war years (1965–1975), military aid—weapons, aircraft, rockets, air defenses, munitions, food, and fuel—was central.

While the number of Soviet military advisers stationed in North Vietnam was fairly small throughout the war (only a few thousand in any given year), these advisers played a vital role in training Vietnamese personnel in the use of advanced weapons such as surface-to-air-missiles (SAMs), radar-controlled antiaircraft guns, and MiG fighters and in repairing and maintaining these sophisticated pieces of equipment. The Vietnamese have acknowledged that a

Soviet missile crew guided the first SA-2 missile to shoot down a U.S. aircraft over North Vietnam (an F-4 downed on July 24, 1965) and that Soviet artillery advisers trained the Vietnamese gun crews who fired the long-range 122-millimeter artillery pieces that pummeled the U.S. base during the 1968 siege of Khe Sanh. While the number of Soviet military personnel killed in action during the Vietnam War was small (less than two dozen), as late as August 19, 1972, a Soviet SAM expert was killed during a U.S. air attack on a Vietnamese SA-2 missile unit near Kep Airfield in North Vietnam.

Economic aid was entirely geared to the war effort. By the 1970s Soviet aid was huge and diverse, amounting to some $1 billion or more each year. It would have been impossible for North Vietnam to have continued the war without this aid. After the North Vietnamese victory in 1975, governmental ineptness led to the near collapse of the economies of both northern and southern Vietnam. The Soviet Union had to send the SRV basic food and oil supplies.

Immediately after the war ended, a more intimate relationship than ever before developed. This was in part the result of a precipitous decline in relations between China and Vietnam. Wars with China and Cambodia proved costly between 1978 and 1979 and drove Vietnam into near total dependency on the Soviet Union. In November 1979 the Soviet Union signed a friendship pact with the SRV in return for which the SRV obtained naval and air bases. Ironically, many of these were former U.S. bases in southern Vietnam. The Soviet presence was everywhere. By the mid-1980s, the relationship had become very close, to the point that Vietnam was considered a Soviet client state.

After the reform-minded Mikhail Gorbachev came to power in 1985, Soviet-Vietnamese relations steadily declined.

Gorbachev enacted major changes in Soviet foreign policy, moving away from militarily and ideologically oriented policies to those based on economics. Furthermore, he achieved a rapprochement with China. Those changes greatly reduced the value of Vietnam to the Soviet Union. In Soviet eyes, Vietnam became just another poor country that drained crucial economic resources. Vietnam, in turn, criticized Gorbachev's wide-ranging political and economic reforms. The collapse of communism in Eastern Europe in 1989 and then in the Soviet Union itself two years later profoundly shocked Vietnamese leaders.

Vietnam now faded from the attention of Russia's new leaders, who now had no ideological affinity toward the country. Economic and military aid completely stopped. Because of Russia's major economic crisis, which did not abate until after the new millennium, trade itself greatly declined and would be conducted only on a basis of full equality and in hard currency. A few Russian entrepreneurs found Vietnam an attractive place to buy cheap consumer goods to sell in Russia, but criminal behavior of some Vietnamese workers and students in Russia caused problems. The two nations continue to have an ambivalent relationship, and it appears unlikely that Moscow will rekindle the ardor of its former relationship with Hanoi. Indeed, Russia's principal strategic and economic interests seem more oriented toward Central and Western Europe and the Middle East.

Michael Share

References

Blagov, Sergei. "Missile Ambushes: Soviet Air Defense Aid." *Vietnam*, August 2001.

Donaldson, Robert, ed. *The Soviet Union and the Third World: Successes and Failures.* Boulder, CO: Westview, 1980.

Edmonds, Robin. *Soviet Foreign Policy: The Brezhnev Years*. Oxford: Oxford University Press, 1983.

Gaiduk, Ilya V. *The Soviet Union and the Vietnam War*. Chicago: Ivan R. Dee, 1996.

Longmire, R. A. *Soviet Relations with South-East Asia: An Historical Survey*. London: Kegan Paul International, 1989.

Lowe, Norman. *Mastering Twentieth-Century Russian History*. Houndsmill, UK: Palgrave, 2002.

MacKenzie, David. *From Messianism to Collapse: Soviet Foreign Policy, 1917–1991*. Fort Worth, TX: Harcourt Brace, 1994.

Missile Branch. *Lich Su Bo Doi Ten Lua Phong Khong, 1965–2005* [History of Air Defense Missile Troops, 1965–2005]. Hanoi: People's Army Publishing House, 2005.

Nguyen Khac Tinh, Tran Quang Hau, Phung Luan, and Bui Thanh Hung. *Phao Binh Nhan Dan Viet Nam: Nhung Chang Duong Chien Dau, Tap II* [People's Artillery of Vietnam: Combat History, Vol. 2]. Hanoi: Artillery Command, 1986.

Pike, Douglas. *Vietnam and the Soviet Union: Anatomy of an Alliance*. Boulder, CO: Westview, 1987.

United States Congress and the Vietnam War

The Vietnam War served as a focal point for American intervention in Southeast Asia to stem the tide of communism within the context of the Cold War. The U.S. Congress, also operating within the parameters of the Cold War, generally followed presidential initiatives in U.S. foreign affairs. However, the Vietnam War sparked an evolving nine-year-long contentious debate within Congress, particularly in the Senate, and between members of Congress and the administrations of presidents Lyndon B. Johnson, Richard M. Nixon, and Gerald R. Ford. This debate was not only marked by multiple shifts in congressional support of the war but also highlighted the tensions between congressional and presidential war-making powers.

Johnson's assumption of the presidency after President John F. Kennedy's assassination in Dallas, Texas, on November 22, 1963, prompted the new president to shore up congressional and public support for his administration. In the realm of foreign policy and national security, Johnson persuaded many of the key Vietnam policy makers in Kennedy's administration to remain on board. As a result, many of Kennedy's policies related to Vietnam remained unexamined, and the U.S. role in Vietnam continued. Johnson confirmed this stance by asserting to a joint session of Congress on November 27, 1963, that the U.S. commitment to the government and the people of the Republic of Vietnam (RVN, South Vietnam) would remain unchanged and that the war in the region had to be won.

The looming 1964 presidential election and his focus on his Great Society initiatives also encouraged Johnson to stay the course in Vietnam. Meanwhile, congressional support in 1964 continued to back Johnson's approach to the Vietnam dilemma except for the loud dissenting voice of Senator Wayne L. Morse (D-OR), who disagreed with even an advisory role in Southeast Asia. Senate Republicans and conservative Democrats fervently supported the president's efforts, as they would generally do throughout his administration. However, other congressional voices, particularly within the Senate Foreign Relations Committee, began to quietly caution Johnson of the dangers underlying U.S. policy toward Vietnam. Senator Michael (Mike) J. Mansfield (D-MT) advised the president to inform the public of the long-term risks associated with staying the course in Vietnam.

The committee's chairman, Senator J. William Fulbright (D-AR), opposed American withdrawal from Vietnam but also called for a reexamination of Cold War assumptions anchoring U.S. foreign policy. Other senators, including George S. McGovern (D-SD), expressed concerns as well but were reluctant to force the issue in light of an election year. Assistant Secretary of State Frederick Dutton's June 1964 memorandum to National Security Advisor McGeorge Bundy summarizing congressional attitudes toward Vietnam confirmed the ambiguity, warning of the Senate's cautionary support of Johnson.

Conditions worsened in Vietnam in the first half of 1964, with increasing control in South Vietnam by the Viet Cong (VC) and desertions from the Army of the Republic of Vietnam (ARVN, South Vietnamese Army). Johnson's response was to augment advisory forces and aid to South Vietnam, all with congressional approval, and to focus attention on the Democratic Republic of Vietnam (DRV, North Vietnam) itself with American naval patrols in the Gulf of Tonkin and the implementation of OPLAN 34A raids along North Vietnam's coast by South Vietnamese forces. The latter triggered a North Vietnamese attack on the U.S. Navy destroyer *Maddox* by North Vietnamese patrol boats on August 1, 1964, and another presumed attack on the *Maddox* and another destroyer, the *C. Turner Joy*, on the stormy night of August 3–4. Johnson used the occasion to retaliate with air strikes against the North Vietnamese and to push the Gulf of Tonkin Resolution through Congress on August 7, with a vote of 98 to 2 in the Senate (with Morse and Senator Ernest Gruening [D-Ala.] predictably dissenting) and a vote of 416 to 0 in the House of Representatives.

The Gulf of Tonkin Resolution focused strictly on the facts of the first and alleged second North Vietnamese attacks and granted the president the support of Congress in taking all necessary steps at the president's discretion to repel armed attacks against the United States and provide assistance, including armed support, to members of the Southeast Asia Collective Defense Treaty. The measure further provided expiration of the resolution dependent upon the president's determination of the security situation in the region as dictated by United Nations (UN) actions or via a concurrent resolution of Congress, whichever came first. Ultimately Johnson used the resolution as a carte blanche to escalate the war in Vietnam dramatically, beginning in 1965.

Although the resolution attracted nearly unanimous support, the debate in the Senate exposed concerns over U.S. involvement in a regional land war and the impact of the situation on U.S.-Soviet relations, which had been warming after passage of the 1963 Limited Test Ban Treaty, as well as the danger of Chinese intervention, which had occurred during the Korean War (1950–1953) with disastrous complications. These concerns were eerily reminiscent of congressional attitudes expressed in Dutton's June memorandum prior to the Gulf of Tonkin Incident. Election-year worries over a potential Barry M. Goldwater Republican administration and fears of an aggressive Goldwater Vietnam policy also colored the response from Democrats and stifled any open criticism of Johnson.

Johnson's decision to escalate American involvement in Vietnam after his 1964 election victory and into 1965 with continued bombing raids and additional ground troops prompted a new debate in Congress. The debate began in February 1965 with a series of speeches on Vietnam by senators, both pro and con, that appeared in Walter Lippmann's highly influential column in the *Washington Post*. These speeches and responses, reflecting yet again senatorial concerns embodied in Dutton's memorandum but also lacking an integrated alternative proposal, signaled that Johnson's Vietnam policy in Southeast Asia was rapidly becoming a major issue. Even so, subsequent to Johnson's decision in April to shift from defensive to offensive operations in the region with the insertion of counterinsurgency troops, a $700 million appropriations bill to support U.S. military needs in Vietnam for fiscal year 1966 was approved by the Senate (88 to 3) and the House (408 to 7) in May 1965. Congress, in spite of growing opposition to Johnson's policies, continued to approve appropriations throughout the Johnson administration so as to negate any public perception of an unwillingness to support the troops. At the same time, Congress was reluctant to call for a unilateral withdrawal.

In late July 1965 Mansfield sent Johnson a memorandum supported by a bipartisan group of senators, including Fulbright. Although not fully unanimous on all points, the senators offered avenues of negotiations for Vietnam, including possible roles for France and the UN. The memorandum pointedly stressed the need for détente with the Soviet Union and the relative unimportance of Vietnam to U.S. interests. Johnson's response on July 28 was to deploy the 1st Cavalry Division (Airmobile) to Vietnam and raise the monthly draft quota. The stakes were raised further in February 1966 with televised hearings of the Senate Foreign Relations Committee on Vietnam. The hearings generated heightened public interest in the war and increased the credibility of the war's congressional critics but also enraged Johnson, who continued to hold fast to his policy of supporting the South Vietnamese government. More importantly, the hearings galvanized Johnson's critics

and transformed the Senate's customary private criticism to a more aggressive approach.

Nevertheless, the lack of a focused conclusion as to what to do next in Vietnam and the variability in public opinion failed to provide congressional critics with immediate leverage to change policy. Indeed, the fiscal year 1967 supplemental authorization for Vietnam amounted to $12.2 billion, on top of the $10.3 billion in regular appropriations. The Clark-Mansfield amendment to the authorization, proposed by senators Mansfield and Joseph S. Clark (D-PA), specified a pledge by Congress of all necessary support of the troops in the field and was passed by a vote of 72 to 19 in the Senate. However, this was coupled with congressional support of the Geneva Accords of 1954 and 1962, implying support of a negotiated settlement through unification efforts, and thus signaled to the administration the notion of compromising with Congress.

The situation began to change in 1967. The coupling of increased anxiety over stresses within the U.S. economy and heightened weekly casualty rates in Southeast Asia caused problems for Democratic senators across the board and further attenuated support for the administration. Their sentiment of the situation was not improved with images of antiwar demonstrations flashing on television screens. The conservative war hawks in both parties were ineffective in rebutting the slide of support because of their own views of Vietnam as a minor issue compared to the larger and more important concerns over a breakdown in civil discipline and the expansion of liberal policies at home. Nonetheless, overall congressional concern over a Communist victory in Southeast Asia still prevailed and checked a complete fracture with the president. The fiscal year 1968 defense appropriations of $22 billion reflected this concern.

The proposed cuts of 10 percent by Morse, cushioned by leeway given to the secretary of defense for specific cuts, only garnered the support of Gruening, Fulbright, Clark, and Stephen M. Young (D-OH). A more limited version of 5 percent cuts subsequently proposed by Morse only picked up the vote of Philip A. Hart (D-MI) and failed to pass.

The television images of the Tet Offensive in January 1968, however, and subsequent Senate hearings in March on the events leading to the Gulf of Tonkin Resolution as well as a grilling of Secretary of State Dean Rusk three weeks later spurred a significant shift in support. Fulbright, the quiet persuader in previous dialogues with the president, now openly decried the costs of the war, both human and monetary, as well as the damage done to America's reputation abroad cast against a political backdrop of troubling domestic issues. Concerned with the widening gulf between the Senate and his policies, Johnson addressed the nation on television on March 31, 1968, espousing his plan to de-escalate certain military operations in Vietnam, seek negotiations for a peaceful resolution, and prevail upon the South Vietnamese government to share more of the fighting and announcing his intention not to run for a second term in the 1968 election.

As Nixon assumed the presidency and responsibility for war policy from Johnson in January 1969, the new president faced a Congress favoring disengagement in Southeast Asia but still reluctant to pave the way for a Communist victory in the region. The problem was how to accomplish both goals. Funding for the war mirrored this tension, with congressional approval of fiscal year 1969 defense appropriations amounting to $25.5 billion in regular appropriations and $1.3 billion in supplemental funds. Nevertheless, Nixon also encountered a more assertive Congress, battle-tested by its struggles with the Johnson administration. This assertiveness was exhibited in several congressional bellwether events throughout the Nixon presidency. Although 1969 witnessed expanded efforts to equip and supply the ARVN as a precursor for American disengagement, otherwise known as Vietnamization, the disclosure of Nixon's secret decision to send raids into neighboring Laos to disrupt North Vietnamese supply routes sparked Senate outrage, particularly from McGovern and Fulbright. These raids contravened the intent of a December 1969 congressional directive sponsored by senators Mansfield, Frank F. Church (D-ID), and John Sherman Cooper (R-KY), to shut the door on using American troops in Laos and Thailand.

The president's April 1970 announcement that he had sent troops into Cambodia to destroy North Vietnamese military forces in that country prompted the Senate to consider the Cooper-Church Amendment to the Foreign Military Sales Act. The amendment proposed U.S. withdrawal from Cambodia by June 30 and prohibited military funding in that country after July 1. In the context of violent antiwar protests in May, a watered-down version was finally passed on June 30 after a vote of 58 to 37 in the Senate.

However, troop withdrawals the same day in accordance with Nixon's planned timetable, along with tabling of the amendment in the House by a vote of 237 to 153, essentially rendered the impact of the amendment moot. The passed amendment was followed by a bipartisan amendment proposed by McGovern and Senator Mark O. Hatfield (R-OR) to halt all funds for the war after December 1970 and withdraw all troops by June 30, 1971. The amendment suffered defeat by a vote of 55 to 39 in the Senate. Even if the amendment had passed, a more prowar House and a Nixon veto would have defeated it. However, the antiwar lobby in the Senate was encouraged by a substantial one-third support.

McGovern and Hatfield were reinvigorated the following year, with polls indicating the president's approval rating on Vietnam hovering near 31 percent and the public's desire for a timetable for final troop withdrawals reaching 72 percent, despite Nixon's existing gradual but small troop withdrawals. The polls reflected a tumultuous spring of 1971 in the halls of Congress. Spurred by the public revealing of the My Lai Massacre, Ron V. Dellums, a Socialist Party representative from northern California's 9th District, created an exhibit of images detailing alleged American war crimes in Vietnam and subsequently called for formal congressional hearings on the subject. The House refused, but Dellums pursued informal hearings of his own in April 1971. The hearings attracted considerable media scrutiny, although much of the evidence and testimony proved sketchy. In the Senate, Fulbright presided over 22 Foreign Relations Committee hearing sessions in April and May to debate legislative proposals for an end to the war.

John F. Kerry, a young Vietnam War veteran and national coordinator of the Vietnam Veterans Against the War, testified before the committee and included accounts rendered by fellow war veterans of war crimes and atrocities committed by both American and enemy troops. McGovern and Hatfield followed the hearings in June with their proposed new amendment to the Military Selective Service Act of 1967, prohibiting funding of U.S. military operations in Indochina after December 31, 1972. With a vote of 55 to 42, the amendment gained only 3 additional votes from the previous year's similar amendment. McGovern

and Hatfield's amendment was accompanied by a House rejection vote of 255 to 158 on an amendment proposed by representatives Lucien N. Nedzi (D-MI) and Charles W. Whalen Jr. (R-OH) to forbid military appropriations in Southeast Asia after the end of the 1971 calendar year.

The reluctance of the Senate to tip the balance to fully seize the reins of its constitutional war policy powers vis-à-vis the president was reinforced in 1972 by Henry A. Kissinger's secret talks with the North Vietnamese and Nixon's visits to China and the Soviet Union that same year. Nixon's autumn 1972 election victory and his January 1973 announcement of an armistice agreement among the combatants in South Vietnam again temporarily checked his critics. However, revelations of the administration's secret bombing campaign in Cambodia (Operation MENU) against People's Army of Vietnam (PAVN, North Vietnamese Army) base areas there and the North Vietnamese–backed Khmer Rouge, occurring amid the throes of the Watergate Scandal and domestic jitters over rising oil prices, weakened the president and finally tipped the balance. Congress swiftly responded by forcing Nixon to end the bombing by August 15, 1973, and prohibited funding of combat operations in the region through supplemental appropriation acts enacted on July 1. Adoption of these restricted funding acts by a vote of 72 to 14 in the Senate and 278 to 124 in the House on one act and a vote of 73 to 16 in the Senate and 266 to 75 in the House on the other act showed how far the pendulum had swung.

Furthermore, Congress passed the War Powers Act on November 7, 1973, checking presidential war-making powers, although the act tellingly failed to apply it to the now-dwindling American military presence in Vietnam. Congress also took a more effective and immediate step beyond its previous restricted funding acts by assuming control of military funding through passage of a veto-busting $21.3 billion defense appropriations bill in the autumn of 1973 with a key provision requiring congressional approval prior to U.S. military assistance extended in Southeast Asia. The measure resoundingly passed with voice votes in both houses.

President Ford, Nixon's successor after his August 1974 resignation as a consequence of the Watergate Scandal, now had to deal with a Congress willing to flex its muscle. For fiscal year 1975, Nixon had requested $1.45 billion in aid to South Vietnam. Congress authorized less than half that ($700 million) for the South Vietnamese government as long as it existed as an entity. Ford subsequently requested a supplemental authorization of $300 million in January 1975 and an additional aid package of $700 million in April, for a total of $1.7 billion for the fiscal year to prop up the tottering South Vietnamese government. Congress rejected both supplemental requests outright. More than $145 billion had been poured into Southeast Asia since the beginning of American involvement in the 1950s, and Congress was finally weary of tossing more money into the morass. The fall of Saigon at the end of April 1975 stopped the authorized $700 million in aid to the South Vietnamese government and effectively ended America's involvement there. After the war ended, Congress seemed far more attuned to presidential uses of military power abroad, and presidents in turn seemed more cognizant of congressional powers vis-à-vis armed conflict.

Mark F. Leep

References

Belasco, Amy, Lynn J. Cunningham, Hannah Fischer, and Larry A. Niksch. *Congressional Restrictions on U.S. Military Operations in Vietnam, Cambodia, Laos, Somalia, and Kosovo: Funding and Non-Funding Approaches*. Washington, DC: Congressional Research Service, January 16, 2007.

Daggett, Stephen. *Military Operations: Precedents for Funding Contingency Operations in Regular or in Supplemental Appropriations Bills*. Washington, DC: Congressional Research Service, June 13, 2006.

Karnow, Stanley. *Vietnam: A History*. 2nd rev. and updated ed. New York: Penguin, 1997.

Mann, Robert. *A Grand Delusion: America's Descent into Vietnam*. New York: Basic Books, 2001.

Stone, Gary. *Elites for Peace: The Senate and the Vietnam War, 1964–1968*. Knoxville: University of Tennessee Press, 2007.

V

Vann, John Paul (1924–1972)

U.S. Army officer and critic of military strategy; U.S. Agency for International Development (USAID) official. John Paul Vann was born on July 2, 1924, in Norfolk, Virginia. He was drafted into the army in 1943 during World War II and trained as a navigator. Vann remained in the service after the war, and when the Army Air Forces became an independent service in 1947 as the U.S. Air Force, Vann transferred to the U.S. Army. After fighting in Korea, he received a degree from Rutgers University in 1955, graduated from the U.S. Army Command and General Staff College in 1958, and earned an MBA from Syracuse University in 1959. He was promoted to lieutenant colonel in 1961.

Vann served his first tour of duty in Vietnam during March 1962–April 1963. Part of his duties included advising an Army of the Republic of Vietnam (ARVN, South Vietnamese Army) infantry division in the Mekong Delta. What he saw in Vietnam dismayed him, particularly in the Battle of Ap Bac (January 1962). Despite what President John F. Kennedy was being told by his military advisers, Vann believed that the war was being lost but that it could be won if the right tactics and military might were applied. When his reports were ignored, he leaked information to journalists covering the fighting in Vietnam. He was then reassigned to the Pentagon, where his words still fell on deaf ears.

After 20 years in the army, Vann retired on July 31, 1963, and began to speak out publicly on the war. He returned to Vietnam in March 1965 as a civilian working for USAID. He was so successful that in 1966 he was made chief of the civilian pacification program for the provinces surrounding Saigon. In 1967 he denounced General William Westmoreland's strategy and warned that the Communists were still a threat; the Tet Offensive of 1968 seemed to support Vann's point of view. Because Vann's critique was aimed at trying to improve the war effort, he was promoted in May 1971 to senior adviser for the Central Highlands and, as a civilian, was given command over U.S. military forces and the civilians in the pacification program. As the senior adviser, Vann had significant influence on the operations of the ARVN units in the area. His position was equivalent to that of a U.S. Army major general, but he was still a civilian. In effect, he was the third most powerful American in Vietnam. After successfully directing the defense against a People's Army of Vietnam (PAVN, North Vietnamese Army) offensive, Vann died in a helicopter crash in the Central Highlands on July 9, 1972.

Vann was a complex and compelling figure. Dedicated to winning the war, he nonetheless openly criticized the American strategy. He condemned indiscriminate bombing of the countryside as cruel and morally wrong. Vann believed America to be the greatest power on earth, a position that it was destined to hold forever and that it should use to bring peace and prosperity to the world. There was much wrong about

John Paul Vann, head of Civil Operations and Rural Development Support (CORDS) in III Corps Tactical Zone, during a tour of Leloi hamlet in March 1968. He would direct all U.S. forces in II Corps during the 1972 NVA Easter Offensive. (Time & Life Pictures/Getty Images)

the war in Vietnam but not the war itself, and he could not accept an American defeat. Indeed, he seemed to embody the American dilemma in Vietnam. Vann was posthumously awarded the Presidential Medal of Freedom. He was also the only civilian to receive the Distinguished Service Cross during the Vietnam War.

Laura Matysek Wood

References

Hunt, Richard A. *Pacification: The American Struggle for Vietnam's Hearts and Minds.* Boulder, CO: Westview, 1995.

McKenna, Thomas P. *Kontum: The Battle to Save South Vietnam.* Lexington: University Press of Kentucky, 2011.

Sheehan, Neil. *A Bright Shining Lie: John Paul Vann and America in Vietnam.* New York: Random House, 1988.

Vo Nguyen Giap (1911–)

Vietnamese leader of the military struggles from 1944 to 1980 against Japan, France, the United States, Cambodia, and China. Vo Nguyen Giap was born on August 25, 1911, to a townswoman, Nguyen Thi Kien, and her husband, Vo Quang Nghiem, in the tiny village of An Xa along the banks of the Kien Giang River, a subdistrict of Quang Ninh, Le Thuy District, in Quang Binh Province in central Annam just north of the 17th Parallel. Giap was the sixth of eight children, the first three having died in infancy.

Giap completed his primary education in local schools and in 1925 moved to Hue to study at the Quoc Hoc, or Lycée Nationale. Regarded by school authorities as an agitator, he was expelled in 1927 and worked

General Vo Nguyen Giap was the military commander of the Viet Minh against the French during the Indochina War. He also commanded the People's Army of Vietnam (North Vietnamese army) against the Americans during the Vietnam War. (Getty Images)

for a time as a journalist. He also joined the Tan Viet Cach Menh Dang (Revolutionary Party for a New Vietnam), which soon split into two factions. Giap allied himself with the Communist wing and thereafter lived a double life as a journalist and a secret revolutionary.

Giap was caught in a police dragnet at the end of 1930 and was sentenced to serve two years at hard labor at Lao Bao, a French prison in the mountains near Laos. There he met his future wife, 15-year-old Nguyen Thi Quang Thai, daughter of a railroad employee in Vinh. Given an early release, Giap moved to Vinh and stayed at the

home of Professor Dang Thai Mai, a former teacher of literature at the Quoc Hoc. There Giap met Mai's daughter, Dang Bich Ha, then a toddler (she was born in 1929), who called him *chu* ("uncle") and would one day became his second wife.

After moving to Hanoi, Giap studied at the Lycée Albert Sarraut, graduating in 1934. Thereupon he accepted a job as teacher of history and French at Lycée Thang Long (Rising Dragon). He simultaneously published a newspaper, *Hon Tre Tap Moi* (Soul of Youth, New Edition), which was shut down by authorities after its fifth issue. Thereupon Giap published *Le Travail* (Work) and initiated at least 11 other short-lived journals. He also began studies at the School of Law of the University of Hanoi, and in 1938 he received his *license en droit* with a concentration in political economy.

Giap joined the Communist Party in 1937 and sometime before April 1939 married Quang Thai. In early 1940 they had a daughter, Hong Anh ("Red Queen of Flowers"). In April 1940 the party ordered him to flee into southern China. He left behind his wife and daughter, never again to see Quang Thai, who was arrested by the French in May 1941 and tortured to death in Hoa Lo ("The Oven") Prison in Hanoi.

Traveling with Pham Van Dong, Giap reached southern China and there met Nguyen Ai Quoc, now calling himself Ho Chi Minh. Under Ho's orders, Giap returned to the mountains of northern Tonkin between 1941 and 1945 and, with his cadre, worked among the hill tribes (Nung, Tho, Man Trang, Man Tien, Tay [Tai], Dao, Hmong, and others), converting them to the anti-French cause. One of his followers, Chu Van Tan, became a leader in the first armed resistance organization, the Army for National Salvation. Meanwhile, Ho organized a new group, the Viet Nam Doc Lap Dong Minh

Hoi (Vietnam Independence League), or Viet Minh. Its rivals for power included the Dang Dai Viet, a nationalist middle-class urban group; the Viet Nam Quoc Dan Dang, an older group founded in 1927 by radical intellectuals; and the Viet Nam Cach Menh Dong Minh Hoi, founded in 1942 under Chinese sponsorship.

Giap's Viet Minh cadres were most successful in enlisting support among both lowland Vietnamese and hill people. He insisted on such a rigid code of conduct for his agents that tribal women began calling them "men without cocks." French efforts between 1942 and 1944 to destroy this fledgling movement came to be called the time of the "white terror."

On December 22, 1944, Giap formed 34 men into the Viet Nam Tuyen Truyen Giai Phong Quan (Vietnam Armed Propaganda Liberation Brigade). The first attacks against the French came on December 24 when Giap's unit struck outposts at Phai Khat and Na Ngan. During a later attack on the town of Thai Nguyen on August 20, 1945, Giap learned that the Japanese had surrendered, and he marched his men into Hanoi. Between August 19 and 30 Ho's Viet Minh grabbed power from the Red River to the Mekong Delta. Giap became minister of the interior of the new Democratic Republic of Vietnam (DRV, North Vietnam) and was later named to the rank of full general and commander of all Viet Minh military forces. Widely recognized as a master logistician, Giap also became adept at tactics and strategy. He drew his understanding of military science from many sources, including patriotic inspiration from his own country's past heroes such as Trung Trac and Trung Nhi, Ly Bon and Ngo Quyen, and Tran Hung Dao and Nguyen Hue. Giap also learned from the writings of Sun Tzu, Mao Zedong, Ho Chi Minh, and Vladimir Lenin. Giap knew of

Napoleon's campaigns and assiduously studied the writings of T. E. Lawrence. From all of these as well as his own field experiences, Giap welded together an approach to combat that confounded his enemies.

Military incidents with the French in Tonkin, particularly at Haiphong, caused Giap to issue a national call to arms on December 19, 1946. Retreating in the face of French strength, by early 1947 the Viet Minh government and Giap's army were once again hiding in the remote fastnesses of North Vietnam. During the next years, Giap put together an army of nearly 300,000 troops and militia and made a series of attacks against French troops and positions, sometimes sustaining horrific casualties. In 1953 he launched a drive into Laos, having already gained control of most of central and North Vietnam outside the coastal lowlands. French military commander General Henri Navarre, seeking a set-piece battle with Giap's forces, chose to commit 10,000 troops to an isolated valley in northwestern Vietnam astride Giap's line of communication to Laos at Dien Bien Phu.

Giap secretly brought recently obtained artillery into the surrounding mountains, a development that the French considered impossible. He also massed 50,000 troops and laid siege for 55 days to French strong points in the valley. The French surrendered on May 8, 1954, and then at Geneva gave up further efforts to control Vietnam north of the 17th Parallel.

Giap also led the military campaign against the Republic of Vietnam (RVN, South Vietnam) and the United States during the 1960s and 1970s. Giap, like Mao, believed that revolutionary warfare against a government passed through three stages: guerrilla warfare, strategic defense, and counteroffensive. Giap was long concerned that the United States might invade North Vietnam and, when he believed his forces strong enough, frequently orchestrated frontal attacks on U.S. positions, as in the Ia Drang Valley (November 1965), at Khe Sanh (January 1968), and in the Tet Offensive (January 1968). Militarily opposed to the latter, he bowed before the greater political influence of Le Duan, General Nguyen Chi Thanh, and their allies in the Politburo. These individuals, all dedicated to the overthrow of the South Vietnamese government, faulted Giap for his reticence to use his units boldly below the 17th Parallel and consistently called for increased military action in South Vietnam.

The Tet Offensive destroyed the Viet Cong (VC) and forced the People's Army of Vietnam (PAVN, North Vietnamese Army) troops to carry the burden of the war. Still, Tet was a strategic victory for the Communists even though it was a tactical defeat. Following Ho's death (September 2, 1969), Giap shared power with Le Duan, who controlled domestic affairs, and Pham Van Dong, who presided over the Foreign Ministry. Giap's goals were to prolong the war, to inflict setbacks to U.S. president Richard Nixon's policy of Vietnamization, and to impose continuing casualties on U.S. troops. Not until 1970 did Giap order new offensives, concentrating on the conquest of southern Laos and destabilization of Cambodia's border region.

In 1972, with some dismay because he believed that the time was not yet ripe, Giap planned his Easter Offensive. The Politburo had called for the offensive, assuming that with U.S. forces all but withdrawn, South Vietnam was ripe for attack. Once again Giap's misgivings were proven correct. Throughout most of South Vietnam, after initial withdrawals, the Army of the Republic of Vietnam (ARVN, South Vietnamese Army) held its positions when buttressed with massive American air strikes. Nixon also ordered extensive bombings of North Vietnam and the mining of Haiphong

Harbor. The PAVN suffered more than 100,000 casualties. Still, when it was over Giap's divisions occupied territory never before controlled, and the terms of the January 1973 peace agreement did not require their removal.

Ironically, although he retained his post of minister of defense, the Politburo then stripped Giap—who had opposed the entire offensive—of his command of the PAVN and gave it to his chief of staff and longtime disciple, General Van Tien Dung. It was Dung who led the Ho Chi Minh Campaign, the final assault on South Vietnam in 1975.

Thereafter Giap's life consisted of a round of visits to countries, most of which were Communist: Cuba, Algeria, the Soviet Union, East Germany, Hungary, Poland, China, Yemen, Madagascar, Mozambique, Ethiopia, Guinea, Benin, Congo, and Angola. Appointed to head the Ministry of Science and Technology, Giap opposed the 1978 Vietnamese invasion of Cambodia and played only a supervisory role in it and in the conflict with China that began in 1979. In 1977 Giap retired as minister of defense, lost his position in the party Politburo in 1982, and in August 1991 was forced to give up his remaining post as vice premier in charge of family planning. Now viewed as a "national treasure," Giap has lived quietly at his villa, appearing on ceremonial occasions but closely watched by his government, which feared that he might lead a military coup against it.

Cecil B. Currey

References

Currey, Cecil B. *Victory at Any Cost: The Genius of Viet Nam's General Vo Nguyen Giap*. Washington, DC: Brassey's, 1997.

Davidson, Phillip A. *Vietnam at War: The History, 1946–1975*. Novato, CA: Presidio, 1988.

Turley, Gerald H. *The Easter Offensive: The Last American Advisors, Vietnam, 1972*. Novato, CA: Presidio, 1985.

Van Tien Dung. *Our Great Spring Victory*. New York: Monthly Review Press, 1977.

Vo Nguyen Giap. *Dien Bien Phu*. 5th ed., rev. and supplemented. Hanoi: Gioi Publishers, 1994.

Vo Nguyen Giap. *Unforgettable Days*. Hanoi: Foreign Languages Publishing House, 1978.

Who's Who in the Socialist Countries. New York: Saur, 1978.

Westmoreland, William Childs (1914–2005)

U.S. Army general and commander of American forces in Vietnam from June 1964 to June 1968. William Childs Westmoreland was born in rural Spartanburg County, South Carolina, on March 26, 1914. Military service was traditional on both sides of young Westmoreland's family. His father, a textile plant manager, had attended the Citadel, and Westmoreland did so for one year before entering the U.S. Military Academy, West Point, in 1932, where he became cadet first captain.

Commissioned a lieutenant of field artillery in 1936, Westmoreland served in various posts in the United States. In 1942 he became a major and commanded an artillery battalion in Tunisia and Sicily, distinguishing himself in the February 1943 Battle of Kasserine Pass. He then served with the 9th Infantry Division in France, where he was promoted to colonel and became division chief of staff. He fought with the division in Germany and after the war commanded a regiment in occupation duties. In 1946, after completing parachute training, he commanded the 504th Parachute Infantry Regiment. From 1947 to 1950, Westmoreland was chief of staff of the 82nd Airborne Division. He then taught at the Army Command and Staff School and the Army War College.

In August 1952 Westmoreland assumed command of the 187th Airborne Regimental Combat Team in Korea, and that November he was promoted to brigadier general. For the next several years he served on the General Staff and was promoted to major general in 1956, after which he commanded the 101st Airborne Division at Fort Campbell, Kentucky. From 1960 to 1963, he served as superintendent at West Point. Promoted to lieutenant general in 1963, Westmoreland returned to Fort Campbell to command the XVIII Airborne Corps. He was then ordered to Vietnam as deputy commander, U.S. Military Assistance Command, Vietnam (MACV).

Westmoreland arrived in Vietnam on January 27, 1964, and in June was named to succeed General Paul D. Harkins as commander of MACV. Westmoreland judged the South Vietnamese to lack a "sense of urgency." His own approach to command in Vietnam was to be one of action, not of contemplation. Secretary of Defense Robert McNamara noted in his memoirs that "Westy possessed neither Patton's boastful flamboyance nor LeMay's stubbornness but shared their determination and patriotism." In August 1964 Westmoreland was promoted to full general; it was now Westmoreland's war.

One characteristic that President Lyndon B. Johnson looked for in his new commander in Vietnam was mental agility and flexibility to adapt to unforeseen events. Few would disagree that Westmoreland brought abundant energy and impeccable standards to his command, but some have criticized his choice of tactics and timing.

The military strategy of search and destroy seemingly was consistent with the political character of limited war in Vietnam, where

Gen. William C. Westmoreland speaks at a news conference in 1967. As commander of U.S. Military Assistance Command, Vietnam between 1964 and 1968, he was instrumental in planning and executing American strategy during the Vietnam War. Tremendous damage was inflicted on Communist forces, but the general, like the United States as a whole, underestimated North Vietnamese resolve to win at any cost. (AP/Wide World Photos)

the United States and the Republic of Vietnam (RVN, South Vietnam) were partners in contesting a Communist insurgency that threatened the viability of the South Vietnamese government. Search-and-destroy operations were designed to deny to the Viet Cong (VC) and the People's Army of Vietnam (PAVN, North Vietnamese Army) the cover and concealment of their jungle bases and to bring their military units to battle. Allied units would enter jungle sanctuaries, search methodically during the day, and occupy strong night-defensive positions, daring the Communists to attack. MACV's approach depended on superior intelligence data and sufficient airmobile combat units to reach the decisive location in time to exploit the opportunity. Search-and-destroy operations were predicated on the assumption that combat in Vietnam had moved from insurgency/guerrilla actions to larger-unit actions.

General Bruce Palmer Jr., who served as commander of II Field Force, Vietnam, and later of U.S. Army, Vietnam, concludes in his book *The 25-Year War* that the chosen American style of war "was tough, risky business, for our troops, moving into and searching a hostile area, being exposed to enemy ambush, mines, and booby traps." Moreover, he points out, this approach surrendered the initiative to the Communists, forcing the allies "to react and dance to the enemy's tune." Both Palmer and Andrew F. Krepinevich Jr. have written that MACV's assumption that large-unit warfare had supplanted the Communists' small-unit guerrilla-style hit-and-run tactics after 1965 was invalid. In 1967 Westmoreland believed that the initiative had firmly switched to the allies, noting that the VC and the PAVN had lost control over large areas and populations.

It may be that the flaw in the U.S. phase (1965–1973) of the war in Vietnam was a poorly conceived grand strategy. Neil Sheehan in *A Bright Shining Lie* says that in prosecuting a war of attrition, "The building of the killing machine had become an end in itself." Grand strategy—the sum of political, economic, military, and other component strategies—is designed to accomplish the purpose of the war. In the most striking way, the chosen military strategy of attrition did not lead directly and resolutely to the political end of the conflict. It is not surprising that General Westmoreland and the MACV staff sought a strategic solution to the growing VC/PAVN capability through the application of U.S. technology and firepower. What is surprising is that they believed that an American-style quick fix could win a protracted war. In many ways, the "other war"—pacification—was the more important stepping stone to an allied victory. American strategists discovered too late that carrying the war to the Communists at the same time as they were attempting to strengthen the South Vietnamese toward national self-sufficiency was like pulling on both ends of a rope simultaneously.

VC/PAVN forces were fighting the Americans and their allies like a seasoned boxer, willing to go the distance by slipping punches when possible and absorbing them with minimum damage when necessary. But through it all the Communists had their eyes on the objective: to frustrate and damage the Americans' will to continue the war. General Westmoreland's warriors had four years in the ring with General Vo Nguyen Giap's unsophisticated but numerous and dedicated troops. Instead of being weakened by attrition, the VC/PAVN seemed to gain in strength and audacity until they suffered enormous losses in their 1968 Tet Offensive.

Explaining that American intelligence had forecast a VC attack, General Westmoreland said that "I made a mistake; I should have called a press conference and made known to the world that we knew this attack was coming." It was clear that after the Tet Offensive the U.S. government, reflecting the impatience and confusion of the American people, began withdrawing the essential moral support and then the resources necessary for victory. It was not entirely Westmoreland's fault, only his misfortune to be the responsible official on the ground in Vietnam. In that regard Harry Summers is probably right that it is unfair to compare General Westmoreland with General Giap because the PAVN commander enjoyed a unity of command that in the American system of war fighting was distributed among many civilian and military authorities.

In July 1968 President Johnson recalled Westmoreland from Vietnam and appointed him U.S. Army chief of staff. As his former deputy, General Creighton Abrams, carried on with the gradual handing-off of the war to the unready and sometimes unwilling South Vietnamese, Westmoreland set his professional skills to work on issues such as the all-volunteer force. In July 1972 Westmoreland retired from the army after more than 36 years of service. In 1976 he published his memoirs, *A Soldier Reports*.

In January 1982 the Columbia Broadcasting System (CBS) and its journalist Mike Wallace aired a television documentary that accused General Westmoreland and his staff of fudging Communist casualty figures to give the appearance of progress and eventual success in Vietnam. As the general put it in his December 1994 interview, "They accused me of basically lying. . . . If there is anything that I cherish, it's character." Westmoreland brought a libel suit against CBS that resulted in a two-and-a-half-month trial and ended with an out-of-court settlement on February 18, 1985. CBS stood by its documentary but issued a statement that it did not mean to impugn General Westmoreland's patriotism or loyalty "in performing his duties as he saw them." Following his retirement, Westmoreland made a brief but unsuccessful foray into politics in search of the Republican nomination for governor of South Carolina. He was a frequent speaker at patriotic events. Westmoreland died on July 18, 2005, in Charleston, South Carolina.

John F. Votaw

References

Furgurson, Ernest B. *Westmoreland: The Inevitable General*. Boston: Little, Brown, 1968.

Herring, George C. "Westmoreland, William Childs." In *Dictionary of American Military Biography*, Vol. 3, edited by Roger Spiller, 1179–1183. Westport, CT: Greenwood, 1984.

Sheehan, Neil. *A Bright Shining Lie: John Paul Vann and America in Vietnam*. New York: Random House, 1988.

Sorley, Lewis. *Westmoreland: The General Who Lost Vietnam*. New York: Houghton Mifflin Harcourt, 2011.

Westmoreland, William C. *A Soldier Reports*. New York: Doubleday, 1976.

Westmoreland, William C. "Vietnam in Perspective." In *Vietnam: Four American Perspectives*, edited by Patrick J. Hearden, 39–57. West Lafayette, IN: Purdue University Press, 1990.

Zaffiri, Samuel. *Westmoreland: A Biography of General William C. Westmoreland*. New York: William Morrow, 1994.

Vietnamese Declaration of Independence (September 2, 1945)

In March 1945 the Japanese arrested French officials and the vast bulk of the French military throughout Indochina. Thus, on August 14, when Japan surrendered unconditionally to the Allies, there was a vacuum in Vietnam into which Nationalist leader Ho Chi Minh and his Viet Minh Nationalist/Communist organization now moved. On August 16 in Hanoi, Ho declared himself president of the provisional government of a "free Vietnam," and three days later the Viet Minh seized power in Hanoi. Emperor Bao Dai abdicated on August 25, and on September 2 in Hanoi, Ho publicly announced the formation of a "Provisional Government of the Democratic Republic of Vietnam" with its capital at Hanoi. Then, in a clear bid to widen his base at home and win Western support abroad, on November 11 Ho dissolved the Indochinese Communist Party (ICP).

"All men are created equal. They are endowed by their Creator with certain inalienable rights; among these are Life, Liberty, and the pursuit of Happiness."

This immortal statement was made in the Declaration of Independence of the United States of America in 1776. In a broader sense, this means: All the peoples on the earth are equal from birth, all the peoples have a right to live, to be happy and free.

The Declaration of the French Revolution made in 1791 on the Rights of Man and the Citizen also states: "All men are born free and with equal rights, and must always remain free and have equal rights."

Those are undeniable truths.

Nevertheless, for more than eighty years, the French imperialists, abusing the standard of Liberty, Equality, and Fraternity, have violated our Fatherland and oppressed our fellow-citizens. They have acted contrary to the ideals of humanity and justice.

In the field of politics, they have deprived our people of every democratic liberty.

They have enforced inhuman laws; they have set up three distinct political regimes in the North, the Center and the South of Vietnam in order to wreck our national unity and prevent our people from being united.

They have built more prisons than schools. They have mercilessly slain our patriots, they have drowned our uprisings in rivers of blood.

They have fettered public opinion, they have practiced obscurantism against our people.

To weaken our race they have forced us to use opium and alcohol.

In the field of economics, they have fleeced us to the backbone, impoverished our people, and devastated our land.

They have robbed us of our rice fields, our mines, our forests, and our raw materials. They have monopolized the issuing of bank-notes and the export trade.

They have invented numerous unjustifiable taxes and reduced our people, especially our peasantry, to a state of extreme poverty.

They have hampered the prospering of our national bourgeoisie; they have mercilessly exploited our workers.

In the autumn of 1940, when the Japanese Fascists violated Indochina's territory to establish new bases in their fight against the Allies, the French imperialists went down on their bended knees and handed over our country to them.

Thus, from that date, our people were subjected to the double yoke of the French and the Japanese. Their sufferings and miseries increased. The result was that from the end of last year to the beginning of this year, from Quang Tri Province to the North of Vietnam, more than two million of our fellow-citizens died from starvation. On March 9, the French troops were disarmed by the Japanese. The French colonialists either fled or surrendered showing that not only were they incapable of "protecting" us, but that, in the span of five years, they had twice sold our country to the Japanese.

On several occasions before March 9, the Viet Minh League urged the French to ally themselves with it against the Japanese. Instead of agreeing to this proposal, the French colonialists so intensified their terrorist activities against the Viet Minh members that before fleeing they massacred a great number of our political prisoners detained at Yen Bay and Cao Bang.

Notwithstanding all this, our fellow citizens have always manifested toward the French a tolerant and humane attitude. Even after the Japanese Putsch of March, 1945, the Viet Minh League helped many Frenchmen to cross the frontier, rescued some of them from Japanese jails, and protected French lives and property.

From the autumn of 1940, our country had in fact ceased to be a French colony and had become a Japanese possession.

After the Japanese had surrendered to the Allies, our whole people rose to regain our national sovereignty and to found the Democratic Republic of Viet-Nam.

The truth is that we have wrested our independence from the Japanese and not from the French.

The French have fled, the Japanese have capitulated, Emperor Bao Dai has abdicated. Our people have broken the chains which for nearly a century have fettered them and have independence for the Fatherland. Our people at the same time have overthrown the monarchic regime that has reigned supreme for dozens of centuries. In its place has been established the present Democratic Republic.

For these reasons, we, members of the Provisional Government, representing the whole Vietnamese people, declare that from now on we break off all relations of a colonial character with France; we repeal all the international obligation that France has so far subscribed to on behalf of Viet-Nam, and we abolish all the special rights the French have unlawfully acquired in our Fatherland.

The whole Vietnamese people, animated by a common purpose, are determined to fight to the bitter end against any attempt by the French colonialists to reconquer their country.

We are convinced that the Allied nations, which at Teheran and San Francisco have acknowledged the principles of self-determination and equality of nations, will not refuse to acknowledge the independence of Viet-Nam.

A people who have courageously opposed French domination for more than eighty years, a people who have fought side by side with the Allies against the fascists during these last years, such a people must be free and independent.

For these reasons, we, members of the Provisional Government of the Democratic Republic of Viet-Nam, solemnly declare to the world that Viet-Nam has the right to be a free and independent country—and in fact it is so already. The entire Vietnamese people are determined to mobilize all their physical and mental strength, to sacrifice their lives and property in order to safeguard their independence and liberty.

Source: Ho Chi Minh, *Selected Works*, Vol. 3 (Hanoi: Foreign Languages Publishing House, 1960–62), 17–21.

Final Declaration of the Geneva Conference on Indochina (July 21, 1954)

This final agreement of the Geneva Conference (May 8–July 21, 1954) regarding Indochina declared Cambodia, Laos, and Vietnam to be independent states. Cambodia and Laos would hold elections in 1955. Vietnam, while recognized as one state, was temporarily divided at the 17th Parallel, with the Democratic Republic of Vietnam (DRV, North Vietnam) to control north of that line and the State of Vietnam (SVN) south of it. Internationally supervised elections to unite the two were fixed for July 1956. During the 300-day period it would take for all North Vietnamese armed forces to leave southern Vietnam and for all French Union forces to leave North Vietnam, civilians could also move from one zone to the other if they so chose.

1. The Conference takes note of the agreements ending hostilities in Cambodia, Laos, and Vietnam and organizing international control and the supervision of the execution of the provisions of these agreements.

2. The Conference expresses satisfaction at the end of hostilities in Cambodia, Laos, and Vietnam; the Conference expresses its conviction that the execution of the provisions set out in the present declaration and in the agreements of the cessation of hostilities will permit Cambodia, Laos, and Vietnam henceforth to play their part, in full independence and sovereignty, in the peaceful community of nations.

3. The Conference takes note of the declarations made by the Governments of Cambodia and Laos of their intention to adopt measures permitting all citizens to take their place in the national community, in particular by participating in the next general elections, which, in conformity with the constitution of each of these countries, shall take place in the course of the year 1955, by secret ballot and in conditions of respect for fundamental freedoms.

4. The Conference takes note of the clauses in the agreement on the cessation of hostilities in Vietnam prohibiting the introduction into Vietnam of foreign troops and military personnel as well as of all kinds of arms and munitions. The Conference also takes note of the declarations made by the Governments of Cambodia and Laos of their resolution not to request foreign aid, whether in war material, in personnel, or in instructors except for the purpose of the effective defense of their territory and, in the case of Laos, to the extent defined by the agreements of the cessation of hostilities in Laos.

5. The Conference takes note of the clauses in the agreement on the cessation of hostilities in Vietnam to the effect that no military base under the control of a foreign State may be established in the regrouping zones of the two parties, the latter having the obligation to see that the zones allotted to them shall not constitute part of any military alliance and shall not be utilized for the resumption of hostilities or in the service of an aggressive policy. The Conference also takes note of the declarations of the Governments of Cambodia and Laos to the effect that they will not join in any

agreement with other States if this agreement includes the obligation to participate in a military alliance not in conformity with the principles of the Charter of the United Nations or, in the case of Laos, with the principles of the agreement on the cessation of hostilities in Laos or, so long as their security is not threatened, the obligation to establish bases on Cambodian or Laotian territory for the military forces of foreign powers.

6. The Conference recognizes that the essential purpose of the agreement relating to Vietnam is to settle military questions with a view to ending hostilities and that the military demarcation line is provisional and should not in any way be interpreted as constituting a political or territorial boundary. The Conference expresses its conviction that the execution of the provisions set out in the present declaration and in the agreement on the cessation of hostilities creates the necessary basis for the achievement in the near future of a political settlement in Vietnam.

7. The Conference declares that, so far as Vietnam is concerned, the settlement of political problems, effected on the basis of respect for the principles of independence, unity, and territorial integrity, shall permit the Vietnamese people to enjoy the fundamental freedoms, guaranteed by democratic institutions established as a result of free general elections by secret ballot. In order to ensure that sufficient progress in the restoration of peace has been made, and that all the necessary conditions obtain for free expression of the national will, general elections shall be held in July 1956 under the supervision of an international commission composed of representatives of the Member States of the International Supervisory Commission, referred to in the agreement on the cessation of hostilities. Consultations will be held on this subject between the competent representative authorities of the two zones from July 20, 1955, onward.

8. The provisions of the agreements on the cessation of hostilities intended to ensure the protection of individuals and of property must be most strictly applied and must, in particular, allow everyone in Vietnam to decide freely in which zone he wishes to live.

9. The competent representative authorities of the North and South zones of Vietnam, as well as the authorities of Laos and Cambodia, must not permit any individual or collective reprisals against persons who had collaborated in any way with one of the parties during the war, or against members of such persons' families.

10. The Conference takes note of the declaration of the Government of the French Republic to the effect that it is ready to withdraw its troops from the territory of Cambodia, Laos, and Vietnam, at the request of the Governments concerned and within periods which shall be fixed by agreement between the parties except in the cases where, by agreement between the two parties, a certain number of French troops shall remain at specified points and for a specified time.

11. The Conference takes note of the declaration of the French Government to the effect that for the settlement of all the problems connected with the reestablishment and consolidation of peace in Cambodia, Laos, and Vietnam, the French Government will

proceed from the principle of respect for the independence and sovereignty, unity and territorial integrity of Cambodia, Laos, and Vietnam.

12. In their relations with Cambodia, Laos, and Vietnam, each member of the Geneva Conference undertakes to respect the sovereignty, the independence, the unity, and the territorial integrity of the above-mentioned States, and to refrain from any interference in their internal affairs.

13. The members of the Conference agree to consult one another on any question which may be referred to them by the International Supervisory Commission, in order to study such measures as may prove necessary to ensure that the agreements on the cessation of hostilities in Cambodia, Laos, and Vietnam are respected.

Source: The Pentagon Papers: The Defense Department History of United States Decisionmaking on Vietnam, Vol. 1. Senator Gravel edition (Boston: Beacon, 1971), 571–573.

President Dwight Eisenhower: Letter to Ngo Dinh Diem (October 23, 1954)

Ngo Dinh Diem was premier of the State of Vietnam (SVN). A Catholic in a predominantly Buddhist country, he had powerful support in the United States. Nonetheless, Diem's hold on power appeared tenuous. Opposing him were other political figures as well as the Binh Xuyen gangsters in Saigon and religious sects that had been armed by the French. Diem also clashed with army chief of staff General Nguyen Van Hinh, who talked openly about a coup. Critical to Diem's survival was U.S. president Dwight D. Eisenhower's decision in October to channel all U.S. aid directly to Diem's government. This greatly upset the French, for it undercut their remaining authority in southern Vietnam. In November Eisenhower sent former U.S. Army chief of staff General J. Lawton Collins to southern Vietnam as special ambassador with authority over all U.S. government agencies in Vietnam. Collins arrived there in early November and stated that Washington would deal only with Diem. At the end of November, Hinh left Vietnam for exile in France.

Dear Mr. President:

I have been following with great interest the course of developments in Vietnam, particularly since the conclusion of the conference at Geneva. The implications of the agreement concerning Vietnam have caused grave concern regarding the future of the country temporarily divided by an artificial military grouping, weakened by a long and exhausting war, and faced with enemies without and by their subversive collaborators within.

Your recent requests for aid to assist in the formidable project of the movement of several hundred thousand loyal Vietnamese citizens away from areas which are passing under a de facto rule and political ideology which they abhor, are being fulfilled. I am glad that the United States is able to assist in this humanitarian effort.

We have been exploring ways and means to permit our aid to Vietnam to be more effective and to make a greater contribution to the welfare and stability of the Government of Vietnam. I am, accordingly, instructing the American Ambassador to Vietnam [Donald R. Heath] to examine with you in your capacity as Chief of Government, how an intelligent program of American aid given directly to your Government can serve to assist Vietnam in its present hour of trial, provided that your Government is prepared to give assurances as to the standards of performance it would be able to maintain in the event such aid were supplied.

The purpose of this offer is to assist the Government of Vietnam in developing and maintaining a strong, viable state, capable of resisting attempted subversion or aggression through military means. The Government of the United States expects that this aid will be met by performance on the part of the Government of Vietnam in undertaking needed reforms. It hopes that such aid, combined with your own continuing efforts, will contribute effectively toward an independent Vietnam endowed with a strong Government. Such a Government would, I hope, be so responsive to the nationalist aspirations of its people, so enlightened in purpose and effective in performance, that it will be respected at home and abroad and discourage any who might wish to impose a foreign ideology on your free people.

Source: "U.S. Aid to Viet-Nam," *Department of State Bulletin* 31(303) (1954): 735–736.

National Security Action Memorandum No. 328 (April 6, 1965)

In early March 1965, U.S. Army chief of staff General Harold K. Johnson had taken a fact-finding trip to Vietnam, and later that month the Joint Chiefs of Staff (JCS) proposed that U.S. forces in the Republic of Vietnam (RVN, South Vietnam) be permitted to undertake a more active combat role. On April 6 President Lyndon Johnson agreed to the JCS request to deploy substantially greater U.S. forces to South Vietnam, including two additional marine battalions, and agreed that all marine units in Vietnam could be employed in a "more active role" as advocated by Military Assistance Command, Vietnam (MACV), commander General William Westmoreland. This change was, however, to be presented to the U.S. public as "wholly consistent with existing policy."

On Thursday, April 1, the President made the following decisions with respect to Vietnam:

1. Subject to modifications in the light of experience, and to coordination and direction both in Saigon and in Washington, the President approved the 41-point program of non-military actions submitted by Ambassador Taylor in a memorandum dated March 31, 1965.
2. The President gave general approval to the recommendations submitted by Mr. Rowan in his report dated March 16, with the exception that the President withheld approval of any request for supplemental funds at this time—it is his decision that this program is to be energetically supported by all agencies and departments and by the reprogramming of available funds as necessary within USIA.
3. The President approved the urgent exploration of the 12 suggestions for covert and other actions submitted by the Director of Central Intelligence under date of March 31.
4. The President repeated his earlier approval of the 21-point program of military actions submitted by General Harold K. Johnson under date of March 14 and re-emphasized his desire that aircraft and helicopter reinforcements under this program be accelerated.
5. The President approved an 18–20,000 man increase in U.S. military support forces to fill out existing units and supply needed logistic personnel.
6. The President approved the deployment of two additional Marine Battalions

and one Marine Air Squadron and associated headquarters and support elements.

7. The President approved a change of mission for all Marine Battalions deployed to Vietnam to permit their more active use under conditions to be established and approved by the Secretary of Defense in consultation with the Secretary of State.

8. The President approved the urgent exploration, with the Korean, Australian, and New Zealand Governments, of the possibility of rapid deployment of significant combat elements from their armed forces in parallel with the additional Marine deployment approved in paragraph 6.

9. Subject to continuing review, the President approved the following general framework of continuing action against North Vietnam and Laos:

We should continue roughly the present slowly ascending tempo of ROLLING THUNDER operations, being prepared to add strikes in response to a higher rate of VC operations, or conceivably to slow the pace in the unlikely event VC slacked off sharply for what appeared to be more than a temporary operational lull.

The target systems should continue to avoid the effective GCI range of MIGS. We should continue to vary the types of targets, stepping up attacks on lines of communication in the near future, and possibly moving in a few weeks to attacks on the rail lines north and northeast of Hanoi.

Leaflet operations should be expanded to obtain maximum practicable psychological effect on the North Vietnamese population.

Blockade or aerial mining of North Vietnamese ports need further study and should be considered for future operations. It would have major political complications, especially in relation to the Soviets and other third countries, but also offers many advantages.

Air operations in Laos, particularly route blocking operations in the Panhandle area, should be stepped up to the maximum remunerative rate.

10. Ambassador Taylor will promptly seek the reactions of the South Vietnamese Government to appropriate sections of this program and their approval as necessary, and in the event of disapproval or difficulty at that end, these decisions will be appropriately reconsidered. In any event, no action into Vietnam under paragraphs 6 and 7 above should take place without GVN approval or further Presidential authorization.

11. The President desires that with respect to the actions in paragraphs 5 through 7, premature publicity be avoided by all possible precautions. The actions themselves should be taken as rapidly as practicable, but in ways that should minimize any appearance of sudden changes in policy, and official statements on these troop movements will be made only with the direct approval of the Secretary of Defense, in consultation with the Secretary of State. The President's desire is that these movements and changes should be understood as being gradual and wholly consistent with existing policy.

Source: The Pentagon Papers as Published by the New York Times (New York: Quadrangle, 1971), 452–453.

Robert McNamara, Secretary of Defense: Excerpt from Memorandum for President Lyndon Johnson (April 21, 1965)

U.S. secretary of defense Robert McNamara and other administration officials met in Honolulu on April 20, 1965, to discuss Vietnam policy and assess military requirements with Military Assistance Command, Vietnam (MACV), commander General William Westmoreland; U.S. ambassador to the Republic of Vietnam (RVN, South Vietnam) Maxwell Taylor; and commander in chief, U.S. Pacific Command, Admiral Ulysses Sharp. Here McNamara sums up that meeting for President Lyndon Johnson and details the U.S. forces that should be sent to Vietnam to bolster U.S. marines and troops from the Republic of Korea (ROK, South Korea) already there. McNamara reports that the conferees are in agreement that after a span of as long as a "year or two," the demonstrated military failure of Communist forces in South Vietnam will break their will to continue the struggle and bring about an acceptable political outcome.

Mr. William Bundy, Mr. McNaughton and I met with Ambassador Taylor, General Wheeler, Admiral Sharp and General Westmoreland in Honolulu on Tuesday, April 20. Following is my report of that meeting:

1. None of them expects the DRV/VC to capitulate, or come to a position acceptable to us, in less than six months. This is because they believe that a settlement will come as much or more from VC failure in the South as from DRV pain in the North, and that it will take more than six months, perhaps a year or two, to demonstrate VC failure in the South.

2. With respect to strikes against the North, they all agree that the present tempo is about right, that sufficient increasing pressure is provided by repetition and continuation. All of them envisioned a strike program continuing at least six months, perhaps a year or more, avoiding the Hanoi–Haiphong–Phuc Yen areas during that period. There might be fewer fixed targets, or more restrikes, or more armed reconnaissance missions. Ambassador Taylor stated what appeared to be a shared view, that it is important not to "kill the hostage" by destroying the North Vietnamese assets inside the "Hanoi do-nut." They all believe that the strike program is essential to our campaign—both psychologically and physically—but that it cannot be expected to do the job alone. They all considered it very important that strikes against the North be continued during any talks.

3. None of them sees a dramatic improvement in the South in the immediate future. Their strategy for "victory" over time, is to break the will of the DRV/VC by denying them victory. Ambassador Taylor put it in terms of a demonstration of Communist impotence, which will lead eventually to a political solution. They see slow improvement in the South, but all emphasized the critical importance of holding on and avoiding—for psychological and morale reasons—a spectacular defeat of GVN or US forces. And they all suspect that the recent VC lull is but the quiet before a storm.

4. To bolster the GVN forces while they are building up, they all recommend the following deployments in addition to the 2,000 Koreans and 33,500 US troops already in-country (including the 4 Marine battalions at Danang-Hue):

- 1 US Army brigade (3 btn) at Bien Hoa/Vung Tau
- 4,000 closing 1 May
- 3 US Marine air sqs + 3 btns at Chu Lai
- 6,200 closing 5 May
- 1 Australian btn at Vun Tau
- 1,250 closing 21 May
- 1 US Army brigade (3 btn) at Qui Nhon/Nha Trang
- 4,000 closing 15 Jn.
- 1 Korean RCT (3 btn) at Quang Ngai
- 4,000 closing 15 Jn.
- Augmentation of various existing forces
- 11,000 already approved
- Logistics troops for previously approved force level
- 7,000 already approved
- Logistics troops for above enclaves and possible 3 divisions
- 16,000 not yet approved
- TOTAL: US 13 btns 82,000
- ROK & ANZAC 4 btns 7,250

5. Possible later deployments, not recommended now, include a US AirMobile division (9 btns-15,800) to Pleiku/Kontum, and I Corps HQ (1,200) to Nha Trang; and even later, the remainder of the Korean division (6 btns-14,500) to Quang Ngai, and the remainder of the Marine Expeditionary Force (3 btns-24,800) to Danang.

Source: Foreign Relations of the United States, 1964–1968: Vietnam, January–June 1965, Vol. 2 (Washington, DC: U.S. Government Printing Office, 1996), 574–575.

Ho Chi Minh: Letter to Lyndon Johnson (February 15, 1967)

On February 15, 1967, in a personal letter to U.S. president Lyndon Johnson, President Ho Chi Minh of the Democratic Republic of Vietnam (DRV, North Vietnam) responds to the U.S. proposal for a bombing halt. In this uncompromising missive, Ho accuses the United States of violating pledges that it had made at the 1954 Geneva Conference, intervening in Vietnamese affairs, and turning the Republic of Vietnam (RVN, South Vietnam) into a U.S. "neocolony and military base." He also accuses the United States of war crimes. The only way to bring about peace is for the United States to cease its "aggression" by immediately halting the bombing of North Vietnam and withdrawing its own and "satellite" troops from South Vietnam, recognizing the National Front for the Liberation of South Vietnam (usually known as the National Liberation Front [NLF]), and permitting the holding of free elections.

Ho does not mention North Vietnam's infiltration of troops into South Vietnam, which the United States had demanded as a precondition to halt the bombing; rather, he says that if the United States is sincere about direct peace talks with the North Vietnamese government, it must first halt unconditionally all bombing of North Vietnam.

To His Excellency Mr. Lyndon B. Johnson, President, United States of America

Excellency, on February 10, 1967, I received your message. Here is my response.

Viet-Nam is situated thousands of miles from the United States. The Vietnamese people have never done any harm to the United States. But, contrary to the commitments made by its representative at the Geneva Conference of 1954, the United States Government has constantly intervened in Viet-Nam, it has launched and intensified the war of aggression in South Viet-Nam for the purpose of prolonging the division of Viet-Nam and of transforming South Viet-Nam into an American neo-colony and an American military base. For more than two years now, the American Government, with its military aviation and its navy, has been waging war against the Democratic Republic of Viet-Nam, an independent and sovereign country.

The United States Government has committed war crimes, crimes against peace and against humanity. In South Viet-Nam a half-million American soldiers and soldiers from the satellite countries have resorted to the most inhumane arms and the most barbarous methods of warfare, such as napalm, chemicals, and poison gases in order to massacre our fellow countrymen, destroy the crops, and wipe out the villages. In North Viet-Nam thousands of American planes have rained down hundreds of thousands of tons of bombs, destroying cities, villages, mills, roads, bridges, dikes, dams and even churches, pagodas, hospitals, and schools. In your message you appear to deplore the suffering and the destruction in Viet-Nam. Permit me to ask you: Who perpetrated these monstrous crimes? It was the American soldiers and the soldiers of the satellite countries. The United States Government is entirely responsible for the extremely grave situation in Viet-Nam.

The American war of aggression against the Vietnamese people constitutes a challenge to the countries of the socialist camp, a threat to the peoples' independent movement, and a grave danger to peace in Asia and in the world.

The Vietnamese people deeply love independence, liberty, and peace. But in the face of the American aggression they have risen up as one man, without fearing the sacrifices and the privations. They are determined to continue their resistance until they have won real independence and liberty and true peace. Our just cause enjoys the approval and the powerful support of peoples throughout the world and of large segments of the American people.

The United States Government provoked the war of aggression in Viet-Nam. It must cease that aggression, it is the only road leading to the re-establishment of peace. The United States Government must halt definitively and unconditionally the bombings and all other acts of war against the Democratic Republic of Viet-Nam, withdraw from South Viet-Nam all American troops and all troops from the satellite countries, recognize the National Front of the Liberation of South Viet-Nam, and let the Vietnamese people settle their problems themselves. Such is the basic content of the four-point position of the Government of the Democratic Republic of Viet-Nam, such is the statement of the essential principles and essential arrangements of the Geneva agreements of 1954 on Viet-Nam. It is the basis for a correct political solution of the Vietnamese problem. In your message you suggested direct talks between the Democratic Republic of Viet-Nam and the United States. If the United States Government really wants talks, it must first halt unconditionally the bombings and all other acts of war against the Democratic Republic of Viet-Nam. It is only after the unconditional halting of the American bombings and of all other American acts of war against the Democratic Republic of Viet-Nam that the Democratic Republic of Viet-Nam and the United States could begin talks and discuss questions affecting the two parties.

The Vietnamese people will never give way to force, it will never accept conversation under the clear threat of bombs.

Our cause is absolutely just. It is desirable that the Government of the United States act in conformity to reason.

Sincerely,

Ho Chi Minh

Source: "President Ho Chi Minh's Reply," *Department of State Bulletin* 56(1450) (1967): 596–597.

President Lyndon Johnson: Excerpt from Address in San Antonio, Texas (September 29, 1967)

In June 1967 two Frenchmen, Dr. Herbert Marcovich and Raymond Aubrac, approached Dr. Henry Kissinger, then a private U.S. citizen and Harvard University professor who was attending a conference in Paris, about establishing contact with the leadership of the Democratic Republic of Vietnam (DRV, North Vietnam) to discuss the possibility of serving as intermediaries between Washington and Hanoi. Aubrac had known Ho since 1946. The Lyndon Johnson administration agreed, and the two Frenchmen traveled to Hanoi in late July to present a new U.S. proposal. The United States would halt the bombing of North Vietnam in return for a pledge from Hanoi to enter into substantive peace talks without Washington insisting on Hanoi's de-escalation of its military effort in the Republic of Vietnam (RVN, South Vietnam). The message did, however, warn against any North Vietnamese effort to "take advantage" of the situation. As it turned out, the North Vietnamese leadership rejected the U.S. offer, which they said still imposed conditions. President Johnson then made the offer public in the course of a speech in San Antonio, Texas, on September 29. The démarche became known as the San Antonio Formula.

Our desire to negotiate peace—through the United Nations or out—has been made very, very clear to Hanoi—directly and many times through third parties.

As we have told Hanoi time and time and time again, the heart of the matter really is this: The United States is willing to stop all aerial and naval bombardment of North Viet-Nam when this will lead promptly to productive discussions. We, of course, assume that while discussions proceed, North Viet-Nam would not take advantage of the bombing cessation or limitation.

But Hanoi has not accepted any of these proposals.

So it is by Hanoi's choice, and not ours and not the rest of the world's, that the war continues.

Why, in the face of military and political progress in the South, and the burden of our bombing in the North, do they insist and persist with the war?

From the many sources the answer is the same. They still hope that the people of the United States will not see this struggle through to the very end. As one Western diplomat reported to me only this week—he had just been in Hanoi—"They believe their staying power is greater than ours and that they can't lose." A visitor from a Communist capital had this to say: "They expect the war to be long, and that the Americans in the end will be defeated by a breakdown in morale, fatigue, and psychological factors." The Premier of North Viet-Nam said as far back as 1962: "Americans do not like long, inconclusive war . . . Thus we are sure to win in the end."

Are the North Vietnamese right about us?

I think not. No. I think they are wrong. I think it is the common failing of totalitarian regimes, that they cannot really understand the nature of our democracy:

- —They mistake dissent for disloyalty;
- —They mistake restlessness for a rejection of policy;
- —They mistake a few committees for a country;
- —They misjudge individual speeches for public policy.

They are no better suited to judge the strength and perseverance of America than the Nazi and the Stalinist propagandists were able to judge it. It is a tragedy that they must discover these qualities in the

American people, and discover them through a bloody war.

And, soon or late, they will discover them.

In the meantime, it shall be our policy to continue to seek negotiations, confident that reason will some day prevail, that Hanoi will realize that it just can never win, that it will turn away from fighting and start building for its own people.

Source: "Answering Aggression in Viet-Nam," *Department of State Bulletin* 57(1478) (1967): 519–522.

General William Westmoreland, Commander of U.S. Forces in Vietnam: Excerpts from National Press Club Address (November 21, 1967)

In mid-November 1967 U.S Military Assistance Command, Vietnam (MACV), commander General William Westmoreland returned to the United States and provided President Lyndon Johnson a decidedly upbeat assessment on the progress of the war. Johnson then asked Westmoreland to make his views public. On November 21 the general appeared before the National Press Club. In his remarks Westmoreland asserts that the United States, the Army of the Republic of Vietnam (ARVN, South Vietnamese Army), and Korean forces are winning the war and that victory is "within our grasp—the enemy's hopes are bankrupt." Westmoreland subsequently told a *Time* interviewer that "I hope they try something, because we are looking for a fight." That fight occurred in the Communist Tet Offensive of late January 1968.

Improving Vietnamese Effectiveness

With 1968, a new phase is now starting. We have reached an important point when the end begins to come into view. What is this third phase we are about to enter?

In Phase III, in 1968, we intend to do the following:

Help the Vietnamese Armed Forces to continue improving their effectiveness.

Decrease our advisers in training centers and other places where the professional competence of Vietnamese officers makes this possible.

Increase our advisory effort with the younger brothers of the Vietnamese Army: the Regional Forces and Popular Forces.

Use U.S. and free-world forces to destroy North Vietnamese forays while we assist the Vietnamese to reorganize for territorial security.

Provide the new military equipment to revitalize the Vietnamese Army and prepare it to take on an ever-increasing share of the war.

Continue pressure on North to prevent rebuilding and to make infiltration more costly.

Turn a major share of frontline DMZ defense over to the Vietnamese Army.

Increase U.S. support in the rich and populated delta.

Help the Government of Viet-Nam single out and destroy the Communist shadow government.

Continue to isolate the guerrilla from the people.

Help the new Vietnamese government to respond to popular aspirations and to reduce and eliminate corruption.

Help the Vietnamese strengthen their policy forces to enhance law and order.

Open more roads and canals.

Continue to improve the Vietnamese economy and standard of living.

The Final Phase

Now for phase IV—the final phase. That period will see the conclusion of our plan to weaken the enemy and strengthen our friends until we become progressively super-fluous. The object will be to show the world that guerrilla warfare and invasion do not pay as a new means of Communist aggression.

I see phase IV happening as follows:

Infiltration will slow.

The Communist infrastructure will be cut up and near collapse.

The Vietnamese Government will prove its stability, and the Vietnamese Army will show that it can handle Viet Cong.

The Regional Forces and Popular Forces will reach a higher level of professional performance.

U.S. units can begin to phase down as the Vietnamese Army is modernized and develops its capacity to the fullest.

The military physical assets, bases and ports, will be progressively turned over to the Vietnamese.

The Vietnamese will take charge of the final mopping up of the Viet Cong (which will probably last several years). The U.S., at the same time, will continue the developmental help envisaged by the President for the community of Southeast Asia.

You may ask how long phase III will take, before we reach the final phase. We have already entered part of phase III. Looking back on phases I and II, we can conclude that we have come a long way.

I see progress as I travel all over Viet-Nam.

I see it in the attitudes of the Vietnamese.

I see it in the open roads and canals.

I see it in the new crops and the new purchasing power of the farmer.

I see it in the increasing willingness of the Vietnamese Army to fight North Vietnamese units and in the victories they are winning.

Parenthetically, I might say that the U.S. press tends to report U.S. actions; so you may not be as aware as I am of the victories won by South Vietnamese forces.

The enemy has many problems:

He is losing control of the scattered population under his influence.

He is losing credibility with the population he still controls.

He is alienating the people by his increased demands and taxes, where he can impose them.

He sees the strength of his forces steadily declining.

He can no longer recruit in the South to any meaningful extent; he must plug the gap with North Vietnamese.

His monsoon offensives have been failures.

He was dealt a mortal blow by the installation of a freely elected representative government.

And he failed in his desperate effort to take the world's headlines from the inauguration by a military victory.

Lastly, the Vietnamese Army is on the road to becoming a competent force. Korean troops in Viet-Nam provide a good example for the Vietnamese. Fifteen years ago the Koreans themselves had problems now ascribed to the Vietnamese. The Koreans surmounted these problems, and so can and will the Vietnamese. . . .

We are making progress. We know you want an honorable and early transition to the fourth and last phase. So do your sons and so do I.

It lies within our grasp—the enemy's hopes are bankrupt. With your support we will give you a success that will impact not only on South Viet-Nam but on every emerging nation in the world.

Source: "Progress Report on the War in Viet-Nam," *Department of State Bulletin* 57(1485) (1967): 785–788.

President Lyndon Johnson: Excerpts from Televised Address (March 31, 1968)

Compounding problems for President Lyndon Johnson, 1968 was an election year. On March 12 in New Hampshire, anti–Vietnam War senator Eugene McCarthy of Minnesota stunned Johnson by winning 42 percent of the vote in that state's Democratic primary (although many of those voting for McCarthy were in fact signaling their displeasure with Johnson for not using greater military force). This prompted antiwar senator Robert Kennedy of New York to join the race. Worried Democratic Party leaders urged the president to do something dramatic to bolster his sagging popularity. On March 31 in a televised address to the nation, Johnson reiterates his Vietnam policies and also announces a halt in the bombing of most of the Democratic Republic of Vietnam (DRV, North Vietnam). Then at the close of his remarks he stuns the nation by announcing that given the nature of the challenges, he cannot in good conscience devote even "an hour" of his time to "personal partisan causes" or to anything other than the "awesome duties" of the presidency and that he will neither seek nor accept another term as president.

Good evening, my fellow Americans. Tonight I want to speak to you of peace in Viet-Nam and Southeast Asia.

No other question so preoccupies our people. No other dream so absorbs the 250 million human beings who live in that part of the world. No other goal motivates American policy in Southeast Asia.

For years, representatives of our Government and others have traveled the world seeking to find a basis for peace talks.

Since last September, they have carried the offer that I made public at San Antonio.

That offer was this: that the United States would stop its bombardment of North Viet-Nam when that would lead promptly to productive discussions—and that we would assume that North Viet-Nam would not take military advantage of our restraint.

Hanoi denounced this offer, both privately and publicly. Even while the search for peace was going on, North Viet-Nam rushed their preparations for a savage assault on the people, the Government, and the allies of South Viet-Nam.

Their attack—during the Tet holidays—failed to achieve its principal objectives.

It did not collapse the elected government of South Viet-Nam or shatter its army, as the Communists had hoped.

It did not produce a "general uprising" among the people of the cities, as they had predicted.

The Communists were unable to maintain control of any of the more than 30 cities that they attacked. And they took very heavy casualties.

But they did compel the South Vietnamese and their allies to move certain forces from the countryside into the cities. They caused widespread disruption and suffering. Their attacks, and the battles that followed, made refugees of half a million human beings.

The Communists may renew their attack any day. They are, it appears, trying to make 1968 the year of decision in South Viet-Nam—the year that brings, if not final victory or defeat, at least a turning point in the struggle.

This much is clear: If they do mount another round of heavy attacks, they will not succeed in destroying the fighting power of South Viet-Nam and its allies.

But tragically, this is also clear: Many men—on both sides of the struggle—will be lost. A nation that has already suffered 20 years of warfare will suffer once again.

Armies on both sides will take new casualties. And the war will go on.

There is no need for this to be so.

There is no need to delay the talks that could bring an end to this long and this bloody war.

Tonight I renew the offer I made last August—to stop the bombardment of North Viet-Nam. We ask that talks begin promptly, that they be serious talks on the substance of peace. We assume that during those talks Hanoi will not take advantage of our restraint.

We are prepared to move immediately toward peace through negotiations. So tonight, in the hope that this action will lead to early talks, I am taking the first step to deescalate the conflict. We are reducing—substantially reducing—the present level of hostilities. And we are doing so unilaterally and at once.

Tonight I have ordered our aircraft and our naval vessels to make no attacks on North Viet-Nam, except in the area north of the demilitarized zone where the continuing enemy buildup directly threatens Allied forward positions and where the movements of their troops and supplies are clearly related to that threat.

The area in which we are stopping our attacks includes almost 90 percent of North Viet-Nam's population and most of its territory. Thus there will be no attacks around the principal populated areas or in the food-producing areas of North Viet-Nam.

Even this very limited bombing of the North could come to an early end if our restraint is matched by restraint in Hanoi. But I cannot in good conscience stop all bombing so long as to do so would immediately and directly endanger the lives of our men and our allies. Whether a complete bombing halt becomes possible in the future will be determined by events.

Our purpose in this action is to bring about a reduction in the level of violence that now exists.

It is to save the lives of brave men and to save the lives of innocent women and children. It is to permit the contending forces to move closer to a political settlement.

And tonight I call upon the United Kingdom and I call upon the Soviet Union, as cochairmen of the Geneva conferences and as permanent members of the United Nations Security Council, to do all they can to move from the unilateral act of deescalation that I have just announced toward genuine peace in Southeast Asia.

Now, as in the past, the United States is ready to send its representatives to any forum, at any time, to discuss the means of bringing this ugly war to an end.

I am designating one of our most distinguished Americans, Ambassador Averell Harriman, as my personal representative for such talks. In addition, I have asked Ambassador Llewellyn Thompson, who returned from Moscow for consultation, to be available to join Ambassador Harriman at Geneva or any other suitable place just as soon as Hanoi agrees to a conference.

I call upon President Ho Chi Minh to respond positively and favorably to this new step toward peace.

But if peace does not come now through negotiations, it will come when Hanoi understands that our common resolve is unshakable and our common strength is invincible.

Tonight, we and the other allied nations are contributing 600,000 fighting men to assist 700,000 South Vietnamese troops in defending their little country.

Our presence there has always rested on this basic belief: The main burden of preserving their freedom must be carried out by them—by the South Vietnamese themselves.

We and our allies can only help to provide a shield behind which the people of South Viet-Nam can survive and can grow and develop. On their efforts—on their determinations and resourcefulness—the outcome will ultimately depend. . . .

The actions that we have taken since the beginning of the year to reequip the South Vietnamese forces; to meet our responsibilities in Korea, as well as our responsibilities in Viet-Nam; to meet price increases and the cost of activating and deploying Reserve forces; to replace helicopters and provide the other military supplies we need—all of these actions are going to require additional expenditures.

The tentative estimate of those additional expenditures is $2.5 billion in this fiscal year and $2.6 billion in the next fiscal year.

These projected increases in expenditures for our national security will bring into sharper focus the Nation's need for immediate action, action to protect the prosperity of the American people and to protect the strength and the stability of our American dollar.

On many occasions I have pointed out that without a tax bill or decreased expenditures next year's deficit would again be around $20 billion. I have emphasized the need to set strict priorities in our spending. I have stressed that failure to act—and to act promptly and decisively—would raise very strong doubts throughout the world about America's willingness to keep its financial house in order.

Yet Congress has not acted. And tonight we face the sharpest financial threat in the post-war era—a threat to the dollar's role as the keystone of international trade and finance in the world. . . .

One day, my fellow citizens, there will be peace in Southeast Asia.

It will come because the people of Southeast Asia want it—those whose armies are at war tonight and those who, though threatened, have thus far been spared.

Peace will come because Asians were willing to work for it—and to sacrifice for it—and to die by the thousands for it.

But let it never be forgotten: Peace will come also because America sent her sons to help secure it.

It has not been easy—far from it. During the past 4–1/2 years, it has been my fate and my responsibility to be Commander in Chief. I lived daily and nightly with the cost of this war. I know the pain that it has inflicted. I know perhaps better than anyone the misgivings that it has aroused.

Throughout this entire long period, I have been sustained by a single principle: that what we are doing now in Viet-Nam is vital not only to the security of Southeast Asia, but it is vital to the security of every American.

Surely we have treaties which we must respect. Surely we have commitments that we are going to keep. Resolutions of the Congress testify to the need to resist aggression in the world and in Southeast Asia.

But the heart of our involvement in South Viet-Nam—under three different Presidents, three separate administrations—has always been America's own security.

And the larger purpose of our involvement has always been to help the nations of Southeast Asia become independent and stand alone, self-sustaining as members of a great world community—at peace with themselves and at peace with all others.

With such an Asia, our country—and the world—will be far more secure than it is tonight.

I believe that a peaceful Asia is far nearer to reality because of what America has done in Viet-Nam. I believe that the men who endure the dangers of battle—fighting there for us tonight—are helping the entire world avoid far greater conflicts, far wider wars, far more destruction, than this one.

The peace that will bring them home some day will come. Tonight I have offered the first in what I hope will be a series of mutual moves toward peace.

I pray that it will not be rejected by the leaders of North Viet-Nam. I pray that they will accept it as a means by which the sacrifices of their own people may be ended. And I ask your help and your support, my fellow citizens, for this effort to reach across the battlefield toward an early peace. . . .

Throughout my entire public career I have followed the personal philosophy that I am a free man, an American, a public servant, and a member of my party, in that order always and only.

For 37 years in the service of our nation, first as a Congressman, as a Senator and as Vice President and now as your President, I have put the unity of the people first. I have put it ahead of any divisive partisanship.

And in these times as in times before, it is true that a house divided against itself by the spirit of faction, of party, of region, of religion, of race, is a house that cannot stand.

There is division in the American house now. There is divisiveness among us all tonight. And holding the trust that is mine, as President of all the people, I cannot disregard the peril to the progress of the American people and the hope and the prospect of peace for all peoples.

So I would ask all Americans, whatever their personal interests or concern, to guard against divisiveness and all its ugly consequences.

Fifty-two months and 10 days ago, in a moment of tragedy and trauma, the duties of this Office fell upon me. I asked then for your help and God's, that we might continue America on its course, binding up our wounds, healing our history, moving forward in new unity, to clear the American agenda and to keep the American commitment for all of our people.

United we have kept that commitment. United we have enlarged that commitment.

Through all time to come, I think America will be a stronger nation, a more just society, and a land of greater opportunity and fulfillment because of what we have all done together in these years of unparalleled achievement.

Our reward will come in the life of freedom, peace, and hope that our children will enjoy through ages ahead.

What we won when all of our people united must not now be lost in suspicion, distrust, selfishness, and politics among any of our people.

Believing this as I do, I have concluded that I should not permit the Presidency to become involved in the partisan divisions that are developing in this political year.

With America's sons in the fields far away, with America's future under challenge right here at home, with our hopes and the world's hopes for peace in the balance every day, I do not believe that I should devote an hour or a day of my time to any personal partisan causes or to any duties other than the awesome duties of this Office—the Presidency of your country.

Accordingly, I shall not seek, and I will not accept, the nomination of my party for another term as your President.

But let men everywhere know, however, that a strong, a confident, and a vigilant America stands ready tonight to seek an honorable peace—and stands ready tonight to defend an honored cause—whatever the price, whatever the burden, whatever the sacrifices that duty may require.

Thank you for listening.

Good night and God bless all of you.

Source: Public Papers of the Presidents of the United States: Lyndon B. Johnson, 1968–69, Book 1 (Washington, DC: U.S. Government Printing Office, 1970), 469–476.

President Richard Nixon: Excerpts from Speech on Vietnamization (November 3, 1969)

Although touted as beginning under President Richard Nixon, Vietnamization—the building up of the armed forces of the Republic of Vietnam (RVN, South Vietnam) and turning more of the war over to them—actually began in the last year of the Lyndon Johnson administration. In the course of this televised address to the American people on November 3, 1969, Nixon traces the history of U.S. involvement in Vietnam and his hopes for Vietnamization. Unfortunately, Vietnamization did not work as hoped. Although the South Vietnamese armed forces were larger and better equipped, the same problems remained: too few qualified officers, poor leadership, inability to maintain sophisticated equipment, and rampant corruption. In the course of this speech, Nixon also enunciates what becomes known as the Nixon Doctrine. The United States will honor its current treaty negotiations and provide a nuclear umbrella for its key allies. In the case of aggression, the United States will provide military and economic assistance only.

Good evening, my fellow Americans.

Tonight I want to talk to you on a subject of deep concern to all Americans and to many people in all parts of the world—the war in Vietnam.

I believe that one of the reasons for the deep division about Vietnam is that many Americans have lost confidence in what their Government has told them about our policy. The American people cannot and should not be asked to support a policy which involves the overriding issues of war and peace unless they know the truth about that policy.

Tonight, therefore, I would like to answer some of the questions that I know are on the minds of many of you listening to me.

How and why did America get involved in Vietnam in the first place? How has this administration changed the policy of the previous administration? What has really happened in the negotiations in Paris and on the battlefront in Vietnam? What choices do we have if we are to end the war? What are the prospects for peace? Now, let me begin by describing the situation I found when I was inaugurated on January 20:

* The war had been going on for 4 years. 1,000 Americans had been killed in action.
* The training program for the South Vietnamese was behind schedule.
* 540,000 Americans were in Vietnam with no plans to reduce the number.
* No progress had been made at the negotiations in Paris and the United States had not put forth a comprehensive peace proposal.
* The war was causing deep division at home and criticism from many of our friends as well as our enemies abroad.

In view of these circumstances there were some who urged that I end the war at once by ordering the immediate withdrawal of all American forces.

From a political standpoint this would have been a popular and easy course to follow. After all, we became involved in the war while my predecessor was in office. I could blame the defeat which would be the result of my action on him and come out as the peacemaker. Some put it to me quite bluntly: This was the only way to avoid allowing Johnson's war to become Nixon's war.

But I had a greater obligation than to think only of the years of my administration and of the next election. I had to think of the effect of my decision on the next generation and on the future of peace and freedom in America and in the world.

Let us all understand that the question before us is not whether some Americans are for peace and some Americans are against peace. The question at issue is not whether Johnson's war becomes Nixon's war.

The great question is: How can we win America's peace?

Well, let us turn now to the fundamental issue. Why and how did the United States become involved in Vietnam in the first place? Fifteen years ago North Vietnam, with the logistical support of Communist China and the Soviet Union, launched a campaign to impose a Communist government on South Vietnam by instigating and supporting a revolution.

In response to the request of the Government of South Vietnam, President Eisenhower sent economic aid and military equipment to assist the people of South Vietnam in their efforts to prevent a Communist takeover. Seven years ago, President Kennedy sent 16,000 military personnel to Vietnam as combat advisers. Four years ago, President Johnson sent American combat forces to South Vietnam.

Now, many believe that President Johnson's decision to send American combat forces to South Vietnam was wrong. And many others—I among them—have been strongly critical of the way the war has been conducted.

But the question facing us today is: Now that we are in the war, what is the best way to end it?

In January I could only conclude that the precipitate withdrawal of American forces from Vietnam would be a disaster not only for South Vietnam but for the United States and for the cause of peace.

For the South Vietnamese, our precipitate withdrawal would inevitably allow the Communists to repeat the massacres which followed their takeover in the North 15 years before. They then murdered more than 50,000 people and hundreds of thousands more died in slave labor camps.

We saw a prelude of what would happen in South Vietnam when the Communists entered the city of Hue last year. During their brief rule there, there was a bloody reign of terror in which 3,000 civilians were clubbed, shot to death, and buried in mass graves.

With the sudden collapse of our support, these atrocities of Hue would become the nightmare of the entire nation—and particularly for the million and a half Catholic refugees who fled to South Vietnam when the Communists took over in the North.

For the United States, this first defeat in our Nation's history would result in a collapse of confidence in American leadership, not only in Asia but throughout the world.

Three American Presidents have recognized the great stakes involved in Vietnam and understood what had to be done.

In 1963, President Kennedy, with his characteristic eloquence and clarity, said:

. . . we want to see a stable government there, carrying on a struggle to maintain its national independence. We believe strongly in that. We are not going to withdraw from that effort. In my opinion, for us to withdraw from that effort would mean a collapse not only of South Vietnam, but Southeast Asia. So we are going to stay there.

President Eisenhower and President Johnson expressed the same conclusion during their terms of office.

For the future of peace, precipitate withdrawal would thus be a disaster of immense magnitude.

A nation cannot remain great if it betrays its allies and lets down its friends.

Our defeat and humiliation in South Vietnam without question would promote recklessness in the councils of those great powers who have not yet abandoned their goals of world conquest.

This would spark violence wherever our commitments help maintain the peace—in the Middle East, in Berlin, eventually even in the Western Hemisphere.

Ultimately, this would cost more lives.

It would not bring peace; it would bring more war.

For these reasons, I rejected the recommendation that I should end the war by immediately withdrawing all of our forces. I chose instead to change American policy on both the negotiating front and battlefront. In order to end a war fought on many fronts, I initiated a pursuit for peace on many fronts. In a television speech on May 14, in a speech before the United Nations, and on a number of other occasions I set forth our peace proposals in great detail.

We have offered the complete withdrawal of all outside forces within 1 year.

We have proposed a cease-fire under international supervision.

We have offered free elections under international supervision with the Communists participating in the organization and conduct of the elections as an organized political force. And the Saigon Government has pledged to accept the result of the elections.

We have not put forth our proposals on a take-it-or-leave-it basis. We have indicated that we are willing to discuss the proposals that have been put forth by the other side. We have declared that anything is negotiable except the right of the people of South Vietnam to determine their own future. At the Paris peace conference, Ambassador Lodge has demonstrated our flexibility and good faith in 40 public meetings.

Hanoi has refused even to discuss our proposals. They demand our unconditional acceptance of their terms, which are that we withdraw all American forces immediately and unconditionally and that we overthrow the Government of South Vietnam as we leave.

We have not limited our peace initiatives to public forums and public statements. I recognized, in January, that a long and bitter war like this usually cannot be settled in a public forum. That is why in addition to the public statements and negotiation I have explored every possible private avenue that might lead to a settlement.

Tonight I am taking the unprecedented step of disclosing to you some of our other initiatives for peace—initiatives we undertook privately and secretly because we thought we thereby might open a door which publicly would be closed.

I did not wait for my inauguration to begin my quest for peace.

Soon after my election, through an individual who is directly in contact on a personal basis with the leaders of North Vietnam, I made two private offers for a rapid, comprehensive settlement. Hanoi's replies called in effect for our surrender before negotiations.

Since the Soviet Union furnishes most of the military equipment for North Vietnam, Secretary of State Rogers, my Assistant for National Security Affairs, Dr. Kissinger, Ambassador Lodge, and I, personally, have met on a number of occasions with representatives of the Soviet Government to enlist their assistance in getting meaningful negotiations started. In addition, we have had extended discussions directed toward that same end with representatives of other governments which have diplomatic relations with North Vietnam. None of these initiatives have to date produced results.

In mid-July, I became convinced that it was necessary to make a major move to break the deadlock in the Paris talks. I spoke directly in this office, where I am now sitting, with an individual who had known Ho Chi Minh on a personal basis for 25 years. Through him I sent a letter to Ho Chi Minh. I did this outside of the usual diplomatic channels with the hope that with the necessity of making statements for propaganda removed, there might be constructive progress toward bringing the war to an end. Let me read from that letter to you now:

Dear Mr. President:

I realize that it is difficult to communicate meaningfully across the gulf of four years of war. But precisely because of this gulf, I wanted to take this opportunity to reaffirm in all solemnity my desire to work for a just peace. I deeply believe that the war in Vietnam has gone on too long and delay in bringing it to an end can benefit no one— least of all the people of Vietnam. . . .

The time has come to move forward at the conference table toward an early resolution of this tragic war. You will find us forthcoming and open-minded in a common effort to bring the blessings of peace to the brave people of Vietnam. Let history record that at this critical juncture, both sides turned their face toward peace rather than toward conflict and war.

I received Ho Chi Minh's reply on August 30, 3 days before his death. It simply reiterated the public position North Vietnam had taken at Paris and flatly rejected my initiative.

The full text of both letters is being released to the press.

In addition to the public meetings that I have referred to, Ambassador Lodge has met with Vietnam's chief negotiator in Paris in 11 private sessions.

We have taken other significant initiatives which must remain secret to keep open some channels of communication which may still prove to be productive.

But the effect of all the public, private, and secret negotiations which have been undertaken since the bombing halt a year ago and since this administration came into office on January 20, can be summed up in one sentence: No progress whatever has been made except agreement on the shape of the bargaining table.

Well now, who is at fault?

It has become clear that the obstacle in negotiating an end to the war is not the President of the United States. It is not the South Vietnamese Government.

The obstacle is the other side's absolute refusal to show the least willingness to join us in seeking a just peace. And it will not do so while it is convinced that all it has to do is to wait for our next concession, and our next concession after that one, until it gets everything it wants.

There can now be no longer any question that progress in negotiation depends only on Hanoi's deciding to negotiate, to negotiate seriously.

I realize that this report on our efforts on the diplomatic front is discouraging to the American people, but the American people are entitled to know the truth—the bad news as well as the good news—where the lives of our young men are involved.

Now let me turn, however, to a more encouraging report on another front.

At the time we launched our search for peace I recognized we might not succeed in bringing an end to the war through negotiation. I, therefore, put into effect another plan to bring peace—a plan which will bring the war to an end regardless of what happens on the negotiating front.

It is in line with a major shift in U.S. foreign policy which I described in my press conference at Guam on July 25. Let me briefly explain what has been described as the Nixon Doctrine—a policy which not only will help end the war in Vietnam, but which is an essential element of our program to prevent future Vietnams.

We Americans are a do-it-yourself people. We are an impatient people. Instead of teaching someone else to do a job, we like to do it ourselves. And this trait has been carried over into our foreign policy. In Korea and again in Vietnam, the United States furnished most of the money, most of the arms, and most of the men to help the people of those countries defend their freedom against Communist aggression.

Before any American troops were committed to Vietnam, a leader of another Asian country expressed this opinion to me when I was traveling in Asia as a private citizen. He said: "When you are trying to assist another nation defend its freedom, U.S. policy should be to help them fight the war but not to fight the war for them."

Well, in accordance with this wise counsel, I laid down in Guam three principles as guidelines for future American policy toward Asia:

* First, the United States will keep all of its treaty commitments.
* Second, we shall provide a shield if a nuclear power threatens the freedom of a nation allied with US or of a nation whose survival we consider vital to our security.
* Third, in cases involving other types of aggression, we shall furnish military and economic assistance when requested in accordance with our treaty commitments. But we shall look to the nation directly threatened to assume the primary responsibility of providing the manpower for its defense.

After I announced this policy, I found that the leaders of the Philippines, Thailand, Vietnam, South Korea, and other nations which might be threatened by Communist aggression, welcomed this new direction in American foreign policy.

The defense of freedom is everybody's business—not just America's business. And it is particularly the responsibility of the people whose freedom is threatened. In the previous administration, we Americanized the war in Vietnam. In this administration, we are Vietnamizing the search for peace.

The policy of the previous administration not only resulted in our assuming the primary responsibility for fighting the war, but even more significantly did not adequately stress the goal of strengthening the South Vietnamese so that they could defend themselves when we left.

The Vietnamization plan was launched following Secretary Laird's visit to Vietnam in March. Under the plan, I ordered first a substantial increase in the training and equipment of South Vietnamese forces.

In July, on my visit to Vietnam, I changed General Abrams' orders so that they were consistent with the objectives of our new policies. Under the new orders, the primary mission of our troops is to enable the South Vietnamese forces to assume the full responsibility for the security of South Vietnam.

Our air operations have been reduced by over 20 percent.

And now we have begun to see the results of this long overdue change in American policy in Vietnam.

After 5 years of Americans going into Vietnam, we are finally bringing American men home. By December 15, over 60,000 men will have been withdrawn from South Vietnam, including 20 percent of all of our combat forces.

The South Vietnamese have continued to gain in strength. As a result they have been able to take over combat responsibilities from our American troops.

Two other significant developments have occurred since this administration took office.

* Enemy infiltration, infiltration which is essential if they are to launch a major attack, over the last 3 months is less than 20 percent of what it was over the same period last year.
* Most important—United States casualties have declined during the last 2 months to the lowest point in 3 years.

Let me now turn to our program for the future.

We have adopted a plan which we have worked out in cooperation with the South Vietnamese for the complete withdrawal of all U.S. combat ground forces, and their replacement by South Vietnamese forces on an orderly scheduled timetable. This withdrawal will be made from strength and not from weakness. As South Vietnamese forces become stronger, the rate of American withdrawal can become greater.

I have not and do not intend to announce the timetable for our program. And there are obvious reasons for this decision which I am sure you will understand. As I have indicated on several occasions, the rate of withdrawal will depend on developments on three fronts.

One of these is the progress which can be or might be made in the Paris talks. An announcement of a fixed timetable for our withdrawal would completely remove any

incentive for the enemy to negotiate an agreement. They would simply wait until our forces had withdrawn and then move in.

The other two factors on which we will base our withdrawal decisions are the level of enemy activity and the progress of the training programs of the South Vietnamese forces. And I am glad to be able to report tonight progress on both of these fronts has been greater than we anticipated when we started the program in June for withdrawal. As a result, our timetable for withdrawal is more optimistic now than when we made our first estimates in June. Now, this clearly demonstrates why it is not wise to be frozen in on a fixed timetable.

We must retain the flexibility to base each withdrawal decision on the situation as it is at that time rather than on estimates that are no longer valid.

Along with this optimistic estimate, I must—in all candor—leave one note of caution. If the level of enemy activity significantly increases we might have to adjust our timetable accordingly.

However, I want the record to be completely clear on one point.

At the time of the bombing halt just a year ago, there was some confusion as to whether there was an understanding on the part of the enemy that if we stopped the bombing of North Vietnam they would stop the shelling of cities in South Vietnam. I want to be sure that there is no misunderstanding on the part of the enemy with regard to our withdrawal program.

We have noted the reduced level of infiltration, the reduction of our casualties, and are basing our withdrawal decisions partially on those factors. If the level of infiltration or our casualties increase while we are trying to scale down the fighting, it will be the result of a conscious decision by the enemy.

Hanoi could make no greater mistake than to assume that an increase in violence will be to its advantage. If I conclude that increased enemy action jeopardizes our remaining forces in Vietnam, I shall not hesitate to take strong and effective measures to deal with that situation.

This is not a threat. This is a statement of policy, which as Commander in Chief of our Armed Forces, I am making in meeting my responsibility for the protection of American fighting men wherever they may be.

My fellow Americans, I am sure you can recognize from what I have said that we really only have two choices open to us if we want to end this war.

* I can order an immediate, precipitate withdrawal of all Americans from Vietnam without regard to the effects of that action.
* Or we can persist in our search for a just peace through a negotiated settlement if possible, or through continued implementation of our plan for Vietnamization if necessary, a plan in which we will withdraw all of our forces from Vietnam on a schedule in accordance with our program, as the South Vietnamese become strong enough to defend their own freedom.

I have chosen this second course. It is not the easy way. It is the right way.

It is a plan which will end the war and serve the cause of peace—not just in Vietnam but in the Pacific and in the world.

In speaking of the consequences of a precipitate withdrawal, I mentioned that our allies would lose confidence in America.

Far more dangerous, we would lose confidence in ourselves. Oh, the immediate reaction would be a sense of relief that our men were coming home. But as we saw the consequences of what we had done, inevitable remorse and divisive recrimination would scar our spirit as a people.

We have faced other crises in our history and have become stronger by rejecting the easy way out and taking the right way in meeting our challenges. Our greatness as a nation has been our capacity to do what had to be done when we knew our course was right.

I recognize that some of my fellow citizens disagree with the plan for peace I have chosen. Honest and patriotic Americans have reached different conclusions as to how peace should be achieved.

In San Francisco a few weeks ago, I saw demonstrators carrying signs reading: "Lose in Vietnam, bring the boys home."

Well, one of the strengths of our free society is that any American has a right to reach that conclusion and to advocate that point of view. But as President of the United States, I would be untrue to my oath of office if I allowed the policy of this Nation to be dictated by the minority who hold that point of view and who try to impose it on the Nation by mounting demonstrations in the street.

For almost 200 years, the policy of this Nation has been made under our Constitution by those leaders in the Congress and the White House elected by all of the people. If a vocal minority, however fervent its cause, prevails over reason and the will of the majority, this Nation has no future as a free society.

And now I would like to address a word, if I may, to the young people of this Nation who are particularly concerned, and I understand why they are concerned, about this war.

I respect your idealism. I share your concern for peace. I want peace as much as you do. There are powerful personal reasons I want to end this war. This week I will have to sign 83 letters to mothers, fathers, wives, and loved ones of men who have given their lives for America in Vietnam. It is very little satisfaction to me that this is only one-third as many letters as I signed the first week in office. There is nothing I want more than to see the day come when I do not have to write any of those letters.

I want to end the war to save the lives of those brave young men in Vietnam.

But I want to end it in a way which will increase the chance that their younger brothers and their sons will not have to fight in some future Vietnam someplace in the world.

And I want to end the war for another reason. I want to end it so that the energy and dedication of you, our young people, now too often directed into bitter hatred against those responsible for the war, can be turned to the great challenges of peace, a better life for all Americans, a better life for all people on this earth.

I have chosen a plan for peace. I believe it will succeed.

If it does succeed, what the critics say now won't matter. If it does not succeed, anything I say then won't matter.

I know it may not be fashionable to speak of patriotism or national destiny these days. But I feel it is appropriate to do so on this occasion.

Two hundred years ago this Nation was weak and poor. But even then, America was the hope of millions in the world. Today we have become the strongest and richest nation in the world. And the wheel of destiny has turned so that any hope the world has for the survival of peace and freedom will be determined by whether the American people have the moral stamina and the courage to meet the challenge of free world leadership.

Let historians not record that when America was the most powerful nation in the world we passed on the other side of the road and allowed the last hopes for peace and freedom of millions of people to be suffocated by the forces of totalitarianism.

And so tonight—to you, the great silent majority of my fellow Americans—I ask for your support.

I pledged in my campaign for the Presidency to end the war in a way that we could win the peace. I have initiated a plan of action which will enable me to keep that pledge.

The more support I can have from the American people, the sooner that pledge can be redeemed; for the more divided we are at home, the less likely the enemy is to negotiate at Paris.

Let us be united for peace. Let us also be united against defeat. Because let us understand: North Vietnam cannot defeat or humiliate the United States. Only Americans can do that.

Fifty years ago, in this room and at this very desk, President Woodrow Wilson spoke words which caught the imagination of a war-weary world. He said: "This is the war to end war." His dream for peace after World War I was shattered on the hard realities of great power politics and Woodrow Wilson died a broken man.

Tonight I do not tell you that the war in Vietnam is the war to end wars. But I do say this: I have initiated a plan which will end this war in a way that will bring us closer to that great goal to which Woodrow Wilson and every American President in our history has been dedicated—the goal of a just and lasting peace.

As President I hold the responsibility for choosing the best path to that goal and then leading the Nation along it. I pledge to you tonight that I shall meet this responsibility with all of the strength and wisdom I can command in accordance with our hopes, mindful of your concerns, sustained by your prayers.

Thank you and goodnight.

Source: Public Papers of the Presidents of the United States: Richard Nixon, 1969 (Washington, DC: U.S. Government Printing Office, 1971), 901–909.

President Richard Nixon: Excerpts from Speech on Cambodia (April 30, 1970)

President Richard Nixon sought to demonstrate U.S. resolve and pressure the Democratic Republic of Vietnam (DRV, North Vietnam) in the Paris negotiations by intervening in Cambodia, the border area of which was adjacent to the Republic of Vietnam (RVN, South Vietnam) and honeycombed with People's Army of Vietnam (PAVN, North Vietnamese Army) supply dumps. This step had long been advocated by the U.S. military but had been rejected by President Lyndon Johnson. The secret bombing of the Cambodian border areas by U.S. B-52 bombers—dubbed Operation MENU—began on March 18, 1969, and extended over a span of 14 months. When this action did not have the desired effect, Nixon authorized the use of ground troops. Beginning on April 14, 1970, Army of the Republic of Vietnam (ARVN, South Vietnamese Army) troops entered Cambodia to destroy PAVN border supply caches. Then, despite opposition from Secretary of Defense Melvin Laird and Secretary of State William Rogers, Nixon authorized the use of American ground forces. The resulting Cambodian Incursion involved 50,000 ARVN and 30,000 U.S. troops. On April 30, Nixon informed the American people by television that U.S. troops were invading Cambodia. Nixon says that this is in response to a request from the South Vietnamese government. It is not an invasion but instead is an incursion, an extension of the war "to protect our men who are in Viet-Nam and to guarantee the continued success of our withdrawal and the Vietnamization programs."

Good evening, my fellow Americans.

Ten days ago, in my report to the Nation on Viet-Nam, I announced a decision to withdraw an additional 150,000 Americans from Viet-Nam over the next year. I said then that I was making that decision despite our concern over increased enemy activity in Laos, in Cambodia, and in South Viet-Nam.

At that time, I warned that if I concluded that increased enemy activity in any of these areas endangered the lives of Americans remaining in Viet-Nam, I would not hesitate to take strong and effective measures to deal with that situation.

Despite that warning, North Viet-Nam has increased its military aggression in all these areas, and particularly in Cambodia.

After full consultation with the National Security Council, Ambassador Bunker, General Abrams, and my other advisers, I have concluded that the actions of the enemy in the last 10 days clearly endanger the lives of Americans who are in Viet-Nam now and would constitute an unacceptable risk to those who will be there after withdrawal of another 150,000.

To protect our men who are in Viet-Nam and to guarantee the continued success of our withdrawal and Vietnamization programs, I have concluded that the time has come for action.

Tonight I shall describe the actions of the enemy, the actions I have ordered to deal with that situation, and the reasons for my decision.

Cambodia, a small country of 7 million people, has been a neutral nation since the Geneva agreement of 1954—an agreement, incidentally, which was signed by the Government of North Viet-Nam.

American policy since then has been to scrupulously respect the neutrality of the Cambodian people. We have maintained a skeleton diplomatic mission of fewer than 15 in Cambodia's capital, and that only since last August. For the previous 4 years, from 1965 to 1969, we did not have any diplomatic mission whatever in Cambodia. And for the past 5 years, we have provided no military assistance whatever and no economic assistance to Cambodia.

North Viet-Nam, however, has not respected that neutrality.

For the past 5 years ... North Viet-Nam has occupied military sanctuaries all along the Cambodian frontier with South Viet-Nam. Some of these extend up to 20 miles into Cambodia. The sanctuaries ... are on both sides of the border. They are used for hit-and-run attacks on American and South Vietnamese forces in South Viet-Nam.

These Communist-occupied territories contain major base camps, training sites, logistics facilities, weapons and ammunition factories, airstrips, and prisoner of war compounds.

For 5 years neither the United States nor South Viet-Nam has moved against these enemy sanctuaries, because we did not wish to violate the territory of a neutral nation. Even after the Vietnamese Communists began to expand these sanctuaries 4 weeks ago, we counseled patience to our South Vietnamese allies and imposed restraints on our own commanders.

In contrast to our policy, the enemy in the past 2 weeks has stepped up his guerrilla actions, and he is concentrating his main forces in these sanctuaries ... where they are building up to launch massive attacks on our forces and those of South Viet-Nam.

North Viet-Nam in the last 2 weeks has stripped away all pretense of respecting the sovereignty or the neutrality of Cambodia. Thousands of their soldiers are invading the country from the sanctuaries; they are encircling the Capital of Phnom Penh. Coming from these sanctuaries ... they have moved into Cambodia and are encircling the Capital.

Cambodia, as a result of this, has sent out a call to the United States, to a number of other nations, for assistance. Because if this enemy effort succeeds, Cambodia would become a vast enemy staging area and a springboard for attacks on South Viet-Nam along 600 miles of frontier, a refuge where enemy troops could return from combat without fear of retaliation.

North Vietnamese men and supplies could then be poured into that country, jeopardizing not only the lives of our own men but the people of South Viet-Nam as well. ...

In cooperation with the armed forces of South Viet-Nam, attacks are being launched this week to clean out major enemy sanctuaries on the Cambodian-Viet-Nam border.

A major responsibility for the ground operations is being assumed by South Vietnamese forces. For example, the attacks in several areas ... are exclusively South Vietnamese ground operations under South Vietnamese command, with the United States providing air and logistical support.

There is one area, however ... where I have concluded that a combined American and South Vietnamese operation is necessary.

Tonight American and South Vietnamese units will attack the headquarters for the entire Communist military operation in South Viet-Nam. This key control center has been occupied by the North Vietnamese and Viet Cong for 5 years in blatant violation of Cambodia's neutrality.

This is not an invasion of Cambodia. The areas in which these attacks will be launched are completely occupied and controlled by North Vietnamese forces. Our purpose is not to occupy the areas. Once enemy forces are driven out of these sanctuaries and once their military supplies are destroyed, we will withdraw.

These actions are in no way directed at the security interests of any nation. Any government that chooses to use these actions as a pretext for harming relations with the United States will be doing so on its own responsibility and on its own initiative, and we will draw the appropriate conclusions.

Now, let me give you the reasons for my decision.

A majority of the American people, a majority of you listening to me, are for the withdrawal of our forces from Viet-Nam. The action I have taken tonight is indispensable for the continuing success of that withdrawal program.

A majority of the American people want to end this war rather than to have it drag on interminably. The action I have taken tonight will serve that purpose.

A majority of the American people want to keep the casualties of our brave men in Viet-Nam at an absolute minimum. The action I take tonight is essential if we are to accomplish that goal.

We take this action not for the purpose of expanding the war into Cambodia, but for the purpose of ending the war in Viet-Nam and winning the just peace we all desire. We have made and we will continue to make every possible effort to end this war through negotiation at the conference table rather than through more fighting on the battlefield. . . .

My fellow Americans, we live in an age of anarchy, both abroad and at home. We see mindless attacks on all the great institutions which have been created by free civilizations in the last 500 years. Even here in the United States, great universities are being systematically destroyed. Small nations all over the world find themselves under attack from within and from without.

If, when the chips are down, the world's most powerful nation, the United States of America, acts like a pitiful, helpless giant, the forces of totalitarianism and anarchy will threaten free nations and free institutions throughout the world.

It is not our power but our will and character that is being tested tonight. The question all Americans must ask and answer tonight is this: Does the richest and strongest nation in the history of the world have the character to meet a direct challenge by a group which rejects every effort to win a just peace, ignores our warning, tramples on solemn agreements, violates the neutrality of an unarmed people, and uses our prisoners as hostages?

If we fail to meet this challenge, all other nations will be on notice that despite its overwhelming power the United States, when a real crisis comes, will be found wanting.

During my campaign for the Presidency, I pledged to bring Americans home from Viet-Nam. They are coming home.

I promised to end this war. I shall keep that promise.

I promised to win a just peace. I shall keep that promise.

We shall avoid a wider war. But we are also determined to put an end to this war. . . .

No one is more aware than I am of the political consequences of the action I have taken. It is tempting to take the easy political path: to blame this war on previous administrations and to bring all of our men home immediately, regardless of the consequences, even though that would mean defeat for the United States; to desert 18 million South Vietnamese people who have put their trust in us and to expose them to the same slaughter and savagery which the leaders of North Viet-Nam inflicted on hundreds of thousands of North Vietnamese who chose freedom when the Communists took over North Viet-Nam in 1954; to get peace at any price now, even though I know that a peace of humiliation for the United States would lead to a bigger war or surrender later.

I have rejected all political considerations in making this decision.

Whether my party gains in November is nothing compared to the lives of 400,000 brave Americans fighting for our country and for the cause of peace and freedom in Viet-Nam. Whether I may be a one-term President is insignificant compared to whether by our failure to act in this crisis the United States proves itself to be unworthy to lead the forces of freedom in this critical period in world history. I would rather be a one-term President and do what I believe is right than to be a two-term President at the cost of seeing America become a second-rate power and to see this nation accept the first defeat in its proud 190-year history.

Source: Public Papers of the Presidents of the United States: Richard Nixon, 1970 (Washington, DC: U.S. Government Printing Office, 1971), 405–410.

Henry Kissinger, National Security Advisor: Excerpt from News Conference (October 26, 1972)

Returning from Saigon, U.S. national security advisor Henry Kissinger held a nationally televised press conference in which he struck a very positive note about the prospects for peace. In this portion of the transcript,

Kissinger glosses over the fundamental objections raised by President Nguyen Van Thieu of the Republic of Vietnam (RVN, South Vietnam), stating only that a half dozen matters needed to be hammered out, including "certain ambiguities," "linguistic problems," and "technical problems." He does not mention that the United States would be presenting substantial demands that will change the character of the document already agreed to and says that it should take no more than one more meeting and "several hours of work" to achieve final agreement.

Now, what is it, then, that prevents the completion of the agreement? Why is it that we have asked for one more meeting with the North Vietnamese to work out a final text? The principal reason is that in a negotiation that was stalemated for five years, and which did not really make a breakthrough until October 8, many of the general principles were clearly understood before the breakthrough, but as one elaborated the text, many of the nuances on which the implementation will ultimately depend became more and more apparent.

It was obvious, it was natural, that when we were talking about the abstract desirability of a cease-fire that neither side was perhaps as precise as it had to become later about the timing and staging of a cease-fire in a country in which there are no clear frontlines. And also the acceptance on our part of the North Vietnamese insistence on an accelerated schedule meant that texts could never be conformed, that English and Vietnamese texts tended to lag behind each other, and that ambiguities in formulation arose that require one more meeting to straighten out.

Let me give you a few examples, and I think you will understand that we are talking here of a different problem than what occupied us in the many sessions I have had with you ladies and gentlemen about the problem of peace in Vietnam, sessions which concerned abstract theories of what approach might succeed.

We are talking here about six or seven very concrete issues that, with anything like the good will that has already been shown, can easily be settled. For example, it has become apparent to us that there will be great temptation for the cease-fire to be paralleled by a last effort to seize as much territory as possible and perhaps to extend operations for long enough to establish political control over a given area.

We would like to avoid the dangers of the loss of life, perhaps in some areas even of the massacre that may be inherent in this, and we therefore want to discuss methods by which the international supervisory body can be put in place at the same time that the cease-fire is promulgated.

The Secretary of State has already had preliminary conversations with some of the countries that are being asked to join this body in order to speed up this process.

Secondly, because of the different political circumstances in each of the Indo-Chinese countries, the relationship of military operations there to the end of the war in Viet-Nam, or cease-fires there in relation to the end of the war in Viet-Nam, is somewhat complex; and we would like to discuss more concretely how to compress this time as much as possible.

There were certain ambiguities that were raised by the interview that the North Vietnamese Prime Minister, Pham Van Dong, gave to one of the weekly journals in which he seemed to be, with respect to one or two points, under a misapprehension as to what the agreement contained, and at any rate, we would like to have that clarified.

There are linguistic problems. For example, we call the National Council of

Reconciliation an administrative structure in order to make clear that we do not see it as anything comparable to a coalition government. We want to make sure that the Vietnamese text conveys the same meaning.

I must add that the words "administrative structure" were given to us in English by the Vietnamese, so this is not a maneuver on our part.

There are some technical problems as to what clauses of the Geneva accords to refer to in certain sections of the document, and there is a problem which was never settled in which the North Vietnamese, as they have pointed out in their broadcast, have proposed that the agreement be signed by the United States and North Viet-Nam—we on behalf of Saigon, they on behalf of their allies in South Viet-Nam.

We have always held the view that we would leave it up to our allies whether they wanted a two-power document or whether they wanted to sign themselves a document that establishes peace in their country. Now, they prefer to participate in the signing of the peace, and it seems to us not an unreasonable proposal that a country on whose territory a war has been fought and whose population has been uprooted and has suffered so greatly—that it should have the right to sign its own peace treaty. This, again, strikes us as a not insuperable difficulty, but its acceptance will require the redrafting of certain sections of the document, and that, again, is a job that will require several hours of work.

We have asked the North Vietnamese to meet with us on any date of their choice. We have, as has been reported, restricted our bombing, in effect, to the battle area in order to show our good will and to indicate that we are working within the framework of existing agreements.

We remain convinced that the issues that I have mentioned are soluble in a very brief period of time. We have undertaken, and I repeat it here publicly, to settle them at one more meeting and to remain at that meeting for as long as is necessary to complete the agreement.

Source: U.S. Congress, Senate, *Background Information Relating to Southeast Asia and Vietnam,* 7th rev. ed. (Washington, DC: U.S. Government Printing Office, 1974), 490–491.

President Richard Nixon: Letter to President Nguyen Van Thieu (November 14, 1972)

President Nguyen Van Thieu of the Republic of Vietnam (RVN, South Vietnam) refused to budge on the peace negotiations. U.S. national security advisor Henry Kissinger urged President Richard Nixon to sign the agreement without him, but the president refused, blaming Hanoi for the impasse. Kissinger has suggested that Nixon rejected implementing the October agreement without Thieu because he would have found it awkward prior to the November 1972 presidential election to risk his support among conservatives who were his political base. In order to regain Thieu's cooperation in the peace negotiations, in November Nixon sent Kissinger's deputy General Alexander Haig to Saigon, and in Operation ENHANCE PLUS the Pentagon turned over massive amounts of military equipment to the South Vietnamese armed forces. In this note to Thieu, Nixon spells out the demands that the United States will make of the negotiators from the Democratic Republic of Vietnam (DRV, North Vietnam) in Paris, including the withdrawal of a number of its troops into North Vietnam, but states that he does not expect all U.S. demands to be met. He also hints at a withdrawal of U.S. assistance if Thieu does not agree to the final text reached.

I was pleased to learn from General Haig that you held useful and constructive discussions with him in Saigon in preparation for Dr. Kissinger's forthcoming meeting with North Vietnam's negotiations in Paris.

After studying your letter of November 11 with great care I have concluded that we have made substantial progress towards reaching a common understanding on many of the important issues before us. You can be sure that we will pursue the proposed changes in the draft agreement that General Haig discussed with you with the utmost firmness and that, as these discussions proceed, we shall keep you fully informed through your Ambassador to the Paris Conference on Vietnam who will be briefed daily by Dr. Kissinger.

I understand from your letter and from General Haig's personal report that your principal remaining concern with respect to the draft agreement is the status of North Vietnamese forces now in South Vietnam. As General Haig explained to you, it is our intention to deal with this problem first by seeking to insert a reference to respect for the demilitarized zone in the proposed agreement and, second, by proposing a clause which provides for the reduction and demobilization of forces on both sides in South Vietnam on a one-to-one basis and to have demobilized personnel return to their homes.

Upon reviewing this proposed language, it is my conviction that such a provision can go a long way towards dealing with your concern with respect to North Vietnamese forces. General Haig tells me, however, that you are also seriously concerned about the timing and verification of such reductions. In light of this, I have asked Dr. Kissinger to convey to you, through Ambassador Bunker, some additional clauses we would propose adding to the agreement dealing with each of these points. In addition, I have asked that Dr. Kissinger send you the other technical and less important substantive changes which General Haig did not have the opportunity to discuss with you because they had not yet been fully developed in Washington. With these proposed modifications, I think you will agree that we have done everything we can to improve the existing draft while remaining within its general framework.

You also raise in your letter the question of participation by other Asian countries in the International Conference. As you know, the presently contemplated composition are the permanent members of the United Nations Security Council, the members of the ICCS, the parties to the Paris Conference on Vietnam and the Secretary General of the United Nations. We seriously considered Cambodian and Laotian participation but decided that these would be unnecessary complications with respect to representation. We do not, however, exclude the possibility of delegations from these countries participating in an observer status at the invitation of the conference. As for Japan, this question was raised earlier in our negotiations with Hanoi and set aside because it inevitably raises the possibility of Indian participation. I have, however, asked that Dr. Kissinger raise this matter again in Paris and he will inform your representative what progress we make on this. What we must recognize as a practical matter is that participation of Japan is very likely to lead to the participation of India. We would appreciate hearing your preference on whether it is better to include both countries or neither of them.

Finally, in respect to the composition of the ICCS, I must say in all candor that I do not share your view that its contemplated membership is unbalanced. I am hopeful that it will prove to be a useful mechanism in detecting and reporting violations of the agreement. In any event, what we both must recognize is that the supervisory mechanism in itself is in no measure as important as our own firm determination to see to it that the agreement works and our vigilance with respect to the prospect of its violation.

I will not repeat here all that I said to you in my letter of November 8, but I do wish to reaffirm its essential content and stress again my determination to work towards an early agreement along the lines of the schedule which General Haig explained to you. I must explain in all frankness that while we will do our very best to secure the changes in the agreement which General Haig discussed with you and those additional ones which Ambassador Bunker will bring you, we cannot expect to secure them all. For example, it is unrealistic to assume that we will be able to secure the absolute assurances which you would hope to have on the troop issue.

But far more important than what we say in the agreement on this issue is what we do in the event the enemy renews its aggression. You have my absolute assurance that if Hanoi fails to abide by the terms of this agreement it is my intention to take swift and severe retaliatory action.

I believe the existing agreement to be an essentially sound one which should become even more so if we succeed in obtaining some of the changes we have discussed. Our best assurance of success is to move into this new situation with confidence and cooperation.

With this attitude and the inherent strength of your government and army on the ground in South Vietnam, I am confident this agreement will be a successful one.

If, on the other hand, we are unable to agree on the course that I have outlined, it is difficult for me to see how we will be able to continue our common effort towards securing a just and honorable peace. As General Haig told you I would with great reluctance be forced to consider other alternatives. For this reason, it is essential that we have your agreement as we proceed into our next meeting with Hanoi's negotiators. And I strongly urge you and your advisors to work promptly with Ambassador Bunker and Our Mission in Saigon on the many practical problems which will face us in implementing the agreement. I cannot over-emphasize the urgency of the task at hand nor my unalterable determination to proceed along the course which we have outlined.

Above all we must bear in mind what will really maintain the agreement. It is not any particular clause in the agreement but our joint willingness to maintain its clauses. I repeat my personal assurances to you that the United States will react very strongly and rapidly to any violation of the agreement. But in order to do this effectively it is essential that I have public support and that your Government does not emerge as the obstacle to a peace which [the] American public now universally desires. It is for this reason that I am pressing for the acceptance of an agreement which I am convinced is honorable and fair and which can be made essentially secure by our joint determination.

Mrs. Nixon joins me in extending our warmest personal regards to Madame Thieu and to you. We look forward to seeing you again at our home in California once the just peace we have both fought for so long is finally achieved.

Source: Foreign Relations of the United States, 1969–1976, Vol. 9 (Washington, DC: U.S. Government Printing Office, 2010), 395–398.

Excerpt from Paris Peace Agreement (January 27, 1973)

On January 23, 1973, the Democratic Republic of Vietnam (DRV, North Vietnam) and the United States concluded a new peace agreement, which was now imposed on the government of the Republic of Vietnam (RVN, South Vietnam). Four parties signed: the United States, South Vietnam, North Vietnam, and the Provisional Revolutionary Government (PRG), the Communist provisional government in South Vietnam. Despite a few cosmetic changes, the agreement was for all practical purposes identical to that signed the previous October. The agreement acknowledges the "independence, sovereignty, unity and territorial integrity of Viet-Nam as recognized by the 1954 Geneva Agreements on Vietnam." This was what Hanoi had argued for years: that Vietnam was one country and that its effort in South Vietnam was not foreign aggression but rather a legitimate struggle for national independence and unity. The agreement provides for a cease-fire, withdrawal of all U.S. troops and advisers from South Vietnam, release of prisoners, the formation of a Council of National Reconciliation and Concord to resolve disagreements between South Vietnam and North Vietnam and organize new general elections, new supervisory machinery (the International Commission of Control and Supervision, consisting of representatives of Canada, Hungary, Poland, and Indonesia), and withdrawal of foreign troops from Laos and Cambodia. The agreement also leaves in place in South Vietnam an estimated 150,000 People's Army of Vietnam (PAVN, North Vietnamese Army) troops.

Agreement on Ending the War and Restoring Peace in Vietnam

The Parties participating in the Paris Conference on Viet-Nam,

With a view to ending the war and restoring peace in Viet-Nam on the basis of respect for the Vietnamese people's fundamental national rights and the South Vietnamese people's right to self-determination, and to contributing to the consolidation of peace in Asia and the world.

Have agreed on the following provisions and undertake to respect and to implement them:

Chapter I The Vietnamese People's Fundamental National Rights

Article 1. The United States and all other countries respect the independence, sovereignty, unity, and territorial integrity of Viet-Nam as recognized by the 1954 Geneva Agreements on Viet-Nam.

Chapter II Cessation of Hostilities— Withdrawal of Troops

Article 2. A cease-fire shall be observed throughout South Viet-Nam as of 2400 hours G.M.T., on January 27, 1973.

At the same hour, the United States will stop all its military activities against the territory of the Democratic Republic of Viet-Nam by ground, air and naval forces, wherever they may be based, and end the mining of the territorial waters, ports, harbors, and waterways of the Democratic Republic of Viet-Nam. The United States will remove, permanently deactivate or destroy all the mines in the territorial waters, ports, harbors, and waterways of North Viet-Nam as soon as this Agreement goes into effect.

The complete cessation of hostilities mentioned in this Article shall be durable and without limit of time.

Article 3. The parties undertake to maintain the cease-fire and to ensure a lasting and stable peace.

As soon as the cease-fire goes into effect:

a. The United States forces and those of the other foreign countries allied with the United States and the Republic of Viet-Nam shall remain in-place pending the implementation of the plan of troop withdrawal. The Four-Party Joint Military Commission described in Article 16 [not included here] shall determine the modalities.

b. The armed forces of the two South Vietnamese parties shall remain in-place. The Two-Party Joint Military Commission described in Article 17 [not included here] shall determine the areas controlled by each party and the modalities of stationing.

c. The regular forces of all services and arms and the irregular forces of the parties in South Viet-Nam shall stop all offensive activities against each other and shall strictly abide by the following stipulations:
   • —All acts of force on the ground, in the air, and on the sea shall be prohibited;
   • —All hostile acts, terrorism and reprisals by both sides will be banned.

Article 4. The United States will not continue its military involvement or intervene in the internal affairs of South Viet-Nam.

Article 5. Within sixty days of the signing of this Agreement, there will be a total withdrawal from South Viet-Nam of troops, military advisers, and military personnel, including technical military personnel and military personnel associated with the pacification program, armaments, munitions, and war material of the United States and those of the other foreign countries mentioned in Article 3 (a). Advisers from the above-mentioned countries to all paramilitary organizations and the police force will also be withdrawn within the same period of time.

Article 6. The dismantlement of all military bases in South Viet-Nam of the United States and of the other foreign countries mentioned in Article 3 (a) shall be completed within sixty days of the signing of this Agreement.

Article 7. From the enforcement of the cease-fire to the formation of the government provided for in Article 9 (b) and 14 of this Agreement, the two South Vietnamese parties shall not accept the introduction of troops, military advisers, and military personnel including technical military personnel, armaments, munitions, and war material into South Viet-Nam.

The two South Vietnamese parties shall be permitted to make periodic replacement of armaments, munitions and war material which have been destroyed, damaged, worn out or used up after the cease-fire, on the basis of piece-for-piece, of the same characteristics and properties, under the supervision of the Joint Military Commission of the two South Vietnamese parties and of the International Commission of Control and Supervision.

Chapter III The Return of Captured Military Personnel and Foreign Civilians, and Captured and Detained Vietnamese Civilian Personnel

Article 8

a. The return of captured military personnel and foreign civilians of the parties shall be carried out simultaneously with and completed not later than the same day as the troop withdrawal mentioned in Article 5. The parties shall exchange complete lists of the above-mentioned captured military personnel and foreign civilians on the day of the signing of this Agreement.

b. The Parties shall help each other to get information about those military personnel and foreign civilians of the parties missing in action, to determine the location and take care of the graves of the dead so as to facilitate the exhumation and repatriation of the remains, and to take any such other measures as may be required to get information about those still considered missing in action.

c. The question of the return of Vietnamese civilian personnel captured and detained in South Viet-Nam will be resolved by the two South Vietnamese parties on the basis of the principles of Article 21 (b) of the Agreement on the Cessation of Hostilities in Viet-Nam of July 20, 1954. The two South Vietnamese parties will do so in a spirit of national reconciliation and concord, with a view to ending hatred and enmity, in order to ease suffering and to reunite families. The two South Vietnamese parties will do their utmost to resolve this question within ninety days after the cease-fire comes into effect.

Chapter IV The Exercise of the South Vietnamese People's Right to Self-Determination

Article 9. The Government of the United States of America and the Government of the Democratic Republic of Viet-Nam undertake to respect the following principles for the exercise of the South Vietnamese people's right to self-determination:

a. The South Vietnamese people's right to self-determination is sacred, inalienable, and shall be respected by all countries.

b. The South Vietnamese people shall decide themselves the political future of South Viet-Nam through genuinely free and democratic general elections under international supervision.

c. Foreign countries shall not impose any political tendency or personality on the South Vietnamese people.

Article 10. The two South Vietnamese parties undertake to respect the cease-fire and maintain peace in South Viet-Nam, settle all matters of contention through negotiations, and avoid all armed conflict.

Article 11. Immediately after the cease-fire, the two South Vietnamese parties will:

- —achieve national reconciliation and concord, end hatred and enmity, prohibit all acts of reprisal and discrimination against individuals or organizations that have collaborated with one side or the other;
- —ensure the democratic liberties of the people: personal freedom, freedom of speech, freedom of the press, freedom of meeting, freedom of organization, freedom of political activities, freedom of belief, freedom of movement, freedom of residence, freedom of work, right to property ownership, and right to free enterprise.

Article 12

a. Immediately after the cease-fire, the two South Vietnamese parties shall hold consultations in a spirit of national reconciliation and concord, mutual respect, and mutual non-elimination to set up a National Council of National Reconciliation and Concord of three equal segments. The Council shall operate on the principle of unanimity. After the

National Council of National Reconciliation and Concord has assumed its functions, the two South Vietnamese parties will consult about the formation of councils at lower levels. The two South Vietnamese parties shall sign an agreement on the internal matters of South Viet-Nam as soon as possible and do their utmost to accomplish this within ninety days after the cease-fire comes into effect, in keeping with the South Vietnamese people's aspirations for peace, independence and democracy.

b. The National Council of National Reconciliation and Concord shall have the task of promoting the two South Vietnamese parties' implementation of this Agreement, achievement of national reconciliation and concord and ensurance of democratic liberties. The National Council of National Reconciliation and Concord will organize the free and democratic general elections provided for in Article 9 (b) and decide the procedures and modalities of these general elections. The institutions for which the general elections are to be held will be agreed upon through consultations between the two South Vietnamese parties. The National Council of National Reconciliation and Concord will also decide the procedures and modalities of such local elections as the two South Vietnamese parties agree upon.

Article 13. The question of Vietnamese armed forces in South Viet-Nam shall be settled by the two South Vietnamese parties in a spirit of national reconciliation and concord, equality and mutual respect, without foreign interference, in accordance with the postwar situation. Among the questions to be discussed by the two South Vietnamese parties are steps to reduce their military effectives and to demobilize the troops being reduced. The two South Vietnamese parties will accomplish this as soon as possible.

Article 14. South Viet-Nam will pursue a foreign policy of peace and independence. It will be prepared to establish relations with all countries irrespective of their political and social systems on the basis of mutual respect for independence and sovereignty and accept economic and technical aid from any country with no political conditions attached. The acceptance of military aid by South Viet-Nam in the future shall come under the authority of the government set up after the general elections in South Viet-Nam provided for in Article 9 (b).

Chapter V The Reunification of Viet-Nam and the Relationship Between North and South Viet-Nam

Article 15. The reunification of Viet-Nam shall be carried out step by step through peaceful means on the basis of discussions and agreements between North and South Viet-Nam, without coercion or annexation by either party, and without foreign interference. The time for reunification will be agreed upon by North and South Viet-Nam.

Pending reunification:

a. The military demarcation line between the two zones at the 17th parallel is only provisional and not a political or territorial boundary, as provided for in paragraph 6 of the Final Declaration of the 1954 Geneva Conference.

b. North and South Viet-Nam shall respect the Demilitarized Zone on either side of the Provisional Military Demarcation Line.

c. North and South Viet-Nam shall promptly start negotiations with a view to reestablishing normal relations in various fields. Among the questions to be negotiated are the modalities of civilian movement across the Provisional Military Demarcation Line.

d. North and South Viet-Nam shall not join any military alliance or military bloc and shall not allow foreign powers to maintain military bases, troops, military advisers, and military personnel on their respective territories, as stipulated in the 1954 Geneva Agreements on Viet-Nam.

[. . .]

Source: "Agreement on Ending the War and Restoring Peace in Vietnam," *Department of State Bulletin* 68(1755) (1973): 169–172.

Vietnam War Chronology

1887	French Indochina is officially created from the consolidation of French possessions in the region.
December 25, 1927	Nguyen Thai Hoc establishes the Viet Nam Quoc Dan Dang (VNQDD, or Vietnam National Party) as the first well-organized nationalist revolutionary party in Vietnam.
February 3, 1930	Ho Chi Minh helps to carry out a fusion of three Vietnamese communist parties into what becomes the Indo-Chinese Communist Party (ICP).
February 10, 1930	French put down an uprising in Yen Bay, northwest of Hanoi, all but destroying the Vietnam Nationalist Party.
September 1940	Japan occupies French Indochina.
May 1941	Ho Chi Minh forms the Viet Nam Doc Lap Dong Minh Hoi (Vietnam Independence League), commonly known as the Viet Minh.
December 22, 1944	With Ho Chi Minh's support, Vo Nguyen Giap sets up an armed propaganda brigade of 34 Vietnamese and begins to attack French outposts in northern Vietnam.
March 9, 1945	The Japanese stage a coup against the French and seize power directly in Vietnam.
March 11, 1945	Tokyo grants Vietnam its independence.
July–August 1945	The Potsdam Conference produces agreement regarding the disarmament of Japanese forces in Indochina at the conclusion of World War II: Chinese

nationalist forces will take surrender of Japanese troops north of, and British south of, the 16th Parallel.

August 16, 1945 In Hanoi, Ho Chi Minh declares himself president of the provisional government of a "free Vietnam."

August 19, 1945 The Viet Minh seize power in Hanoi.

August 24, 1945 In Saigon, Viet Minh leader Tran Van Giau declares the insurrection under way in the south.

August 27, 1945 Ho Chi Minh convenes his first cabinet meeting at Hanoi.

September 2, 1945 Ho Chi Minh publicly announces the formation of a "Provisional Government of the Democratic Republic of Vietnam" (DRV, later known as North Vietnam) with its capital at Hanoi.

September 13, 1945 In accordance with the Potsdam Agreements, 5,000 British troops arrive in southern Indochina.

September 14, 1945 Chinese nationalist troops arrive to disarm Japanese troops north of the 16th Parallel.

September 22, 1945 French troops return to Vietnam, seeking to regain control of Indochina.

October 25, 1945 Jacques-Philippe Leclerc begins the reconquest of Indochina for France, predicting it will take about a month for "mopping-up operations."

November 11, 1945 In a bid to widen his base at home and win Western support abroad, Ho Chi Minh dissolves the ICP.

February 28, 1946 The Franco-Chinese Accords secure Chinese withdrawal from northern Vietnam; the Chinese leave the following month.

March 6, 1946 The Ho-Sainteny Agreement is signed, setting the future relationship between the DRV and France. The DRV agrees to a French military presence in the north to protect French lives and property. In exchange, France recognizes the DRV as a free state and agrees to a referendum in the south to see if it wishes to join the DRV as a unified state, although no date for the vote is specified.

May 1946	Ho Chi Minh travels to France for negotiations.		Viet Minh positions near the Chinese border
June 1, 1946	In a meeting at Fontainebleau with Ho Chi Minh, French high commissioner for Indochina Georges Thierry d'Argenlieu subverts the Ho-Sainteny Agreement by pronouncing in Saigon the establishment of the "Republic of Cochin China."	**March 8, 1949**	Paris concludes the Elysée Agreements with former Vietnamese emperor Bao Dai, creating the State of Vietnam, and Paris concedes that Vietnam is in fact one country.
		July 1, 1949	The State of Vietnam is formally established.
November 20, 1946	A French naval blockade of the port city of Haiphong prompts fighting between Vietnamese and French forces that lasts until November 22.	**January 14, 1950**	Ho Chi Minh declares that the DRV is the only legal government of Vietnam. The People's Republic of China formally recognizes the DRV and agrees to furnish military assistance to the Viet Minh.
November 23, 1946	Although fighting has stopped, French troops are ordered to attack Vietnamese military installations, and casualty estimates range from 200 to 20,000 with continual fighting until November 28.	**May 8, 1950**	The United States announces plans to extend economic and military aid to the French in Indochina.
December 19, 1946	Full-scale fighting erupts in Vietnam, beginning the Indochina War.	**July 26, 1950**	U.S. president Harry Truman signs legislation providing $15 million in aid to the French war effort in Indochina.
October 7, 1947	French forces launch Operation LEA, a series of attacks on	**October 10, 1950**	The U.S. Military Assistance and Advisory Group (MAAG) is established in Saigon.

December 23, 1950   The United States signs a mutual defense assistance agreement with France, Vietnam, Cambodia, and Laos.

September 7, 1951   The United States signs an agreement with the State of Vietnam to provide economic assistance.

March 13, 1954   The siege of the French entrenched positions at Dien Bien Phu officially begins with a heavy Viet Minh bombardment.

April 29, 1954   U.S. president Dwight D. Eisenhower announces that the United States will not intervene militarily in Indochina.

May 7, 1954   The last French troops surrender at Dien Bien Phu, officially ending the battle.

May 8, 1954   The Indochina phase of the Geneva Conference begins.

June 18, 1954   Bao Dai selects Ngo Dinh Diem as the new premier of the State of Vietnam.

July 7, 1954   Diem officially forms his new government, which claims to encompass all of Vietnam.

July 21, 1954   The Geneva Conference issues three cease-fire agreements and one final declaration; Vietnam is temporarily divided into northern and southern zones pending nationwide elections to be held in 1956.

October 9, 1954   French forces complete their evacuation of Hanoi.

October 24, 1954   Eisenhower writes to Diem and promises direct assistance to his government, now in control of South Vietnam.

February 12, 1955   MAAG takes over responsibility from the French for training and organizing the State of Vietnam Army.

May 10, 1955   Diem formally requests U.S. military advisers.

July 19, 1955   The DRV government proposes the naming of representatives for a conference to negotiate general elections as called for in 1954 Geneva

	Agreement to the State of Vietnam government.
July 20, 1955	The State of Vietnam government rejects the proposal on the grounds that elections in the DRV would not be free.
August 9, 1955	The State of Vietnam government declares it will not enter into negotiations with the DRV government regarding elections as long as the northern Communist government continues.
October 23, 1955	After Bao Dai tries to remove him as premier, Diem organizes a carefully managed referendum, which results in a publicized 98 percent vote in his favor.
October 26, 1955	Using these referendum results as justification, Diem proclaims the Republic of Vietnam (RVN, South Vietnam) with himself as president.
April 6, 1956	South Vietnam again declares that it is a "non-signatory to the Geneva Agreements" and "continues not to recognize their provisions."
April 26, 1956	France officially abolishes its high command in Indochina.
May 11, 1956	The DRV once more proposes convening a conference regarding elections, which is again rejected by South Vietnam.
July 20, 1956	Deadline set by the 1954 Geneva Conference for elections, yet no elections are held.
September 14, 1956	The last French troops leave Saigon.
October 26, 1956	A new South Vietnamese constitution is created, heavily weighted toward control by the executive branch. This apparent reform is largely a sham, as Diem increasingly subjects South Vietnam to authoritarian rule.
January 1959	The Vietnamese Workers' Party Central Committee declares its support for armed insurrection in South Vietnam, although it states that this should remain secondary to the "political struggle."

April 4, 1959 — Eisenhower commits the United States to maintaining South Vietnam as a separate national entity.

July 8, 1959 — Two U.S. servicemen are killed in a Communist attack on Bien Hoa, the first Americans to die in the Vietnam War.

September 26, 1959 — An attack by the 2nd Liberation Battalion on units of the 23rd Division of the Army of the Republic of Vietnam (ARVN, South Vietnamese Army) leads U.S. and South Vietnamese officials to begin referring to the rebels as "Viet Cong," pejorative for "Vietnamese communists."

September 1959 — The Third Vietnamese Workers' Party Congress approves a program of violent overthrow of the Diem government. There are now two tasks at hand: carrying out a "socialist revolution" in the north and "liberating the South."

November 11–12, 1960 — In Saigon, members of the South Vietnamese Army surround the presidential palace in an effort to force Diem to institute reforms, a new government, and more effective prosecution of the war; Diem outmaneuvers them by agreeing to a long list of reforms—including freedom of the press, a coalition government, and new elections—until he can bring up loyal units and defeat the coup, whose members flee to Cambodia.

December 20, 1960 — Hanoi establishes the National Front for the Liberation of South Vietnam, usually known as the National Liberation Front (NLF); designed to replicate the Viet Minh as an umbrella nationalist organization, it reaches out to all those disaffected with Diem.

December 31, 1960 — There are now some 900 U.S. military personnel in South Vietnam.

May 15, 1961 — The U.S. State Department announces that it will increase MAAG personnel beyond the Geneva limit.

May 9–15, 1961	U.S. vice president Lyndon B. Johnson visits Saigon. Although expressing private reservations about Diem, he publicly hails him the "Winston Churchill of Southeast Asia."
September 18, 1961	A VC battalion besieges the provincial capital of Phuoc Vinh, 60 kilometers north of Saigon. During the month of August, there were 41 engagements between government troops and the VC in South Vietnam.
October 18, 1961	Diem declares a state of national emergency.
November 22, 1961	National Security Action Memorandum No. 111 authorizes U.S. commitment of additional helicopters, transport planes, and warplanes, as well as personnel to carry out training and actual combat missions.
December 6, 1961	The U.S. Joint Chiefs of Staff (JCS) authorize Operation FARM GATE, which allows U.S. personnel and aircraft to undertake combat missions if at least one Vietnamese national is carried on board the strike aircraft for training purposes.
December 8, 1961	Washington issues a report accusing North Vietnam of aggression against South Vietnam and warning of a "clear and present danger" of Communist victory.
December 11, 1961	The ferry carrier USNS *Card* arrives in Saigon with the 8th and 57th Transportation Companies, the first U.S. helicopter units sent to Vietnam.
January 12, 1962	Operation RANCH HAND—the spraying of defoliant herbicides in South Vietnam—begins.
February 1962	The 39th Signal Battalion, a communication unit, is the first unit of regular U.S. ground forces to arrive in Vietnam.
February 3, 1962	The "Strategic Hamlet" program begins in South Vietnam.
February 6, 1962	The U.S. Military Assistance Command, Vietnam (MACV) is

established, commanded by General Paul D. Harkins and tasked with directing the U.S. war effort.

February 27, 1962 Diem survives another coup attempt when Republic of Vietnam Air Force (VNAF, South Vietnamese Air Force) pilots try to kill him and his brother Ngo Dinh Nhu by bombing and strafing the presidential palace; dozens of Diem political opponents disappear, and thousands more are sent to prison camps.

May 1962 Communist forces gain control of a large area of Laos.

December 31, 1962 Some 11,300 U.S. military personnel are now in South Vietnam.

January 2, 1963 South Vietnamese forces suffer a humiliating defeat at the Battle of Ap Bac in the Mekong Delta southwest of Saigon.

May 8, 1963 Buddhists riot in Hue protesting the South Vietnamese government's ban on flying the flag of the World Fellowship of Buddhists; South

Vietnamese riot police kill eight demonstrators, including some children, leading to widespread Buddhist demonstrations throughout South Vietnam.

June 11, 1963 Elderly Buddhist monk Thich Quang Duc publicly burns himself to death to protest the South Vietnamese government's policies.

August 20, 1963 Diem declares martial law.

August 21, 1963 South Vietnamese Special Forces attack Buddhist pagodas; many are damaged and over 1,400 Buddhists are arrested.

August 22, 1963 Henry Cabot Lodge replaces Frederick Nolting as U.S. ambassador to South Vietnam.

October 2, 1963 As a result of the recent violence against Buddhists and other opponents of the Diem government, Washington decides to suspend a large portion of South Vietnam's economic aid, which is a clear signal to those planning a coup against Diem.

November 1, 1963 A military coup led by Duong Van Minh, Ton That Dinh, and Tran Van Don overthrows the Diem government.

November 2, 1963 Both Diem and Nhu, whom U.S. leaders assumed would be given safe passage out of the country, are murdered; the coup leaders set up a provisional government, suspend the constitution, and dissolve the National Assembly.

December 1963 The North Vietnamese leadership decides to send regulars from the People's Army of Vietnam (PAVN, North Vietnamese Army) to South Vietnam.

January 16, 1964 Lyndon B. Johnson, now president, authorizes covert operations against North Vietnam (OPLAN 34A); such operations, to be conducted by South Vietnamese forces supported by the United States, and beginning in February, will gather intelligence and conduct sabotage to destabilize the country.

January 30, 1964 Major General Nguyen Khanh ousts the South Vietnamese government headed by Duong Van Minh; U.S. officials, caught by surprise, promptly hail Khanh as the new leader because he promises to rule with a strong hand.

March 1964 Secretary of Defense Robert McNamara visits South Vietnam and vows U.S. support for Khanh.

April 1964 North Vietnamese Army regulars begin to infiltrate South Vietnam.

June 9, 1964 In response to operations in Laos conducted by Communist Pathet Lao and North Vietnamese forces, the United States begins Operation BARREL ROLL, a bombing campaign to support Royal Laotian Army and CIA-trained Hmong irregular forces.

June 20, 1964 General William C. Westmoreland replaces Harkins as MACV commander.

July 7, 1964 General Maxwell D. Taylor arrives in

	South Vietnam as the new U.S. ambassador.
July 30–31, 1964	South Vietnamese naval forces, using American swift boats, carry out commando raids against islands off the North Vietnamese coast, and North Vietnam accuses the United States and South Vietnam of an "extremely serious" violation of 1954 Geneva Agreements.
August 2, 1964	North Vietnamese torpedo boats attack the U.S. destroyer *Maddox* on patrol in international waters in the Gulf of Tonkin.
August 4, 1964	The *Maddox* and the *C. Turner Joy* claim that they have been attacked by North Vietnamese patrol boats, and Johnson orders U.S. air strikes against "gunboats and certain supporting facilities in North Vietnam."
August 7, 1964	Congress passes the Tonkin Gulf Resolution, authorizing "all necessary steps, including the use of armed force" in Southeast Asia.

September 1964	Westmoreland initiates HOP TAC, a pacification operation in six provinces around Saigon.
September 30, 1964	The first major antiwar demonstrations in the United States are held at the University of California, Berkeley.
November 1, 1964	Communist forces attack Bien Hoa Air Base, killing five U.S. military personnel and destroying six B-57 bombers.
December 14, 1964	Operation BARREL ROLL begins with U.S. planes attacking "targets of opportunity" in northern Laos.
December 24, 1964	Two Americans are killed when Viet Cong sappers bomb U.S. billets in Saigon.
December 31, 1964	There are now some 23,300 U.S. military personnel in South Vietnam.
February 7, 1965	Communists attack U.S. installations at Pleiku, and in retaliation, U.S. aircraft strike targets in North Vietnam (Operation FLAMING DART).
February 15, 1965	China threatens to enter the war if the

United States invades North Vietnam.

February 18, 1965 South Vietnamese Army and Marine units oust Khanh in a bloodless coup.

February 27, 1965 The U.S. State Department issues report detailing North Vietnamese "aggression."

February 28, 1965 U.S. and South Vietnamese officials announce that Johnson has decided to begin reprisal attacks against North Vietnam to secure a negotiated settlement.

March 2, 1965 Operation ROLLING THUNDER, the U.S.–South Vietnamese bombing campaign against North Vietnam, begins.

March 8, 1965 9th Marine Expeditionary Brigade lands at Red Beach, north of Da Nang.

April 1965 The United States begins Operation STEEL TIGER, an air interdiction campaign over the Ho Chi Minh Trail in the northern panhandle of Laos.

April 7, 1965 Johnson announces that the United States is willing to hold "unconditional discussions" with North Vietnam and suggests a $1 billion economic aid program for Southeast Asia.

April 8, 1965 North Vietnamese premier Pham Van Dong rejects Johnson's offer and announces a four-point position on peace, including settlement of South Vietnam's internal affairs "in accordance with the program of the National Liberation Front of South Vietnam, without any foreign interference."

April 21, 1965 A regiment of the 325th PAVN Division is identified in South Vietnam, proving that main force North Vietnamese units are now operating south of the DMZ.

May 1965 The U.S. Navy begins Operation MARKET TIME to interdict Communist surface traffic in South Vietnamese coastal waters.

May 3, 1965	The U.S. Army's 173rd Airborne Brigade arrives in South Vietnam and immediately begins combat operations in III Corps Tactical Zone.
May 13–18, 1965	Six-day U.S. bombing pause over North Vietnam.
June 16, 1965	McNamara announces new troop deployments to South Vietnam, bringing U.S. troop strength there to 70,000 men.
June 18, 1965	The ARC LIGHT campaign begins as B-52 bombers strike Communist targets within South Vietnam.
July 8, 1965	Lodge is reappointed as U.S. ambassador to South Vietnam.
October 15–16, 1965	The student-run National Coordinating Committee to End the War in Vietnam sponsors nationwide demonstrations in some 40 U.S. cities.
November 14–17, 1965	The U.S. 1st Cavalry Division fights a major battle with North Vietnamese forces in the Ia Drang Valley.

November 27, 1965	A march for peace in Vietnam draws 15,000 to 35,000 marchers in Washington, D.C.
December 1965	Operation TIGER HOUND, U.S. Air Force strikes against targets in southern panhandle of Laos, begins, and the ARC LIGHT campaign by B-52s is extended to include Laos.
December 24, 1965	The United States begins a second pause in the bombing of North Vietnam in an effort to get North Vietnam to negotiate.
January 1966	The Cu Chi Tunnels, used by the Viet Cong as shelter and to transport troops and supplies, are discovered by American forces.
January 25–March 6, 1966	U.S. 1st Cavalry Division, South Vietnamese and Korean forces conduct Operation MASHER/WHITE WING/THANG PHONG II in Binh Dinh Province, the largest search-and-destroy operation to date.
January 31, 1966	U.S. air strikes resume against North Vietnam.

February 1, 1966 The UN Security Council meets to consider a U.S. draft resolution calling for an international conference to bring about peace in South Vietnam and Southeast Asia.

February 2, 1966 North Vietnam rejects the UN action on Vietnam.

April 12–14, 1966 After a number of demonstrations and strikes, the South Vietnamese National Directorate promises elections for a constituent assembly within three to five months, and antigovernment demonstrations come to an end.

July 30–August 5, 1966 U.S. aircraft intentionally strike targets in the demilitarized zone (DMZ) for the first time.

September 11, 1966 The promised assembly elections are held in South Vietnam, although many decry them as "completely crooked."

October 1966 The U.S. Navy begins Operation SEA DRAGON, the interdiction of Communist supply vessels in coastal waters off North Vietnam.

December 2–5, 1966 U.S. bombers raid truck depots, rail yards, and fuel dumps in the immediate vicinity of Hanoi, with additional air strikes occurring near Hanoi on December 14–15.

December 26, 1966 U.S. officials admit that U.S. planes have "accidentally struck civilian areas while attempting to bomb military targets."

December 31, 1966 There are now some 385,300 U.S. military personnel in South Vietnam.

January 8–26, 1967 About 16,000 U.S. soldiers from the 1st and 25th Infantry Divisions, 173rd Airborne Brigade, and 11th Armored Cavalry Regiment join 14,000 South Vietnamese troops in the conduct of Operation CEDAR FALLS, the first corps-sized operation in the war.

February 22– May 14, 1967 Operation JUNCTION CITY, largest Allied operation to date, is conducted by 22 U.S. battalions and 4 ARVN battalions (nearly 25,000 troops) in Tay Ninh Province, near the Cambodian border.

April 15, 1967 Massive antiwar demonstrations are held in cities across the United States.

May 1, 1967 Ellsworth Bunker replaces Lodge as U.S. ambassador to South Vietnam.

September 3, 1967 After months of turmoil between civilian and military leaders, Nguyen Van Thieu and Nguyen Cao Ky are elected president and vice president, respectively, of South Vietnam.

September 11, 1967 Heavy U.S. air strikes are conducted on Haiphong and its suburbs in an effort to isolate the port from Hanoi.

October 12–14, 1967 Heavy U.S. air strikes are conducted against Haiphong shipyards and docks.

October 21–23, 1967 Some 50,000 Americans rally against the war in Washington, D.C., and march on the Pentagon.

December 30, 1967 The South Vietnamese government announces a 36-hour Lunar New Year (Tet) truce.

January 1, 1968 North Vietnam announces that it "will hold talks with the United States" after it has "unconditionally" halted bombing and "other acts of war" against North Vietnam.

January 21, 1968 Communist forces begin a siege of the U.S. Marine base at Khe Sanh near the DMZ.

January 30, 1968 The first premature attacks in Communist Tet Offensive commence at Da Nang, Pleiku, Nha Trang, and nine other cities in central South Vietnam.

January 31, 1968 The main thrust of the Tet Offensive begins, which includes Saigon and Hue, 5 of 6 autonomous cities, 36 of 44 provincial capitals, and 64 of 245 district capitals. The attacks—in both timing and magnitude—catch U.S. and South Vietnamese forces off guard. Although the Tet Offensive proves to be a tactical disaster for the Communists, its psychological impact has important effects on U.S. support for the war.

February 7, 1968 North Vietnamese troops overrun a U.S. Army Special Forces camp at Lang Vei, southwest of Khe Sanh.

February 20, 1968 The U.S. Senate Foreign Relations Committee begins hearings on the 1964 Gulf of Tonkin incident in which Senators J. William Fulbright and Wayne Morse charge the Defense Department with withholding information on U.S. naval activities in the gulf that might have provoked North Vietnam.

February 25, 1968 South Vietnamese and U.S. forces recapture Hue after 25 days of occupation by Communist troops.

February 26, 1968 The first mass graves are discovered in Hue. One authority estimates that Communist forces may have killed as many as 5,700 people in Hue during their occupation of the city.

February 27, 1968 CBS news anchorman Walter Cronkite, who had just returned from Saigon and Hue, declares the war a "bloody stalemate" and advises the United States to seek a negotiated end to the war.

March 16, 1968 A platoon from Company C, 1st Battalion, 20th Infantry, 11th Infantry Brigade (Light) of the 23rd (Americal) Division, commanded by Lieutenant William L. Calley, massacres between 200 and 500 unarmed civilians in the hamlet of My Lai.

March 31, 1968 Johnson announces a bombing halt over North Vietnam except for "the area north of the demilitarized zone." He calls on North Vietnam to agree to peace talks and announces that he will not be seeking reelection.

April 3, 1968 North Vietnam offers to send representatives to meet with U.S. officials "with a view to determining with the American side the unconditional cessation of the U.S.

bombing raids and all other acts of war against the Democratic Republic of Vietnam so that talks may start." Johnson agrees.

April 8, 1968 Siege of Khe Sanh is lifted when elements of the U.S. 1st Cavalry Division reach the Marine base, opening Route 9 to ground traffic.

April 26, 1968 Massive antiwar demonstrations occur on college campuses across the United States, including some 200,000 protesters in New York City.

May 5–13, 1968 The second large-scale Communist offensive of the year occurs. Although it is smaller than Tet, Communists strike some 119 targets.

May 12, 1968 U.S.–North Vietnamese preliminary peace talks open in Paris.

May 25–June 4, 1968 The third widespread Communist offensive of the year is conducted.

June 27, 1968 U.S. troops withdraw from their base at

Khe Sanh after a 77-day siege.

July 3, 1968 General Creighton Abrams replaces Westmoreland as commander of MACV.

October 31, 1968 Johnson announces an end to ROLLING THUNDER—the complete cessation of "all air, naval, and artillery bombardment of North Vietnam" as of November 1.

November 2, 1968 Thieu states that South Vietnam will not attend the Paris negotiations because of the inclusion of NLF representatives.

November 12, 1968 The United States threatens it might proceed with the Paris negotiations without the participation of the South Vietnamese government.

November 27, 1968 South Vietnam announces that it will take part in the Paris peace talks—after the United States reiterates its nonrecognition of the NLF as a separate entity.

December 23, 1968 The NLF representative in

Paris, Tran Buu Kiem, rejects direct negotiations between the NLF and the South Vietnamese government and insists on talks only with Washington.

December 31, 1968 There are now some 536,000 U.S. military personnel in South Vietnam.

January 25, 1969 Four-party peace talks begin in Paris.

February 23–24, 1969 Communist forces launch mortar and rocket attacks on some 115 targets in South Vietnam, including the cities of Saigon, Da Nang, Hue, and the U.S. base at Bien Hoa.

March 18, 1969 Operation MENU, the secret U.S. air strikes inside Cambodia by B-52 bombers, begins and will continue until May 26, 1970.

March 19, 1969 Secretary of Defense Melvin Laird proclaims the "Vietnamization" of the war.

March 26, 1969 Women Strike for Peace, the first large anti–Vietnam War rally during the administration of Richard Nixon, occurs in Washington, D.C.

March 27, 1969 In Paris, the U.S. and South Vietnamese negotiators declare that a peace settlement must include withdrawal of all North Vietnamese "regular and subversive forces" from Laos, Cambodia, and South Vietnam.

April 5–6, 1969 Antiwar protests occur in a number of U.S. cities.

April 30, 1969 Peak U.S. military strength in South Vietnam is reached with 543,482 personnel.

May 10–20, 1969 As part of Operation APACHE SNOW, U.S. paratroopers and South Vietnamese troops engage a North Vietnamese regiment on Ap Bia Mountain, which becomes known as "Hamburger Hill" after savage fighting results in heavy casualties for both sides.

May 12, 1969 Communist forces launch the largest number of attacks throughout South Vietnam since the 1968 Tet Offensive.

May 14, 1969 In his first major speech on Vietnam, Nixon proclaims an eight-point peace proposal that calls for simultaneous withdrawal of U.S. troops and "all non-South Vietnamese forces" from South Vietnam.

June 8, 1969 At a meeting with President Thieu on Midway Island, Nixon announces that the United States will withdraw 25,000 troops from South Vietnam by August, the first step in "Vietnamization," the process of turning the responsibility for the war over to the South Vietnamese.

June 10, 1969 The Provisional Revolutionary Government of the Republic of South Vietnam (PRG) is formed by the NLF and other pro-NLF, anti-RVN organizations and individuals.

July 25, 1969 Nixon proclaims the Nixon Doctrine, which states that non-Communist Asian nations will now have to bear the brunt of their defense from conventional, non-nuclear attacks and will be responsible for their own internal security.

September 2, 1969 Ho Chi Minh dies in Hanoi.

October 15, 1969 National Moratorium antiwar demonstrations occur across the United States, involving hundreds of thousands of people.

November 3, 1969 In a major address on Vietnam, Nixon appeals to the "silent majority" of Americans and argues that a "precipitate withdrawal" would lead to a "disaster of immense magnitude."

November 15, 1969 Antiwar demonstration at the Washington Monument, the largest in the capital to date, draws some 250,000 people.

November 16, 1969 The U.S. Army announces its investigation into charges that U.S. forces shot more than 100 Vietnamese civilians in My Lai village in March 1968.

November 24, 1969 Lieutenant Calley is ordered to stand trial for the premeditated

murder of 109 Viet-
namese civilians at
My Lai.

December 1, 1969 The first military
draft lottery since
1942 is held at
Selective Service
headquarters.

March 13, 1970 Cambodian leaders
demand that Viet-
namese Communist
troops withdraw
from the country
immediately, and
they sack the North
Vietnamese embassy
in Phnom Penh.

March 17, 1970 Cambodian troops,
supported by South
Vietnamese artillery,
attack Vietnamese
Communist sanctua-
ries along the
Cambodia-Vietnam
border.

March 18, 1970 The Cambodian
National Assembly
deposes Prince Siha-
nouk, declaring Gen-
eral Lon Nol the
interim chief of state.
Thieu announces his
hope of working
with the new Cam-
bodian government
to control Commu-
nist border activity.

March 23, 1970 In Beijing, Sihanouk
announces that he
will form a "national
union government"

and "national libera-
tion army." North
Vietnam and the
Pathet Lao declare
their support.

March 27–28, 1970 South Vietnamese
forces, supported by
the United States,
launch their first
major attack against
Communist base
areas in Cambodia.

March 28, 1970 Washington announces that U.S. troops
will be permitted, on
the judgment of field
commanders, to
cross into Cambodia
in response to enemy
threats, but insists
that this does not
mean a widened war.

April 4, 1970 The largest demon-
stration in favor of
U.S. involvement in
Vietnam to date is
held in Washington,
D.C.

April 5, 1970 Two South Vietnamese Army battalions
push more than
10 miles into Cam-
bodia, this time with-
out U.S. air support.

April 8, 1970 Vietnamese Communist troops drive back
Cambodian govern-
ment forces in heavy
fighting some nine
miles from the South
Vietnamese border.

April 11, 1970   Cambodian government troops begin the massacre of several thousand Vietnamese civilians living in southeast Cambodia. Some 40,000 Vietnamese in Phnom Penh are sent to concentration camps.

April 20, 1970   Nixon announces his intention to withdraw 150,000 U.S. troops over the next year.

April 21, 1970   South Vietnamese troops cross the Cambodian border for the third time in one week to attack Communist base areas.

April 30, 1970   Nixon announces that U.S. troops are attacking Communist sanctuaries in Cambodia, one objective being the Communist Central Office of South Vietnam headquarters in the Fishhook area some 50 miles northwest of Saigon. Widespread antiwar protests erupt on U.S. college campuses.

May 3, 1970   The Pentagon confirms that the United States has conducted heavy bombing of targets in North Vietnam, the first major bombing of the country since the November 1968 bombing halt.

May 4, 1970   The Kent State Massacre occurs when Ohio National Guardsmen fire on antiwar student demonstrators at Kent State University, killing 4 and wounding 11.

May 6, 1970   Some 200 college campuses across the United States shut down to protest the war and events at Kent State.

May 9, 1970   Some 75,000 to 100,000 people gather in Washington, D.C., in a hastily organized protest against the U.S. invasion of Cambodia.

May 12, 1970   South Vietnam announces that on May 9, South Vietnamese and U.S. warships began a blockade of some 100 miles of Cambodian coastline to prevent Communist resupply by sea.

May 20, 1970	Some 100,000 people demonstrate in New York City in support of Nixon's Indochina policy.		withdrawal of U.S. forces, unconditional release of prisoners of war (POWs), and a political solution reflecting the will of the South Vietnamese people.
May 26, 1970	Operation MENU ends.		
June 24, 1970	The U.S. Senate repeals the Tonkin Gulf Resolution in vote of 81 to 10.	**October 8, 1970**	Communist delegations in Paris reject Nixon's proposal, insisting instead on the unconditional withdrawal of U.S. forces from Indochina.
June 30, 1970	U.S. forces end two months of operations inside Cambodia, although some South Vietnamese forces remain there. The U.S. Senate approves the Cooper-Church Amendment, aimed at limiting future presidential action in Cambodia.	**November 20–21, 1970**	U.S. forces raid the Son Tay POW compound 25 miles from Hanoi, but find no U.S. personnel there.
September 1, 1970	The U.S. Senate rejects the McGovern-Hatfield Amendment that sets a deadline of December 31, 1971, for complete withdrawal of U.S. forces from South Vietnam.	**December 10, 1970**	Nixon warns North Vietnam that he will resume the bombing of North Vietnam if fighting in South Vietnam intensifies.
		December 31, 1970	There are now some 334,600 U.S. military personnel in South Vietnam.
October 7, 1970	Nixon announces a five-point proposal to end the war based on an established cease-fire in South Vietnam, Laos, and Cambodia. He proposes eventual	**January 1, 1971**	Congress forbids the use of U.S. ground troops in Laos and Cambodia, although it does not prohibit the use of airpower there.
		February 8, 1971	South Vietnamese forces invade southern Laos.

Dubbed Operation LAM SON 719, the incursion's goal is the disruption of the Communist supply and infiltration network. The operation is supported by U.S. airpower and artillery.

March 24, 1971 LAM SON 719 ends precipitously. South Vietnamese forces capture extensive Communist supplies but sustain heavy casualties. Many U.S. helicopters are also lost.

March 29, 1971 Calley is found guilty of the premeditated murder of 22 Vietnamese civilians at My Lai. He is sentenced to life in prison, which is later reduced to ten years. In 1974, however, he is paroled.

April 16, 1971 Nixon announces that a residual U.S. force will remain in Vietnam as long as it is needed in order for the South Vietnamese "to develop the capacity for self-defense."

April 24, 1971 More than 200,000 people participate in a Washington rally to protest the war.

May 31, 1971 In Paris, the United States secretly proposes a deadline for withdrawal of all American troops to North Vietnam in return for the repatriation of American prisoners and a cease-fire.

June 13, 1971 The *New York Times* begins publication of the Pentagon Papers, a heretofore secret Pentagon analysis of the three-decades-long U.S. involvement in Indochina.

June 26, 1971 North Vietnam offers to release American prisoners at the same time as civilian prisoners and the withdrawal of U.S. forces, but insists that the United States also abandon support of Thieu.

June 30, 1971 The U.S. Supreme Court rules that the Pentagon Papers may be published.

August 20, 1971 Retired South Vietnamese general Duong Van Minh, the only opposition candidate in South Vietnam's presidential election, withdraws from the race, charging that it is rigged in Thieu's favor.

October 3, 1971	Thieu is elected to another four-year term as president of South Vietnam.	
October 11, 1971	Washington proposes free elections in South Vietnam to be organized by an independent body representing all political forces in the south, with Thieu resigning one month before elections.	
December 26–30, 1971	U.S. aircraft resume the bombing of North Vietnam, mounting heavy attacks.	
January 2, 1972	Nixon announces that U.S. forces will continue to withdraw from South Vietnam, but that 35,000 U.S. troops will remain until the release of all U.S. POWs.	
January 25, 1972	Nixon reveals the details of secret trips taken by National Security Advisor Henry Kissinger to the Paris peace talks and the text of the October 11, 1971, U.S. peace proposal.	
January 26, 1972	North Vietnam rejects the latest U.S. peace proposal.	
March 23, 1972	Washington announces the indefinite	

suspension of the Paris peace talks until the Communists agree to "serious discussions" of predetermined issues.

March 30, 1972 North Vietnamese forces launch their Spring, or Easter, Offensive, the largest Communist military action since 1968. On Good Friday, 130,000 North Vietnamese troops in 14 divisions and 26 separate regiments conduct a coordinated attack on three fronts.

April 4–June 9, 1972 The Battle of Kontum in the Central Highlands takes place.

April 6, 1972 The United States resumes the heavy bombing of North Vietnam.

April 7–June 18, 1972 The Battle of An Loc takes place.

April 15, 1972 The United States resumes the bombing of military targets in the vicinity of Hanoi and Haiphong, the first such strikes in four years.

April 15–20, 1972 Widespread antiwar demonstrations occur across the United States.

April 22, 1972	Antiwar demonstrators hold marches and rallies throughout the United States to protest the renewed bombing of North Vietnam.	**May 8–12, 1972**	A wave of antiwar protests sweeps across the United States.
April 27, 1972	The Paris peace talks resume.	**June 1972**	General Fred Weyand replaces Abrams as commander of MACV.
May 1, 1972	South Vietnamese forces and U.S. advisers abandon Quang Tri, the northernmost provincial capital of South Vietnam, following five days of heavy fighting.	**June 18, 1972**	Siege of An Loc is broken; President Thieu flies in to congratulate his troops.
		June 28, 1972	Nixon announces that no more draftees will be sent to Vietnam unless they volunteer for such duty.
May 4, 1972	Citing a "complete lack of progress," the United States and South Vietnam announce an indefinite halt to the Paris peace talks.	**July 13, 1972**	Formal peace talks resume in Paris.
		August 28, 1972	Nixon announces an end to the military draft by July 1973.
May 8, 1972	Nixon announces the mining of all North Vietnamese ports, the interdiction of rail and other communications, and air strikes against military targets in North Vietnam (Operation LINEBACKER I), until the return of U.S. POWs and the establishment of an internationally supervised cease-fire throughout Indochina.	**September 15, 1972**	South Vietnamese forces retake Quang Tri.
		September 26–27, 1972	Kissinger holds additional secret talks in Paris with North Vietnamese representative Le Duc Tho.
		October 8, 1972	Tho presents a draft peace agreement proposing that two separate administrations remain in South Vietnam and negotiate general elections.

October 19–20, 1972 Kissinger meets with Thieu in Saigon. Thieu opposes draft treaty provisions that allow North Vietnamese troops to remain in place in South Vietnam. Nixon announces a halt in bombing of North Vietnam above the 20th Parallel. He also sends a message to North Vietnamese premier Pham Van Dong confirming that the agreement is complete and pledging that it will be signed by the two foreign ministers on October 31, although he seeks clarification on several points.

October 23, 1972 A U.S. message to Hanoi requests further negotiations, citing difficulties with Saigon.

October 26, 1972 North Vietnam announces that secret talks in Paris have produced a tentative agreement to end the war; Henry Kissinger declares, "Peace is at hand."

November 1, 1972 Thieu publicly objects to provisions in the draft agreement permitting North Vietnamese troops to remain in South Vietnam and providing for a three-segment "administrative structure" to preside over political settlement and elections.

November 16, 1972 Nixon sends a letter to Thieu pledging to press North Vietnam for the changes demanded by Thieu.

November 20–21, 1972 Kissinger and Tho begin another round of secret negotiations near Paris.

December 13, 1972 The Paris peace talks deadlock.

December 18–29, 1972 The United States renews the bombing of the Hanoi–Haiphong area (Operation LINEBACKER II, also known as the "Christmas bombing"), using B-52s as well as fighter-bombers.

December 22, 1972 Washington announces that the bombing of North Vietnam will continue until Hanoi agrees to negotiate "in a spirit of good will and in a constructive attitude."

December 30, 1972 Washington announces an end to the bombing north of the

20th Parallel and that negotiations between Kissinger and Tho will resume on January 2, 1973.

December 31, 1972 There are now only approximately 24,000 U.S. military personnel in South Vietnam.

January 8–12, 1973 Kissinger and Tho resume private negotiations in Paris.

January 15, 1973 Nixon announces an end to all U.S. offensive military action against North Vietnam.

January 20, 1973 Nixon sends an ultimatum to Thieu regarding signing the peace agreement.

January 23, 1973 Kissinger and Tho present an initial peace agreement in Paris, by which a cease-fire would begin on January 27 and all POWs would be released within 60 days.

January 25, 1973 The foreign ministers of the United States, North Vietnam, the RVN, and the PRG formally sign two-party and four-party versions of the peace agreement.

January 27, 1973 The cease-fire goes into effect, although

both sides violate it. Laird announces an end to the military draft.

February 12, 1973 The release of U.S. POWs begins in Hanoi.

February 17, 1973 Washington and Hanoi issue a joint communiqué announcing an agreement to establish a Joint Economic Commission to develop economic relations, particularly U.S. contributions to "healing the wounds of war" in North Vietnam.

February 21, 1973 A peace agreement is signed in Laos. The United States halts bombing there.

March 15 and 28, 1973 Nixon threatens to take unilateral action to force North Vietnam to suspend or reduce its use of the Ho Chi Minh Trail network to move military equipment into South Vietnam.

March 29, 1973 The last U.S. POWs leave Hanoi, and the last U.S. troops leave South Vietnam. MACV headquarters is disestablished.

April 3, 1973 A joint communiqué from Nixon and

Thieu charges Communist violations of the cease-fire agreement by infiltration and warns that continued violations "would call for appropriately vigorous reactions."

April 25, 1973 RVN and PRG delegations offer incompatible proposals for a political settlement.

May 10, 1973 The U.S. House of Representatives passes a second supplemental appropriations bill with an amendment deleting the authorization for the transfer of $430 million by the Defense Department for the bombing of Cambodia. Another amendment prohibits the use of funds for combat activities in or over Cambodia by U.S. forces.

June 9, 1973 Although Kissinger and Tho negotiate a new agreement for the implementation of the Paris peace agreement, fighting in South Vietnam reaches its highest level since mid-February.

June 29, 1973 The U.S. House of Representatives

passes a compromise bill with an August 15 deadline to halt all bombing of Cambodia and adds North and South Vietnam to areas included in ban on combat activities.

July 26, 1973 The U.S. House of Representatives passes the Foreign Assistance Bill after agreeing to an amendment prohibiting the use of funds to aid in the reconstruction of North Vietnam unless specifically authorized by Congress.

August 14, 1973 The U.S. bombing of Cambodia ends, bringing to a halt all U.S. military activity in Indochina.

September 10, 1973 The RVN protests the construction of air bases in the PRG zone on the basis that it has control of all air space over South Vietnam.

October 1973 North Vietnamese leaders decide on a new offensive in the south with a projected final victory in 1976.

October 1, 1973 Thieu declares that Communists are

planning a spring 1974 "general offensive" and calls for "preemptive attacks."

October 3–7, 1973 VNAF planes carry out heavy raids against the PRG zone in Tay Ninh Province, beginning a bombing campaign throughout the Third Military Region.

October 15, 1973 The leadership of Communist forces in South Vietnam issues an order to begin counterattacks on RVN bases and other points of its choosing in retaliation for Saigon's earlier offensive operations.

October 16, 1973 Kissinger and Tho are awarded the Nobel Prize for Peace. Kissinger accepts, but Tho declines the award until such time as "peace is truly established" in Vietnam.

November 7, 1973 Congress overrides Nixon's veto of the War Powers Act, which limits the president's power to commit U.S. armed forces abroad without congressional approval.

November 15, 1973 Congress passes the Military Procurement Authorization bill that prohibits funds for any U.S. military action in any part of Indochina.

February 1974 RVN forces launch major offensive operations against PRG areas in Quang Ngai Province and the Cu Chi–Trang Bang area west of Saigon.

March 1974 The Communist Party's Central Military Committee passes a resolution stating that if the United States and the RVN "do not implement the agreement," it must "destroy the enemy and liberate the South." This month sees the heaviest fighting in South Vietnam since the cease-fire.

March 22, 1974 In the last major political initiative by either side in the war, the PRG offers to hold elections within one year of establishment of a National Council of

	National Reconciliation and Concord.
April 4, 1974	The U.S. House of Representatives rejects Nixon's request to increase military aid to the RVN.
April 11, 1974	The South Vietnamese Army evacuates its base at Tong Le Chan, having been surrounded by Communist troops since the cease-fire.
April 12, 1974	RVN representatives withdraw from the Paris talks on political reconciliation with the PRG.
May 13, 1974	The PRG delegation suspends its participation in the Paris political talks.
July–August	Communist forces regain major areas of the provinces of Quang Nam and Quang Ngãi in the first major offensive in the lowlands.
August 6, 1974	The U.S. House of Representatives cuts military aid appropriations for South Vietnam from $1 billion to $700 million.
October 1974	The Communist political and military leadership in Vietnam concludes that

	the United States is unlikely to intervene and could not save the Thieu regime even if it did.
October 8, 1974	The PRG calls on public figures and organizations in South Vietnam to work for the overthrow of the Thieu government and the establishment of a new regime in Saigon.
December 13, 1974	Communist forces begin an attack on Phuoc Long Province north of Saigon.
December 31, 1974	There are now only approximately 50 U.S. uniformed military personnel in South Vietnam.
January 6, 1975	Communist forces take Phuoc Binh, the capital of Phuoc Long Province.
January 8, 1975	Communist forces seize all of Phuoc Long Province. The United States does not intervene with airpower.
March 10, 1975	Communist forces attack and seize Ban Me Thuot in South Vietnam's Central Highlands, opening their Spring Offensive called "Campaign 275."

March 12, 1975	Ban Me Thuot falls to Communist forces.		ordered to leave South Vietnam.
March 14, 1975	South Vietnamese forces begin a withdrawal from the Central Highlands.	**April 17, 1975**	In Cambodia, Khmer Rouge forces seize control of Phnom Penh.
March 15, 1975	South Vietnamese forces begin a retreat from Kontum and Pleiku, which soon becomes a debacle.	**April 21, 1975**	Thieu resigns. Vice President Tran Van Huong becomes president.
March 19, 1975	Communist forces attack and capture Quang Tri City. The retreat of South Vietnamese forces from Da Nang turns into a rout.	**April 26, 1975** **April 28, 1975**	The Communist assault on Saigon begins. Huong resigns. Duong Van Minh, who helped overthrow Diem in 1963, becomes president.
March 26, 1975	Hue falls to Communist troops. Da Nang, flooded with refugees, is already under rocket attack.	**April 29, 1975**	Operation FREQUENT WIND, the full evacuation of U.S. personnel from South Vietnam, takes place. Having been delayed for too long, the operation takes place under chaotic circumstances. All U.S. personnel are evacuated, but only a fraction of South Vietnamese thought to be at risk are evacuated.
March 30, 1975	Da Nang falls to the Communists. Hanoi orders General Van Tien Dung to push toward Saigon in what will be known as the Ho Chi Minh Campaign.		
April 9–22, 1975	The Battle for Xuan Loc, the capital of Long Khanh Province and a strategically important location for the defense of Saigon, takes place.	**April 30, 1975**	Communist forces capture Saigon, for all practical purposes bringing the Vietnam War to a close.
April 16, 1975	All "unneeded" Americans are		

Bibliography

Adler, Bill. *Letters from Vietnam*. New York: Presidio Press, 2004.

Ahern, Thomas L. *Vietnam Declassified: The CIA and Counterinsurgency*. Lexington: University Press of Kentucky, 2009.

Allison, William Thomas. *Military Justice: The Rule of Law in an American War*. Lawrence: University Press of Kansas, 2007.

Alvarez, Everett, Jr., and Anthony S. Pitch. *Chained Eagle*. New York: Dell, 1989.

Anderson, Charles B. *The Grunts*. San Rafael, CA: Presidio, 1976.

Anderson, David L., *The Columbia Guide to the Vietnam War*. New York: Columbia University Press, 2004.

Anderson, David L., ed. *The Columbia History of the Vietnam War*. New York: Columbia University Press, 2011.

Anderson, David L., ed. *The Human Tradition in the Vietnam Era*. Wilmington, DE: Scholarly Resources, 2000.

Anderson, David L., ed. *Shadows on the White House: Presidents and the Vietnam War, 1945–1975*. Lawrence: University Press of Kansas, 1993.

Anderson, David L., and John Ernst, eds. *The War That Never Ends: New Perspectives on the Vietnam War*. Lexington: University Press of Kentucky, 2007.

Anderson, William C. *Bat-21*. Englewood Cliffs, NJ: Prentice Hall, 1980.

Andradé, Dale. *America's Last Vietnam Battle: Halting Hanoi's 1972 Easter Offensive*. Lawrence: University Press of Kansas, 2001.

Andradé, Dale. *Ashes to Ashes: The Phoenix Program and the Vietnam War*. Lanham, MD: Lexington Books, 1990.

Andradé, Dale. *Spies and Commandos: How America Lost the Secret War In North Vietnam*. Lawrence: University Press of Kansas, 2000.

Andradé, Dale. *Trial by Fire: The 1972 Easter Offensive, America's Last Vietnam Battle*. New York: Hippocrene Books, 1995.

Appy, Christian G. *Working-Class War: American Combat Soldiers & Vietnam*. Chapel Hill: University of North Carolina Press, 1993.

Arlen, Michael. *Living-Room War*. 1969; reprint, New York: Syracuse University Press, 1997.

Arnett, Peter. *Live from the Battle Field: From Vietnam to Baghdad, 35 Years in the World's War Zones*. New York: Simon and Schuster, 1994.

Atkinson, Rick. *The Long Gray Line: The American Journey of West Point's Class of 1966*. New York: Holt Paperbacks, 2009.

Balaban, John. *Remembering Heaven's Face: A Moral Witness in Vietnam*. New York: Poseidon, 1991.

Ball, George W. *The Past Has Another Pattern*. New York: Norton, 1982.

Baritz, Loren. *Backfire: A History of How American Culture Led Us into Vietnam and Made Us Fight the Way We Did*. New York: Morrow, 1985.

Barrett, David M. *Uncertain Warriors: Lyndon Johnson and His Vietnam Advisers*.

Lawrence: University Press of Kansas, 1993.

Bartholomew-Feis, Dixee R. *The OSS and Ho Chi Minh: Unexpected Allies in the War Against Japan*. Lawrence: University Press of Kansas, 2006.

Bass, Thomas A. *Vietnamerica: The War Comes Home*. New York: Soho Press, 1996.

Beidler, Philip D. *American Literature and the Experience of Vietnam*. Athens: University of Georgia Press, 1982.

Belknap, Michael R. *The Vietnam War on Trial: The My Lai Massacre and the Court-Martial of Lieutenant Calley*. Lawrence: University Press of Kansas, 2002.

Bergerud, Eric M. *The Dynamics of Defeat. The Vietnam War in Hau Nghia Province*. Boulder, CO: Westview, 1991.

Bergerud, Eric M. *Red Thunder, Tropic Lightning: The World of a Combat Division in Vietnam*. Boulder, CO: Westview, 1993.

Berman, Larry. *Lyndon Johnson's War: The Road to Stalemate in Vietnam*. New York: Norton, 1989.

Berman, Larry. *No Peace, No Honor: Nixon, Kissinger, and Betrayal in Vietnam*. New York: Free Press, 2001.

Berman, Larry. *Perfect Spy: The Incredible Double Life of Pham Xuan An, Time Magazine Reporter and Vietnamese Communist Agent*. New York: HarperCollins, 2007.

Berman, Larry. *Planning a Tragedy: The Americanization of the War in Vietnam*. New York: Norton, 1982.

Berman, William C. *William Fulbright and the Vietnam War: The Dissent of a Political Realist*. Kent, OH: Kent State University Press, 1988.

Bey, Douglas. *Wizard 6, a Combat Psychiatrist in Vietnam*. College Station: Texas A&M University Press, 2006.

Bigeard, General Marcel. *Pour une parcelle de gloire*. Paris: Plon, 1976.

Bigler, Philip. *Hostile Fire: The Life and Death of First Lieutenant Sharon Lane*. Arlington, VA: Vandamere, 1996.

Billings-Yun, Melanie. *Decision against War: Eisenhower and Dien Bien Phu, 1954*.

New York: Columbia University Press, 1988.

Bilton, Michael, and Kevin Sim. *Four Hours in My Lai*. New York: Penguin, 1992.

Blair, Anne E. *Lodge in Vietnam: A Patriot Abroad*. New Haven, CT: Yale University Press, 1995.

Bodard, Lucien. *The Quicksand War: Prelude to Vietnam*. Boston: Little, Brown, 1967.

Botkin, Richard. *Ride the Thunder: A Vietnam War Story of Honor and Triumph*. Los Angeles: WND Books, 2009.

Bowman, John S, ed. *The World Almanac of the Vietnam War*. New York: Pharos Books, 1985.

Brace, Ernest C. *A Code to Keep: The True Story of America's Longest-Held Civilian Prisoner of War*. New York: St. Martin's, 1988.

Bradley, Mark Philip. *Vietnam At War*. Oxford: Oxford University Press, 2009.

Bradley, Mark Philip, and Marilyn B. Young, eds. *Making Sense of the Vietnam Wars: Local, National and Transnational Perspectives*. New York: Oxford University Press, 2008.

Braestrup, Peter. *Big Story: How the American Press and Television Reported and Interpreted the Crisis of Tet 1968 in Vietnam and Washington*. Novato, CA: Presidio, 1994.

Brigham, Robert K. *ARVN: Life and Death in the South Vietnamese Army*. Lawrence: University Press of Kansas, 2006.

Broughton, Jack. *Going Downtown: The War against Hanoi and Washington*. New York: Pocket Books, 1990.

Browne, Malcolm. *Muddy Boots and Red Socks: A Reporter's Life*. New York: Crown, 1993.

Browne, Malcolm. *The New Face of War*. Indianapolis: Bobbs-Merrill, 1965.

Bryan, C. D. B. *Friendly Fire*. New York: Putnam, 1976.

Bui Diem, with David Chanoff. *In the Jaws of History*. Boston: Houghton, Mifflin, 1987.

Bui Tinh. *From Enemy to Friend*. Annapolis, MD: Naval Institute Press, 2002.

Burchett, Wilfred G. *The Furtive War: The United States in Vietnam and Laos*. New York: International Publishers, 1963.

Burkett, B. G., and Glenna Whitley. *Stolen Valor: How the Vietnam Generation Was Robbed of Its Heroes and Its History*. Dallas: Verity, 1998.

Butler, David. *The Fall of Saigon: Scenes from the Sudden End of a Long War*. New York: Simon and Schuster, 1985.

Buttinger, Joseph. *The Smaller Dragon: A Political History of Vietnam*. New York: Praeger, 1958.

Buzzanco, Robert. *Masters of War: Military Dissent and Politics in the Vietnam Era*. New York: Cambridge University Press, 1996.

Cable, Larry E. *Conflict of Myths: The Development of American Counterinsurgency Doctrine and the Vietnam War*. New York: New York University Press, 1988.

Cady, John F. *The Roots of French Imperialism in Eastern Asia*. Ithaca, NY: Cornell University Press, 1954.

Cao Van Vien and Dong Van Khuyen. *Reflections on the Vietnam War*. Indochina Monographs. Washington, DC: U.S. Army Center of Military History, 1980.

Capps, Walter H., ed. *The Vietnam Reader*. New York: Routledge, 1991.

Caputo, Philip. *A Rumor of War*. New York: Holt, Rinehart and Winston, 1977.

Carroll, James. *An American Requiem: God, My Father, and the War That Came between Us*. New York: Houghton Mifflin, 1996.

Castle, Timothy N. *One Day Too Long: Top Secret Site 85 and the Bombing of North Vietnam*. New York: Columbia University Press, 1999.

Catton, Philip E. *Diem's Final Failure: Prelude to America's War in Vietnam*. Lawrence: University Press of Kansas, 2002.

Chandler, David P. *The Tragedy of Cambodian History: Politics, War, and Revolution since 1945*. New Haven, CT: Yale University Press, 1991.

Chanoff, David, and Doan Van Toai. *Portrait of the Enemy*. New York: Random House, 1986.

Chapuis, Oscar M. *A History of Vietnam: From Hong Bang to Tu Duc*. Westport, CT: Greenwood, 1995.

Chapuis, Oscar M. *The Last Emperors of Vietnam: From Tu Duc to Bao Dai*. Westport, CT: Greenwood, 2000.

Charlton, Michael, and Anthony Moncrieff. *Many Reasons Why: The American Involvement in Vietnam*. New York: Hill and Wang, 1978.

Charton, Pierre. *Indochine 1950: La tragédie de l'évacuation de Cao Bang*. Paris: Société de production littéraire, 1975.

Chen, King C. *China's War with Vietnam, 1979: Issues, Decisions, and Implications*. Stanford, CA: Hoover Institute Press, 1987.

Chomsky, Noam. *Rethinking Camelot: JFK, the Vietnam War, and U.S. Political Culture*. Boston: South End, 1993.

Clayton, Anthony. *Three Marshals of France: Leadership after Trauma*. London: Brassey's, 1992.

Clifford, Clark, with Richard Holbrooke. *Counsel to the President: A Memoir*. New York: Random House, 1991.

Clodfelter, Mark. *The Limits of Air Power: The American Bombing of North Vietnam*. New York: Free Press, 1989.

Clodfelter, Mark. *Vietnam in Military Statistics: A History of the Indochina Wars, 1772–1991*. Jefferson, NC: McFarland, 1995.

Coan, James P. *Con Thien: The Hill of Angels*. Tuscaloosa: University of Alabama Press, 2004.

Coedès, Georges. *The Making of South East Asia*. Translated by H. M. Wright. Berkeley: University of California Press, 1966.

Colby, William. *Honorable Men: My Life in the CIA*. New York: Simon and Schuster, 1978.

Colby, William, with James McCargar. *Lost Victory: A Firsthand Account of America's Sixteen-Year Involvement in Vietnam*. Chicago: Contemporary Books, 1989.

Coleman, J. D. *Incursion: From America's Chokehold on the NVA Lifelines to the Sacking of the Cambodian Sanctuaries*. New York: St. Martin's Press, 1991.

Coleman, J. D. *Pleiku: The Dawn of Helicopter Warfare in Vietnam.* New York: St. Martin's, 1988.

Conboy, Kenneth J., and James Morrison. *Shadow War: The CIA's Secret War in Laos.* Boulder, CO: Paladin, 1995.

Corfield, Justin. *The History of Vietnam.* Westport, CT: Greenwood, 2008.

Cosmas, Graham A., Terrence P. Murray, William R. Melton, and Jack Shulimson. *U.S. Marines in Vietnam: Vietnamization and Redeployment, 1970–1971.* Washington, DC: History and Museums Division, Headquarters, U.S. Marine Corps, 1986.

Cummings, Dennis J. *The Men behind the Trident: Seal Team One in Vietnam.* Annapolis, MD: Naval Institute Press, 1997.

Currey, Cecil B. *Edward Lansdale: The Unquiet American.* Boston: Houghton Mifflin, 1988.

Currey, Cecil B. *Victory at Any Cost: The Genius of Viet Nam's General Vo Nguyen Giap.* Washington, DC: Brassey's, 1997.

Cutler, Thomas J. *Brown Water, Black Berets: Coastal and Riverine Warfare in Vietnam.* Annapolis, MD: Naval Institute Press, 1988.

Daddis, Gregory A. *No Sure Victory: Measuring U.S. Army Effectiveness and Progress in the Vietnam War.* New York: Oxford University Press, 2011.

Dalloz, Jacques. *The War in Indo-China, 1945–54.* Savage, MD: Barnes and Noble, 1990.

Dang Van Viet. *Highway 4: The Border Campaign (1947–1950).* Hanoi: Foreign Languages Publishing House, 1990.

Davidson, Phillip A. *Vietnam at War: The History, 1946–1975.* Novato, CA: Presidio, 1988.

Dawson, Alan. *55 Days: The Fall of South Vietnam.* Englewood Cliffs, NJ: Prentice Hall, 1977.

Deac, Wilfred P. *Road to the Killing Fields: The Cambodian War of 1970–1975.* College Station: Texas A&M University Press, 1997.

DeBenedetti, Charles, with Charles Chatfield. *An American Ordeal: The Antiwar Movement of the Vietnam Era.* Syracuse, NY: Syracuse University Press, 1990.

De Folin, Jacques. *Indochine, 1940–1955: La fin d'un rêve.* Paris: Perrin, 1993.

DeForest, Orrin, and David Chanoff. *Slow Burn: The Rise and Bitter Fall of American Intelligence in Vietnam.* New York: Simon and Schuster, 1990.

De Gaulle, Charles. *The War Memoirs of Charles de Gaulle,* Vol. 3, *Salvation, 1944–1946.* Translated by Richard Howard. New York: Simon and Schuster, 1960.

Denton, Jeremiah A., with Ed Brandt. *When Hell Was in Session.* New York: Reader's Digest, 1976.

Devillers, Philippe. *Histoire du Vietnam de 1940 à 1952.* Paris: Editions de Seuil, 1952.

Dillard, Walter Scott. *Sixty Days to Peace: Implementing the Paris Peace Accords, Vietnam 1973.* Washington, DC: National Defense University, 1982.

Dommen, Arthur J. *Conflict in Laos: The Politics of Neutralization.* Rev. ed. New York: Praeger, 1971.

Dommen, Arthur J. *The Indochinese Experience of the French and Americans: Nationalism and Communism in Cambodia, Laos, and Vietnam.* Bloomington: Indiana University Press, 2001.

Dong Van Khuyen. *The Republic of Vietnam Armed Forces.* Washington, DC: U.S. Army Center of Military History, 1980.

Donovan, David. *Once a Warrior King: Memories of an Officer in Vietnam.* New York: McGraw-Hill, 1985.

Dooley, Thomas A. *Deliver Us from Evil: The Story of Viet Nam's Flight to Freedom.* New York: Farrar, Straus and Cudahy, 1956.

Duiker, William J. *The Communist Road to Power in Vietnam.* 2nd ed. Boulder, CO: Westview, 1996.

Duiker, William J. *Historical Dictionary of Vietnam.* Metuchen, NJ: Scarecrow, 1989.

Duiker, William J. *Ho Chi Minh: A Life.* New York: Hyperion, 2000.

Duiker, William J. *The Rise of Nationalism in Vietnam, 1900–1911.* Ithaca, NY: Cornell University Press, 1976.

Duiker, William J. *Vietnam: Revolution in Transition.* 2nd ed. Boulder, CO: Westview, 1995.

Duncanson, Dennis J. *Government and Revolution in Vietnam.* New York: Oxford University Press, 1968.

Ebert, James R. *A Life in a Year: The American Infantryman in Vietnam, 1965–1972.* Novato, CA: Presidio, 1993.

Edelman, Bernard, ed. *Dear America: Letters Home from Vietnam.* New York: Norton, 1985.

Ellsberg, Daniel. *Papers on the War.* New York: Simon and Schuster, 1972.

Ellsberg, Daniel. *Secrets: A Memoir on Vietnam and the Pentagon Papers.* New York: Viking Penguin, 2002.

Elwood-Akers, Virginia. *Women War Correspondents in the Vietnam War, 1961–1975.* Metuchen, NJ: Scarecrow, 1988.

Emerson, Gloria. *Winners and Losers: Battles, Retreats, Gains, Losses, and Ruins from the Vietnam War.* New York: Random House, 1976.

Engelmann, Larry. *Tears before the Rain: An Oral History of the Fall of South Vietnam.* New York: Oxford University Press, 1990.

Esper, George, and the Associated Press. *The Eyewitness History of the Vietnam War, 1961–1975.* New York: Ballantine Books, 1983.

Fall, Bernard B. *Hell in a Very Small Place: The Siege of Dien Bien Phu.* New York: Lippincott, 1966.

Fall, Bernard B. *Last Reflections on a War.* Garden City, NY: Doubleday, 1967.

Fall, Bernard B. *Street without Joy: The French Debacle in Indochina.* Rev. ed. Mechanicsburg, PA: Stackpole Books, 1994.

Fall, Bernard B. *The Two Viet-Nams: A Political and Military Analysis.* 2nd rev. ed. New York: Praeger, 1967.

Fall, Bernard B. *Viet-Nam Witness, 1953–66.* New York: Praeger, 1966.

Fall, Dorothy. *Bernard Fall: Memories of a Soldier-Scholar.* Washington, DC: Potomac Books, 2006.

FitzGerald, Frances. *Fire in the Lake: The Vietnamese and the Americans in Vietnam.* Boston: Little, Brown, 1972.

Ford, Harold P. *CIA and the Policymakers: Three Episodes, 1962–1968.* Washington DC: CIA Center for the Study of Intelligence, 1988.

Franklin, H. Bruce. *M.I.A. or Mythmaking in America: How and Why Belief in Live POWs Has Possessed a Nation.* New Brunswick, NJ: Rutgers University Press, 1993.

Frankum, Ronald B., Jr. *Like Rolling Thunder: The Air War in Vietnam, 1964–1975.* New York: Rowman and Littlefield, 2005.

Freeman, James M. *Hearts of Sorrow: Vietnamese-American Lives.* Stanford, CA: Stanford University Press, 1989.

Frier, Gilles. *Les trois guerres d'Indochine.* Lyon: Presses Universitaires de Lyon, 1993.

Fry, Joseph A. *Debating Vietnam: Fulbright, Stennis, and Their Senate Hearings.* New York: Rowman and Littlefield, 2006.

Gabriel, Richard A., and Paul L. Savage. *Crisis in Command: Mismanagement in the Army.* New York: Hill and Wang, 1978.

Gaddis, John L. *The Cold War: A New History.* New York: Penguin, 2006.

Gaiduk, Ilya V. *The Soviet Union and the Vietnam War.* Chicago: Ivan R. Dee, 1996.

Gardner, Lloyd C. *Pay Any Price: Lyndon Johnson and the Wars for Vietnam.* Lanham, MD: Ivan R. Dee, 1997.

Gargus, John. *The Son Tay Raid: American POWs in Vietnam Were Not Forgotten.* College Station: Texas A&M University Press, 2007.

Garland, Albert N., ed. *A Distant Challenge: The U.S. Infantryman in Vietnam, 1967–1972.* Nashville: Battery, 1983.

Garnier, Francis. *Voyage d'exploration en Indo-Chine, 1866–88.* Paris: Editions la Découverte, 1985.

Gilbert, Marc Jason, and William Head. *Why the North Won the Vietnam War.* New York: Palgrave Macmillan, 2002.

Gillespie, Robert M. *Black Ops Vietnam: The Operational History of MACVSOG.* Annapolis, MD: Naval Institute Press, 2011.

Glasser, Ronald J. *365 Days.* New York: G. Braziller, 1971.

Glenn, Russell W. *Reading Athena's Dance Card: Men against Fire in Vietnam.* Annapolis, MD: Naval Institute Press, 2000.

Goff, Stanley, and Robert Sanders, with Clark Smith. *Brothers: Black Soldiers in the Nam.* Novato, CA: Presidio, 1982.

Goldman, Peter, and Tony Fuller. *Charlie Company: What Vietnam Did to Us.* New York: Morrow, 1983.

Goldstein, Gordon M. *Lessons in Disaster: McGeorge Bundy and the Path to War in Vietnam.* New York: Times Books, 2008.

Gole, Henry G. *General William E. DePuy: Preparing the Army for Modern War.* Lexington: University Press of Kentucky, 2008.

Gottlieb, Sherry Gershon. *Hell No, We Won't Go! Resisting the Draft during the Vietnam War.* New York: Viking, 1991.

Gould, Lewis L. *1968: The Election That Changed America.* Chicago: Ivan R. Dee, 1993.

Grant, Zalin. *Survivors.* New York: Norton, 1975.

Gras, Yves. *Histoire de la Guerre d'Indochine.* Paris: Éditions Denoël, 1992.

Greene, Bob. *Homecoming: When the Soldiers Returned from Vietnam.* New York: Putnam, 1989.

Greene, John Robert. *The Presidency of Gerald R. Ford.* Lawrence: University Press of Kansas, 1995.

Grey, Jeffrey, Peter Pierce, and Jeff Doyle. *Australia's Vietnam War.* College Station: Texas A&M Press, 2002.

Groom, Winston, and Duncan Spencer. *Conversations with the Enemy: The Story of Pfc. Robert Garwood.* New York: Putnam, 1983.

Gruner, Elliott. *Prisoners of Culture: Representing the Vietnam POW.* New Brunswick, NJ: Rutgers University Press, 1993.

Guilmartin, John F. *A Very Short War: The Mayaguez and the Battle of Koh Tang.* College Station: Texas A&M University Press, 1995.

Gustainis, J. Justin. *American Rhetoric and the Vietnam War.* New York: Praeger, 1993.

Hackworth, David H., and Eihys England. *Steel My Soldiers' Hearts.* New York: Touchstone, 2003.

Hackworth, Colonel David H., and Julie Sherman. *About Face: The Odyssey of an American Warrior.* New York: Simon and Schuster, 1989.

Halberstam, David. *The Best and the Brightest.* New York: Random House, 1972.

Halberstam, David. *Ho.* Lanham, MD: Rowman and Littlefield, 2007.

Halberstam, David. *The Making of a Quagmire: America and Vietnam during the Kennedy Era.* Rev. ed. Lanham, MD: Rowman and Littlefield, 2008.

Hamilton-Merritt, Jane. *Tragic Mountains: The Hmong, the Americans, and the Secret Wars for Laos, 1942–1992.* Bloomington: Indiana University Press, 1993.

Ha Mai Viet. *Steel and Blood: South Vietnamese Armor and the War for Southeast Asia.* Annapolis, MD: Naval Institute Press, 2008.

Hammel, Eric. *Fire in the Streets: The Battle for Hue, Tet, 1968.* Chicago: Contemporary Books, 1991.

Hammel, Eric. *Khe Sanh: Siege in the Clouds; An Oral History.* New York: Crown, 1989.

Hammer, Ellen J. *A Death in November: America in Vietnam, 1963.* New York: Dutton, 1987.

Hammer, Ellen J. *The Struggle for Indochina.* Stanford, CA: Stanford University Press, 1954.

Hammond, William M. *Public Affairs: The Military and the Media, 1962–1968.* Washington DC: Department of the Army, 1988.

Hammond, William M. *Public Affairs: The Military and the Media, 1968–1973*. Honolulu: University Press of the Pacific, 2002.

Hargrove, Thomas R. *A Dragon Lives Forever: War and Rice in Vietnam's Mekong Delta, 1969-1991*. Bloomington, IN: Authorhouse, 2003.

Hathorn, Reginald. *Here Are the Tigers: The Secret Air War in Laos*. Mechanicsburg, PA: Stackpole Books, 2008.

Hayslip, Le Ly, and Jay Wurts. *When Heaven and Earth Changed Places: A Vietnamese Woman's Journey from War to Peace*. New York: Doubleday, 1989.

Head, William, and Lawrence E. Grinter, ed. *Looking Back on the Vietnam War: A 1990's Perspective on the Decisions, Combat, and Legacies*. Westport, CT: Greenwood, 1993.

Heineman, Kenneth J. *Campus Wars: The Peace Movement at American State Universities in the Vietnam Era*. New York: New York University Press, 1993.

Hellman, John. *American Myth and the Legacy of Vietnam*. New York: Columbia University Press, 1986.

Hemingway, Albert. *Our War Was Different: Marine Combined Action Platoons in Vietnam*. Annapolis, MD: Naval Institute Press, 1994.

Herr, Michael. *Dispatches*. New York: Knopf, 1977.

Herring, George C. *America's Longest War: The United States and Vietnam, 1950–1975*. 4th ed. New York: McGraw-Hill, 2001.

Herring, George C. *LBJ and Vietnam: A Different Kind of War*. Austin: University of Texas Press, 1994.

Herrington, Stuart A. *Silence Was a Weapon: The Vietnam War in the Villages; A Personal Perspective*. Novato, CA: Presidio, 1982.

Hersh, Seymour M. *Cover-Up: The Army's Secret Investigation of the Massacre at My Lai 4*. New York: Random House, 1972.

Hersh, Seymour M. *My Lai 4: A Report on the Massacre and Its Aftermath*. New York: Random House, 1970.

Hess, Gary. R. *Vietnam: Explaining America's Lost War*. Hoboken, NJ: Wiley-Blackwell, 2008.

Hickey, Gerald Cannon. *Window on a War: An Anthropologist in the Vietnam Conflict*. Lubbock: Texas Tech University Press, 2002.

Higham, Charles. *The Archaeology of Mainland Southeast Asia*. Cambridge: Cambridge University Press, 1989.

Hoang Hai Van and Tan Tu. *Pham Xuan An: A General of the Secret Service*. Hanoi: Gioi Publishers, 2003.

Hoang Van Thai. *How South Vietnam Was Liberated*. Hanoi: Gioi Publishers, 1996.

Hobson, Chris. *Vietnam Air Losses: United States Air Force, Navy, and Marine Corps Fixed-Wing Aircraft Losses in Southeast Asia, 1961–1973*. Hinckley, UK: Midland Publishing, 2001.

Hoffmann, Stanley. *Primacy or World Order: American Foreign Policy since the Cold War*. New York: McGraw-Hill, 1978.

Ho Khang. *The Tet Mau Than 1968 Event in South Vietnam*. Hanoi: Gioi Publishers, 2001.

Holm, Tom. *Strong Hearts, Wounded Souls: Native American Veterans of the Vietnam War*. Austin: University of Texas Press, 1996.

Ho Mai Viet. *Steel and Blood: South Vietnamese Armor and the War for Southeast Asia*. Annapolis, MD: Naval Institute Press, 2008.

Hooper, Edwin B., Dean C. Allard, and Oscar P. Fitzgerald. *The United States Navy and the Vietnam Conflict*, Vol. 1, *The Setting of the Stage to 1959*. Washington, DC: U.S. Navy, Naval History Division, 1976.

Hubbell, John G., Andrew Jones, and Kenneth Y. Tomlinson. *P.O.W.: A Definitive History of the American Prisoner-of-War Experience in Vietnam, 1964–1973*. New York: Reader's Digest, 1976.

Hunt, Richard A. *Pacification: The American Struggle for Vietnam's Hearts and Minds*. Boulder, CO: Westview, 1995.

Huynh, Jade Ngoc Quang. *South Wind Changing*. St. Paul, MN: Graywolf, 1994.

Isaacs, Arnold R. *Vietnam Shadows: The War, Its Ghosts, and Its Legacy.* Baltimore: Johns Hopkins University Press, 1997.

Isaacs, Arnold R. *Without Honor: Defeat in Vietnam and Cambodia.* Baltimore: Johns Hopkins University Press, 1983.

Isaacson, Walter. *Kissinger: A Biography.* New York: Simon and Schuster, 1992.

Jensen-Stevenson, Monika, and William Stevenson. *Kiss the Boys Goodbye: How the United States Betrayed Its Own POWs in Vietnam.* New York: Dutton, 1990.

Johnson, Lyndon B. *The Vantage Point: Perspectives of the Presidency, 1963–1969.* New York: Holt, Rinehart and Winston, 1971.

Jones, Charles. *Boys of '67.* Mechanicsburg, PA: Stackpole, 2006.

Kahin, George McT. *Intervention: How America Became Involved in Vietnam.* New York: Knopf, 1986.

Kane, Rod. *Veteran's Day.* New York: Orion Books, 1989.

Karnow, Stanley. *Vietnam: A History.* 2nd rev. and updated ed. New York: Penguin, 1997.

Katsiaficas, George N., ed. *Vietnam Documents: American and Vietnamese Views of the War.* New York: M. E. Sharpe, 1992.

Kelley, Michael P. *Where We Were in Vietnam: A Comprehensive Guide to the Firebases, Military Installations and Naval Vessels of the Vietnam War, 1945–75.* Central Point, OR: Hellgate, 2002.

Kerrey, Bob. *When I Was a Young Man: A Memoir.* New York: Harcourt Brace, 2002.

Kimball, Jeffrey P., ed. *To Reason Why: The Debate about the Causes of Involvement in the Vietnam War.* Philadelphia: Temple University Press, 1990.

Kimball, Jeffrey P., ed. *Nixon's Vietnam War.* Lawrence: University Press of Kansas, 2002.

King, Peter, ed. *Australia's Vietnam: Australia in the Second Indochina War.* Boston: Allen and Unwin, 1983.

Kinnard, Douglas. *The War Managers.* Hanover, NH: University Press of New England, 1977.

Kirk, Donald. *Wider War: The Struggle for Cambodia, Thailand, and Laos.* New York: Praeger, 1971.

Kissinger, Henry. *White House Years.* Boston: Little, Brown, 1979.

Kissinger, Henry. *Years of Upheaval.* Boston: Little, Brown, 1982.

Kolko, Gabriel. *Anatomy of a War: Vietnam, the United States, and the Modern Historical Experience.* New York: Pantheon, 1985.

Kovic, Ron. *Born on the Fourth of July.* New York: McGraw-Hill, 1976.

Krall, Yung. *A Thousand Tears Falling: The True Story of a Vietnamese Family Torn Apart by War, Communism, and the CIA.* Atlanta: Longstreet, 1995.

Krepinevich, Andrew F., Jr. *The Army and Vietnam.* Baltimore: Johns Hopkins University Press, 1986.

Krohn, Charles A. *The Lost Battalion of Tet: Breakout of the 2–12 Cavalry at Hue.* Annapolis, MD: Naval Institute Press, 2008.

Kutler, Stanley I., ed. *Encyclopedia of the Vietnam War.* New York: Scribner, 1996.

Lacouture, Jean. *Ho Chi Minh: A Political Biography.* New York: Random House, 1968.

Lamb, Christopher Jon. *Belief Systems and Decision Making in the Mayaguez Crisis.* Gainesville: University of Florida Press, 1988.

Lam Quang Thi. *Hell in An Loc: The 1972 Easter Invasion and the Battle That Saved South Vietnam.* Denton: University of North Texas Press, 2009.

Lam Quang Thi. *The Twenty-Five Year Century: A South Vietnamese General Remembers the Indochina War to the Fall of Saigon.* Denton: University of North Texas Press, 2001.

Lane, Mark. *Conversations with Americans.* New York: Simon and Schuster, 1970.

Lang, Daniel. *Casualties of War.* New York: McGraw-Hill, 1969.

Langguth, A. J. *Our Vietnam: The War, 1954–1975*. New York: Simon and Schuster, 2000.

Lanning, Michael Lee, and Dan Cragg. *Inside the VC and NVA: The Real Story of North Vietnam's Armed Forces*. College Station: Texas A&M University Press, 2008.

Lansdale, Edward Geary. *In the Midst of Wars: An American's Mission to Southeast Asia*. New York: Harper and Row, 1972.

Larsen, Stanley Robert, and James Lawton Collins Jr. *Allied Participation in Vietnam*. Vietnam Studies Series. Washington, DC: Department of the Army, U.S. Government Printing Office, 1975.

Larzelere, Alex. *The Coast Guard at War: Vietnam, 1965–1975*. Annapolis, MD: Naval Institute Press, 1997.

Laurence, John. *The Cat From Hue: A Vietnam War Story*. New York: PublicAffairs, 2001.

Le Gro, William E. *Vietnam from Cease-Fire to Capitulation*. Washington, DC: U.S. Army Center of Military History, 1981.

Lepre, George. *Fragging: Why U.S. Soldiers Assaulted Their Officers in Vietnam*. Lubbock: Texas Tech University Press, 2011.

Le Thanh Khoi. *Histoire du Viet Nam des origines à 1858*. Paris: Sudestasie, 1981.

Lien-Hang T, Nguyen. *Hanoi's War: An International History of the War for Peace in Vietnam*. Chapel Hill: The University of North Carolina Press, 2012.

Lifton, Robert Jay. *Home from the War: Vietnam Veterans, Neither Victims nor Executioners*. New York: Simon and Schuster, 1973.

Lind, Michael. *Vietnam: The Necessary War: A Reinterpretation of America's Most Disastrous Military Conflict*. New York: Touchstone, 1999.

Logevall, Fredrik. *Choosing War: The Lost Chances for Peace and the Escalation of the War in Vietnam*. Berkeley: University of California Press, 1999.

Luu Van Loi and Nguyen Anh Vu. *Le Duc Tho–Kissinger Negotiations in Paris*. Hanoi: Gioi Publishers, 1996.

Ly Quy Chung, ed. *Between Two Fires: The Unheard Voices of Vietnam*. New York: Praeger, 1970.

Macdonald, Peter. *Giap: The Victor in Vietnam*. New York: Norton, 1993.

MacGarrigle, George L. *Combat Operations: Taking the Offensive, October 1966 to October 1967*. Washington, DC: Center of Military History, U.S. Army, 1998.

Maclear, Michael. *The Ten Thousand Day War: Vietnam, 1945–1975*. New York: St. Martin's, 1981.

MacPherson, Myra. *Long Time Passing: Vietnam and the Haunted Generation*. New York: Doubleday, 1984.

Maneli, Mieczyslaw. *The War of the Vanquished*. New York: Harper and Row, 1969.

Mangold, Tom, and John Penycate. *The Tunnels of Cu Chi*. New York: Random House, 1985.

Maraniss, David. *They Marched into Sunlight: War and Peace, Vietnam and America, October 1967*. New York: Simon and Schuster, 2003.

Marolda, Edward J. *By Sea, Air, and Land: An Illustrated History of the U.S. Navy and the War in Southeast Asia*. Washington, DC: Naval Historical Center, Department of the Navy, 1994.

Marolda, Edward J., and Oscar P. Fitzgerald. *The United States Navy and the Vietnam Conflict: From Military Assistance to Combat, 1959–1965*, Vol. 2. Washington, DC: Naval Historical Center, 1986.

Marr, David G. *Vietnam 1945: The Quest for Power*. Berkeley: University of California Press, 1995.

Marr, David G. *Vietnamese Tradition on Trial, 1920–1945*. Berkeley: University of California Press, 1981.

Marshall, Kathryn. *In the Combat Zone: An Oral History of American Women in Vietnam, 1966–1975*. Boston: Little, Brown, 1987.

Marshall, S. L. A. *Ambush*. New York: Cowles, 1969.

Marshall, S. L. A. *Battles in the Monsoon: Campaigning in the Central Highlands,*

South Vietnam, Summer, 1966. New York: William Morrow, 1967.

Marshall, S. L. A. *Bird: The Christmastide Battle*. New York: Cowles, 1968.

Marshall, S. L. A. *West to Cambodia*. New York: Cowles, 1968.

Marshall, S. L. A., and David Hackworth. *DA Pam 525–2 Vietnam Primer*. Washington, DC: U.S. Government Printing Office, 1967.

Mason, Robert. *Chickenhawk*. New York: Viking, 1983.

Maslowski, Peter, and Don Winslow. *Looking for a Hero: Staff Sergeant Joe Ronnie Hooper and the Vietnam War*. Lincoln: University of Nebraska Press, 2009.

Mauer, Harry. *Strange Ground: Americans in Vietnam, 1945–1975, an Oral History*. New York: Henry Holt, 1989.

McCallum, Jack E. *Military Medicine: From Ancient Times to the 21st Century*. Santa Barbara, CA: ABC-CLIO, 2003.

McCarthy, Mary. *The Seventeenth Degree*. New York: Harcourt, Brace, Jovanovich, 1974.

McCloud, Bill. *What Should We Tell Our Children about Vietnam*. Norman: University of Oklahoma Press, 1989.

McConnell, Malcolm. *Inside the Hanoi Secret Archives: Solving the MIA Mystery*. New York: Simon and Schuster, 1995.

McDermott, Mike. *True Faith and Allegiance*. Tuscaloosa: The University of Alabama Press, 2012.

McKenna, Thomas P. *Kontum: The Battle to Save South Vietnam*. Lexington: University Press of Kentucky, 2011.

McMaster, H. R. *Dereliction of Duty: Lyndon Johnson, Robert McNamara, the Joint Chiefs of Staff, and the Lies That Led to Vietnam*. New York: HarperCollins, 1997.

McNab, Chris, and Andy Weist. *The Illustrated History of the Vietnam War*. San Diego: Thunder Bay, 2000.

McNamara, Robert S., with Brian VanDeMark. *In Retrospect: The Tragedy and Lessons of Vietnam*. New York: Vintage Books, 1995.

McNeill, Ian. *To Long Tan: The Australian Army and the Vietnam War, 1950–1966*. St. Leonards, New South Wales: Allen and Unwin/Australian War Memorial, 1993.

Metzner, Edward P. *More Than a Soldier's War: Pacification in Vietnam*. College Station: Texas A&M University Press, 1995.

Metzner, Edward P., Huynh Van Chinh, Tran Van Phuc, and Le Nguyen Binh. *Reeducation in Postwar Vietnam: Personal Postscripts to Peace*. College Station: Texas A&M University Press, 2001.

Michel, Marshall L., III. *Clashes: Air Combat over North Vietnam, 1965–1972*. Annapolis, MD: Naval Institute Press, 1997.

Michel, Marshall L., III. *The Eleven Days of Christmas: America's Last Vietnam Battle*. San Francisco: Encounter Books, 2002.

Military History Institute of Vietnam. *Victory in Vietnam: The Official History of the People's Army of Vietnam, 1954–1975*. Lawrence: University Press of Kansas, 2002.

Miller, John G. *The Bridge at Dong Ha*. Annapolis, MD: Naval Institute Press, 1996.

Moïse, Edwin E. *Historical Dictionary of the Vietnam War*. New York: Scarecrow Press, 2001.

Moïse, Edwin E. *Tonkin Gulf and the Escalation of the Vietnam War*. Chapel Hill: University of North Carolina Press, 1996.

Moore, Harold G., and Joseph L. Galloway. *We Are Soldiers Still: A Journey back to the Battlefields of Vietnam*. New York: Harper, 2008.

Moore, Harold G., and Joseph L. Galloway. *We Were Soldiers Once . . . and Young: Ia Drang—The Battle That Changed the War in Vietnam*. New York: Random House, 1992.

Morgan, Joseph G. *The Vietnam Lobby: The American Friends of Vietnam, 1955–1975*. Chapel Hill: University of North Carolina Press, 1997.

Morgan, Ted. *Valley of Death: The Tragedy at Dien Bien Phu That Led America into the Vietnam War*. New York: Random House, 2010.

Morrison, Wilbur H. *The Elephant and the Tiger: The Full Story of the Vietnam War*. New York: Hippocrene Books, 1990.

Moss, George. *Vietnam: An American Ordeal*. 2nd ed. Englewood Cliffs, NJ: Prentice Hall, 1994.

Moyar, Mark. *Phoenix and the Birds of Prey: The CIA's Secret Campaign to Destroy the Viet Cong*. Annapolis, MD: Naval Institute Press, 1997.

Moyar, Mark. *Triumph Forsaken: The Vietnam War, 1954–1965*. New York: Cambridge University Press, 2006.

Murphy, Edward F. *Dak To: The 173rd Airborne Brigade in South Vietnam's Central Highlands, June–November 1967*. Novato, CA: Presidio, 1993.

Murphy, Edward F. *The Hill Fights: The First Battle of Khe Sanh*. New York: Random House, 2003.

Murphy, John. *Harvest of Fear: A History of Australia's Vietnam War*. Boulder, CO: Westview, 1994.

Nalty, Bernard C. *The War against Trucks: Aerial Interdiction in Southern Laos, 1968–1972*. Washington, DC: Air Force History and Museums Program, U.S. Air Force, 2005.

Neilands, J. B., et al. *Harvest of Death: Chemical Warfare in Vietnam and Cambodia*. New York: Free Press, 1972.

Newman, John M. *JFK and Vietnam: Deception, Intrigue, and the Struggle for Power*. New York: Warner Books, 1992.

Newman, John M. *Vietnam War Literature: An Annotated Bibliography of Imaginative Works about Americans Fighting in Vietnam*. 3rd ed. Lanham, NJ: Scarecrow, 1996.

Ngo Quang Truong. *Territorial Forces*. Washington, DC: U.S. Army Center of Military History, 1981.

Nguyen Cao Ky. *Twenty Years and Twenty Days*. New York: Stein and Day, 1976.

Nguyen Khac Vien. *The Long Resistance, 1858–1975*. Hanoi: Foreign Languages Publishing House, 1975.

Nguyen Khac Vien. *Vietnam: A Long History*. Hanoi: Foreign Languages Publishing House, 1987.

Nguyen Tien Hung and Jerrold L. Schechter. *The Palace File*. New York: Harper and Row, 1986.

Nichols, John B., and Barrett Tillman. *On Yankee Station: The Naval Air War over Vietnam*. Annapolis, MD: Naval Institute Press, 1987.

Nixon, Richard M. *No More Vietnams*. New York: Arbor House, 1985.

Nixon, Richard M. *The Real War*. New York: Warner, 1980.

Nixon, Richard M. *RN: The Memoirs of Richard Nixon*. New York: Grosset and Dunlap, 1978.

Nolan, Keith William. *Battle for Hue: Tet, 1968*. Novato, CA: Presidio, 1983.

Nolan, Keith William. *The Battle for Saigon: Tet, 1968*. Novato, CA: Presidio, 1996.

Nolan, Keith William. *House to House: Playing the Enemy's Game in Saigon, May 1968*. St. Paul, MN: Zenith, 2006.

Nolan, Keith William. *Into Laos: The Story of Dewey Canyon II/Lam Son 719, Vietnam 1971*. Novato, CA: Presidio, 1986.

Nolan, Keith William. *Ripcord: Screaming Eagles under Siege, Vietnam 1970*. Novato, CA: Presidio, 2000.

Nolting, Frederick. *From Trust to Tragedy: The Political Memoirs of Frederick Nolting, Kennedy's Ambassador to Diem's Vietnam*. New York: Praeger, 1988.

Novosel, Michael J. *Dustoff: The Memoir of an Army Aviator*. Novato, CA: Presidio, 1999.

O'Ballance, Edgar. *The Wars in Vietnam, 1954–1980*. Rev. ed. New York: Hippocrene Books, 1981.

Oberdorfer, Don. *TET! The Turning Point in the Vietnam War*. Baltimore: Johns Hopkins University Press, 2001.

O'Brien, Tim. *If I Die in a Combat Zone*. New York: Delacorte, 1973.

Olson, James S., ed. *Dictionary of the Vietnam War*. New York: Greenwood, 1988.

Olson, James S., and Randy Roberts. *Where the Domino Fell: America and Vietnam, 1945–1990.* New York: St. Martin's, 1991.

Olson, James S., and Randy Roberts. *The Vietnam War: Handbook of the Literature and Research.* Westport, CT: Greenwood, 1993.

An Outline History of the Vietnam Workers' Party, 1930–1975. Hanoi: Foreign Languages Publishing House, 1978.

Palmer, General Bruce, Jr. *The 25-Year War: America's Military Role in Vietnam.* Lexington: University Press of Kentucky, 1984.

Palmer, Dave R. *Summons of the Trumpet: U.S.-Vietnam in Perspective.* San Rafael, CA: Presidio, 1995.

Palmer, Laura. *Shrapnel in the Heart: Letters and Remembrances from the Vietnam Memorial.* New York: Random House, 1987.

Patti, Archimedes L. A. *Why Viet Nam? Prelude to America's Albatross.* Berkeley: University of California Press, 1980.

Pearson, Willard. *The War in the Northern Provinces, 1966–1968.* Washington, DC: Department of the Army, 1975.

Pedroncini, Guy, and General Philippe Duplay, eds. *Leclerc et l'Indochine.* Paris: Albin Michel, 1992.

Personalities of the South Vietnam Liberation Movement. New York: Commission for Foreign Relations of the South Vietnam National Front for Liberation, 1965.

Peterson, Michael E. *The Combined Action Platoons: The U.S. Marines' Other War in Vietnam.* New York: Praeger, 1989.

Pham Cao Duong. *Lich Su Dan Toc Viet Nam,* Quyen I, *Thoi K Lap Quoc* [History of the Vietnamese People, Vol. I, The Making of the Nation]. Fountain Valley, CA: Truyen Thong Viet, 1987.

Phillips, Rufus. *Why Vietnam Matters: An Eyewitness Account of Lessons Not Learned.* Annapolis, MD: Naval Institute Press, 2008.

Phillips, William R. *Night of the Silver Stars: The Battle of Lang Vei.* Annapolis, MD: Naval Institute Press, 1997.

Philpott, Tom. *Glory Denied: The Saga of Jim Thompson, America's Longest-Held Prisoner of War.* New York: Norton, 2001.

Pike, Douglas. *A History of Vietnamese Communism, 1923–1978.* Stanford, CA: Hoover Institute Press, 1978.

Pike, Douglas. *Viet Cong: The Organization and Techniques of the National Liberation Front of South Vietnam.* Cambridge, MA: MIT Press, 1966.

Pimlot, John, ed. *Vietnam: The Decisive Battles.* New York: Booksales, 2004.

Pisor, Robert. *The End of the Line: The Siege of Khe Sanh.* New York: Norton, 1982.

Plaster, John. *SOG: The Secret Wars of America's Commandos in Vietnam.* New York: Simon and Schuster, 1997.

Porch, Douglas. *The French Foreign Legion: A Complete History of the Legendary Fighting Force.* New York: HarperCollins, 1991.

Porter, Gareth. *A Peace Denied: The United States, Vietnam, and the Paris Agreement.* Bloomington: Indiana University Press. 1975.

Prados, John, ed. *In Country: Remembering the Vietnam War.* Lanham, MD: Ivan R. Dee, 2011.

Prados, John. *The Blood Road: The Ho Chi Minh Trail and the Vietnam War.* New York: Wiley, 1999.

Prados, John. *Vietnam: The History of an Unwinnable War, 1945–1975.* Lawrence: University Press of Kansas, 2009.

Prados, John, and Ray W. Stubbe. *Valley of Decision: The Siege of Khe Sanh.* Boston: Houghton Mifflin, 1991.

Pratt, John Clark, ed. *Vietnam Voices: Perspectives on the War Years, 1941–1982.* New York: Viking, 1984.

Pribbenow, Merle L., and William J. Duiker. *Victory in Vietnam: The Official History of the People's Army of Vietnam.* Lawrence: University Press of Kansas, 2002.

Prochnau, William. *Once upon a Distant War: David Halberstam, Neil Sheehan, Peter Arnett—Young War Correspondents and Their Early Vietnam Battles.* New York: Vintage Books, 1995.

Puller, Lewis B., Jr. *Fortunate Son: The Autobiography of Lewis B. Puller, Jr.* New York: Grove Weidenfeld, 1991.

Pyle, Richard, and Horst Faas. *Lost over Laos: A True Story of Tragedy, Mystery, and Friendship.* Cambridge, MA: Da Capo, 2003.

Quang X. Pham. *A Sense of Duty: My Father, My American Journey.* New York: Ballantine Books, 2005.

Race, Jeffrey. *War Comes to Long An: Revolutionary Conflict in a Vietnamese Province.* Berkeley: University of California Press, 1972.

Randle, Robert F. *Geneva 1954: The Settlement of the Indochinese War.* Princeton, NJ: Princeton University Press, 1969.

Randolph, Stephen P. *Powerful and Brutal Weapons: Nixon, Kissinger, and the Easter Offensive.* Cambridge: Harvard University Press, 2007.

Reardon, Carol. *Launch the Intruders: A Naval Attack Squadron in the Vietnam War, 1972.* Lawrence: University Press of Kansas, 2005.

Robbins, Christopher. *Air America.* New York: Putnam, 1979.

Rotter, Andrew, ed. *Light at the End of the Tunnel: A Vietnam War Anthology.* New York: St. Martin's, 1991.

Rowe, John Crowe, and Rick Berg, ed. *The Vietnam War and American Culture.* New York: Columbia University Press, 1991.

Roy, Jules. *The Battle of Dienbienphu.* New York: Harper and Row, 1965.

Rusk, Dean. *As I Saw It.* Edited by Daniel S. Papp. New York: Norton, 1990.

Sack, John. *M.* New York: New American Library, 1966.

Safer, Morley. *Flashbacks: On Returning to Vietnam.* New York: Random House, 1990.

Sainteny, Jean. *Histoire d'une Paix Manquée: Indochine, 1945–1947.* Paris: Amiot-Dumont, 1953.

Sainteny, Jean. *Ho Chi Minh and His Vietnam: A Personal Memoir.* Chicago: Cowles, 1972.

Salisbury, Harrison E., ed. *Vietnam Reconsidered: Lessons from a War.* New York: Harper and Row, 1984.

Santoli, Al, ed. *Everything We Had: An Oral History of the Vietnam War by Thirty-Three American Soldiers Who Fought It.* New York: Random House, 1981.

Santoli, Al, ed. *Leading the Way—How Vietnam Veterans Rebuilt the U.S. Military: An Oral History.* New York: Ballantine Books, 1994.

Santoli, Al, ed. *To Bear Any Burden: The Vietnam War and Its Aftermath in the Words of Americans and Southeast Asians.* New York: Dutton, 1985.

Schell, Jonathan. *The Military Half.* New York: Knopf, 1968.

Schell, Jonathan. *The Village of Ben Suc.* New York: Knopf, 1967.

Scholl-Latour, Peter. *Death in the Rice Fields: An Eyewitness Account of Vietnam's Three Wars, 1945–1979.* New York: St. Martin's, 1985.

Schreadley, R. L. *From the Rivers to the Sea: The United States Navy in Vietnam.* Annapolis, MD: Naval Institute Press, 1992.

Schwenkel, Christina. *The American War in Contemporary Vietnam: Transnational Remembrance and Representation.* Bloomington: Indiana University Press, 2009.

Shultz, Richard H., Jr. *The Secret War against Hanoi.* New York: HarperCollins, 1999.

Schulzinger, Robert D. *A Time for Peace: The Legacy of the Vietnam War.* New York: Oxford University Press, 2006.

Schulzinger, Robert D. *A Time for War: The United States and Vietnam, 1941–1975.* New York: Oxford University Press, 1997.

Scruggs, Jan C., and Joel L. Swerdlow. *To Heal a Nation: The Vietnam Veterans Memorial.* New York: Harper and Row, 1985.

Sevy, Grace, ed. *The American Experience in Vietnam: A Reader.* Norman: University of Oklahoma Press, 1989.

Shapley, Deborah. *Promise and Power: The Life and Times of Robert McNamara.* Boston: Little, Brown, 1993.

Sharp, Ulysses S. Grant. *Strategy for Defeat: Vietnam in Retrospect.* San Rafael, CA: Presidio, 1978.

Shaw, John M. *The Cambodian Campaign: The 1970 Offensive and America's Vietnam War.* Lawrence: University Press of Kansas, 2005.

Shawcross, William. *Sideshow: Kissinger, Nixon, and the Destruction of Cambodia.* New York: Simon and Schuster, 1979.

Shay, Jonathan. *Achilles in Vietnam: Traumatic Stress and the Undoing of Character.* New York: Antheneum, 1994.

Sheehan, Neil. *A Bright Shining Lie: John Paul Vann and America in Vietnam.* New York: Random House, 1988.

Sheppard, Don. *Riverine: A Brown-Water Sailor in the Delta, 1967.* Novato, CA: Presidio, 1992.

Shkurti, William J. *Soldiering on in a Dying War: The True Story of the Firebase Pace Incidents and the Vietnam Drawdown.* Lawrence: University Press of Kansas, 2011.

Showalter, Dennis E., and John G. Abert, eds. *An American Dilemma: Vietnam, 1964–1973.* Chicago: Imprint Publications, 1993.

Shulimson, Jack. *U.S. Marines in Vietnam, 1965.* Washington, DC: History and Museums Division, Headquarters, U.S. Marine Corps, 1978.

Shulimson, Jack. *U.S. Marines in Vietnam, 1966: An Expanding War.* Marine Corps Vietnam Series. Washington, DC: History and Museums Division, Marine Corps Historical Center, U.S. Marine Corps Headquarters, 1982.

Shulimson, Jack, Leonard A. Blasiol, Charles R. Smith, and David A. Dawson. *U.S. Marines in Vietnam: The Defining Year, 1968.* Washington, DC: History and Museums Division, Headquarters, U.S. Marine Corps, 1997.

Shulimson, Jack, and Charles M. Johnson. *U.S. Marines in Vietnam: The Landing and the Buildup.* Washington, DC: History and Museums Division, Headquarters, U.S. Marine Corps, 1977.

Sigler, David Burns. *Vietnam Battle Chronology: U.S. Army and Marine Corps Combat Operations, 1965–1973.* Jefferson, NC: McFarland, 1992.

Simpson, Howard R. *Dien Bien Phu: The Epic Battle America Forgot.* Washington, DC: Brassey's, 1994.

Simpson, Howard R. *Tiger in the Barbed Wire: An American in Vietnam, 1952–1991.* Washington, DC: Brassey's, 1992.

Smith, Winnie. *American Daughter Gone to War: On the Front Lines with an Army Nurse in Vietnam.* New York: Morrow, 1992.

Snepp, Frank. *Decent Interval: An Insider's Account of Saigon's Indecent End.* New York: Random House, 1977.

Solis, Gary D. *Son Thang: An American War Crime.* Annapolis, MD: Naval Institute Press, 1997.

Sorley, Lewis. *A Better War: The Unexamined Victories and Final Tragedy of America's Last Years in Vietnam.* New York: Harcourt, Brace, 1999.

Sorley, Lewis. *Thunderbolt: General Creighton Abrams and the Army of His Times.* 2nd ed. Bloomington: Indiana University Press, 2008.

Sorley, Lewis. *Westmoreland: The General Who Lost Vietnam.* New York: Houghton Mifflin Harcourt, 2011.

Spector, Ronald H. *Advice and Support: The Early Years, 1941–1960.* United States Army in Vietnam Series. Washington, DC: U.S. Army Center of Military History, 1983.

Spector, Ronald H. *After Tet: The Bloodiest Year in Vietnam.* New York: Free Press, 1993.

Stanton, Shelby L. *Green Berets at War: U.S. Army Special Forces in Southeast Asia, 1956–1975.* Novato, CA: Presidio, 1985.

Stanton, Shelby L. *The Rise and Fall of an American Army: The U.S. Ground Forces in Vietnam, 1965–1975.* Novato, CA: Presidio, 1985.

Stanton, Shelby L. *U.S. Army and Allied Ground Forces in Vietnam Order of Battle.* Washington, DC: U.S. News Books, 1981.

Steinman, Ron. *The Soldiers' Story: Vietnam in Their Own Words*. New York: B&N, 2009.

Stevens, Fitzgerald. *The Trail*. New York: Garland, 1993.

Stockdale, James B. *A Vietnam Experience: Ten Years of Reflection*. Stanford, CA: Hoover Institute Press, 1984.

Sullivan, John F. *Of Spies and Lies: A CIA Lie Detector Remembers Vietnam*. Lawrence: University Press of Kansas, 2002.

Summers, Harry G. *Historical Atlas of the Vietnam War*. Boston: Houghton Mifflin, 1995.

Summers, Harry G. *On Strategy: A Critical Analysis of the Vietnam War*. Novato, CA: Presidio Press 1995.

Swift, Earl. *Where They Lay: Searching for America's Lost Soldiers*. New York: Houghton Mifflin, 2003.

Takiff, Michael. *Brave Men, Gentle Heroes: American Fathers and Sons in World War II and Vietnam*. New York: William Morrow, 2003.

Taylor, John M. *General Maxwell Taylor: The Sword and the Pen*. New York: Doubleday, 1989.

Taylor, Keith Weller. *The Birth of Vietnam*. Berkeley: University of California Press, 1983.

Taylor, General Maxwell D. *Swords and Plowshares*. New York: Norton, 1972.

Telfer, Gary L. *U.S. Marines in Vietnam: Fighting the North Vietnamese, 1967*. Washington, DC: History and Museums Division, Headquarters, U.S. Marine Corps, 1984.

Terry, Wallace. *Bloods: An Oral History of the Vietnam War by Black Veterans*. New York: Random House, 1984.

Thompson, Virginia. *French Indo-China*. New York: Octagon Books, 1968.

Timberg, Robert. *The Nightingale's Song*. New York: Touchstone, Simon and Schuster, 1996.

Toczek, David M. *The Battle of Ap Bac, Vietnam: They Did Everything but Learn from It*. Annapolis, MD: Naval Institute Press, 2007.

Todd, Olivier. *Cruel April: The Fall of Saigon*. New York: Norton, 1987.

Tourison, Sedgwick D. *Project Alpha: Washington's Secret Military Operations in North Vietnam*. New York: St. Martin's, 1997.

Tourison, Sedgwick D. *Talking with Victor Charlie: An Interrogator's Story*. New York: Ivy, 1991.

Tran Van Nhut. *An Loc: The Unfinished War*. Lubbock: Texas Tech University Press, 2009.

Trujillo, Charley, ed. *Soldados: Chicanos in Viet Nam*. San Jose, CA: Chusma House, 1990.

Truong Nhu Tang, with David Charnoff and Doan Van Toai. *A Viet Cong Memoir: An Inside Account of the Vietnam War and Its Aftermath*. New York: Harcourt Brace Jovanovich, 1985.

Tuchman, Barbara W. *The March of Folly: From Troy to Vietnam*. New York: Knopf, 1984.

Tucker, Spencer C. *Vietnam*. Lexington: University Press of Kentucky, 1999.

Turley, Gerald H. *The Easter Offensive: The Last American Advisors, Vietnam, 1972*. Novato, CA: Presidio, 1985.

U.S. Department of State. *Aggression from the North: The Record of North Viet-Nam's Campaign to Conquer South Viet-Nam*. Washington, DC: U.S. Government Printing Office, 1965.

Valentine, Douglas. *The Phoenix Program*. New York: Morrow, 1990.

Valette, Jacques. *La Guerre d'Indochine, 1945–1954*. Paris: Armand Colin, 1994.

VanDeMark, Brian. *Into the Quagmire: Lyndon Johnson and the Escalation of the Vietnam War*. New York: Oxford University Press, 1991.

Van Devanter, Lynda. *Home before Morning: The Story of an Army Nurse in Vietnam*. New York: Beaufort Books, 1983.

Veith, George J. *Black April: The Fall of South Vietnam 1973–75*. New York: Encounter Books, 2012.

Vo Nguyen Giap. *"Big Victory, Great Task." North Viet-Nam's Minister of Defense*

Assesses the Course of the War. New York: Praeger, 1968.

Vo Nguyen Giap. *Dien Bien Phu*. 5th ed., rev. and supplemented. Hanoi: Gioi Publishers, 1994.

Vo Nguyen Giap. *The Military Art of People's War: Selected Writings of Vo Nguyen Giap*. Edited with an introduction by Russell Stetler. New York: Monthly Review Press, 1970.

Vo Nguyen Giap. *Viet Nam People's War Has Defeated U.S. War of Destruction*. Hanoi: Foreign Languages Publishing House, 1969.

Vo Nguyen Giap. *People's War People's Army: The Viet Cong Insurrection Manual for Underdeveloped Countries*. New York: Praeger, 1962.

Vo Nguyen Giap. *Unforgettable Months and Years*. Translated by Mai Elliott. Ithaca, NY: Cornell University Press, 1975.

Vo Nguyen Giap and Huu Mai. *Dien Bien Phu: Rendezvous with History, a Memoir*. Hanoi: Gioi Publishers, 2004.

Vo Nguyen Giap and Huu Mai. *Duong Toi Dien Bien Phu* [The Road to Dien Bien Phu]. Hanoi: People's Army Publishing House, 2001.

Vo Nguyen Giap and Huu Mai. *Fighting under Siege: Reminiscences*. Hanoi: Gioi Publishers, 2004.

Vo Nguyen Giap and Huu Mai. *The General Headquarters in the Spring of Brilliant Victory*. Hanoi: Gioi Publishers, 2002.

Walt, Lewis W. *Strange War, Strange Strategy: A General's Report on Vietnam*. New York: Funk and Wagnalls, 1976.

Warr, Nicholas. *Phase Line Green: The Battle for Hue, 1968*. Annapolis, MD: Naval Institute Press, 1997.

Wells, Tom. *The War Within: America's Battle over Vietnam*. Berkeley: University of California Press, 1994.

Westmoreland, William C. *A Soldier Reports*. New York: Doubleday, 1976.

Wexler, Sanford. *The Vietnam War: An Eyewitness History*. New York: Facts on File, 1992.

Wheeler, John. *Touched with Fire: The Future of the Vietnam Generation*. New York: F. Watts, 1984.

Whitlow, Robert H. *U.S. Marines in Vietnam: The Advisory & Combat Assistance Era, 1954–1964*. Washington, DC: History and Museums Division, Headquarters, U.S. Marine Corps, 1977.

Whitlow, Robert, Jack Shulimson, and Gary L. Telfer. *U.S. Marines in Vietnam: An Anthology and Annotated Bibliography, 1954–1973*. Washington, DC: History and Museums Division, Headquarters, U.S. Marine Corps, 1985.

Wiest, Andrew, Mary Kathryn Barbier, and Glenn Robins, eds. *America and the Vietnam War: Re-examining the Culture and History of a Generation*. New York: Routledge, 2010.

Wiest, Andrew. *Vietnam's Forgotten Army: Heroism and Betrayal in the ARVN*. New York: New York University Press, 2007.

Wiest, Andrew, ed. *Rolling Thunder in a Gentle Land: The Vietnam War Revisited*. Oxford, UK: Osprey, 2006.

Wilcox, Fred A. *Waiting for an Army to Die: The Tragedy of Agent Orange*. New York: Random House, 1983.

Wilkins, Warren. *Grab Their Belts to Fight Them: The Viet Cong's Big-Unit War against the U.S., 1965–1966*. Annapolis, MD: Naval Institute Press, 2011.

Willbanks, James H. *Abandoning Vietnam: How America Left and South Vietnam Lost Its War*. Lawrence: University Press of Kansas, 2004.

Willbanks, James H. *The Battle of An Loc*. Bloomington: Indiana University Press, 2005.

Willbanks, James H. *The Tet Offensive: A Concise History*. New York: Columbia University Press, 2007.

Willbanks, James H. *Thiet Giap! The Battle of An Loc, April 1972*. Fort Leavenworth, KS: Combat Studies Institute, 1993.

Willbanks, James H. *Vietnam War Almanac*. New York: Facts on File, 2009.

Willenson, Kim. *The Bad War: An Oral History of the Vietnam War*. New York: New American Library, 1987.

Williams, Reese. *Unwinding the Vietnam War: From War into Peace.* Seattle: Real Comet, 1987.

Williams, William Appleman, Thomas McCormick, Lloyd Gardner, and Walter LaFaber, eds. *America in Vietnam: A Documentary History.* New York: Norton, 1989.

Windrow, Martin. *The Last Valley: Dien Bien Phu and the French Defeat in Vietnam.* London: Weidenfeld and Nicolson, 2004.

Winters, Francis X. *The Year of the Hare: America in Vietnam, January 25, 1963–February 15, 1964.* Athens: University of Georgia Press, 1997.

Wirtz, James J. *The Tet Offensive: Intelligence Failure in War.* Ithaca, NY: Cornell University Press, 1991.

Wittman, Sandra M. *Writing about Vietnam: The Literature of the Vietnam Conflict.* Boston: G. K. Hall, 1989.

Wolff, Tobias. *In Pharaoh's Army: Memories of the Lost War.* New York: Knopf, 1994.

Wyatt, Clarence R. *Paper Soldiers: The American Press and the Vietnam War.* 2nd ed. Chicago: University of Chicago Press, 1995.

Young, Marilyn B. *The Vietnam Wars, 1945–1990.* New York: HarperCollins, 1991.

Zabecki, David T. ed. *Vietnam: A Reader.* New York: ibooks, 2002.

Zaffiri, Samuel. *Hamburger Hill: The Brutal Battle for Dong Ap Bia, May 11–20, 1969.* Novato, CA: Presidio, 1988.

Zaffiri, Samuel. *Westmoreland: A Biography of General William C. Westmoreland.* New York: William Morrow, 1994.

Zaroulis, N. C., and Gerald Sullivan. *Who Spoke Up? American Protest against the War in Vietnam, 1963–1975.* Garden City, NY: Doubleday, 1984.

Zhai, Qiang. *China and the Vietnam Wars, 1950–1975.* Chapel Hill: University of North Carolina Press, 2000.

Zumwalt, Elmo, Jr. *On Watch: A Memoir.* New York: Quadrangle/New York Times Books, 1976.

Zumwalt, Elmo, Jr., and Elmo Zumwalt III, with John Pekkanen. *My Father, My Son.* New York: Macmillan, 1986.

Spencer C. Tucker, Sandra M. Wittman, and James H. Willbanks

Editor and Contributors List

Editor

Lieutenant Colonel James H. Willbanks, PhD, United States Army (Ret.)
Director, Department of Military History
U.S. Army Command and General Staff College

Contributors

Lacie A. Ballinger
Collections Manager
Fort Worth Museum of Science and History

Dr. John L. Bell, Jr.
Department of History
Western Carolina University

Dr. David M. Berman
School of Education
Department of Curriculum
and Education
University of Pittsburgh

Dr. Robert K. Brigham
Department of History
Vassar College

Peter W. Brush
Librarian
Vanderbilt University

Lauraine Bush
Independent Scholar

Thomas R. Carver
Independent Scholar

Dr. David Coffey
Professor and Chair
Department of History and Philosophy
University of Tennessee at Martin

Dr. Cecil B. Currey
University of South Florida

Elizabeth W. Daum
Independent Scholar

Dr. Paul S. Daum
Department of History
New England College

Dr. Arthur J. Dommen
The Indochina Institute
George Mason University

Dr. Joe P. Dunn
Department of History and Politics
Converse College

R. Blake Dunnavent
Department of History
LSU Shreveport

Dr. Bruce Elleman
History Department
Texas Christian University

Dr. Arthur T. Frame
Professor of Strategy and
Operational Warfare
U.S. Army Command and General Staff
College

Charles J. Gaspar
Department of Humanities and
Communication Arts
Brenau University

John M. Gates
Department of History
Wooster College

John Robert Greene
Department of History
Cazenovia College

Dr. William P. Head
Historian/Chief, WR-ALC Office of
History
U.S. Air Force

Second Lieutenant Lincoln Hill
Department of History
U.S. Air Force Academy

Dr. Richard A. Hunt
Center for Military History

Dr. Arnold R. Isaacs
Independent Scholar

Dr. Richard L. Kiper
Independent Scholar

Dr. William M. Leary
Department of History
University of Georgia

Mark F. Leep
Independent Scholar

Dr. Edwin E. Moïse
Department of History
Clemson University

Dr. Jerry Morelock
Colonel, U.S. Army, Retired
Editor in Chief, *Armchair General Magazine*

Dr. Michael R. Nichols
Department of History
Tarrant County College

Dr. Paul G. Pierpaoli, Jr.
Fellow
Military History, ABC-CLIO, LLC

Dr. Michael Richards
Department of History
Sweet Briar College

Dr. Barney J. Rickman III
Valdosta State University

Dr. John D. Root
Lewis Department of Humanities
Armour College
Illinois Institute of Technology

Dr. Rodney J. Ross
Senior Professor of History/
Geography
Harrisburg Area Community College

Dr. David C. Saffell
Department of History and Political
Science
Ohio Northern University

Dr. Claude R. Sasso
William Jewell College

Dr. Michael Share
Department of History
University of Hong Kong

Dr. Lewis Sorley
Independent Scholar

Dr. James E. Southerland
Brenau University

Dr. Richard D. Starnes
Department of History
Western Carolina University

Dr. Kenneth R. Stevens
Department of History
Texas Christian University

Adam J. Stone
Independent Scholar

Dr. Brenda J. Taylor
Department of History
Texas Wesleyan University

Dr. Earl H. Tilford, Jr.
Army War College

Dr. Spencer C. Tucker
Senior Fellow
Military History, ABC-CLIO, LLC

Dr. John F. Votaw
Independent Scholar

Dr. James H. Willbanks
Department of Military History
U.S. Army Command and General
Staff College

Sandra M. Wittman
Library Services
Oakton Community College

Dr. Laura Matysek Wood
Department of Social Sciences
Tarrant County College

Clarence R. Wyatt
Pottinger Professor of History and Special
Assistant to the President Centre College

Dr. David T. Zabecki
Major General
Army of the United States, Retired

Index

About the Editor

Dr. James H. Willbanks is the General of the Army George C. Marshall Chair of Military History and Director of the Department of Military History at the U.S. Army Command and General Staff College, Fort Leavenworth, Kansas. He is a retired Army officer with 23 years' service in various infantry and staff assignments, including a tour as an adviser with a South Vietnamese infantry regiment during the 1972 North Vietnamese Easter Offensive. He holds a BA in history from Texas A&M University, and an MA and PhD in history from the University of Kansas. He is the author of several books on the Vietnam War, including *Abandoning Vietnam*, *The Battle of An Loc*, and *The Tet Offensive: A Concise History*. He is also the editor of *America's Heroes: Medal of Honor Recipients from the Civil War to Afghanistan*.